IMMIGRANT AND REFUGEE
CHILDREN AND FAMILIES

Immigrant and Refugee Children and Families

CULTURALLY RESPONSIVE PRACTICE

Alan J. Dettlaff and Rowena Fong

EDITORS

COLUMBIA UNIVERSITY PRESS   NEW YORK

COLUMBIA UNIVERSITY PRESS
Publishers Since 1893
New York   Chichester, West Sussex

cup.columbia.edu
Copyright © 2016 Columbia University Press
All rights reserved

Library of Congress Cataloging-in-Publication Data

Names: Dettlaff, Alan J., editor. | Fong, Rowena, editor.
Title: Immigrant and refugee children and families : culturally responsive practice / edited by
    Alan J. Dettlaff and Rowena Fong.
Description: New York : Columbia University Press, 2016. | Includes index. | Description based
    on print version record and CIP data provided by publisher; resource not viewed.
Identifiers: LCCN 2015046227 (print) | LCCN 2015042951 (ebook) | ISBN 9780231541794
    (electronic) | ISBN 9780231172844 (cloth : alk. paper) | ISBN 9780231172851 (pbk.)
Subjects: LCSH: Social work with immigrants—United States. | Social work with children—
    United States. | Immigrants—Services for—United States. | Immigrant children—Services
    for—United States. | Refugee children—Services for—United States. | Family services—
    United States.
Classification: LCC HV4010 (print) | LCC HV4010 .I396 2016 (ebook)
LC record available at http://lccn.loc.gov/2015046227

Columbia University Press books are printed on permanent and durable acid-free paper.
This book is printed on paper with recycled content.
Printed in the United States of America

Cover design: Kathleen Lynch

References to websites (URLs) were accurate at the time of writing.
Neither the author nor Columbia University Press is responsible for URLs
that may have expired or changed since the manuscript was prepared.

TO VULNERABLE IMMIGRANT AND REFUGEE CHILDREN, FAMILIES,
AND COMMUNITIES, AND THE PROVIDERS, PRACTITIONERS, AND
POLICYMAKERS WHO TIRELESSLY ADVOCATE ON THEIR BEHALF

IN 2013, the United Nations reported that the number of international migrants worldwide had reached 232 million, up from 175 million in 2000. The number one destination of these immigrants—mostly from Latin America, Africa, and Asia—is the United States. This is not the first time that our country has been the journey's end for immigrants and refugees, but this is by far the largest wave of humanity that has taken enormous risks to seek the American Dream of security, happiness, and opportunity. Motivating these vast streams of migrants are poverty, famine, war, civil disintegration, community violence, genocide, and government-sponsored repression. Migrants embark on journeys of epic proportions whether we look at them as members of large groups or as individuals. We know that migrants and their children leave harrowing conditions in their home countries. The circumstances can be familial, such as domestic violence at the hands of cruel abusers who, if not aided, are abetted by police, who turn a blind eye or take payments to remain silent. The threats can also be local, wherein armed gangs, militants, or tribal rivals rob and beat parents, sexually assault and abduct their daughters, and conscript their preteen and teenage sons into service to commit unspeakable crimes. Threats can also be large national or cultural ordeals, such as religious persecution, government repression, and imprisonment or disappearance. These premigration traumas push migrants to flee, even at the risk of losing their lives.

Then come the journeys of escape—the perimigration experiences, the physical and emotional hardships of finding a way to safety. Whether we are talking about the thousands of migrants who board unsafe vessels to cross oceans to safe harbors—many losing their lives, the survivors watching the horrors—or about the migratory passages on foot, atop trains, in buses, or in the sunbaked trailers of trucks, the dreadful journey is almost as painful as the situations they leave behind. It compounds the hurts and sorrows migrants feel when forced into exile from their native countries.

Arrival in a new country brings a certain relief, whether thanks to the coast guards, navies, and private ships that bring these migrants to safety or to the border patrols into whose arms they fall. These are the happiest moments. But they are often short lived, for what might follow is detention in a refugee camp or detention center. For how long? Days? Months? Years? "Will we be returned?" they worry. "Will we be given asylum?" the refugee asks. Here begin the postmigration stresses, strains, and disappointments of tens of thousands of immigrants and refugees. Seldom do these weary travelers find welcome wagons when they arrive at their final destination. Too often, the places they go to are unprepared to receive them, and frequently there is vocal public opposition, even violence, against them. Like all major traumas, these disappointments will be passed from generation to generation.

This important new volume addresses the critical life-saving issues that face the United States when tired, traumatized refugees and immigrants appear on our shores or our borders, or are resettled across our land by nongovernmental organizations. The book's chapters add to our understanding of the history, policies, and federal immigration practices that influence the work with immigrants and refugees. We cannot practice, advocate, or change policies without understanding how our immigration system operates or what its priorities are. Appreciating the cultures of our New Americans is as important as helping them resettle and assisting them through the shock waves and rewards of acculturation. Any professional practice with immigrants and refugees—be it social work, medicine, nursing, psychiatry, pharmacy, or education—can only succeed if it takes into account the histories, cultures, and migratory experiences of the clients served. From sound practices, burnished over time and shared among caring colleagues, we are better able to change systems that need changing and innovate when we encounter the obsolete.

No one person, system, or nation can stop the violence, oppression, unrest, social decay, or tyrannical regimes that force parents to pack rucksacks, take their children's hands, and head into an uncharted exodus. What we can do, and this book is a superb resource for doing it, is to be prepared to help these parents, their children, and their children's children live rich, fulfilling lives.

Luis H. Zayas
University of Texas at Austin

CHANGES IN IMMIGRATION PATTERNS and trends over the past two decades have considerably shifted the demographic profile of the United States. Not only has the number of foreign-born immigrants living in the United States increased, but also a larger proportion of this foreign-born population consists of children and families. In 2010, foreign-born immigrants represented 12.9 percent of the total U.S. population (Grieco et al., 2012). Most adult immigrants are not U.S. citizens, and many are undocumented. As of 2010, nearly twelve million undocumented immigrants lived in the United States, representing approximately 30 percent of the total foreign-born population (Passel & Cohn, 2011). Children with at least one foreign-born parent represent more than one fourth (26 percent) of all children in the United States (Fortuny, Capps, Simms, & Chaudry, 2009). Most children of immigrants (87 percent) were born in the United States and are U.S. citizens. However, 44 percent of all children of immigrants live in families where neither parent is a U.S. citizen, and nearly one third live in mixed-status families, in which the children are citizens but at least one parent is not (Fortuny et al., 2009).

When immigrant and refugee children come to the attention of social service systems—including the child welfare, juvenile justice, education, physical health, and mental health systems—they are at increased vulnerability of experiencing negative outcomes because of barriers associated with their immigration and refugee status, as well as language barriers, cultural misunderstandings, and a lack of culturally responsive service providers. Given the rapid and increasing growth of the immigrant and refugee populations in the United States, it is imperative that these systems be equipped to respond to the needs of immigrant and refugee children and families to ensure positive outcomes regarding their health and well-being. Yet, few resources exist to prepare social workers and other helping professionals to understand these issues and to communicate across systems to provide culturally responsive services. Professionals also need to recognize the potential barriers to culturally responsive practice and learn to approach service delivery from a perspective of cultural humility. To achieve this, professionals need more information on the barriers and challenges facing immigrant and refugee children and families and on specific strategies that can be used to address these challenges across systems. Further, given the diversity within the immigrant and refugee populations, both in immigration status and country of origin, professionals need additional information on the unique challenges that exist for these diverse groups as well as strategies to address these challenges. This text is designed to provide students, educators, policymakers, practitioners, and administrators with new knowledge and strategies that will build the capacity of the intersecting child welfare, juvenile justice, education, physical health, and mental health systems to provide culturally responsive services to immigrant and refugee children and families.

This text begins with a comprehensive overview of the policy and legal landscape impacting immigrant and refugee children and families in the United States in order to provide an understanding of the barriers and challenges to well-being that result from state and federal policies. In part 2, the text addresses the unique needs, challenges, and issues of five racial and ethnic groups of immigrants and refugees. These five populations represent the ten countries with the greatest number of immigrants, and these immigrants represent 90 percent of all immigrants residing in the United States. This section also provides an understanding of the history, patterns, and reasons for migration among these groups as well as supplying the context of their cultural values and norms in order to promote culturally responsive practice. Part 2 also explores issues of diversity that exist within these major ethnic groups. In part 3, we explore the unique challenges and opportunities that are present within five major social service systems—child welfare, juvenile justice, education, physical health, and mental health—along with cross-system strategies to improve the responses of these systems to immigrant and refugee children and families. The text concludes in part 4

with an example of advocacy efforts in one system to promote positive outcomes for immigrant and refugee children and families, as well as future
directions for policy, practice, and research.

REFERENCES

Fortuny, K., Capps, R., Simms, M., & Chaudry, A. (2009). *Children of immigrants: National and state characteristics.* Retrieved from http://www.urban
.org/publications/411939.html

Grieco, E. M., Acosta, Y. D., de la Cruz, G. P., Gambino, C., Gryn, T., Larson,
L. J., . . . Walters, N. P. (2012). *U.S. Census Bureau: The foreign-born population in the United States: 2010.* Retrieved from http://www.census.gov/prod
/2012pubs/acs-19.pdf

Passel, J., & Cohn, D. (2011). *Unauthorized immigrant population: National and
state trends, 2010.* Retrieved from http://www.pewhispanic.org/files/reports
/133.pdf

IMMIGRANT AND REFUGEE
CHILDREN AND FAMILIES

PART 1

U.S. Immigration and Refugee Systems and the Federal Policy Landscape

CHAPTER 1

Introduction

▸ ALAN J. DETTLAFF, ROWENA FONG,
and CAITLIN O'GRADY

IN 2013, the foreign-born population of the United States reached a historic high of more than 41 million (Zong & Batalova, 2015). However, transnational migration to the United States is not a new phenomenon. In fact, since the founding of the United States, migration has been an integral component of the country's history (Jaggers, Gabbard, & Jaggers, 2014). Who migrates to the United States, and why do they undertake this journey? This chapter will explore these questions, first by providing a theoretical overview of the factors driving migration and then by discussing trends in migration patterns during specific periods of U.S. history. After exploring these questions, the chapter concludes by considering how a historical understanding of migration patterns can inform social work practice with the present foreign-born population.

FACTORS DRIVING MIGRATION: A THEORETICAL OVERVIEW

In order to develop a comprehensive understanding of the factors influencing migration from an individual's country of origin, it is necessary to draw on theories spanning a range of disciplines (Brettell & Hollifield, 2008). Economic theory, for example, suggests that "push" factors such as poor living conditions, lack of employment opportunities, and low wages drive individuals to leave their country of origin, whereas "pull" factors such as available employment and higher wages influence decisions to migrate to a specific receiving country (Brettell & Hollifield, 2008; Massey, Durand,

& Malone, 2003). Economic factors in isolation, however, do not suffi-ciently explain individuals' decisions to migrate (Brettell & Hollifield, 2008; Massey et al., 2003). Political conditions within a sending country also largely influence migration patterns. In countries with weak systems of governance, individuals and families may undertake the migration jour-ney because the government in their country of origin lacks the necessary infrastructure to provide services essential to their well-being (Betts, 2011). Individuals' migration decisions are influenced by internal conditions within their country of origin as well as by the extent to which social capi-tal is available to migrants in a receiving country (Brettell & Hollifield, 2008; Massey et al., 2003). Massey et al. identify migrant networks as the primary form of social capital driving migration to a specific receiving country, and they define migrant networks as "sets of interpersonal ties that connect migrants, former migrants, and nonmigrants at places of ori-gin and destination through reciprocal ties of kinship, friendship, and shared community origin" (Massey et al., 2003, p. 19). This definition sug-gests that when there is an established community of individuals of shared cultural and national heritage in a receiving locale, there is a greater likeli-hood of subsequent migration. New migrants entering a community where there is an established network of support have more resources available to navigate the cultural context of their new country of residence, thus easing the transition to life in the receiving country (Massey et al., 2003). The term *immigrants* is used to identify individuals who migrate from their country of origin to a new country of residence for reasons such as those listed here.

DISTINGUISHING BETWEEN VOLUNTARY AND FORCED MIGRATION

The previous section framed migration as a decision that individuals make voluntarily, but it should also be noted that there are cases where individu-als are forced to migrate as a result of government-sponsored violence and persecution directed at them because of their membership in a specific tar-get group (Zolberg, Suhrke, & Aguayo, 1989). In these cases, the interna-tional community acknowledges a need for special protection (Zolberg et al., 1989). Individuals escaping persecution in their country of origin may seek temporary protection in a neighboring country and request permission to permanently resettle in a third country as a *refugee*. Individuals are identified as *refugees* if they are unable to return to their country of origin because of persecution or the threat of persecution and are granted permission while abroad to resettle in a host country (Burt & Batalova, 2014). Refugees resettling in the United States are able to apply for lawful permanent resident (LPR) status one year after their admission to the United States (Burt & Batalova, 2014). In 2012, 58,179 individuals were resettled in the United States under refugee status (Burt & Batalova, 2014).

Refugees are granted protected status before arriving in their country of resettlement, but forced migrants may also arrive in a country where they wish to resettle without having been granted this protected status. Such migrants are identified as *asylees*, signifying that they have not been granted refugee status before resettling but instead subsequently request protection upon their arrival (Burt & Batalova, 2014). Asylees do not enter their new country of residence with protected legal status, and therefore they must prove before an immigration court that fear of persecution prevents their return to their country of origin.

The international community distinguishes between *immigrants, refugees*, and *asylees*, but the literature suggests that in practice these distinctions are not always clear (Betts, 2011). Even among individuals not formally recognized as refugees or asylees, material deprivations or a lack of security that will threaten their survival if they remain in their country of origin may force them to migrate (Betts, 2011). Whether migrants are identified as *immigrants, refugees*, or *asylees*, it is important to recognize the complexity of factors driving their migration journey to their new country of residence.

U.S. MIGRATION TRENDS: A HISTORICAL OVERVIEW

An analysis of migration patterns throughout U.S. history illustrates the ways in which multiple factors converge to influence the migrations of specific populations in distinct sociopolitical contexts. This section will offer a brief history of migration flows to the United States from the time of its founding to the present, emphasizing the factors that influenced the migrations of specific populations during distinct periods of U.S. history.

Migration in the Late Eighteenth Through Late Nineteenth Centuries

In the immediate aftermath of U.S. independence in the late eighteenth century, the U.S. government welcomed migrants as a strategy to populate their newly founded territory and to help their economy prosper. Jaggers et al. (2014) refer to this period from 1776 through 1881 as the Open Door era, signifying that there was little to no emphasis on regulating migration flows during this period. The individuals and families who undertook the migration journey to the United States during this period were primarily European: between 1790 and 1892, more than 16 million Europeans migrated to the United States, of whom approximately 90 percent were from the northern European countries of Germany, Great Britain, Ireland, and the Scandinavian region (Bankston & Hidalgo, 2006). Asian migration to the United States also began toward the end of this period, with the first Chinese immigrants arriving in California at the start of the Gold Rush era in 1849 (Paik, Kula, Saito, Rahman, & Witenstein, 2014). Migration to the United States during this period was motivated largely by the lure of employment opportunities and opportunities for economic and social advancement (Bankston & Hidalgo, 2006).

The Beginning of Immigration Regulation

Although the U.S. government welcomed immigrants to help the country prosper after its founding, it began to place regulations on migration flows in the late nineteenth century as the immigrant population continued to grow (Jaggers et al., 2014). Jaggers et al. (2014) define the period from 1882 through 1916 as the Era of Regulation and identify such regulation as largely a result of concerns that increased migration would pose a threat to the country's national and cultural identities. Chinese immigrants in particular were impacted by nativist discrimination, which culminated in the passage of the Chinese Exclusion Act of 1882 (Jaggers et al., 2014; Paik et al., 2014). In response to the fear that Chinese laborers were taking away job opportunities from U.S.-born citizens, the Chinese Exclusion Act of 1882 barred all skilled and unskilled Chinese laborers from entering the United States. The legislation also imposed barriers that made it increasingly difficult for Chinese immigrants who were not laborers to enter the country, thus, by the turn of the twentieth century, largely decreasing the number of Chinese who made the migration journey to the United States (Jaggers et al., 2014; Paik et al., 2014).

In addition to legislation restricting Chinese migration, the U.S. government began to establish ports of entry to process immigrants arriving in the United States. First, Ellis Island in New York was established to process immigrants arriving from Europe, and later Angel Island was established in San Francisco, California, in 1910 to process immigrants arriving from Asia (Jaggers et al., 2014). During the period of these initial regulations, the majority of individuals migrating to the United States continued to be of European origin, although there was a demographic shift from northern Europe to southern and eastern Europe (Bankston & Hidalgo, 2006). From 1901 to 1910, Austria-Hungary, Russia, and Italy were the countries that sent the most immigrants to the United States (Wasem, 2013). Economic factors continued to motivate migration during this period, although a growing number of eastern European migrants, particularly Jewish migrants from Russia, came to the United States to escape political and religious persecution (Bankston & Hidalgo, 2006). In 1910, a growing number of Mexican migrants also began to enter the United States, to escape the violence resulting from the Mexican Revolution (Bankston & Hidalgo, 2006).

The Escalation of Immigration Restriction

The continuing flow of migrants to the United States, and the changing demographics of the migrant population, spurred increased nativist fears and stricter attempts to limit the number and types of individuals entering the United States (Jaggers et al., 2014). Jaggers et al. (2014) characterize these increased regulatory efforts as reflecting an Era of Restriction, which they estimate to have spanned the period from 1917 through 1964. This period of increased restriction began with the Immigration Act of 1917, which both prohibited illiterate individuals over the age of 16 from entering the country and imposed an $8 head tax on all immigrants (Jaggers et al., 2014; Rosales, 2000). The Immigration Act of 1917 was followed in 1924 by legislation that granted entry to the United States according to a nationality-based quota system, which allotted 96 percent of all designated entries to individuals from European countries and prohibited all non-white

Asian migrants from entering the United States (Hernandez, 2010; Rosales, 2000). Because of the necessity of Mexican labor to keep the U.S.
economy strong, Mexicans were exempt from the quota system (Hernandez, 2010; Rosales, 2000). As a result of this restrictive legislation, from 1921
through 1930, migration was predominantly from Europe and Mexico, with
Germany, Canada, Italy, and Mexico sending the most migrants during this
period (Wasem, 2013).

With the onset of the Great Depression in 1929 and the resulting scar-
city of employment, the U.S. government became increasingly concerned
with limiting migration flows. Whereas the U.S. economy had previously
relied on Mexican labor, this demand reversed during the era of the Great
Depression, and the climate in the United States became increasingly hostile to Mexican immigrants (Rosales, 2000). In an effort to curb Mexican
migration, particularly Mexican immigrants who entered the United
States without documents, the government passed legislation in 1929 that
punished individuals caught for a second time without documents with a
fine of $1,000 and a prison term of one year (Rosales, 2000). The political
climate remained hostile to immigrants until the onset of World War II,
when the number of males sent to fight overseas created a labor shortage in
the United States (Rosales, 2000). As migration from Europe dramatically
decreased during World War II (Rumbaut, 1994), the U.S. government
responded to this labor shortage by entering into a formal agreement with
the Mexican government that allowed Mexican men who met specified age
and physical health requirements to enter the United States legally on a
temporary basis as guest workers (Boehm, 2008; Donato, 1994; Gamboa,
1987; Hernandez, 2010; Rosas, 2011). This program, known as the Bracero
program, remained in effect from 1942 through 1964 (Boehm, 2008; Donato,
1994; Gamboa, 1987; Hernandez, 2010; Rosas, 2011). Although adult males
meeting the specified age and health requirements were given legal authorization to work in the United States, demands for labor and unstable economic conditions in Mexico led to a rise in undocumented immigration to
the United States among ineligible males, women, and children from Mexico who sought the same economic opportunities as Bracero laborers (Hernandez, 2006, 2010). This rise in undocumented immigration led to increased enforcement activities on the part of the U.S. government. A 1954
campaign known as Operation Wetback was the most notable enforcement activity of this period. The intent of this highly publicized campaign

was to intensify enforcement efforts, with the aim of demonstrating to the Mexican immigrant community that "illegal" immigration would not be tolerated (Hernandez, 2006, 2010). The period that Jaggers et al. (2014) define as the Era of Restriction is thus characterized both by legislation restricting entry into the United States based on country of origin and by increased efforts to curb and punish "illegal" immigration.

Changing Trends in Migration Flows: 1965 to the Present

Research suggests that migration flows to the United States changed significantly after 1965 as a result of national legislation that ended the nationality-based quota system (Jaggers et al., 2014). Rather than allocating immigrant visas on the basis of national origin, the Immigration and Nationality Act of 1965 allocated 300,000 immigrant visas per year, including 170,000 visas allocated for migrants from the Eastern Hemisphere. Allocations according to hemisphere were eliminated in 1978 (Jaggers et al., 2014). Changing migration patterns were influenced not only by these legislative changes but also by official recognition of the need to grant special protection to individuals fleeing persecution in their country of origin. Although the United Nations' 1951 Convention Relating to the Status of Refugees formally defined the plight of refugees and acknowledged the responsibility of the international community in granting protection to this category of migrants (Zolberg et al., 1989), the United States' acknowledgment of the plight of refugees can be traced to the Refugee Act of 1980. The Refugee Act of 1980 officially adopted the United Nations' definition of refugee and established the Office of Refugee Resettlement to coordinate resettlement efforts (Kennedy, 1981; Office of Refugee Resettlement, n.d.). The establishment of this formalized system for admitting refugees to the United States, coupled with the elimination of the nationality-based quota system, led to demographic shifts in the national origin of individuals migrating to the United States.

Reflecting these changing demographic trends in migration patterns, statistics indicate that from the 1960s to the present, the majority of migrants arrived in the United States from Latin America and Asia (Jaggers et al., 2014; Rumbaut, 1994; Wasem, 2013). In contrast to 1940, when only 13 percent of immigrants were arriving from Latin America and Asia and 86 percent were arriving from Canada and Europe, by 1990, less than

13 percent of the immigrant population were arriving from Canada and Europe and 84 percent were arriving from Asia and Latin America (Rumbaut, 1994). Although the role of legislative changes in shifting patterns of migration flows cannot be ignored, Rumbaut (1994) suggests that the reasons for the changing demographics are more complex. Changes in migration patterns can also be attributed to internal conditions within sending countries in the post–World War II era (Rumbaut, 1994). In order to better understand the changing migration flows and complexity of factors driving migration during this period, the following sections will more closely examine migration to the United States by geographic region.

MIGRATION FROM LATIN AMERICA, 1965 TO THE PRESENT

Data suggest that for each decade between 1981 and 2010, Mexico has been the country sending the most immigrants to the United States (Wasem, 2013). From 1991 to 2000, El Salvador was also among the top seven sending countries, and both El Salvador and Colombia were among the top ten sending countries from 2001 to 2010 (Wasem, 2013). As previously discussed, there has been a long history of migration from Mexico to the United States, fueled by labor demand (Rosales, 2000). Rumbaut states that these historical ties continue to drive migration, noting that "decades of active agricultural labor recruitment . . . preceded the establishment of chain migrations of family members and eventually of large and self-sustaining migratory social networks" (Rumbaut, 1994, p. 597). Referring back to our theoretical overview of the factors influencing decisions to migrate, it is evident that although factors such as economic instability and lack of employment opportunities may drive individuals to emigrate from Mexico, Mexicans are also influenced in their decision to migrate to the United States by factors such as geographic proximity, knowledge of employment opportunities, and the presence of migrant networks that can provide social support and facilitate the process of navigating a new cultural context.

   In order to understand factors driving migration to the United States from Central and South American countries, it is necessary to understand the political climate of the post–World War II era. With the conclusion of World War II came growing tensions between the communist regimes of the East and capitalist countries of the West, with the United States and the Soviet Union vying for the promotion of their political and economic systems throughout Latin America (Sewell, 2008). With Soviet efforts to establish economic and political relationships throughout the region came reciprocal efforts on the part of the U.S. government to establish ties with Latin American countries that would promote their own economic and political interests (Sewell, 2008). Thus, Latin American countries throughout the region were exposed both to communist and capitalist political ideals and were the subjects of substantial intervention from both the United States and the Soviet Union. The result was widespread political instability throughout the region. Guatemala, El Salvador, and Nicaragua all provide telling case examples. In the case of Guatemala, the U.S.-backed overthrow of leftist president Jacobo Arbenz Guzmán in 1954 led to the installation of a military dictatorship, resulting in the deaths of 150,000 to 160,000 people and the disappearance of 40,000 to 45,000 others (Figueroa Ibarra, 2006). Similarly, for more than a decade in the latter half of the twentieth century, El Salvador was the site of civil war between the military-led government, backed by the United States, and a unified front of leftist guerrilla forces (Allison & Alvarez, 2012). In Nicaragua, conflict between the Somoza dictatorship and the leftist Sandinista National Liberation Front led to the overthrow of the Somoza dictatorship in 1979 (Schroeder, 2005). In the wake of this violence pervading the region, migration from Latin America to the United States increased as individuals fled the conflicts that threatened their lives and livelihoods in their countries of origin.

Latin American countries affected by Cold War violence transitioned to democratic governments in the late twentieth century, but a lack of infrastructure has continued to undermine the security of citizens in countries throughout the region (Arias & Goldstein, 2010). Because law enforcement entities are often unable to address acts of violence effectively, gangs and paramilitary forces pose serious security risks to residents (Arias & Goldstein, 2010). The security risks throughout the region, particularly in El Salvador, Guatemala, and Honduras, are reflected in the recent influx of unaccompanied minor children seeking asylum in the United States because of escalating gang violence in their country of origin (United Nations High Commissioner for Refugees, 2014). The recent increase in the number of Central American children fleeing violence and persecution has led the U.S. State Department (2015) to establish an in-country refugee/parole processing program for minors in Honduras, El Salvador, and Guatemala, in an effort to increase the number of children arriving in the United States with protected status.

MIGRATION FROM THE CARIBBEAN, 1965 TO THE PRESENT

Migration flows from the Caribbean to the United States also increased considerably in the latter half of the twentieth century. More than half a million Cubans migrated to the United States in the 1960s, and this number increased to almost 800,000 in the 1970s (Portes & Grosfoguel, 1994). In addition, in each decade between 1981 and 2010, the Dominican Republic has been among the top countries sending immigrants to the United States (Wasem, 2013). Although not among the top sending countries, Jamaica and Haiti have also contributed to migration flows from this region (Portes & Grosfoguel, 1994). Portes and Grosfoguel state that the long history of U.S. economic intervention in the Caribbean has contributed to migration flows, although internal conditions within specific sending countries spurred migration at distinct intervals:

> The effect of overwhelming external hegemony was the creation of insular economies molded entirely by North American interests and the emergence of local societies profoundly dependent in their political and cultural outlook. This orientation established the broad framework for subsequent U.S.-bound migration, although the actualization of each individual outflow responded to specific circumstances. (Portes & Grosfoguel, 1994, p. 52)

In the case of Cuba, the Cuban Revolution, which led to the establishment of Fidel Castro's communist regime, resulted in the influx of middle- and upper-class Cuban migrants who sought political refuge in the United States in the 1960s and 1970s (Portes & Grosfoguel, 1994). The composition of the Cuban population migrating to the United States began to change in the 1980s, when individuals began to arrive in the United States in larger numbers as a result of more difficult economic circumstances (Portes & Grosfoguel, 1994). A large influx of Cuban refugees to the United States closely followed the passage of the Refugee Act of 1980 (Gordon, 1987; Kennedy, 1981).

Initial migration from the Dominican Republic and Haiti was also driven by political circumstances. The first wave of Dominican migration to the United States occurred during the political upheaval following the assassination of dictator Rafael Leónidas Trujillo in 1961 and increased during the 1970s and 1980s because of worsening economic conditions (Portes & Grosfoguel, 1994). Migrants from the Dominican Republic were primarily individuals from the urban working class. In the case of Haiti, the first wave of migrants arrived in the United States seeking refuge from the dictatorship of François Duvalier. Although these individuals were primarily from the middle class, individuals who were experiencing harder economic circumstances soon joined this first wave of migrants. In the case of Jamaica, factors influencing migration were of a different nature than those of the Dominican Republic and Haiti. Policies in Great Britain that restricted the entry of Jamaican immigrants, coupled with efforts by the United States to recruit Jamaican laborers and professionals, led to increased migration from Jamaica to the United States. Jamaican immigrants included laborers recruited to work on sugar plantations in Florida, as well as individuals entering the personal service sector and professionals, primarily nurses, recruited to address U.S. labor demands (Portes & Grosfoguel, 1994). The diversity of the migrant population from the Caribbean region again illustrates how a convergence of factors, including economic conditions, labor demands, ties with the United States, and internal political conditions in sending countries, all drive migration.

MIGRATION FROM ASIA, 1965 TO THE PRESENT

Paik et al. (2014) discuss the importance of recognizing the unique sociopolitical contexts influencing migration from distinct Asian regions in order to understand migration flows from Asia in the post–World War II era. In the case of the Philippines, Rumbaut (1994) discusses how the nation's colonial ties to the United States influenced individuals' decisions to migrate. Rumbaut (1994) states that, throughout U.S. history, these colonial ties have led to active recruitment of Filipino laborers, and, as in the case of Mexico, this has facilitated the establishment of migrant networks that drive subsequent migration. Ties between the United States and the Philippines can help explain the fact that the Philippines was the country sending the second largest number of immigrants to the United States in each decade between 1981 and 2010 (Wasem, 2013).

Another explanation for the patterns of migration to the United States from other Asian regions is U.S. involvement and intervention in the

sending countries (Rumbaut, 1994). Paik et al. (2014) state that a large influence on the increase in Korean migration to the United States after the
1950s was U.S. intervention in the Korean War. India was also among the
countries sending the most immigrants to the United States from 1981
through 2010 (Wasem, 2013). This wave of immigrants from India was
largely comprised of skilled professionals (Paik et al., 2014), and U.S. involvement in India in the form of foreign aid and technical assistance is
thought to contribute to migration decisions among professionals in search
of opportunities for economic advancement (Rumbaut, 1994). The United
States was also a resettlement location for Southeast Asian refugees from
Vietnam, Laos, and Cambodia after their governments fell to communist
regimes in 1975 (Gordon, 1987). Rumbaut points out that the post-1970 influx of Vietnamese political refugees arriving in the United States can be
understood as "a dialectical legacy of the U.S. role in the Indochina War"
(Rumbaut, 1994, p. 598) during the Cold War era. Although the number
of Vietnamese refugees entering the United States has decreased in recent
decades, Southeast Asian refugees continue to comprise a sizable percentage of the U.S. refugee population (Burt & Batalova, 2014). Recent statistics indicate that refugees from the Southeast Asian country of Burma have
constituted the largest group of refugees resettled in the United States over
the past decade (Burt & Batalova, 2014). This brief overview of patterns of
Asian migration from the mid-1960s through the present thus suggests
that, similar to migration patterns observed in Latin America and the
Caribbean, increased migration to the United States was influenced by
a convergence of factors related to economic conditions, internal political
conditions within sending countries, and ties between sending countries
and the United States, often related to U.S. foreign policy and patterns of
intervention in the sending countries.

MIGRATION FROM AFRICA, 1965 TO THE PRESENT

Although African countries have not been among the top senders of immigrants to the United States from the 1960s to the present, it is still noteworthy that migration from Africa increased throughout the latter half of
the twentieth century (Rumbaut, 1994). In the late twentieth and early
twenty-first centuries, the largest numbers of African migrants have been
arriving in the United States from Nigeria and Ethiopia, followed by

Ghana, Egypt, Kenya, Morocco, Somalia, South Africa, Sudan, and Liberia (Bankston & Hidalgo, 2006). Although this population of migrants includes immigrants in search of employment opportunities, a significant number of Africans enter the United States as refugees fleeing violent conflict and political instability in their countries of origin. Estimates suggest that almost 115,000 African refugees entered the United States between 1990 and 2003 (Bankston & Hidalgo, 2006). Somalis have comprised the third largest group of refugees resettled in the United States over the past decade, and the African countries of Somalia, Democratic Republic of the Congo, Eritrea, Sudan, and Ethiopia were all among the top ten countries sending refugees in 2012 (Burt & Batalova, 2014).

MIGRATION FROM THE MIDDLE EAST, 1965 TO THE PRESENT

Although the Middle East is not a top region sending immigrants, the overall number of Middle Eastern immigrants to the United States has increased over the past several decades (Auclair & Batalova, 2013). Iraqis comprise the largest population of immigrants from the region, whereas immigrants from Saudi Arabia and Yemen represent the fastest-growing Middle Eastern immigrant populations (Auclair & Batalova, 2013). Iraq and Iran were also among the top ten countries sending refugees in 2012 as a result of political instability and violence (Auclair & Batalova, 2013; Burt & Batalova, 2014). It is important to be aware of the negative attention that Middle Eastern migrants in the United States have received since the attacks on September 11, 2001 (Auclair & Batalova, 2013).

THE NEED FOR CULTURALLY RESPONSIVE PRACTICE WITH IMMIGRANT AND REFUGEE CHILDREN AND FAMILIES

Culturally responsive practice involves using the cultural knowledge and experiences of diverse clients to inform the ways in which social work practitioners engage, assess, and intervene with them. It acknowledges that the social worker does not have a full understanding of another person's culture, and it places the social worker in the role of learner, to learn about the client's culture and to use this information in the practice. It also acknowledges the legitimacy and importance of another's culture and unique cultural experiences. In this way, culturally responsive practice is a very individualized approach to social work practice.

The previous sections have illustrated that migration is a complex phenomenon that presents unique and individualized challenges for the children and families undertaking the migration journey. Not only may children and families have experienced trauma in their country of origin that motivated their departure, but upon their arrival in the United States, they are also faced with the task of navigating an unfamiliar cultural context, often with limited support. At the same time, immigrant and refugee children and families often experience increased barriers to accessing supportive services because of the limited availability of services that are culturally and linguistically responsive. An awareness of the unique experiences of immigrant and refugee children and families is an essential first step in providing services that address the needs of this population in a culturally responsive manner.

Culturally responsive practice is necessary, but it requires a determined commitment and dedicated focus to learn about differences between the different ethnic groups and even within a single ethnic group (Dettlaff & Fong, 2012; Fong, 2003; Lum, 2011). Ethnicity is not the only diverse factor to be conscious of; religious differences, such as Muslim practices, also need to be considered with cultural humility (Gallardo, 2014; Ortega & Faller, 2011). A goal of this book is to provide you with insight into the unique experiences of this population, as well as information on culturally responsive strategies for addressing their needs, giving you the necessary tools to support immigrant and refugee children and families in your practice.

CONCLUSION: IMPLICATIONS FOR SOCIAL WORK PRACTICE IN THE PRESENT

The information presented in this chapter suggests not only that the foreign-born population in the United States has reached a historic high (Zong & Batalova, 2015) but also that the U.S. immigrant population is becoming increasingly diverse in terms of their country of origin, legal status, employment and educational backgrounds, and reasons for migration (Rumbaut, 1994). The new immigrant population faces an increasingly hostile climate in the aftermath of the terrorist attacks of September 11,

2001, as increased emphasis on national security has resulted in the perception that immigrants pose a threat to the security of U.S.-born citizens (Burt & Batalova, 2014; Castles & Miller, 2009). Current stalemates in passing legislation on comprehensive national immigration reform reflect a political climate in which the issue of immigration is polarized and emotionally charged (Giovagnnoli, 2013). In this polarized political climate, decisions on how to address the needs of the immigrant population and facilitate their integration into U.S. society are left to individual states, which leads to diversity in service accessibility and the rights that immigrants are afforded according to the state in which they reside (Jaggers et al., 2014). This information suggests not only that there is considerable diversity among the immigrant population arriving in the United States but also that there are marked differences in their postarrival reception and experience depending on the geographic region in which they settle.

An understanding of both the heterogeneity of the immigrant population and the diversity of their experiences upon their arrival in the United States is essential for effective social work practice with this population. In turn, an understanding of the historical factors contributing to present migration patterns, as well as knowledge of the complex circumstances that lead individuals to migrate, is the first step toward informing effective practice. It is for these reasons that this book has begun with a theoretical overview of why people migrate and a historical overview of trends in migration patterns throughout history. As you continue to progress through this book and learn more about current policies and effective practices for serving the immigrant and refugee populations, it will be beneficial to contextualize this information within the historical backdrop that has been provided.

KEY TERMS

ASYLEES Migrants who have not been granted refugee status before resettling but subsequently request protection upon arrival in the new country.

CHINESE EXCLUSION ACT OF 1882 A law that barred all skilled and unskilled Chinese laborers from entering the United States.

CULTURAL HUMILITY The practice of offering services to diverse clients with a sense of humility in learning about their cultural values, beliefs, and protocols.

CULTURALLY RESPONSIVE PRACTICE   The process and practice of social work
practitioners, researchers, policymakers, administrators, and advocates acquiring knowledge and skills about diversity components of cultures.

REFUGEES   Individuals who are unable to return to their country of origin
because of persecution or the threat of persecution and who have been granted
permission while abroad to resettle in a host country.

STUDY QUESTIONS

1 What are the differences between an immigrant, a refugee, and an asylee?
2 What are the two kinds of migration, and how do they differ from one
another?
3 What are migrant networks, and why are they important?
4 What are some of the reasons that contribute to migration journeys?
5 What is cultural humility, and how does it promote culturally responsive
practice?

ADDITIONAL RESOURCES

First Focus Center for the Children of Immigrants: http://firstfocus.org
/issues/children-of-immigrants/

Immigrant Legal Resource Center: http://www.ilrc.org

Migration Policy Institute: http://www.migrationpolicy.orgOffice of Refugee
Resettlement: http://www.acf.hhs.gov/programs/orr

Unaccompanied Children's Services Program of the Office of Refugee
Resettlement: http://www.acf.hhs.gov/programs/orr/programs/ucs

REFERENCES

Allison, M. E., & Alvarez, A. M. (2012). Unity and disunity in the FMLN. *Latin
American Politics & Society, 54*(4), 89–118.

Arias, D., & Goldstein, D. (2010). Violent pluralism: Understanding the new
democracies of Latin America. In D. Arias and D. Goldstein (Eds.), *Violent democracies in Latin America* (pp. 1–34). Durham, NC: Duke University Press.

Auclair, G., & Batalova, J. (2013). Middle Eastern and North African immigrants
in the United States. Retrieved from http://www.migrationpolicy.org/article
/middle-eastern-and-north-african-immigrants-united-states

Bankston, C. L., & Hidalgo, D. A. (Eds.). (2006). *Immigration in U.S. history* (Vols. 1–2). Pasadena, CA: Salem.

Betts, A. (2011). *Survival migration: Failed governance and the crisis of displacement.* Ithaca, NY: Cornell University Press.

Boehm, D. A. (2008). "Now I am a man and a woman!": Gendered moves and migrations in a transnational Mexican community. *Latin American Perspectives, 35*(1), 16–30.

Brettell, C. B., & Hollifield, J. F. (2008). Introduction. In C. B. Brettell and J. F. Hollifield (Eds.), *Migration theory: Talking across disciplines* (2nd ed., pp. 1–30). New York, NY: Routledge.

Burt, L., & Batalova, J. (2014). Refugees and asylees in the United States. Retrieved from http://www.migrationpolicy.org/article/refugees-and-asylees-united -states

Castles, S., & Miller, M. J. (2009). *The age of migration: International population movements in the modern world* (4th ed.). New York, NY: Palgrave Macmillan.

Dettlaff, A., & Fong, A. (Eds.). (2012). *Child welfare practice with immigrant children and families.* New York, NY: Routledge Taylor and Francis.

Donato, K. M. (1994). Policy and Mexican migration to the United States, 1942– 92. *Social Science Quarterly, 75*(4), 705–729.

Figueroa Ibarra, C. (2006). The culture of terror and Cold War in Guatemala. *Journal of Genocide Research, 8*(2), 191–208.

Fong, R. (Ed.). (2003).*Culturally competent practice with immigrant and refugee children and families.* New York, NY: Guilford.

Gallardo, E. (Ed.). (2014). *Developing cultural humility: Embracing race, privilege, and power.* Los Angeles, CA: Sage.

Gamboa, E. (1987). Braceros in the Pacific Northwest: Laborers on the domestic front, 1942–1947. *Pacific Historical Review, 56*(3), 378–398.

Giovagnnoli, M. (2013). Overhauling immigration law: A brief history and basic principles of reform. Retrieved from http://www.immigrationpolicy .org/perspectives/overhauling-immigration-law-brief-history-and-basic -principles-reform

Gordon, L. W. (1987). Southeast Asian refugee migration to the United States. *Center for Migration Studies Special Issues, 5*(3), 153–173.

Hernandez, K. L. (2006). The crimes and consequences of illegal immigration: A cross-border examination of Operation Wetback, 1943 to 1954. *Western Historical Quarterly, 37*(4), 421–444.

——. (2010). *Migra! A history of the U.S. Border Patrol*. Berkeley: University of California Press.

Jaggers, J., Gabbard, W. J., & Jaggers, S. J. (2014). The devolution of U.S. immigration policy: An examination of the history and future of U.S. immigration policy. *Journal of Policy Practice, 13*(1), 3–15.

Kennedy, E. M. (1981). Refugee Act of 1980. *International Migration Review, 15*(1–2), 141–156.

Lum, D. (2011). *Culturally competent practice: A framework for understanding diverse groups and justice issues*. Belmont, CA: Brooks/Cole.

Massey, D. S., Durand, J., & Malone, N. J. (2003). *Beyond smoke and mirrors: Mexican immigration in an era of economic integration*. New York, NY: Russell Sage Foundation.

Office of Refugee Resettlement. (n.d.). History. Retrieved from http://www.acf.hhs.gov/programs/orr/about/history

Ortega, R., & Faller, K. (2011). Training child welfare workers from an intersectional cultural humility perspective: A paradigm shift. *Child Welfare, 90*, 27–49.

Paik, S. J., Kula, S. M., Saito, L. E., Rahman, Z., & Witenstein, M. A. (2014). Historical perspectives on diverse Asian American communities: Immigration, incorporation, and education. *Teachers College Record, 116*(8), 1–45.

Portes, A., & Grosfoguel, R. (1994). Caribbean diasporas: Migration and ethnic communities. *Annals of the American Academy of Political and Social Science, 533*, 48–69.

Rosales, F. A. (Ed.). (2000). *Testimonio: A documentary history of the Mexican-American struggle for civil rights*. Houston, TX: Arte Público.

Rosas, A. E. (2011). Breaking the silence: Mexican children and women's confrontation of Bracero family separation, 1942–1964. *Gender & History, 23*(2), 382–400.

Rumbaut, R. G. (1994). Origins and destinies: Immigration to the United States since World War II. *Sociological Forum, 9*(4), 583–621.

Schroeder, M. J. (2005). Bandits and blanket thieves, communists and terrorists: The politics of naming Sandinistas in Nicaragua, 1927–36 and 1979–90. *Third World Quarterly, 26*(1), 67–86.

Sewell, B. (2008). A perfect (free-market) world? Economics, the Eisenhower administration, and the Soviet economic offensive in Latin America. *Diplomatic History, 32*(5), 841–868.

United Nations High Commissioner for Refugees. (2014). *Children on the run: Unaccompanied children leaving Central America and Mexico and the need for*

international protection. Retrieved from http://www.unhcrwashington.org
/sites/default/files/1_UAC_Children on the Run_Full Report.pdf

U.S. State Department. (2015). *In-country refugee/parole processing for minors in
Honduras, El Salvador, and Guatemala (Central American Minors—CAM).*
Retrieved from http://www.acf.hhs.gov/programs/orr/resource/in-country
-refugee-parole-processing-for-minors-in-honduras-el-salvador-and-guatemala
-central-american-minors-cam

Wasem, R. E. (2013). *U.S. immigration policy: Chart book of key trends* (Congressional Research Service Publication No. 7-5700). Retrieved from http://www
.fas.org/sgp/crs/homesec/R42988.pdf

Zolberg, A. R., Suhrke, A., & Aguayo, S. (1989). *Escape from violence: Conflict and
the refugee crisis in the developing world.* New York, NY: Oxford University
Press.

Zong, J., & Batalova, J. (2015). Frequently requested statistics on immigrants and
immigration in the United States. Retrieved from http://www.migrationpolicy
.org/article/frequently-requested-statistics-immigrants-and-immigration
-united-states/

CHAPTER 2

Overview of the U.S. Immigration System

▸ *ELIZABETH FRANKEL*

THE HISTORY OF U.S. IMMIGRATION LAW is marked by two competing philosophies. The first is best described by Emma Lazarus's famous words inscribed on the Statue of Liberty: "Give us your tired, your poor, your huddled masses yearning to breathe free, the wretched refuse of your teeming shore. Send these, the homeless, tempest-tost to me, I lift my lamp beside the golden door." Written in 1883, these words reflect the nation's attitude in the early years following U.S. independence (Gordon, Mailman, & Yale-Loehr, 2015). At that time, U.S. society had a liberal philosophy toward immigration, where immigrant laborers and settlers were encouraged to come to the United States and help build and protect this new country (Gordon et al., 2015). Immigrants—most of whom were Europeans arriving largely from Ireland, Germany, France, and England—were generally welcomed during this time, and the government did little to regulate immigration (Gordon et al., 2015).

Beginning in the 1830s, the dominant immigrant groups migrating to the United States shifted, and with that shift came a change in attitude toward these newcomers (Fuchs & Martin, 2012). First, beginning in that decade, there was a large increase in Irish immigrants fleeing the potato famines and economic hardship (Fuchs & Martin, 2012). Between 1820 and 1880, millions of Irish Catholics left Europe and immigrated to the United States in search of economic opportunity (Weissbrodt & Danielson, 2011). Around the mid-nineteenth century, there was a wave of German Catholic immigrants migrating to the United States following the depressions in Europe (Weissbrodt & Danielson, 2011). Finally, the discovery of gold in California in 1848, combined with the Taiping Rebellion in China from 1850 to 1864, caused a large number of Chinese laborers to immigrate to California (Hing, 1993). The arriving immigrants began to compete with U.S. laborers for jobs (Fuchs & Martin, 2012). Furthermore, since the United States was largely Protestant at that time, the new arrivals, many of whom were Catholic, were not well received (Weissbrodt, 1998). These changes triggered an explosion of racial and religious prejudice and class conflict. New immigrants became the targets of physical and verbal attacks (Fuchs & Martin, 2012). With this new attitude came a new philosophy toward immigration that was highly restrictionist, emphasizing the need to protect U.S. borders and place limits on those allowed to enter the country (Fuchs & Martin, 2012). This anti-immigrant sentiment culminated in the passage of the Chinese Exclusion Act of 1882, an openly racist law, which prohibited the admission of all Chinese laborers to the United States (Fuchs & Martin, 2012).

Following suit, in 1924, Congress passed the National Origins Act, designed to maintain the ethnic status quo by creating quotas for each nation based on the percentage of people of that nationality living in the United States at the time of the 1890 Census (Fuchs & Martin, 2012). Use of the 1890 Census was openly discriminatory, allowing higher entry rates for immigrants from northern and western Europe while lowering quotas for the "new" immigrants from southern and eastern Europe (Fuchs & Martin, 2012). As a result of the National Origins Act, during World War II, the United States turned away thousands of refugees seeking protection from Nazi Germany because allowing them entry would have exceeded the requisite quotas (Fuchs & Martin, 2012).

In 1952, Congress passed the Immigration and Nationality Act (INA), combining all previous immigration laws into one statute (Fuchs & Martin, 2012). Although the INA has been amended substantially over the years, it remains the law governing immigration in the United States. The 1952 INA established a system of preference categories for immigrants with family in the United States—U.S. citizens or lawful permanent residents (LPRs)—and for those with skills needed in the labor market (Fuchs & Martin, 2012). The INA prescribed numerical limits for each category of immigrant and left the national origins quota system in effect (Fuchs & Martin, 2012; Gordon et al., 2015). It was not until 1965 that amendments to the Immigration and Nationality Act abolished the national origins quotas (Fuchs & Martin, 2012; Gordon et al., 2015). In its place, the amendments established a cap of 160,000 for those emigrating from the Eastern Hemisphere (with a limit of no more than 20,000 per country) and 120,000 on those emigrating from the Western Hemisphere (without per-country limits) (Fuchs & Martin, 2012; Gordon et al., 2015). Eventually, in 1978, legislation was passed combining the caps on those emigrating from both hemispheres to a worldwide total of 290,000 (Fuchs & Martin, 2012).

In the 1970s and 1980s, the United States saw a dramatic increase in the migration of undocumented immigrants to the United States (Weissbrodt, 1998). In 1986, Congress passed the Immigration Reform and Control Act (IRCA), which sought to deter future unauthorized immigration by creating a system of sanctions for employers who hired undocumented workers while at the same time creating a path to status for the millions of immigrants living in the United States unlawfully. Through IRCA, undocumented immigrants who had been living in the United States as of January 1, 1982, were able to obtain conditional legal status and eventually status as legal permanent residents after passing certain tests, similar to the current naturalization requirements. The Immigration Reform and Control Act also had provisions for the legalization of certain agricultural workers. As a result of IRCA, 2.7 million undocumented immigrants were able to obtain lawful immigration status (Martin, 2012). The Immigration Reform and Control Act remains the most extensive legalization program ever passed by Congress. Since IRCA, Congress has at times passed legislation allowing the legalization of certain nationalities, but nothing as extensive as IRCA has been passed (Legomsky & Rodriguez, 2015).

One problem with IRCA was that, although it allowed the legalization of many undocumented immigrants living in the United States, it did not provide for the admission of family members of those legalized (Martin, 2012). Because those legalized under IRCA were disproportionately from Mexico, and there were per-country limits placed on family-based immigration for relatives of lawful permanent residents, the wait time for family members grew substantially (Martin, 2012). In response to this problem, among others, Congress passed the Immigration Act of 1990 (Martin, 2012). The Immigration Act of 1990 increased the numerical ceilings for immigrant admissions to 480,000 for family-based immigrants (up from 216,000) and to 140,000 for employment-based immigrants (up from 54,000) (Gordon et al., 2015; Martin, 2012). It also created a lottery system that awards visas randomly to applicants from countries with low admission rates (Gordon et al., 2015). Finally, it granted legal residence to thousands of spouses and minor children of those who received status under IRCA (Weissbrodt, 1998).

Throughout the 1990s, anti-immigrant sentiment escalated (Gordon et al., 2015). In 1996, Congress passed three bills that together drastically swept back many protections and rights held by immigrants. First, the Anti-terrorism and Effective Death Penalty Act (AEDPA), passed in the aftermath of the Oklahoma City bombings, greatly expanded the grounds for deportation of noncitizens convicted of crimes. That same year, Congress passed the Personal Responsibility and Work Opportunity Reconciliation Act (welfare reform), which reversed prior law, making LPRs ineligible for federal benefits, including food stamps and supplemental security income. Finally, Congress passed the Illegal Immigration Reform and Immigrant Responsibility Act of 1996 (IIRIRA), the most sweeping bill to roll back protections for undocumented immigrants and lawful permanent residents. This legislation further expanded the grounds for removal of noncitizens, limited paths to relief from removal, and introduced expedited procedures for deporting noncitizens. After 1996, there was little change to U.S. immigration law until the Homeland Security Act, passed in the wake of the September 11, 2001, attacks and described later in this chapter.

Beginning in the early twenty-first century, many state and local governments started to pass laws seeking to restrict the rights of immigrants living within their borders. Most famously, in 2010, Arizona passed the controversial Senate Bill 1070 (SB 1070), which consisted of numerous provisions aimed at identifying undocumented immigrants living within the state of Arizona, including making it a state crime to apply for work without authorization or to fail to carry "an alien registration document." One of the most controversial provisions of the law required that, during a lawful stop, detention, or arrest, state and local law enforcement attempt to determine an individual's immigration status when there is "reasonable suspicion" that the individual is in the country unlawfully. In 2012, the U.S. Supreme Court struck down many of the provisions in Arizona's SB 1070, but it upheld the provision allowing law enforcement to question an individual's immigration status during a routine stop (*Arizona v. United States*, 2012). Since the passage of Arizona's SB 1070, many other states have followed suit, passing similar legislation aimed at identifying noncitizens living within state borders.

Today, with millions of undocumented immigrants living in the shadows, it is largely recognized that our immigration system needs reform. Yet, there is great debate over what those reforms should look like. There is constant tension between securing U.S. borders and the desire to protect vulnerable groups, including children, families, and those seeking humanitarian protection. Although many people hope that federal reform is on the horizon, it is unclear what that reform will look like and when it will happen.

THE KEY FEDERAL AGENCIES TASKED
WITH ENFORCING U.S. IMMIGRATION LAW

The Immigration and Naturalization Service (INS) was established in 1933, and for 70 years it served as the primary agency tasked with immigration enforcement (Aleinikoff, Martin, Motomura, & Fullerton, 2012). As such, the INS had a myriad of functions, including the inspection of immigrants arriving at U.S. borders and ports of entry, the prosecution and removal of individuals present in the United States without proper documentation, and the processing of applications for asylum and other immigration benefits.

The events of September 11, 2001, triggered a dramatic restructuring of agencies responsible for homeland security (Aleinikoff et al., 2012). In 2002, Congress passed the Homeland Security Act, which dissolved the INS and transferred most of its functions to the U.S. Department of Homeland Security (DHS). The DHS is a cabinet-level department of the U.S. government and is charged with protecting the United States from threats that can occur both within and outside its borders, including terrorism and natural disasters (Aleinikoff et al., 2012). As a result of the Homeland Security Act, the former functions of the INS were divided among three separate agencies within DHS: (1) Customs and Border Protection (CBP), (2) Immigration and Customs Enforcement (ICE), and (3) U.S. Citizenship and Immigration Services (USCIS) (Aleinikoff et al., 2012). The immigration courts are housed in a separate branch of government, the Department of Justice. The following section outlines the functions of these federal agencies with regard to immigration enforcement.

CUSTOMS AND BORDER PROTECTION
AND IMMIGRATION AND CUSTOMS ENFORCEMENT

Customs and Border Protection and Immigration and Customs Enforcement are the two primary agencies charged with immigration enforcement. The first is responsible for border security, enforcing hundreds of U.S. laws and regulations, including those related to trade, drugs, and immigration (Aleinikoff et al., 2012, pp. 242–243). It posts officers at official land, air, and sea ports of entry and is responsible for apprehending individuals attempting to enter the United States without authorization (Aleinikoff et al., 2012, pp. 242–243). Most undocumented immigrants are first apprehended by CBP authorities near the U.S.-Mexico border.

In contrast to CBP, ICE focuses primarily on interior immigration enforcement (Aleinikoff et al., 2012). Apprehensions by ICE may take place through raids at factories, restaurants, or other places that employ large numbers of immigrants, on public transportation, or in private homes (Legomsky et al., 2015). In addition, ICE may be notified by state or local law enforcement when immigrants are arrested through the criminal process (Legomsky et al., 2015). The Office of Enforcement and Removal Operations (ERO) is the primary enforcement arm of ICE and is responsible for the identification, apprehension, and deportation of removable aliens from the United States (Aleinikoff et al., 2012). It oversees a vast network of adult detention facilities (Aleinikoff et al., 2012).

U.S. CITIZENSHIP AND IMMIGRATION SERVICES

U.S. Citizenship and Immigration Services (USCIS) is the administrative and service branch of DHS (Aleinikoff et al., 2012, pp. 246–248). It processes immigrant visa petitions and applications for U.S. citizenship, as well as asylum and refugee applications. Its officers, who are not necessarily attorneys, then adjudicate these claims for relief. Many of the forms of immigration relief described in Section IV, including affirmative asylum applications, T visas (for victims of human trafficking), U visas (available to victims of certain crimes who cooperate with law enforcement and are able to obtain a certification from law enforcement verifying that they participated in the detection, investigation, or prosecution of criminal activity), and SIJS (Special Immigrant Juvenile Status), are adjudicated by

USCIS. Generally, proceedings before USCIS are less adversarial than in immigration court. Noncitizens either may present their claims for relief entirely on paper or may have an interview with a USCIS officer. There is no judge or ICE trial attorney present to cross-examine an individual during a USCIS interview.

IMMIGRATION COURTS

The immigration courts are housed within the Department of Justice Executive Office for Immigration Review (EOIR). As explained in more detail in the next section, once apprehended, many noncitizens are placed in removal (deportation) proceedings. These proceedings are heard by immigration judges around the country. The proceedings are adversarial, with an attorney from the ICE Office of Chief Counsel prosecuting the case on behalf of the Department of Homeland Security. Immigration judges make decisions about whether noncitizens are subject to removal and whether an individual qualifies for certain forms of relief from removal.

LEGAL RIGHTS AFFORDED IMMIGRANTS
UPON APPREHENSION

Once an individual is apprehended, ICE or CBP may offer the person the option of Voluntary Departure (INA § 240B, 8 U.S.C.A. § 1229c, 2015). Voluntary Departure means that the noncitizen may leave the United States without incurring the fines and penalties typically attached to an order of removal. By contrast, a noncitizen ordered removed faces anywhere from a 10 year to a lifetime bar from returning. Individuals granted Voluntary Departure may later return legally to the United States and will not face any penalty for having previously entered unlawfully. However, by taking a Voluntary Departure, the individual forgoes the opportunity to appear before an immigration judge and argue that he has a right to remain in the United States. An individual who does not initially accept Voluntary Departure may be afforded another opportunity before the immigration court; however, there are no guarantees that ICE will agree to a Voluntary Departure at a later date.

If an individual either is not offered or does not accept a Voluntary Departure, then DHS will typically serve the noncitizen with a Notice to

Appear (NTA), placing the individual in removal proceedings (INA §239, 8 U.S.C.A. § 1229, 2015; 8 C.F.R. § 239, 2015). The Department of Homeland Security must then file the Notice to Appear with the immigration court, and the immigration court will send notice of the date of the first master calendar hearing on the case. A master calendar hearing is a short status hearing, where the respondent may be asked to plead to the allegations in the Notice to Appear. If a noncitizen is seeking certain forms of relief from removal, the court will schedule an individual hearing on the case. Because of backlogs in the immigration courts, subsequent hearings may be scheduled years after the initial master calendar hearing.

The Department of Homeland Security must also decide whether to place an apprehended immigrant in detention pending the outcome of removal proceedings. In some cases, the noncitizen may be subject to mandatory detention; this is typically the case for those accused of committing crimes that render the person removable (INA § 236(c), 8 U.S.C.A. § 1226(c), 2015). If an individual is not subject to mandatory detention, then ICE has discretion to decide whether to detain the individual with or without bond or to release the individual on conditional parole (INA § 236(a), 8 U.S.C.A. § 1226(a), 2015). The Department of Homeland Security is typically required to make these decisions within 48 hours of apprehension (8 C.F.R. § 287.3(d), 2015).

The Department of Homeland Security retains enormous discretion with regard to enforcement-related decisions, including whether to stop and question an individual, whether to serve an NTA, and whether to place the individual in detention. In August 2013, ICE issued a directive with the goal of ensuring that immigration enforcement does not unnecessarily break apart families or undermine parental rights (U.S. Immigration and Customs Enforcement, 2013). The policy provides that ICE should pay special attention to cases involving parents or legal guardians who are caretakers involved in child welfare proceedings or who have U.S. citizen or LPR children. The directive provides that "ICE will maintain a comprehensive process for identifying, placing, monitoring, accommodating, and removing alien parents or legal guardians of minor children while safeguarding their parental rights."

Although noncitizens are recognized as having certain due process protections, namely the right to a hearing before an immigration judge, noncitizens do not have a right to counsel at government expense. As a result, even though proceedings are adversarial and the government is represented by counsel, many noncitizens—including families and children—appear in immigration court alone.

SPECIAL PROVISIONS FOR UNACCOMPANIED IMMIGRANT CHILDREN

Unaccompanied immigrant children are children who have come to the United States alone, without a parent or guardian. Until recently, the number of unaccompanied children arriving in the United States each year remained fairly low at approximately 8,000 children a year (U.S. Department of Health and Human Services, 2014). The number started to rise steadily in 2011, and in 2014, approximately 57,000 unaccompanied immigrant children were placed in federal custody, the highest number to date (U.S. Department of Health and Human Services, 2014).

When a child is apprehended by Customs and Border Patrol or Immigration and Customs Enforcement, the agency must first determine whether the child is an "unaccompanied alien child"—a legal term of art meaning that the child is under 18 years of age, without lawful status, and without a parent or legal guardian available to provide care at that time (Homeland Security Act § 462(g)(2), 6 U.S.C. § 279(g)(2), 2002). If the child is determined to be unaccompanied, CBP or ICE has 72 hours to transfer the child to the custody of the Department of Health and Human Services (HHS) Office of Refugee Resettlement (ORR), the federal agency charged with the care and custody of unaccompanied minors (William Wilberforce Trafficking Victims Protection Reauthorization Act [TVPRA] § 235(b)(3), 8 U.S.C. § 1232(b)(3), 2008).

The Office of Refugee Resettlement contracts with local nonprofits that run the facilities that house unaccompanied immigrant children (U.S. Department of Health and Human Services, 2015). Initially, the children are placed in shelters or more secure detention facilities around the country. There are three general types of ORR facilities, ranging from the least restrictive to the most restrictive:

- Shelter care: This is the most common facility, with the lowest level of security and the highest number of children per staff. In some locations, ORR-funded "shelter care" is a kind of short-term group home.

- Staff-secure: These facilities have higher security and a higher staff-to-child ratio. They are for children identified as having behavioral issues or juvenile delinquency histories, or those considered flight risks.
- Secure: These facilities are generally state-run juvenile detention facilities, with which ORR contracts on a per-child basis. These facilities are supposed to be limited to children who pose an unacceptable flight risk or a risk to themselves or others.

The Office of Refugee Resettlement also operates therapeutic facilities, or contracts for services with state or county residential treatment centers, for children with significant mental health needs. While the children are in its care, ORR must provide them with basic necessities, including food and clothing. It must also provide the children with education, medical care, recreational time, and telephone contact with family members.

In 2008, Congress passed the William Wilberforce Trafficking Victims Protection Reauthorization Act (TVPRA), which modified the responsibilities of HHS toward unaccompanied immigrant children. Pursuant to the TVPRA, ORR must promptly place children in the least restrictive setting that is in the best interests of the child (TVPRA, § 235(c)(2), 8 U.S.C. § 1232(c)(2), 2015). A child should only be placed in a secure facility if it has been determined that the child poses a danger to self or others or has been charged with certain criminal or juvenile delinquency offenses. The placement of a child in a secure facility should be reviewed on a monthly basis.

For most children in ORR care, the ultimate goal is release to family members in the United States. Before placing a child with relatives or others, HHS must first determine that such person or entity is capable of providing for the child's physical and mental well-being and that the placement is safe (TVPRA, § 235(c)(3)(A), 8 U.S.C.A. § 1232(c)(3)(A), 2015). The determination must include verification of the proposed custodian's relationship to the child, and an independent finding that the individual has not engaged in any activity that would indicate a potential risk to the child. For children with no family in the United States, ORR also has some long-term foster care placements for children who have been identified as qualifying for legal relief to remain in the United States.

Like adults, immigrant children have no right to counsel at government expense; however, the TVPRA does require that ORR provide *access* to counsel for unaccompanied children in their care (TVPRA, § 235(c)(5), 8 U.S.C.A. § 1232(c)(5), 2015). As a result, ORR currently provides funding for legal service providers around the country to give Know Your Rights presentations and legal screenings to the children. The legal service providers are also able to represent some of the children in care; however, resources for direct representation remain limited, with many nonprofits relying on the services of pro bono attorneys at large law firms.

PATHS TO LAWFUL STATUS FOR CHILDREN AND FAMILIES

CASE STUDY: EMILIA

Emilia, now 15 years old, was brought to the United States from Mexico by her mother in 2001, when she was just a small child. Emilia grew up in Chicago and is currently in high school.

Emilia has never met her father, who abandoned her mother before Emilia was born. When Emilia was 5 years old, her mother married a U.S. citizen. Emilia's stepfather has a drinking problem and is physically abusive to both Emilia and her mother. Emilia's stepfather threatened to call immigration if Emilia's mother ever tried to leave him, so Emilia's mother is terrified to try and get help.

One night, Emilia's mother and stepfather were fighting and a neighbor overheard and called the police. When the police arrived, the officer could tell that something was wrong, but Emilia's mother would not share anything with the police and told the officer that she did not want to press charges. The officer was concerned about Emilia and called Child Protective Services. Emilia was removed from her mother's care and placed in a foster home.

After spending time with Emilia, the social worker assigned to her case was able to gather more information about Emilia's life. The social worker learned that even though Emilia has spent her whole life in the United States, she remains undocumented. The social worker also learned more about the abuse by Emilia's stepfather. A few months earlier, Emilia accompanied her mother to the hospital one night after her stepfather knocked out her mother's tooth. While at the hospital, the police questioned Emilia's mother, who told them about the abuse. The police made a report, and then a social worker at the hospital helped Emilia and her mother find a domestic violence shelter to spend the night. Emilia thought that her mother would finally leave her stepfather; however, the next day Emilia's mother changed her mind and told the police that she did not want to press charges.

Emilia's social worker realizes that Emilia needs to speak with an immigration attorney to assess her ability to apply for lawful status in the United States. The social worker reaches out to an attorney, who assesses Emilia's case and finds the following:

1   Special Immigrant Juvenile Status. Emilia may be able to obtain Special Immigrant Juvenile Status (SIJS), a form of status available to children who have been abused, abandoned, or neglected by one or both of their parents and for whom it is not in their best interests to return to their country of origin.

2   U Visa. Both Emilia and her mother may be able to obtain a U visa, a visa available to victims of certain crimes who cooperate with law enforcement and are able to obtain a certification from law enforcement verifying that they participated in the detection, investigation, or prosecution of criminal activity. If Emilia's mother applies for a U visa, Emilia would also qualify as a derivative. Alternatively, if Emilia decides to report her stepfather's abuse to the police, Emilia may be able to obtain a U visa as the primary applicant.

3   Violence Against Women Act (VAWA).* Emilia's mother may be able to obtain status pursuant to the Violence Against Women Act (VAWA), based on the abuse she suffered at the hands of her U.S. citizen spouse. Emilia's mother will have to demonstrate that she was physically battered or subject to extreme cruelty by her U.S. citizen husband and that the abuse occurred in the United States. If Emilia's mother obtains status through VAWA, Emilia would also qualify for status as a derivative applicant.

4   Deferred Action for Childhood Arrivals (DACA). Emilia would be eligible for DACA. Unlike the other forms of relief described here, DACA would not provide Emilia with a path to lawful status in the United States; however, she would not be subject to deportation for a period of two years, and she would be granted work authorization. Deferred Action for Childhood Arrivals is available to young people who are currently at least 15 years old, came to the United States before turning 16 years old, were present in the United States and under the age of 31 as of June 15, 2012 (when DACA was announced), have resided in the United States

continuously since June 15, 2007, are currently in school, and do not have certain criminal convictions or otherwise pose a threat to national security.

*Family-Based Immigration and VAWA: It is important to note that VAWA would allow Emilia's mother to adjust her status from within the United States, without having to leave. This is an important exception to the laws that typically apply to family-based immigration and adjustment of status. Because Emilia's mother initially entered the United States without inspection, if she tried to adjust her status to lawful permanent resident based solely on her marriage to a U.S. citizen (not through VAWA), she would first have to leave the United States to process her lawful permanent residence abroad. Furthermore, because she has been in the United States unlawfully for many years, when she leaves the United States she will trigger a 10-year bar from returning. This means that Emilia's mother would have to wait at least 10 years to enter the United States lawfully, unless she could obtain a waiver. The Violence Against Women Act offers an exception and would allow Emilia's mother to adjust her status lawfully, without first having to leave the United States and without triggering the 10-year bar.

The majority of immigrants come to the United States either through family or through employment-based petitions. Others are granted humanitarian protection, including asylum, T visas (for victims of human trafficking), or other forms of relief. With the exception of "nonimmigrant visas," which never provide a path to lawful permanent resident status, once an individual is granted an immigrant visa, the noncitizen may apply for status as a lawful permanent resident (LPR) after some designated period of time. An LPR (also known as a green card holder) has the right to permanently live in the United States as long as the individual meets certain requirements. Specifically, LPRs must reside in the United States, file income taxes, register with the Selective Service, and obey the laws of the United States. If an LPR commits a crime, he or she is at high risk of losing status.

An individual who has been an LPR for five years becomes eligible to apply for naturalization (status as a U.S. citizen) (INA § 316, 8 U.S.C.A. § 1427, 2015). The following are some of the basic requirements necessary to naturalize (INA § 312(a), 8 U.S.C.A. § 1423(a), 2015; INA § 316, 8 U.S.C.A. § 1427, 2015):

1 Residency in the United States. The applicant must have resided in the United States continuously for both the five years preceding the filing of the application and for the period from filing to grant of naturalization.

2 Good moral character. The applicant must demonstrate good moral character.

3 Age. The applicant must be 18 years of age or older.

4 Language. With some limited exceptions, the applicant must show "an understanding of the English language, including an ability to read, write, and speak words in ordinary usage."

5 Civics. The applicant must possess "a knowledge and understanding of the fundamentals of the history, and of the principles and form of government, of the United States."

6 Citizenship Oath. The applicant must take a citizenship oath declaring allegiance to the U.S. Constitution and renouncing all allegiances with foreign governments.

Naturalization from LPR to U.S. citizen is the most common way for individuals to become citizens after they turn 18. However, it is important to note that there are two other ways to acquire U.S. citizenship: (1) citizenship by birth; and (2) citizenship by descent (INA § 301(a), 8 U.S.C.A. § 1401(a), 2015). Under U.S. law, anyone born on U.S. soil is a U.S. citizen. Furthermore, anyone who has a parent that is a U.S. citizen at the time of birth may be a citizen by descent. For citizenship by descent, there are certain additional residency and physical presence requirements in order for the parent to pass down citizenship to the child.

The following section provides an overview of the most common paths to lawful permanent resident status and U.S. citizenship. This brief overview should not be considered comprehensive. There are many factors that could disqualify an individual from obtaining relief or that could prohibit the noncitizen from adjusting to lawful permanent residence (for example, having committed certain crimes). Moreover, this summary does not include all forms of relief; it is simply meant to provide a basic overview of the forms of immigration relief most commonly available to children and families. It is always best practice to consult with a reputable immigration attorney. One can be found through the American Immigration Lawyers Association (AILA).

FAMILY-BASED IMMIGRATION

An individual with a family member who is a U.S. citizen or lawful permanent resident may be eligible for a family-based immigrant visa (INA § 201, 8 U.S.C.A. § 1151, 2015; INA § 203(a), 8 U.S.C.A. § 1153(a), 2015). Eligibility for this type of visa depends on the relationship between the noncitizen beneficiary and the sponsoring family member, and on the sponsor's status as either a U.S. citizen or an LPR. Children and spouses of a U.S. citizen, and parents of a U.S. citizen 21 years of age or older, are eligible for visas as "immediate relatives." Those considered immediate relatives of U.S. citizens are not subject to the yearly numerical limits on family-based visas and therefore do not face the lengthy waits that many other family-based immigrants are subject to.

Applicants whose visa applications are based on other family relationships with a U.S. citizen or LPR are eligible for Limited Family-Based Immigrant visas. Unlike Immediate Relative petitions, there are strict caps on the number of visas available each year under each Limited Family-Based Immigrant classification group, with no more than 480,000 visas issued in any given year. If more applications are received in a given year than the number of eligible visas (which is almost always the case), they will be awarded on a first-come, first-served basis determined by the filing date of the petition. The waiting lists for some classifications of visas are so long that it can take years—even decades—to receive the visa.

Table 2.1 summarizes who is eligible to apply for these two categories of family-based visas. A "child" is defined as 21 years old or younger and unmarried. This category can include adopted children who meet certain requirements. "Sons and daughters" are over 21 years of age. In cases where the family member abroad has a spouse or child, those individuals can be included on the family-based petition.

To apply for a family-based visa, the visa applicant is *not* the noncitizen but is actually the family member (called the "petitioner"). The noncitizen is considered the "beneficiary" of the relative's application. The noncitizen must have the sponsoring relative file a Form I-130 with the Department of Homeland Security demonstrating that he or she is a U.S. citizen or LPR and has the required relationship to the intended immigrant. If the application is approved, the noncitizen can then apply for permanent residence based on the visa petition.

TABLE 2.1 Eligibility Criteria for Family-Based Visas

SPONSOR'S IMMIGRATION STATUS	FAMILIAL RELATIONSHIP
U.S. citizen (immediate relative visa)	Spouse of a U.S. citizen Child of a U.S. citizen Parent of a U.S. citizen (provided the U.S. citizen is 21 years old)

U.S. citizen or LPR (limited family-based visa)	Unmarried sons and daughters of
	  U.S. citizens
	Spouse of an LPR
	Child of an LPR
	Married sons and daughters of U.S. citizens
	Brothers and sisters of U.S. citizens
	  (provided the U.S. citizen is 21 years old)

Source: https://travel.state.gov/content/visas/en/immigrate/family/family-preference.html

It is important to note that for noncitizens who initially entered the United States unlawfully, there are serious limitations on their ability to adjust their status based on an approved family-based visa petition (INA § 212(a)(6), 8 U.S.C.A. § 1182(a)(6), 2015). Such individuals are generally unable to adjust their status within the United States, and they must return to their countries of origin in order to process their family-based petition. However, upon leaving the United States, these individuals may trigger lengthy bars to reentry (3 or 10 years) as a penalty for their unlawful presence in the United States (INA § 212(a)(9), 8 U.S.C.A. § 1182(a)(9), 2015). If the noncitizen has any criminal history, the bars from returning may be permanent. There is a waiver available for those who can demonstrate extreme hardship to a U.S. citizen or lawful permanent resident spouse or parent (INA § 212(a)(9)(B)(v), 8 U.S.C.A. § 1182(a)(9), 2015); however, this is a high burden, and waivers are not easily granted. These limitations would also apply to noncitizens seeking adjustment of status through employment-based immigration; however, most of the humanitarian-based forms of relief have waivers that allow adjustment of status even if the noncitizen initially entered the United States unlawfully.

EMPLOYMENT-BASED IMMIGRATION

Individuals with certain skills that are considered desirable for the U.S. economy are able to immigrate to the United States on the basis of having

TABLE 2.2 Preference Categories for Employment-Based Immigration

PREFERENCE CATEGORY	QUALIFYING INDIVIDUALS
First preference: Priority workers	Immigrants with extraordinary ability in the sciences, arts, education, business, or athletics Professors and researchers who are outstanding Certain multinational executives and managers
Second preference: Advanced degrees	Professionals holding advanced degrees Individuals with exceptional ability in the sciences, arts, or business
Third preference: Skilled workers, professionals, and others	Individuals capable of performing certain "skilled labor" with two years of training Professionals with a B.A. only "Unskilled labor" for which qualified U.S. workers are not available
Fourth preference: Special immigrants	This category grants a special benefit to certain categories of workers, including religious workers or long-term U.S. government employees as defined in INA § 101(a)(27)(C) through (M)
Fifth preference: Employment creation	Individuals engaging in a new commercial enterprise in which they have invested $1,000,000 and hired at least 10 full-time U.S. workers

Source: https://www.uscis.gov/working-united-states/permanent-workers

a sponsoring employer (INA § 201(d), 8 U.S.C.A. § 1151(d), 2015; INA § 203(b), 8 U.S.C.A. § 1153(b), 2015). There are 140,000 slots for employment-based immigrant visas, and there are five preference categories. For the second and third preference categories, an employer must obtain a labor certification from the Department of Labor demonstrating that (1) able, willing, and qualified American workers are not available and (2) the applicant's employment will not adversely affect the wages and working conditions of similarly employed U.S. workers.

Every year since the current system went into effect in 1990, the family program as a whole has been oversubscribed, whereas the employment program as a whole has been undersubscribed. However, there are often backlogs for applicants for second preference petitions from China and India and for all third preference category petitions. Table 2.2 gives the five preference categories for employment-based immigration.

To apply for an employment-sponsored visa, the employer is the petitioner and the noncitizen is the beneficiary. As in the case of a family-based petition, if the application is approved, the noncitizen can then apply for permanent residence based on the visa petition.

HUMANITARIAN-BASED IMMIGRATION

Although employment and family-based immigration remain the two predominant means of immigration to the United States, much attention is often paid to the much smaller number of visas granted for humanitarian reasons. If granted a form of humanitarian protection such as asylum or a T visa, immigrants, even those who entered the United States unlawfully, may be allowed to remain in the United States and eventually become lawful permanent residents.

Asylum

Asylum is a form of protection granted to individuals in the United States who meet the legal definition of a "refugee," meaning that they have been persecuted in their home country, or fear they will be persecuted, on account of their race, religion, nationality, membership in a particular social group, or political opinion (INA § 101(a)(42), 8 U.S.C.A. § 1101(a)(42), 2015; INA § 208, 8 U.S.C.A. § 1158, 2015). Unlike the U.S. refugee program, which provides protection to refugees identified *outside* the United States by bringing them to the United States for resettlement, asylum provides protection to qualified applicants who are already inside the United States or are seeking entry into the United States at a port of entry. There are no quotas on the number of individuals who may be granted asylum each year. After one year, individuals who are granted asylum are eligible to apply to adjust their status to that of a lawful permanent resident.

Ani is a child from Sudan who fled after his father and older brother were murdered for failing to join a militia group. Ani fears that as the oldest boy in the home, he would be forced to join the militia or be killed if he were returned to Sudan. He does not support the political goals of the militia; moreover, he believes his religion prohibits his participation in the militia. Despite this, he knows that his own government will be unable to protect him from the militia, just as it was unable to protect his father and brother. Ani has a claim for asylum.

Applicants for asylum must demonstrate both a subjective and an objective fear of persecution in their home country (*Matter of Acosta*, 1985). In other words, an applicant must demonstrate that he or she is afraid of persecution (subjective fear) and that the fear is reasonable, or well founded (objective fear). The term persecution is not specifically defined in the Immigration and Nationality Act. Over time, however, many courts have interpreted the meaning of persecution to include "either a threat to the life or freedom of, or the infliction of suffering or harm upon, those who differ in a way regarded as offensive" (*Matter of Acosta*, 1985). Common characteristics of persecution include detention, arrest, interrogation, prosecution, imprisonment, illegal searches, confiscation of property, surveillance, beatings, or torture (*Mitev v. INS*, 1995). Furthermore, the persecution must have been perpetrated by the government or by an entity the government will not or cannot control (*Matter of Acosta*, 1985).

An individual must demonstrate that the persecution suffered was on account of the applicant's (1) race, (2) religion, (3) national origin, (4) political opinion, or (5) membership in a social group. In recent years, the "social group" category has become a particularly complex area of asylum law. Generally, members of a social group must share an "immutable characteristic" such as gender, race, family ties, or shared past experience (*Matter of Acosta*, 1985). Of late, some courts have heightened this threshold by requiring applicants for asylum to demonstrate that their social group is also "particular" and "socially distinct" (*Matter of M-E-V-G-*, 2014; *Matter of W-G-R-*, 2014). In the past, applicants had established asylum based on their membership in social groups consisting of former child soldiers, young women who were members of a certain tribe who have not been subject to female genital mutilation but who oppose the practice, and students (*Lukwago v. Ashcroft*, 2003; *Matter of Kasinga*, 1996; *Matter of Villalla*, 1990).

Generally, there are two paths to asylum in the United States:

- *Affirmative*: For people who are not in immigration court removal proceedings.
- *Defensive*: For people who have been placed in immigration court removal proceedings.

In the affirmative process, an asylum seeker files an application with USCIS and is given an appointment to present his or her case to an asylum officer in a nonadversarial interview. If a noncitizen has been placed in removal proceedings, then that individual must apply for asylum before the immigration court rather than before USCIS. Applying for asylum in immigration court is a more adversarial process than the affirmative process, with a trial attorney representing the Department of Homeland Security, which prosecutes the case.

An applicant must file an affirmative asylum application within one year of entering the United States unless that individual can demonstrate extraordinary circumstances for failing to file within that time. In 2008, the law was amended to exempt unaccompanied alien children from the one-year filing deadline (TVPRA § 235(d)(7), 2008; INA § 208(a)(2)(E), 8 U.S.C.A. § 1158(a)(2)(E), 2015).

Until 2009, children in removal proceedings—including those detained by ORR—were required to seek asylum in front of an immigration judge in defensive, adversarial immigration court proceedings. However, the law was changed in 2008 to allow unaccompanied immigrant children to first apply for asylum affirmatively with USCIS (TVPRA § 235(d)(7), 2008; 8 U.S.C.A. § 1232(d)(7), 2015). This means that the child will first seek asylum through an affirmative interview with USCIS and, in the meantime, the child's immigration court case is generally "continued" or put on hold. If USCIS does not grant asylum, the child can still pursue the asylum claim in front of the immigration judge. This essentially gives the child two chances to prove the case and gives the child a more child-friendly, nonadversarial setting in which to start.

Finally, if an immigrant child has a parent applying for refugee status or asylum, the child may qualify as a derivative beneficiary, whether the child is in or outside the United States. The child must file for these benefits within two years from the date that the parent entered the United States.

T and U Visas

The Victims of Trafficking and Violence Prevention Act of 2000 created the T and U visas for noncitizen victims of crimes (INA § 101(a)(15)(T), 8 U.S.C. § 1101(a)(15)(T), 2015; 8 C.F.R. § 214.11, 2015; INA § 101(a)(15)(U), 8 U.S.C. § 1101(a)(15)(U), 2015; INA § 214(p), 8 U.S.C.A. § 1184(p), 2015; 8 C.F.R. §§ 212.17, 214.14, 2015). Both visas are designed to provide legal status to noncitizens who assist authorities in the investigation of trafficking or other specified crimes.

The T visa was created to address the problem of international human trafficking by providing trafficking victims with a defense against removal from the United States (U.S. Department of Justice, 2002). The most recent statistics provided by the U.S. Department of State identified approximately 50,000 victims of human trafficking worldwide (U.S. Department of State, 2014). This does not include the thousands of people who were never identified. Many victims of human trafficking are women or minors (U.S. Department of State, 2014).

In order to apply for a T visa, an applicant must prove that he or she is a victim of "severe trafficking" in persons, either for sex or labor. Specifically, a "severe form of trafficking of persons" is defined (Victims of Trafficking and Violence Protection Act of 2000 § 103(8), 22 U.S.C. § 7102(9), 2015; 28 § C.F.R. 1100.25, 2015) as

1   the purpose of a commercial sex act, which was induced by force, fraud, or coercion, or occurred when the person had not reached 18 years of age; or
2   the purpose of labor or services, which were induced by force, fraud, or coercion for the purpose of subjecting the person to involuntary servitude, peonage, debt bondage, or slavery.

T visa applicants must be physically present in the United States, and those over the age of 18 must comply with reasonable requests by law enforcement to assist in the investigation or prosecution of traffickers. Finally, T visa applicants must demonstrate that they will suffer extreme hardship involving unusual and severe harm if returned to their home country.

Arnold was taken from his mother in Liberia and brought to the United States when he was 7 years old. At the time, Arnold was told that he was coming to the United States to be adopted by a family, but the man who brought him here failed to obtain a visa and told customs officials that Arnold was his son. The same man forced Arnold to live in the back room of his small hair-braiding shop. During the day, Arnold was expected to clean the shop, and he was not allowed to attend school. In three years, Arnold left the shop just a few times—never unattended. Arnold has not spoken with his mother since he left Liberia, and he fears that she has died. He has no other adults to care for him in his home country. Arnold would have a claim for a T visa.

The U visa is designed for noncitizens who are the victims of certain se-rious crimes *that occur within the United States*. Applicants for a U visa must have suffered substantial physical or mental abuse as a result of crimi-nal activity, must have information about the criminal activity, and must par-ticipate in the detection, investigation, or prosecution of such criminal activity. Only victims of certain crimes are eligible to apply for a U visa. "Qualifying crimes" include rape; torture; trafficking; incest; domestic violence; sexual assault; abusive sexual contact; prostitution; sexual exploita-tion; female genital mutilation; being held hostage; peonage; involuntary ser-vitude; slave trade; kidnapping; abduction; unlawful criminal restraint; false imprisonment; blackmail; extortion; manslaughter; murder; felonious as-sault; witness tampering; obstruction of justice; perjury; or attempt, conspir-acy, or solicitation to commit any of the above-mentioned crimes.

In order to obtain a U visa, an applicant must obtain a certification from a law enforcement agency, prosecutor, or judge attesting that the nonciti-zen has participated in or will participate in the detection, investigation, or prosecution of the crime. However, these officials are not required to pro-vide this certification. In some jurisdictions, local law enforcement agen-cies have simply refused to provide law enforcement certifications, even when a crime victim has fully participated to the best of his or her ability in an investigation. Their reasons for refusing to cooperate vary: they may not believe the victim has been sufficiently helpful, they may mistakenly be-lieve a conviction (rather than investigation) is required before the certifi-cation can be signed, or they may refuse as part of a broader anti-immigrant strategy. Other law enforcement agencies, including Child Protective Ser-vices, understand the value of supporting immigrants who have come for-ward to report crimes and assist in the identification and prosecution of criminals.

Nina is a 16-year-old child from Honduras who was smuggled into the United States in 2008. The men who smuggled Nina held her, and dozens of other indi-viduals, in a drop house in the United States against her will until her family paid additional ransom money to the smugglers. While in the drop house, Nina wit-nessed one of the smugglers kill a man who was not able to pay the ransom. The smugglers sexually harassed Nina and threatened her with sexual abuse as a

(CONTINUED)

means of controlling her. When immigration authorities discovered Nina, she reported what she saw to federal officers and identified one of the men who was part of the smuggling ring. Nina then testified in the trial against the smuggling ring. Nina would have a claim for a U visa.

Applications for both U and T visas are submitted in writing to USCIS instead of to an immigration judge. Individuals who are granted a U or a T visa may remain in the United States for up to four years; in some cases, that period may be extended. After three years, U or T visa holders may apply for lawful permanent resident status. U and T visa grantees who are over 21 years of age may apply for their spouses and children. Grantees under the age of 21 may also petition for their parents, unmarried siblings under the age of 18, and spouses and children.

Violence Against Women Act (VAWA)

In 1994, Congress passed the Violence Against Women Act. As explained earlier, normally when a family-based visa petition is filed, the U.S. citizen or LPR is the petitioner. The Violence Against Women Act recognized that many immigrants remain in abusive relationships because of a fear that they would be deported without the support of their U.S. citizen or LPR spouse, parent, or child. Therefore, VAWA created an exception, allowing victims of domestic violence to self-petition for relief by applying independently, without turning to the abusive relative for sponsorship (INA § 204(a)(1)(A)(iii) & (iv), 8 U.S.C.A. § 1154(a)(1)(A)(iii) & (iv), 2015). In order to qualify for relief under VAWA, the noncitizen must also show that (1) he or she has resided with the abusive citizen or LPR at some point either inside or outside the United States (this includes visits), (2) the noncitizen has good moral character; and (3) the noncitizen currently resides in the United States (there are some exceptions to this requirement). Children under 14 are presumed to have good moral character. Furthermore, if a child was not abused but the child's parent was abused by a U.S. citizen or lawful permanent resident spouse, the child may qualify for relief as a derivative VAWA beneficiary.

In order to petition for relief under VAWA, a noncitizen must file an I-360 petition with USCIS, with supporting documentation. A decision will be made by USCIS on the basis of the paper application. The benefits of a grant of relief under VAWA include immediate employment authorization, the ability to remain in the United States, and the ability to adjust status to that of lawful permanent resident.

HUMANITARIAN RELIEF UNIQUE TO CHILDREN

Special Immigrant Juvenile Status

In 1990, Congress enacted legislation providing a pathway to citizenship, known as Special Immigrant Juvenile Status (SIJS), for immigrant children who have been abused, abandoned, or neglected (INA § 101(a)(27)(J); 8 U.S.C. § 1101(a)(27)(J), 2015). The process for seeking SIJS involves both a state court and a federal government component, and it is important to note that the state and federal systems may not be complementary or cooperative with one another. The process can be summarized as follows:

• *Step 1*: The child seeks an order from a state court judge (typically dependency proceedings in juvenile court or guardianship proceedings in probate court) finding that (1) reunification with one or both of the child's parents is not viable because of abuse, neglect, or abandonment or a similar basis under state law and (2) it is not in the child's best interests to return to the home country. This order is known as a "predicate" order.
• *Step 2*: The child includes this predicate order in an SIJS petition (or I-360 form) filed with USCIS. The child must be under 21 on the date the SIJS petition is filed with USCIS and must be unmarried. In some cases, USCIS may interview the child, whereas in others USCIS will decide based on the paper filing only.
• *Step 3*: The child applies for lawful permanent resident (LPR) status. Children in immigration court removal proceedings will submit an application for adjustment of status to the immigration court once the SIJS petition is approved. Otherwise, the SIJS petition and the adjustment of status application can be filed concurrently with USCIS.

There is no requirement that the abuse, neglect, or abandonment have occurred in the United States.

> Angela was born in Guatemala. When Angela was very young, her father died and her mother left her in the care of her elderly grandmother. When Angela was 13, her grandmother became gravely ill, leaving Angela with no one in Guatemala to take care of her. Angela's mother made arrangements for Angela to be smuggled into the United States. Although Angela made it across the border safely, she was victimized by both her mother and stepfather after her arrival. Angela's mother abused her physically. Angela's stepfather abused her sexually, forcing himself on Angela, and her mother did nothing to try to stop him. Angela would have a claim for Special Immigrant Juvenile Status.

Children who receive SIJS are immediately eligible to adjust their status to lawful permanent residency, thus enabling them to live and work permanently in the United States, to qualify for federal financial aid and other benefits, and to travel in and out of the United States. Note, however, that not every child who meets the criteria for SIJS spelled out here is able to adjust their status. Some children, particularly those with adult criminal convictions or those who have been involved in drug trafficking, may not qualify to adjust their status even if USCIS approves their SIJS petitions.

Children granted an SIJS-based adjustment of status cannot subsequently petition to bring parents to the United States, even a parent who was not named as an abuser. It is important that children understand this consequence of filing for SIJS, because some children do not want to be prevented from facilitating reunification with their parents, even parents who have mistreated them. It is also important to keep in mind that it can be difficult for some children to speak against a parent to an attorney, judge, or any of the other stakeholders who need to hear the child's story.

Deferred Action for Childhood Arrivals

Immigration and Customs Enforcement (ICE) is a prosecuting agency that bears discretion in deciding who to place in removal proceedings. It may refrain from initiating, or may terminate, removal proceedings in particularly sympathetic cases. Although ICE has long held a practice of exercising prosecutorial discretion, in June 2012 the government expanded its policy.

On June 15, 2012, President Obama announced a policy called "Deferred Action for Childhood Arrivals" (DACA) (Napolitano, 2012), which applies to the same population of youths that would have been impacted by the DREAM Act. The DREAM Act stands for the Development, Relief and Education of Alien Minors Act. It is a bipartisan bill that was originally introduced in August 2001 by Democratic Senator Dick Durbin of Illinois and Senator Orrin Hatch, a Republican from Utah. The DREAM Act would have provided a path to lawful permanent residency and eventually citizenship for individuals between the ages of 12 and 35, of good moral character, who came to the United States before the age of 16, had resided in the United States for at least five years, and had graduated from high school, obtained a GED, or been accepted into a college or university. Since its original introduction in 2001, the DREAM Act has been reintroduced—with certain changes—in 2009, 2010, and 2011. Each time, it failed to pass.

Unlike the DREAM Act, DACA is a more limited remedy for undocumented children. Also unlike the DREAM Act, DACA provides no path to lawful status in the United States; it simply provides that the government will not initiate removal proceedings against an individual for a period of two years and will allow the person to work in the United States with authorization. In order to qualify for DACA, an applicant must show that he or she:

1   is at least 15 years old and was under the age of 31 as of June 15, 2012;
2   came to the United States before the sixteenth birthday;
3   has continuously resided in the United States since June 15, 2007;
4   had no lawful status on June 15, 2012;
5   was physically present in the United States on June 15, 2012;
6   is currently in school, has graduated or has obtained a certificate of completion from high school, has obtained a general equivalency diploma (GED), or is an honorably discharged veteran of the Coast Guard or Armed Forces of the United States; and
7   has not been convicted of a felony, significant misdemeanor, or three or more other misdemeanors, and does not otherwise pose a threat to national security or public safety.

On November 20, 2014, President Obama announced an expanded deferred-action program that would permit Deferred Action for Parents of U.S. Citizens and Lawful Permanent Residents (DAPA) and would expand the existing DACA program (Johnson, 2014). On February 16, 2015, a federal district court in the Southern District of Texas temporarily blocked the DAPA and expanded DACA program from being implemented. At the time of this writing, the DAPA/DACA expansion remains tied up in litigation and unavailable to anyone who may qualify; however, the following is a summary of how the expanded DACA program would change the original requirements.

1. Under the original DACA program, an individual must have been under the age of 31 as of June 15, 2012. The expanded program would eliminate this age cap.
2. Under the original DACA program, a person must have resided in the United States continuously since June 15, 2007. The expanded program would require continuous residency since January 1, 2010.
3. Under the original DACA program, deferred action and employment authorization are issued for a two-year period, and people who receive DACA must apply to renew their deferred-action status every two years. Under the expanded program, the two-year period would be expanded to a three-year period.

Since the DACA program was initiated in 2012, hundreds of young people have been granted deferred action through this program.

CONCLUSION

Immigration law in the United States is a highly complex and constantly evolving field. In fact, the Supreme Court has analogized the Immigration and Nationality Act to the tax code in its intricacy. Despite that, our laws are narrowly drawn, and they frequently provide no path to lawful immigration status for many wishing to live and work in the United States. The family-based system has been critiqued as a form of nepotism, while in practice the lengthy backlogs often mean that families are kept apart for years or even decades. The employment-based system provides few opportunities for unskilled workers, making this route impossible for those less privileged. And the humanitarian protections available, although laudable in their aims, often fail to protect those most in need of protection.

Each year, the number of mixed-status families—families whose members have different immigration statuses—continues to grow. And, each year, thousands of parents are deported, leaving behind children who are U.S. citizens. Although most agree that the current system is in need of reform, the question of how to fix the system is highly divisive. Some recommend enhanced border security, harsher penalties for breaking the law, and greater internal enforcement. Others suggest providing a path to status for the hundreds of thousands of undocumented immigrants who have lived, worked, and paid taxes in the United States for years. President Obama, unable to pass comprehensive immigration reform, has instead exercised his authority to introduce policy changes aimed at protecting children and families and focusing enforcement efforts on those who have committed serious crimes or pose a threat to society. However, with a new administration, these policies could quickly change, or disappear altogether. Consequently, the future of our immigration system remains uncertain.

Ultimately, our immigration laws, which dictate who we allow in and who we keep out, reflect the value choices of our nation. But when this system results in the long-term or permanent separation of parents and children, we must question whether we have made the right choices. If we want a system that truly protects the most vulnerable, then legislative reform that broadens the paths to lawful immigration status is imperative.

KEY TERMS

DEPARTMENT OF HOMELAND SECURITY The U.S. Department of Homeland Security (DHS) is a cabinet-level department of the U.S. government and is charged with protecting the United States from threats that can occur both within and outside its borders, including terrorism and natural disasters. There are three agencies within DHS that handle immigration matters: (1) Customs and Border Protection (CBP), (2) Immigration and Customs Enforcement (ICE), and (3) U.S. Citizenship and Immigration Services (USCIS).

FAMILY-BASED IMMIGRATION Immigration based on a familial relationship with a U.S. citizen or lawful permanent resident. Family-based immigration accounts for the majority of immigrants who come to the United States each year.

LAWFUL PERMANENT RESIDENT (LPR) An LPR (also known as a green card holder) has the right to permanently live in the United States as long as the individual meets certain requirements. Specifically, LPRs must reside in the United States, file income taxes, register with the Selective Service, and obey the laws of the United States. After five years of residency, an LPR is eligible to naturalize and become a U.S. citizen.

UNACCOMPANIED ALIEN CHILD A legal term of art meaning that the child is under 18 years of age, without lawful status, and without a parent or legal guardian available to provide care at that time.

VIOLENCE AGAINST WOMEN ACT (VAWA) This federal law provides a path to lawful status for noncitizens who have been abused by a spouse or parent who is either a U.S. citizen or lawful permanent resident or by a child who is a U.S. citizen.

STUDY QUESTIONS

1 What are the requirements for an individual to obtain asylum in the United States?
2 What are the requirements to naturalize and become a U.S. citizen?
3 What relatives can a U.S. citizen petition to bring to the United States through family-based immigration?
4 How does the remedy provided by Deferred Action for Childhood Arrivals (DACA) differ from the other types of legal relief discussed in this chapter?
5 When applying to enter the United States as a second or third preference category employment-based immigrant, the petitioner must obtain a labor certification from the Department of Labor. What does the petitioner have to demonstrate to obtain a labor certification?

ADDITIONAL RESOURCES

American Bar Association Commission on Immigration: http://www .americanbar.org/groups/public_services/immigration.html
The Commission directs the Association's efforts to ensure fair treatment and full due process rights for immigrants and refugees within the United States.
Bridging Refugee Youth and Children's Services: http://www.brycs.org

Mission: Bridging Refugee Youth and Children's Services (BRYCS) strengthens the capacity of refugee-serving and mainstream organizations across the United States to ensure the successful development of refugee children, youths, and their families by increasing information sharing and promoting collaboration at the local, state, regional, and national levels.

First Focus Center for the Children of Immigrants: http://firstfocus.org/issues/children-of-immigrants/

Mission: Children of immigrants are affected every day by policy choices on immigration, education, health care, and a range of other issues. And because one fourth of children in America today are children of immigrants, those choices shape America's future. The First Focus Center for the Children of Immigrants challenges policymakers to ensure that all children and families, regardless of immigration status, have the opportunity to live the American Dream.

Immigrant Legal Resource Center: http://www.ilrc.org

Mission: The Immigrant Legal Resource Center (ILRC) is a national nonprofit resource center that provides legal training, educational materials, and advocacy to advance immigrant rights. The mission of the ILRC is to work with and educate immigrants, community organizations, and the legal sector to continue to build a democratic society that values diversity and the rights of all people.

PBS Series: The New Americans: http://www.pbs.org/independentlens/newamericans/

This series by executive producer Steve James tells five stories of immigrants migrating from their homelands—Nigeria, the West Bank, the Dominican Republic, Mexico, and India—to the United States. The filmmakers followed the subjects over a four-year period. In telling these five stories, the filmmakers sought to reflect as much as possible the racial, geographic, and economic diversity of the current immigrant experience.

REFERENCES

8 C.F.R. § 212.17 (2015).

8 C.F.R. § 214.11 (2015).

8 C.F.R. § 214.14 (2015).

8 C.F.R. § 239 (2015).

8 C.F.R. § 287.3(d) (2015).

28 C.F.R. § 1100.25 (2015).

Aleinikoff, T. A., Martin, D. A., Motomura, H., & Fullerton, M. (Eds.). (2012). *Immigration and citizenship process and policy* (7th ed.). St. Paul, MN: West Publishing.

Antiterrorism and Effective Death Penalty Act (AEDPA), Pub. L. No. 104-132, 110 Stat. 1214 (1996).

Arizona v. United States, 132 S. Ct. 2492 (2012).

Fuchs, L., & Martin, S., United States Select Commission on Immigration and Refugee Policy. (2012). Staff report: Immigration and U.S. history—the evolution of the Open Society. In T. A. Aleinikoff, D. A. Martin, H. Motomura, & M. Fullerton (Eds.), *Immigration and citizenship process and policy* (7th ed., pp. 3–24). St. Paul, MN: West Publishing. (Originally published 1981)

Gordon, C., Mailman, S., & Yale-Loehr, S. (2015). Immigration law and procedure, §§ 2.02–2.04. In S. H. Legomsky & C. M. Rodriguez (Eds.), *Immigration and refugee law and policy* (6th ed., pp. 13–24). St. Paul, MN: West Publishing. (Originally published 2011, LexisNexis Matthew Bender)

Hing, B. O. (1993). *Making and remaking Asian America through immigration policy, 1850–1990.* Stanford, CA: Stanford University Press.

Homeland Security Act § 462, 6 U.S.C. § 279 (2002).

Illegal Immigrant Reform and Immigrant Responsibility Act (IIRIRA), Pub. L. No. 104-208, 110 Stat. 3009-546 (1996).

Immigration and Nationality Act (INA) § 101(a)(15)(T), 8 U.S.C. § 1101(a)(15)(T) (2015).

INA § 101(a)(15)(U), 8 U.S.C. § 1101(a)(15)(U) (2015).

INA § 101(a)(27)(J); 8 U.S.C. § 1101(a)(27)(J) (2015).

INA § 101(a)(42), 8 U.S.C.A. § 1101(a)(42) (2015).

INA § 201, 8 U.S.C.A. § 1151 (2015).

INA § 203, 8 U.S.C.A. § 1153 (2015).

INA § 204, 8 U.S.C.A. § 1154 (2015).

INA § 208, 8 U.S.C.A. § 1158 (2015).

INA § 212, 8 U.S.C.A. § 1182 (2015).

INA § 214, 8 U.S.C.A. § 1184 (2015).

INA § 236, 8 U.S.C.A. § 1226 (2015).

INA § 239, 8 U.S.C.A. § 1229 (2015).

INA § 240B, 8 U.S.C.A. § 1229c (2015).

INA § 301, 8 U.S.C.A. § 1401 (2015).

INA § 312, 8 U.S.C.A. § 1423 (2015).

INA § 316, 8 U.S.C.A. § 1427 (2015).

Immigration Reform and Control Act (IRCA), Pub. L. No. 99-603; 100 Stat. 3359 (1986).

Johnson, J. C., Secretary of Homeland Security. (2014, November 20). Exercising prosecutorial discretion with respect to individuals who came to the United States as children and with respect to certain individuals who are the parents of U.S. citizens or permanent residents. Retrieved from http://www.dhs.gov/sites/default/files/publications/14_1120_memo_deferred_action.pdf

Legomsky, S. H., & Rodriguez, C. M. (Eds.). (2015). *Immigration and refugee law and policy* (6th ed.). St. Paul, MN: West Publishing.

Lukwago v. Ashcroft, 329 F.3d 157, 178–789 (3rd Cir. 2003).

Martin, S. (2012). A nation of immigrants. In T. A. Aleinikoff, D. A. Martin, H. Motomura, & M. Fullerton (Eds.), *Immigration and citizenship process and policy* (7th ed., pp. 24–34). St. Paul, MN: West Publishing. (Originally published 2010, Cambridge University Press)

Matter of Acosta, 19 I. & N. Dec. 211 (B.I.A. 1985), modified on other grounds by Matter of Mogharrabi, 19 I. & N. 439 (B.I.A. 1987).

Matter of Kasinga, 21 I. & N. Dec. 357, 365–66 (B.I.A. 1996).

Matter of M-E-V-G-, 26 I. & N. Dec. 227 (BIA 2014).

Matter of Villalla, 20 I. & N. Dec. 142 (BIA 1990).

Matter of W-G-R-, 26 I. & N. Dec. 208 (BIA 2014).

Mitev v. INS, 67 F.3d 1325, 1330 (7th Cir. 1995).

Napolitano, J., Secretary of Homeland Security. (2012, June 15). Exercising prosecutorial discretion with respect to individuals who came to the United States as children. Retrieved from http://www.dhs.gov/xlibrary/assets/s1-exercising-prosecutorial-discretion-individuals-who-came-to-us-as-children.pdf

Personal Responsibility and Work Opportunity Reconciliation Act, Pub. L. No. 104-193, 110 Stat. 2015 (1996).

U.S. Department of Health and Human Services, Administration of Children and Family Services, Office of Refugee Resettlement. (2014). Fact sheet. Retrieved from https://www.acf.hhs.gov/sites/default/files/orr/fact_sheet.pdf

——. (2015). *About unaccompanied children's services.* Retrieved from http://www.acf.hhs.gov/programs/orr/programs/ucs/about

U.S. Department of Justice. (2002). *Department of Justice issues T visa to protect women, children, and all victims of human trafficking.* Retrieved from http://www.usdoj.gov/opa/pr/2002/January/02_crt_038.htm

U.S. Department of State. (2014). *Trafficking in persons report*. Retrieved from http://www.state.gov/documents/organization/226844.pdf

U.S. Immigration and Customs Enforcement. (2013). *Facilitating parental interests in the course of civil immigration enforcement activities*. Retrieved from http://www.ice.gov/doclib/detention-reform/pdf/parental_interest_directive _signed.pdf

Victims of Trafficking and Violence Protection Act of 2000, § 103, 22 U.S.C. § 7102 (2015).

Violence Against Women Act (VAWA), Pub. L. No. 103-322, H.R. 3355, Title IV, § 40001-40703 (1994).

William Wilberforce Trafficking Victims Protection Reauthorization Act (TVPRA) § 235, 8 U.S.C.A. § 1232 (2015).

CHAPTER 3

Federal Policy Implications for Immigrant Children and Families

PUBLIC BENEFIT LAWS AND IMMIGRATION REFORM

▸ *WENDY CERVANTES*

FEDERAL POLICY DEBATES on immigration in the United States have often neglected to consider the best interests of children, despite the fact that children of immigrants represent the fastest-growing segment of the U.S. child population (Chaudry & Fortuny, 2010). As a result, children and families frequently suffer the consequences of federal laws that not only fail to reflect their needs but also often undermine their health and safety. The increase in unauthorized immigration from the early 1990s through the 2000s fueled federal policy responses aimed at curbing the flow of unauthorized immigrants, ramping up enforcement measures, and restricting access to public benefits for authorized and unauthorized immigrants alike. These policies have had direct consequences for immigrant and refugee families, the communities they live in, and the programs that serve them. In the years ahead, the challenge for policymakers will be to find solutions that address the unauthorized population currently residing in the United States as well as future flows while at the same time ensuring that these policies promote the well-being of children who will be a critical segment of the future U.S. workforce.

There are many areas of federal policy that impact immigrant and refugee families, including legislation dealing with trafficking, health care, and education. This chapter will focus on two major areas of federal policy impacting immigrant and refugee families, including public benefit laws and federal efforts to address the estimated 11.7 million unauthorized immigrants currently living in the United States. This chapter will provide an overview of immigrant and refugee eligibility for federal public benefit programs, including the impact on access to benefits of the Personal Responsibility and Work Opportunity Reconciliation Act (PRWORA) and the Illegal Immigration Reform and Immigrant Responsibility Act (IIRIRA). Recent legislative and administrative proposals to address the unauthorized population will also be discussed, as well as how these various policies can impact the way in which systems serve children.

IMMIGRANT ELIGIBILITY AND ACCESS
TO FEDERAL PUBLIC BENEFITS

Immigrants, including those that are lawfully present, face restrictions in accessing federal means-tested benefits, many of which have proven critical in reducing child poverty and supporting economic stability, food security, and health for low-income families (Chaudry & Fortuny, 2010; Hernandez & Napierala, 2013; Yoshikawa & Kholoptseva, 2013). Rules regarding immigrant and refugee eligibilities for public benefits are complicated and vary by program as well as by state. Factors determining eligibility include the individual's current immigration status, the length of time that status has been maintained, the date the individual entered the United States, and the criteria applied by the individual's state of residence (Broder, 2005). In some cases, the individual's age may also be a factor, such as for children under the age of 18.

IMPACT OF FEDERAL LAWS ON IMMIGRANT ELIGIBILITY

Historically, noncitizens have faced restrictions in accessing assistance from federal public benefit programs. For example, unauthorized immigrants and individuals on temporary visas have never been eligible for programs such as the Supplemental Nutrition Assistance Program (SNAP), nonemergency Medicaid, Supplemental Security Income (SSI), and Temporary Assistance for Needy Families (TANF). The Personal Responsibility and Work Opportunity Reconciliation Act (PRWORA) of 1996 significantly impacted public benefit eligibility for lawfully present immigrants, with immigrant participation in benefit programs dropping significantly in subsequent years. Despite legislative changes to restore some previous eligibility categories, the law's chilling effect in deterring immigrants from seeking critical benefits remains largely intact (Broder, 2005).

Before 1996, lawfully present immigrants who met the general income and family composition requirements were able to access federal means-tested programs in the same way as U.S. citizens. After the law's implementation, most lawfully present immigrants were subject to restrictions and waiting periods for federal means-tested programs, including SSI, SNAP, nonemergency Medicaid, TANF, and the State Children's Health Insurance Program (SCHIP).

PRWORA also created two categories of immigrants for the purposes of determining program eligibility, including "qualified" immigrants and "not qualified" immigrants. "Qualified" immigrants include lawful permanent residents (LPRs), refugees, and other individuals granted asylum, as well as specific entrants such as Cuban and Haitian entrants and conditional entrants, and certain vulnerable populations such as victims of trafficking and victims of abuse. "Nonqualified immigrants," including unauthorized immigrants and some lawfully present immigrants, are generally prohibited from receiving federal public benefits. The terms "qualified" and "nonqualified" can often be misleading, given that the law restricts access to federal programs between the two groups (Broder & Blazer, 2011). The welfare law also created an arbitrary cutoff date for eligibility purposes, distinguishing between individuals who entered the United States before and after the enactment of the law on August 22, 1996, and prohibiting postenactment "qualified" immigrants from eligibility for federal means-tested programs for the first five years of their "qualified" status, also known as the "five year ban" (Fortuny, Hernandez, & Chaudry, 2010).

The exceptions within each category of eligibility are complicated, further contributing to confusion. Since the inception of the welfare law, "not qualified" immigrants remain eligible for emergency Medicaid if they otherwise meet their state's Medicaid requirements. Unauthorized children and other children who fall under "not qualified" remain eligible for all school lunch programs, and currently all states provide access to the Special Supplemental Program for Women, Infants, and Children (WIC) (Broder, 2005). Within the "qualified" group, certain categories of immigrants, such as refugees, asylees, specific entrants, and other immigrants considered "humanitarian immigrants" are exempt from the five-year waiting period (Broder & Blazer, 2011). For a full list of federal means-tested programs and current eligibility requirements, please see table 3.1.

TABLE 3.1 Overview of Immigrant Eligibility for Key Federal Means-Tested Programs

PROGRAM	LAWFUL PERMANENT RESIDENTS (AGE 18 AND OVER)	LAWFUL PERMANENT RESIDENTS (UNDER AGE 18)	LAWFUL PERMANENT RESIDENTS (PREGNANT WOMEN)	REFUGEES, ASYLEES, VICTIMS OF TRAFFICKING, OTHERS[a]	LAWFULLY PRESENT INDIVIDUALS	UNDOCUMENTED IMMIGRANTS (INCLUDING CHILDREN AND PREGNANT WOMEN)
	IF ENTERED THE UNITED STATES ON OR AFTER AUGUST 22, 1996:					
SNAP	Not eligible until after five-year waiting period or have credit for 40 quarters of work	Eligible	Not eligible until after five-year waiting period or have credit for 40 quarters of work	Eligible	Not eligible	Not eligible
Medicaid	Not eligible until after five-year waiting period[b]	State option[c] to provide without a five-year waiting period[b]	State option to provide without a five-year waiting period[b]	Eligible[d]	State option for children under 21 and pregnant women only	Eligible only for emergency Medicaid
CHIP	Not eligible until after five-year waiting period	State option to provide without a five-year waiting period[c]	State option to provide without a five-year waiting period	Eligible	State option for children under 21 and pregnant women only[c]	Not eligible[f]

TANF	Not eligible until after five-year waiting period	Not eligible until after five-year waiting period[g]	Not eligible until after five-year waiting period[g]	Eligible[d]	Not eligible	Not eligible
SSI	Not eligible until after five-year waiting period and have credit for 40 quarters of work or meet another exception	Not eligible until after five-year waiting period and have credit for 40 quarters of work or meet another exception	Not eligible until after five-year waiting period and have credit for 40 quarters of work	Only eligible during first seven years after status is granted	Not eligible	Not eligible

Source: This is a modified version of a table published by the National Immigration Law Center on January 29, 2013, entitled "A Quick Guide to Immigrant Eligibility for ACA and Key Federal Means-tested Programs," available at www.nilc.org.

a Also includes Cuban/Haitian entrants, Amerasian immigrants, Iraqi or Afghan special immigrants, and individuals granted withholding of deportation or removal.

b In a few states, they remain ineligible after five years unless they have credit for 40 quarters of work history or are a veteran, active duty military, or his or her spouse or child.

c Eligible if receiving federal foster care.

d A few states terminate Medicaid to humanitarian immigrants after a seven-year period and/or TANF after a five-year period.

e Currently, 29 states have elected to provide Medicaid/CHIP to children, regardless of date of entry.

f Five states and several counties in California use state funds to provide medical coverage for children regardless of immigration status.

g At least a dozen states use their maintenance of effort funds to provide TANF without a waiting period.

Federal legislation passed in subsequent years restored eligibility for certain federal programs to immigrant children and other vulnerable populations. For example, the 2002 Farm Security and Rural Investment Act restored eligibility for the SNAP program to "qualified" children by removing the five-year waiting period, although it maintained that "not qualified" children would remain ineligible for the program. In 2009, the Children's Health Insurance Program Reauthorization Act (CHIPRA) provided states the option to waive the five-year ban for "lawfully residing" children and pregnant women, enabling states to provide federally funded health coverage to these populations regardless of their date of entry (Broder & Blazer, 2011). To date, more than half the states have taken up the option to provide health care to lawfully present immigrant children and pregnant women.

Other federal immigration laws also create additional restrictions on immigrants' access to federal programs. For example, immigration authorities have long had the authority to deny an immigrant from entering the United States if it is determined that the individual may become a "public charge," which is defined as an individual "who is likely to become primarily dependent on the government for subsistence, as demonstrated by either the receipt of public cash assistance for income maintenance or institutionalization for long-term care at government expense." Public charge determinations are based on the assessment of various factors, including an immigrant's health, education, income, and other factors, such as affidavits of support (Broder & Blazer, 2011). Affidavits of support were established under the Illegal Immigration Reform and Immigrant Responsibility Act of 1996 (IIRIRA), which required family members in the United States to sign these affidavits on behalf of individuals who did not pass the public charge test on their own. Sponsors must demonstrate strict income levels and agree to repay any means-tested public benefit the sponsored individual may have received (Broder & Blazer, 2011).

The 1996 immigration and welfare laws also require agencies to "deem" the income of an immigrant's sponsor as well as the sponsor's spouse in determining an immigrant's eligibility for federal means-tested benefits (Broder & Blazer, 2011). These "deeming rules" apply until the immigrant obtains U.S. citizenship or approximately 10 years of work history (40 quarters) in the United States, thereby further delaying access to programs in some cases.

PRACTICE IMPLICATIONS OF IMMIGRANT
BARRIERS TO FEDERAL BENEFITS

Research has consistently shown that immigrant families use public benefits at lower rates than their native-born counterparts, despite their large share of the low-income population (Fortuny & Chaudry, 2011; Hernandez & Napierala, 2013). Children in immigrant families are more likely than children in native families to live in families with incomes below the federal poverty level, despite the fact that they are significantly more likely to live in low-income families with working parents (Chaudry & Fortuny, 2010; Hernandez & Napierala, 2013). This is because the average median hourly wage for immigrant parents is lower than that of native parents ($18 versus $14), although this varies greatly by country of origin, education level, and immigration status (Chaudry & Fortuny, 2010). Unauthorized parents generally have the lowest incomes, with many earning lower than the minimum wage and enduring poor work conditions (Yoshikawa, 2011). Despite their income eligibility, children of immigrants are less likely than children of natives to participate in federal programs like SNAP (Chaudry & Fortuny, 2010). It is important to note that U.S. citizen children with immigrant parents are also less likely than U.S. citizen children of native parents to participate in programs like SNAP and CHIP (Capps & Fortuny, 2006; Kenney, Lynch, Cook, & Phong, 2010).

Several studies have also documented the reasons for low use of public benefits by immigrants, including lack of knowledge about the programs among immigrants, confusion among immigrants and service providers alike regarding the eligibility rules, and language and cultural barriers (Capps & Fortuny, 2006; Hernandez & Napierala, 2013; Yoshikawa & Kholoptseva, 2013). Because each federal program has its own set of eligibility rules, a mixed-status family (where there may be a range of immigration statuses, including at least one U.S. citizen child and one unauthorized parent) may be faced with a situation in which a U.S. citizen child may qualify for a benefit, whereas an LPR child may need to wait five years, and an unauthorized adult may be ineligible altogether. Because of different standards applied by each state, it is also possible that when an immigrant moves from one state to another, the individual's eligibility for a particular benefit may also change. Thus, it is not uncommon for an immigrant to wrongfully assume he or she is ineligible for a benefit or for a service provider to wrongfully deny an immigrant a benefit to which he or she is entitled.

For mixed-status families, there also is often a reluctance to engage with government authorities because of fear of putting family members at risk of deportation. Research on mixed-status families shows that this reluctance is also increased when programs require proof of income, as is the case with federal means-tested programs (Yoshikawa & Kholoptseva, 2013). Fear of authorities is also increased in states with high rates of immigration enforcement as a result of federal partnerships with local police to apprehend unauthorized immigrants as well as in states that have passed anti-immigrant legislation. For example, an unauthorized parent may be reluctant to seek services for a U.S. citizen child despite the child being eligible, because of fear of being turned over to immigration authorities. State anti-immigrant legislation, such as the bills passed recently in Arizona and Alabama, included provisions requiring health and human service providers to document the immigration status of individuals who apply for public benefits, including programs that do not require the verification of immigration status (Baxter, 2012). Many of these restrictions were overturned on constitutional grounds, such as the provision in the Alabama law requiring that schools document the immigration status of children and parents. Nonetheless, the result was still a chilling effect on immigrant use of benefits in those states.

CASE STUDY

Navigating Complex Eligibility Rules: Gina's Mixed-Status Family

Gina is a single mother of three children, who came to Georgia from Guatemala to join her sister after Gina's husband died in a workplace accident. Gina eventually remarried another undocumented immigrant from Guatemala and had a third child, who is a U.S. citizen by birth. As a nanny working in the informal market, Gina helps support her family on approximately $200 a week. She worries a lot about her children not receiving the services they need, and she was once scared that if she took any of her children to the doctor she could get in trouble or have her children taken away because of her own immigration status. Ever since Georgia passed an immigration law in 2011, Gina has been reluctant to seek public benefits for her children.

CASE STUDY (*CONTINUED*)

Her two oldest children, a daughter who is 17 and a son who is 13, are undocumented as well. The 17-year-old daughter joined an immigrant youth group in her
high school during the past year, and with their support she was able to obtain
temporary legal status through the 2012 Deferred Action for Childhood Arrivals
(DACA) program. With high school graduation right around the corner, the oldest
daughter is considering working for a year to help out her family, as she is the
only one who has permission to work legally. Neither she nor her 13-year-old
brother has access to federally funded health care. Her brother is also too young
to apply for the DACA program and will have to wait until he is 15 to apply. Their
younger sister, who is a 9-year-old U.S. citizen, has access to the Children's
Health Insurance Program (CHIP) and all other federal means-tested benefits.
Despite being the youngest, she is the only one who talks about potentially going
to college, because, as a U.S. citizen and resident of Georgia, she would qualify for
in-state tuition and therefore does not have to worry about leaving her family. Despite being siblings and growing up in the same home, Gina's children have access
to very different benefits and therefore also have very different plans for their
respective futures.

As previously mentioned, there also remain concerns among immigrants
that use of certain federal benefits may have immigration consequences,
such as limiting an individual's ability to sponsor other family members in
the future or creating negative consequences for one's sponsor. For example, confusion regarding the types of benefits that put an individual at risk
of becoming a public charge continue to deter immigrants from applying
for benefits, despite efforts by government agencies to clarify that use of
certain noncash benefits, such as health care, do not make an individual a
public charge (Broder & Blazer, 2011).

The limited access to critical safety net programs by immigrant children
and families raises concerns not only for their overall health and well-being
but also for their potential for entering systems such as the child welfare or
juvenile justice systems. Research consistently shows that poverty is one of
the greatest predictors for system involvement (Capps & Fortuny, 2006).
For service providers, the federal laws governing immigrant and refugee
benefit eligibilities also have implications for the extent to which providers

are able to connect children and families to available benefits. In addition to the need for strong language-access mechanisms and training in culturally responsive practice, it is important that agencies provide updated guidance to staff on the current policies in their state.

Research has also shown that immigrants are more likely to access benefits in community-based settings that they are traditionally comfortable with rather than through government agencies (Crosnoe et al., 2012). Schools, faith-based institutions, and community-based organizations have all demonstrated success in providing the immigrant community with information about the importance and availability of benefit programs (Crosnoe et al., 2012; Vericker, Fortuny, Finegold, & Ozdemir, 2010). For example, research shows that immigrants are more likely to access the WIC program not only because of its availability to all immigrants regardless of status but also because the program is often administered at community-based centers and even within some schools (Vericker et al., 2010).

Finally, research also shows that outreach to immigrant communities is essential in ensuring that immigrants are aware of the programs that both they and their children are eligible for. Unlike refugees, who often must engage with government entities and other service providers on a regular basis, immigrants, especially those who are unauthorized, are less likely to engage with such agencies and have access to this type of information. Thus, models such as the *promotora* model, which focuses on immigrant educators ("*promotoras*") going out into the community to share information about health needs and available resources, are especially effective in ensuring that the immigrant community is educated about how to access certain benefits (Flores, 2012).

LOOKING AHEAD: FUTURE ELIGIBILITY POLICIES

When Congress made these sweeping changes to immigration and welfare laws, the stated reasons for doing so were "to encourage self-sufficiency and to remove an extra incentive for coming to the United States" and also to defray costs (Broder, 2005). However, these goals neglected to weigh the short- and long-term impacts on children and families. Although advocates have worked to reverse some of the negative impacts of the 1996 laws, it has become increasingly difficult in the current political climate to expand eligibility or even maintain current eligibility. As public sentiment over unauthorized immigration has become increasingly divided, there have been efforts by policymakers to further restrict immigrants' access to federal benefits and income supports, including legislative proposals to prevent U.S. citizen and LPR children in mixed-status families from receiving the Additional Child Tax Credit (ACTC) and to deter children in mixed-status families from accessing SNAP benefits (Curran & Cervantes, 2011).

Access to federal means-tested benefits has also been a controversial topic in recent deliberations on comprehensive immigration reform, with targeted efforts by Congress to ensure that newly legalized immigrants will face very long waiting periods before being able to access federal programs. The Obama administration's 2014 immigration actions also have similarly come under attack, encountering attempts to block the programs altogether as well as criticism of the ability of those who benefit from the programs to access earned income supports such as the Earned Income Tax Credit (EITC).

PROTECTING THE CHILD TAX CREDIT FOR IMMIGRANT FAMILIES

The Child Tax Credit (CTC) is a tax credit specifically designed to help working parents offset the costs of raising children, and its refundable portion, the Additional Child Tax Credit (ACTC), is available to families who meet certain income requirements. Currently, immigrant parents are able to claim the CTC and ACTC when they file their taxes using either a Social Security Number (SSN) or an Individual Taxpayer Identification Number (ITIN), which is a tax identification number provided to those who do not qualify for an SSN. In recent years, there have been several legislative proposals introduced in Congress to require an SSN in order to claim the CTC and ACTC, and such proposals have the potential to push millions of children living in immigrant families further below the poverty line. The average immigrant household that receives the ACTC earns just $21,000 a year. Without the ACTC, these families would be denied an average refund of $1,500, money that is often used on food, rent, and other basic needs.

FEDERAL EFFORTS TO ADDRESS THE UNAUTHORIZED POPULATION

Currently, 5.1 million children, 4.1 million of whom are U.S. citizens, live in immigrant families with at least one unauthorized parent, and less than

1 million children are unauthorized themselves and continue to face uncertain futures (Capps, Fix, and Zong, 2016). Only reforms to current immigration law that provide a path to citizenship, which must be enacted by federal legislation, can provide unauthorized immigrants and their families with permanent relief and long-term economic opportunities. Pending federal legislative action, the executive branch of the government has taken steps to address the impact of enforcement measures on families through reforms to the immigration enforcement system, changes to the legal immigration system, and the introduction of programs aimed at providing temporary relief to certain segments of the unauthorized population, including those who entered the United States as children and those who are parents of U.S. citizens and LPRs.

FEDERAL IMMIGRATION REFORM

Policymakers of both major political parties recognize that the current U.S. immigration system is in need of reform and that whatever legislation is passed must incorporate a solution for addressing the 11.7 million undocumented immigrants currently estimated to be living in the United States. Policymakers also recognize the need to update the legal immigration system to ensure that the system is able to meet future immigration flows. Since the last sweeping immigration reform law was passed in 1986, Congress has fallen short in subsequent attempts to pass new legislation.

The most recent attempt occurred during the 113th Congress, with the passage of the bipartisan Border Security, Economic Opportunity, and Immigration Modernization Act of 2013 by the U.S. Senate on June 27, 2013. The bill included several important provisions directly impacting children and families, including (1) an earned pathway to citizenship for unauthorized immigrants as well as a unique, more expedient pathway for certain unauthorized immigrants who entered the United States as children; (2) provisions to protect children and families impacted by immigration enforcement measures, including the ability of parents to make decisions regarding their child's care throughout the detention and removal process as well as requirements for state child welfare agencies to help promote reunification of children in foster care with detained or deported parents; (3) updates to the family reunification system, including the elimination and expansion of certain categories as well as the lifting of visa caps on others; (4) changes in immigration law to take into account the potential impact on children in critical removal and inadmissibility decisions, such as providing immigration judges with discretion to consider hardship to children when determining whether to order a parent removed; and (5) additional protections for unaccompanied immigrant children, including improved screening mechanisms and access to federally funded legal representation (Cervantes, 2013). Although many of the bill's provisions promoted the best interests of children in immigrant families, it is important to note that the bill still failed to address concerns regarding newly legalized immigrants' access to benefits, as all immigrants having "provisional status" would remain ineligible for federal means-tested benefits and would have to wait an additional five years once they obtained LPR status, thus leading to eligibility waiting periods as long as 13 years (Cervantes, 2013).

The House of Representatives ultimately did not take up the bill, nor did the House advance any immigration reform legislation of its own. Thus, the urgency for comprehensive immigration reform remains, with millions of families still separated every day by an outdated family-based immigration system and many family members still at risk of detention and deportation (Cervantes & Gonzales, 2013).

THE DREAM ACT

In recent years, there have also been efforts in the U.S. Congress to advance legislation to provide a path to citizenship for undocumented youths living in the United States, both through stand-alone legislation and as part of comprehensive immigration reform. The Development, Relief and Education for Alien Minors Act (DREAM Act) is a federal bill that has been introduced in various versions since its first introduction in 2001 by Senators Dick Durbin and Orrin Hatch.

Although the specific provisions of the DREAM Act change with each version introduced, the core components of the bill include a path to citizenship for certain undocumented youths who came to the United States as children, had resided in the United States for a set amount of time before the bill's passage, and have completed some higher education and/or military service. Previous versions of the bill required youths to have entered the

United States before the age of 16, and many versions have set an age cap for eligibility, an exception being the most recent version, which was included in the Senate's 2013 comprehensive immigration reform bill.

Several versions of the DREAM Act have also addressed higher education access issues, such as repeal of Section 505 of the 1996 IIRIRA law, which prohibits states from providing in-state tuition or other benefits to unauthorized students based on state residency without also providing the same benefit to U.S. citizen students who are not residents of the state. As a result, states could be deterred from providing in-state tuition rates to undocumented students. Some versions of the DREAM Act have also provided limited access to higher education assistance, specifically federal loans and work-study, to help defray the high cost of tuition because many unauthorized students come from low-income families (Gonzales & Bautista, 2014; Lindsey, 2013). To date, 18 states have enacted their own legislation to provide in-state tuition rates to undocumented students through the development of a range of residency requirements for in-state tuition purposes (such as requiring that a student attend a local high school for a set number of years), with Texas being the first state to pass such a bill, in 2001 (Lindsey, 2013).

Historically, the DREAM Act has been a bipartisan bill, and it has gained increasing public support in recent years with the rise of the undocumented youth movement, which has propelled youths, commonly referred to as "DREAMers," to reveal their undocumented status, share their stories with the public, and mobilize on behalf of policy change (Gonzalez & Bautista, 2014; Lindsey, 2013). In 2010, the DREAM Act was brought to a vote for the first time as a stand-alone bill, and although it passed the House of Representatives in a historic bipartisan vote during the lame-duck session, it later fell five votes short in the Senate.

FEDERAL ADMINISTRATIVE REFORMS

Because of inaction on federal legislation, administrative immigration reforms have become increasingly important in providing undocumented immigrant families with some form of interim relief. The Obama administration has introduced various reforms to minimize the harmful impact of immigration enforcement on children and families and to provide temporary legal status to certain segments of the undocumented population, including the introduction of two targeted deferred action programs in late 2014.

Deferred Action for Childhood Arrivals

On June 15, 2012, President Obama introduced the Deferred Action for Childhood Arrivals program (DACA), which was implemented the following August. The original 2012 DACA program provided a renewable two-year reprieve from deportation and granted work authorization to certain youths who arrived in the United States as children. To be eligible for the 2012 program, an individual must meet the following requirements: (1) have entered the United States before the age of 16 and been younger than 31 years old on the date of the policy's announcement; (2) been at least 15 years old at the time of application; (3) lived in the United States for five continuous years before the program's announcement; (4) obtained a high school diploma or general equivalency diploma (GED), been honorably discharged from the Armed Services or Coast Guard, or be currently enrolled in school; and (5) passed a background check and possess no felony, significant misdemeanor, or three or more nonsignificant misdemeanor charges. Shortly after the policy's implementation, the Obama administration later clarified that DACA beneficiaries were *not* to be considered "lawfully present" for the purposes of health care, thereby making DACA beneficiaries ineligible for federally funded health care programs.

The Migration Policy Institute estimates that 2.1 million people could potentially be eligible for the 2012 DACA program, with 1.2 million immediately eligible and others needing to wait to meet minimum-age or academic requirements (Batalova, Hooker, & Capps, 2014). As of January 2015, more than 720,000 immigrant youths had applied for DACA, and more than 685,000 applications had been approved (U.S. Citizenship and Immigration Services, 2015). In an analysis of the first two years of the program, the UnDACAmented research project found that DACA had significantly impacted the lives of beneficiaries by fostering a greater number of economic and educational opportunities (Gonzales & Bautista, 2014). Nearly 60 percent of DACA beneficiaries surveyed had obtained a new job and a driver's license, nearly half had opened their first bank account, and more than a third had obtained their first credit card (Gonzales & Bautista, 2014). Although DACA also expanded educational opportunities by providing increased access to in-state tuition rates and campus employment, barriers to financing a higher education remained for many (Gonzalez & Bautista, 2014). Of those who are eligible for DACA but have not applied, parenthood, economic hardship (making it difficult to pay the $465 application fee), and distrust of government agencies were all stated as reasons for not applying for the program (Gonzales & Bautista, 2014).

CASE STUDY

A DREAMer's Journey: Nelly's Story

Nelly traveled to New York City from Mexico with her mother and siblings when she was 13 years old. She struggled for many years to catch up with her peers in school because of her limited English and her evening job, which she needed to help out her parents with bills. Ultimately, she was able to overcome the odds and become the first from her family to attend college. She attended a small community college in Indianapolis on a part-time basis, where she was able to access in-state tuition and was awarded a few small scholarships. Nelly pursued a degree in early childhood education while working full-time at a supermarket, despite the fact that it was unclear if she would ever be able to work legally in the field of her choice. She graduated in 2013, one year after President Obama announced the Deferred Action for Childhood Arrivals (DACA) program. She obtained her DACA status and work permit shortly after her graduation and was able to secure a job in a dual-language pre-kindergarten program right away because of her training and bilingual skills. She was also able to obtain a driver's license for the first time and open a bank account. Nelly says, "My hard work and those who believed in me helped me get closer to my dream. And it was ultimately DACA that made my dream come true."

Despite the success of DACA in expanding the economic and social mobility of its beneficiaries, the program's temporary nature deters some from applying, and others are similarly waiting for a more permanent option, such as immigration reform (Gonzalez & Bautista, 2014). The educational requirements and cost also remain barriers to those who are unable to enroll in school because of family responsibilities or other economic barriers. The extent to which community organizations and school personnel are able to conduct outreach in immigrant communities and assist potential DACA applicants with the application process also impacts application and approval rates. However, even with increased participation in the program, a permanent solution for DACA beneficiaries and their families still depends on legislative change that can provide a path to citizenship.

Following the failure of the House of Representatives to move forward with immigration reform legislation in 2014, President Obama signaled that his administration would be taking administrative steps to improve the immigration system. On November 20, 2014, he announced his administration's most robust administrative immigration reforms to date, known as the "Immigration Accountability Executive Actions." The new actions included expansion of the 2012 Deferred Action for Childhood Arrivals program. The revised program removes the arbitrary age cap of the 2012 program, meaning that those who met all the other requirements but were "aged out" of the previous program would now be able to apply. The revised program also modifies the previous requirement of continuous presence from June 15, 2007, to January 1, 2010, and extends the two-year term of the program to three years. Implementation of the expanded DACA program is still pending, but it has been estimated that up to 300,000 DREAMers may benefit from the program's expansion (Capps & Rosenblum, 2014).

Deferred Action for Parents of Americans and Lawful Permanent Residents (DAPA)

The Obama administration's immigration actions include a new deferred action program for the parents of U.S. citizens and LPRs, known as the Deferred Action for Parents of Americans and Lawful Permanent Residents (DAPA) program. Similar to the DACA program, the DAPA program provides a renewable three-year reprieve from deportation and work authorization for those who are eligible. To be eligible for the program, an individual must (1) be the parent of a U.S. citizen or LPR (regardless of qualifying son's or daughter's age); (2) have continuously resided in the United States since January 1, 2010; and (3) pass a background check and have no felony, significant misdemeanor, or three or more nonsignificant misdemeanor charges.

It has been estimated that up to 3.3 million parents of minor U.S. citizen and LPR children growing up in the United States could benefit from the DAPA program (Capps & Rosenblum, 2014). Children whose parents qualify for the program will no longer need to live in fear of being separated from a parent as a result of deportation, and their economic security and overall well-being have the potential to greatly improve on account of their parents obtaining work authorization. Research reveals that many undocumented parents work in low-wage, unstable jobs and are often forced to work multiple jobs, leaving them little time to focus on nurturing their child's education and overall development (Yoshikawa, 2011; Yoshikawa & Kholoptseva, 2013). Parents who benefit from the program will be better able to secure stable employment, earn higher wages, and have more time to focus on parenting (Suro, Suarez-Orozco, & Canizales, 2015; Cervantes 2014). By obtaining Social Security numbers and paying taxes, working parents who meet the necessary income requirements will also have access to the Earned Income Tax Credit, a proven tool for lifting families out of poverty (Center on Budget and Policy Priorities, 2015). An analysis by the Center for American Progress estimates that beneficiaries of DAPA could see an increase of 6 percent to 10 percent in earned wages, and another analysis estimates that as many as 40,000 children in California alone could be lifted out of poverty as a result of their parents obtaining DAPA (Oakford, 2014a; Pastor, Sanchez, & Carter, 2015).

Expansion of Provisional Waiver Program

The 2014 executive immigration actions also include expansion of the 2013 provisional unlawful presence program. This program aims to enable certain individuals who have been unlawfully present in the United States for more than 180 days to apply for a "waiver" to overcome the reentry barriers that have historically forced individuals to be separated from family members for several years as they wait to qualify for an immigrant visa. The new provisional waiver program enables applicants to apply for a waiver "stateside" while in the United States and requires their departure only when they need to appear for a visa interview with a consulate official abroad. The 2013 provisional waiver program was restricted to the spouses, parents, and certain children of U.S. citizens (who were unmarried, at least 17 years of age, and under the age of 21). Under the new executive actions, the stateside waiver will now also be available to the sons and daughters of U.S. citizens regardless of the son's or daughter's age as well as to the spouses, sons, and daughters of LPRs. These changes are expected to prevent the unnecessary separation of families as they wait for approval of an immigrant visa (Cervantes, 2014).

Immigration Enforcement Reforms Focused on Family Unity

The Obama administration has also implemented important immigration enforcement reforms in recent years to address concerns regarding the detrimental impact of detention and deportation on children and families. Department of Homeland Security (DHS) data reveal that more than 72,410 parents of U.S. citizen children had been deported in 2013, with even higher numbers in previous years (Foley, 2014). The collateral damage to children left behind has been well documented by several studies that demonstrate that separation from a parent because of immigration enforcement measures, or even the fear of losing a parent, significantly harms a child's mental and physical health, academic performance, and economic security (Capps, Casteneda, Chaudry, & Santos, 2007; Dreby, 2012; Satinsky, Hu, Heller, & Farhang, 2013).

In 2011, Immigration and Customs Enforcement (ICE) Assistant Secretary John Morton issued a memorandum directing the agency to prioritize removal of those who pose a threat to national security or have committed certain crimes and/or specific immigration violations, such as those who crossed the border in the previous three years (U.S. Immigration and Customs Enforcement, 2011a). That guidance was followed by another memorandum, commonly referred to as the "prosecutorial discretion memo," which delineated the categories of individuals that were to be considered for prosecutorial discretion (U.S. Immigration and Customs Enforcement, 2011b). Many of the detention reforms that followed in subsequent years focused on developing screening mechanisms and tools to enable ICE to identify certain vulnerable populations, such as pregnant or nursing parents as well as parents of minor U.S. citizen or LPR children, and determine their eligibility for release (Butera & Cervantes, 2013).

In August 2013, ICE announced a policy known as the "parental interest directive" to address barriers facing detained and deported parents involved with the child welfare system. The directive establishes guidelines for detained parents with children in the child welfare system to help facilitate communication between child welfare agencies and immigration enforcement agencies as well as facilitate a parent's ability to attend relevant court proceedings, meet case plan requirements, and make arrangements for children at the time of removal (U.S. Immigration and Customs Enforcement, 2013). The directive also allows for the limited use of humanitarian parole for parents outside the United States who may need to be physically present for a termination of parental rights (TPR) hearing. In early 2015, the Department of Health and Human Services Administration for Children and Families issued an information memorandum to state and local child welfare agencies to help ensure compliance with the ICE parental interest directive and provide guidance on other strategies to better facilitate reunification of system-involved children with detained or deported parents (U.S. Department of Health and Human Services, Administration for Children and Families, 2015).

The 2014 immigration executive actions also included revisions to enforcement priorities and policies. For example, ICE's enforcement priorities were further narrowed to target felons, national security threats, and recent border crossers who entered after January 1, 2014, including parents and children who entered the U.S. to seek refuge from violence in Central America (Rosenblum, 2015). The executive actions also included the end of the controversial jail-based immigration enforcement program known as the Secure Communities program. The Secure Communities program required screening of all individuals apprehended by law enforcement for possible immigration violations, which often resulted in longer detention for the individual, pending further investigation by immigration authorities. Although the stated goal of Secure Communities and other law enforcement–based programs was to target "serious criminals" for immigration enforcement, analysis of DHS removal statistics revealed that the program also resulted in the deportation of many parents and other individuals for very minor offenses (Kohli, Markowitz, & Chavez, 2011). It is expected that the Secure Communities program will be replaced by another criminal justice screening program, called the Priority Enforcement Program (PEP), but the practice of broadly issuing "detainers" and holding individuals who have not been charged with a crime is expected to be discontinued.

IMPLEMENTATION OF ADMINISTRATIVE
IMMIGRATION REFORMS

Shortly after the announcement of the immigration executive actions, state and federal policymakers quickly reacted to both oppose and approve the reforms. This reaction included federal legislative action to restrict funding to DHS, and a lawsuit by several states to block the new deferred action programs. On February 16, 2015, a federal district court in Texas filed a preliminary injunction to temporarily block implementation of the expanded DACA program and new DAPA program. On February 23, 2015, the U.S. Department of Justice responded to the decision by appealing it and making an emergency stay request, which would have allowed the programs to move forward pending the consideration of a full appeal. The emergency stay was later denied, and the Fifth Circuit Court of Appeals affirmed the district court's order. On January 19, 2016, the Supreme Court agreed to hear the case, and a final decision is expected in late June 2016. At the time of writing, the 2014 deferred action programs remain stalled.

Even if the immigration accountability executive actions are fully implemented at a later date, the ultimate success of these new programs will depend on the extent to which eligible applicants are able to enroll in the new programs and fully integrate into civic life. Additionally, the whole range of executive actions are only expected to provide relief for approximately half of the U.S. undocumented population, leaving millions at risk of deportation. The new deferred action programs, like the 2012 DACA program, also fall short of providing beneficiaries with a path to citizenship or full access to federal safety net programs, such as CHIP and SNAP. Advocates for children and families also remain concerned that, even in light of the new administrative actions, the Obama administration continues to prioritize the detention and deportation of individuals who have recently entered the country, including children and families entering the United States in order to escape violence in Central America. Thus, it is clear that the only permanent solution for the U.S. undocumented population remains for Congress to pass immigration reform legislation that includes a path to citizenship.

CONCLUSION

Just as the 1996 immigration and reform laws created long-term implications for immigrant and refugee families by impacting access to benefits, federal policy decisions in the years ahead will largely determine the long-term well-being of immigrant and refugee children in the United States. Complex immigration rules create challenges for potential beneficiaries as well as service providers and put children at risk of being denied critical benefits they are entitled to. Thus, it is important that policymakers be intent on incorporating the unique needs of immigrant and refugee children into policy discussions focused on strengthening federal safety net programs and reforming the U.S. immigration system. In the coming years, Congress will have the opportunity to reconsider legislation on a wide range of child-specific issues, such as child nutrition programs, welfare reform, and education reform. Because of the increase in unaccompanied immigrant children in recent years, Congress may also be considering changes to the 2008 Trafficking Victims Protections Reauthorization Act as well as other legislative reforms dealing with Central American refugees (Cervantes & Mathur, 2014). Finally, the outcome of the pending 2014 immigration executive actions is likely to influence the future of federal immigration reform, an issue that will continue to be a legislative priority for policymakers, both Democrat and Republican, as the Hispanic and Asian electorate, which is increasingly comprised of naturalized immigrant voters and children of immigrants, continues to grow in political power (Oakford, 2014b).

As federal policymakers consider these various legislative immigration proposals, they will have an opportunity either to further undermine the health and well-being of immigrant and refugee children or work to promote these children's best interests by implementing policies proven to strengthen outcomes for all children. Given that children in immigrant families will continue to comprise a significant segment of the increasingly diverse U.S. child population and future workforce, the impact of these policy decisions will have implications for the nation as a whole.

KEY TERMS

LAWFUL PERMANENT RESIDENT (LPR)   Under U.S. immigration law, any person not a citizen of the United States who is residing in the United States under legally recognized and lawfully recorded permanent residence as an immigrant. Also known as a "green card holder."

NATURALIZED CITIZEN   LPRs who have undergone the naturalization process to become U.S. citizens. LPRs must reside in the United States for five or more years and meet other requirements, including a background check and citizenship test. LPRs married to U.S. citizens can naturalize in three years, and some specific categories may be eligible for naturalization sooner than that.

NONQUALIFIED IMMIGRANT An immigrant outside the qualified immigrant category. This includes persons with temporary protected status, those seeking asylum, other lawfully present immigrants (such as students), and unauthorized immigrants.

QUALIFIED IMMIGRANT A foreign-born person who is eligible to receive federal public benefits and falls into one of the following categories:

- LPRs
- Asylees
- Refugees
- Persons paroled in the United States for a period of at least one year
- Persons granted withholding of deportation
- Persons granted conditional entry (before April 1, 1980)
- Cuban and Haitian entrants
- Amerasian immigrants
- Victims of severe human trafficking (since 2000, victims of trafficking and their derivative beneficiaries have been eligible for federal benefits)
- Battered spouses and children (with a pending or approved spousal visa or self-petition under the Violence Against Women Act)

UNAUTHORIZED IMMIGRANT An immigrant who has not received permission to live or work in the United States.

STUDY QUESTIONS

1 In what ways do federal public benefit laws inhibit immigrant and refugee families from accessing benefits? Why is immigrant eligibility for benefits such a delicate political issue?

2 What can service providers do to ensure that immigrants and refugees are connected to public benefits?

3 How do federal public benefit and immigration laws uniquely impact mixed-status families?

4 What is the potential impact of federal bills such as comprehensive immigration reform and the DREAM Act on family and child well-being?

5 What federal administrative policies have been announced in recent years, and how can these policies help improve outcomes for immigrant families? What are their limitations?

ADDITIONAL RESOURCES

Center on Immigration and Child Welfare (research, practice, and policy resources focused on immigrant and refugee children involved in the child welfare system): http://www.cimmcw.org

First Focus Center for the Children of Immigrants (information on various federal policy issues impacting children in immigrant families): http://www.firstfocus.org

Migration Policy Institute (data and research on immigrant and refugee communities): http://www.migrationpolicy.org

National Immigration Law Center (information on various federal policy issues impacting low-income immigrants and refugees, including public benefits): http://www.nilc.org

National Resource Center for Permanency and Family Connections (resources on how to ensure safety, permanency, and well-being for immigrant families): http://www.hunter.cuny.edu/socwork/nrcfcpp/info _services/immigration-and-child-welfare.html

REFERENCES

Batalova, J., Hooker, S., & Capps, R. (2014). *DACA at the two-year mark: A national and state profile of youth eligible and applying for deferred action.* Washington, DC: Migration Policy Institute.

Baxter, T. (2012). *Alabama's immigration disaster: The harshest law in the land harms the state's economy and society.* Washington, DC: Center for American Progress.

Broder, T. (2005). Immigrant eligibility for public benefits. In G. P. Adams (Ed.), *Immigration and nationality law handbook 2005–06* (pp. 759–786). Washington, DC: American Immigration Lawyers Association.

Broder, T., & Blazer, J. (2011). Overview of immigrant eligibility for federal programs. Washington, DC: National Immigration Law Center.

Butera, E., & Cervantes, W. (2013). Family unity in the face of immigration enforcement: Past, present, and future. In S. D. Phillips, Y. Lincroft, A. J. Dettlaff, L. Bruce, & W. Cervantes (Eds.), *Children in harm's way: The intersection of the criminal justice, immigration enforcement, and child welfare system.* Washington, DC: Jointly published by The Sentencing Project and First Focus.

Capps, R., Casteneda, R. M., Chaudry, A. J., & Santos, R. (2007). *Paying the price: The impact of immigration raids on America's children.* Washington, DC: Urban Institute.

Capps, R., Fix, M., & Zong, J. (2016). *A profile of U.S. children with unauthorized parents.* Washington, DC: Migration Policy Institute.

Capps, R., & Fortuny, K. (2006). *Immigration and child and family policy.* Washington, DC: Urban Institute.

Capps, R., & Rosenblum, M. (2014). *Executive action for unauthorized immigrants: Estimates of the populations that could receive relief.* Washington, DC: Migration Policy Institute.

Center on Budget and Policy Priorities. (2015). *Policy basics: The earned income tax credit.* Fact sheet. Retrieved from http://www.cbpp.org/cms/?fa=view&id=2505

Cervantes, W. (2013). *Immigration reform and the implications for children and families: An analysis of the Senate immigration reform bill.* Washington, DC: First Focus.

——. (2014). *A step forward: Immigration executive actions & our nation's children.* Washington, DC: First Focus.

Cervantes, W., & Gonzales, R. (2013). *The cost of inaction: Why children can't wait for immigration reform.* Washington, DC: First Focus Center for the Children of Immigrants.

Cervantes, W., & Mathur, R. (2014). *Legal protections for children in the Trafficking Victims Protection Act.* Washington, DC: First Focus Center for the Children of Immigrants.

Chaudry, A. J., & Fortuny, K. (2010). *Children of immigrants: Economic well-being.* Washington, DC: Urban Institute.

Crosnoe, R., Pedroza, J., Purtell, K., Fortuny, K., Perreira, K., Ulvestad, K., . . . Chaudry, A. (2012). *Promising practices for increasing immigrants' access to Health and Human Services.* Washington, DC: U.S. Department of Health and Human Services, Assistant Secretary for Planning and Evaluation.

Curran, M., & Cervantes, W. (2011). *The important role of the Child Tax Credit in reducing child poverty.* Washington, DC: First Focus.

Dreby, J. (2012). *How today's immigration enforcement policies impact children, families, and communities: A view from the ground.* Washington, DC: Center for American Progress.

Flores, G. (2012). Community health workers, *promotores,* and parent mentors: Innovative community-based approaches in improving the health and health-care of children. In *Big ideas 2012: Children in the Southwest* (pp. 154–162). Washington, DC: First Focus.

Foley, E. (2014, June 25). Deportation separated thousands of U.S. citizen children from deported parents in 2013. *Huffington Post.* Retrieved from http://www.huffingtonpost.com/2014/06/25/parents-deportation_n_5531552.html

Fortuny, K., & Chaudry, A. (2012). *Overview of immigrants' eligibility for SNAP, TANF, Medicaid, and CHIP.* Washington, DC: U.S. Department of Health and Human Services, Office of the Assistant Secretary for Planning and Evaluation, Office of Human Services Policy.

Fortuny, K., & Chaudry, A. J. (2011). *A comprehensive review of immigrant access to Health and Human Services.* Washington, DC: Urban Institute.

Fortuny, K., Hernandez, D. J., & Chaudry, A. J. (2010). *Young children of immigrants: The leading edge of America's future.* Washington, DC: The Urban Institute.

Gonzales, R., & Bautista, A. M. (2014). *Two years and counting: Assessing the growing power of DACA.* Washington, DC: American Immigration Council.

Hernandez, D. J., & Napierala, J. S. (2013). *Diverse children: Race, ethnicity, and immigration in America's new non-majority generation.* New York, NY: Foundation for Child Development.

Kenney, G. M., Lynch, V., Cook, A., & Phong, S. (2010). Who and where are the children yet to enroll in Medicaid and the Children's Health Insurance Program? *Health Affairs, 29,* 1920–29.

Kohli, A., Markowitz, P., & Chavez, L. (2011). *Secure communities by the numbers: An analysis of demographics and due process.* Berkeley, CA: Chief Justice Earl Warren Institute on Law and Social Policy, University of California, Berkeley, Law School.

Lindsey, K. (2013). *Access to education: Challenges and opportunities for immigrant students.* Washington, DC: First Focus Center for the Children of Immigrants.

National Immigration Law Center. (2013, January 29). *A quick guide to immigrant eligibility for ACA and key federal means-tested programs.* Table. Retrieved from www.nilc.org

Oakford, P. (2014a). *Administrative action on immigration reform: The fiscal benefits of temporary work permits.* Washington, DC: Center for American Progress.

——. (2014b). *The Latino electorate by generation: The rising influence of children of immigrants.* Washington, DC: Center for American Progress.

Pastor, M., Sanchez, J., & Carter, V. (2015). *The kids aren't alright—but they could be: The impact of deferred action for parents of Americans and lawful permanent residents (DAPA) on children.* Los Angeles: University of Southern California Dornsife Center for the Study of Immigrant Integration.

Rosenblum, M. (2015) *Understanding the potential impact of executive action on immigration enforcement.* Washington, DC: Migration Policy Institute.

Satinsky, S., Hu, A., Heller, J., & Farhang, L. (2013). *Family unity, family health: How family-focused immigration reform will mean better health for children and families.* Oakland, CA: Human Impact Partners.

Suro, R., Suarez-Orozco, M., & Canizales, S. (2015). *Removing insecurity: How American children will benefit from President Obama's executive action on immigration.* Los Angeles: Tomás Rivera Policy Institute at the University of Southern California and the Institute for Immigration, Globalization, and Education at the University of California-Los Angeles.

U.S. Citizenship and Immigration Services. (2015). *Number of I-821D, consideration of deferred action for childhood arrivals by fiscal year, quarter, intake, biometrics and case status: 2012–2014* [Dataset]. Retrieved from http://www.uscis .gov/tools/reports-studies/immigration-forms-data/data-set-deferred-action -childhood-arrivals

U.S. Department of Health and Human Services, Administration for Children and Families. (2015). *Case planning and service delivery for families with parents and legal guardians who are detained or deported by immigration enforcement.* Information memorandum. Washington, DC: Author.

U.S. Immigration and Customs Enforcement. (2011a). *Civil immigration enforcement priorities for the apprehension, detention, and removal of aliens.* Agency memo. Available at: https://www.ice.gov/doclib/news/releases/2011 /110302washingtondc.pdf

———. (2011b). *Exercising prosecutorial discretion consistent with the civil immigration enforcement priorities of the agency or the apprehension, detention, and removal of aliens.* Agency memo. Available at: https://www.ice.gov/doclib/secure -communities/pdf/prosecutorial-discretion-memo.pdf

———. (2013). *Facilitating parental interests in the course of civil immigration enforcement actions.* Agency memo. Retrieved from https://www.ice.gov/parental -interest

Vericker, T., Fortuny, K., Finegold, K., & Ozdemir, S. B. (2010). *Effects of immigration on WIC and NSLP caseloads.* Washington, DC: Urban Institute.

Yoshikawa, H. (2011). *Immigrants raising citizens: Undocumented parents and their young children.* New York: Russell Sage Foundation.

Yoshikawa, H., & Kholoptseva, J. (2013). *Unauthorized immigrant parents and their children's development: A summary of the evidence.* Washington, DC: Migration Policy Institute.

CHAPTER 4

Immigration Enforcement and Its Impact on Immigrant Children and Families

▸ *DAVID B. THRONSON*

U.S. IMMIGRATION LAW IMPACTS FAMILY INTEGRITY in profound ways, serving in some instances as a pathway to unify families and in others as a force to separate them. In reaching these outcomes that are so directly consequential for family integrity, immigration law shares common ground with family law and child welfare law, which also shape decisions about where children and families live. But immigration law and family law systems operate in very different spaces, with underlying goals and values that are quite distinct and often irreconcilable. When families fall outside rigid lines drawn by immigration law, the enforcement of immigration law may override otherwise commendable decisions about who will live where and with whom, often in ways that conflict with core societal and legal values about family.

Immigration law does play a central role in assisting certain qualifying families in obtaining lawful immigration status for family members, and this aspect of immigration law contributes to the impression that the promotion of family unity is one of immigration law's key values. When this pro-family perception is coupled with prevalent negative and dehumanizing stereotypes that unauthorized immigrants are "illegal," it is not uncommon to see as a result the assumption that parents who are unauthorized immigrants or who face deportation simply must be bad people and probably bad parents. Otherwise, why would these parents not just stand in line in our family-friendly immigration system and obtain lawful immigration status? If this is a good family, why would immigration law operate in a way that separates it? Further, when immigration law is enforced through the arrest and detention of parents, often in traumatic circumstances witnessed by their children, a narrative of parental and family unworthiness can be reinforced not only outside the family but also within it.

Missing from this picture is the unacknowledged reality that immigration law has a deeply rooted disregard for family. Immigration law privileges only a subset of families while it fails to provide pathways for many families and family members to obtain lawful immigration status. Contrary to popular perception, U.S. immigration law does not provide a line to stand in for every person who might wish to live with his or her family lawfully in the United States. This is true even for immigrants with U.S. citizen spouses and U.S. citizen children. The divisions that immigration law draws every day in extending lawful status to some and deporting others operate independently of notions of family values or values regarding the importance of parenting that are central in other realms of society and law.

In understanding the ways in which immigration enforcement impacts families and children, it is critical to begin with an understanding of the manner in which immigration law approaches children and families.

IMMIGRATION LAW'S TREATMENT OF CHILDREN AND FAMILIES

At first glance, U.S immigration law appears to promote family unity because it has a vast and complicated system of family-sponsored immigration and avenues for derivative immigration of the family members of certain immigrants who qualify for immigration benefits (8 U.S.C. § 1151(b)(2)(A)(i) (2015); 8 U.S.C. § 1151(c) (2015); 8 U.S.C. § 1153(a) (2015); 8 U.S.C. § 1153(d) (2015)). Indeed, reports of U.S immigration law often attribute to it the goal of keeping families intact (Sanger, 1987). This perception most plainly conflicts with the reality of immigration law when a family member faces deportation from the United States, but even more important are tensions in the basic family immigration framework that operate less obviously but effectively bar families from living together in conformity with immigration law even before enforcement efforts may come to bear.

Before turning to efforts to deport or prevent the entry of immigrants who lack lawful immigration status, it is vital to examine the underlying immigration law that privileges some immigrants with lawful status, making them secure, while leaving others subject to harsh enforcement and increasingly difficult barriers to entry. In other words, immigration law establishes a framework for lawful immigration that narrows the pool of persons and families that will be subject to deportation through the allocation of lawful immigration status to some and the withholding of this status from others. The limited role of family in determining who will obtain lawful status, and thus exemption from some of the harshest provisions of immigration law, is often misunderstood.

In determining who is permitted to immigrate to the United States lawfully, it is widely overlooked that immigration law is very much about determining when U.S. citizens and legal permanent residents can create immigration rights in others. In delineating who is empowered to sponsor and thus generate immigration rights in certain family members, immigration law privileges specified families and relationships while devaluing others. A narrow set of personal choices about family are empowered, whereas others are rejected.

The Immigration and Nationality Act's family-sponsored immigration provisions permit U.S. citizens and legal permanent residents to petition for immigrant visas for certain family members (8 U.S.C. § 1151(b)(2)(A)(i); 8 U.S.C. § 1153(a) (2015)). A "petitioner," a U.S. citizen or person having lawful permanent residence, files for a "beneficiary," a person wishing to immigrate. The law presumes the beneficiary is waiting outside the country. If the principal beneficiary has a spouse or children, in some instances the spouse or children may acquire immigration status as derivatives (8 U.S.C. § 1153(d) (2015)). This system empowers petitioners with lawful immigration status to regulate the flow of immigration status from themselves to qualifying relatives and their dependents.

Immigration law assigns varying priorities to family-sponsored immigration petitions based on the immigration status of the petitioner and the relationship between the petitioner and the beneficiary (8 U.S.C. § 1151(b) (2); 8 U.S.C. § 1153(a) (2015)). Citizens of the United States are allowed to petition for their spouses, children, siblings, and parents (8 U.S.C. § 1153(a); 8 U.S.C. § 1151(b)(2)(A)(i) (2015)). Petitioners with lawful permanent residence may petition only for unmarried children and spouses (8 U.S.C. § 1153(a) (2015)).

Under this system, citizen petitions receive priority over lawful permanent resident petitions. Petitions based on familial relationships deemed closer are privileged over those based on less favored family relationships (Demleitner, 2003; Kelly, 2001; Motomura, 1995; Romero, 2005; Zug, 2009). Petitions of citizens for their spouses and unmarried minor children are not subject to numerical limits, and thus there are no backlogs for these categories (8 U.S.C. § 1151(b) (2015)). Petitions based on relationships that are less favored, including those between a legal permanent resident parent and a child, are subject to annual numerical limitations, and extensive backlogs of many years can develop. The petitions that receive the lowest priority are those based on the relationship between adult citizens and their siblings, and backlogs can extend for decades. Because immigration laws recognize "certain family ties but not others, and then rank those ties in order of importance . . . [they] indicate which relationships matter the most in the eyes of the state. In short, laws relating to the family inherently embody normative ideals" (Huntington, 2009, p. 413). In the absence of a qualifying relative with a qualifying status, family relationships play no role in determining eligibility to obtain lawful immigration status.

In limiting the family relationships that it recognizes, immigration law undermines family arrangements for caretaking and support of children that diverge from nuclear family norms. Immigration law's restrictive use of a narrow construct of family effectively "negates other prevalent family configurations which make up functional families, such as single-parent households, grandparent-grandchild households, same-sex couples, polygamous marriages, and extended family configurations" (King, 2010, p. 515; see Edwards, 2013, regarding recent developments for same-sex couples). This approach ignores the lived reality of millions of children in the United States who "grow up in families in which care is not provided exclusively by two heterosexual opposite-sex parents. Instead, caregivers increasingly include gay and lesbian families, single parent or 'cohabiting' parent families, families with grandparents (either as primary caregivers or in addition to primary caregivers), and various other formations" (Kavanagh, 2004, p. 91).

The failure to recognize nontraditional families in immigration law can create different impacts across racial and ethnic lines. Ignoring grandparents who care for their grandchildren in immigration law can have a particularly harsh impact on Latino populations because "Hispanic grandparents are the largest population of noncitizen caregiver grandparents" (Zug, 2009, p. 242). In using a limited construction of family, immigration law adopts "a false construct of human society, cultural constructions, and racial and ethnic prejudices" (King, 2010, p. 515).

Immigration law not only privileges some families over others but also treats children in a manner that is at odds with other systems. First, for immigration purposes, children can be recognized as a "child" only if they meet the criteria of a "particularly exhaustive" statutory definition (*INS v. Hector*, 1986; see also 8 U.S.C. § 1101(b)(1) (2015)). This definition works to exclude many children born out of wedlock and older adopted children (*INS v. Hector*, 1986; see also 8 U.S.C. § 1101(b)(1) (2015)). As in the broader family context, functional relationships outside formal statutory confines are ignored (Motomura, 1995, p. 43). For example, even when a woman's "relationship with her nieces closely resembles a parent-child relationship, [the courts] are constrained to hold that Congress, through the plain language of the statute, precluded this functional approach to defining the word 'child'" (*INS v. Hector*, 1986, pp. 90–91). Although courts have noted that with regard to "the technical definition of 'child' contained within this statute . . . it could be argued that the line should have been drawn at a different point . . . these are policy questions entrusted exclusively to the political branches of our Government" (*INS v. Hector*, 1986, p. 89, citing *Fiallo v. Bell*, 1977). This formalistic approach fails to account for choices outside the child's control about who can and will provide care for the child, and contrasts with the treatment of children in other areas of law. "To be sure, the [Immigration and Nationality Act's] definition of 'child' may be far out of step with the times, and may have particularly deleterious effects on aliens whose culture's definition of 'family' is legitimately broader than the traditional definition of those related by blood or adoption" (*Dorado v. Gonzalez*, 2006, p. 902).

Family-sponsored immigration provides no benefits to children because they are children. "To the extent that the framework for family-sponsored and derivative immigration tends to achieve family integrity, it does so by ceding control over a child's status to parents and by denying opportunities for children to achieve legal status as children without their parents" (Thronson, 2006, p. 1182). If the child has a recognized relationship with the "right" parent, who advances successfully through the maze of immigration law, the child may benefit. But, other than as a dependent of the "right" parent, the major paths to acquiring lawful immigration provide no special recognition or rights to children as individuals or on the basis of their status as children.

Immigration law values families in which a family member has status, but not all such families. Those in which an adult holds status are privileged, and those in which children hold status are not. In its focus on the adults in children's lives rather than the children themselves, immigration law fails to recognize children as individuals. In limiting the group of adults in children's lives who matter for purposes of immigration law, the perspective of the child is devalued further.

This asymmetric treatment of adults and children is also evident beyond eligibility for immigration, as other provisions of immigration law grant significance to family relationships. Even in situations where a person is eligible for an immigration visa, grounds for inadmissibility still may preclude a beneficiary from being able to immigrate to the United States (8 U.S.C. § 1182 (2015)). For example, immigration law bars for three years the reentry of people who leave the United States after remaining here unlawfully for more than 180 days (8 U.S.C. § 1182(a)(9)(B)(i)(I) (2015)). Those who remain in the United States unlawfully for a year or more and then leave are barred from reentry for 10 years (8 U.S.C. § 1182(a)(9)(B)(i)(II) (2015)). This means that even people who are eligible for immigrant status based on a qualifying family relationship but have been in the country unlawfully for more than a year are barred from consular process to obtain lawful permanent resident status without facing a 10-year wait outside the country. This is of central importance to those who entered the country without inspection and on that basis have been barred from having their immigration petition processed in the United States through a process known as adjustment of status (8 U.S.C. § 1255(a)–(c) (2015)). The hardship imposed by these statutory provisions has a heightened impact on families with members from Mexico and Central America, regions that are overrepresented among those who entered without inspection (Pew Hispanic Center, 2006, p. 4).

Immigration law does acknowledge the hardship that a bar to admission for 3 or 10 years can impose, but in providing a waiver to these grounds of inadmissibility, only hardships faced by adult family members (i.e., spouses and parents) are relevant (8 U.S.C. § 1182(a)(9)(B)(v), (2015)). Hardships that will affect children are irrelevant under the statute (8 U.S.C.

§ 1182(a)(9)(B)(v) (2015)). Here again, by writing the reality of immigrant families and children out of the immigration law framework, immigration law restricts families from successfully navigating the immigration system to regularize the immigration status of all family members. This, in turn, creates the pool of persons and families that will be impacted most directly and deeply by deportation because they are not able to obtain lawful status.

Family plays a similarly limited role in mounting a defense to deportation from the United States. For example, persons without lawful immigration status who are placed in removal proceedings may apply for cancellation of the removal if they meet a number of criteria, including having been physically present in the United States for 10 years and being of good moral character (INA § 240A, 8 U.S.C. § 1229b (2015)). To qualify, they also must prove that removal would cause "exceptional and extremely unusual hardship" to a legal permanent resident or U.S. citizen spouse, parent, or child (INA § 240A, 8 U.S.C. § 1229b (2015)). The standard here is high and is difficult to satisfy. Cancellation applicants must not only have qualifying family members but must also demonstrate hardship "substantially different from, or beyond that which would normally be expected from the deportation of an alien with close family members here" (In re *Monreal-Aguinaga*, 2001).

This means that the expected hardship that the deportation of a family member will cause is irrelevant. Mere separation between parents and children left behind in the United States is not "exceptional and extremely unusual hardship" because "deportation rarely occurs without personal distress and emotional hurt" (*Sullivan v. INS*, 1985). Family separation is "simply one of the common results of deportation or exclusion [that] are insufficient to prove extreme hardship" (*Jimenez v. INS*, 1997). Because this harm is anticipated, immigration law considers it irrelevant and insufficient to merit relief from deportation.

To argue that children will accompany the deported parent fares no better. Diminished access to health care, education, and economic opportunities for U.S. citizen children raised in other countries is also an anticipated outcome of deportation and thus does not meet the "exceptional and extremely unusual hardship" standard (*Jimenez v. INS*, 1997). "Congress has never accepted the theory that minor American-born children of deportable aliens must, or even should, remain in the United States, and that living with their deportable parents in their home country would result in 'extreme hardship' to them" (In re *Piggot*, 1974).

Across determinations of eligibility for lawful status, waivers of inadmissibility grounds, and relief from deportation, immigration law stands in stark contrast to mainstream values and approaches in other areas of law, such as family law, where the centrality of children's interests in legal decisions regarding family is well established. For example, the "custody law in every state in the United States... embraces the 'best interests' standard" (Blair & Weiner, 2005). Immigration law routinely ignores the best interests of children and families. It anticipates and accepts that significant hardship inevitably will result from the enforcement of immigration law.

SHIFTING IMMIGRATION ENFORCEMENT PRIORITIES

Efforts to enforce immigration law constantly evolve, and they have shifted in abrupt ways over relatively short time spans. Each new push alters the risk for people living in the United States without authorization. Changes in the geographic locus of enforcement activity, for example from border areas to interior regions, not only impact which immigrants feel the direct brunt of enforcement policies but also disrupt long-standing patterns of migration. Shifts in target priorities, from workplaces to homes, have a particular impact on the size and nature of enforcement actions. Decisions about how to prioritize enforcement resources based on individual characteristics of immigrants, such as criminal backgrounds or previous immigration law violations, alter the allocation of time and resources for enforcement and move individual immigrants closer or further from the focal point of enforcement. And changes in collaborations with other institutions, particularly police, alter pipelines that channel immigrants into deportation processes. As enforcement priorities and patterns shift, so do the fortunes of immigrants and their families.

Across the various shifts in tactics and targets, the past several decades have seen a steady and significant increase in immigration enforcement and spending on enforcement. The budget for the Border Patrol was $568 million in 1996, $1.5 billion in 2003, and $3.5 billion by 2012 (U.S. Border Patrol, 2013). The expenditures did yield results in terms of the sheer number of deportations, as annual removals increased from approximately

70,000 in 1996 to 420,000 in 2012 (Rosenblum & Meissner, 2014, p. 1). At the same time, it led to changes in long-standing patterns of cyclical migration. When the government began to increase its efforts to control U.S. borders, crossings became more difficult and risky. Increased border enforcement, coupled with the relatively low interior enforcement of the day, meant that risks of deportation after arrival were not as high as the risks of being caught crossing a border (Reza, 2004).

The combination of tougher border enforcement and relatively lax interior enforcement discouraged past patterns of seasonal migration and resulted in more permanent patterns of settlement as undocumented immigrants who managed to enter the United States chose to remain rather than risk an attempt at cyclical migration. From 1986 to 2010, the probability that a Mexican immigrant would return to Mexico within a year after entering the United States fell from 60 percent to 8 percent (Klein, 2013). As cyclical migration diminished, the size of the undocumented population in the United States grew, prompting the government to increase immigration enforcement resources in the country's interior.

Enforcement in the late 1990s and early 2000s was characterized by workplace raids, which were often large, dramatic events that simultaneously impacted hundreds of immigrants and their families and disrupted entire communities (Capps, Castaneda, Chaudry, & Santos, 2007). Given the scale of these events, workplace raids resulted in "crisis scenarios in terms of the care arrangements for the hundreds of children who temporarily lost their parents . . . [and led] to a general sense of chaos and fear" (Capps et al., 2007, p. 34). Reports of one major raid indicate that at times the "situation deteriorated further toward outright panic," and families hid "in their basements or closets for days" (Capps et al., 2007, p. 34). The shift to interior enforcement more generally contributed to a climate of fear among immigrants, who often are settled in communities far from borders. Therefore, they might not previously have felt targeted by immigration law enforcement.

More recently, massive workplace raids have given way to more targeted enforcement. These events are of smaller scale and generate less media coverage. In moving from the indiscriminate dragnets of large workplace raids, there has been increased use of home raids and a "new worksite enforcement strategy prioritizing investigation and prosecution of 'egregious' employers who drive the demand for unauthorized immigration"

(Immigration Policy Center, 2015). Although the pace of deportations has slowed, it has not ceased, and indeed it has risen to record levels.

A primary method of increased interior enforcement has involved coordination between immigration enforcement officials and state and local law enforcement officials. Under so-called 287(g) agreements and a broader program known as Secure Communities, local law enforcement officials engaged in screening and detaining immigrants with whom they came into contact, often for low-level offenses and before prosecution and conviction for such charges. Although these programs resulted in high numbers of immigration enforcement actions, they never managed to focus resources on persons involved in serious criminal behavior. In the words of Jeh Johnson, secretary of the Department of Homeland Security:

> The goal of Secure Communities was to more effectively identify and facilitate the removal of criminal aliens in the custody of state and local law enforcement agencies. But the reality is the program has attracted a great deal of criticism, is widely misunderstood, and is embroiled in litigation; its very name has become a symbol for general hostility toward the enforcement of our immigration laws. Governors, mayors, and state and local law enforcement officials around the country have increasingly refused to cooperate with the program, and many have issued executive orders or signed laws prohibiting such cooperation. A number of federal courts have rejected the authority of state and local law enforcement agencies to detain immigrants pursuant to federal detainers issued under the current Secure Communities program. (U.S. Department of Homeland Security, 2014)

In 2014, Secretary Johnson discontinued the program, replacing it with a new program, the Priority Enforcement Program, which is intended to focus on individuals actually convicted of specified crimes and minimize the use of detainers (U.S. Department of Homeland Security, 2014). Time will tell if this meets the goal of targeting resources at serious criminal offenders and avoids pulling people with minor crimes and traffic offenses into its nets.

The demise of Secure Communities coincided with attempts to increase the use of discretion in immigration enforcement. In 2010 and 2011, the director of Immigration and Customs Enforcement issued various memoranda outlining criteria for the use of prosecutorial discretion in all phases of civil immigration enforcement. These attempted to establish categories of immigrants on which to focus enforcement resources, including those who pose a national security or public safety risk, recent entrants and fugitives, and criminals with serious criminal convictions. Factors that would count favorably in the exercise of discretion included the length of time in the United States, whether the person was brought to the United States as a child, and service in the U.S. military (Morton, 2011). On November 20, 2014, to further consolidate and reconcile policies on discretion, a single enforcement-priorities memorandum was released that is binding on all DHS agencies.

More formal efforts to exercise discretion have the potential to provide relief to immigrant children lacking lawful immigration status. Many young unauthorized immigrants brought to the United States as youths are potentially eligible for relief under the Deferred Action for Childhood Arrivals (DACA) program, for which up to 1.9 million unauthorized immigrants may qualify (Batalova, Hooker, & Capps, 2013). This effort, along with an expansion that would reach undocumented parents, is the subject of intense litigation, and continuing implementation efforts are likely to face major delays.

In the meantime, most of the undocumented population has no viable option to obtain lawful immigration status under current law and remains subject to apprehension and removal. Still, even with increased border presence and interior enforcement, government enforcement efforts will result in the deportation of only a very small portion of the unauthorized immigrant population in the United States. With resources to deport about 400,000 persons per year, the government at best will remove less than 4 percent of the more than 11 million estimated undocumented immigrants in the United States. Millions of immigrants, without regard to their immigration status, have regular employment and have established homes in the United States. As the Supreme Court long ago remarked, the presence of a population lacking authorized immigration status in the United States is quite established (*Plyler v. Doe*, 1982).

This hardly means that all is well for undocumented immigrants and their families. The convergence of an immigration system that denies pathways to lawful status to many family members, increased immigration enforcement and anti-immigrant rhetoric, and a large population built up over decades and firmly established has led to the rise of a society characterized by mixed-status families. This development has serious implications for child and family well-being.

MIXED-STATUS FAMILIES AND THE EFFECTS
OF IMMIGRATION ENFORCEMENT ON CHILDREN

Enforcement of immigration laws has a great influence on national demographics as immigrants settle in the United States. Given the reduction in cyclical migration, many immigrants ultimately deported are not newcomers to the United States. A 2006 study found that some 70 percent of those charged with being removable had lived in the United States for more than a decade. The median length of residence was 14 years (Rosenblum & McCabe, 2014; Transactional Records Access Clearinghouse, 2006). As immigrants settle in the United States, one principal means of integration is through family formation, and the rise of mixed-status families is the obvious result. The limited relevance of family in immigration matters contributes greatly to the resulting demographics of the nation's immigrant population, influencing the large number of mixed-status families, families in which not all family members share the same immigration or citizenship status (Fix & Zimmermann, 1999, p. 2).

Children in immigrant families now account for nearly one fourth of all children in the United States (Hernandez & Cervantes, 2011, p. 6). The majority of children in immigrant families (59 percent) have at least one parent who is a U.S. citizen (Hernandez, 2009). Still, with the population of unauthorized immigrants now estimated at 11.7 million (Hoefer, Rytina, & Baker, 2011), there are 5.5 million children who have at least one parent lacking lawful immigration status (Passel & Cohn, 2011). Of these 5.5 million children, 4 million are U.S. citizens (Passel & Cohn, 2011). Bringing adults into the picture, almost 9 million people live in families with at least one unauthorized immigrant (Passel & Cohn, 2009, p. 8). An estimated 3.8 million parents of U.S. citizen children lack lawful immigration status, meaning that parents of U.S. citizen children are 37 percent of the adult unauthorized immigrant population (Passel & Cohn, 2009). Of immigrants who actually were deported, many are separated from their U.S.-born children. Between July 2010 and September 2012, an estimated 205,000 deportees were the parent of at least one child who was a U.S. citizen, yielding an estimated annual average of approximately 90,000 deportations of the parents of U.S. citizens (Wessler, 2012a, 2012b). Immigration enforcement activities are traumatic for those arrested and for witnesses alike, especially children who witness the arrests of parents or other relatives

(Hendricks, 2007). Following a caregiver's deportation, "many children face traumatic circumstances and insecure care" (Capps et al., 2007, p. 37). According to "[c]hild psychology experts . . . children suffer most from the disruption of armed agents coming into their homes and taking away their parents—and sometimes themselves. Children can experience stress, depression and anxiety disorders" (Hendricks, 2007). Moreover, "children who witness their parents being taken into custody lose trust in their parents' ability to keep them safe and begin to see danger everywhere" (Hendricks, 2007). "The most destabilizing impact on the children of arrestees following worksite enforcement actions came from the separation and fragmentation of families" (Capps et al., 2007, p. 42). For children, "emotional trauma . . . followed separation from one or both parents" (Capps et al., 2007, p. 50). Younger children cannot understand the concept of immigration law, and any "sudden separation [is] considered personal abandonment" (Capps et al., 2007, p. 51).

When the parent who is arrested is a working parent, he or she is often the person in the family who is most integrated into U.S. society, so the connection with the broader society is diminished (Capps et al., 2007). In addition, a parent's deportation removes that parent's earnings from the household, creating "a more unstable home environment and remov[ing] one of the main strengths in immigrant families—the presence of two parents" (Capps et al., 2007, p. 41).

Following mass immigration enforcement raids where the raids were a shared experience across entire communities, the events caused "some degree of polarization between Latino immigrants and other community residents" (Capps et al., 2007, p. 51). Children experience social isolation when they are "harassed by other children or branded as criminals because their parents were arrested" (Capps et al., 2007, p. 52). Children exhibited increased absenteeism in schools (WCCO–CBS Minnesota, 2007). Following one large raid, at school "[m]any children exhibited outward signs of stress . . . [and] lost their appetites, ate less, and lost weight" (WCCO–CBS Minnesota, 2007).

Even outside the deportation context, the immigration status of family members is not without consequence, especially for citizen children of unauthorized immigrants, who often find themselves effectively stateless. These children face barriers not encountered by children in nonimmigrant families, as many "policies that advantage or disadvantage noncitizens are likely to have broad spillover effects on the citizen children who live in the great majority of immigrant families" (Fix & Zimmermann, 1999, p. 2).

Unsurprisingly, immigration status impacts the economic status of children and families, and children of immigrants are "1.5 times more likely than children in native-born families to live in a family with an income below the official federal poverty threshold, at 27.8 percent versus 18.6 percent" (Hernandez & Cervantes, 2011, p. 9). Citizen children in immigrant families commonly do not receive the needed benefits for which they are eligible as individuals. Benefits for children are often obtained only through a parent's initiative, and parents who are ineligible themselves may be inhibited in seeking benefits for which their children qualify (Fix & Zimmermann, 1999, p. 3). When parents are deterred from seeking benefits for their children, "inequalities in access within families have been created informally through the actions of parents and public program staff . . . resulting in a hierarchy of citizen children's access to social benefits, which is ordered by their parent's citizenship and immigration status" (Leiter, McDonald, & Jacobson, 2006, p. 18). Children of immigrants "are substantially more likely than children with U.S.-born parents to be poor, have food-related problems, live in crowded housing, lack health insurance, and be in fair or poor health" (Capps et al., 2007, p. 5).

Even though citizen children are often eligible for benefits without regard to their parents' status, citizen children of immigrant parents access public benefits at a lower rate than that for children born to citizen parents (Fix & Passel, 2002). This fact alone undermines myths that immigrants are drawn to the United States by the availability of public assistance (Fix & Passel, 2002). Since the passage of welfare reform legislation in 1996, many social benefits laws now differentiate between citizens and noncitizens, including those noncitizens with legal immigration status, reducing the overall availability of benefits to immigrant families (Personal Responsibility and Work Opportunity Reconciliation Act of 1996, Pub. L. No. 104-193, § 412, 110 Stat. 2105, 2269–2270, 1996). When citizenship status limits eligibility and only some family members are eligible for benefits, citizen children who live "in households with noncitizens . . . suffer the disadvantage of . . . reduced overall household resources" (Fix & Zimmermann, 1999, p. 2).

Immigration law's limitations on achieving lawful status and the possible imposition of family-separating deportation have a constant effect on immigrant families. Without lawful status or hopes for a pathway to such status, "fear of deportation haunts many immigrants. They know that they can be torn away from established lives, family, friends, and community in an instant for lacking the proper immigration papers or for even something as minor as failing to file a change of address form with the U.S. government within ten days of moving" (Johnson, 2007, p. 46). Living with family members who lack authorized immigration status means living with the constant fear that a family member will face deportation.

IMMIGRATION LAW AND FAMILY LAW IN TENSION

The ever present possibility of deportation and the lack of pathways to regularize the presence of large numbers of persons in mixed-status families not only impact the economic realities of families but also complicate interactions between immigrant families and other societal institutions and legal systems. Family courts, for example, are called on to make custody determinations that are challenged by the context of immigration laws and enforcement when a parent is deported or when parents in immigrant families divorce. In such instances, courts and other involved parties can view the immigration status of parents and children as a tempting, though questionable, area of inquiry for family courts struggling to make difficult determinations about the interests of children.

Appellate courts that have addressed whether immigration status per se can affect child custody have rejected the notion outright. For example, the Nevada Supreme Court ruled that without regard to their immigration status, parents stand "on equal footing...when asserting their right to custody of their children" (*Rico v. Rodriguez*, 2005). In rejecting the argument that a father "should be denied custody solely because of his immigration status," a court in Washington observed that the "due process and equal protection provisions prevent denying an illegal immigrant custody based on that ground" (In re *Parentage of Florentino*, 2002). The notion that parents without authorized immigration status have diminished rights in the parent–child relationship, commonly raised by a parent with status, is flatly without basis.

This commonsense constitutional rule does not make the family court's job easy in the face of immigration law realities. In a common situation, where immigration law blocks the appropriate family law outcome of a child staying with a parent in the United States, developing alternatives to maintain the parent–child relationship can create new challenges to the expertise and resources of family courts. One challenge is to question the routine assumptions of social workers and courts that U.S. citizen children of parents facing deportation must remain in the United States.

CASE STUDY: MERCEDES SANTIAGO-FELIPE

There is no inherent reason that parents forced by immigration law to leave the country can no longer care for their children. For example, Mercedes Santiago-Felipe, an immigrant from Guatemala, lived in Grand Island, Nebraska, with her two U.S. citizen children. She speaks "a Mayan Indian dialect . . . and speaks no English and very little Spanish" (In re *Interests of Mainor T.*, 2004). In 2001, she was arrested for slapping her 6-year-old son, her children were taken into "protective custody," and the "record indicates that after Mercedes was arrested and incarcerated for 'child abuse,' the then Immigration and Naturalization Service (INS) placed a hold on her through the Hall County jail because she was an illegal alien" (In re *Interests of Mainor T.*, 2004). Misdemeanor charges of abuse ultimately were dismissed, and the Nebraska Foster Care Review Board later "found that the children were inappropriately removed from the home" given that "a 'slap on the face' was insufficient evidence to support a finding that [her son] was in imminent danger and that no evidence supported a finding that [her daughter] was in danger" (In re *Interests of Mainor T.*, 2004). Further, the review board noted that Santiago-Felipe was offered no services to prevent removal, such as a parenting class, a family support worker, or therapy. Despite the board's ultimate conclusion, Santiago-Felipe's encounter with Child Protective Services was hardly inconsequential.

Santiago-Felipe received no legal counsel or advice that she could contest her removal and that she had valid claims to legal status in the United States, and she was deported two months after being taken into custody. During her two months of detention in a building next door to the county courthouse, "although the children had asked to see Mercedes . . . [she] had no visitation with them" (In re *Interests of Mainor T.*, 2004). Also, despite knowledge of the social workers, the guardian ad litem, and ultimately the judge that Santiago-Felipe was held next door by immigration officials, the county court proceeded in her absence with hearings to adjudicate the fate of the children (In re *Interests of Mainor T.*, 2004).

As the matter unfolded, the case plan that was developed contained "no goals or tasks related to reunification, including attempts to establish contact with Mercedes" (In re *Interests of Mainor T.*, 2004). Later, on appeal, the state asserted that "at the time of the removal of the children from the Appellant she could not care for them. . . . The Appellant was deported out of the country" (In re Interests of Mainor T., 2004). The guardian ad litem in the case argued on appeal that Santiago-Felipe could not "rehabilitate herself . . . due to her immigration status and deportation" (In re *Interests of Mainor T.*, 2004).

In May 2002, the state "filed a motion to terminate Merecedes' parental rights to her children, alleging as its sole basis for termination of those rights that the children had been in out-of-home placement for 15 or more months of the most recent 22 months" (In re *Interests of Mainor T.*, 2004). The next month, the court entered an order terminating Santiago-Felipe's parental rights, with an added finding that the children had been abandoned (In re *Interests of Mainor T.*, 2004).

On appeal, the Nebraska Supreme Court determined that "plain error permeate[d] the entire proceedings and that such error denied fundamental fairness to Mercedes" (In re *Interests of Mainor T.*, 2004). The termination of Santiago-Felipe's parental rights "was fundamentally unfair, denied Mercedes due process in these proceedings, and is plain error" (In re *Interests of Mainor T.*, 2004). The state "cannot prove that termination of parental rights is in a child's best interests by implementing a case plan that precludes a parent's compliance" (In re *Interests of Mainor T.*, 2004). Further, the court found there was "nothing in the record to show that Mercedes left the United States voluntarily and, by doing so, intentionally withheld from her children her presence, care, love, protection, or maintenance" (In re *Interests of Mainor T.*, 2004). Finally, more than three years after her separation from her children, Santiago-Felipe was able to return to the Unites States and was reunited with her children in Grand Island, Nebraska (O'Hanlon, 2004).

Immigration issues can complicate family and child custody matters, but immigration law can never be allowed to override fundamental rights to family integrity. A parent's "location abroad presents many challenges for any child welfare agency assigned by the state to oversee the welfare of the child" (Boye, 2004, p. 1517). There are "many unavoidable obstacles, including information disadvantages, financial limitations, cultural differences, communication barriers, and the involvement of multiple judicial systems" (Boye, 2004, p. 1517). When immigration law does not allow a parent to return to the United States, cross-border difficulties are compounded, but they are not insurmountable. Certainly, the imperative to preserve the parent–child relationship requires efforts to overcome these barriers. In this context, the impact of immigration law is felt throughout family court and child welfare systems that must deal with the aftermath of immigration law's disruption of living arrangements that often were serving the interests of families and children quite well.

Parents who are detained by immigration authorities pending removal proceedings face daunting obstacles in maintaining their role as parents and participating in child welfare proceedings for children left behind. The Parental Interests directive announced in 2013 corrects some of the problems faced by Mercedes Santiago-Felipe. It instructs enforcement agents to find alternatives to detention for parents of minor children and requires U.S. Immigration and Customs Enforcement to keep parents who are detained close to home so family members can visit. The directive also allows deported parents to return for custody hearings (U.S. Immigration and Customs Enforcement, 2013). Immigration detention policies and practices are often the source of barriers to parent participation, but family courts also contribute by failing to demand means to communicate with and ensure the participation of detained parents. Better outcomes are not likely without strong leadership from family courts. This requires efforts on the part of child welfare workers as well as the cooperation of immigration officials in upholding parents' constitutional rights to participate in proceedings involving their children.

CONCLUSION

Immigration law and enforcement efforts play an outsized role in shaping the lives of many immigrants and immigrant families. Understanding that immigration law does not embody an effort to assess the interests of children and families in reaching its conclusions about who is permitted to remain in the United States is a critical first step to ensuring that the family integrity rights of families and children are not undermined in other systems. Common notions of immigration law as being family friendly give way under closer scrutiny because the complexities of immigration law work to reunite a subset of families while they simultaneously work to separate many more. Under U.S. immigration law, having a family member who is a U.S. citizen or lawful permanent resident often is not relevant, and it is never sufficient to guarantee that family members lacking lawful immigration status have a pathway to regularizing status. This is true even in situations where the enforcement of immigration law may result in significant hardship to families and children.

Immigration law enforcement patterns and priorities are in constant flux. Increased border security, coupled with the lack of viable pathways for immigrants to regularize their status, has given rise to a large population of mixed-status families. The threat of deportation, though statistically unlikely for immigrants not involved with the criminal justice system, still looms large not just for immigrants themselves but also for others in mixed-status families. The uncertainty that the possibility of deportation creates can alter family dynamics and create barriers to full participation in society. In instances where enforcement activity directly impacts a family, confusion and emotional trauma are common. When immigration enforcement actions take place, it is not the immigration system but families and other legal systems that are left to resolve the problems that are created.

Indeed, many of the contradictions and challenges that lie at the intersections of immigration law and family law find their way into family courts and child welfare system interactions with immigrant families. The knowledge that immigration law devalues basic notions of family independence and decision making is important because it highlights the need to prevent immigration law concerns from eclipsing the critical values that animate family law and child welfare systems.

KEY TERMS

ALIEN Any individual who is not a U.S. citizen or U.S. national, regardless of whether the person has lawful immigration status.

CITIZEN A citizen is a person who legally belongs to a country and has the full rights and protection of that country. Under the fourteenth amendment to the U.S. Constitution, "All persons born or naturalized in the United States, and subject to the jurisdiction thereof, are citizens of the United States and of the State wherein they reside." This means that children born in the

United States are U.S. citizens without regard to the status of their parents. Other persons may acquire citizenship, but statutes govern the acquisition of citizenship by children of U.S. citizens under certain conditions and by naturalization.

LAWFUL PERMANENT RESIDENT A person who is permitted to live and work in the United States indefinitely, often referred to as "LPR" or as a "green card holder." Lawful permanent residents have many of the rights of U.S. citizens but may not vote and may be subject to deportation based on certain violations of the law.

MIXED-STATUS FAMILY A family in which not all family members share the same immigration or citizenship status.

REMOVAL Removing a person from the United States to another country. Before 1996, U.S. law used the distinct terms "deportation" and "exclusion" to describe the removal of a person from the United States under immigration law, depending on whether a person had entered the United States or was considered to be at the border. Reforms to immigration law in 1996 formally consolidated procedures for deportation and exclusion into a single process under the name removal, but the older terms remain in common use.

STUDY QUESTIONS

1 Explain how immigration laws contribute to the number of mixed-status families in the United States.
2 How do immigration enforcement actions impact children and families?
3 Identify instances where immigration laws and policies diverge from the treatment of children and families in other areas.
4 What challenges arise for social workers and family court systems related to immigration?
5 How could immigration enforcement policies and practices be reformed to protect families?

ADDITIONAL RESOURCES

American Bar Association Center on Children and the Law, Child Welfare and Immigration: http://www.americanbar.org/groups/child_law/what _we_do/projects/immigration.html

Center for Public Policy Studies, *Immigration Resources*:

http://www.centerforpublicpolicy.org/index.php?s=16420

Immigration Policy Center, Unaccompanied Children: A Resource Page:
http://www.immigrationpolicy.org/just-facts/unaccompanied-children
-resource-page

National Immigrant Women's Advocacy Project, *Resource Library and
Technical Assistance Center*: http://niwaplibrary.wcl.american.edu/

Women's Refugee Commission, Parental Rights & Family Unity: https://
womensrefugeecommission.org/programs/migrant-rights/parental-rights

REFERENCES

8 U.S.C. § 1101(b)(1) (2015).

8 U.S.C. § 1151(b)(2)(A)(i) (2015).

8 U.S.C. § 1151(c) (2015).

8 U.S.C. § 1153(a) (2015).

8 U.S.C. § 1153(d) (2015).

8 U.S.C. § 1182 (2015).

8 U.S.C. § 1229b (2015).

8 U.S.C. § 1255(a)–(c) (2015).

Batalova, J., Hooker, S., & Capps, R. (with Bachmeier, J. D., & Cox, E.). (2013). *Deferred action for childhood arrivals at the one-year mark: A profile of currently eligible youth and applicants*. Washington, DC: Migration Policy Institute.

Blair, M. D., & Weiner, M. H. (2005). Resolving parental custody disputes—a comparative exploration. *Family Law Quarterly, 39,* 247–266.

Boye, A. R. (2004). Making sure children find their way home: Obliging states under international law to return dependent children to family members abroad. *Brooklyn Law Review, 69,* 1515–1553.

Capps, R., Castaneda, R. M., Chaudry, A., & Santos, R. (2007). *Paying the price: The impact of immigration raids on America's children*. Washington, DC: Urban Institute. Retrieved from http://www.urban.org/uploadedPDF/411566_immigration_raids.pdf

Demleitner, N. V. (2003). How much do Western democracies value family and marriage? Immigration law's conflicted answers. *Hofstra Law Review, 32,* 273–310.

Dorado v. Gonzalez, 202 F. App'x 898, 899 (6th Cir. 2006).

Edwards, B. P. (2013). Welcoming a post-DOMA world: Same-sex spousal petitions and other post-Windsor immigration implications. *Family Law Quarterly, 47,* 173–189.

Fiallo v. Bell, 430 U.S. 787, 798 (1977).

Fix, M. E., & Passel, J. S. (2002). *Lessons of welfare reform for immigrant integration*. Washington, DC: Urban Institute. Retrieved from http://www.urban .org/url.cfm?ID=900497

Fix, M. E., & Zimmermann, W. (1999). *All under one roof: Mixed-status families in an era of reform*. Report. Washington, DC: Urban Institute. Retrieved from http://www.urban.org/UploadedPDF/409100.pdf

Hendricks, T. (2007, April 27). The human face of immigration raids in Bay Area: Arrests of parents can deeply traumatize children caught in the fray, experts argue. *San Francisco Chronicle*. Retrieved from http://www.sfgate.com/news /article/The-human-face-of-immigration-raids-in-Bay-Area-2598853.php

Hernandez, D. J. (2009, March). *Generational patterns in the U.S.: American community survey and other sources*. Paper presented at a national conference on children and adolescents from immigrant families, "The immigrant paradox in education and behavior: Is becoming American a developmental risk?" Providence, RI.

Hernandez, D. J., & Cervantes, W. D. (2011). *Children in immigrant families: Ensuring opportunity for every child in America*. Report. Washington, DC: First Focus. Retrieved from http://fcd-us.org/sites/default/files/First%20Focus%20 -%20Children%20in%20Immigrant%20Families.pdf

Hoefer, M., Rytina, N., & Baker, B. (2012). *Estimates of the unauthorized immigrant population residing in the United States: January 2011*. Washington, DC: Department of Homeland Security, Office of Immigration Statistics. Retrieved from www.dhs.gov/sites/default/files/publications/ois_ill_pe _2011.pdf

Huntington, C. (2009). Happy families? Translating positive psychology into family law. *Virginia Journal of Social Policy and the Law, 16*, 385–424.

Immigration and Nationality Act (INA) § 240A (2015).

Immigration Policy Center. (2015). *A guide to the immigration accountability executive action*. Retrieved from http://www.immigrationpolicy.org/special-reports /guide-immigration-accountability-executive-action.

In re Interests of Mainor T., 674 N.W.2d 442 (Neb. 2004).

In re Monreal-Aguinaga, 23 I. & N. Dec. 56, 65 (BIA 2001).

In re Parentage of Florentino, 113 Wash. App. 1002, 2002 WL 1825422 at *5, n.11 (Wash. App. Div. 2 Aug. 9, 2002).

In re Piggot, 15 I. & N. Dec. 129, 131 (BIA 1974).

INS v. Hector, 479 U.S. 85 (1986).

Jimenez v. INS, 116 F.3d 1485 (9th Cir. 1997).

Johnson, K. R. (2007). *Opening the floodgates: Why America needs to rethink its borders and immigration laws.* New York: New York University Press.

Kavanagh, M. M. (2004). Rewriting the legal family: Beyond exclusivity to a care-based standard. *Yale Journal of Law and Feminism, 16,* 83–142.

Kelly, L. (2001). Family planning, American style. *Alabama Law Review, 52,* 955–960.

King, S. M. (2010). U.S. immigration law and the traditional nuclear conception of family: Toward a functional definition of family that protects children's fundamental human rights. *Columbia Human Rights Law Review, 41,* 509–567.

Klein, E. (2013, August 14). "Who're you going to believe on immigration? Mark Krikorian or your lying eyes?" *The Washington Post.* Retrieved from http://www.washingtonpost.com/blogs/wonkblog/wp/2013/08/14/whore-you-going-to-believe-on-immigration-mark-krikorian-or-your-lying-eyes/

Leiter, V., McDonald, J. L., & Jacobson, H. T. (2006). Challenges to children's independent citizenship: Immigration, family and the state. *Childhood, 13,* 11–27.

Morton, J. (2011). *Exercising prosecutorial discretion consistent with the civil immigration enforcement priorities of the Agency for the Apprehension, Detention, and Removal of Aliens.* Memorandum for all field office directors, all special agents in charge, all chief counsel, U.S. Immigration and Customs Enforcement. Retrieved from http://www.ice.gov/doclib/secure-communities/pdf/prosecutorial-discretion-memo.pdf

Motomura, H. (1995). The family and immigration: A roadmap for the Ruritanian lawmaker. *American Journal of Comparative Law 43,* 511–544.

O'Hanlon, K. (2004, December 2). Guatemalan woman regains custody of kids. Associated Press. Retrieved from http://www.boston.com/news/nation.articles/2004/12/02

Passel, J. S., & Cohn, D. (2009, April 14). *A portrait of unauthorized immigrants in the United States.* Washington, DC: Pew Hispanic Center. Retrieved from http://www.pewhispanic.org/2009/04/14/a-portrait-of-unauthorized-immigrants-in-the-united-states/

——. (2011). *Unauthorized immigrant population: National and state trends.* Washington, DC: Pew Hispanic Center. Retrieved from http://www.pewhispanic.org/2011/02/01/unauthorized-immigrant-population-brnational-and-state-trends-2010/

Personal Responsibility and Work Opportunity Reconciliation Act of 1996, Pub. L. No. 104-193, § 412, 110 Stat. 2105, 2269–2270 (1996).

Pew Hispanic Center. (2006, May 22). *Modes of entry for the unauthorized migrant population*. Fact sheet. Retrieved from http://pewhispanic.org/files/fact sheets/19.pdf

Plyler v. Doe, 457 U.S. 202, 210 (1982).

Reza, H. G. (2004, August 4). Border patrol faces new limits in inland empire. *Los Angeles Times*, p. B1.

Rico v. Rodriguez, 120 P.3d 812, 818 (Nev. 2005).

Romero, V. C. (2005). Asians, gay marriage, and immigration: Family unification at a crossroads. *Indiana International and Comparative Law Review, 15*, 337–346.

Rosenblum, M. C., & McCabe, K. (2014). *Deportation and discretion: Reviewing the record and options for change*. Washington, DC: Migration Policy Institute. Retrieved from http://www.migrationpolicy.org/research/deportation-and-discretion-reviewing-record-and-options-change

Rosenblum, M. C., & Meissner, D. (2014). *The deportation dilemma: Reconciling tough and humane enforcement*. Washington, DC: Migration Policy Institute. Retrieved from http://www.migrationpolicy.org/research/deportation-dilemma-reconciling-tough-humane-enforcement

Sanger, C. (1987). Immigration reform and control of the undocumented family. *Georgetown Immigration Law Journal, 2*, 296–297.

Sullivan v. INS, 772 F.2d 609, 611 (9th Cir. 1985).

Thronson, D. B. (2006). Choiceless choices: Deportation and the parent–child relationship. *Nevada Law Journal, 6*, 1165–1214.

Transactional Records Access Clearinghouse (TRAC). (2006). *How often is the aggravated felony statute used?* Retrieved from http://trac.syr.edu/immigration/reports/158

U.S. Border Patrol. (2013). *Enacted border patrol program budget by fiscal year*. Retrieved from http://www.cbp.gov/sites/default/files/documents/BP%20Budget%20History%201990-2013.pdf

U.S. Department of Homeland Security. (2014). *Exercising prosecutorial discretion with respect to individuals who came to the United States as children and with respect to certain individuals who are the parents of U.S. citizens or permanent residents* [Agency Memo]. Retrieved from http://www.dhs.gov/sites/default/files/publications/14_1120_memo_deferred_action.pdf

U.S. Immigration and Customs Enforcement. (2013, August 23). *Facilitating parental interests in the course of civil immigration enforcement activities*. Retrieved from www.ice.gov/doclib/detention-reform/pdf/parental_interest_directive_signed.pdf

WCCO–CBS Minnesota. (2007, February 12). *School enrollment down following swift raids*. Retrieved from http://www.alipac.us/f12/school-enrollment-down -following-swift-raids-50107/

Wessler, S. F. (2012a). Nearly 205K deportations of parents of U.S. citizens in just over two years. *Color Lines News for Action*. New York, NY: Applied Research Center. http://www.colorlines.com/archives/2012/12/us_deports_more_than _200k_parents.html

———. (2012b, December 17). Primary data: Deportations of parents of U.S. citizen kids. *Color Lines News for Action*. New York, NY: Applied Research Center. http://colorlines.com/archives/2012/12/deportations_of_parents_of_us-born _citizens_122012.html

Zug, M. (2009). Deporting grandma: Why grandparent deportation may be the next big immigration crisis and how to solve it. *U.C. Davis Law Review, 43,* 193–252.

PART 2

Major Immigrant and Refugee Populations in the United States

CHAPTER 5

Latino Immigrant and Refugee Children and Families

▸ ALAN J. DETTLAFF, MICHELLE JOHNSON-MOTOYAMA,
and E. SUSANA MARISCAL

LATINOS ARE THE LARGEST, most ethnically diverse, and fastest-growing segment of the U.S. population, following several decades of increased migration coupled with decreased emigration. Between 2000 and 2010, the Latino population, consisting of persons from Mexico, Cuba, the Dominican Republic, Central America, South America, and other Latin countries, grew by 43 percent, more than 4 times the growth rate of the total U.S. population (Ennis, Ríos-Vargas, & Albert, 2011). As of 2010, Latinos represented 16.3 percent of the total U.S. population, an increase of 15.2 million people since 2000. Further, Latino children represented nearly one fourth of all children in the United States, comprising 24 percent of all children under the age of 18. By 2050, the Latino population's share of the total population is expected to nearly double, reaching 30 percent of the total population. Thus, nearly one in three U.S. residents would be Latino (U.S. Bureau of the Census, 2008).

Among Latino adults, 52 percent are foreign-born immigrants who migrated to the United States (Pew Hispanic Center, 2012). However, among Latino children, only 8 percent are foreign born (Pew Hispanic Center, 2012). Yet it is important to note that although the large majority of Latino children are born in the United States, more than half (52 percent) of Latino children have at least one immigrant parent (Fry & Passel, 2009). Overall, the Latino population is relatively youthful compared with other racial and ethnic groups in the United States: the median age of Latinos in the United States in 2010 was 27, compared with 42 for whites, 32 for blacks, and 35 for Asians (Pew Hispanic Center, 2012).

Important differences also exist between native and foreign-born children with regard to population size and distribution. Whereas children comprise 49.5 percent of the native-born Latino population, only 7.4 percent of foreign-born Latinos are children (Pew Hispanic Center, 2012). The age distributions of native and foreign-born children also differ. The age distribution of U.S.-born Latino children is shaped like a pyramid, with younger children represented among the largest age groupings. The pyramid is inverted for immigrant children: older children form the largest age groupings, whereas younger children represent a very small proportion of the total foreign-born Latino child population (Pew Hispanic Center, 2010). Older immigrant children tend to be disproportionately male, reflecting the gendered nature of migration patterns from Latin American countries to the United States (Pew Hispanic Center, 2010).

Geographically, more than three quarters of the Latino population live in the South (36 percent) or the West (41 percent), with more than half of the Latino population in the United States residing in just three states— California, Texas, and Florida (Ennis et al., 2011). A similar pattern exists among foreign-born Latinos. However, recent trends in migration patterns suggest that immigrants who once settled in large urban centers are now moving to destinations in suburban and rural communities with little history or experience with immigrants. As a result, over the past 10 years, states in the Midwest, Rocky Mountains, and Southeast have experienced more than a 200 percent increase in their immigrant populations (Fortuny, Capps, Simms, & Chaudry, 2009).

HISTORY AND REASONS FOR MIGRATION

Although circumstances leading to immigration vary among families, most families choose to migrate because the financial or political situation in their own country has left them with no other option (Segal & Mayadas, 2005). For families living in poverty in their country of origin, the decision to migrate is often based on financial necessity, with families migrating in search of greater wages and increased job opportunities in order to improve the living conditions of the family (Jennissen, 2007).

For many immigrant families, the immigration experience denotes a significant life crisis that contains both opportunities and risks. For undocumented immigrants, as well as for asylum seekers and refugees, the initial act of leaving one's own country and entering the United States can be dangerous, with many immigrants experiencing violence, robbery, and sexual assault during the immigration process (Solis, 2003). For many families, immigration may occur in several phases, resulting in children who are separated from parents and other siblings for extended periods until economic conditions are stable enough for all children to join the family. The stress associated with the initial stage of immigration can result in depression and anxiety, and individuals who experience significant trauma during immigration may develop symptoms of posttraumatic stress disorder (Smart & Smart, 1995). Further compounding these difficulties is the possibility of preexisting psychological concerns that may worsen as a result of the immigration experience (Finno, Vidal de Haymes, & Mindell, 2006).

Once in the new country, families continue to experience stress resulting from language barriers, unfamiliar customs, and the loss of previously established support systems (Hancock, 2005; Solis, 2003). Many of the challenges new immigrants face are tangible (e.g., finding employment, shopping, paying bills, navigating school and medical systems), and each of these challenges can result in further anxiety and stress (Segal & Mayadas, 2005). Undocumented immigrants may experience additional stress, as they live with ongoing fear of discovery and deportation. These immigrants may have difficulty obtaining employment, and they are vulnerable to many forms of exploitation, particularly by employers, who may use their undocumented status as leverage to pay below-market wages or to refuse payment once the work is completed.

UNACCOMPANIED ALIEN CHILDREN

In recent years, the United States has experienced an unprecedented wave of children traveling alone through Mexico, without parents or other family members, and arriving at the southern border. The number of these children apprehended by the U.S. Department of Homeland Security (DHS) has increased from an average of 6,500 per year before 2011 to an estimated 60,000 to 90,000 children in 2014. Although in 2011 unaccompanied children were mostly teenage boys, the numbers of girls and of children under 12 have also steadily increased. The majority of children are arriving from three Central American countries— Honduras, Guatemala, and El Salvador—as well as Mexico, and have multiple and

UNACCOMPANIED ALIEN CHILDREN   (CONTINUED)

complex reasons for leaving their homes, including violence perpetrated by criminals, gangs, and drug cartels; severe deprivation and poverty; abuse in their homes; illness, physical decline, or death of caregivers; and increased opportunities for education and employment.

Yet, despite these threats to safety, most of these children are apprehended and promptly returned to Mexico after less than a day or two in the United States. This has raised many questions about the role of the United States in ensuring the safety of these children, as well as calls to assist in addressing the humanitarian concerns in their countries of origin that have led to this unprecedented wave of migration. In response to this crisis, the Center on Immigration and Child Welfare has recommended the following strategies to ensure the safety of unaccompanied alien children (Center on Immigration and Child Welfare, 2014):

- Improving screening mechanisms for children apprehended at the border, such as requiring U.S. Customs and Border Protection to contract with child welfare professionals to conduct screening interviews with children.
- Ensuring that children's due process rights are upheld as stipulated by U.S. immigration laws and agreements. Due process should not be compromised by the current practice of "priority dockets," an accelerated immigration court process. Children should receive timely legal orientation, legal services, and legal representation in court. Currently, immigrant children are treated as adults in U.S. immigration courts, in contrast to the treatment of children in all other U.S. courts, where their needs are addressed as paramount concerns.
- Never placing children who have been abused, neglected, or abandoned, or are classified as dependent children, in facilities with, or primarily used for, juvenile or adult offenders.
- Allowing adequate time to identify and carefully screen potential U.S. sponsors, including parents and other family members, before placement.
- Providing follow-up services for all children placed with sponsors in the United States to promote their long-term safety, placement stability, and well-being.
- Working in partnership with governments in countries of origin to develop safe repatriation and reintegration programs for returned children and developing strategies to address the root causes of the violence and instability that cause children to flee.

CULTURAL VALUES AND CONFLICTS
WITH U.S. VALUE SYSTEMS

Although Latinos are a highly diverse group, they share certain values as a result of their shared history of Spanish colonization and the influence of the Catholic Church (Gonzalez, 2000). *Familismo* is considered one of the most important cultural values across Latino populations and is particularly relevant to the context of practice with children and families. This value involves a strong identification and attachment with nuclear and extended families, along with a deep sense of family commitment, involvement, and responsibility. The family offers emotional security and a sense of belonging to its members, and it is the unit to which individuals turn for help in stressful or difficult situations. When family members are in need, others will help, particularly those in stable situations. Similarly, when parents are experiencing challenges that affect their ability to adequately parent their children, it is expected that the extended family will provide assistance. For immigrant families, a strong sense of family responsibility and parents' desires for a better life for their children often underlie many families' reasons for immigration. The challenges associated with immigration may cause strain within families at times, but the family may draw considerable strength and pride from their accomplishments, particularly among parents who are able to meet the needs of their children in the midst of ongoing challenges.

Many Latinos also share a common faith, with Catholicism being the predominant religion among most Latinos (Sanchez & Jones, 2010). This faith is deeply rooted in Latino culture, and although it may be expressed differently and with different levels of participation in organized activities, the values and practices of the Catholic Church have important cultural significance for many Latinos. As with their sense of family responsibility, faith can be an important source of strength for many Latino families.

Among some Latino families, views concerning gender and gender roles may also be present and impact families' interactions with certain systems. Latino families are commonly associated with traditional gender roles in which wives assume a relatively submissive role to their husbands. Although there is some research that suggests these views are becoming less common, other research indicates that these traditional views have an influence over certain behaviors and interactions among Latinos (e.g., Flores, Eyre, &

Millstein, 1998; Raffaelli & Ontai, 2004). However, research also suggests that upon families' immigration to the United States, traditional notions of gender may be considerably challenged because of differing cultural norms as well as economic considerations that may require women to enter the workforce and men needing to accept additional responsibilities for child care and housework (Coltrane, Parke, & Adams, 2004). However, whereas immigrant women who are employed in the United States generally experience greater autonomy and independence, men often experience the opposite (Pessar, 1999). This situation is further compounded when men struggle with unemployment, as this may increase the risk for relationship conflict (Aldarondo, Kaufman, & Jasinski, 2002; Cunradi, Caetano, & Schafer, 2002).

Although parenting styles are influenced by a number of factors, including culture, class, and education, for immigrant families, parenting styles are further influenced by their level of acculturation and the unique goals and experiences of each family (Mendez, 2006). Parenting styles are based on cultural practices and attitudes, such as beliefs about the value of punishment and the use of punitive disciplinary strategies to correct behavior. Although norms concerning acceptable child rearing and punishment vary by culture, a number of studies have documented the use of authoritarian parenting styles and corporal punishment as a disciplinary strategy prevalent among immigrant parents (e.g., Frias-Armenta & McCloskey, 1998). When combined with other stressors, such as poverty and acculturative stress, this parenting style may result in harsh physical discipline that can lead to involvement by child welfare systems (Earner, 2007).

Differences in parenting expectations may also place immigrant children and families at risk of involvement with child welfare systems. For example, the use of sibling caretaking, in which older children are responsible for the supervision and socialization of younger children, is a common child care practice in many cultures outside the United States and among recent immigrants (Hafford, 2010). However, this may be interpreted as neglect or inadequate supervision in the United States depending on the circumstances and laws of the state (Zielewski, Malm, & Geen, 2006). Similarly, newly arrived immigrant parents who are unfamiliar with U.S. child-rearing norms and laws may leave children unattended for short periods, potentially placing them at additional risk for child welfare system involvement because of allegations of neglect (Fontes, 2005).

DIVERSITY AMONG LATINOS

Although Latinos share a colonial past, a common language, and certain similar values, they are a highly diverse group, representing more than 20 countries of origin, with distinct cultural values, traditions, and worldviews. This section provides a glimpse of the rich and varied mix of cultures, histories, and characteristics of the Latino population in the United States. Several factors contribute to the heterogeneity that exists among Latinos, particularly country of origin, how many generations they have been in the United States, and immigration status.

Country of Origin

A national survey revealed that about half of all Latinos identify themselves first based on country of origin and then as either Hispanic (33 percent) or Latino (14 percent) (Taylor, Lopez, Martinez, & Velasco, 2012). This preference is defined as ethnic identity, the ethnic component within the self-concept, which influences psychosocial adjustment and coexists and evolves together with other identities and roles. The self-described family ancestry or place of birth in the 2010 Census provides information about the countries of origin of Latinos in the United States (table 5.1). According to these data, Latinos of Mexican (63 percent), Puerto Rican (9.2 percent), and Cuban (3.5 percent) origin or descent represent the nation's three largest Hispanic groups. Although a similar breakdown was found in the 2013 American Community Survey, the differences identified reflect the rapid growth of certain groups, such as Latinos of Salvadoran and Dominican origin (Stepler & Brown, 2015). Indeed, the Salvadoran population grew by 152 percent from 2000 to 2010, Dominicans by 85 percent, Guatemalans by 180 percent, and Colombians by 93 percent (Ennis et al. 2011).

This diversity is further reflected in the states and communities in which Latinos reside. California and Texas are among the five states with the largest Latino populations both in number (14.5 and 10 million, respectively) and as a percentage of the population (almost 40 percent in both cases). Other states with the largest numbers of Latinos are Florida (4.5 million), New York (3.6 million), and Illinois (2.1 million), whereas New Mexico (47 percent), Arizona (30 percent), and Nevada (27 percent) have the biggest share of Latinos among the population (Krogstad & Lopez, 2014a).

TABLE 5.1 U.S. Hispanic Population by Country of Origin

ORIGIN GROUP	2010 U.S. CENSUS		2013 AMERICAN COMMUNITY SURVEY	
	POPULATION (IN THOUSANDS)	SHARE (%)	POPULATION (IN THOUSANDS)	SHARE (%)
Mexican	31,798	63.0	34,582	64.1
Puerto Rican	4,624	9.2	5,121	9.5
All other Hispanic	3,452	6.8	1,666	3.1
Cuban	1,786	3.5	1,985	3.7
Salvadoran	1,649	3.3	1,975	3.7
Dominican	1,415	2.8	1,788	3.3
Guatemalan	1,044	2.1	1,304	2.4
Colombian	909	1.8	1,072	2.0
Spaniard	635	1.3	746	1.4
Honduran	633	1.3	790	1.5
Ecuadorian	565	1.1	686	1.3
Peruvian	531	1.1	628	1.2
Nicaraguan	348	0.7	380	0.7
Argentinean	225	0.4	176	0.3
Venezuelan	215	0.4	247	0.5
Panamanian	165	0.3	176	0.3
Chilean	127	0.3	150	0.3
Costa Rican	126	0.3	137	0.3
Bolivian	99	0.2	122	0.2
Uruguayan	57	0.1	57	0.1
Other Central American	32	0.1	41	0.1
Other South American	22	<0.1	32	0.1
Paraguayan	20	<0.1	23	<0.05

Sources: Adapted from Lopez, M., and Dockterman, D. (2011). U.S. Hispanic country of origin counts for nation, top 30 metropolitan areas. Washington, DC: Pew Research Center, and from R. Stepler and A. Brown, Statistical portrait of Hispanics in the United States, 1980–2013 (Washington, DC: Pew Research Center, 2015). Copyright 2015 Pew Research Center.

Latinos of Mexican origin are by far the dominant group in many metropolitan areas. For example, in San Antonio, Texas, Mexicans comprise 91.3 percent of all Latinos. In Chicago, nearly eight of every ten (79.2 percent) of the area's Latinos and more than half (58.1 percent) of the Atlanta area's Latinos are of Mexican origin. However, other groups are dominant in other urban areas. For example, Puerto Ricans are the largest Latino group in the New York area (29.4 percent), Cubans are the largest group in the Miami area (50.9 percent), and Salvadorans are the largest group in the Washington, DC, area (33.7 percent) (Lopez & Dockterman, 2011). As these figures suggest, it is not uncommon for Latinos from multiple countries of origin to reside in the same communities. For example, Puerto Ricans are the largest Latino group (28.0 percent) in the Boston area, followed by Dominicans (23.2 percent), Salvadorans (10.8 percent), Guatemalans (7.9 percent), Mexicans (6.9 percent), and Cubans (2.1 percent), with a large population (21.0 percent) comprising "other" backgrounds (Lopez & Dockterman, 2011).

Generation in the United States

The family histories of some Latinos in the United States extend back as many as 16 generations, while other Latinos may be newcomers who are just crossing the border today (Camarillo, 2007). In 2000, 40 percent of Latinos were first-generation immigrants. Over one quarter (28 percent) of Latinos were of the second generation (U.S. born with at least one foreign-born parent), and another third (32 percent) were third generation or higher (U.S. born with U.S.-born parents) (Suro & Passel, 2003). However, the Latino population has been changing dramatically over the past decade as births have outpaced immigration as a key source of growth. The Latino immigrant population boomed from 4.2 million to 14.1 million between 1980 and 2000 and decreased to 6.6 million between 2000 and 2012. In contrast, there were 9.6 million Latino births in the United States between 2000 and 2012, accounting for 60 percent of the Latino population growth (Krogstad & Lopez, 2014a). Today, three in five Latinos are U.S. born (Morin, 2009).

Most Latinos in the United States speak Spanish (82 percent), which facilitates connections with their cultures of origin as well as between different Latino communities (Taylor et al., 2012). However, number of generations in the United States may be associated with changes in cultural orientation and social location as reflected in language use and preference, educational attainment, intermarriage, and household income level. For example, first-generation or immigrant Latinos account for most of those in the United States who speak Spanish. The second generation is fundamentally bilingual, whereas the third or higher generations speak predominantly English (Suro & Passel, 2003). In fact, coinciding with the rise of U.S.-born Latinos, English proficiency increased from 59 percent to 68 percent from 2000 to 2013. First-generation Latinos tend to have lower levels of education when compared with other generations: about half of Latino immigrants had at least a high school diploma, compared to more than three quarters of their U.S.-born counterparts (82 percent). Indeed, the share of second-generation Latinos with at least a college degree surpassed that of Latinos overall (21 percent vs. 15 percent). Similarly, household income levels are greater for U.S.-born Latinos than for immigrants. In 2012, median household income for a household of three was $34,600 for Latino immigrants, compared with $48,400 for second-generation Latinos (Cohn, Gonzalez-Barrera, Passel, & Livingston, 2013). Also, the home ownership rate is higher for second-generation Latinos than for Latino immigrants. First-generation Latinos also tend to marry within their ethnic group, which occurs less frequently among U.S.-born Latinos regardless of their generation. When compared with Latino immigrants, who intermarry at a relatively low rate (8 percent), intermarriage is much more common among the second (32 percent) and the third or higher (57 percent) generations.

Second-generation Latinos are notably young, with a median age of 28; 57 percent are younger than 18. They are mainly the product of mass immigration from Latin America that began in the 1960s. Latino adults of third and higher generation are likely to be descendants of families that came from Latin America many generations ago, and in some cases they would have been living in U.S. territories when those areas were incorporated as new states. Their median age is 39 (Cohn et al., 2013).

Immigration Status

Among Latinos, immigration to the United States is predominately economically driven. Other reasons for migration include political instability and repression, war-related hardship and persecution, natural disasters, family conflict, persecution related to sexual orientation, and status as a highly trained professional (Cohn et al., 2013; Organista, 2007). For Latinos, the process of immigration to the United States is often characterized by loss, trauma, fear, and isolation. These experiences vary depending on country of origin, type of migration, and individual motivations (Glick, 2010; Rumbaut, 1994).

Immigration status and citizenship are tied to legal rights, access to services, and entitlement to benefits. Of the 40.2 million foreign-born individuals who were in the United States in 2010, nearly three quarters were legal immigrants (72 percent), which includes naturalized citizens, permanent residents, and legal temporary migrants, and more than one quarter (28 percent) were unauthorized or without documentation (Passel & Cohn, 2011). Although Mexicans comprise the majority of unauthorized immigrants, their proportion has decreased in recent years from 58 percent in 2009 to 52 percent in 2012 (Cohn et al., 2013; Passel & Cohn, 2011). About a quarter of unauthorized immigrants are from Central America; this proportion has held steady in recent years. Nearly two thirds of unauthorized immigrants have lived in this country for at least 10 years, and nearly half are parents of minor children (Taylor et al., 2011). Unauthorized immigrants represent a particularly vulnerable population given risks of deportation and exploitation, restricted access to health and social services, and the experience of discrimination (Hancock, 2005; Padilla & Perez, 2003; Solis, 2003; Smart & Smart, 1995).

No less than 9 million people are part of "mixed-status" families that include at least one unauthorized adult and at least one U.S.-born child (Taylor et al., 2011). In 2012, there were 4 million unauthorized immigrant adults, of which 3.7 million did not have protection from deportation under Deferred Action for Childhood Arrivals (DACA) or under the Temporary Protected Status (TPS) program. Policies that impact unauthorized immigrants are likely to have spillover effects on U.S.-born family members. For example, restricted access to means-tested programs such as food stamps may contribute to food insecurity among children in mixed-status families (Fix & Passel 1999, 2002; Fix & Zimmerman, 2001; Van Hook & Balisteri, 2006). Additionally, children in mixed-status families tend to have less access to health insurance and experience further barriers to health care access when compared with families with two U.S.-born parents (Capps, Fix, Ost, Reardon-Anderson, & Passel, 2004; Douglas-Hall & Koball, 2004; Ku & Matani, 2001).

BARRIERS THAT CONTRIBUTE TO CROSS-SYSTEM INVOLVEMENT

Similar to other historically marginalized populations, Latino children of immigrants and their families are at disproportionate risk of experiencing a number of psychosocial problems, including poverty (Lopez & Velasco, 2011), low educational attainment (Fry, 2010; Lopez, 2009), exposure to violence (Frias & Angel, 2005; Mariscal, 2013), and health concerns (Finch, Hummer, Kolody, & Vega, 2001; Finch & Vega, 2003).

Poverty

The primary psychosocial problem impacting Latinos is poverty. As of 2010, more than one in four (26.6 percent) U.S. Latinos lived in poverty, the highest this rate has been since 1993, and an increase of more than 5 percent since 2007 (DeNavas-Walt, Proctor, & Smith, 2011). Among children in the United States, more Latino children are living in poverty than for any other racial or ethnic group. In 2010, Latino children represented 37.3 percent (6.1 million) of all poor children, whereas 30.5 percent were white and 26.6 percent were African American (Lopez & Velasco, 2011). The Latino child poverty rate increased by 6.4 percent, compared with a 4.6 percent increase for black children and a 2.3 percent increase for white children. The impact of the Great Recession was evident in a rapid increase in the Latino unemployment rate (11.1 percent in 2011), a sharp wealth decrease, and a sharp increase in food insecurity (32.1 percent) (Lopez & Velasco, 2011).

Particularly impacted were 4.1 million Latino children of immigrants, with a poverty rate of 40.2 percent in 2010 (9.4 percent increase). Most of these children (86.2 percent) were born in the United States. Whereas two thirds (67.6 percent) of Latino children living in poverty had at least one immigrant parent, 10.8 percent of white and 13.3 percent of black impoverished children had immigrant parents (Lopez & Velasco, 2011). The impact of the Great Recession on Latino children of immigrants also varied depending on their parents' educational attainment and family composition. Half of the Latino children of immigrants living in poverty had parents who were married (53.7 percent), and 82.3 percent had low levels of education (e.g., completed high school or less) (Lopez & Velasco, 2011).

Educational Attainment

Latinos face several challenges regarding educational attainment, including lower reading and mathematics achievement than white and Asian middle school students (Lopez, 2009); higher high school dropout rates (13 percent) than white (4 percent) or black (8 percent) students (U.S. Department of Education, National Center for Education Statistics, 2014); and lower school enrollment rates (33 percent) than the overall population (42 percent) for ages 18 and 24 (Lopez, 2009).

Although most young Latinos (88 percent) and their parents (77 percent) consider college education important for getting ahead in life, their aspirations do not match their educational attainment. This is particularly true for Latino immigrants, who are about half (11 percent) as likely as U.S.-born Latinos (21 percent) to hold a college degree (Cohn et al., 2013). Two major gaps persist for Latinos. The first gap corresponds to young adults' aspirations to get a college degree, with lower educational aspirations among Latinos (48 percent) than among non-Latino whites (60 percent). The second and more important gap corresponds to young Latino immigrants and U.S.-born Latinos, with 60 percent of the share of U.S.-born Latinos expecting to get at least a college degree versus 29 percent of immigrant Latinos (Lopez, 2009).

Additionally, adolescent and adult Latino immigrants face unique educational barriers, including age at immigration, schooling in country of origin, language barriers, pressing economic needs, and immigration status (American Council of Education, 2011). For instance, Mexican immigrant youths who arrived in the United States later in their lives (33 percent) were more likely to drop out of school than those who arrived in early childhood (8 percent). Latino immigrants who had schooling problems in their country of origin were also likely either to never enroll or to drop out of school. Language barriers are an important barrier to educational attainment; 7 in 10 Latino immigrant adults who did not complete high school reported not speaking English well, if at all (American Council of Education, 2011).

Pressing economic needs are common among Latino immigrants; they were more likely than U.S.-born Latinos to be supporting a family (29 percent vs. 17 percent), either in the United States or in their country of origin. Indeed, 64 percent of Latino immigrants versus 21 percent of U.S.-born Latinos reported supporting family in their country of origin (Lopez, 2009). High tuition costs and low-wage jobs make it difficult for Latino immigrants to pursue further education. Immigration status can make all these challenges even more difficult, placing unauthorized immigrants at a greater disadvantage. Because of these unique educational barriers, Latino immigrants are not likely to access traditional educational programs and services.

Exposure to Violence

Although between 17 percent and 45 percent of Latinas experienced intimate partner violence (IPV) at least once in their lives (Frias & Angel, 2005), some studies have reported higher rates of IPV among U.S.-born Latinas. Higher sexual coercion rates (29.4 percent vs. 12 percent) and rates of psychological abuse (92.9 percent vs. 72.6 percent) were reported among U.S.-born Latinas when compared with Latina immigrants. Findings regarding the prevalence of physical violence are inconsistent (Frias & Angel, 2005; Hazen & Soriano, 2007). Lower lifetime rates of IPV were also found among Mexican immigrant women when compared with Mexican American women (7–12 percent and 10–31 percent, respectively) (Aldarondo et al., 2002). However, the age at migration seems to influence IPV rates. If foreign-born Latinas migrated at age 15 or earlier, they were at a greater risk than U.S.-born Latinas for IPV, even after controlling for English proficiency (Frias & Angel, 2005).

Social isolation, smaller social networks, language barriers, lack of information, fear of deportation, racism, and previous experiences with law enforcement in their countries of origin prevent Latina immigrants from seeking help (Frias & Angel, 2005; Hass, Dutton, & Orloff, 2000; Moracco, Hilton, Hodges, & Frasier, 2005; Perilla, Bakeman, & Norris, 1994; Welland & Ribner, 2008). For instance, a study revealed that those Latinas with immigration status stability were more likely to call the police; yet police did not take immigrant Latinas' calls seriously, did not provide a language interpreter, and had low arrest rates (Ammar, Orloff, Dutton, & Aguilar-

Hass, 2005). However, IPV not only affects Latinas; it negatively impacts Latino children and adolescents as well.

Estimates suggest that between 1.1 million and 3.3 million Latino children and adolescents are exposed to IPV in the United States every year (Mariscal, 2013). These children are likely to be exposed to multiple violent incidents, which may include different degrees of severity, intensity, and child involvement. Childhood exposure to IPV negatively impacts several functioning domains, including physical health, mental health, social relationships, academic performance, and juvenile justice involvement (Mariscal, 2013; Osofsky, 2003). In addition, these children are 15 times more likely than children not exposed to IPV to experience physical abuse and neglect (Osofsky, 2003).

Studies using the National Survey of Child and Adolescent Well-being (NSCAW), conducted with families involved with the child welfare system, reported that Latino children were the most likely to experience physical abuse (22 percent) and that school-age Latina girls had higher rates of exposure to intimate partner violence than African American and white girls (Simmel, 2011). Regarding the types of substantiated maltreatment, Latino children of immigrants are almost 6 times more likely than children of second-generation Latinos to be sexually abused and more than 20 times more likely than children of U.S.-born Latinos to experience physical neglect (Dettlaff & Earner, 2010).

CASE STUDY: ELENA

Elena is a 23-year-old Mexican woman with a nine-month-old daughter. She has lived in the United States for 10 years but has undocumented immigration status. Elena is seeking services from a faith-based social services agency after an incident of domestic violence between herself and her daughter's father, Carlos, a 30-year-old U.S. citizen of Mexican descent.

Elena came to the United States with her parents when she was 13 years old. She dropped out of school at age 17 so that she could work to better support her parents, as well as extended family in Mexico. Elena met Carlos through a mutual friend, and they began dating two years ago. Several months after they started dating, Elena became pregnant. Although this was unplanned, there was never a question of terminating the pregnancy, and Elena and Carlos became engaged and moved into a small, one-bedroom apartment. After their daughter, Olivia, was born, their situation became very stressful. Elena was staying home to care for the baby, and Carlos was working two jobs to pay their rent and other expenses. When Carlos came home from work, Elena would try to sleep for a few hours, but Carlos was also tired from working all day. When Olivia was six months old, she was diagnosed with colic, which further prevented Elena and Carlos from getting much sleep. Carlos began to get frustrated about his long hours and lack of sleep, and he and Elena began to fight often. The fights soon became physical.

During one incident, Carlos struck Elena while she was holding the baby, and they both fell to the floor. Olivia was unhurt, but Elena had a large bruise on her face that their neighbors noticed. One neighbor encouraged Elena to call the police, but she refused—she was afraid she would be arrested because of her immigration status and become separated from Olivia. She also feared that if she were deported, she would lose custody of Olivia permanently, as Olivia was a U.S. citizen. During the most recent incident of violence, Elena fled with Olivia to a friend's home. This friend said they could stay for a short time, but she also had young children and was concerned that Carlos would find them. This friend arranged for Elena to seek services from a neighborhood agency affiliated with her church.

1　In conducting an assessment, what issues need to be addressed?

2　What interventions would you suggest for Elena and Olivia?

3　How might Elena's undocumented immigration status impact the services she receives?

4　How would you address Elena's fears of discovery and potential deportation?

LATINO PARADOXES IN HEALTH

Epidemiologic or health paradoxes refer to trends in the health of Latinos that document positive health outcomes, despite adversity (Acevedo-Garcia & Bates, 2008). Multiple studies have documented health outcomes that are better among Latino immigrants when compared with non-Latino racial or ethnic groups and U.S.-born Latinos (Franzini, Ribble, & Keddie,

2001; Hayes-Bautista, 2002; Jasso, Massey, Rosenzweig, & Smith, 2004; Palloni & Arias, 2004; Palloni & Morenoff, 2001). For example, infant mortality and infant low birth weight (<2,500 grams, or <5.5 pounds) are important measures of infant health and are associated with a range of physical and cognitive disabilities across the person's life span. In general, the prevalence of infant mortality and low birth weight among Latinos is lower than for African American and white infants (MacDorman & Mathews, 2008). What is considered "paradoxical" is that many Latinos have socioeconomic profiles that place other racial or ethnic groups at risk for poor infant health because of factors such as low household income, limited access to medical care, and low rates of prenatal care utilization. Moreover, groups that tend to be the most socioeconomically disadvantaged within the Latino population, such as immigrants, often have healthier infants than their U.S.-born counterparts (Johnson & Marchi, 2009).

However, the initial advantages observed in Latino children do not persist for certain indicators. For example, when compared with African Americans and whites, Latino children are less likely to be fully immunized and more likely to have tuberculosis (Zambrana & Logie, 2000). With regard to oral health, compared with other racial or ethnic groups, Mexican American children are more likely to have dental cavities and less likely to have them treated or filled (Flores et al., 2002). Latino youths face a disproportionate burden of risks for diabetes and obesity in adulthood (Acevedo-Garcia & Bates, 2008). Among adolescents, Latino teen pregnancy decreased by 34 percent in recent years, representing the largest decline among any racial or ethnic group. Yet, Latinos have the highest rate of teen pregnancy and adolescent birth rate, with 49.9 births per 1,000 women aged 15 to 19, compared with 47.4 for African Americans and 21.8 for whites (Hamilton, Martin, & Ventura, 2012). Latino youths are the least likely to report using condoms when compared with African Americans and whites, placing them at the greatest risk of teenage pregnancy, sexually transmitted diseases, and adult HIV/AIDS (Cubbin, Santelli, Brindis, & Braveman, 2005). Regarding substance use, studies suggest that Latino immigrants have more positive health behaviors, particularly related to substance use and mental health outcomes, when compared with their U.S.-born counterparts (Alegría et al., 2007; Grant et al., 2004; Vega, Alderete, Kolody, & Aguilar-Gaxiola, 1998).

Different arguments have been made to explain Latino paradoxes in the health literature: the presence of cultural and/or social protective factors, immigrant selection, and artifacts of data. Cultural and/or social protective factors arguments highlight the social support families receive through social networks, strong cultural ties, religiosity, cultural values such as *familismo*, and salutary health behaviors (Hayes-Bautista, 2002). The protective factors argument often implies an acculturation hypothesis, which suggests that the Latino immigrant families' protective factors will erode with time spent in the United States and across generations. The immigrant selection argument suggests that so-called paradoxes result from the processes that bring to the United States Latino immigrants who are healthier than their counterparts who stay behind (Palloni & Morenoff, 2001). Finally, some researchers suggest that paradoxical patterns may stem from data artifacts such as undercounts of morbidity and mortality, inconsistent ways of defining Latino identity, and the underreporting of health problems among Latinos (Franzini, Ribble, & Keddie, 2001; Jasso et al., 2004; Palloni & Morenoff, 2001). Given the limited ability of most studies to account for all of these possible explanations, the question of Latino health paradoxes is far from settled. As such, the paradoxes observed in some areas of Latino health should not lead professionals to overlook the considerable barriers that face the Latino population.

RESULTING EFFECTS AND SYSTEM INVOLVEMENT

Consistent with these poor outcomes, Latinos are disproportionately overrepresented in a number of systems, such as child welfare and justice.

Justice System

Latino youths represent approximately 19 percent of all youths aged 10 to 17, yet they represent 25 percent of youths who are incarcerated (Saavedra, 2010). Of further concern, the share of Latino youths under 18 who were held in adult prisons increased from 12 percent to 20 percent from 2000 to 2008, while during the same period, the share of white and African American youths in adult facilities decreased (Saavedra, 2010). Latino youths also receive harsher treatment than white youths, even when they are charged with the same offense. For example, in every offense category, the admission rate for Latinos with no prior convictions was higher than for white youths (5 times higher for violent offenses, and 13 times higher for drug offenses). Also, the average length of incarceration was higher for Latino youths than for any other racial or ethnic group (Villarruel et al., 2002). In addition to Latino youths' involvement with the juvenile justice and adult criminal justice systems, their involvement with the Immigration and Naturalization Service may result in incarceration, deportation, and permanent separation from families (Villarruel et al., 2002). In recent years, there has been a dramatic increase in the number of unaccompanied children (e.g., traveling without a parent or guardian, although they may have traveled with another relative) who have crossed the U.S. border without authorization. The number of children apprehended by the U.S. Department of Homeland Security increased from 39,000 in 2013 to 47,000 in 2014. Although the majority of unaccompanied children apprehended were teenagers (91 percent in 2013 versus 84 percent in 2014), the number of apprehensions among children age 12 and younger increased by 117 percent. Most of these children are Hondurans, Salvadorans, and Guatemalans, who are likely fleeing poverty and violence (Krogstad, Gonzalez-Barrera, & Lopez, 2014).

Child Welfare

In the child welfare system, Latino children are slightly underrepresented at the national level. As of 2010, they represented 18.3 percent of children in foster care compared with 20.1 percent of children in the general population (Summers, Wood, & Russell, 2012). More than a third (36 percent) of Latino children involved with the child welfare system have an immigrant parent, whereas two thirds have a U.S.-born parent. Latino children of immigrants represent 5.2 percent of all children involved with the child welfare system, and nearly four out of five (79.6 percent) of these children are U.S. born. Children of U.S.-born Latinos tend to be younger than children of immigrants (Dettlaff & Earner, 2010). Compared with children of U.S.-born Latinos, children of immigrants were more likely to be living in a two-parent home with their biological father present and less likely to have a grandparent present in the home. Latino immigrant caregivers were more likely to report living in a safe neighborhood and having helpful neighbors. They were also more likely to have an intellectual or cognitive impairment, poor parenting skills, or a recent history of arrest, yet they were less likely than Latino U.S.-born caregivers to abuse drugs. However, no group differences were found regarding the remaining risk factors identified in these families, including the use of excessive discipline, domestic violence, low social support, and difficulty meeting basic needs (Dettlaff & Earner, 2010). Additionally, high stress in the family (58 percent) and poor parenting skills (26 percent) were the most important family risk factors for parents of U.S.-born Latinos, whereas parents of immigrant Latino children were 3 times as likely to use "excessive discipline" (47 percent vs. 14 percent) as parents of U.S.-born Latinos (Dettlaff & Johnson, 2011).

Nevertheless, Latino children and families are frequently treated as a homogenous group, with little understanding being demonstrated of the potential differences between groups, their characteristics, or particular risk factors present in their families. Latino families, particularly Latino unauthorized immigrants, involved with the child welfare system, for instance, tend to underutilize basic services, even if their children are U.S. born and entitled to them. Of the 37 percent of Latino families that were referred to concrete services, only 17 percent actually received services as a result of a referral. Service underutilization depicts the serious challenges to receiving needed services that these families face because of issues surrounding immigration status, language and cultural barriers, and lack of caseworker competence to work with immigrant populations. In fact, language barriers can lead to inaccurate assessment of problems and needs and to miscommunication that ultimately can influence decision making (Finno-Velazquez, 2014).

It is necessary that child welfare agencies conduct a thorough assessment of the strengths and protective factors that may be present in immigrant Latino families involved with the child welfare system. For instance, a powerful strength that can be used as a motivating factor in service delivery is the Latino immigrant parents' desire to provide a better future for their children (Dettlaff & Earner, 2010). Likewise, Latino values, such as maternal monitoring, can be another source of strength (Mariscal, 2013). Additionally, immigrant communities can be a resource to build networks to support Latino immigrant families and enhance children's safety and well-being (Dettlaff & Earner, 2010). Social workers have the opportunity to connect immigrant families to a range of supportive services to which they may not have access otherwise.

Health

In addition to Latinos' overrepresentation in certain systems, significant disparities impact Latinos' access to other systems and receipt of services, particularly those concerning their physical health and mental health. Health care use among Latinos is low, with only 70 percent of Latino adults reporting that they had seen a doctor in the past year, compared with 83 percent of white adults (Schiller, Lucas, Ward, & Peregoy, 2012). The youthfulness of the Latino population in the United States contributes to its healthiness, particularly among adult Latino immigrants. Fewer adult Latinos who are neither legal permanent residents nor U.S. citizens had a regular health care provider (34 percent) or missed work because of illness or injury (42 percent) (Livingston, 2009).

Among racial and ethnic groups, Latinos are the least likely to have health insurance coverage. Nationally, the uninsured rate among Latinos is 31 percent, compared with 12 percent for whites and 20.5 percent for African Americans (National Council of La Raza, 2012). Generational status plays an important role in health care access among Latinos (Brotanek, Halterman, Auinger, & Weitzman, 2005; Burgos, Schetzina, Dixon, & Mendoza, 2005). Compared with U.S.-born Latinos (17 percent), Latino immigrants (39 percent) are more than twice as likely to lack health insurance. Also, more Latino immigrant children (34 percent) than U.S.-born Latinos (12 percent) and U.S. children (9 percent) lacked insurance (Krogstad & Lopez, 2014b). Additional barriers to health care access include cultural differences, availability of bilingual health professionals, and perceived discrimination within the health care system (Friedman et al., 2005; Smedley, Stith, & Nelson, 2003). Discrimination within the health care system was perceived to be associated with language barriers (46 percent), inability to pay for care (43 percent), racial discrimination (37 percent), and medical history (25 percent) (Livingston, 2009).

Mental Health

Immigration status and acculturation are important factors that influence Latino mental health. Rates for most mental health disorders are significantly lower among Latino immigrants (23.8 percent) than among U.S.-born Latinos (36.8 percent). Among Latino immigrants, rates were higher among those who migrated before age 13 (29 percent) or after age 34 (28 percent) compared with those who migrated at other ages (21.5 percent). Latinos with low English proficiency, an indicator of acculturation, had lower rates than those with high English proficiency, except for anxiety among men and depression among women. Additionally, mental health disorder rates also vary by country of origin. For instance, Puerto Ricans (39.0 percent) have the highest overall prevalence rate for mental illness, compared with Mexicans and Cubans (both 28.4 percent) and the rest of Latinos (27 percent) (Alegría et al., 2007).

Unauthorized Latino immigrants experience additional stressors, such as the threat of or having had a previous history with deportation and isolation (National Council of La Raza, 2005). Also, the immigration process can be a traumatic experience for many Latino immigrants. As Latino immigrant families endure contextual stresses in the migration and settlement process, they tend to develop coping skills through the dynamic balance of change and continuity. Meaning and hopefulness are essential for the development of resilience among these families. These families "attempt to restore meaning and purpose in life in the midst of multiple ambiguous losses through family connectedness, family rituals, awareness of social marginalization, and belief of spiritual systems" (Falicov, 2002, p. 278). Long-held beliefs and spiritual systems can inform a family's meaning making and its ability to deal with adversity. For example, cultural values contribute to Latinos' acceptance of suffering and adversities as part of life (cargar la cruz—bear the cross). By believing that little in life is in their hands, "mastery of the possible" (Falicov, 2002, p. 281), what can be solved is solved and what cannot is accepted.

Few Latinos with a mental health disorder seek mental health services (less than 1 in 11), particularly among Latino immigrants (1 in 20). Similarly, a number of studies have found that Latino youths are significantly less likely than both white and African American youths to receive needed mental health services (Hough et al., 2002; Kataoka, Zhang, & Wells, 2002). Research has suggested that barriers to the receipt of mental health services among Latino youths may include differing cultural values and beliefs concerning mental health treatment (Ho, Yeh, McCabe, & Hough, 2007), cultural differences in the interpretation of children's behaviors (Roberts, Alegría, Roberts, & Chen, 2005; Zimmerman, Khoury, Vega, Gil, & Warheit, 1995), or a lack of culturally appropriate services available to Latino families (Gudiño, Lau, & Hough, 2008; Lopez, Bergren, & Painter, 2008). Latino attitudes and the stigma associated with mental illness can discourage the use of services. For instance, depression may be mistaken for nervousness (*"ataque de nervios"*) or tiredness. Privacy, expressed in the proverb *"los trapos sucios se lavan en casa"* ("One must wash their dirty laundry at home"), implies that problems should not be discussed outside the family. For this reason, many Latinos rely first on their family, traditional healers, churches, or community during a mental health crisis (National Council of La Raza, 2005). Additional barriers to receipt of mental health services that Latinos face include lack of information on where to seek treatment, lack of transportation to treatment centers, and lack of bilingual and culturally responsive providers (Aguilar-Gaxiola et al., 2002).

Special Education

Within the educational system, although Latino children are proportionately represented among children identified with a learning disability and in need of special education services, they are underrepresented among children participating in gifted and talented programs (3.57 percent vs. 7.47 percent for whites). Latino males are overrepresented among youths receiving disciplinary actions, including suspensions and expulsions (U.S. Department of Education, Office of Civil Rights, 2012).

Latino immigrants also face language and cultural barriers to accessing special education services. Many Latino immigrant families do not know how to access public resources or how to prepare their children for higher education; these challenges become even greater for families who do not speak English. Indeed, one of the largest educational attainment gaps exists between English learners and English speakers. Although schools provide special linguistic programs to support English learners, the specific contents of these programs vary greatly. More importantly, the gap between English learners and native speakers persists, and increases over the years, even after the child has exited the linguistic program. For example, compared with native speakers' reading scores, English learners scored 30 points lower in fourth grade, 45 points lower in eighth grade, and 52 points lower in twelfth grade (American Psychological Association, 2012). A national survey conducted by the Pew Research Center identified the views of both

Latino adults and youths regarding the major reasons that Latino students underperform in school as follows: lack of parental involvement, teachers' different cultural backgrounds, students' limited English skills, and students' failure to work as hard as other students do. In addition, this survey identified the reasons provided by Latinos to end their education either during or right after high school. Among the most important reasons were needing to support their family (74 percent), having poor English skills (50 percent), disliking school (40 percent), and not needing further education in order to work (40 percent) (Lopez, 2009).

Because Latino children, especially Latino immigrants, are overrepresented in the lower end of the academic achievement distribution, they are underrepresented in the gifted and talented programs. Improving Latino immigrant children's academic performance is likely to impact their representation in gifted and talented programs. In addition, the special education needs of Latino English learners may be masked behind their low English proficiency (American Psychological Association, 2012).

IMPACTS OF FEDERAL POLICIES

The history of Latinos as an ethnic minority in the United States was forged primarily through American colonization and the annexation of formerly Mexican lands in the U.S. Southwest during the nineteenth century (Camarillo, 2007). Basic socioeconomic and political structures were transformed in the 1900s through the rapid influx of whites, the commercialization of land, and shifts from a pastoral system to a wage-based economy (Telles & Ortiz, 2008). The failure of the Mexican economy in 1907, followed by the decade-long Mexican Revolution that began in 1910, sparked a period of mass authorized immigration to the United States, which continued until the Great Depression of 1929. Over time, the U.S. economy has become increasingly intertwined with the Mexican economy and increasingly reliant on workers from Mexico. At the same time, the United States has continued to impose more legal limits on immigration from Mexico, particularly in the wake of the Great Recession of 2007–2009.

The Mexican-origin population is more likely to be of low socioeconomic status when compared with other Latino subgroups. This is largely because of the diverse political and economic legacies of Latino country-of-origin groups but is also shaped by historical racist practices and discriminatory immigration policies. For example, whereas Mexican immigrants in the United States were often poor and came in search of better economic opportunities, Cubans who came to the United States were members of a prosperous middle class who feared the consequences of a takeover by Fidel Castro and were later able to use their skills, networks, and U.S. political support to integrate into the middle class.

Today, more Latino children than any other racial or ethnic group are living in poverty, a product of high birth rates to Latina immigrants and declining economic opportunities for families (Lopez & Velasco, 2011). Recent policies targeting immigration have exacerbated these patterns by restricting immigrants' access to services and programs while limiting their rights. For example, California Proposition 187 was a 1994 ballot initiative that sought to prohibit undocumented residents from receiving health care, public education, and other social services in the state (Gibbs & Bankhead, 2001). This initiative was later overturned by a district court decision in 1995, just before the passage of the Personal Responsibility and Work Opportunity Reconciliation Act of 1996 (PRWORA), which restricted the eligibility of undocumented immigrants, as well as many legal immigrants, for a variety of public programs. For example, most legal permanent residents became ineligible for (a) means-tested public benefit programs for five years after receiving permanent residence and (b) Medicare and Social Security for 10 years after receiving permanent residence. National and local evaluations suggest that the restrictions embedded in these initiatives successfully reduced immigrant families' participation in public programs along with the participation of refugees, citizen children, and other populations whose eligibility was not restricted (Borjas, 2011; Fix & Passel, 2002; Zimmerman & Fix, 1998). For example, decreases in the utilization of prenatal care among foreign-born women were recorded, as were a number of preventable deaths to individuals who avoided medical treatment because of fear of immigration authorities (Mizoguchi, 1999). It has also been found that immigrants avoid social services and other public programs because they fear becoming a "public charge," a consideration in determining inadmissibility or adjustment in immigration status (Fix & Passel, 1999).

In 1996, the Illegal Immigration Reform and Immigrant Responsibility Act expanded the definition of an "aggravated felony" and created a new process to speed the deportation of immigrants without a formal hearing

(Ewing, 2012). Also in 1996, the Antiterrorism and Effective Death Penalty Act was passed, allowing the detention and deportation of non-U.S. citizens on the basis of "secret evidence." In the wake of the terrorist attacks of 9/11, the federal government has instituted a number of measures that conflate antiterrorism concerns with renewed attempts to control unauthorized immigration at the federal and local levels (Ewing, 2012). The enforcement of federal immigration laws to control undocumented immigration has played a crucial role in the significant increase in the number of incarcerated Latino federal offenders. The number of Latinos sentenced in federal courts quadrupled between 1991 and 2007, and immigration offenses accounted for 48 percent of these sentences. In 2007, Latinos represented 40 percent of all sentenced federal offenders, nearly one third of federal incarcerated inmates (Lopez & Light, 2009).

On the one hand, Latinos have been "relegated to virtual invisibility" (Perea cited in Morin, 2009, p. 6) because their history in the United States is largely absent from the public eye. On the other hand, more than 66 percent of news stories about Latinos focus on crime, illegal immigration, and terrorism (Morin, 2009), adding to public misperceptions while fueling prejudice, discrimination, and social injustice.

Immigration policy in the United States remains a contentious issue at the forefront of political and social debate. In recent years, the challenges associated with implementing federal comprehensive immigration reform have led to myriad state and local policies directed at immigrants. Approximately 500 immigration-related bills were introduced by state legislators after the collapse of comprehensive immigration reform in 2007, and by 2008, the number of proposed immigration-related bills had tripled to 1,562 (Catholic Legal Immigration Network, 2015). These developments have had important implications for the health and well-being of Latino children and families, particularly immigrants from Mexico and Central America, who comprise the majority of the 11 million immigrants in the United States who are undocumented.

Although Latino children and families are impacted by many different policies on a day-to-day basis, aggressive immigration enforcement through programs housed under the federal Agreement of Cooperation in Communities to Enhance Safety and Security (ACCESS), and the immigration relief options that have been established through executive orders by President Barack Obama discussed in chapters 3 and 4 of this volume, are among the most salient.

CULTURALLY RESPONSIVE STRATEGIES
TO ADDRESS CHALLENGES

Culturally responsive assessment of immigrant Latino children and families is critical given the diversity within this population and the range of factors that may be contributing to their involvement with service systems. Culturally responsive practice with immigrant Latino families requires that practitioners clearly assess the history, values, and traditions of these families as well as how these values and traditions influence these families' thoughts and behaviors. Cultural values shape the ways in which families view their problems, accept responsibility, and respond to interventions. Thus, practitioners should expend considerable effort learning about the cultural background, values, and traditions of each family in order to understand the dynamics of the family system and understand family concerns through the cultural lens of the family. Practitioners should understand these cultural factors before having any discussions with clients concerning possible interventions.

Assessment of immigrant families requires particular attention, as professionals may make assessments by filtering information through their own cultural lens. This could result in inaccurate assessments of the issues, making families vulnerable to bias. Cultural bias can affect immigrant families when personal values, cultural differences, and professional judgments influence decision making, resulting in misinterpretation or misdiagnosis of the presenting issues. Thus, when conducting assessments of immigrant Latino families, providers should be aware of the probable influence of their own cultural values and biases, and they should make an effort to understand the dynamics of the situation through the cultural lens of the immigrant family.

Careful assessment of immigrant Latino families is also important because of the likely impact of acculturative stress within families. Whereas acculturation refers to the internal process of change experienced by immigrants upon exposure to a new culture (Padilla & Perez, 2003), acculturative stress refers to the stress that results directly from the acculturative process (Berry, Kim, Minde, & Mok, 1987). Upon migration, individuals face a multitude of challenges as they attempt to navigate the new culture. Acculturative stress results when individuals lack the necessary skill or means to interact and be successful in the new environment (Berry et al., 1987). For many immigrants, the acculturative stress experienced following immigration is lifelong, pervasive, and intense. Language barriers, lack of employment, loss of social support, inadequate financial resources, and discrimination experienced in the new culture are all factors associated with acculturative stress (Berry, 2005).

Following assessment, it is important to remember that families' experiences with immigration and acculturation will continue to affect service delivery. In general, families who experience greater amounts of acculturative stress will be less likely to be able to engage in the development of new skills or resources that are necessary for addressing the issues they are facing. It is also less likely that these families will be able to draw on existing strengths and coping abilities to address these issues effectively because of the stress they are experiencing. As a result, issues of acculturative stress and the associated anxiety experienced by immigrant families must be addressed first in order for long-term change to result. Thus, literature on intervention with Latino immigrant families stresses the importance of interventions that increase social support and reduce isolation (Denner, Kirby, Coyle, & Brindis, 2003; Fontes, 2002). Social support has been shown to reduce stress and provide the protective factors that are necessary to minimize the negative effects of acculturative stress (Denner et al., 2003).

CULTURALLY RESPONSIVE INTERVENTIONS

The importance of cultural responsiveness has been widely emphasized when developing and implementing interventions with immigrant Latino children and families (e.g., Dettlaff & Rycraft, 2010; Hall, 2001; Hodge, Jackson, & Vaughn, 2010). Despite this, surprisingly little research on the effectiveness of culturally responsive interventions with immigrant Latino populations has been conducted. Additionally, the notion of what makes an intervention culturally responsive has varied widely across studies. However, an emerging body of research has begun to identify a number of factors that may facilitate positive outcomes among this population. These factors typically involve some form of cultural adaptation that seeks to incorporate aspects of the target population's culture into a given intervention. This can occur either in the structure and process of service delivery or in the content of the intervention itself.

Adaptations concerning the structure and process of service delivery can involve either aspects associated with the service provider or aspects associated with the space and/or location in which the intervention is delivered. At the service provider level, perhaps of primary importance to practice with immigrant Latino children and families is the provision of services in their preferred language. That language barriers between patients and providers contribute to health disparities is well established in the research literature (e.g., Jacobs, Agger-Gupta, Chen, Piotrowski, & Hardt, 2003). Specific concerns include delay or denial of services, decreased likelihood of follow-up care, problems with medication management, underutilization of preventative services, and misdiagnosis of symptoms (Brach & Fraser, 2000; Gandhi et al., 2000; Jacobs, Shepard, Suaya, & Stone, 2004). In contrast, studies have shown that language concordance increases patient satisfaction, self-reported health status, and adherence to both medication and follow-up care (Freeman et al., 2002; Perez-Stable, Napoles-Springer, & Miramontes, 1997). Even for families that may speak English, it is important to recognize that they may prefer to receive services in their native language, particularly when the information or service provided concerns their health and well-being or that of their children. And although it may not always be possible for direct service providers to provide services in a family's native language, the use of professional interpreters has consistently been associated with improved outcomes in health settings (Karliner, Jacobs, Chen, & Mutha, 2007).

Ethnic matching between providers and service recipients may also contribute to positive outcomes (e.g., Casas, Vasquez, & Ruiz de Esparza, 2002; Vasquez, 2007). Providers having the same ethnicity as the client may be more likely to understand the culture-specific values or norms of the client, resulting in a more effective assessment and intervention plan. Service recipients may also have increased trust in discussing or disclosing certain issues when working with providers who share the same ethnicity. The space and/or location in which interventions are provided to facilitate cultural responsiveness may also be considered. For example, provision of services within immigrant communities may facilitate access as well as maintain connections to recipients' communities and cultural norms, both of which may facilitate positive outcomes.

In developing or adapting the content of interventions to facilitate cultural responsiveness, Resnicow, Braithwaite, Ahluwalia, & Baranowski (1999) distinguish between *surface structure* and *deep structure*. The former involves tailoring the materials and messages of an intervention to observable social and behavioral characteristics of the population, whereas the latter integrates into the content of the intervention the cultural, psychological, social, and historical factors of the target population that influence behaviors. For example, surface structure tailoring may involve using photographs of people or places with which the target population can identify or integrating into the intervention language, music, or foods specific to the target population. In contrast, deep structure tailoring would involve integrating into the content of the intervention unique cultural values that promote well-being.

Surface structure tailoring is necessary to facilitate receptivity, comprehension, and acceptance of the message involved in the intervention (Resnicow et al., 1999), whereas deep structure tailoring is necessary to convey salience and to determine program impact (Resnicow et al., 1999). This level of tailoring involves understanding how members of the target population perceive and understand the causes or issues associated with the concern, as well as their perceptions regarding the determinants of specific behaviors. Thus, the intervention demonstrates an appreciation for how cultural values, religion, family, and historical experiences shape the ways in which individuals behave and respond to interventions. For example, Gloria and Peregoy (1996) discuss the importance of integrating values such as *simpatia* (sympathy), *personalismo* (personalism), *familismo* (familial ties), *hembrismo* (brotherhood), *verguenze* (pride), and *espiritismo* (spiritualism) into prevention programs.

SPOTLIGHT: PROMISING PRACTICE INVOLVING CULTURAL ADAPTATIONS
AND ETHNIC MATCHING

Safe Care

Safe Care is an evidence-based, behavioral parent-training program that targets risk factors for child physical abuse and neglect. The program involves an 18–20-week in-home intervention designed to improve parent communication and problem solving, improve parent–child and parent–infant bonding, and enhance home safety and health care skills, with the ultimate goal of preventing child abuse and neglect. In a number of studies with a general population, Safe Care has demonstrated efficacy in preventing the first incidence of maltreatment and in reducing repeat maltreatment (Chaffin, Hecht, Bard, Silovsky, & Beasley, 2012; Gershater-

Molko, Lutzker, & Wesch, 2003). A culturally adapted version of Safe Care is currently being implemented in San Diego County with Latino parents, many of whom are immigrants. Preliminary research has examined client perceptions of adherence, the working alliance between the parent and practitioner, and overall satisfaction with the program. Findings show that perceptions of service delivery were consistent for Latino and non-Latino clients, suggesting that adaptations made to engage Latino and Spanish-speaking parents can be done without compromising adherence to the model. Provider-client ethnic match and service receipt in Spanish were associated with more positive perceptions of adherence and satisfaction among Latino parents (Finno-Velasquez, Fettes, Aarons, & Hurlburt, 2014).

COLLABORATIONS ACROSS SYSTEMS

When Latino immigrant and refugee children and families become involved in health and social service systems, collaboration across systems is essential in meeting the complex needs of these families. Often, service delivery to immigrant and refugee families is complex and fragmented, resulting in families not receiving needed services. Further, for many families, their immigration status presents an immediate crisis that they may need to address before they can turn their attention to the issues that led to their involvement with the system. Service delivery can be aided through collaborative relationships across systems and immigrant service providers who work as a team to meet the complex needs of these families.

Collaboration with legal systems may also be necessary to assist families in resolving immigration-related issues, as it is unlikely that practitioners in health and social services systems will have the knowledge or skills to address these issues. Collaborations with immigration attorneys or legal advocacy organizations can be established to ensure that families have access to needed legal resources as part of their overall service plan. In some instances, collaborators across systems may pursue legislative actions to address unique challenges that are impacting immigrant families involved in their systems.

CROSS-SYSTEM COLLABORATIONS RESULTING
IN LEGISLATIVE ACTION

Through collaborations across systems, several states have made strides in developing policies in response to the complex and often devastating impacts of immigration enforcement on immigrant children and families. California's Reuniting Immigrant Families Act, Senate Bill 1064 (2012), authorizes courts to provide an extension in the family reunification period in child welfare cases involving detained or deported parents and prohibits immigration status alone from being used as a disqualifying factor in determining a caregiver's suitability to be a placement resource for a child. The California Call for Kids Act, Assembly Bill 2015 (2012), reinforces existing state penal code requirements, requiring two additional phone calls for custodial parents at time of arrest for the purposes of making child care arrangements, and requiring that language-accessible signs regarding the rights to phone calls be posted in facilities (Cervantes, 2014). In Maryland, legislation was passed to ensure that all eligible abused, abandoned, or neglected children may obtain lawful permanent residence through Special Immigrant Juvenile Status (SIJS) through age 21 instead of 18 (Cervantes, 2014).

CONCLUSION

Although the Latino immigrant population is diverse in culture and country of origin, a number of systemic barriers that may contribute to poor outcomes across health and social service systems impact Latino immigrants in the United States. Strategies are needed that address these barriers, particularly as they negatively affect the health and well-being of vulnerable children and families. Specifically:

1   Policies are needed that ensure that practitioners receive adequate training on the issues and experiences affecting immigrant populations. Training needs to be developed by experts and needs to incorporate follow-up activities to facilitate transfer of learning.
2   Programs are needed that focus on recruitment and retention of bilingual and bicultural practitioners.
3   Research is needed to evaluate training outcomes and bilingual and bicultural recruitment and retention efforts.

4 Culturally responsive interventions are needed that use the latest empirical information available to incorporate cultural adaptations and facilitate positive outcomes.

5 Policies are needed that promote cross-system collaboration to address the complex cross-system challenges experienced by immigrant children and families.

6 Community outreach positions are needed within health and social service systems to develop connections with immigrant communities and service providers.

7 Research is needed to evaluate the effectiveness of collaborations across systems and make recommendations for improvement.

KEY TERMS

ACCULTURATION An internal change process that occurs when individuals from one culture are continuously exposed to another culture, with this exposure resulting in changes to the original cultural and behavioral patterns of the group. This process includes not only behavioral changes but also changes to value systems, developmental processes, and cultural norms. How individuals acculturate and the level to which they acculturate vary according to the value systems, roles, personality styles, and developmental processes of the individual.

ACCULTURATIVE STRESS Distinct from acculturation, acculturative stress refers to the stress that results from the acculturative process as individuals navigate a new culture and make decisions about the level to which they will integrate into the new culture.

FAMILISMO A value or quality shared by many Latinos that refers to a strong orientation toward family and places high value on marriage, child rearing, and commitment to family members. This extends beyond the nuclear family to extended family members across multiple generations, as well as unrelated family members such as godparents.

LATINO A word used to describe people who are from—or whose ancestors are from—Mexico, Puerto Rico, Cuba, Central and South America, and other Latin American and/or Spanish cultures. The term is sometimes used interchangeably with Hispanic (e.g., Hispanic or Latino), although there are regional differences in the use of these terms within the United States, as well as criticisms about the use and origins of both terms.

UNACCOMPANIED ALIEN CHILDREN A term used to classify undocumented immigrant children who enter the United States unaccompanied by a parent or other adult guardian.

STUDY QUESTIONS

1 What is acculturative stress, and how might it contribute to Latino families' involvement within systems?
2 What strengths related to their migration experience might exist within Latino immigrant families?
3 How might individual bias impact the assessment of Latino immigrant families?
4 What systemic issues can impact the services provided to Latino immigrant families by health and social service systems?
5 What barriers may prevent Latino immigrant families from accessing services they need from health and social service systems?

ADDITIONAL RESOURCES

Immigrant Legal Resource Center: http://www.ilrc.org
Migration Policy Institute: http://www.migrationpolicy.org
National Research Center on Hispanic Children and Families: http://www .childtrends.org/nrc/
Pew Research Center: Hispanic Trends: http://www.pewhispanic.org
Unaccompanied Children's Services Program of the Office of Refugee Resettlement: http://www.acf.hhs.gov/programs/orr/programs/ucs

REFERENCES

Acevedo-Garcia, D., & Bates, L. M. (2008). Latino health paradoxes: Empirical evidence, explanations, future research, and implications. In H. Rodriguez, R. Saenz, & C. Menjivar (Eds.), *Latino/as in the United States: Changing the face of America* (pp. 101–113). New York: Springer.
Aguilar-Gaxiola, S. A., Zelezny, L., Garcia, B., Edmondson, C., Alejo-Garcia, C., & Vega, W. A. (2002). Mental health care for Latinos: Translating research into action: Reducing disparities in mental health care for Mexican Americans. *Psychiatric Services, 53*(12), 1563–1568.

Aldarondo, E., Kaufman, G. K., & Jasinski, J. (2002). A risk marker analysis of wife assault in Latino families. *Violence Against Women, 8*, 429–454.

Alegría, M., Mulvaney-Day, N., Woo, M., Torres, M., Gao, S., & Oddo, V. (2007). Correlates of past-year mental health service use among Latinos: Results from the National Latino and Asian American Study. *American Journal of Public Health, 97*(1), 76–83.

American Council of Education. (2011). *By the Numbers: ACE report identifies educational barriers for Hispanics.* Washington, DC: Author.

American Psychological Association. (2012). Ethnic and racial disparities in education: Psychology's contributions to understanding and reducing disparities. Washington, DC: Author.

Ammar, N., Orloff, L., Dutton, M. A., & Aguilar-Hass, G. (2005). Calls to police and police response: A case study of Latina immigrant women in the USA. *International Journal of Police Science and Management, 7*(4), 230–244.

Berry, J. W. (2005). Acculturation: Living successfully in two cultures. *International Journal of Intercultural Relations, 29*, 697–712.

Berry, J. W., Kim, U., Minde, T., & Mok, D. (1987). Comparative studies of acculturative stress. *International Migration Review, 21*, 491–511.

Borjas, G. J. (2011). Poverty and program participation among immigrant children. *The Future of Children, 21*, 247–266.

Brach, C., & Fraser, I. (2000). Can cultural competency reduce racial and ethnic disparities? A review and conceptual model. *Medical Care Research Review, 57*, 181–217.

Brotanek, J. M., Halterman, J., Auinger, P., & Weitzman, M. (2005). Inadequate access to care among children with asthma from Spanish-speaking families. *Journal of Health Care for the Poor and Underserved, 16*, 63–73.

Burgos, A. E., Schetzina, K. E., Dixon, L. B., & Mendoza, F. S. (2005). Importance of generational status in examining access to and utilization of health care services by Mexican American children. *Pediatrics, 115*, 322–330.

Camarillo, A. M. (2007). Mexico. In M. Waters, & R. Ueda (Eds.), *The new Americans: A guide to immigration since 1965* (pp. 504–517). Cambridge, MA: Harvard University Press.

Capps, R., Fix, M., Ost, J., Reardon-Anderson, J., & Passel, J. (2004). *The health and well-being of young children of immigrants.* Washington, DC: Urban Institute.

Casas, J. M., Vasquez, M., & Ruiz de Esparza, C. A. (2002). Counseling the Latina/o: A guiding framework for a diverse population. In P. B. Pederson, J. G.

Draguns, W. J. Lonner, & J. E. Trimble (Eds.), *Counseling across cultures* (pp. 133–160). Thousand Oaks, CA: Sage.

Catholic Legal Immigration Network. (2015). *State and local immigration project.* Retrieved from https://cliniclegal.org/programs/advocacy/state-and-local

Center on Immigration and Child Welfare. (2014). *Statement on the welfare of unaccompanied children.* Retrieved from http://cimmcw.org/wp-content /uploads/2014/06/MCWNN-Statement-on-Unaccompanied-Immigrant -Children-August-2014.pdf

Cervantes, W. (2014). *Family unity & immigration enforcement: Policies impacting child welfare.* Washington, DC: First Focus Center for the Children of Immigrants.

Chaffin, M., Hecht, D., Bard, D., Silovsky, J. F., & Beasley, W. H. (2012). A statewide trial of the SafeCare home-based services model with parents in Child Protective Services. *Pediatrics, 129,* 509–515.

Cohn, D., Gonzalez-Barrera, A., Passel, J. S., & Livingston, G. M. (2013). Demographic portrait of adult children of immigrants. In *Second-generation Americans: A portrait of the adult children of immigrants.* Washington, DC: Pew Research Center. Retrieved from http://www.pewsocialtrends.org/2013/02 /07/chapter-2-demographic-portrait-of-adult-children-of-immigrants/

Coltrane, S., Parke, R. D., & Adams, M. (2004). Complexity of father involvement in low-income Mexican American families. *Family Relations, 53,* 179–189.

Cubbin, C., Santelli, J., Brindis, C. D., & Braveman, P. (2005). Neighborhood context and sexual behaviors among adolescents: Findings from the national longitudinal study of adolescent health. *Perspectives on Sexual Reproduction and Health, 37*(3), 125–134.

Cunradi, C. B., Caetano, R., & Schafer, J. (2002). Socioeconomic predictors of intimate partner violence among white, black, and Hispanic couples in the United States. *Journal of Family Violence, 17,* 377–389.

DeNavas-Walt, C., Proctor, B. D., & Smith, J. C. (2011). *U.S. Census Bureau, current population reports (P60-239), income, poverty, and health insurance coverage in the United States: 2010.* Washington, DC: U.S. Government Printing Office.

Denner, J., Kirby, D., Coyle, K., & Brindis, C. (2003). The protective role of social capital and cultural norms in Latino communities: A study of adolescent births. In M. Aguirre-Molina & C. M. Molina (Eds.), *Latina health in the United States: A public health reader.* San Francisco, CA: Jossey-Bass.

Dettlaff, A. J., & Earner, I. (2010). *Latino children of immigrants in the child welfare system: Findings from the National Survey of Child and Adolescent Well-*

being. Englewood, CO: Migration and Child Welfare National Network, American Humane Association.

Dettlaff, A. J., & Johnson, M. A. (2011). Child maltreatment dynamics among immigrant and U.S. born Latino children: Findings from the National Survey of Child and Adolescent Well-being (NSCAW). *Children and Youth Services Review, 33*(6), 936–944.

Dettlaff, A. J., & Rycraft, J. R. (2010). Adapting systems of care for child welfare practice with immigrant Latino children and families. *Evaluation and Program Planning, 33,* 303–310.

Douglas-Hall, A., & Koball, H. (2004). *Children of recent immigrants: National and regional trends.* New York: National Center for Children in Poverty, Columbia University.

Earner, I. (2007). Immigrant families and public child welfare: Barriers to services and approaches for change. *Child Welfare, 86*(4), 63–91.

Ennis, S. R., Ríos-Vargas, M., & Albert, N. G. (2011, May). *The Hispanic population: 2010.* Washington, DC: U.S. Bureau of the Census.

Ewing, W. A. (2012). *Opportunity and exclusion: A brief history of U.S. immigration policy.* Washington, DC: Immigration Policy Center, American Immigration Council.

Falicov, C. (2002). Ambiguous loss: Risk and resilience in Latino immigrant families. In M. Suarez-Orozco & M. Paez (Eds.), *Latinos remaking America* (pp. 274–288). Los Angeles: University of California Press.

Finch, B. K., Hummer, R. A., Kolody, B., & Vega, W. A. (2001). The role of discrimination and acculturative stress in the physical health of Mexican-origin adults. *Hispanic Journal of Behavioral Sciences, 23,* 399–429.

Finch, B. K., & Vega, W. A. (2003). Acculturation stress, social support, and self-rated health among Latinos in California. *Journal of Immigrant Health, 5*(3), 109–117.

Finno, M., Vidal de Haymes, M., & Mindell, R. (2006). Risk of affective disorders in the migration and acculturation experience of Mexican Americans. *Protecting Children, 21*(2), 22–35.

Finno-Velazquez, M. (2014). *Barriers to support service use for Latino immigrant families reported to Child Welfare: Implications for policy and practice.* Los Angeles: University of Southern California School of Social Work.

Finno-Velasquez, M., Fettes, D. L., Aarons, G. A., & Hurlburt, M. S. (2014). Cultural adaptation of an evidence-based home visitation programme: Latino clients' experiences of service delivery during implementation. *Journal of Children's Services, 9,* 280–294.

Fix, M., & Passel, J. (1999). *Trends in non-citizens' and citizens' use of public benefits following welfare reform: 1994–1997.* Washington, DC: The Urban Institute.

Fix, M., & Passel, J. (2002) *The scope and impact of welfare reform's immigrant provisions.* Washington, DC: The Urban Institute.

Fix, M., & Zimmermann, W. (2001). All under one roof, mixed status families in an era of reform. *International Migration Review, 35*(134), 397–419.

Flores, E., Eyre, S., & Millstein, S. G. (1998). Sociocultural beliefs related to sex among Mexican American adolescents. *Hispanic Journal of Behavioral Sciences, 20,* 60–82.

Flores, G., Fuentes-Afflick, E., Barbot, O., Carter-Pokras, O., Claudio, L., Lara, M., . . . & Weitzman, M. (2002). The health of Latino children: Urgent priorities, unanswered questions, and a research agenda. *The Journal of the American Medical Association, 288*(1), 82–90.

Fontes, L. A. (2002). Child discipline and physical abuse in immigrant Latino families: Reducing violence and misunderstanding. *Journal of Counseling and Development, 80,* 31–40.

——. (2005). *Child abuse and culture: Working with diverse families.* New York, NY: Guilford.

Fortuny, K., Capps, R., Simms, M., & Chaudry, A. (2009). *Children of immigrants: National and state characteristics.* Retrieved from Urban Institute website: http://www.urban.org/publications/411939.html

Franzini, L., Ribble, J. C., & Keddie, A. M. (2001). Understanding the Hispanic paradox. *Ethnicity and Disease, 11*(3), 496–518.

Freeman, G. K., Rai, H., Walker, J. J., Howie, J. G., Heaney, D. J., & Maxwell, M. (2002). Non-English speakers consulting with the GP in their own language: A cross-sectional survey. *British Journal of General Practice, 52,* 36–38.

Frias, S. M., & Angel, R. J. (2005). The risk of partner violence among low-income Hispanic subgroups. *Journal of Marriage and Family, 67*(3), 552–564.

Frias-Armenta, M., & McCloskey, L. A. (1998). Determinants of harsh parenting in Mexico. *Journal of Abnormal Child Psychology, 26,* 129–139.

Friedman, J. Y., Anstrom, K. J., Weinfurt, K. P., McIntosh, M. Bosworth, H. B., Oddone, E. Z., . . . & Schulman, K. A. (2005). Perceived racial/ethnic bias in healthcare in Durham County, North Carolina: A comparison of community and national samples. *North Carolina Medical Journal, 66,* 267–275.

Fry, R. (2010). *Hispanics, high school dropouts and the GED.* Washington, DC: Pew Research Center.

Fry, R., & Passel, J. S. (2009). *Latino children: A majority are U.S.-born offspring of immigrants*. Retrieved from the Pew Hispanic Center website: http://pew hispanic.org/files/reports/110.pdf

Gandhi, T. K., Burstin, H. R., Cook, E. F., Puopolo, A. L., Haas, J. S., Brennan, T. A., & Bates, D. W. (2000). Drug complications in outpatients. *Journal of General Internal Medicine, 15*, 149–154.

Gershater-Molko, R. M., Lutzker, J. R., & Wesch, D. (2003). Project SafeCare: Improving health, safety, and parenting skills in families reported for and at-risk for child maltreatment. *Journal of Family Violence, 18*, 377–386.

Gibbs, J. T., & Bankhead, T. (2001). *Preserving privilege: California politics, propositions, and people of color*. Westport, CT: Praeger.

Glick, J. E. (2010). Connecting complex processes: A decade of research on immigrant families. *Journal of Marriage and Family, 72*(3), 498–515.

Gloria, A. M., & Peregoy, J. J. (1996). Counseling Latino alcohol and other substance users/abusers: Cultural considerations for counselors. *Journal of Substance Abuse Treatment, 13*, 119–126.

Gonzalez, J. (2000). *Harvest of empire: A history of Latinos in America*. New York, NY: Penguin.

Grant, B., Stinson, F., Hasin, D., Dawson, D., Chou, S., & Anderson, K. (2004). Immigration and lifetime prevalence of DSM-IV psychiatric disorders among Mexican Americans and non-Hispanic whites in the United States: Results from the National Epidemiologic Survey on Alcohol and Related Conditions. *Archives of General Psychiatry, 61*(12), 1226–1233.

Gudiño, O. G., Lau, A. S., & Hough, R. L. (2008). Immigrant status, mental health need, and mental health service utilization among high-risk Hispanic and Asian Pacific Islander youth. *Child Youth Care Forum, 37*, 139–153.

Hafford, C. (2010). Sibling caretaking in immigrant families: Understanding cultural practices to inform child welfare practice and evaluation. *Evaluation and Program Planning, 33*, 294–302.

Hall, G. C. N. (2001). Psychotherapy research with ethnic minorities: Empirical, ethical, and conceptual issues. *Journal of Consulting and Clinical Psychology, 69*, 502–510.

Hamilton, B. E., Martin, J. A., & Ventura, S. J. (2012). *Births: Preliminary data for 2011*. Hyattsville, MD: National Center for Health Statistics.

Hancock, T. (2005). Cultural competence in the assessment of poor Mexican families in the rural southeastern United States. *Child Welfare, 84*, 689–711.

Hardina, D. (2014). Deferred action, immigration, and social work: What should social workers know? *Journal of Policy Practice, 13*(1), 30–44.

Hass, G. A., Dutton, M. A., & Orloff, L. E. (2000). Lifetime prevalence of violence against Latina immigrants: Legal and policy implications. *Domestic Violence: Global Responses, 7*, 93–113.

Hayes-Bautista, D. E. (2002). The Latino health research agenda for the twenty-first century. In M. M. Suarez-Orozco & M. Paez (Eds.), *Latinos remaking America* (pp. 215–235). Berkely: University of California Press.

Hazen, A. L., & Soriano, F. I. (2007). Experiences with intimate partner violence among Latina women. *Violence Against Women, 13*(6), 562–582.

Ho, J., Yeh, M., McCabe, K., & Hough, R. L. (2007). Parental cultural affiliation and youth mental health service use. *Journal of Youth and Adolescence, 36*, 529–542.

Hodge, D. R., Jackson, K. F., & Vaughn, M. G. (2010). Culturally sensitive interventions for health behaviors among Latino youth: A meta-analytic review. *Children and Youth Services Review, 32*, 1331–1337.

Hough, R. L., Hazen, A. L., Soriano, F. I., Wood, P. A., McCabe, K., & Yeh, M. (2002). Mental health services for Latino adolescents with psychiatric disorders. *Psychiatric Services, 53*, 1556–1562.

Jacobs, E. A., Agger-Gupta, N., Chen, A. H., Piotrowski, A., & Hardt, E. J. (2003). *Language barriers in healthcare settings: An annotated bibliography of the research literature.* Woodland Hills: The California Endowment.

Jacobs, E. A., Shepard, D. S., Suaya, J. A., & Stone, E. (2004). Overcoming language barriers in health care: Costs and benefits of interpreter services. *American Journal of Public Health, 94*, 866–869.

Jasso, G., Massey, D. S., Rosenzweig, M. R., & Smith, J. P. (2004). Immigrant health selectivity and acculturation. In N. B. Anderson, R. A. Bulatao, & B. Cohen (Eds.), *Critical perspectives on racial and ethnic differences in health in late life* (pp. 227–266). Washington, DC: The National Academies Press.

Jennissen, R. (2007). Causality chains in the international migration systems approach. *Population Research and Policy Review, 26*, 411–436.

Johnson, M. A., & Marchi, K. S. (2009). Segmented assimilation theory and perinatal health disparities among women of Mexican descent. *Social Science & Medicine, 69*(1), 101–109.

Karliner, L. S., Jacobs, E. A., Chen, A. H., & Mutha, S. (2007). Do professional interpreters improve clinical care for patients with limited English proficiency? A systematic review of the literature. *Health Services Research, 42*, 727–754.

Kataoka, S. H., Zhang, L., & Wells, K. B. (2002). Unmet need for mental health care among U.S. children: Variation by ethnicity and insurance status. *American Journal of Psychiatry, 159*, 1548–1555.

Krogstad, J. M., Gonzalez-Barrera, A., & Lopez, M. H. (2014). *Children 12 and under are fastest growing group of unaccompanied minors at U.S. border.* Washington, DC: Pew Research Center.

Krogstad, J. M., & Lopez, M. H. (2014a). *Hispanic nativity shift: U.S. births drive population growth as immigration stalls.* Washington, DC: Pew Research Center.

——. (2014b). *Hispanic nativity shift: U.S. Hispanic immigrants more likely to lack health insurance than U.S.-born.* Washington, DC: Pew Research Center.

Ku, L., & Matani, S. (2001). Left out: Immigrants' access to health care and insurance. *Health Affairs, 20*(1), 247–256.

Livingston, G. (2009). *Hispanics, health insurance and health care access.* Washington, DC: Pew Research Center.

Lopez, C., Bergren, M. D., & Painter, S. G. (2008). Latino disparities in child mental health services. *Journal of Child and Adolescent Psychiatric Nursing, 21,* 137–145.

Lopez, M., & Dockterman, D. (2011). *U.S. Hispanic country of origin counts for nation, top 30 metropolitan areas.* Washington, DC: Pew Research Center.

Lopez, M. H. (2009). *Latinos and education: Explaining the attainment gap.* Washington, DC: Pew Research Center.

Lopez, M. H., & Light, M. T. (2009). *A rising share: Hispanics and federal crime.* Washington, DC: Pew Research Center.

Lopez, M. H., & Velasco, G. (2011). *Childhood poverty among Hispanics sets record, leads nation: The toll of the Great Recession.* Washington, DC: Pew Research Center.

MacDorman, M. F., & Mathews, T. J. (2008). Recent trends in infant mortality in the United States. *NCHS Data Brief,* 1–8.

Mariscal, E. S. (2013). *Personal and environmental protective factors contributing to the resilience of Latino adolescents exposed to intimate partner violence: Findings from the National Survey of Child and Adolescent Well-being II.* Lawrence: University of Kansas.

Mendez, J. A. O. (2006). Latino parenting expectations and styles: A literature review. *Protecting Children, 21*(2), 53–61.

Mizoguchi, N. (1999). Proposition 187: California's anti-immigrant statute. In E. J. Kramer, S. L. Ivey, & Y. Ying (Eds.). *Immigrant women's health: Problems and solutions* (pp. 65–78). San Francisco, CA: Jossey-Bass.

Moracco, K. E., Hilton, A., Hodges, K. G., & Frasier, P. Y. (2005). Knowledge and attitudes about Intimate Partner Violence among immigrant Latinos in rural North Carolina. *Violence Against Women, 11*(3), 337–352.

Morin, J. L. (2009). *Latino/a rights and justice in the United States*. Durham, NC: North Carolina Academic Press.

National Council of La Raza. (2005). Critical disparities in Latino mental health: Transforming research into action. Washington, DC: Author.

———. (2012). *Fast facts: Latinos and health care*. Retrieved from http://www.nclr .org/images/uploads/publications/FastFacts_LatinosandHealthCare2012 .pdf

Organista, K. (2007). *Solving Latino psychosocial and health problems: Theory, practice, and populations*. Hoboken, NJ: John Wiley & Sons.

Osofsky, J. D. (2003). Prevalence of children's exposure to domestic violence and child maltreatment: Implications for prevention and intervention. *Clinical Child and Family Psychology Review, 6*(3), 161–170.

Padilla, A., & Perez, W. (2003). Acculturation, social identity, and social cognition: A new perspective. *Hispanic Journal of Behavioral Sciences, 25*(1), 35–55.

Palloni, A., & Arias, E. (2004). Paradox lost: Explaining the Hispanic adult mortality advantage. *Demography, 41*(3), 385–415.

Palloni, A., & Morenoff, J. D. (2001). Interpreting the paradoxical in the Hispanic paradox: Demographic and epidemiologic approaches. *Annals of the New York Academy of Sciences, 954*, 140–174.

Passel, J. S., & Cohn, D. (2011). *Unauthorized immigrant population: National and state trends, 2010*. Washington, DC: Pew Hispanic Center.

Perez-Stable, E. J., Napoles-Springer, A., & Miramontes, J. M. (1997). The effects of ethnicity and language on medical outcomes of patients with hypertension or diabetes. *Medical Care, 35*, 1212–1219.

Perilla, J., Bakeman, R., & Norris, F. (1994). Culture and domestic violence: The ecology of abused Latinas. *Violence and Victims, 9*(4), 325–339.

Pessar, P. R. (1999). Engendering migration studies: The case of new immigrants in the United States. *American Behavioral Scientist, 42*, 577–600.

Pew Hispanic Center. (2010). *Statistical profiles of the Hispanic and foreign-born populations in the U.S.* Washington, DC: Author.

———. (2012). *Statistical portrait of Hispanics in the United States, 2010*. Washington, DC: Author.

Raffaelli, M., & Ontai, L. L. (2004). Gender socialization in Latino/a families: Results from two retrospective studies. *Sex Roles, 50*, 287–299.

Resnicow, K., Braithwaite, R., Ahluwalia, J., & Baranowski, T. (1999). Cultural sensitivity in public health: Defined and demystified. *Ethnicity and Disease, 9*, 10–21.

Roberts, R. E., Alegría, M., Roberts, C. R., & Chen, I. G. (2005). Mental health problems of adolescents as reported by their caregivers: A comparison of European, African, and Latino Americans. *Journal of Behavioral Health Services & Research, 32*, 1–13.

Rumbaut, R. G. (1994). Origins and destinies: Immigration to the United States since World War II. *Sociological Forum, 9*, 583–621.

Saavedra, J. D. (2010). *Just the facts: A snapshot of incarcerated Hispanic youth* [fact sheet]. Washington, DC: National Council of La Raza.

Sanchez, T. W., & Jones, S. (2010). The diversity and commonalities of Latinos in the United States. In R. Furman & N. Negi (Eds.), *Social work practice with Latinos: Key issues and emerging themes* (pp. 31–44). Chicago, IL: Lyceum Books.

Schiller, J. S., Lucas, J. W., Ward, B. W., & Peregoy, J. A. (2012). *Summary health statistics for U.S. adults: National Health Interview Survey, 2010*. Washington, DC: National Center for Health Statistics.

Segal, U., & Mayadas, N. (2005). Assessment of issues facing immigrant and refugee families. *Child Welfare, 84*, 563–583.

Simmel, C. (2011). Demographic profiles of children reported to the child welfare system. *Journal of Public Child Welfare, 5*, 87–110.

Smart, J., & Smart, D. (1995). Acculturative stress of Hispanics: Loss and challenge. *Journal of Counseling and Development, 73*, 390–396.

Smedley, B., Stith, A. Y., & Nelson, A. R. (Eds.). (2003). *Unequal treatment: Confronting racial and ethnic disparities in health care*. Washington, DC: Institute of Medicine.

Solis, J. (2003). Re-thinking illegality as a violence against, not by, Mexican immigrants, children, and youth. *Journal of Social Sciences, 59*, 15–31.

Stepler, R., & Brown, A. (2015). *Statistical portrait of Hispanics in the United States, 1980–2013*. Washington, DC: Pew Research Center.

Summers, A., Wood, S., & Russell, J. (2012). *Disproportionality rates for children of color in foster care*. Reno, NV: National Council of Juvenile and Family Court Judges.

Suro, R., & Passel, J. S. (2003). *The rise of the second generation: Changing patterns in Hispanic population growth*. Washington, DC: Pew Research Center.

Taylor, P., Lopez, M. H., Martinez, J., & Velasco, G. (2012). *When labels don't fit: Hispanics and their views of identity*. Washington, DC: Pew Research Center.

Telles, E. E., & Ortiz, V. (2008). *Generations of exclusion: Mexican Americans, assimilation and race*. New York: Russell Sage Foundation.

U.S. Bureau of the Census. (2008). *An older and more diverse nation by midcentury.* Retrieved from http://www.census.gov/Press-Release/www/releases/archives /population/012496.html

U.S. Department of Education, & National Center for Education Statistics. (2014). *The condition of education 2014 (NCES 2014-083): Status dropout rates.* Fast Facts. Washington, DC: Author.

U. S. Department of Education, Office of Civil Rights. (2012). *The transformed civil rights data collection—March 2012 data summary.* Retrieved from http:// www2.ed.gov/about/offices/list/ocr/data.html

Van Hook, J., & Balisteri, K. S. (2006). Ineligible parents, eligible children: Food stamps receipt, allotments, and food insecurity among children of immigrants. *Social Science Research, 35*(1), 228–251.

Vasquez, M. J. (2007). Cultural differences and the therapeutic alliance: An evidence-based analysis. *American Psychologist, 62*, 878–885.

Vega, W.A., Alderete, E., Kolody, B., & Aguilar-Gaxiola, S. (1998). Illicit drug use among Mexicans and Mexican Americans in California: The effects of gender and acculturation. *Addiction, 93*, 1839–1850.

Villarruel, F. A., Walker, N. E., Minifee, P., Rivera-Vazquez, O., Peterson, S., & Perry, K. (2002). Donde está la justicia? A call to action on behalf of Latino and Latina youth in the U.S. justice system. East Lansing: Michigan State University, Institute for Children, Youth, and Families.

Welland, C., & Ribner, N. (2008). *Healing from violence: Latino men's journey to a new masculinity.* New York: Springer.

Zambrana, R. E., & Logie, L. A. (2000). Latino child health: Need for inclusion in the U.S. national discourse. *American Journal of Public Health, 90*(12), 1827–1833.

Zielewski, E. R., Malm, K., & Geen, R. (2006). Children caring for themselves and child neglect: When do they overlap? Washington, DC: Urban Institute.

Zimmerman, R. S., Khoury, E. L., Vega, W. A., Gil, A. G., & Warheit, G. J. (1995). Teacher and parent perceptions of behavior problems among a sample of African American, Hispanic, and non-Hispanic white students. *American Journal of Community Psychology, 23*, 181–197.

Zimmerman, W., & Fix, M. E. (1998). *Declining immigrant applications for Medi-Cal and welfare benefits in Los Angeles County.* Washington, DC: The Urban Institute.

CHAPTER 6

Asian and Pacific Islander Immigrant and Refugee Children and Families

▸ HALAEVALU F. OFAHENGAUE VAKALAHI, OFA KU'ULEI
LANIMEKEALOHA HAFOKA, *and* ROWENA FONG

REGARDLESS OF WHETHER ASIANS and Pacific Islanders seek refuge in the United States because of danger or dreams, the relocation experience can be physically, mentally, and culturally taxing for each individual, family, and community. These experiences can also produce numerous opportunities for growth and for positive contributions to both the original culture and the new one. The immigration and refugee experiences, although individually unique, have often created vulnerabilities and challenges for Asian and Pacific Islander children and families related to unfavorable socioeconomic, education, physical health, and mental health outcomes (Bronstein & Montgomery, 2011; Kassebaum et al., 1995; Le, 2002). The accumulation of stress and distress often experienced by refugee and immigrant children and families can contribute to higher levels of psychological distress, symptoms of current and posttraumatic stress disorder, depression, and other emotional and behavioral problems (Bronstein & Montgomery, 2011). Experiences of Asian and Pacific Islander immigrants and refugees in the United States have multiple layers of complexity that are inter- and intragenerational and transnational, and often impact the dynamics of navigating one's original and new cultural values, beliefs, practices, and languages (Bush, Bohon, & Kim, 2005; Lewis, 2008; Wong, 2008). Historically, for Asians and Pacific Islanders, the immigration and refugee experiences have produced negative outcomes for some but also a higher quality of life for others.

Examining Asians and Pacific Islanders in this chapter as a group separate from other immigrant groups, including those from other parts of the Asia-Pacific region, is warranted, given their unique cultures and lived immigration experiences. Furthermore, building on historically important yet aggregated literature and limited data on Asian and Pacific Islanders as a combined group, this chapter provides a platform for further dialogue that advocates for disaggregation of Asians and Pacific Islanders as unique groups; a closer examination, meaning more accurate data, of the different needs resulting from the refugee and immigration experiences separately; and development of more best practices that embrace dual cultures and communities and culturally responsive practices in multiple systems and across disciplines. This chapter will contribute to an extremely limited literature on a large and heterogeneous immigrant group that continues to be marginalized, underrepresented, and underserved, and this discussion in turn is intended to inform more culturally responsive strategies and approaches for Asians and Pacific Islanders.

DEFINITIONS

Immigrant is defined as an individual who chooses to relocate to another country for multiple reasons, including education, employment, family reunification, advancement, and/or better quality of life. The choice to relocate may be the result of a basic desire to seek a better way of life and not necessarily be because of war or violence. For many Asian and Pacific Islander (API) immigrants to the United States, the sense of interdependency in their culture of origin has contributed positively to the preservation of many indigenous cultural values, beliefs, and practices while they integrate new cultural lifeways. This collective worldview can enhance understanding of the immigration experience and inform responses to micro- and macro-level roadblocks resulting from immigration (Hafoka, 'Uluʻave, & Hafoka, 2014).

Refugee, on the other hand, refers to an individual forced out of his or her homeland because of war, disaster, political upheaval, or religious or ethnic tragedies (Fong, 2004). Social, economic, and legal factors assist governments in determining benefits and access to resources, thus differentiating between these two groups. However, these factors may also be the reasons for seeking refuge in another country. According to the United Nations High Commissioner for Refugees (2012), a refugee is

> any person who, owing to a well-founded fear of being persecuted for reasons of race, religion, nationality, membership of a particular social group, or political opinion, is outside the country of his nationality, and is unable to or, owing to such fear, is unwilling to avail himself of the protection of that country.

Although seemingly comprehensive, this definition fails to recognize the importance of national identity; in this case, of Asian and Pacific Islanders (API). These criteria can also be used as a mechanism for discriminatory decisions on entry, granting privileges to certain countries and during specific periods of time. Likewise, this definition seems to undermine the human experience related to war and danger, and the importance of one's homeland, thus disregarding the fact that seeking refuge is a complex issue beyond being a personal experience (United Nations High Commissioner for Refugees, 2012).

DEMOGRAPHIC PATTERNS AND WITHIN-GROUP DIVERSITY

According to the U.S. Bureau of the Census (2010), the foreign-born population includes immigrants and refugees, specifically naturalized citizens, lawful permanent residents, refugees, asylees, legal nonimmigrants, and undocumented persons. The foreign-born population in the United States numbers in the millions and will continue to grow as scientific and technological advancements facilitate relocation, and social conditions compel repositioning. In the United States today, there are multiple generations of Asian and Pacific Islander Americans who are either first-generation immigrants and refugees or descendants of immigrants and refugees. Consideration of intergenerational preservation and transference of cultural lifeways from first to second and subsequent generations of Asian and Pacific Islanders in the United States is critical for educators, policymakers, practitioners, and other professionals (Fong, 2004; Vakalahi, Godinet, & Fong, 2006). This generational dynamic offers a unique opportunity for developing more comprehensive responses to the needs of Asian and Pacific Islander immigrants and refugees.

Asian American Immigrants and Refugees

In this chapter, Asian American immigrants and refugees include specifically first-generation immigrants and refugees or descendants of immigrants
and refugees from East Asia (China, Japan, and Korea) and Southeast Asia
(Cambodia, Indonesia, Laos, Malaysia, Philippines, Thailand, and Vietnam). As described by the U.S. Bureau of the Census, foreign-born Asian
Americans are predominantly from Southeast and East Asia, specifically
from the Philippines, India, and China, and large numbers of them live in
states such as California, New York, and Texas. About 75 percent of Hawaii's
immigrants are from Asia. Numbering more than 10 million and accounting for 28 percent of the immigrant population, Asian Americans are the
second largest immigrant group in the United States. The 1965 U.S. Immigration and Nationality Act facilitated their increase in number. Of the
undocumented immigrants in 2010, about 11 percent were Asians (U.S.
Bureau of the Census, 2010; Xie & Goyette, 2004).

Furthermore, between 2001 and 2010, there were 248,956 Asian American refugees, which is about 47 percent of the approximately 528,000 refugee arrivals during that period. About 43 percent of these Asian refugees
were granted asylum in the United States, and almost 53 percent (62,350) of
the 118,684 Asian asylees were Chinese (Batalova, 2011). Also, more than 3
million foreign-born Asians received permanent residency in the United
States between 2001 and 2010, whereas more than 250,000 were naturalized
citizens in 2010. Additionally, between 2000 and 2009, more than 80 percent
of Asian immigrants were of working age, and they were more likely
than U.S.-born Asian men to be in the civilian labor force. Those employed
were more likely to be in highly skilled occupations such as technology,
management, science, and engineering. In the medical field, 58 percent of
immigrant physicians and surgeons were Asian immigrants, whereas
52 percent of immigrant registered nurses were Asian. In 2009, Asian immigrant women outnumbered Asian men. More than 50 percent of Asian
immigrants were fluent in English, and about half of those 25 years of age
and older had a bachelor's or higher degree. As an aggregate, with some
variation by country of birth, Asian Americans excelled in almost all areas,
including higher education, English language proficiency, and high-level
occupations. Overall, Asian immigrants were less likely to live in poverty,
compared with all immigrant populations (U.S. Bureau of the Census,

2010; U.S. Department of Homeland Security, 2010; Passel & Cohn, 2011; Ruggles et al., 2010).

Pacific Islander Immigrants and Refugees

In contrast to Asian immigrants and refugees, the story of Pacific Islanders reflects greater disadvantages related to education, economics, and health. Historical and emerging information that affirms such disadvantaged status partly justifies the need for disaggregated data and ethnicity-specific solutions.

Pacific Islanders in the United States are originally from Polynesia (e.g., Tonga, Tahiti), Micronesia (e.g., Marshall Islands), and Melanesia (e.g., Papua New Guinea). Pacific Islanders, an extremely diverse and multiracial group, are one of the fastest-growing racial groups in the United States. Similar to other communities of color, Pacific Islanders experienced their highest growth between 2000 and 2010, in which there were about 672,923 Pacific Islanders in the United States, the majority residing in Hawaii, California, Utah, Nevada, Alaska, and throughout the western United States (U.S. Bureau of the Census, 2006–2010). Some Pacific Islanders are from countries without a legal connection to the United States, which means that they must apply for legal permanent resident status in order to migrate to the United States. Other Pacific Islanders are from countries with political agreements with the United States, including those who are U.S. nationals because they are residents of U.S. territories and those who live in countries under the Compact of Free Association (COFA) agreement. Immigrants under COFA receive employment permits but may not be eligible to receive public benefits immediately upon arrival in the United States (Empowering Pacific Islander Communities, 2014). Climate change is the most critical threat to refugees in the Pacific Islands; however, because the United Nations Convention on the Status of Refugees does not include displacement caused by climate change, Pacific Islanders are often excluded under this category. Asylum for political and human rights reasons is, on the other hand, relevant for Pacific Islanders.

Immigration and refugee status are complex but critical realities for Pacific Islanders, including those who are undocumented. The lack of linguistically and culturally responsive programs generates additional challenges in navigating complex systems and accessing necessary services. For

TABLE 6.1 Demographic Characteristics of Asian Americans
and Pacific Islanders

	ASIAN AMERICANS (SINGLE RACE)	PACIFIC ISLANDERS (SINGLE RACE)
Median age	35.4	28.9
Homeowners[a]	58%	48%
Median household income	$67,022	$52,776
Low income[a]	26%	35%
Living in poverty	11.1%	18.8%
Without health insurance	18%	17%
High school diploma or more	85%	87%
Bachelor's degree or more	50%	14%
Graduate or professional degree	20%	4%

Source: Adapted from Facts for features. Asian/Pacific American heritage month (Washington, DC: U.S. Bureau of the Census, 2007 and 2010).
[a] U.S. Bureau of the Census 2007 figures. All other data U.S. Bureau of the Census, 2010.

instance, Pacific Islanders struggle to obtain access to higher education and to remain in school once they get there. Approximately 18 percent of Pacific Islanders have at least a bachelor's degree (see table 6.1), with Marshallese and Samoans having the lowest numbers, and Tongan and Samoan freshmen have below average admission rates. Likewise, diseases such as heart disease, cancer, diabetes, and obesity disproportionately impact Pacific Islanders, a situation that is complicated by the lack of access to culturally responsive services, extreme lack of health insurance (nearly one in five Pacific Islanders do not have health insurance), cost (about 18 percent did not see a doctor in 2012 because of cost), language barrier (most speak other languages, higher than average rate of limited English proficiency), and undocumented immigration status. Suicide deaths among Pacific Islanders also increased, by 170 percent between 2005 and 2010 (Empowering Pacific Islander Communities, 2014; U.S. Bureau of the Census, 2010).

Economic woes have also negatively impacted Pacific Islanders, who have higher than average poverty rates and larger than average household sizes because of their common cultural practice of intergenerational living. Unaffordable and overcrowded housing, in particular, can contribute to negative consequences in children's behavioral and mental health. Hernandez,

Denton, and Blanchard (2011) found that there is a 34 percent chance of living in overcrowded housing among Pacific Islanders. Confounding the housing issue is the 123 percent increase in the unemployment rate and 56 percent increase in the number of Pacific Islanders living in poverty. The disproportionate number of incarcerated Pacific Islanders, particularly in California and Utah, likewise contributes to the disenfranchised experiences of Pacific Islander immigrants and refugees (Empowering Pacific Islander Communities, 2014; U.S. Bureau of the Census, 2010).

There are multiple roadblocks associated with the immigration experience, including language barriers, cultural dissonance, poverty, and unavailability of economic opportunities. However, despite overwhelming challenges, Pacific Islanders contribute positively to the U.S. economy through small business ownership and by working in accommodation and food services, retail, and health care. They also contribute to American civic life as politicians, veterans, and a potentially large but unrecognized voting constituency. Pacific Islanders continue to promote education as a mechanism to alleviate unfavorable financial and social conditions (Harmon, Oosterbeek, & Walker, 2003). Using a collective and integrative approach that integrates indigenous Pacific Islander cultures and American life would potentially turn the curve of negative consequences for Pacific Islander Americans more in their favor (Hafoka et al., 2014).

HISTORY, PATTERNS, AND REASONS FOR MIGRATION

Asian and Pacific Islanders migrate to the United States primarily for the same reasons of a deep desire for a better quality of life and socioeconomic and educational opportunities for themselves and their families. Pacific Islanders commonly obtain legal immigrant status through family sponsorship, whereas Asians commonly obtain it through family and employer sponsorships. Compared with other immigrants, Asians are more likely to have employer sponsorship (Pew Research Center, 2014).

Federal policies past and present have had major impacts on the quality of life of Asian and Pacific Islander immigrant and refugee children as well as on the economic success of their families. Immigration system reform or lack thereof continues to impact immigrants and refugees, who consistently struggle with poverty, economic distress, poor housing, underemployment, inadequate education, confusion about the role of child welfare laws in rearing children, and increased parental stress resulting from generational disconnect and cultural duality. Nonetheless, federal policies have also facilitated task forces and initiatives such as the White House Initiative on Asian Americans and Pacific Islanders, which created a strategic plan for disaggregating data, funding education, promoting community engagement and entrepreneurship, growing a well-equipped workforce that is representative of the cultures and communities in the United States, and integrating immigrants and refugees linguistically and culturally into appropriate social service systems (Muñoz & Rodriguez, 2015).

In the area of federal policies, a core facilitator of migration into the United States among Asians and Pacific Islanders has been the U.S. Immigration and Nationality Act of 1965. The considerable increase in the number of Asian immigrants and refugees in particular is a direct result of this federal policy, which removed national origin quotas that historically privileged European immigrants (Migration Policy Institute, 2014). This federal legislation allowed the mass migration of Chinese, Korean, Filipino, Asian Indian, Vietnamese, Laotian, and Cambodian refugees, with the exception of those of Japanese heritage. Since 1965, there has been high demand for educated and skilled workers. Asian immigrants have responded to this call, which has led to the use of the title "model minority" to describe the Asian American community (Xie & Goyette, 2004).

Before 1965, low-wage workers had been recruited from various Asian countries, which led to blatant discrimination and racial violence against these immigrants. In the 1840s and 1850s, Chinese immigrants migrated to Hawaii and then to the continental United States. By 1860, there were about 35,000 Chinese in the continental United States. Seeking a refuge from war as well as better economic opportunities, the largest portion of the Chinese immigrant pool consisted of men who were temporary manual workers hired when white workers were on strike. Similarly, in 1898, Filipino immigrants began migrating to the United States to seek agricultural work. In the 1900s, Japanese immigrants migrated to Hawaii to work on the plantations, and these immigrants accounted for 43 percent of the population of Hawaii in 1920. During World War II, more than 100,000 Japanese from California and adjacent regions were placed in internment camps (Xie & Goyette, 2004).

Fawcett and Arnold (1987) have suggested that factors other than federal legislation and workforce demands influenced the rapid growth in

Asian immigrants. These included the fact that the Philippines was formerly under the protection of the United States and was one of its trading partners, so this economic dependency contributed tremendously to the migration of Filipinos into the United States. Among Koreans, political and military dependency, as well as marriage to American soldiers and adoption of Korean children, contributed to their mass migration into the United States. Both for Asians and for Pacific Islanders, mass migration was also facilitated by scholarships available to international students who would earn an education in the United States and return to their home countries. Upon completion of a degree, many of these graduates did not return to their home countries.

Pacific Islanders are among the most recent immigrants to the United States and numbered about 365,000 in the U.S. Census in 1980 and 1990. Many Pacific Islanders are first-generation Americans, whereas others have been in the United States for three generations. Regardless of generation, Pacific Islander culture is strongly preserved and passed on through intergenerational relationships. Among Pacific Islander immigrants and refugees, the nuances of historical trauma (Hurdle, 2002) resulting from the dual experiences of colonization and immigration past and present must be taken into consideration by the practitioners, policymakers, and community organizers who make decisions about responses to the needs of this population. Immigrant children and their families, more so for Pacific Islanders than for Asians, often experience overwhelming levels of stress because of unemployment, underemployment, lack of housing, and poor health. These result from their lower socioeconomic status, lower parental education level, and lower-wage jobs (Yoshihama, 2001). Among undocumented workers, added stress and fear of exposure are daily realities (Child Trends, 2007; Lassetter & Callister, 2009). Pacific Islanders are the most politically, educationally, and economically disadvantaged group in the United States (U.S. Bureau of the Census, 2007, 2010).

Today, the systems that serve immigrants and refugees are more restrictive, as a result of social conditions such as terrorism, mass shootings, economic crises, and other human tragedies. This social climate has resulted in a more hostile and anti-immigrant environment (Androff, Ayon, Becerra, & Gurrola, 2011), thus affirming the significance of social support networks and safety nets in Asian and Pacific Islander communities for each new wave of immigrants. Immigration as a civil law technically mandates that overstayed and undocumented immigrants are by law entitled to better living conditions than prisoners or detainees (American Civil Liberties Union, 2007). Because undocumented immigrants are seen to be breaching a contract, not breaking a law, they are tried accordingly. However, recent changes have opened the door for federal and state law enforcement entities to criminalize the enforcement of immigration policy, charging undocumented individuals as criminals by linking them to social security fraud and identity theft, which are felonies that may land an individual in prison. Additionally, law enforcers across the United States are pushing for restrictions on access to education, social services, and public benefits for undocumented individuals (Androff, Ayon, Becerra, & Gurrola, 2011). These are the realities of Asian and Pacific Islander undocumented immigrants.

CULTURAL VALUES, BELIEFS, AND PRACTICES

The diversity in the Asian and Pacific Islander foreign-born population mirrors the differences, and similarities, of their cultural heritages, economic conditions, political systems, religious practices, and languages. Foreign-born Asian and Pacific Islanders have contributed positively to American society through their strong sense of family and filial piety, sacrifice for the collective good, harmony, inclusiveness and reciprocity, spiritual connectedness, and deep commitment to passing on these legacies through intergenerational connections as a foundation on which to live across space and time (Taufe'ulungaki, 2008; Vakalahi & Fong, 2014; Vakalahi & Godinet, 2014; Westervelt, 1910). For instance, ensuring inclusiveness and collectivity in the family and community are fundamental cultural lifeways in indigenous Asian and Pacific Islander cultures that have been preserved and passed on to generations of Asians and Pacific Islanders in the United States. These lifeways are reflected in access to the large extended family, social supports, intergenerational relations, and transnational connections. Giving and receiving resources and wealth unconditionally, accepting shared responsibility for each other, and embracing interdependency in the family and community are also central to the identity of Asian and Pacific Islander immigrants (Fong, 2011; Lee, 1997; McDermott, Tseng, & Maretzki, 1980; Mokuau, 1991; Vakalahi & Godinet, 2014).

With major growth in the migration of Asians and Pacific Islanders, their dual and multiple cultural identities, transnational identities, and relationships have become important for identifying and responding to their needs in the United States. Although unique in their own right, Asians and Pacific Islanders collectively have shared cultural elements that would inform responsive policies, practices, and research, such as conceptualizing responses holistically and spiritually; embracing the family as the center of life, with unconditional love for children and respect for elders; and cultivating community as the frame for one's identity (Fong & Furuto, 2001).

Examples of Cultural Conflicts

Ensuring effective multisystemic examination of and responses to the needs of Asian and Pacific Islander immigrant and refugee children and families requires a balanced and coherent intersection and integration of dual and multiple cultural lifeways. Such balance in the formulation of culturally responsive services to needs by systems such as education, social services, physical and mental health, and others is imperative to the well-being of Asian and Pacific Islander children and their families and communities. An example of conflicting cultural lifeways between Asian and Pacific Islander culture and U.S. majority culture is on health care policies. Policies on informed consent and advanced directives that are common practices in majority individualistic cultures may be challenging to collectivist cultures such as Asians and Pacific Islanders, in which all decisions are made collaboratively in families and communities in order to accommodate the needs and expectations of the group. Whereas majority culture encourages making decisions individually, Asian and Pacific Islander cultures expect an individual to seek the input and guidance of the family in making a decision. In many Asian and Pacific Islander cultures, the eldest member, most often the eldest son, is delegated the responsibility of decision making. Likewise, filial piety or family obligation speaks to the collective obligation and responsibility of the younger generation for the older generation. Therefore, the health care option of placing an elder in a nursing or group home is not an acceptable option in collectivist cultures such as those of Asians and Pacific Islanders (Long & Long, 1982; McLaughlin & Braun, 1998). Similarly, the common use of folk medicine in Asian and Pacific Islander communities also raises questions about these health policies and their enforcement.

Child rearing is another issue of possible conflict for Asians and Pacific Islanders. In other words, what one culture may deem abusive may be defined as discipline in another culture. Asians and Pacific Islanders some-times struggle with adjusting to child-rearing methods required by the U.S. legal system. It is incumbent on professionals to have a clear understanding of cultural practices and norms that may assist in correctly identifying and treating child abuse cases. For example, some Southeast Asian parents use "coining" (rubbing of coins) or "cupping" (cupping of skin) on their children as therapy; however, these methods leave noticeable bruises on the children (Yeatman, Shaw, Barlow, & Barlett, 1976). Professionals such as teachers report these practices to officials as child maltreatment or child abuse. Al-though the law is explicit on the mandatory obligation for professionals to report child abuse, coining or cupping practices have not proven to be med-ically harmful for children and may in fact have psychological benefits (Nguyen, Nguyen, & Nguyen, 1987).

CASE STUDY: LI HUA AND FANG MING

Li Hua, age 30, and Fang Ming, age 32, a couple married for five years, are immi-grants from China. Both are students at the local university and are studying to get their PhDs. They have been reported having loud and violent quarrels. Other residents in their married student housing complex are complaining that their ar-guments are becoming more violent, and residents are beginning to fear that Li Hua might harm herself or be harmed by Fang Ming. Concerns about their 3-year-old daughter, Mei Jun, are being voiced because the couple's neighbors in the married student complex have recently seen bruise marks on Mei Jun's arms and legs. The resident adviser in the married student housing complex, suspect-ing child abuse, decides to report Li Hua and Fang Ming to Child Protective Ser-vices (CPS), and an initial investigation begins.

The CPS worker visits the Chinese couple and begins to ask questions about the couple's situation and the reasons for the loud and violent arguments. Fang Ming blames Li Hua, saying that her duty is to become pregnant and have a son. The traditional Chinese values of having a male heir weigh on Fang Ming, who gets pressure from his parents in China. Fang Ming is very disappointed that their only child is a daughter, as the former One Child Policy in China allowed only one child. Fang Ming had hoped that by coming to the United States, his wife would become pregnant and they could have a son. But Li Hua is far too inter-ested in pursuing her PhD and does not want to have another child. She has neglected Mei Jun, who bruises easily when she falls on the playground at the child development center at the university. Teachers have also wondered if child abuse is occurring in the home.

In handling this case, CPS workers need to address the possible issues of domestic violence and child abuse. But they also need to be culturally responsive and understand the macro-level population policies of China that limit couples in having children, putting undue pressure on the wife to make choices between the interests of self, husband, and in-laws, as well as national birth control policies. If CPS workers did not understand the restrictions of the One Child Policy and the tensions it causes for families like that of Li Hua, Fang Ming, and Mei Jun, they may make decisions affecting the family that might not only be unhelpful but also have negative outcomes. In dealing with this case, the CPS worker needs to know that there are differences in Chinese couples who come from mainland China, Hong Kong, or Taiwan and that national or government family policies do affect family and individual choices, resulting in possible negative consequences.

CHALLENGES RELATED TO CROSS-SYSTEM INVOLVEMENT

Involvement in multiple social service systems can produce negative outcomes for children and families from all walks of life. For Asian and Pacific Islander refugees and immigrants, involvement in multiple social service systems, such as child welfare, physical and mental health, justice, education, and other institutions, have often produced devastating outcomes given the multiple layers of traumatic experiences, acculturative stress, and physical and mental health disparities that accompany migration outside one's country of origin.

The challenges of cross-system involvement are generally defined in terms of systemic infrastructure, practices, and workforce. In terms of infrastructure, challenges in cross-system partnership originate in the disconnection in communication between systems. Asian and Pacific Islander immigrant and refugee children and families are involved with social service systems that often do not communicate consistently, lack transparency, struggle with the coordination of services, and are not funded sufficiently to provide responsive services. The historical difficulty in agreeing on a collective mission across all social service systems and the lack of relevant policies also make accountability for outcomes of services difficult. The complexity and complications of coordinating these systems have resulted in very few cross-system initiatives, and these are often disjointed and underfunded and are seldom successful. Consequently, these systems become sources of risk, and the outcomes for these immigrant and refugee children and families are worse in comparison with those of other Americans (Kashim & Vakalahi, 2010).

Regarding practices, it is often challenging to ensure that the conceptualization of cross-system initiatives is based specifically on Asian and Pacific Islander cultures. The manner in which collaborations across systems are conceptualized is critical for responding to the need for trauma-informed services for Asian and Pacific Islander children and families who have experienced traumatic events of family and community loss and living in a foreign system (Adams, 2010; Cooper, Masi, Dababnah, Aratani, & Knitzer, 2007). The difficulties of encountering a system foreign to these newcomers as well as the co-occurring issues of trauma warrant more collaboration across systems (Ryan & Testa, 2005).

In terms of workforce, the knowledge base on effective cross-system collaboration that takes into consideration the lives of immigrants and refugees is sparse, and culturally and linguistically responsive professional skills are often lacking. The professional workforce in these partnerships across systems does not reflect the need for trained social workers who make decisions based on values and ethics and have experience in advocacy and in navigating multiple social service systems (Hollingsworth, 2009) for immigrants and refugees. The workforce is also lagging behind the need for linguistically experienced social work professionals who can navigate multiple social systems and cultures of Asian and Pacific Islander children and families.

CULTURALLY RESPONSIVE STRATEGIES
TO ADDRESS CHALLENGES

A number of evidence-based intervention strategies have been used with Asian and Pacific Islander immigrants and refugees in the United States, with some succeeding and others failing. The following are examples of strategies grounded in cultural values of family, community, reciprocity, and collectivity. As the general literature shows, effective and sustained culturally responsive strategies must be framed and defined by the target culture. For instance, in Asian cultures, body, mind, and spirit are the foundational elements of culturally responsive physical health and mental health practices. Mindfulness of the significance of relationships is central to working effectively with Asian immigrants and refugees.

Similarly, an example for Pacific Islanders is the Pacific Conceptual Framework (Family and Community Services, 2014), which was developed using a Pacific epistemology to respond to issues of family violence and promotion of family well-being in New Zealand by using a strengths-based perspective. Although this overarching framework has not been used in the United States, Pacific Islanders developed it for Pacific Islanders, including those in the diaspora. This overarching framework comes from the following: Turanga Māori—Cook Islander; Vuvale Doka Sautu—Fijian; Koe Fakatupuolamaoui he tau Magafaoua Niu—Niuean; le tōfā mamao—Samoan; Toku fou Tiale—Tuvalu; Fofola e fala kae talanoa e kainga—Tongan; and Kāiga Māopoopo—Tokelauan. True to its cultural core, this framework was built on values and practices of inclusiveness, reciprocity, collectivity, interconnectedness, and interdependency to achieve balance in relationships, interactions, and transactions (Family and Community Services, 2014). Framework fundamentals that would inform practice include that family is central; fluency in the language is critical for change; rituals and relationships contribute to well-being; and ethnicity-specific practice is imperative (Family and Community Services, 2014).

Built on this overarching framework are a number of Pacific indigenous practice approaches, including Ifoga (Jantzi, 2001), an indigenous Samoan healing practice emphasizing reconciliation; Fakalelei (Jantzi, 2001), a Tongan holistic healing practice; Pola and Uku (Mafile'o, 2005), a community practice approach; Seitapu (Pulotu-Endemann et al., 2007), a culturally responsive mental health practice approach; Fa'afaletui (Tamasese, Peteru, & Waldegrave, 1997) and Talanoa ile l'a (Faleolo, 2013), approaches for working with youths; Family Group Conferencing (Wilcox et al., 1991), for family preservation; E Kaveinga (Crummer, 1998), a child welfare approach; Fonofale (Pulotu-Endemann, 2002), a model of health using an image of a house to represent important factors in healthy development; Ho'oponopono (Pukui, Haertig, & Lee, 1972), for family conflict resolution; and Popao (Fotu & Tafa, 2009), that cultural identity strengthens mental health.

Overall, specific practice implications for Asian and Pacific Islander immigrants and refugees are grounded in deeply rooted cultural values that clarify understanding in times of conflict as well as inform assessment, planning, and selection of appropriate interventions. As discussed previously, in selecting appropriate conceptual frameworks and relevant practice interventions for working with Asians and Pacific Islanders, there are important factors that must be considered by professionals: the significance of historical experiences and consequences of colonization and immigration; the need for a linguistically competent workforce; the importance of understanding the multicultural and multigenerational embeddedness of behavior changes and the reality of transnationalism and transculturalism in this population; the centrality of family and community as originators or buffers for shame and stigma relative to mental health services; and the importance of assessment tools that take into account the roles of church, culture, community, and family.

COLLABORATIONS ACROSS SYSTEMS

Loss of family and challenges of acculturative stress among Asian and Pacific Islander immigrants and refugees warrant collaborations across systems (Luster et al., 2009). Migration, voluntary or forced, can be an extremely traumatic experience for children and their families, and subsequently a possible source of risk factors for delinquency, poor health, health disparities, stress, and so forth. Partnerships across systems can be a key to creating trauma-informed social service systems (Adams, 2010; Cooper et al., 2007; Ryan & Testa, 2005).

Children are socialized and nurtured in families and communities, so creating social service systems that respond effectively to the needs of children in their families and communities is imperative. Generally, collaboration across systems is an inherent part of the immigration experience, as reflected across the continuum of grassroots partnerships within local communities to national collaborations (Stewart, 2013). For Asian and Pacific Islander immigrants and refugees, partnerships between families, communities, and social service systems are critical for creating culturally responsive systems of care and enabling better access to resources in order to meet needs. Collaboration across systems can be a complex and complicated process of bringing together siloed entities, which sometimes contributes to negative experiences among consumers. However, such collaboration also presents opportunities for growth and progress in the lives of immigrant and refugee children and families. Collaboration across social service systems such as child welfare, physical and mental health, juvenile justice, education, and other institutions can better inform comprehensive services and programs for Asian and Pacific Islander immigrants and refugees (Luster et al., 2009; Nash & Bilchik, 2009). Collaborations across systems can and have produced primarily positive outcomes (Stewart, 2013).

For instance, partnerships among multiple systems are a powerful means for placing pressure on decision makers to disaggregate data as the foundation for effective work with Asian and Pacific Islander immigrants and refugees. Accurate, current, and disaggregated data are imperative for moving the national agenda on improving the outcomes of Asian and Pacific Islander immigrants and refugees. Disaggregation of data is necessary to address the decades of trivialization of the outcomes of Asian and Pacific Islanders who were struggling as individuals and families yet in aggregate were dubbed "model minorities" (White House Initiative on Asian Americans and Pacific Islanders, 2009).

Furthermore, collaboration across systems offers the opportunity for hybrid and integrated strategies and approaches to the needs of Asian and Pacific Islander immigrants and refugees. For example, the integration of modern medicine and indigenous healing can generate culturally and linguistically responsive approaches to the physical and mental health of Asian and Pacific Islander children and families. Reciprocity between cultures of origin and new cultures can better inform the social service system in receiving and assisting new immigrants and refugees. Moreover, collaboration across systems can facilitate sharing of scarce resources and advocacy for equal access to services and resources urgently needed by immigrants and refugees. Alignment of social service systems to support culturally responsive ideologies that produce best practices can better respond to the needs of Asian and Pacific Islander children and families struggling with the immigration and refugee experiences (Empowering Pacific Islander Communities, 2014).

Additionally, partnerships across systems contribute to the reconceptualization of children and families within the immigration and refugee experiences and to engaging strengths-based services that contribute to healthy outcomes. An ecosystems perspective that engages children and families holistically across the various social service systems is important. Putting these children and families front and center in the conversation about and creation of best practices is critical. The collective commitment of child welfare, physical and mental health, education, and justice system professionals can change the negative perceptions of immigrants and refugees and thereby facilitate equitable access to needed resources. Collaboration across systems can be a powerful means of advocating for policies that ensure funding, resources, and equal access, as well as employee training on appropriate decision making for offering a strong system of care tailored for Asian and Pacific Islander immigrants and refugees (Empowering Pacific Islander Communities, 2014; Stewart, 2013; Wiig & Tuell, 2004, 2008).

SPOTLIGHT: IMMIGRANT AND REFUGEE SERVICES

Services for Asian and Pacific Islander immigrants and refugees are limited, underresourced, and often fused with services offered to the general public or general Asian and Pacific Islander population. Although services exist, their quality and quantity do not always meet the demand. Nonetheless, there are organizations that have institutionalized the commitment to serving Asian and Pacific Islander immigrants and refugees despite scarce resources and the growing U.S. anti-immigration climate. A few are highlighted here.

Asian Association of Utah

Improving quality of life for refugees and immigrants in Utah

Founded in 1977, Asian Association of Utah is a private, non-profit, community-based organization located in Salt Lake City, Utah. From its beginnings of supporting Asian immigrants and refugees in terms of reducing barriers and increasing opportunities, Asian Association of Utah has served over 2,000 refugees and immigrants from around the world each year over the past 37 years toward independence and self-sufficiency. Services offered by Asian Association of Utah include case management, employment, counseling and mental health treatment, English classes, after-school tutoring, and other services needed by immigrant and refugee individuals and families. Asian Association of Utah has been successful in creating networks of support for clients, which in turn has positively impacted the community in which they live.

Source: http://aau-slc.org/about-us/history-and-mission

Asian and Pacific Islander American Health Forum

Founded in 1986 and located in San Francisco, California, and Washington, DC, Asian and Pacific Islander American Health Forum (APIAHF) provides leadership

and advocacy for health equity, fairness, and justice among AA and NHPI communities in the U.S. and its territories and affiliated jurisdictions. APIAHF mobi-
lizes AA and NHPI communities collectively to positively influence health
policies through the provision of funding, training, technical assistance, and
consultation.

Source: http://www.apiahf.org

Asian and Pacific Islander Coalition on HIV/AIDS

The primary mission of APICHA is to facilitate access to healthcare for vulnerable Asian and Pacific Islanders living in New York City and Manhattan. Embodied
by the slogan "We care," APICHA advocates for dignity and respect for all people
regardless of their circumstances in life, particularly the "others" including those
from the LGBT community and individuals living with HIV/AIDS. Grounded on
core values of cultural competency, advocacy, respect, leadership, compassion,
courage, and stewardship, APICHA embraces the calling to facilitate health and
well-being of all community members regardless of circumstance.

Source: http://www.apicha.org/apicha/main.html

Asian Pacific Islander Legal Outreach

Framed by the necessity of culturally and linguistically competent services for
marginalized API communities in the Bay Area (San Francisco and Oakland),
Asian Pacific Islander Legal Outreach (formerly Nihonmachi Legal Outreach) was
founded in 1975 as a community-based, social justice organization. APILO provides legal, social, and educational services to combat domestic violence, violence against women, immigrant rights, elder abuse, human trafficking, and
other challenges in the API communities.

Source: http://www.apilegaloutreach.org/index.html

May: Asian-Pacific American Heritage Month

Visibility and acceptance of immigrants was the expected outcome when Congress established Asian-Pacific American Heritage Month. This heritage month
honors the sacrifice of early API pioneers, provides a platform that acknowledges
the existence of API communities, and provides grounds for achievements of
dreams and goals in a new home country.

CONCLUSION

Implications for research, practice, policy, and education regarding Asian and Pacific Islander immigrants and refugees are many. However, it is a daunting task to provide a complete portrait of a vastly diverse, culturally evolving, and tremendously resilient Asian and Pacific Islander population. Nonetheless, our hope is that this chapter will facilitate the dialogue and next steps in responding to the needs of this American population. Refugee and immigration status are systemic in nature, and their impacts can be comprehensively positive or negative for individuals, families, and communities. As such, a clearer picture is needed that requires up-to-date, accurate, and disaggregated data on the physical and mental health and socioeconomic status of Asian and Pacific Islander immigrants and refugees by distinct ethnic and racial group.

For children and youths, there is a need to focus on facilitating higher educational achievement, particularly among Pacific Islanders, as a mechanism for higher socioeconomic status. Alternative and innovative models of practice in institutions of higher learning that facilitate admission, retention, and graduation will be key. These targeted higher education efforts and mentoring into careers are imperative.

For families and communities, political and civic engagement is important for current and future generations to survive and thrive. Cultivating the natural entrepreneurial spirit of Asian and Pacific Islander immigrants will also yield positive socioeconomic outcomes, particularly as this population begins to recover economically.

As stated, legal status is a major factor that helps or hinders progress for Asian and Pacific Islander immigrants and refugees. As such, policymakers and advocates on behalf of immigrants and refugees must begin the process of developing comprehensive and compassionate immigration reform. In light of current events, mandatory training for the law enforcement community should be included in this plan for reform in order to fairly and equally protect the civil rights of Asian and Pacific Islander immigrants and refugees in the United States.

Finally, professionals need to cultivate partnerships with immigrant and refugee groups to develop competencies in knowledge and skills to provide quality, respectful, culturally and linguistically responsive services.

In summary, recommendations for culturally responsive practice with and advocacy for Asian and Pacific Islanders include:

1 Disaggregated data are urgently needed to inform decision making, given the differences in cultures and immigration experiences and their relationship to socioeconomic, education, and health outcomes.

2 Immediate attention to the high levels of immigration-related psychological distress, posttraumatic stress disorder, depression, and other emotional and behavioral problems is warranted.

3 Recognize the fact that these communities operate on dual sets of cultural values, beliefs, practices, and languages.

4 Integrating into practice the fundamentals of family and filial piety is central, spirituality and relationships contribute to well-being, and ethnicity-specific practice is imperative.

5 Consider the consequences of colonization and immigration, the importance of understanding the multicultural and multigenerational embeddedness of behavior changes, and the reality of transnationalism and transculturalism.

6 There is a need for a linguistically competent workforce; fluency in the immigrant's language is critical for change.

7 Consider the importance of assessment tools that take into account the roles of church, culture, community, and family.

8 There are existing opportunities for hybrid and integrated strategies and approaches.

9 Acknowledge the fact that Asian and Pacific Islander communities contribute to the economy through small business ownership and by working in the accommodation, food service, retail, and health care industries, and that they also contribute civically in politics, as veterans, and as a potentially large but unrecognized voting constituency.

KEY TERMS

CHINA'S ONE CHILD POLICY A population control policy passed in the People's Republic of China in 1979 allowing married couples officially and legally to birth one child. Modifications to the policy in 2014 allow two children.

FILIAL PIETY A traditional Asian cultural value where, even as adults, children, particularly the eldest son, are under the obligation of caring for parents and putting their needs first, before themselves and other family members.

"MODEL MINORITIES" A coined term used stereotypically and falsely to denote that among all the ethnic minority groups, the Asians and Pacific Islanders were the models of success and achievement.

PACIFIC CONCEPTUAL FRAMEWORK A framework using a Pacific epistemology of inclusiveness, reciprocity, collectivity, interconnectedness, and interdependency to achieve balance in relationships, interactions, and transactions in order to respond from a strengths-based perspective to issues of family violence and promotion of family well-being in New Zealand.

PACIFIC ISLANDERS Persons originally from Polynesia, Micronesia, and Melanesia.

STUDY QUESTIONS

1 What culturally responsive assessment tools can be used to work effectively with Asian and Pacific Islander immigrant and refugee children and families?

2 What are the culturally and linguistically responsive services available specifically for Asian and Pacific Islander immigrants and refugees?

3 What are the impacts of the colonization and immigration experiences on dual-cultured Asian and Pacific Islander children?

4 What is the role of cultural strengths in collaborations across systems?

5 What are the strategies for positioning the issues of immigrants and refugees in the efforts for immigration reform?

ADDITIONAL RESOURCES

Asian and Pacific Island Wellness Center: http://www.apiwellness.org/home.html

Asian and Pacific Islander American Health Forum: http://www.apiahf.org

Asian and Pacific Islander Coalition on HIV/AIDS: http://www.apicha.org/apicha/main.html

Asian and Pacific Islander Institute on Domestic Violence: http://www.apiahf.org/apidvinstitute/default.htm

Asian Pacific Islander Legal Outreach: http://www.apilegaloutreach.org /index.html

Foundation for Education: http://www.youtube.com/watch?v=iLfEI_L3ynE

Higher education: http://www.youtube.com/watch?v=vNJSc6UKKhI

Pacific Island Ethnic Art Museum: http://www.pieam.org/

Pacific Islanders in Communication: http://www.piccom.org/

Pacific Islands Forum Secretariat: http://www.forumsec.org/index.cfm

U.S. Bureau of the Census: http://www.census.gov/population/www /socdemo/race/api.html

U.S. Census on Native Hawaiians and Pacific Islanders: http://www.youtube .com/watch?v=P4ycBZW-NoU

REFERENCES

Adams, E. (2010). *Healing invisible wounds: Why investing in trauma-informed care for children makes sense.* Washington, DC: Justice Policy Institute.

American Civil Liberties Union. (2007). *Overview of U.S. Immigration Detention and International Human Rights Law on the Use of Detention in the U.S.* Washington, DC: Author.

Androff, D. K., Ayon, C., Becerra, D., & Gurrola, M. (2011). US immigration policy and immigrant children's well-being: The impact of policy shifts. *Journal of Sociology and Social Welfare, 38,* 77.

Batalova, J. (2011). Asian immigrants in the United States. Retrieved from http:// www.migrationpolicy.org/article/asian-immigrants-united-states-1

Bronstein, I., & Montgomery, P. (2011). Psychological distress in refugee children: A systematic review. *Clinical Child and Family Psychology Review, 14*(1), 44–56.

Bush, K. R., Bohon, S. A., and Kim, H. K. (2005). Adaptation among immigrant families: Resources and barriers. In P. C. McKenry and S. J. Price (Eds.), *Families and change: Coping with stressful events and transitions* (3rd ed., pp. 307–332). Thousand Oaks, CA: Sage.

Child Trends. (2007). *Child indicators, summer 2007.* http://www.childtrends .org/?publications=the-child-indicator-summer-2007

Cooper, J. L., Masi, R., Dababnah, S., Aratani, Y., & Knitzer, J. (2007). *Strengthening policies to support children, youth, and families who experience trauma.* New York, NY: Columbia University, National Center for Children in Poverty.

Crummer, A. (1998). E kaveinga: A Cook Islands model of social work practice. Auckland, New Zealand: Children, Young Persons & Their Families Service.

Empowering Pacific Islander Communities. (2014). *Native Hawaiians and Pacific Islanders: A community of contrasts*. Retrieved from http://empoweredpi.org/wp-content/uploads/2014/06/A_Community_of_Contrasts_NHPI_US_2014-1.pdf

Faleolo, M. M. (2013). Cultural authentication in social work education: A balancing act. In C. Noble, M. Henrickson, and I. Y. Han, *Social work education: Voices from the Asia Pacific* (2nd ed., pp. 105–132). Sydney, Australia: Sydney University Press.

Family and Community Services. (2014). *The Pacific conceptual framework*. Retrieved from http://www.familyservices.govt.nz/working-with-us/programmes-services/pasefika-proud/pacific-cultural-frameworks.html.

Fawcett, J. T., & Arnold, F. (1987). Explaining diversity: Asian and Pacific immigration systems [Special issue]. *Center for Migration Studies, 5*(3), 453–473.

Fong, R. (2011). Cultural competence with Asian Americans. In D. Lum (Ed.), *Culturally competent practice: A framework for understanding diverse groups and justice issues* (4th ed., pp. 333–357). Belmont, CA: Brooks Cole.

Fong, R. (Ed.). (2004). *Culturally competent practice with immigrant and refugee children and families*. New York, NY: Guilford Press.

Fong, R., & Furuto, S. (Eds.). (2001). *Culturally competent social work practice: Skills, interventions and evaluation*. Boston, MA: Allyn & Bacon.

Fotu, M., & Tafa, T. (2009). The Popao model: A Pacific recovery and strength concept in mental health. *Pacific Health Dialogue, 15*(1), 164–170.

Hafoka, M. P., ʻUluʻave, M. F., & Hafoka, I. (2014). Double bind: The duality of Tongan-American identity. In H. F. O. Vakalahi & M. Godinet (Eds.), *Transnational Pacific Islander Americans and social work: Dancing to the beat of a different drum* (pp. 127–138). Washington, DC: NASW.

Harmon, C., Oosterbeek, H., & Walker, I. (2003). The returns to education: Microeconomics. *Journal of Economic Surveys, 17*(2), 115–156.

Hernandez, D. J., Denton, N. A., & Blanchard, V. L. (2011). Children in the United States of America: A statistical portrait by race-ethnicity, immigrant origins, and language. *Annals of the American Academy of Political and Social Science, 633*(1), 102–127.

Hollingsworth, R. (2009). The role of institutions and organizations in shaping radical scientific innovations. In L. Magnusson and J. Ottosson (Eds.), *The evolution of path dependence* (pp. 139–165). Northampton, MA: Edward Elgar.

Hurdle, D. E. (2002). Native Hawaiian traditional healing: Cultural based interventions for social work practice. *Social Work (NASW)*, *47*(2), 183–192.

Jantzi, V. E. (2001). *Restorative justice in New Zealand: Current practice, future possibilities*. Retrieved from http://www.massey.ac.nz/~wtie/articles/vern.htm

Kashim, S., & Vakalahi, H. F. O. (2010). Children, youth, and families in dual jurisdictions: An analysis of the emerging literature. *Michigan Child Welfare Law Journal*, *12*(2), 7–18.

Kassebaum, G., Lau, C. W. S., Kwack, D., Leverette, J., Allingham, E., & Marker, N. (1995). *Identifying disproportionate representation of ethnic groups in Hawaii's juvenile justice system: Phase one*. Honolulu: Center for Youth Research, Social Science Research Institute, University of Hawaii-Manoa.

Lassetter, J. H., & Callister, L. C. (2009). The impact of migration on the health of voluntary migrants in western societies. *Journal of Transcultural Nursing*, *20*(1), 93–104.

Le, T. (2002). Delinquency among Asian/Pacific Islanders: Review of literature and research. *The Justice Professional*, *15*(1), 57–70.

Lee, E. (1997). *Working with Asian Americans: Guide for clinicians*. New York, NY: Guilford.

Lewis, D. C. (2008). Types, meanings and ambivalence in intergenerational exchanges among Cambodian refugee families in the United States. *Ageing and Society*, *28*(5), 693–726.

Long, S., & Long, B. (1982). Curable cancers and fatal ulcers: Attitudes toward cancer in Japan. *Social Science and Medicine*, *16*, 2101–2108.

Luster, T., Saltarelli, A. J., Rana, M., Qin, D. B., Bates, L., & Burdick, K. (2009). The experiences of Sudanese unaccompanied minors in foster care. *Journal of Family Psychology*, *23*(3), 386–395.

Mafile'o, T. A. (2005). *Tongan metaphors of social work practice: Hangē ha Pā kuo Fa'u'* (Doctoral dissertation, Massey University, Palmerston North, New Zealand). Available from Massey Research Online at http://hdl.handle.net/10179 /1697

McDermott, J. F., Jr., Tseng, W., & Maretzki, T. W. (1980). *People and cultures of Hawaii: A psychocultural profile*. Honolulu: The University Press of Hawaii.

McLaughlin, L. A., & Braun, K. L. (1998). Asian and Pacific Islander cultural values: Considerations for health care decision making. *Health & Social Work*, *23*(2), 116–126.

Migration Policy Institute. (2014). *Asian immigrants in the United States*. Retrieved from http://www.migrationpolicy.org/article/asian-immigrants-united-states

Mokuau, N. (Ed.). (1991). *Handbook of social services for Asian and Pacific Islanders*. New York, NY: Greenwood.

Muñoz, C., & Rodriguez, L. (2015). *Strengthening communities by welcoming and integrating immigrants and refugees*. Retrieved from https://www.whitehouse.gov/blog/2015/04/15/strengthening-communities-welcoming-and-integrating-immigrants-and-refugees

Nash, M., & Bilchik, S. (2009, Winter). Child welfare and juvenile justice—two sides of the same coin, part II. *Juvenile and Family Justice Today*, 23–25.

Nguyen, N., Nguyen, P. H., & Nguyen, L. H. (1987). Vietnamese families: Traditional medical practice vs. child abuse. Mimeographed paper.

Passel, J. S., & Cohn, D. (2011). *Unauthorized immigrant population: National and state trends, 2010*. Washington, DC: Pew Hispanic Center.

Pew Research Center. (2014). *The risk of Asian Americans*. Retrieved from http://www.pewsocialtrends.org/2012/06/19/the-rise-of-asian-americans/2/#chapter-1-portrait-of-asian-americans

Pukui, M. K., Haertig, E. W., & Lee, C. A. (1972). *Nānā i ke Kumu: Look to the source* (Vol. 1). Honolulu, HI: Hui Hānai.

Pulotu-Endemann, F. K. (2002). Consequences of alcohol and other drug use: Fonofale. Retrieved from www.alcohol.org.nz/resources/publications/ALAC_drug_Manual_Chapter_4.pdf

Pulotu-Endemann, F. K., Suaali'i-Sauni, T., Lui, D., McNicholas, T., Milne, M., & Gibbs, T. (2007). *Seitapu Pacific mental health and addiction cultural & clinical competencies framework*. Auckland, New Zealand: The National Centre of Mental Health Research and Workforce Development.

Ruggles, J. S., T. A., Genadek, K., Goeken, R., Schroeder, M. B., and Sobek, M. (2010). Integrated Public Use Microdata Series: Version 5.0 [Machine-readable database]. Minneapolis: University of Minnesota.

Ryan, J. P., & Testa, M. K. (2005). Child maltreatment and juvenile delinquency: Investigating the role of placement and placement instability. *Children and Youth Services Review, 27*, 227–249.

Stewart, M. (2013). *Cross-system collaboration*. Los Angeles, CA: National Center for Child Traumatic Stress. Retrieved from http://www.njjn.org/uploads/digital-library/NCTSN_Cross-system-collaboration_Macon-Stewart_September-2013.pdf

Tamasese, K., Peteru, C., & Waldegrave, C. (1997). Ole Taeao Afua, The New Morning: A qualitative investigation into Samoan perspectives on mental health and culturally appropriate services. A research project carried out by The Family Centre, Wellington. Funded by the Health Research Council of New Zealand.

Taufe'ulungaki, A. (2008). "Fonua": Reclaiming Pacific communities in Aotearoa. Conference presentation, LotuMoui. Auckland, New Zealand: Counties-Manukau District Health Board.

United Nations High Commissioner for Refugees. (2012). *Convention relating to the status of refugees.* Retrieved from http://www.unhcr.org/pages/49da0e466 .html

U.S. Bureau of the Census. (2006–2010). *American Community Survey.* Retrieved from http://www.census.gov/prod/cen2010/briefs/c2010br-12.pdf

——. (2007). *Facts for features. Asian/Pacific American heritage month.* Retrieved from http://www.census.gov/Press-Release/www/releases/archives/facts_for _features_special_editions/009714.html

——. (2010). *Facts for features. Asian/Pacific American heritage month.* Retrieved from https://www.census.gov/newsroom/releases/archives/facts_for_features _special_editions/cb10-ff07.html

U.S. Department of Homeland Security, Office of Immigration Statistics. (2010). *Yearbook of immigration statistics.* Various tables. Washington, DC: Author.

Vakalahi, H. F. O., & Fong, R. (2014). Social work practice with Asian and Pacific Islander Americans. In K. Corcoran (Ed.), *Social Workers' Desk Reference (3rd Ed.)* (pp 993–997). New York, NY: Oxford University Press.

Vakalahi, H. F. O., & Godinet, M. (2014). *Transnational Pacific Islander Americans and social work: Dancing to the beat of a different drum.* Washington, DC: NASW.

Vakalahi, H. F. O., Godinet, M., & Fong, R. (2006). Pacific Islander Americans: Impact of colonization and immigration. In R. Fong, R. G. McRoy, & C. O. Hendricks (Eds.), *Intersecting child welfare, substance abuse, and family violence.* Washington, DC: Council on Social Work Education.

Westervelt, W. D. (1910). *Legends of Maui—a demi god of Polynesia and of his mother Hina.* Honolulu: The Hawaiian Gazette.

White House Initiative on Asian Americans and Pacific Islanders. (2009). Retrieved from http://www.ed.gov/edblogs/aapi/aapi-data-disaggregation/

Wiig, J. K., & Tuell, J. A. (2004, rev. 2008). *Guidebook for juvenile justice and child welfare system coordination and integration: A framework for improved outcomes.* Washington, DC: Child Welfare League of America Press.

Wilcox, R., Smith, D., Moore, J., Hewitt, A., Allan, G., Walker, H., Ropata, M., Monu, L., & Featherstone, T. (1991). *Family decision making & family group conference*. Lower Hutt, New Zealand: Practitioners' Publishing.

Wong, M. (2008). *Impact of intergenerational differences on Chinese Americans in family therapy: A qualitative study* (PhD dissertation, Texas Woman's University, Denton, TX).

Xie, Y., & Goyette, K. A. (2004). *A demographic portrait of Asian Americans*. New York, NY: Russell Sage Foundation.

Yeatman, G., Shaw, C., Barlow, M., & Barlett, G. (1976). Pseudobattering in Vietnamese children. *Pediatrics, 58*, 616–618.

Yoshihama, M. (2001). Immigrants-in-context framework: Understanding the interactive influence of socio-cultural contexts. *Evaluation and Program Planning, 24*, 307–318.

CHAPTER 7

South Asian Immigrant and Refugee Children and Families

▸ UMA A. SEGAL

SOCIAL WORK PRIDES ITSELF on being particularly sensitive to diversity and being alert and responsive to cultural differences among people and their life experiences. Nevertheless, like other professions, it tends to group together *immigrants* and *refugees*, and like the U.S. Bureau of the Census, it still sees cultures in terms of geographic blocks. As is evident from the preceding chapters in this volume, immigrants and refugees differ substantially in a number of areas but most specifically in their reasons for migration, with the former generally being voluntary immigrants in search of better opportunities and the latter migrating involuntarily because of fears of persecution if they remained in their home countries.

At least seven nations are grouped together as composing the subcontinent of South Asia: Bangladesh, Bhutan, India, the Maldives, Nepal, Pakistan, and Sri Lanka, although Afghanistan (actually South West Asia) and Myanmar (South East Asia) are also included in this group (http://www.unicef.org/infobycountry/southasia.html). There are some, perhaps even several, similarities in the cultures and experiences of peoples from these countries, but in reality, their homelands, demographic characteristics, and primary reasons for migrating to the United States from each of these countries may be strikingly different. Therefore, the processes of adaptation and integration may vary substantially. Given this reality, this chapter will provide a general overview of the South Asian population in the United States but will tend to focus on the larger immigrant groups from this region, suggesting that one may be able to generalize, with caution, to other immigrants from the area. Table 7.1 provides an indication of the

TABLE 7.1 Population Increase (2010–2013)

YEARS	2010	MID-2013	INCREASE	IMMIGRANTS & U.S.-BORN CHILDREN
Afghanistan	61,906	70,000	13.08%	
Bangladesh	148,326	204,000	27.30%	270,000
Bhutan	420	—	—	
India	1,654,272	2,061,000	19.70%	2,600,000
Myanmar	64,004	98,000	34.70%	
Nepal	39,991	88,000	54.60%	
Pakistan	288,011	339,000	15.00%	455,000
Sri Lanka	34,572	53,000	34.80%	
Source	**IOM**[a]	**MPI**[b]		**MPI**

[a] http://www.iom.int/cms/en/sites/iom/home/about-migration/world-migration.html
[b] http://www.migrationpolicy.org/programs/data-hub/maps-immigrants-and-emigrants-around
-world

growth of the immigrant population from this region in the period 2010–2013, and when one considers the U.S.-born offspring, the numbers are even greater.

These numbers indicate that although the Pakistani and Bangladeshi migrations are sizable, they lag far behind migration from India. Given statistics from the United Nations High Commissioner for Refugees (2015), it is apparent that, barring those from Afghanistan, the majority of the individuals from South Asia are immigrants, not refugees, so the focus of this chapter will be on those who have migrated voluntarily to the United States from these countries. Afghanistan and Myanmar will not be included in this discussion, as they are outside the South Asian block, and since the groups in the United States from Bhutan, Nepal, and Sri Lanka are relatively small at this time, the major focus will be on the three largest populations: the Indians (who compose the third largest immigrant group in the United States after the Mexicans and the Chinese), the Pakistanis, and the Bangladeshis. One exception, however, is the Bhutanese refugees who have come to the United States via Nepal, to which they fled in the 1990s. Although table 7.1 indicates the presence of about 88,000 Nepalese, there are in reality more than 75,000 individuals who are Bhutanese of

Nepalese origin but who became stateless persons when their citizenship was revoked.

The international legal definition of a stateless person is "a person who is not considered as a national by any State under the operation of its law." No country claims this individual as a citizen. Some people become stateless when they lose citizenship, whereas others are born into situations where they are not eligible for citizenship (http://www.unhcr.org/pages/49c3646c158.html).

Recent reports by the Migration Policy Institute (2014) indicate that the three larger South Asian *diaspora* populations in the United States—the Indians, the Pakistanis, and the Bangladeshis—are composed of relatively young individuals. They are better educated than the general U.S. population and have higher household income levels, although, of the three groups, the academic and economic achievements of the Indian group are substantially higher than those of most other immigrant groups in the United States and also above those of the native-born population. Although these South Asian groups are dispersed throughout the country, the highest numbers are found in California, New York, and Texas. Significant numbers of Indians are also found in New Jersey, and Florida and Michigan are major residences for those from Bangladesh.

Although the tendency is to focus on immigrant children and families (particularly on working-age adults), the United States may need to prepare itself for the graying of South Asians. Many who arrived during the 1990s and 2000s are uprooting their aging parents so that they may care for them. These aging parents, often moved against their will and divorced from familiar environments, become dependent economically, socially, and physically. Conversely, South Asian immigrants of the mid-twentieth century are aging themselves, but they are fiercely independent, refusing to live with their children and beginning to move into Western retirement communities. However, they have not thought, as a group, about their health care and chronic needs correlated with the aging process (Shibusawa & Mui, 2010).

This chapter complements chapter 6, on Asian and Pacific Islanders, and suggests that although in the general census East Asians, Southeast Asians, and Pacific Islanders are grouped together with South Asians, despite some shared cultural norms, the latter populations are significantly different from the former three, both in their homelands and in the United States. Most significantly, the centuries of colonization of South Asia by the British have had a lasting effect, both negative and positive, but that has introduced these countries to the English language and, along with it, the cultures of the West. Perhaps for this reason, researchers Hofstede (1980), in his study of cultural commonalities, and House and Javidan (2004), in their "GLOBE" study, found that South Asian countries, particularly India, did not fit neatly into any cultural clusters, including those of the "Far East." In fact, they were found to function in "independent" cultural groups, suggesting that despite their strong cultural connections to their homeland, South Asians are generally likely to adapt to different environments and adopt patterns of behavior as necessary in their host environments. Furthermore, perhaps because of immigration laws in the United States and the continuing visa preference system, those migrating to the United States from most of South Asia thus far have tended to be more educated and skilled than those migrating from other parts of Asia, as is reflected in the 2010 Census data (Migration Policy Institute, 2014).

HISTORY AND REASONS FOR MIGRATION

South Asians have migrated across the globe for centuries and for a variety of reasons, but primarily in search of better economic opportunities, and until 1947, when India won its independence from Britain, the three countries of focus here, India, Pakistan, and Bangladesh (then East Pakistan), were one nation. South Asian labor migration to the West began in the colonial period, and although the United States was relatively inaccessible because of distance and expense, a small South Asian wave did arrive at the beginning of the twentieth century. Although India is a complex of ethnic diversity, most immigrants then were unskilled or agricultural workers from the northern state of Punjab. These Sikh men were from agricultural communities and had reputations for strength and valor, making them ideally suited to agricultural work. This period of migration that began in 1901 was short lived, lasting only about eight years, as the entry of Asians was restricted by the U.S. Congress in 1909 and prohibited in 1924.

In 1965, recognizing the U.S. need for a larger skilled labor force, President Lyndon Johnson signed the Immigration and Nationality Act of 1965 (Hart-Celler Act, INS, Act of 1965, Publication L. 89–236: http://library

.uwb.edu/guides/usimmigration/79%20stat%20911.pdf) abolishing immigration quotas and liberalizing immigration. This law removing discrimination based on nationality threw open the doors of the country, and skilled South Asian, particularly Indian, immigrants began arriving in record numbers in the mid-1960s. This flow has continued steadily, and the size of the South Asian population in North America, both by immigration and by birth, is substantial. In the last 10 years, about 47 percent have come on the employment-based visa, about 50 percent either through family sponsorships or as immediate relatives of U.S. citizens, and a very small percentage, 3 percent, under refugee status (Migration Policy Institute, 2014).

Most refugees in the United States from South Asia are from Bhutan, via Nepal, where they fled in the early 1990s in the wake of the Bhutanese government's decision to resurrect the Bhutanese culture. It revoked their citizenship and expelled all non-Bhutanese, and more specifically, the Lhotsampas, the Bhutanese who were Hindu and of ethnic Nepali origin. In 2007, the United States formally began accepting Bhutanese refugees from Nepal, indicating a cap of 60,000, but by 2014, it had resettled 75,000 individuals (http://timesofindia .indiatimes.com/world/rest-of-world/60000-Bhutanese-refugees-resettled-in -US/articleshow/16277856.cms; and http://www.iom.int/cms/en/sites/iom/home /news-and-views/press-briefing-notes/pbn-2014/pbn-listing/us-resettles -75000-bhutanese-ref.html).

Furthermore, estimates from the Department of Homeland Security (Hoefer, Rytina, & Baker, 2012) indicate that the seventh largest unauthorized immigrant group in 2011 was from India, numbering about 240,000, and because several South and Central American countries do not require entry visas, many pay smugglers to bring them in through Mexico and Central America (Fagen, 2013; López, 2011). Frequently, these smuggled individuals apply for asylum, claiming political persecution, but the veracity of their claims is questionable (Gonzales, 2013). Three years later, by the end of 2014, the number of unauthorized immigrants from India had almost doubled, to 450,000 (Pew Research Center, 2015). Despite peoples' tendency to believe that all immigrants living in the United States illegally are smuggled in, the largest numbers from South Asia enter legally but fail to leave the country when their visas expire; these immigrants are known as "overstays."

Ways to become unauthorized:

- Overstaying visas after their expiration
- Losing jobs under the H-1B temporary work visa status
- Dependent leaving an abusive H-1B visa holder
- Trafficked domestic or sex worker
- Losing asylum cases

Little is known about the success of unauthorized immigrants and the extent to which information about them is integrated into the general literature about this population. However, the website http://southasiandiaspora .tumblr.com/ publishes autobiographical South Asian immigrant stories and is replete with stories of unauthorized immigrants, many of them young adults struggling with concerns about marginalization, apprehension, deportation, or access to higher education. Mixed-status families, those in which some of the members are legal residents and others are here without the requisite papers, are plentiful (Guillermo, 2014), and although there is little literature about the South Asian mixed family specifically, there is sufficient knowledge about such families in other communities (Passel & Cohn, 2011). Parents are often unauthorized, whereas their children are born in the United States and therefore are U.S. citizens. Frequently, some of the children are born abroad, whereas others are citizens by birth. Occasionally, parents are here legally but their adult children come to visit and overstay their visas. Mixed-status families have members that face disparate difficulties because of differential access to resources (health, education, employment, welfare), resulting in practical, social, and emotional stresses among family members.

Since the terror attacks on New York and Washington on September 11, 2001, South Asians in general and Muslim South Asians in particular have been harassed by the authorities, often those in the regions in which they live. If South Asians are Muslim and unauthorized and are apprehended, their immediate deportation is probable.

CULTURAL VALUES AND CONFLICTS
WITH U.S. VALUE SYSTEMS

Although South Asian groups, including those from Nepal, Bhutan, and Sri Lanka, differ substantially among themselves in a number of ways—history, economic views, religion, political process—they do share several sociocultural values that serve to determine goals, guide behavior, and maintain harmony and avoid conflict. With clearly defined rules of conduct in given situations and with specific individuals, much ambiguity is removed, and interactions are predictable when these behavioral norms are followed. However, although these traditional norms are not substantially different from those found among East and Southeast Asian communities, adherence to them may have become diluted in recent years (Chung, 1992).

With increasing globalization and also worldwide westernization, the concepts of individuality, freedom of choice and of speech, pursuit of opportunity and happiness, democracy, and having a voice are becoming increasingly universal. So, although South Asians in the United States may, to a large extent, still subscribe to the norms identified in table 7.2, these norms have been modified over the years and with successive generations. This is also true among many South Asians who may not have left their homelands. Furthermore, these are not uniquely Asian values; these are important to varying degrees in *all* societies. Thus, regardless of ethnicity and background, all groups fall along a continuum in the significance they place on these values in circumscribing behavior. Thus, one may diagram the significance of respect for authority on a continuum as in figure 7.1.

Despite the influence of national culture in determining individuals' behavior (Segal, Segal, & Niemczycki, 1993), immigrants' values are influenced by those of the host country and the opportunities and obstacles it offers. The second and subsequent generations are generally bicultural, living in their immigrant homes but comfortable in the majority society (Segal, 2002). Adaptation has seen norm modification in traditional familial, gender, and generational interactions among South Asians. Females increasingly work outside the home, parents evidence a more equal partnership in household functioning, child rearing, and decision making (Yeung, 2013), and children are more outspoken and self-directed. Although living in a society with different values can conflict with traditional beliefs, raising angst for immigrant families around the world, South Asian immigrants

TABLE 7.2 South Asian Cultural Norms

NORM	DESCRIPTION
Filial piety	Respect, honor, love, and obedience children owe their parents throughout their lives.
Direction of parent–child communications	Reflects parental guidance and direction of the lives of their children.
Self-control and emotional restraint	Restraint in emotional expression to avoid exhibitionism and the inappropriate drawing of attention to oneself or one's group.
Respect for authority	Ascribed authority is not questioned.
Defined roles and expectations	Social roles and expectations are clearly defined based on age, gender, and relationship.
Shame as a behavioral influence	Behavior is a reflection of the entire group; hence misbehavior brings shame to all. Shame is a mechanism for controlling behavior.
Inconspicuousness	Necessity of moderation in ideas, expectations, and behaviors to avoid bringing attention to oneself.
Awareness of social milieu	The situation guides behavior and dictates what is expected based on time and place.
Fatalism	Although one can establish goals and directions, one's fate is predestined.
Communal responsibility	Successes and failures are experienced by the entire community, so the community has a vested interest in all individuals and their actions.
High regard for the elderly	With age comes wisdom, and status increases with longevity.
Centrality of family relationships	The family is the central focus of the individual, and intrafamily relationships and occurrences, both positive and negative, are handled within its boundaries.

have been known to integrate socially, culturally, and politically into the nations to which they migrate (Rao, 2013).

The South Asian population in the United States is relatively educated and affluent (Whatley & Batalova, 2013), and the South Asian experience with colonization and exposure to the West have prepared the middle classes for some aspects of American society. Most South Asian immigrants of the last two decades are well versed in the English language and through it have some exposure to American culture. However, it is faulty to assume that acculturation is ever easy. There are indeed differences in

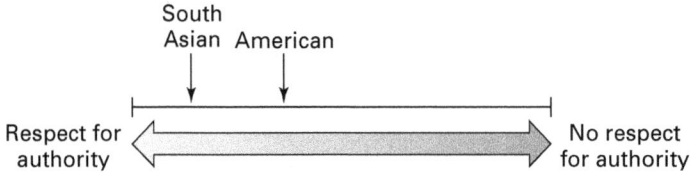

FIGURE 7.1 Values across cultures

norms, behaviors, and attitudes, as well as in more tangible areas, such as food, clothing, and entertainment. This makes adaptation difficult even in the best of circumstances. The absence of traditional supports of family, friends, and one's own society exacerbates difficulties. Nevertheless, most voluntary immigrants are highly resilient and usually develop contexts in which they not only survive but flourish (Segal, Elliott, & Mayadas, 2010).

Cultural differences and conflicts, although troubling to immigrants, do not severely affect their sense of identity. They usually perceive themselves, and are perceived by others, as being South Asian, although, when they return to their homelands, they find they have inexplicably changed and are seen by the natives in South Asia as being American (Segal, 2014). The second generation, on the other hand, often struggles with recognizing its identity, having been born American but with South Asian parents. In addition, although members of the second generation may never have been to the home country, phenotypically they are set apart from their American counterparts. The third generation is likely to experience fewer identity conflicts and usually perceives itself as very much an integral part of the host culture (Tu, 2010). Thus, the first generation has few identity conflicts, the second generation stands with one foot in each culture, often attempting to forge a new one, but home culture influence is greatly diluted for the third generation, which self-identifies as American.

Ever the land of opportunity and immigration, the United States has always had to deal with ethnic and cultural diversity. Although most immigrants were Caucasian, concepts of assimilation and the "melting pot" were possible, as the second and subsequent generations could be easily absorbed into the majority society and become indistinguishable. However, with the increasing diversity brought to the country by people of color from Asia, South America, and Africa, the phenotypic "other" is no longer so readily absorbed, regardless of attempts to become "American." Thus, it is essential that the dominant American society seek to understand ethnic diversity and multiculturalism and the ethnocultural variations in the country. It is virtually impossible for people of color to assimilate into the society, because they are always identifiable as "other"; nevertheless, they are now a sizable segment of the population.

Increasing globalization and the ease and speed of transnational communication have enhanced awareness and appreciation of cultural differences. With more respect and acceptance accorded to diversity, second-generation immigrants may not feel as great a need to reject their cultural heritage. This is apparent in the number of South Asian high school students who have joined ethnic youth groups in several urban metropolitan areas. In addition to providing social support for each other, these youths often assume responsibility for increasing awareness about the South Asian culture communities. In colleges, South Asian clubs are becoming more evident, and South Asian festivals are celebrated on several university campuses.

EXPLANATION OF DIVERSITY WITHIN GROUPS

South Asians hail from the same region, but there are substantial differences across countries and within each country. The Migration Policy Institute's (2014) report suggests that the socioeconomic backgrounds of immigrants from South Asia are similar, perhaps because U.S. immigration and immigrant policies circumscribe the conditions under which individuals may immigrate, ensuring that the majority of those who receive entry visas from South Asia are able to contribute to the enhancement of the economy of the country. Hence, although a large segment of the population in South Asia is not educated, affluent, or skilled, the majority entering the United States have these qualifications and are clearly not a microcosm of their homelands.

Between 1965 and 1985, most entrants into the United States from South Asia were granted work visas, but as naturalized immigrants began to sponsor relatives or workers needed for their businesses and ethnic enterprises, the level of education and affluence of South Asians coming to the country began to change. Hence, South Asians are now more diverse in socioeconomic status and achievement; several have careers in academia, medicine, and technology, but there is a sizable group that is employed in lower-wage jobs in the hospitality and retail industries as well as in trans-portation, and approximately 50 percent of those from Bangladesh, 33 percent from Pakistan, and 25 percent from India are LEP (limited English profi-cient) (South Asian Americans Leading Together, 2014).

DRUM (Desis Rising Up and Moving), an organization based in New York, was established to provide a voice for South Asian low-wage workers, both autho-rized and unauthorized. An excellent video on this population and its children is available at

https://www.youtube.com/watch?v=yMuqb2uS6dQ#t=210.

India received its independence from the British in 1947, and at the same time, East and West Pakistan were carved out of India as two parts of an Islamic nation. After the 1971 war in which India fought West Pakistan on behalf of East Pakistan, the latter separated from Pakistan to form the nation of Bangladesh. India, the world's largest secular democracy, has a population of 1.2 billion people and is a land composed of several cultures, languages (more than 14 with a substantial number of speakers), types of art, and terrains, all combined in relative harmony. Several faiths reflect the Indian population and provide diversity in worldview. Hinduism is the majority religion (80.5 percent), although given the size of the population, Muslims (13.4 percent), Christians (2.3 percent), Sikhs (1.9 percent), and others (1.9 percent) are also well represented (Central Intelligence Agency, 2014). With 196.2 million residents, the majority (96.4 percent) Muslim, Pakistan is also a federal republic, but with an Islamic law influence. Never-theless, its residents are also ethnically diverse, speaking at least six different languages (Central Intelligence Agency, 2014). Likewise, Bangladesh, with a population of 166.3 million, is a Muslim nation (89.5 percent), with a Hindu minority (9.6 percent). However, it is culturally homogenous, with 98 percent speaking Bengali (Central Intelligence Agency, 2014).

Thus, it is clear that South Asians are a diverse group even within specific nations. Perhaps this allows them to adapt readily when they move out-side the region, as they have been wont to do for centuries. Hofstede (1980), in his study of cultural differences that was instrumental in help-ing identify commonalities among nations, found that Indians fit in the

"independent" category and were able to adapt to environmental expectations. More recently, Sharma (2011) reported that in a study of expatriate
professionals, Indians scored highest on the variables measuring open-
mindedness, which may correlate with adaptability, at least for this South
Asian subgroup.

It is expected that the ethnic diversity found in South Asia would be
reflected also in the immigrant population in the United States. Socioeconomic status also influences culture, and since those admitted to the
United States usually have the human and social resources for success, this
is reflected in the profile of entrants. There is diversity in characteristics
such as disability and sexual orientation (Segal, 2010), although the topic
is seldom studied in the United States.

BARRIERS RELATED TO CROSS-SYSTEM INVOLVEMENT

Overall, the overwhelming perception, both by South Asians and by the
host population, is that individual South Asians are well adjusted physically, socially, and mentally. Despite this general perception and South Asian
achievements, transnational and transcultural adaptation is often a difficult
and painful process, and becoming acculturated is a lifelong process (Segal,
2014). Barriers to access and utilization of the several resources and services
available in the United States can be myriad, ranging from economic, to
social, to cultural. These barriers may be a consequence of the infrastructure itself and the inability of South Asians to navigate the system, reflect
South Asians' lack of appreciation of the benefits of the services, be intrinsic to cross-cultural differences, or the services may not be a priority to
which hard-earned resources or limited time should be allocated.

The success of South Asians and the image of the "model minority" often obscure poor access to resources, particularly health care (South Asian
Americans Leading Together, 2012), social problems such as isolation of
the elderly (Brown, 2009), conjugal violence and intergenerational turbu-
lence (Khinduka, 1992), and poverty (Balgopal, 1995), which are experienced by significant numbers of South Asians. Since South Asians have
projected the model minority image, have apparently acclimated themselves, and have not voiced their needs, their issues have been marginalized.
This group, which prefers to keep concerns within the family, has not
sought social service assistance, even in the absence of a viable and proxi-

mate family network. Since most South Asians do not attract social service attention, the myth of the model minority is perpetuated, and few researchers in the social and behavioral sciences assess their experiences or make recommendations for how best to work with them or address their needs.

Health Care Services

South Asian Americans Leading Together (SAALT) (2012) reported that South Asians experience a range of health issues, as do other populations, including cardiovascular disease, various cancers, diabetes, and reproductive and sexual disorders. However, linguistic and cultural barriers, as well as immigrant eligibility restrictions, prevent access and deter utilization of services, and approximately 20 percent of all South Asians lack health coverage, and 40 percent of those under the age of 65 feel they do not have a primary health resource to meet their needs (South Asian Americans Leading Together, 2012). Communication between patient and health care provider involves both language and cultural competence, and health disparities related to ethnicity include an array of factors, not least among them the lack of understanding of cultural variations between provider and patient that affect attitudes and behaviors (Thomas, Fine, & Ibrahim, 2004). Older South Asian immigrants, like all aging groups, have an increased need for the use of medical services; however, several barriers impede utilization and/or compliance. A recent study (Lai & Surood, 2013) that surveyed 220 South Asians over the age of 55 identified four major barriers: cultural incompatibility between patient and physician, personal attitudes regarding the use of services, administrative problems, and other circumstantial challenges. The most significant barriers were associated with the personal attitudes of patients, and these predicted less favorable physical and mental health. An interesting recommendation regarding treatment of depression among South Asians is based on findings of a correlation between depression and experience of social, family, or relationship issues. Leung, Cheung, and Tsui (2012) suggest that this group will step forward for mental health assistance if these symptoms are reframed as reactions to family or social issues rather than as mental health issues.

In addition, research shows that academic institutions still are not consistently preparing health care professionals to recognize the effects of culture on patient care and often the ensuing health disparities (Okoro,

Odedina, & Smith, 2012). Patients also evidence variable appreciation of the opportunities offered by health care providers. Ahmad et al. (2005) found that women, particularly those who had immigrated less than five years earlier, evidenced several stress-inducing factors and limited coping strategies, as most felt they had lost social supports and had experienced economic uncertainty, a lowered social position, a lifestyle that was mechanical and routinized, and dramatic changes in food, access to health care, and climate variations. They were unaware of mental health services and did not use their health care providers as resources.

Some individual researchers and organizations are beginning to address health issues among South Asians, particularly in geographical areas that have larger numbers of these immigrants. Gany et al. (2012), for example, have long recognized that South Asian health behaviors and needs may differ from those of other groups. They provide health camps at South Asian places of worship and at South Asian festivals to educate and screen patients in the New York area. However, research and outreach efforts, though growing, are still in the early stages, and it remains to be seen when these trends will spread across the nation.

Gerontological Concerns

Increasing information on older immigrants is now becoming available, and as the elderly population of South Asians, the retired and widowed parents of immigrants, arrive to assist with their grandchildren or to be supported by their children, they find themselves increasingly isolated (Brown, 2009). Usually financially dependent on their offspring and separated from their peers in India, they find little to occupy them while their children and grandchildren pursue their respective occupations. Since South Asians tend not to live in ethnic enclaves, access to other elderly South Asians is practically nonexistent. Furthermore, even if access were possible, given the diversity of cultures within South Asian countries, these elders may have little in common with each other.

Social Services

Research on South Asian elders is relatively new; however, more is known about younger groups of South Asians and some issues with which they grapple. The subjugation of women and the long-term effects of patriarchal attitudes that South Asian cultures have carried to the United States are aptly captured in the poignant story written by a young, second-generation woman about her mother's experience, in which she stated, "When my Indian mom divorced my dad, she became an outcast. It also saved her life" (Sandhu, 2015).

The prevalence of domestic violence is apparent, as shelters for battered South Asian women have been established around the country. Although the affluence of South Asian immigrants in the United States camouflages their many problems, Manavi, a shelter that provides protection and assistance to victims of domestic violence, was established in New Jersey in 1985. Since then, other shelters have opened to provide assistance to South Asian women in New York (Sakhi), Chicago (Apna Char), Philadelphia (SEWAA), Washington, DC (ASHA), Dallas (Chetna), and St. Louis (SAWERA), and these are but a few among numerous others. For many years, patriarchies have perceived women and children as the property of males, to be controlled by violence and subjugation, and family violence is neither culture specific nor class specific (Dobash & Dobash, 1992). Lee (2013) proposes that although the occurrence of domestic violence among Asians is surprising, given the myth surrounding this group, the perpetuation of this violence is also a product of social system inequality and the lack of funding for organizations providing ethnic-targeted services.

CASE STUDY: DHIRAJ

Thirty-five-year-old IT professional Dhiraj has an H1-B visa, a nonimmigrant visa that permits U.S. companies to hire professionals with special skills the company needs and that are in short supply in the country. Large contingents of IT professionals have been working in the United States with these visas. Dhiraj is working in a large metropolitan area, where he lives with his 33-year-old wife, Anita, and their 10-year-old twins, Raj (a boy) and Rani (a girl). Anita and the children are on dependent visas, and the family has been in the United States for approximately 18 months. Anita became bored staying home and has begun an unlicensed babysitting service in her home for up to four children at a time.

Dhiraj works close to 60 hours a week; however, his income is good, and he and his family are able to live satisfactorily on his salary. He sends 5 percent of his income to his parents in India each month. The children appear happy at school and appear to be doing well academically. Anita, on the other hand, is unhappy, misses her husband's extended family, with whom they had lived until they moved to the United States, and is not accustomed to the household chores of cooking, cleaning, and doing the laundry, as there was a household staff that took care of these responsibilities when they lived in India. Nannies cared for the children, and general oversight of the children was also shared among others in the family. Anita is not used to the intensity of the parent-child contact in the United States. She is just beginning to learn how to drive, and is frustrated and scared, but she knows this is essential if she is to be independent.

About a year after they had moved to the United States, Dhiraj began feeling substantial stress from his 60-hour workweek, although he enjoyed his job. In addition, since Anita had no help in the house and, because she does not drive, was also rather isolated from the community and culture, her needs for help and attention began to further strain Dhiraj's already stressed nerves. He did not understand why, if Anita was home all day, she could not manage the household chores or care for the children, and why she did not show much interest in housework. The food was tasteless, the house was usually less than clean, and piles of both dirty and clean laundry were found in every room. Dhiraj further wondered why Anita wasted her time babysitting when she could be taking care of the house. She kept complaining that she was unhappy in the United States and wanted to go home, and despite his pointing out that they were living a good life and were doing well financially, she was getting increasingly despondent. Raj and Rani were becoming increasingly "Americanized," and Anita felt she was not able to manage them. They frequently challenged her, and she felt they did not respect her.

One day, Anita called a domestic violence hotline. She said she had been seeing its advertisement on television for several months, and she had finally built up the courage to call. She indicated the typical cycle of violence. Dhiraj began pushing her out of his way when she came to him with a question or request. These pushes soon began escalating to shouting at her and striking her, as he accused her of not understanding all that he was doing for the family. The pushing had begun about eight months earlier, and now Anita finds she fears his return from work each day. She is terrified about having made the hotline call, as she fears that he will become more violent. As she came to the United States on a dependent visa, she does not have a visa of her own. She is afraid that if she tries to leave him, she will have no means of support for herself or for her children, and, in any case, she is afraid that she will be deported. Although she wants to return to her homeland, she does not want the disgrace of deportation.

The domestic violence intervention program associated with the hotline has had no experience with South Asian women. In fact, the practitioners thought that the South Asian community did not engage in such behavior. Did Kumagai and Strauss (1983) not find that the cultures of the South Asians and the Japanese protect women from being subjected to domestic violence? Based on their research, there is no domestic violence in these two cultures.

Because this metropolitan area has a relatively small South Asian community, the community has not developed parallel social services, and there are no majority programs that specifically serve this group of "New Americans." The American social services see South Asians rather infrequently, and although they do provide some training on Asian Americans generally, they have not sought to include the distinction of South Asian cultures in their diversity training.

In working with Anita, the social workers at this program must assess which situations are universals and which are unique to the South Asian cultures and, further, which are specific to this particular family. They will need to explore the following:

1 What information does the social worker need about immigration and immigrant laws to work with this client?
2 What are the implications of immigration on family dynamics for this client?
3 What are the implications of the way in which the country perceives and responds to this population?
4 What are the implications for this family?
5 To what extent is general knowledge about domestic violence applicable to the South Asian context?
6 What cultural factors must be taken into account when working with this client?
7 How can social workers rapidly learn enough about the culture to be able to help this client?
8 What are some of the stressors facing Dhiraj?
9 What are some of the stressors affecting Anita?

10 How, if at all, may the children be affected?

11 Although there are no South Asian social service agencies, what resources may there be in the South Asian community?

12 What are realistic options for Anita?

Since the number of elderly South Asians in the United States is still relatively low, since violence against women (and children) is hidden from public view, and since South Asians have been most concerned about the enculturation of their children, social services have focused on difficulties in parent–child relationships. Even within these areas, the issues addressed have been those of autonomy, mate selection, and career choice (Ahmad-Stout & Nath, 2013). There appears to be no information about teen pregnancies, abortion, or sexually transmitted diseases (including HIV/AIDS) among South Asians. There is little knowledge of the extent of drug use or substance abuse, although these are significant problems in India, and although there may be a sizable lesbian, gay, bisexual, and transgendered (LGBT) South Asian population in the United States, as is evident in advertisements of publications in *India Abroad* and the presence of LGBT organizations such as Trikone (San Francisco), TrikoneChicago (Chicago), Satrang (Los Angeles), and SALGA-NYC (New York), the population is relatively unacknowledged by the South Asian community, as well as by researchers and service providers.

Service Utilization

South Asians traditionally rely on family networks to provide social, emotional, and financial support. When they lose these supports through migration, and because seeking help from "outsiders" is considered shameful, South Asians often struggle in silence. For example, the American Community Survey reported that the poverty rate for South Asian families in 2008 was 5.2 percent, and although that is lower than the overall rate of 9.6 percent, it is not insignificant. Limited income has placed additional burdens on and increased the isolation of families who are not aware of external sources of support and emergency assistance. Failure in the United States is especially devastating to immigrants who migrate to improve their economic condition, and the result is often depression, alcohol abuse, psychosomatic problems, marital conflict, and even suicide (Balgopal, 1988).

Thus, the major barriers to South Asian integration and effective utilization of mainstream services, including welfare services, may be the following: (1) the myth of the "model minority," which precludes physical health, mental health, and social service organizations from identifying South Asians as target clients, (2) lack of funding for programs and services for South Asians, (3) lack of preparedness of mainstream organizations to provide culturally and linguistically responsive services to South Asians, (4) inability of South Asians to acknowledge problems in the community, and (5) social and cultural barriers to service utilization by South Asians. Not mentioned in most discussions of cultural competence is the need to address discrimination in the delivery of services. Along with the cultural and linguistic barriers Asian immigrants may face, discrimination against them is also prevalent. Clough, Lee, and Chae (2013) reported findings of interpersonal and institutionalized discrimination in the health care system that added to the intrinsic barriers of working across cultures.

In some ways, all Asians constitute a unique minority in the United States—they are not perceived as an "oppressed" minority, and therefore discrimination against them is relatively unchecked. The most openly kept secret that is evidence of discrimination is the college admissions quota system (Golden, 2012; Unz, 2012). In addition, mainstream organizations do not have programs and services or specific practice strategies that focus on this population, although one recent publication, albeit from Canada, discusses a finding about South Asians in the child protection system: that South Asians wished to learn more about the protection of children and also sought assistance not only for the child but for the entire family (Maiter & Stalker, 2011).

Outreach efforts often overlook South Asians, and there appears to be a general belief that Asian agencies and organizations will take care of their own. Relatively little appears to be included in the diversity efforts of human service organizations. Thus, the issue of communicating or collaborating across services seems to be moot. Physical health, mental health, child welfare, juvenile justice, and education systems in the United States must first recognize that this group of immigrants needs the mainstream's services before they will engage in outreach efforts and seek to become culturally and linguistically responsive and collaborate with each other. This need must also be corroborated by South Asians through their responsiveness to outreach measures and utilization of the services.

IMPACT OF FEDERAL POLICIES ON IMMIGRANT
AND REFUGEE CHILDREN AND FAMILIES

It is important to distinguish between federal immigration policies and federal immigrant policies. The former provide regulations about who the country will allow to enter, why these people are admitted, and who the country keeps out and why. Most immigration policies dealing with admission into the United States revolve around the (1) labor needs of the country, (2) family reunification, or (3) humanitarianism.

> For unauthorized immigrants, none of these policies are relevant. They are often permanently separated from their families, with no possibility of their legal entry. Likewise, travel back to the homeland is impossible, as it would preclude reentry. The link that follows provides a moving account of one unauthorized Nepalese man's complex of reasons for not being able to be with his family in his homeland.
>
> http://india.blogs.nytimes.com/2013/11/01/the-life-of-an-undocumented-south-asian -immigrant/?_r=0

Immigrant policies that address issues of integration focus on developing protocol and resources to ensure that once immigrants and refugees have crossed the border, they are able to integrate and become self-sustaining members of the society. Thus, the question for immigrant policies is, once they are in, how do we help immigrants to integrate? What resources do we allow them to access? Do we place stipulations on accessing resources? Although there are some federal immigrant policies, all states also have the right to develop their own policies related to immigrant integration.

Once immigrants are in the United States legally, federal integration policies allow them access to (1) education, (2) citizenship after a waiting period, (3) intermarriage, and (4) home ownership. The primary benefit of citizenship, not available to immigrants who are not naturalized, is the right to vote. On July 4, 2014, President Barack Obama once again spoke about the significance of immigrants for the welfare of the nation and the importance of ensuring that they are integrated into society. Values of equality and opportunity allow the nation to provide programs that enhance integration efforts (see http://www.whitehouse.gov/the-press-office/2014/07/16 /fact-sheet-strengthening-communities-welcoming-all-residents), and South

Asians are also able to avail themselves of these resources, if they are pointed in that direction.

Camarota (2011) provides an overview of welfare use by immigrants, and although welfare use is high among some immigrant groups, it is very low for Indians and moderate for Pakistanis and other Asians; the highest use is by Mexicans and other Central Americans.

Welfare use by South Asians is relatively low because, overall, the group is socioeconomically more successful than other immigrant groups. Application to Medicaid is often made by caregiver children for their aging parents, who may not have worked long, or at all, in the U.S. economy. However, lack of knowledge about resources and rights also lowers resource utilization.

Camarota (2011) assessed any welfare program, whether cash assistance, food assistance, housing assistance, or Medicaid, and found that the program used most frequently by South Asians appears to be Medicaid. However, since the 1996 Welfare Reform Act, immigrants no longer have access to these "means-tested" programs, namely food stamps for adults, Temporary Assistance for Needy Families (TANF), Medicaid (nonemergency), the Children's Health Insurance Program (CHIP), and Supplemental Security Income (SSI).

CULTURALLY RESPONSIVE STRATEGIES TO ADDRESS CHALLENGES AND CROSS-SYSTEM COLLABORATION

Most South Asians are loath to utilize the services of formal human service agencies, although they usually have little aversion to health care programs. Mental health problems tend to manifest themselves as psychosomatic ailments such as chronic headaches, backaches, dizziness, and weakness. Generally, psychological and emotional difficulties receive little recognition as being legitimate, and physical health is comprehendible, but it is unusual to find the somaticization of mental health issues. Social service use is on the increase, as schools and physicians are making referrals when they identify individuals and families experiencing untoward distress. Mobilization of the family's natural network along with formal service delivery programs has been the most effective form of service delivery.

Knowledge about the South Asian community has come a long way, and practitioners are much more aware of difficulties facing this group of immigrants and its progeny. However, the tendency has been to help the family adapt and acclimatize itself to its new environment and the norms of the host country, and to help it deal with cultural conflicts, particularly in relation to the U.S.-born generation. Most people move for economic reasons, and acceptance of foreigners is based primarily on the same reason; however, so much more is involved. Neither immigrant nor host really appreciates the impact of immigration and the ramifications for the immigrant of movement to an alien land and for the host of accepting onto its shores people who are strikingly different from its own population.

With voluntary immigrants, such as in the case of the South Asian migrating to the United States, host countries feel little responsibility to ease adaptation. Without access to orientation programs, voluntary immigrants navigate the new culture of the United States, its norms, and its infrastructure on their own. No social programs mitigate the loneliness of new immigrants, help them connect with others from their home country, or help them learn about cultural differences. Most immigrants are unprepared for the several unanticipated differences between themselves and the native-born population and may neither have the tools to cope nor know how to seek assistance. Thus, for example, when aging parents begin evidencing dementia or adolescents engage in behaviors traditionally considered unacceptable, families may struggle on their own, unaware of resources in the United States and too embarrassed to seek help in their community. Lai & Surood (2013) also propose, based on the findings of their research, that since personal attitudes of immigrants can impede the effectiveness of service delivery, prevention efforts may include culturally appropriate strategies to provide South Asians with information to overcome these attitudes so that they can better access and utilize services.

Effective strategies for intervention may include outreach efforts that focus on the following:

1   Providing education to the community through its own ethnic organizations regarding physical health, mental health, education, and

(CONTINUED)

culture in the United States, and regarding social, emotional, and familial
challenges in the immigration and adaptation process.

2   Identification of majority society resources that can help immigrants
cope with and/or ameliorate these difficulties.

3   Ensuring that service providers are *well versed* in the immigration
process and the immigrant/refugee experience and have some familiarity
with South Asian cultures.

Social work well recognizes the significance of context, realizing that
the difficulty of adjustment is at the juncture at which the client (individual, family, group, etc.) interacts with the environment. This may necessitate changes by the client or to the environment, or both. Practitioners
should assess what levels of social work require their attention—the micro,
mezzo, or macro—to help them provide effective intervention services to
their clients of Indian origin (Segal, 2012). Models of intervention and
practice literature, however, show very little focus on cross-system processes dealing particularly with the South Asian population. This is not
surprising, as there is little in the majority literature that focuses at all on
the needs of this group, either within or across systems.

Often, becoming sufficiently knowledgeable about the immigrant experience as well as getting a broad overview of South Asian culture is a good
beginning, and immigrants themselves are a good source for this information. However, in the process of being culturally responsive, it is essential to bear in mind that the human condition ensures that we are more
similar than we are different, facing several of the same opportunities and
hurdles and having similar psychological, emotional, and practical responses as we traverse life's journey. In providing services, focusing only on
differences or associating all experience with migration may increase barriers more often than it alleviates difficulties. Furthermore, it is important to
recognize that issues facing the South Asian community go beyond what
much research has focused on. Intrafamilial difficulties, particularly between parents and children, have received a great deal of attention in the
research literature and are related specifically to adaptation to U.S. social
norms, child rearing, dating and marriage, and career choice. Although it

is important to be aware of these issues, it is also clear that these are concerns that are similar for all immigrants, regardless of origin or destination country, and it is also clear that this is not all that is required in working with South Asians.

Reaching South Asians and engaging them in using social service resources to which they are entitled may require special approaches. Traditionally, health care has been the only nonfamilial service acceptable for use. The family/extended family network is considered appropriate and sufficient to meet all other needs. Hence, when the natural supports are diluted because of migration, families find themselves isolated, yet unwilling to access the societal resources that are available through governmental and nonprofit organizations. Although there are non-ethnic organizations around the country that do provide services to South Asians, there is a dearth of literature about them. Outreach provided as education is an effective mechanism for entry into the community.

With this sizable population, one must also address economic security, health and well-being, conjugal violence, and substance abuse, as well as aging, retirement, health care, and end-of-life issues. Thus, the focus must be on the lifespan. These emerging concerns have received little research attention. Furthermore, no research or practice attention has been directed toward the lesbian, gay, bisexual, and transgendered in this immigrant population or to their families, and there have been no outreach efforts targeting them.

Social work and social services must step back from the image of South Asians, and all Asians in general, as the "model minority," meaning successful and well adapted. The fact that they do not seek services is erroneously interpreted as not needing services. With South Asian service programs burgeoning around the country, it is evident that this population does require intervention, but expecting these needs to be fulfilled by South Asian services or for the group to rely only on services provided by the community itself is short-sighted, inefficient, redundant, and impractical.

Appropriate social work services must realize that the issues that plague South Asians are those that plague all human beings. The immigration experience adds another dimension, and cultural differences complicate

matters. However, the fundamental issues that require the attention of social work differ little among people. There seems to be no literature that
indicates that the U.S. social services have been particularly aware of or interested in the South Asian population or in addressing its needs, especially
because South Asians have tended not to live in ethnic enclaves, although a
few have emerged in Queens, New York, and in Edison, New Jersey. This
author published what was an elementary yet considered seminal article in
1991 (Segal, 1991), and it is sadly telling that attention to this group is lacking if that article is still used as a foundation for publications on understanding South Asians.

CONCLUSION

This chapter has provided an overview of the South Asian population in
the United States that recognizes the great deal of ethnic, cultural, and
socioeconomic diversity between countries and also within them. Afghanistan and Myanmar were omitted from the discussion, as they are not
really a part of South Asia. In addition, the experience of the Afghan
group, for a variety of sociocultural, sociopolitical, and socioeconomic
reasons, is vastly different from that of South Asians, and little has been
written about the population from Myanmar, where the immigration flow
to the United States is new and the numbers are relatively low. The population numbers are largest for immigrants from India, Pakistan, and Bangladesh, respectively, and most statistical and research information about
the South Asian community has been drawn from these three groups
and, most frequently, from the Indian immigrant group (Inman, Devdas,
Spektor, & Pendse, 2014).

Overall, the South Asian population is successful and self-sufficient.
However, this overall well-being of the population camouflages the difficulties some individuals and families experience. In addition, because of
the image of success, South Asians usually do not benefit from outreach
efforts or general public and private infrastructure resources, even in navigating the obstacles of life experienced by all individuals. Despite their success and level of acculturation, through the journey of life, when they least
expect it, immigrants are faced with cultural, social, and structural norms
that differ from those with which they are unfamiliar, and they may not

have resources to help them navigate these differences. The social services have failed to recognize this not only for the South Asian immigrant family but also for all immigrants who have been in the United States for a substantial period of time. Adaptation at a superficial or visible level does not necessarily reflect attitude, intrinsic understanding, or behavioral change. This may be the core of some of the problems South Asians face in accessing and receiving culturally responsive services.

It is now time to identify what the profession can do to address xenophobia of and by immigrant groups, including those from South Asia, and (1) prepare existing programs and services to meet the needs of all immigrants, (2) provide orientation programs to help new *voluntary* immigrants integrate into the country, and (3) provide opportunities for longer established immigrants to adapt to emerging issues as they care for their aging parents, cope with their own acute and chronic health needs, or plan for retirement. In professional practice, much lip service is given to the development of networks and cross-disciplinary collaborations. However, there appear to have been few concerted efforts by the several professions to collaborate in providing services to immigrants, particularly those from South Asia.

The ideal entry into the South Asian community is through naturally occurring human service processes. Most families have school-aged children, and most individuals use the services of health care facilities. Professionals in these two human service programs, namely teachers and physicians, are ideally placed to connect South Asians to resources they may require. In addition, the teacher is highly revered in South Asian culture, and the physician is highly valued as an authority. Thus, referrals made by these two professionals are likely to result in follow-through by South Asians.

Teachers have made referrals to social workers or mental health services, identifying the child as being the beneficiary of intervention services. Since the family sees itself as being intrinsic to the child's well-being, this can be an effective conduit into family therapy. Likewise, physicians can make referrals to the mental health services, especially since there is a tendency among South Asians to somaticize stresses, as in South Asian communities physical issues are generally considered more acceptable than mental health ones. The health care system and the educational system, both normally used by all families, can also be used to help South Asians acclimatize to U.S. culture and adapt to the norms of behavior.

RECOMMENDATIONS FOR WORKING WITH SOUTH ASIAN IMMIGRANT AND REFUGEE FAMILIES

1   Recognize that most issues with which South Asians grapple are similar to those all populations face (health, education, employment, relationships).
2   Recognize that the common issues may be exacerbated by the specific immigrant experience and the immigrant's culture (Segal, 2002, 2014).
3   Utilize the community's resources as mediators/vehicles for education and outreach. Several festivals include booths and activities, so a booth can be used to disseminate information.
4   Include community leaders in the training of service providers.
5   Ask clients to provide insight into their national, regional, and family cultures and norms.
6   Mobilize the family's natural network, as families are greatly interested in assisting in the welfare of their own but may not have the knowledge or skills to do so.
7   When working with a particular individual, provide a holistic perspective that assesses and develops intervention at the familial level.
8   Do not fix what is not broken, but avoid "political correctness" or cultural sensitivity that deems all norms acceptable. For instance, if a family chooses to educate its sons but not allow its daughters to access higher education, it would not be inappropriate to explore reasons for this and provide alternative perspectives.
9   Recognize that there is a balance, or a difference, between legal and culturally or socially acceptable behaviors.
10 Reframe mental health issues as issues related to addressing family concerns.
11 Recognize that when an opinion is sought, the clients want an opinion or suggestion. They do not necessarily want to spend a lot of time "starting with where the client is" and being self-reflective and finding their own solutions. They want guidance.
12 Recognize that the issues that immigrants and refugees face change and evolve with their longevity in the country, and acclimatization is not a one-time, or one-period, occurrence.

Social work has painstakingly begun to appreciate the presence and impact of globalization and immigration in the United States and to recognize that these also have substantial implications for the profession. Workers must be prepared for a growing immigrant population, whether it be from South Asia or elsewhere. Just as politicians are beginning to recognize that the South Asian population is worth courting because of its size and overall economic power, the human service organizations will need to become cognizant of the growing problems and issues facing this population, which, unattended, can also in time impact the larger society.

KEY TERMS

DIASPORA   A group that is living outside its country of origin and is dispersed in several other nations.

ENCULTURATION   The acquisition and internalization of the norms, attitudes, and values of a culture different from one's own.

FILIAL PIETY   The respect for, obedience to, and responsibility owed by children to their parents throughout their lives.

"MODEL MINORITY"   A term now used to describe Asian Americans, who are seen as well adjusted and successful. It had its origins in the civil rights movement, when Asians were held up as models to African Americans because they contributed to society and did not make waves.

SOUTH ASIA   The region in the southern part of Asia composed of the following seven nations: Bangladesh, Bhutan, India, the Maldives, Nepal, Pakistan, and Sri Lanka.

STUDY QUESTIONS

1   Identify three ways in which India, Pakistan, and Nepal are different from each other.
2   What are five issues facing South Asian immigrants in their relationships with their children?
3   What forms of cultural conflicts or misunderstandings may immigrants feel as they age in the United States?
4   How can mainstream social services engage in outreach efforts to the South Asian population?
5   What measures can social services take to minimize xenophobia of and by South Asians?

ADDITIONAL RESOURCES

DRUM (Desis Rising Up and Moving: A South Asian Organizing Center): http://www.drumnyc.org/

IOM (International Organization for Migration): http://www.iom.int and http://www.iom.int/cms/en/sites/iom/home/about-migration/world-migration.html

MPI (Migration Policy Institute): http://www.migrationpolicy.org and http://www.migrationpolicy.org/programs/data-hub/maps-immigrants-and-emigrants-around-world

SAALT (South Asian Americans Leading Together): http://saalt.org/

UNICEF (United Nations International Children's Emergency Fund). (2009). *A matter of magnitude: The impact of the economic crisis on women and children in South Asia.* http://www.unicef.org/rosa/Latest_Matter_of_magnitude.pdf

REFERENCES

Ahmad, F., Shik, A., Vanza, R., Cheung, A. M., George, U., & Stewart, D. E. (2005). Voices of South Asian women: Immigration and mental health. *Women & Health, 40*(4), 113–130.

Ahmad-Stout, D. J., & Nath, S. R. (2013). South Asians in college counseling. *Journal of College Student Psychotherapy, 27*(1), 43–61.

Balgopal, P. R. (1988). Social networks and Indian American families. In C. Jacobs and D. D. Bowles (Eds.), *Ethnicity and race: Critical concepts in social work* (pp. 18–33). Silver Springs, MD: National Association of Social Workers.

——. (1995). Indian Americans. In R. L. Edwards (Ed.), *Encyclopedia of social work* (19th ed., pp. 256–260). Washington, DC: National Association of Social Workers Press.

Brown, P. L. (2009, August 31). Invisible immigrants, old and left with "nobody to talk to." *The New York Times.* Retrieved from http://www.nytimes.com/2009/08/31/us/31elder.html?pagewanted=all&_r=0

Camarota, S. A. (2011). Welfare use by immigrant households with children: A look at cash, Medicaid, housing, and food programs. Washington, DC: Center for Immigration Studies. Retrieved from http://www.cis.org/sites/cis.org/files/articles/2011/immigrant-welfare-use-4-11.pdf

Central Intelligence Agency (2014). *World fact book*. Retrieved from https://www
.cia.gov/library/publications/the-world-factbook/geos/in.html

Chung, D. K. (1992). Asian cultural commonalities: A comparison with mainstream
American culture. In S. M. Furuto, R. Biswas, D. K. Chung, K. Murase, &
F. Ross Sheriff (Eds.), *Social work practice with Asian Americans* (pp. 27–44).
Newbury Park, CA: Sage.

Clough, J., Lee, S., & Chae, D. H. (2013). Barriers to health care among Asian immigrants in the United States: A traditional review. *Journal of Health Care of
the Poor and Underserved, 24*(1), 384–403.

Dobash, R. E., & Dobash, R. P. (1992). *Women, violence and social change*. New
York, NY: Routledge.

Fagen, C. (2013, November 19). Illegal immigrants from India stream into US
from Mexico. *Newsmax*. Retrieved from http://www.newsmax.com/US
/India-immigrants-US-Mexico/2013/11/19/id/537570/

Gany, F., Levy, A., Basu, P., Misra, S., Silberstein, J., Bari, S., . . . Leng, J. C. F.
(2012). Culturally tailored health camps and cardiovascular risk among South Asian
immigrants. *Journal of Health Care of the Poor and Underserved, 23*(2), 615–625.

Golden, D. (2012, February 2). Harvard targeted in U.S. Asian-American discrimination probe. *Bloomberg News*. Retrieved from http://www.bloomberg
.com/news/2012-02-02/harvard-targeted-in-u-s-asian-american-discrimi
nation-probe.html

Gonzales, D. (2013, September 8). Arizona sees surge of asylum seekers from
India. *USA Today*. Retrieved from http://www.usatoday.com/story/news
/nation/2013/09/08/ariz-sees-surge-of-asylum-seekers-from-india/2781025

Guillermo, E. (2014, December 1). Numbers reveal how Asian undocumented
remain hidden in America. *NBC News*. Retrieved from http://www.nbcnews
.com/news/asian-america/numbers-reveal-how-asian-undocumented-remain
-hidden-america-n256076

Hoefer, M., Rytina, N., & Baker, B. (2012). *Estimates of the unauthorized immigrant population residing in the United States: January 2011*. Washington, DC:
Office of Immigration Statistics. Retrieved from https://www.dhs.gov/sites
/default/files/publications/ois_ill_pe_2011.pdf

Hofstede, G. (1980). *Culture's consequences*. Beverly Hills, CA: Sage.

House, R. J., & Javidan, M. (2004). Overview of GLOBE. In R. J. House, P. J.
Hanges, M. Javidan, P. W. Dorfman, & V. Gupta (Eds.), *Culture, leadership,
and organizations: The GLOBE study of 62 societies* (pp. 9–26). Thousand Oaks,
CA: Sage.

Inman, A. G., Devdas, L., Spektor, V., & Pendse, A. (2014). Psychological research on South Asian Americans: A three-decade content analysis. *Asian American Journal of Psychology.* http://dx.doi.org/10.1037/a0035633

Khinduka, S. K. (1992). Foreword. In S. M. Furuto, R. Biswas, D. K. Chung, K. Murase, and F. Ross-Sheriff (Eds.), *Social work practice with Asian Americans* (pp. vii–ix). Newbury Park, CA: Sage.

Kumagai, F., & Strauss, M. (1983). Conflict resolution tactics in Japan, India, and the USA. *Journal of Comparative Family Studies, 14*(3), 377–392.

Lai, D. W. L., & Surood, S. (2013). Effect of service barriers on health status of aging South Asian immigrants in Calgary, Canada. *Health & Social Work, 38*(1), 41–50.

Lee, M. (2013). Breaking barriers: Addressing structural obstacles to social service provision for Asian survivors of domestic violence. *Violence Against Women, 19*(11), 1350–1369. Published online before print December 23, 2013, doi: 10.1177/1077801213514486

Leung, P., Cheung, M., & Tsui, V. (2012). Asian Indians and depressive symptoms: Reframing mental health help-seeking behavior. *International Social Work, 55,* 53–70.

López, J. (2011, May 17). Illegal immigration pipeline from South Asia to US passes through Guatemala. *Fox News Latino.* Retrieved from http://latino.foxnews.com/archive/julie-lpez/index.html

Maiter, S., & Stalker, C. (2011). South Asian immigrants' experience of child protection services: Are we recognizing strengths and resilience? *Child & Family Social Work, 16,* 138–148.

Migration Policy Institute (2014). *Select diaspora populations in the United States.* Retrieved from http://migrationpolicy.org/research/select-diaspora-populations-united-states

Okoro, O. N., Odedina, F. T., & Smith, W. T. (2012). Clinical cultural competency and knowledge of health disparities among pharmacy students. *American Journal of Pharmacy Education, 76*(3), 40–46.

Passel, J. S., & Cohn, D. (2011). *Unauthorized immigrant population: National and state trends, 2010.* Washington, DC: Pew Hispanic Center. Retrieved from http://pewhispanic.org/files/reports/133.pdf

Pew Research Center. (2015). *Unauthorized immigrants: Who they are and what the public thinks.* Retrieved from http://www.pewresearch.org/key-data-points/immigration/.

Rao, A. (2013). *The Indian diaspora—past, present, and future.* Retrieved from https://www.tie.org/article/indian-diaspora-past-present-and-future-ashok-rao

Sandhu, G. (2015, February 5). *The World Post*. Retrieved from http://www
.huffingtonpost.com/gursimran-sandhu/indian-divorce-mom-saved-life_b
_6574426.html?ncid=txtlnkusaolp00000592

Segal, M. N., Segal, U. A., & Niemczycki, M. A. P. (1993). Value network for cross-
national marketing management: A framework for analysis and application.
Journal of Business Research, 27, 65–84.

Segal, U. A. (1991). Cultural variables in Asian Indian families. *Families in Society,*
11, 233–241.

——. (2002). *A framework for immigration: Asians in the United States.* New York,
NY: Columbia University Press.

——. (2010). The Indian American family. In R. Wright, C. H. Mindel, R. W.
Habenstein, & T. V. Tran (Eds.), *Ethnic families in America* (Vol. 5, pp. 388–
419). New York, NY: Prentice-Hall.

——. (2012). Working with immigrants and refugees. In R. Link & L. Healy
(Eds.), *Handbook of international social work* (pp. 73–80). New York, NY: Oxford University Press.

——. (2014). Human rights and migration. In K. Libal, M. Berthold, R. Thomas, &
L. Healy (Eds.), *Advancing human rights in social work education* (pp. 435–
453). Washington, DC: Council on Social Work Education.

Segal, U. A., Elliott, D., & Mayadas, N. S. (2010). The immigration process.
In U. A. Segal, D. Elliott, & N. S. Mayadas (Eds.), *Immigration worldwide*
(pp. 3–16). New York, NY: Oxford University Press.

Sharma, E. (2011). Global adjustment perspectives of Indian professionals. *Global*
Business Review, 12, 87–97. doi:10.1177/097215091001200106

Shibusawa, T., & Mui, A. C. (2010). Health status and health services utilization
among older Asian Indian immigrants. *Journal of Immigrant and Minority*
Health, 12(4), 527–533.

South Asian Americans Leading Together (SAALT). (2012). *Promote policies and*
practices that address the health needs of South Asians. Retrieved from http://
saalt.org/wp-content/uploads/2012/09/Health-Care.pdf

——. (2014). *Demographic information.* Retrieved from http://saalt.org/south
-asians-in-the-us/demographic-information/

Thomas, S. B., Fine, M. J., & Ibrahim, S. A. (2004). Health disparities: The importance of culture and health communication. *American Journal of Public*
Health, 94(12), 2050.

Tu, J. (2010). *Explaining the labour market outcomes of first, second and third gen-*
eration immigrants in Canada. Discussion paper series Forschungsinstitut zur

Zukunft der Arbeit, No. 5128. Retrieved from http://nbn-resolving.de/urn: nbn:de:101:1-201010132836

United Nations High Commissioner for Refugees. (2015). *2015 UNHCR country operations profile–Afghanistan*. Retrieved from http://www.unhcr.org/cgi-bin /texis/vtx/page?page=49e486eb6&submit=GO

Unz, R. (2012, December 19). Statistics indicate an Ivy League Asian quota. *The New York Times*. Retrieved from http://www.nytimes.com/roomfordebate /2012/12/19/fears-of-an-asian-quota-in-the-ivy-league/statistics-indicate-an -ivy-league-asian-quota

Whatley, M., & Batalova, J. (2013). Indian immigrants in the United States. *Migration Information Source*. Washington, DC: Migration Policy Institute. Retrieved from http://www.migrationinformation.org/USFocus/display.cfm?ID=962

Yeung, W-J. J. (2013). Asian fatherhood. *Journal of Family Issues, 34*(2), 143–160.

CHAPTER 8

African Immigrant and Refugee Children and Families

▸ MARGARET LOMBE, CHIEDZA MUFUNDE,
and HARRIET MABIKKE

THE HISTORY OF AFRICAN migration to the United States is deeply rooted in the trans-Atlantic slave trade, which brought large numbers of Africans to North America as forced migrants in the sixteenth and nineteenth centuries. Indeed, considerable voluntary migration of Africans to the United States did not begin until the 1980s (Osirim, 2008). Data suggest that the population of African-born persons in the United States was just under 200,000 in the 1980s but continued to increase steadily through the 1990s. In fact, between 2000 and 2010, the number of legal African immigrants grew to about 1.5 million, suggesting that, in that single decade, more Africans arrived voluntarily in the United States than were brought to North America during the trans-Atlantic slave trade. Current estimates indicate that Africans make up about 3.9 percent of the country's 38.5 million immigrants (Osirim, 2008; U.S. Department of State, 2014). This number is projected to increase. Alongside immigrants, the proportion of refugees from the African continent migrating to the United States has also risen. According to Immigration and Naturalization Service (INS) records, one third of all refugees to the United States between 2000 and 2005 were from Africa (U.S. Department of Homeland Security, 2007).

Despite their "common place of origin," there is much diversity among African immigrants. Indeed, Africa is a land of many cultures and languages. It is the second largest continent (after Asia), covering about 20.2 percent of the earth's land, and has 54 countries. It is home to more than one billion people, comprising roughly 14 percent of the world's population, and represents more than 3,000 different ethnic groups, speaking approximately

2,000 languages. The diversity among African immigrants is informed primarily by sociodemographic characteristics, country of origin, reason for migrating, and socioeconomic status. This complexity in fact defines the welfare and experiences of people in this group within the United States. Understanding the complexity that characterizes the African immigrant is essential in developing culturally responsive services and practices.

In this chapter, we provide an overview of the experiences of the African immigrant in the United States. We start by presenting the demographic characteristics of African immigrants, trace the group's history of migration to the United States, identify patterns of settlement, and examine reasons for migrating. Further, we make an attempt to explore their cultural values and conflicts with the mainstream American value systems, if any, along with challenges encountered by African immigrants as they engage with the American socioeconomic system. We also address the social cost of this engagement to the immigrant. In addition, the chapter touches on the impact of federal policies on the immigrant. We limit our attention to health care, education, and labor force participation. The chapter concludes by offering culturally responsive strategies for addressing the challenges identified.

DEMOGRAPHIC PATTERNS

Despite the many generalizations that have been put forth about the African immigrant, the identity of people in this group remains largely unknown. In this section, we attempt to rectify this apparent gap in knowledge. The term "African immigrant" is used to refer to people of African descent who have voluntarily moved to the United States, and does not include Africans of European ancestry. Refugees moving to escape civil strife, famine, and other social vices are often placed in the African immigrant group. The majority of immigrants of African descent come from West African countries such as Ghana, Nigeria, Senegal, Sierra Leone, Liberia, and Mali (U.S. Department of State, 2014; Wilson, 2003). The countries of East and North Africa are also prominent countries of origin. The refugee population is likely to be from South Sudan, Somalia, and Ethiopia (U.S. Department of State, 2014).

Generally, perhaps because of ease of travel/mobility and related factors, African immigrants are likely to be male (about 55 percent) (Priority Africa Network, 2013; Wilson, 2003). This picture, however, is slowly changing, as more women are moving to the United States from Africa. On average, their age distribution at arrival in the United States falls between 25 and 45 years. It is important to note that, during the past few years, the proportion of older immigrants has increased considerably. This may be explained in part by the proportion of resources this group commands and in part by the family reunification policies that have allowed immigrant citizens to reunite with their family members, including parents. The marital status of these immigrants, however, has remained constant over time. People in this group are more likely to be single—either never married, divorced, or widowed.

Individuals classified as immigrants of African ancestry exhibit a wide range of educational and occupational backgrounds and may include professionals as well as unskilled laborers. According to U.S. Census data, African immigrants are one of the most highly educated groups in the United States (Dixon, 2006; U.S. Department of State, 2014). Compared with other immigrant groups, they are likely to have a college degree or to have completed some years of college. This is explained in part by the reason for migration and in part by the emphasis placed on educational attainment for social status and upward mobility. With respect to occupation, more than one third of African immigrants work in professional jobs, and some are found in managerial positions as well as in the service industry. A significant proportion are unemployed. Despite the higher median earnings reported by the group, one in every five African-born immigrants lives in poverty (Dixon, 2006). This observation suggests that although Africans are well educated as a group, they may not always be able to translate that education into professional jobs in the United States. Instead, they may end up in low-paying jobs in the service industry.

Familial networks and sense of community are important for the African immigrant, with the "we" often taking precedence over the "I." Indeed, the spirit of *convivencia* and/or *Ubuntu* forms the essence of being African. It exemplifies much more than coexistence. It suggests that my humanity is caught up with and is inextricably bound to yours—we can only be human together. In a sense, it recognizes that I am human because I belong. It also embraces the compassion and toughness that are inherent in the collective (Bhengu, 2006). For many immigrants, the family and community are the central support system, providing assistance when needed. Social service agencies, although important, are often seen as secondary.

Religion and spirituality are at the core of family life. In general, African immigrants are spiritual and embrace a wide range of religious beliefs, practices, and traditions. Christianity, Islam, and various traditional African religions are commonly practiced faiths. Although there are no clear patterns to depict the religious affiliation of the African immigrant, the history of slavery, colonization, and evangelization influenced conversion to both Islam and Christianity. For example, people from coastal cities such as Dakar, Mombasa, and Timbuktu that came into direct contact with Arab traders are likely to practice Islam. On the other hand, people in the interior of Africa, who encountered the Christian missionaries, are more likely to embrace Christianity. In the African way of life, religion and culture are deeply intertwined.

The fact that culture varies not only from one country to another but within individual countries, among tribes and religious groups, introduces an element of complexity that is not well understood by many social service providers. For the African immigrant, culture not only is expressed through art, music, and oral literature but is also reinforced through religious as well as social behavior and norms. Indeed, among the Bembas of northern Zambia, one of the burial rituals requires that the dead be buried facing east, the direction in which the sun rises. The assumption is that this enables easy transition into the land of their ancestors. It is also not uncommon to place the personal property of the deceased, including eating utensils, walking sticks, blankets, and other useful items, in the grave. The belief surrounding this practice is that ensuring the comfort of the dead on their journey will minimize the likelihood of their return to the land of the living. Furthermore, naming procedures dictate that a child be named after an ancestor. If a child so named cries for days, this is interpreted as a sign that either the child or the person the child is named after has rejected the name. These practices, which are deeply ingrained in African culture, may be practiced regardless of one's religious affiliation.

With respect to utilization of social services, most immigrants of African descent are likely to have minimal engagement with social service agencies. A number of factors may explain this observation. These include the presence of familial networks, which are charged with providing support when it is needed. Moreover, immigrants in this group are more likely to trust such networks and honor the principle of reciprocity, which defines their interactions. Another factor relates to the challenges involved in accessing and navigating formal systems in the United States. Indeed, time constraints may be an issue for many immigrants, who may be trying to adjust to the demands of their new country. In the case of health care, the main challenge concerns the incongruence between the health care system in the home country and that in the United States. Generally, unlike the health care system in the United States, which is primarily preventative, health care in many African countries is reactionary. Care is sought only when one is in need of medical attention. Furthermore, to the African immigrant, the idea of mental health, counseling, and therapy may be foreign and may carry a stigma. In fact, even among family members, mental health needs or issues are rarely discussed.

The foregoing overview serves to underscore the fact that although social service providers and the American public rarely acknowledge it, there is much diversity among African immigrants. This may range from basic elements such as skin tone, country of origin, and level of education to more complex elements, such as ethnicity, reasons for migrating, and culture. Acknowledging this complexity may be essential to working with this population. As a matter of fact, the "one size fits all" approach may not be effective. Working with African immigrants may also require a thorough understanding of the individual and social resources the immigrant commands. This may include level of education, vocational skills, fluency in the language of the host country, and economic resources, along with social networks. Without a doubt, the ease of transition into the host country is likely to be determined by the factors identified in this discussion. Individuals with the human and social capital necessary to navigate and access social services may find transition smoother.

HISTORY, PATTERNS, AND REASONS FOR MIGRATION

The social reality behind the migration of people of African descent to the United States is often masked by stereotypes depicting Africa as a "dark" continent and its people as impoverished, uneducated, residing in poor villages, and victims of mass starvation, who flee their home countries to escape their desperate situation. The reality, however, is that Africans, like other immigrants, move for reasons that are best classified under two main categories: personal and sociopolitical (Matory, 2001). Common among the personal motivators are:

- Educational advancement
- Economic opportunities
- Family reunification

Many people in this category are likely to start their journey with the intention of returning to their home countries. This reality, however, has slowly changed, as many African immigrants are now seeking permanent residence in the United States. In fact, available data suggest that a considerable proportion of African immigrants were naturalized U.S. citizens (about 46.1 percent) in 2010. The data also point to the growing number of individuals of African ancestry who are living in the country without legal residency (Priority Africa Network, 2013). The low incentive to return to the country of origin has been connected to familial expectations, levels of enculturation, political instability, and lack of opportunities in the country of origin. These factors, coupled with the perception that U.S. immigration policies are more friendly than the tighter European Union immigration restrictions, have made the United States a likely destination for Africans (Gordon, 1998; Takougang, 2002).

For many others, political instability along with civil unrest in their home country act as "push" factors, encouraging individuals with skills and resources to emigrate from their home country. Individuals in this group are likely to have experienced acute suffering, including drastic curtailment of human rights. Indeed, many Africans who come to the United States as refugees have lived through and are affected by the remnants of war, poverty, and disease. Many have lived in refugee camps or other communal settings for extended periods of time. A considerable proportion of children may have even participated in war as child soldiers and may have been sexually abused, tortured, victimized, and imprisoned.

It is important to note that regardless of the reason for coming to the United States, African immigrants and refugees are connected to their home countries in many ways. As a group, they act as goodwill ambassadors, advocating for their home countries. For example, in the recent case of Ebola, the Liberian community in Boston initiated fund-raising ventures and engaged in lobbying for action to help fight the epidemic. Immigrants also contribute millions to the economies of African countries through remittances (World Bank, 2014).

As observed, the history of African migration to the United States is connected to the trans-Atlantic slave trade of the sixteenth and nineteenth centuries. Indeed, the first Africans arrived in the United States in chains. Since then, a lot has changed—there has been a new wave of migration, which has been linked to policies such as the Immigration and Nationality Act of 1965, also known as the Hart-Celler Act (Pub. L. No. 89–236, 79 Stat. 911, enacted June 30, 1968) and the 1986 Immigration Reform and Control Act, as well as the Diversity Visa Program, which was introduced as part of the 1990 Immigration Act. Specifically, the 1965 act enabled establishment of the Immigration and Nationalization Act (Family Unification & Refugee Law), paving the way for many Africans to come to the United States. The 1986 Immigration Reform and Control Act has made it possible for undocumented immigrants, including those from the African continent, who were already living in the United States to apply for permanent residency. Further, the Diversity Visa Program, an agenda that promoted immigration from previously underrepresented countries and regions of the world, is said to allow up to 50,000 "qualified" individuals (including Africans) annually to migrate to the United States through a lottery process (U.S. Department of State, 2014).

With respect to patterns of migration, a considerable number of Africans in the United States came to the country as refugees. It is important to point out that Africa is home to about 3.6 million refugees, accounting for approximately 20 percent of the global refugee population. Since 1980, more than 200,000 African refugees have been admitted to the United States for permanent resettlement. Indeed, about one third (32.9 percent) of the 60,680 refugees and asylees admitted to the United States in 2007 were from Africa. Estimates from 2013 place the figure at roughly 16,000 out of a total of 69,926. Please note that, for fiscal year 2013, Africa used up its refugee admission quota, which was set at 15,950 out of the total refugee admission ceiling of 70,000 authorized by the president (U.S. Department of State, 2014). Projections for the 2015 fiscal year have been set at 70,000, with a ceiling of 17,000 for the African region (see table 8.1 for additional data).

Most of the people in this group come from countries engulfed by protracted civil wars. In fact, data on the admission of refugees suggest that the top five countries of origin for African-born refugees and asylees admitted into the United States include Somalia [4,884 (2010), 7,608 (2013)], Democratic Republic of Congo [3,174 (2010), 2,563 (2013)], Eritrea [2,570 (2010), 1,824 (2013)], Sudan [558 (2010), 2,160 (2013)], and Ethiopia [668 (2010), 765 (2013)] (U.S. Department of State, 2014). There is great diversity in this group—it consists of people from 30 African countries. Generally, African refugees are more likely to be young (with an average age of 19 years for Congo, 22 years for Somalia, 23 years for Eritrea and Ethiopia, and 27 years for Sudan). By gender, the group is primarily male (75.6 percent male for Sudan, 59.9 percent for Eritrea, and 54.1 percent for Somalia and Ethiopia).

Unlike their immigrant counterparts, people in this group are less likely to have a college degree and more likely to be limited English proficient (LEP). Although refugees receive employment authorization upon arrival and are encouraged to become employed as soon as possible, people in this group often end up in low-paying entry-level jobs, even if they have high-level skills or education. Hence, they are likely to end up living in poverty.

As noted earlier, the majority of African immigrants come from West and East Africa, representing 43 percent (647,200) and 35 percent (530,000) of the total, respectively. Central and Southern Africa combined accounted for 14 percent of the 1,503,400 immigrants. Further, according to data from the U.S. Bureau of the Census (2014), the countries with the largest immigrant presence in the United States were Nigeria (243,500, or 16 percent of the total), Ethiopia (195,800, or 13 percent), Ghana (149,400, or 10 percent), Egypt (137,799, or 9 percent), and Kenya (110,700, or 7 percent). Available data also suggest that this number continues to grow each year (see table 8.1).

TABLE 8.1 African Immigrant and Refugee Populations in the United States, 1980–2013

PERIOD	NUMBER OF IMMIGRANTS (CUMULATIVE TOTAL)	NUMBER OF REFUGEES (ADMISSION CEILING)
1980	129,900	955
1990	264,800	—
2000	690,800	17,328 (15,000?)
2010	1,326,600	13,305 (15,500)
2013	1,503,400	15,950 (15,980)

Sources: U.S. Bureau of the Census *American Community Survey* (2000); U.S. Bureau of the Census (2006, 2010, and 2013).

SETTLEMENT PATTERNS

Although African immigrants can be found in many towns and cities throughout the United States, major cities such as New York, Chicago, Minneapolis, Los Angeles, Atlanta, and the Washington, DC area continue to attract the largest numbers of immigrants. Indeed, current estimates indicate that the greater New York, Washington, DC and Atlanta metropolitan areas are the U.S. cities with the greatest numbers of immigrants of African ancestry. These three metropolitan areas accounted for about 26 percent of African immigrants in the United States. Further, evidence suggests that the population of African-born immigrants continues to grow in major cities across the United States. For example, between 2000 and 2010, the African foreign-born population increased by 111.1 percent in Texas, 110 percent in Virginia, 100.1 percent in Maryland, 40.3 percent in California, and 35.9 percent in New York. These cities are likely to remain magnets for African immigrants because of the presence of friends and relatives who are able to provide a temporary residence and other social supports until the newcomer is able to get situated (Office of Refugee Settlement, 2004; Singer, 2004).

Big cities tend to be home to large proportions of immigrants of African descent, and many are inclined to turn to ethnic enclaves within these cities. Examples of these include Little Senegal in West Harlem, the Concourse Village section of the West Bronx, and Little Ethiopia in Los Angeles. This is not uncommon among other groups of immigrants—familiar examples include Chinatown, Little Italy, and Irish communities in New York, and predominantly Latino communities in Los Angeles and Miami. Such communities are not only essential for stability and cohesion but are also key for economic participation and may provide the immigrant with an entry to economic opportunities that are unavailable in the mainstream.

African immigrants permeate all aspects of life in their areas of residency. They are doctors, lawyers, professors, engineers, students, cab drivers, clerks, security guards, and chefs (U.S. Bureau of the Census, 2014; Venters & Gany, 2011). The skill set that the immigrant commands, for the most part, tends to define the immigrant's experiences while navigating public attitudes and social policies in the receiving country. Indeed, the capital the immigrant brings to the process plays a major role in affecting how the individual engages with bureaucratic systems such as arranging visas, locating housing, obtaining work permits, and dealing with school systems, to mention just a few areas.

CULTURAL VALUES AND CONFLICTS WITH U.S. VALUE SYSTEMS

There is a tendency to treat the African immigrant community as a homogeneous group. This is problematic in that, as observed earlier, there is great diversity within the group in terms of socioeconomic characteristics, demographics, and country of origin, among other areas. Despite this, there are many common elements within this group. It is imperative that social service providers have a comprehensive understanding of the diversities and commonalities of the African immigrant if they are to be effective in working with this population. In this discussion, we highlight four areas of diversity: (1) colonial history and experience; (2) regional diversity; (3) cultural diversity; and (4) religion. Alongside this, attention is devoted to three elements generally shared by people of African origin: (1) sense of family; (2) communalism; and (3) respect for authority.

WITHIN-GROUP DIVERSITY

Colonial History and Experience

Before the arrival of the Europeans, Africa's contact with foreigners had for the most part been limited to Arabs through the trans-Saharan trade and the Swahili coastal settlements in East Africa. The colonization of Africa by the Europeans that culminated in the Scramble for Africa left an indelible mark on Africa and its people. At the height of the Scramble, about 90 percent of the continent had fallen under European control, with only Abyssinia (present-day Ethiopia) and Liberia still independent (Magdoff, 2014). Indeed, many countries on the African continent share a common history of colonization either directly or indirectly. A number of European countries, including France, Britain, Germany, and Portugal, were beneficiaries of colonialism. The influence of the colonial legacy is still felt today in many African countries, most notably in language and culture. For example, the official languages used in formal institutions in many

African countries are a reflection of this colonial history. Notably, most of West Africa uses French as its official language, whereas parts of East and Southern Africa use English. The Arab culture in the coastal cities of East Africa is a legacy of the Arab influence. The high level of proficiency in the English language, which characterizes the African immigrant in the United States, is also tied to a painful history of colonization. Immigrants from French-speaking Africa may not exhibit this fluency. In a sense, therefore, the "one size fits all" approach may not be effective when working with this group.

Regional Diversity

Service providers need to be aware that although they may come from the same continent, the African immigrant population is diverse in terms of regions, countries within a region, and whether immigrants are from a rural or an urban area. For instance, in terms of cuisine and dress, West Africans tend to share a similar culture that is unique to the region. Concepts such as Harambee may resonate more with Kenyans, and Ujamaa more with Tanzanians, than with Ugandans, although all three people may be classified as East Africans. It is important to realize as service providers that, based on regional diversity, approaches that might be effective for immigrants from a certain region might not be as effective with a group from a different region. For instance, immigrants from West Africa may be viewed as aggressive based on their manner of speech: their tendency to speak at a higher pitch. Rites of passage defining maturity and even death also vary considerably within different regions and countries in Africa. Indeed, even within the same country, different ethnic groups may mark these rites with different ceremonies.

There is also a divide between rural and urban among African immigrants that is defined by the location of origin. Indeed, the experiences of "city-grown Africans" may be different from those of "village-raised Africans." Generally speaking, immigrants from rural areas tend to have a different outlook than their counterparts from urban areas. Some cultural values might be stronger within the rural-raised population, requiring that a social worker probe more to get answers when providing services. Service providers may need to desist from assuming that all Africans fit the stereotype of poor, uneducated, and unsophisticated.

Cultural Diversity

As indicated earlier, Africa is home to a multitude of cultures and languages. Because of this diversity, immigrants from the same country may feel little attachment to each other, let alone to another immigrant from a distant part of the continent. Tribalism tends to run deep in some African countries. African immigrants from countries that are deeply tribalistic may identify themselves first as members of a certain tribe or clan before being members of their country of origin. It is not uncommon to hear phrases like, "My people were Bemba before they became Zambians." This awareness is important for service providers as they design interventions for people in this group. Indeed, interventions designed with the assumption of cohesion among people from the same country or region may not be effective.

Religion

Religious diversity is another aspect defining immigrants of African descent. Immigrants from North Africa tend to follow Muslim traditions, whereas those from Central, East, and Southern Africa are likely to be Christians. Traditional religions are still practiced to a lesser extent.

Although culture and religion are deeply intertwined, culture overrides religion where there is a conflict. In order to be effective in providing service, social workers need to realize that what might look odd or even illegal to a westerner might be acceptable and indeed encouraged in some African cultures. This is especially relevant when providing services to immigrant families. For instance, in some African societies, children are taught as a sign of respect not to look elders directly in the eye when being talked to. This may be contradictory to acceptable behavior in the United States, where looking one in the eye during verbal interactions is encouraged. Based on gender, some ethnic groups may treat their children differently, with preference given to the boy child. While this may not be desirable or encouraged, understanding this phenomenon may empower the service provider to intervene from a point of sensitivity. There is also the issue of polygamy, which is illegal in the United States but widely practiced in Africa, especially in Muslim communities. Female genital mutilation (FGM) may be a contentious issue: the practice is illegal in the Western world but viewed as a rite of passage for young girls in some African tribes. Although service providers might not have answers, especially for such complex issues, being aware of them is important in that it may provide a platform for engagement.

Inspired by this diversity, African immigrants irrespective of their country of origin are bound together by a rich African culture and cultural values that are rooted in the spirit of *convivencia*, and/or *Ubuntu*, which suggests that my humanity is caught up with and is inextricably bound to yours, and thus we can only be human together (Bhengu, 2006). In fact, the spirit of *Ubuntu* guides interactions among people of African descent. In the following section, we highlight three aspects of life that are generally shared by people of African descent: (1) sense of family; (2) communalism; and (3) respect for authority.

Sense of Family

Togetherness and obligation to family, both nuclear and extended, are shared elements in the African immigrant community. The African family, as is the case in other collective cultures, embraces much more than the nuclear family; it encompasses members of the extended family. The extended family may include parents, siblings, grandparents, aunts and uncles, cousins, and many others. In this system, the head of the family has an obligation to treat children within the family equally regardless of biological connection. Indeed, some tribes, such as the Ganda tribe of Uganda, have no word for uncle or aunt; for them, father and mother are used to denote one's parents as well as uncles and aunts.

In the extended family, respect tends to be bestowed according to age, with grandparents commanding the highest level of respect. Understanding the family dynamics is essential for service providers working with this group. This may help reduce misunderstandings with respect to norms guiding relationships and interactions. For instance, raising the offspring of extended family members is acceptable in some African societies. It is seen as a way of strengthening ties within the extended family. It is not uncommon for parents to send their children to live with relatives for extended periods of time. It is also important to appreciate the fact that since the extended family and the community as a whole are involved in nurturing the child, they also have the responsibility to correct and discipline the child.

Service providers need to be aware that an African immigrant's child may be raised differently from an American child. Whereas American children are generally encouraged to be independent, the African child, on the other hand, is guided and nurtured through life until such time as the child is deemed to have become an adult. Indeed, among the Maasai of Kenya and Gisu of eastern Uganda, the end of childhood is marked by an initiation ceremony, such as circumcision. There is also the issue of disciplining a child. What might be viewed as corporal punishment in the United States may be an acceptable mode of discipline for the immigrant family.

In working with immigrant families, service providers may also need to be aware of culturally assigned roles. For instance, some African cultures require that the wife take responsibility for household chores such as cooking, cleaning, and taking care of the children. Asking a husband to do so may be viewed as emasculation. It is also important to note that, in African culture, silence is not antisocial. Indeed, African culture encourages silence if one has nothing constructive to say. Sharing personal information, especially with strangers, is frowned on in many African societies. To be effective, a service provider may need to probe more for answers when working with the immigrant population, especially if the questions are of a personal nature and involve the family.

Communalism

African immigrants, just like their brothers and sisters in Africa, value communalism as well as the security and identity community provides. In a typical African community, people are valued as human beings irrespective of their social status. Vulnerable groups, such as the young, older adults, the sick, and people with disabilities, are considered a communal responsibility. In many African societies, the raising of children is seen as a communal responsibility, hence the adage "it takes a village to raise a child." Fear of public criticism acts as a strong deterrent to members of the community that might otherwise be tempted to neglect their responsibilities to their immediate and extended families and the entire community.

To be effective service providers, practitioners may need to appreciate that, in times of need, many African immigrants are likely to rely on the extended family and their community for support. Social welfare and government aid are often the last resort. Community is seen by some as the primary source of support, and, as such, some immigrants may not sign up for social security benefits even when they qualify. Working through churches or mosques, for instance, may be a more effective strategy in reaching out to immigrants of African ancestry.

Respect for Authority

Common among African immigrants is their respect for authority. In traditional African society, authority rests mainly with the elderly, who are held in high esteem: old age is revered. Older people, for the most part, are given the power to discipline children and the responsibility to resolve community disputes. In the United States, immigrants of African ancestry generally tend to have high regard for authority entities such as teachers, the police, and judicial systems. In dealing with these bodies, because of cultural norms pertaining to respect of authority, African immigrants may be submissive in their approach. Submission, in some instances, such as when dealing with the police, may be perceived as an admission of guilt, lack of drive, or even indifference. This may also be evident in employment situations, where the immigrant may fail to look a potential employer in the eye during a job interview, fail to be assertive in negotiations, and even agree with things they do not fully understand to avoid conflict. The attitude observed may be attributed to cultures that discourage aggressiveness; cultures that frown on assertiveness are cultures that value acquiescence. This knowledge may be of value to service providers working with immigrants in a variety of settings, including schools and health care institutions.

CHALLENGES RELATED TO CROSS-SYSTEM INVOLVEMENT

Before and upon their arrival in the United States, African immigrants interface with various U.S. systems; depending on their specific situation, immigrants are likely to be exposed to the U.S immigration system through the visa application process as well as at the port of entry. Furthermore, the circumstances leading to migration also shape the types of obstacles that immigrants are likely to encounter when accessing social services. For example, immigrants who do not possess permanent residency are not eligible for public benefits and benefits from federally funded programs. Further, although resettled African refugees qualify for benefits from the federal government, these benefits vary widely and are determined by the state of residency (Bruno, 2011). Generally, like other immigrants, Africans face many challenges in interacting with many systems, including health care, education, and the labor force, which are critical in shaping the experiences of immigrants at various stages of their settling in the United States. In the following sections, we highlight some challenges experienced by the African immigrant.

Health Care

Adjusting to a new culture is a long process for both voluntary immigrants and refugees/asylum seekers entering the country, and this adjustment requires support from multiple systems. Mainly because of its complexity, the health care system in the United States is among the systems that immigrants of African descent either completely avoid or deal with only when faced with life-threatening challenges. Issues of access and quality of health insurance continue to be prevalent among immigrant families. In 2007, about 33.2 percent of all immigrants—authorized and unauthorized—did not have health insurance (Camarota, 2009). Furthermore, because of their overrepresentation in low-paying jobs with limited opportunities for obtaining health insurance, African immigrants report lower health care utilization. Indeed, scholars have observed that despite the high levels of education that characterize people in this group, African immigrants are more likely to be found in jobs that do not provide health insurance (Venters & Gany, 2011). The lower rates of access to health insurance among African immigrants account for the high rates of use of emergency health services for primary health needs. Another factor that has been linked to underutilization of health care (in particular, mental health services) by African immigrants is the fact that mental health, counseling, and therapy are seen as foreign practices that carry a stigma. Furthermore, the African immigrant may have difficulty conceptualizing and adequately discussing mental health needs and concepts such as trauma, stress, and depression. Given that the population of African immigrants is growing rapidly, it is critical for the health care system to effectively cater to the needs of this population. This may require understanding the inhibitors and facilitators to access. In addition, a lack of legal status is also generally associated with a lack of private health insurance coverage, which in turn is connected to precarious employment and lower wages, along with limited use of health care services (Capps, McCabe, & Fix, 2011).

Education

Immigrants encounter challenges with respect to the education system. Most of these have to do with navigating the system, often with little information, as well as dealing with different expectations with regard to the education of their children. Many parents in this group struggle to effectively engage with the education system (public schools for the most part). The American school system expects that parents will play an active role in the education of their offspring (Priority Africa Network, 2013). The reality for many parents may be that they work multiple jobs and lack the time to invest in the expected engagement. For some, language may be a barrier inhibiting participation in school-related activities. Others may lack the skills to advocate effectively with teachers and administrators on behalf of their children.

African immigrants seeking refuge in the United States face another layer of challenges as they attempt to integrate into a new culture of "normalcy" from war-torn countries. For example, refugees from Somalia report the lowest levels of formal education compared with any other immigrant group and experience multiple layers of challenges as they attempt to integrate into the mainstream in the United States (Capps et al., 2011).

Labor Force Participation

One of the major challenges experienced in the area of labor force participation is underemployment. The underemployment of highly skilled African immigrants has been documented and has been explained by factors such as recent date of arrival, difficulty in transferring home-country credentials, and labor market discrimination (Capps et al., 2011). In a study analyzing the new dimensions of African immigrant communities and organizations in Washington, DC New York, and Atlanta, the disparity between the immigrant's high educational attainment and low-skill, low-wage jobs in which they were employed was identified as a major concern (Priority Africa Network, 2013). This discussion highlights the difficult and complex process of transferring foreign credentials, the discrimination inherent in the U.S. labor market, and how these factors contribute to high levels of underemployment among immigrants of African ancestry. Economic insecurity and the need to work and support their families in the United States and home countries force high numbers of African immigrants to work in low-paying jobs, often in the service industry. For example, a survey of African immigrants in Minnesota found that 44 percent of African workers surveyed held an unskilled labor or service job, compared with a rate of 24 percent for the age-adjusted general population workforce (Venters & Gany, 2011). Frustrated professional aspirations and economic insecurity have been cited as factors underlying the many social, psychological, and behavioral challenges that African immigrant families face.

IMPACT OF FEDERAL POLICIES ON IMMIGRANTS OF AFRICAN DESCENT

Immigrants are nested in communities that are governed by laws and policies; hence they experience the consequences of prevailing laws and regulations. Prevailing immigration policies have a more direct and concentrated impact on the lives of the African immigrant. Indeed, these have been the basis for political debates in the United States, especially in the past few years. The primary point of contention has been U.S. border security versus demands for cheap labor. Largely because of reasons related to proximity, the African immigrant, although affected by these policies, has not been engaged in the debate on the issue. Their lack of voice in this discourse is a matter of concern; however, this topic is beyond the scope of the current discussion, which is limited to understanding the effects of immigration policies on the African immigrant. Generally, three policies have had the most impact on immigrants of African descent:

1 The Illegal Immigration Reform and Immigrant Responsibility Act of 1996 (IIRIRA)
2 The REAL ID Act (2005)
3 The immigrant provisions of the 1996 Welfare Reform Act, and the Personal Responsibility and Work Opportunity Reconciliation Act (PRWORA)

The Illegal Immigration Reform and Immigrant Responsibility Act of 1996 (IIRIRA) made drastic changes to asylum law, immigration detention, criminal immigration, and many forms of immigration relief. The REAL ID Act (2005) created more restrictions on political asylum, severely curtailed habeas corpus relief for immigrants, increased immigration enforcement mechanisms, altered judicial review, and imposed federal restrictions on the issuance of state driver's licenses to immigrants and others.

The immigrant provisions of the 1996 Welfare Reform Act and the Personal Responsibility and Work Opportunity Reconciliation Act (PRWORA) have made most legal immigrants ineligible for publicly funded services such as Medicaid for the first five years of residence (undocumented immigrants were already ineligible), although states can preserve eligibility by fully funding these services themselves. PRWORA also extends the period of time that sponsors' income can be deemed available to immigrants and therefore counted as income for means-tested programs such as Medicaid. Finally, the law requires that state or local governments providing benefits to undocumented immigrants must pass a law to affirmatively establish their eligibility. These restrictions, aimed at discouraging immigrants likely to seek public benefits from entering the United States, have shifted responsibility away from the government and onto the newcomers.

CULTURALLY RESPONSIVE STRATEGIES TO ADDRESS CHALLENGES FACED BY AFRICAN IMMIGRANTS

Social workers play a critical role in the integration process of immigrants in general. Cultural differences and misunderstandings may result as individuals, families, and communities attempt to feel at home and develop the capital needed to deal with new structures and systems. As they navigate this process, immigrants and refugees are likely to encounter social work practitioners. This makes it imperative for (the) practitioners working with this group to deliver culturally appropriate responses. We limit our reflection on these issues to areas related to challenges immigrants are likely to encounter as they try to make sense of their new reality. These include (1) education, (2) health care, (3) labor force participation, and (4) integration.

Education

Challenges experienced with respect to education may include language barriers, lack of skills to navigate the education system, and cultural elements (e.g., fear of or respect for authority) inhibiting parents' ability to advocate for their child. Implementation of culturally responsive strategies in this regard may start with an acknowledgment of potential challenges. The focus should be on building partnerships with parents, who are indeed the first educators for many children in this group. This could involve creating community-based approaches that emphasize the role of parents in education. To create a strong alliance between parents and teachers, teachers and school-based social work practitioners may need to be educated on the child's specific needs, including language. Indeed, participation in school-related activities, especially for parents with limited English-language proficiency, might be enhanced by using translation services. This in turn may have a positive effect on the education outcomes of immigrant children.

Health Care

Generally, immigrants are identified as a vulnerable population, especially with respect to access to inadequate health care. Factors related to vulnerability in this area are many and complex. Broadly put, these include socioeconomic background; immigration status; level of English proficiency; federal, state, and local policies; residential location; and stigma coupled with marginalization. Evidence suggests that African immigrants generally tend to have lower rates of health insurance, have minimal health care use, and receive lower quality care (Capps et al., 2011; Venters & Gany, 2011). Addressing the health care needs of immigrants in this group could take into consideration the sources of the vulnerabilities experienced. Connection to a community-based organization or a faith-based organization (one of the key sources of social support for the African immigrant) may be an important avenue for addressing health care needs of this group. Such an avenue offers immigrants of African descent a platform for addressing challenges such as mental health. It also presents opportunities to learn about the American health care system. Further, it has the potential to reduce the stigma and marginalization that impact access to health care and give involved parties confidence in speaking about their needs and concerns.

As observed, providers working with African immigrants experience challenges in delivering care, identifying appropriate resources, and understanding the cultural needs of their clients. Likewise, clients served may also experience barriers that may limit their access and even compromise the quality of care received. A number of programs have sprung up to address the unique health needs of this group. We present here a brief overview of one such program: Becoming Empowered Africans through Improved Treatment of Diabetes, Hepatitis B, and HIV/AIDS (BEAT IT!) (Shire et al., 2012).

> Becoming Empowered Africans through Improved Treatment of Diabetes, Hepatitis B, and HIV/AIDS (BEAT IT!) is facilitated by the Center on Health Disparities at Adventist HealthCare. The program was developed through an award funded by the Office of Minority Health Resource Center's National African Immigrant Project. Its primary objective is to promote health care among African immigrants. Targeting the greater Washington, DC and surrounding areas, the program offers individuals and families skills in disease self-management and provides training to assist health care providers in delivering culturally appropriate care.

Employment

Evidence suggests that African immigrants, despite their high levels of education, are likely to be unemployed or be employed in low-income jobs, often in the secondary labor market. Culturally responsive approaches focusing on reducing underemployment and facilitating access to well-paying (mainstream) jobs could consider providing career-related assistance and training. This assistance could include academic recertification, especially for highly qualified immigrants to be able to work in the United States. Another component to this could be the incorporation of lessons in the English language to help improve proficiency. Indeed, it is well documented that English-language proficiency is a critical indicator of success at obtaining a job in the United States. Community-based centers and libraries may offer English lessons for immigrants with limited capabilities in the English language. Social service programs could also link immigrants to the various community-based resources that African immigrants can utilize. Furthermore, effective strategies could include training to facilitate familiarity with the U.S. labor market. Job training and retraining programs along with job fairs targeting immigrant communities have been known to be effective (see, e.g., Fix, Papademetriou, & Sumption, 2013).

Refugee Integration

In the particular case of refugees, isolation is seen as one of the primary concerns. Social service providers working with this group could focus attention on providing assistance with refugee integration and other supportive services. An example of a holistic program that offers social support to the African immigrant to mitigate the challenges posed by lack of access to social systems is the Somali Development Center (SDC), which targets Somalis and other African immigrants. Core services provided by this program include housing assistance, health care and public benefits, support for citizenship preparation, English language instruction, basic literacy instruction, employment training for youths and adults, and interpretation and advocacy in courtrooms.

COLLABORATIONS ACROSS SYSTEMS

Immigrants are nested in communities. Indeed, agencies and programs both within and outside their communities affect the lives of individual immigrants and households. Primary among the systems influencing the lives of immigrants are the health, child welfare, justice, and school systems. For example, a caregiver may experience depression related to factors such as legal status, marital conflict, and even trauma. The mental health of the caregiver has the potential to negatively impact the welfare of children within the household. Therefore, in a way, caregiver depression may be seen as a health concern with far-reaching consequences for the immigrant household. Moreover, in the case of refugee children, poor academic performance and involvement with the juvenile justice system may be a manifestation of the trauma experienced by the child. Addressing this may require understanding of the ecosystem within which the immigrant is nested, meaning the resources and constraints available to and experienced by the immigrant.

In recent years, there has been an acknowledgment of the fact that welfare is a product of the intersection of multiple systems. Hence, coordination of services is said to be essential in improving outcomes and strengthening the support system individuals and households, including immigrants, have to interact with (Adams, 2010; Stewart, 2013). Also, coordinating services has the potential to positively influence the integrity of agencies and programs. Collaborations across systems may occur at multiple levels, including among public agencies, between public and private agencies, within communities, and/or within families. It often requires cross-system dialogue, resource mapping, and increased communication, interaction, and coordination across systems that typically function independently. At the heart of this collaboration is the individual/household—the recipient of services (see figure 8.1).

Four main techniques reported to be essential for fostering and sustaining cross-system collaboration and communication include cross-system training, regular meetings of collaborative partners, a cross-system learning collaboration for service providers, and cross-system facilitators. Involvement of the immigrant and institutions (e.g., the church) that are

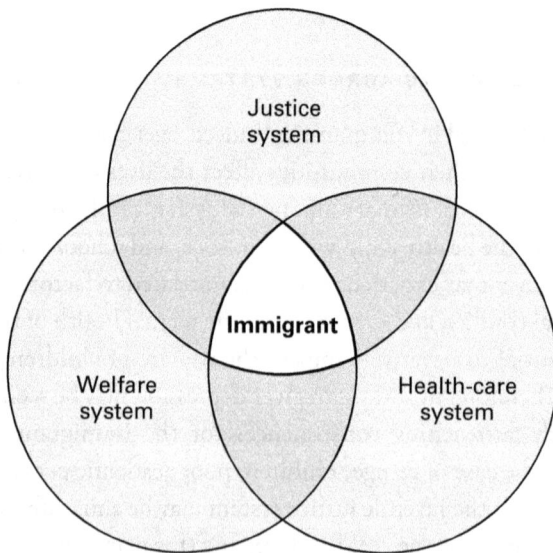

FIGURE 8.1   The intersection of systems with which the
immigrant interacts

central to their welfare may be important for effective collaboration. Another aspect of this, which is often ignored, is assessment and evaluation of the collaboration. This is important in providing guidance on how diverse community agencies, organizations, and individuals can join together to form a web of support for immigrant households and create safe, healthy environments in which children can thrive.

We now provide a case study to help illustrate the unique challenges experienced by immigrant families as they attempt to engage with multiple systems. We present a series of questions to help guide the discussion.

CASE STUDY: THE EL SCEWAMALA FAMILY

John (37 years old) and his wife Lucy (33 years old) emigrated from Uganda 13 years ago. They are both undocumented, having overstayed their visitors' visas after they came to visit John's cousin for her wedding. In Uganda, John was a teacher, and Lucy was a nurse. Lucy has not been able to enroll in school or take recertification exams for nursing because they cannot afford it and also because of the fear of exposing their immigration status. They have three children: 9-year-old daughter Jessica and 4-year-old twin boys Kato and Wasswa. John works two shifts as a security guard, is rarely home, and sleeps a lot when he is home. Lucy stays home to care for the twins. Jessica attends elementary school.

Recently, Lucy has been experiencing severe pain in her lower abdomen. The pain seems to intensify at night, and she can barely get up in the morning. Although the children all have Mass Health coverage, she and John do not have any health insurance, as they are ineligible for the federal health insurance program because of their immigration status. John's job does not provide health insurance. Lucy has been seeing a herbalist from the Ugandan community, but for two weeks, the pain has been unbearable. She is scared of going to the hospital, as they may bring up her immigration status. She is afraid of being deported.

What bothers Lucy most, however, is Jessica. She has become too Americanized. Although all her children were born in the United States, Lucy wants them to keep their Ugandan cultural identity, especially Jessica, whom Lucy hopes will marry a nice Ugandan boy one day. At home, Lucy talks to her children in Luganda, takes them to a Ugandan church, and cooks her favorite Ugandan dish, *matoke* and *binyebwa*, almost daily. Every year, over the Labor Day weekend, Ugandans in the United States have a convention, and Lucy makes sure she takes the children to learn about Ugandan culture.

Although the twins are obedient, lately Jessica has become impossible. She hates Ugandan food, preferring the food served at the school cafeteria, especially hot dogs and pizza. She says that church is boring because they pray in Luganda, and that Luganda embarrasses her among her friends at school. Lucy wishes Jessica would dress more appropriately for school and get rid of those cut-off jeans she loves so much.

Jessica comes home from school and finds that her mother has cooked *matoke* and *binyebwa* again! She refuses to eat the food and asks her mother to make her a hamburger instead. Lucy shouts at Jessica that she is spoiled, ungrateful, and if she wants a hamburger she should make it herself, because Lucy does not know how to make hamburgers and is not about to learn. Their next door neighbor, whose child goes to the same school as Jessica, hears the argument and privately talks to the school social worker about Jessica's apparent abuse and neglect and the welfare of the two other children in the home. She reports that Jessica seems neglected because Jessica's parents do not attend her extracurricular activities. She has had to drive Jessica to school activities herself on numerous occasions. She suspects that Lucy physically abuses Jessica. The school social worker talks to Jessica's teacher, who informs her that Jessica's parents have never volunteered to be room parents and rarely respond to letters sent home with Jessica.

Mother's Perspective

1 Lucy fears that her children are becoming "Americanized" and in the process are losing not only their identity as Ugandans but their attachment to the community as well.
2 Lucy is unprepared for the change in family dynamics—the reversal in the parent and child roles because Jessica seems to understand the new culture better. The idea of asking their child for assistance in navigating American culture makes Lucy and John feel inadequate as parents.
3 Because she is undocumented, Lucy fears deportation and therefore avoids becoming involved in the classroom or in Jessica's other activities because she may be asked questions.
4 In Lucy's native Uganda, teachers had control over students when at school; parents were not required to be involved in their children's education.

CASE STUDY (CONTINUED)

5 Lucy hates the level of personal involvement required to raise children and take care of a home in the United States. In Uganda, they had maids to take care of the children and the home.

6 Lucy finds herself at the intersection of the communal "it takes a village to raise a child" and the individualistic approach to raising children. She had hoped that her neighbors would take a more supportive rather than policing role in raising the children.

7 Lucy feels the absence of communal support, which is compounded by John's limited involvement in raising the children.

8 Lucy fears that the children do not understand that most of the decisions she and John make are ruled by their immigration status.

Father's Perspective

1 John does not understand why Lucy cannot take care of the children and the home. After all, she is home all day—she is the primary caregiver. He sees his role as provider, not as caregiver.

2 Although John lives in the United States, he still sees himself and his children as Ugandans. Preserving this identity is important to him.

3 John is anxious about his perceived loss of control and authority over his household in the Ugandan community.

4 John, too, wishes his new community would be involved with his children in a more positive way.

Child's Perspective

1. Jessica is frustrated at navigating the expectations of the different identities—American versus Ugandan.

2. Jessica struggles to make sense of being "other." She just wants to be normal.

3. Jessica struggles with internalizing the inferiority associated with being African.

4. Jessica struggles with the shame of having parents who are perceived as not fitting in.

Social work practitioners working with families such as the Scewamalas need to be aware of the complexities of their situations and experiences. Indeed, there may not be any easy fixes. The following recommendations may be useful:

1. Social workers should facilitate access to social networks in order to reduce social isolation for immigrants of African descent. Alongside this, space should be created for families to talk about issues that affect them, such as child rearing, challenges presented by their children, and immigration status.

2. Social work practitioners should make an effort to expose African immigrants to what mainstream America considers acceptable disciplinary practices. At the same time, practitioners should pay attention to the "hows" and "whys" behind the parenting styles exhibited by African immigrants.

3. Effort should be devoted to exposing immigrant parents to the idea that the child has a perspective that needs to be heard, respected, and valued.

4. Social work practitioners may need to advocate for enculturation so that children gain exposure to African culture but also learn to appreciate the dominant culture. This could help children gain an appreciation of the duality of their identity.

5. Social workers should assist the school system in appreciating the fact that lack of parental involvement in school activities does not necessarily mean disinterest in children's education. Attention could go into exploring the "why."

6. Social workers in community-based organizations, including churches, should devote time and resources to assisting immigrant parents in understanding the complexity of the schooling experience of children in the United States. African immigrant parents may not be aware of the emphasis that school systems put on social and extracurricular activities.

7. Social work practitioners may need to encourage and expose immigrant parents of African descent to appreciate the legal responsibility of parenting, especially as it relates to discipline.

8. Community-based organizations should create space where children are made aware of the challenges African immigrant parents may experience as they parent in a different cultural context.

CONCLUSION

This chapter set out to provide an overview of the experiences of African immigrants in the United States. It is common knowledge that the issue of immigration has been high on the social and political agendas of countries of the Northern Hemisphere in recent years. In the United States, the focus has been on immigrants from the Americas and people classified as "undocumented." Only recently has attention begun to focus on the African immigrant. Understanding experiences of the African immigrant begins with an appreciation of the fact that the first Africans to come to the United States arrived in chains; this point is significant to the experiences of the immigrant. Other factors of note relate to the diversities inherent within the group with respect to country of origin, history, motivation for migration, and resources commanded by the immigrant, to mention a few. These factors influence the interaction of immigrants with the peoples and systems of the host country as well as their welfare. Awareness of the complexity that characterizes the experiences of the African immigrant is essential in developing culturally responsive services and practices.

Culturally responsive strategies for working with immigrants of African ancestry may incorporate the following points.

1. Acknowledging the similarities and differences within the group may be an important consideration. As has been observed, African immigrants are not a homogenous group, so the "one size fits all" approach may prove problematic when working with families in this group.
2. Another consideration may relate to the practitioner's self-acknowledgment of his or her own biases with respect to immigrants of African descent. This has the potential to alleviate misunderstandings and mistrust between the African immigrant and social service providers.
3. Challenges experienced by immigrant families may be many and complex. Culturally appropriate responses may be guided by the social work maxim to start where the person is. This could mean providing time and space to allow collective exploration of the issue at hand. Starting with a clear articulation of problems or concerns from the immigrant's point of view may be useful. It may also require an appreciation of things the immigrant considers important for well-being and functioning. These may

include family, religion, and sense of community. Using these in interventions may be helpful.

4. It is well understood that language might represent a barrier to interaction with institutions in the United States. This is especially the case with refugees, immigrants with lower levels of education, and immigrants from non–English-speaking countries. The noted barrier could be reduced or eliminated by providing ESL training, where possible. The use of translators and other interventions geared toward reducing communication barriers may prove helpful.

5. Another point worth considering is the need for immigrant families to navigate U.S. systems. A meaningful starting point may be training focused on helping these families understand federal and state laws that are designed to support the integration of immigrants. Social workers may also need to familiarize themselves with these frameworks in order to offer adequate support to this group.

6. Further, in order to be effective, social service providers need to know the rights and services African immigrants may be entitled to. This is especially true for undocumented immigrants who may be living under the constant fear of deportation. They may not know, for instance, that all children, regardless of their legal status, have a right to equal access to K–12 public school programs or that, regardless of their immigration status, they are entitled to emergency medical care under the Federal Emergency Medical Treatment and Labor Act.

7. Knowing that immigrants, especially the undocumented, tend to be afraid of situations that may reveal their immigration status, such as dealing with the police, the school systems, and even the health care system, social workers could try to alleviate this fear by providing a safe environment as well as limiting questions requiring revelation of one's immigration status.

8. Finally, it is important to understand that responding to the needs of immigrant families may require creativity. Indeed, it may necessitate playing multiple roles, such as resource provider, advocate, and resource locator.

KEY TERMS

COMMUNALISM Strong commitment or loyalty to the interests of one's family and ethnic group for the benefit of society. It is seen as a conceptual framework and foundation for African value, thought, and belief systems. It is embodied in popular African sayings such as "it takes a village to raise a child" and is expressed in strong social ties, collective obligation, and mutual decision making.

HARAMBEE Swahili word for "pulling together." It is used mostly in Kenya, as a rallying cry for community engagement. The term calls for collective action on fund-raising and other self-help undertakings.

REMITTANCES Transfer of money by an individual in a foreign country to people in the country of origin. Remittances constitute a significant portion of the GDP of many countries of the Southern Hemisphere and have recently received considerable attention worldwide.

TRIBALISM A state of being organized in, or advocating for, the interests of a tribe or tribes. It implies a way of thinking or behaving in which people are more loyal to their tribe than to any other entity, including their country. Tribalism invokes possession of a strong sense of cultural and ethnic identity by members of one tribe or group. The Kikuyus in Kenya and the Ganda people in Uganda are examples of tribal societies.

UJAMAA An ideology promoted by Mwalimu Julius Nyerere (president of Tanzania from 1962 to 1985). Its focus is on poverty reduction through collective socioeconomic development. It emphasizes community engagement and a sense of "brotherhood."

STUDY QUESTIONS

1 Identify three or four barriers immigrants of African descent are likely to encounter as they attempt to utilize social services in the United States. For each of the barriers identified, propose approaches to help overcome them.

2 Discuss challenges that a social service provider is likely to encounter when working with this population.

3 Identify three major policies that may have the biggest impacts on the lives of immigrants of African descent. Discuss how and why the policies identified are likely to have the said impacts.

4 As a social service provider, explain how you would effectively advocate for immigrants of African descent in the following areas:
   a. Employment for parents
   b. Children's education

c. Access to health care

d. Navigating local and federal policies

5 Overall, do you feel prepared to engage with this population? Discuss potential challenges.

ADDITIONAL RESOURCES

Articles on working with African immigrants in the United States include:

Condon, P. (2006, February 17). Minnesota leads nation in Somali immigrants. Minneapolis Public Radio. Retrieved from http://minnesota .publicradio.org/display/web/2006/02/17/somalipop/

Grieco, E. (2004, September). The African foreign born in the United States. In *Migration Information Source: US in Focus*. Washington, DC: Migration Policy Institute. Retrieved from http://www.migrationinformation.org /Usfocus/display.cfm?ID=250

Nyang, S. (n.d.) *The African immigrant family in the United States of America: Challenges and opportunities*. Retrieved from http://www.africamigration .com/Issue%205/Articles/HTML/Sulayman-Nyang_The-African -Immigrant-in-the-USA.htm

Semple, K. (2008, October 15). A Somali influx unsettles Latino meatpackers. *The New York Times*. Retrieved from http://www.nytimes.com/2008/10/16 /us/16immig.html?ref=us;

Some useful websites include:

African Community Health Initiatives: http://www.africancommunityhealth initiatives.org/what-we-do.html

Massachusetts Immigrant and Refugee Advocacy (MIRA) Coalition: http://www.miracoalition.org/

The National African Immigrant Project: http://minorityhealth.hhs.gov /omh/content.aspx?id=9093&lvl=2&lvlid=16

REFERENCES

Adams, E. (2010). *Healing invisible wounds: Why investing in trauma-informed care for children makes sense*. Washington, DC: Justice Policy Institute.

Bhengu, M. J. (2006). *Ubuntu: The essence of democracy.* Toronto, Canada: Novalis Press.

Bruno, A. (2011). Congressional Research Service, U.S. Refugee Resettlement Assistance 6-15. Retrieved from http://www.fas.org/sgp/crs/row/R41570.pdf

Camarota, S. (2009). *Facts on immigration and health insurance.* Center for Immigration Studies. Retrieved from http://cis.org/HealthCare-Immigration

Capps, R., McCabe, K., & Fix, M. (2011). *Diverse streams: African migration to the United States.* Washington, DC: Migration Policy Institute.

Dixon, D. (2006). *Characteristics of the African born in the United States.* Retrieved from http://www.migrationpolicy.org/article/characteristics-african-born-united-states/

Fix, M., Papademetriou, D. G., & Sumption, M. (2013). *Immigrants in a changing labor market: Responding to economic needs.* Washington, DC: Migration Policy Institute.

Gordon, A. (1998). The new diaspora: African immigration to the United States. *Journal of Third World Studies, 15*(1), 79–103.

Immigration in America. (2008). Retrieved from http://immigrationinamerica.org/327-african-immigrants.html?newsid=327

Magdoff, H. (2014). Colonialism, Western. In *Encyclopædia Britannica.* Retrieved from http://www.britannica.com/topic/colonialism

Matory, J. L. (2001). Africans in the United States. *Footsteps: African American History and Heritage Magazine,* 6–9.

Office of Refugee Resettlement. (2004). *Report to the Congress FY 2004.* Retrieved from http://archive.arf.hhs.gov/programs/orr/data/arc_

Osirim, M. J. (2008). African women in the new diaspora: Transnationalism and the (re) creation of home. *African and Asian Studies, 7,* 367–394.

Priority Africa Network. (2013). *Dimensions of the new diaspora: African immigrant communities & organizations in New York, Washington, D.C., and Atlanta.* Retrieved from http://ccis.ucsd.edu/wp-content/uploads/WP_189.pdf

Shire, A. M., Sandhu, D. S., Kaiya, J. K., Oseini, A. M., Ju Dong, Y., Chaiteerakij, R., & Roberts, L. R. (2012). Viral hepatitis among Somali immigrants in Minnesota: Association of hepatitis C with hepatocellular carcinoma. *Mayo Clinic Proceedings, 87*(1), 17–24.

Singer, A. (2004). *The rise of new immigrant gateways.* Washington, DC: Brookings Institution.

Somali Development Center (SDC). http://www.sdcboston.org

Stewart, M. (2013). *Cross-system collaboration.* Los Angeles, CA: National Center for Child Traumatic Stress.

Takougang, J. (2002). *Contemporary African immigrants to the United States.* Retrieved from http://www.africamigration.com/archive_02/j_takougang.htm

U.S. Bureau of the Census. (2000). *American Community Survey.* Retrieved from http://census.org/acs/www/by~year/2000/

——. (2014). *The foreign-born population from Africa: 2008–2012.* Washington, DC: Author. Retrieved from http://www.census.gov/content/dam/Census /library/publications/2014/acs/acsbr12-16.pdf

U.S. Department of Homeland Security, Office of Immigration Statistics. *2007 Yearbook of Immigration Statistics.* Retrieved from http://www.dhs.gov/ximgtn /statistics/publications/LPR07.shtm

U.S. Department of State. (2014). *Proposed refugee admissions for fiscal year 2014. Report to the Congress.* Retrieved from http://www.state.gov/documents /organization/219137.pdf

Venters, H., & Gany, F. (2011). African immigrant health. *Journal of Immigrant and Minority Health, 13*(2), 333–344.

Wilson, J. (2003). *African born residents of the United States.* Retrieved from http://www.migrationpolicy.org/article/african-born-residents-united-states

World Bank. (2014). *Migration and development brief.* Retrieved from http:// siteresources.worldbank.org

CHAPTER 9

Middle Eastern Immigrant and Refugee Children and Families

▶ ALTAF HUSAIN, AYAT NASHWAN,
  and STEPHENIE HOWARD

GEOPOLITICAL AND SOCIOPOLITICAL events of the twenty-first century have brought to light the inextricable links between the United States and the Middle East region generally but especially with people in America who trace their ancestry to the Middle East. There is tremendous racial, ethnic, religious, linguistic, and socioeconomic diversity within this population, and this diversity is addressed briefly in this chapter. However, the scope of the chapter will be limited to presenting more substantive information on Middle Eastern immigrants and refugees who, in addition to being predominantly Arabic speaking, are Muslim by faith. Given this scope, terms such as Middle Eastern and Arab will be used interchangeably to orient social work students, educators, researchers, and practitioners to immigrants and refugees in the United States who speak Arabic as either a first or second language and who self-identify as Muslim. Nobles and Sciarra note that although not all Arabs are Muslims and not all Muslims are Arabs, one cannot "overestimate" the impact on the Arab world of Islamic teachings and culture—so much so that "religion is not just one aspect of life but its center, affecting all activity, thought and feeling" (Nobles & Sciarra, 2000, p. 183).

This chapter is divided into eight sections. The first section presents information on demographic patterns such as the trends in their growth by numbers and by states with the highest concentrations of this population. Given evidence of the arrival of Middle Easterners into the United States as far back as the late 1800s, the history, patterns, and historic and contemporary reasons for their migration are discussed in the second section.

The third section presents an overview of Middle Eastern cultural values and both perceptions and realities of conflicts with U.S. value systems. The fourth section addresses diversity within the group. The fifth section addresses challenges related to cross-system involvement that arise partly because of Arabs' lack of familiarity with various health and human service systems as well as practitioners' lack of familiarity with immigrants and refugees of Middle Eastern origin. The sixth section presents an overview of the impact of federal policies on this population. The seventh and eight sections present culturally responsive strategies to address challenges Arabs face as well as examples of collaborations across systems.

DEMOGRAPHIC PATTERNS

According to the 2010 American Community Survey (ACS) (U.S. Bureau of the Census, 2010), there were 1,967,219 people in the United States who identify themselves as having Arabic-speaking ancestry. At the turn of the century, Nobles and Sciarra asserted that the "number of Arab immigrants to North America is growing . . . and unofficial estimates place the number of Arab Americans at closer to three million" (Nobles & Sciarra, 2000, p. 184). The Arab American Institute (AAI), based in Washington, DC estimates the Arab American population at 3,665,789 (Arab American Institute Foundation, 2012). The difference of more than 1.7 million between the ACS and the AAI counts is noteworthy and is explained to a great degree by the methods used by the federal government to categorize people of Middle Eastern descent. Consider the classification of "White" as a "person having origins in any of the original peoples of Europe, the Middle East, or North Africa" (U.S. Bureau of the Census, 2015). Under this designation, individuals who self-identify as Lebanese, Arab (general designation), or Moroccan (North Africa) continue to be counted as "White."

Even with regard to foreign policy and diplomatic relations, differences about who to include as Middle Eastern or Arab abound. The Bureau of Near Eastern Affairs (NEA) in the U.S. Department of State includes under its purview a range of nations within both the Middle East and North Africa, such as Algeria, Bahrain, Egypt, Iran, Iraq, Israel, Jordan, Kuwait, Lebanon, Libya, Morocco, Oman, Palestinian Territories, Qatar, Saudi Arabia, Syria, Tunisia, United Arab Emirates, and Yemen. The most detailed analysis of demographic patterns is based on the 2000 Census and appears in a report by Brittingham and De La Cruz (2005) entitled, *We the People of Arab Ancestry in the United States*. Highlights from the report include:

- One out of four Arabs in the United States reported having Lebanese ancestry.
- After the Lebanese, these ancestries were the most commonly reported in the United States: Egyptian (123,000), Syrian (76,000), Palestinian (62,000), Jordanian (36,000), Moroccan (30,000), and Iraqi (29,000).
- There was a higher percentage of men among Arabs (57 percent) than there were among the total U.S. population (49 percent).
- The same gender difference was quite pronounced for the 20 to 49 age group, with 31 percent of Arab men being from this age group compared with only 22 percent of men in the total population being from this age group.
- The likelihood of being married was much higher among Arabs (61 percent) than among the total U.S. population (54 percent), while conversely Arabs were less likely (13 percent) to be separated, widowed, or divorced compared with the total population (19 percent).
- Nearly half (46 percent) of Arabs were citizens by birth, and even among those who were foreign born, the rates of naturalization were proportionally higher than among the population as a whole.
- Compared with the percentage of the total population with bachelor's degrees (24 percent), the proportion of Arabs with a bachelor's degree was nearly twice that (41 percent).

Although during the earliest period of migration (from the late 1800s until the 1920s) Arabs were mostly engaged in trade and moving about from town to town, those who arrived following the 1965 immigration reforms (see the section on "Impact of Federal Policies") were more likely to be professionals and to settle down in a handful of states. The Arab American Institute estimates that the largest Arab populations are found in California (nearly 600,000), New York, Michigan, Florida, and Texas (Arab American Institute Foundation, 2012).

HISTORY, PATTERNS, AND REASONS FOR MIGRATION

Among the non-European immigrants to the United States, Arabs can be categorized as being one of the oldest immigrant groups. Their reasons for migration parallel those of other immigrant groups, ranging from fleeing persecution to seeking economic gain. Although there is evidence that some of the enslaved West Africans spoke Arabic (Diouf, 1998), they were never categorized as "Arabs" or "Middle Easterners." Based on historic and current demographic data, there have been at least four periods in American history when immigrants from the Middle East arrived in the United States (Erickson & Al-Timimi, 2004). The first period includes those whose migration started in 1870 and ended in the early 1920s, when immigration from non-Western European nations was essentially halted by the passage of immigration legislation in 1924. The second period includes those migrating after World War II mostly as students and also those entering the United States following the immigration reforms of 1965. The third period includes those people entering from 1965 until the end of the twentieth century. A fourth period of Arab migration is now discernable as having started following the terrorist attacks of September 11, 2001, and the subsequent war declared on Iraq in early 2003.

FIRST WAVE

Sizable numbers of Middle Easterners, mostly farmers and merchants, did not start arriving in the United States until the 1870s; however, "Middle Eastern" was not a category used at the time by the U.S. government (Haddad, 2004). Until 1899, U.S. officials categorized as Turkish citizens almost anyone arriving from lands ruled by the Ottoman Empire (Marvasti & McKinney, 2004). Owing mostly to their white skin and intense efforts within the United States to ensure Anglo conformity among all immigrants, the Arabs of the first wave assimilated in unprecedented ways. Describing the process of their assimilation and their contribution to American society at the time, Haddad notes:

> Their names were anglicized, Muhammad became Mo, Rashid became Dick, Mojahid became Mark, and Ali was recognized as Al. They dug ditches, laid down railroad tracks, peddled. . . . Their children went to public schools and worked in factories. They enlisted in the American military during the First and Second World Wars and served with distinction. (Haddad, 2004, pp. 4–5)

SECOND WAVE

Partly as a result of shifts in American perceptions of immigration and partly because of international events, a second wave of Arab immigrants arrived in the United States following the demise of the Ottoman Empire in 1922. Ottoman rule was replaced throughout the Middle East by various colonial powers, especially Britain and France. As World War II engulfed most of Europe, the strategic placement as well as vast resources of lands of the Middle East and North Africa served as bases for the colonial powers. The struggles between indigenous peoples of those lands and the colonial powers also displaced hundreds of thousands of people. Following World War II, the United States made strategic calculations to recruit mostly young Arab males of newly independent nations to attend American colleges (Haddad, 2004). Still others, such as the Palestinians, came mostly as families displaced by the creation of present-day Israel in 1948. Most of these families continued the pattern of the first wave of Middle Easterners by settling down in the northeastern and midwestern states.

THIRD WAVE

In the wake of historic civil rights legislation passed in 1964 and 1965, the United States also overhauled the immigration system by abolishing the 1924 national origins quota. Perhaps the largest migration of Arabs from the Middle East and North Africa occurred following the landmark immigration legislation passed in 1965. In addition, Arabs also migrated to the United States as a result of the displacement of people caused by regional instability in the Middle East arising from at least three major conflicts: (1) the 1967 Arab-Israeli war; (2) the onset of civil unrest and ultimately civil war in Lebanon in 1975; and (3) the beginnings of the Iranian Revolution in 1978 (Marvasti & McKinney, 2004). There was a marked difference in the sociodemographic characteristics of the immigrants that comprised the third wave: they were mostly seeking higher education or were established professionals, came from countries in which Islam was the dominant religion, and included among them dissidents and thought leaders who promoted a strong pan-Arab identity (Haddad, 2004). Erickson and Al-Timimi (2004) assert that those who comprised the third period of migration were likely to experience greater difficulty in being incorporated into American society compared with Arab immigrants from the first two periods of immigration.

FOURTH WAVE

The last decade of the twentieth century and the start of the twenty-first century have witnessed the continued arrival of Arabs in the United States. However, this has also been a period in which more refugees from this region have been resettled in various parts of America. The Iran-Iraq war and the U.S. wars against Iraq in the early 1990s and then again starting in 2003 have resulted in the internal, regional, and international migrations of hundreds of thousands of men, women, children, and elderly. Of particular concern to social workers should be the sheer scope of this displacement as estimated by the United Nations High Commissioner for Refugees (UNHCR):

> UNHCR estimated that 4.5 million Iraqis had been displaced both before and after the 2003 US invasion—2.2 million crossing the border and 2.3 million remaining internally displaced within Iraq. In February 2007, UN High Commissioner for Refugees António Guterres declared the exodus of Iraqis the largest population shift in the Middle East since the displacement of Palestinians following the establishment of the state of Israel in 1948. (O'Donnell & Newland, 2008, p. 3)

Monumental events related to the Arab Spring, and specifically the start of the civil war in Syria in 2011 and the war in Yemen in spring 2015, have resulted in the displacement of millions of Arabs. Despite a genuine desire by the Office of Refugee Resettlement to accept Iraqi Christians and Muslims, Syrians, and most recently Yemenis, the rates of arrival of these refugee groups in the United States have been very slow as a result of intensified screening and security measures introduced by the Department of Homeland Security. Auclair and Batalova report that in the first decade of the twenty-first century, "the fastest-growing immigrant groups from the Middle East and North Africa region were Sudanese (149 percent increase from 18,600 to 46,300), Saudis (149 percent increase from 27,800 to 69,200), and Yemenis (110 percent increase from 19,600 to 41,200)" (Auclair & Batalova, 2013, "Size, Distribution and Growth," para. 4). Within these groups, the Saudis traditionally prefer to return to Saudi Arabia, the Yemenis have historically settled in America, and the Sudanese increasingly call America home.

CULTURAL VALUES AND CONFLICTS
WITH U.S. VALUE SYSTEMS

For Middle Eastern immigrants and refugees, cultural values are often rooted in religious teachings, whether it is Christianity, Judaism, or Islam (Nobles & Sciarra, 2000). Christian and Jewish immigrants from this region may experience some conflict with U.S. value systems, but, for the most part, there tends to be alignment in values since the U.S. value system is essentially rooted in the Judeo-Christian tradition. The likelihood that value conflicts will arise is much greater for Muslims generally, because religion is not subsumed as a part of culture but serves as the basis for cultural values. Kohls summarized well the major U.S. and Middle Eastern cultural values and indicated the extent to which there is a conflict between the two sets of values (see table 9.1).

TABLE 9.1   U.S. Cultural Values Contrasted with Middle Eastern
            Cultural Values

U.S. CULTURAL VALUES	MIDDLE EASTERN CULTURAL VALUES
Personal control over the environment/ responsibility	Fate/destiny
Change seen as natural and positive	Stability/tradition/continuity
Time and its control	Human interaction
Equality/fairness	Hierarchy/rank/status
Individualism/independence	Group's welfare/dependence
Self-help/initiative	Birthright inheritance
Competition	Cooperation
Future orientation	Past orientation
Action/work orientation	"Being" orientation
Informality	Indirectness/ritual/"face"
Practicality/efficiency	Idealism/theory
Materialism/acquisitiveness	Spiritualism/detachment

On the surface, the two columns of table 9.1 appear to show mostly conflict between the U.S. cultural values and Middle Eastern cultural values. The reality is that the differences between the two value systems are attributable more to the basis of each system of values and less to the values themselves. For example, Kohls (1988) attributes the importance of wanting to exercise personal control over one's environment and taking responsibility for the environment as a U.S. cultural value, whereas focusing much more on fate and destiny is a quality attributed to Middle Easterners. This delineation regrettably mimics what Orientalists have (incorrectly) been writing for centuries. An unshakable belief in the omniscience and omnipotence of the Divine and a belief in divine predestination is seen by Middle Easterners as a prerequisite to any human exertion of personal and collective effort to achieve a goal (see the text box "Everything Is God's Will").

EVERYTHING IS GOD'S WILL

Fatima is an ailing widow who is a naturalized citizen of the United States. Her brother entered the United States to visit her and is now out of status, living as an undocumented immigrant. Fatima laments her failing health but accepts her illness as God's will and wants to keep praying for healing. The social worker should not misinterpret Fatima's desire to pray as being mutually exclusive of efforts to help Fatima seek medical treatment. Praying to the Divine for assistance is not fatalism; it is a concomitant realization of the limits of human endeavors. Therefore, accepting the outcome of human efforts is a reflection of Divine Will. Fatima's resistance to seeking professional intervention may be unrelated to fatalism. On a more practical level, she may fear that involvement in the health system will bring scrutiny of her family members who have a mixed immigration status.

Similarly, having a spiritual outlook for Middle Easterners may present as being seemingly detached from worldly desires. This appearance of detachment emanates directly from the importance given by Arabs to the afterlife while not forgetting their responsibility to live a full life on earth. The value U.S. society places on time and its control stands in contrast to the emphasis Arabs place on human interaction and the formation of strong relationships, which is why a social worker might experience tremendous frustration during the assessment phase or the first meeting with an Arab if the bulk of that meeting time is spent on what the social worker might interpret as small talk. However, for the Arabs, that small talk serves as a trust-building exercise.

Next, we present some of these cultural values and the perceived and real conflicts of those values with the U.S. value system. In particular, the importance Middle Easterners accord the role of faith and religion, as well as collectivism, are elaborated on at length since they permeate and to a great extent serve as the sources of the other cultural values.

ROLE OF FAITH AND RELIGION

An especially pronounced conflict with the U.S. value system occurs for those Middle Easterners who self-identify as religious and proclaim that their religion is essentially their way of life (see the case study "You're in America now, so look like an American"). As Nobles and Sciarra emphasize, "though not all Arabs are Muslims, or Muslims Arab, it is hard to overestimate the influence of Islam on the Arab world" (Nobles & Sciarra, 2000, p. 183).

For immigrants and refugees from this region, much like those earlier Eastern European immigrants about whom Oscar Handlin wrote in his 1951 work *The Uprooted*, religion is very much a way of life and is not relegated to religious services on a particular day of the week or to a major religious holiday once or twice a year. Thus, every major decision, most activities of daily living, and relationships between family members and between the individual and society at large are all aspects of an Arab's life, which are either directly governed by or at least impacted by religious teachings (Nobles & Sciarra, 2000). A conflict arises both because of the lessening emphasis placed on institutionalized religion in American society and because of the bright boundary that exists regarding the role religion should play in the public domain (Zolberg & Woon, 1999).

CASE STUDY: "YOU'RE IN AMERICA NOW, SO LOOK LIKE AN AMERICAN"

Sarah, a Muslim immigrant from Palestine, was naturalized as a U.S. citizen following her marriage to a Palestinian American. She was educated in Palestine and is working at a part-time job while she improves her English skills. Her understanding of modest apparel leads her to cover her hair with the *hijab* when she is serving as a cashier at the local grocery store. Her American employer may request that Sarah remove the *hijab* while at work. His request could reflect either a broader societal understanding of the role of culture and religion or a more xenophobic attitude toward immigrants and refugees. His reactions could range from "you can believe whatever you want, but don't bring those beliefs to work" to "you're in America now, so look like an American." In this case, the employer assumes wrongly that the wearing of the *hijab* is a preference. For Sarah, a more deep-rooted conflict would arise because, according to her understanding, her wearing of the *hijab* is a matter of obeying God's order. There are clear implications for Sarah's psychosocial well-being since her conflict is between obeying God and obeying her employer, who, if he chooses to discontinue her employment, could exacerbate her precarious financial well-being. Potentially complicating matters further, were Sarah an undocumented immigrant or a member of a family with mixed immigration status, she might feel even more vulnerable about the consequences of disobeying her employer.

RELIGION, CULTURE, AND THE HELPING RELATIONSHIP

The impact of adherence to religious teachings in daily life also permeates the helping relationship. For example, the Arab client may relegate mental, emotional, and physical healing to the realm of prayer, or the interactions between clients and social workers of opposite genders may be guided by religiously mandated concerns for modesty and privacy. Christian and Muslim Arabs use *Allah* or *Ilah* to refer to God, so for clients who self-identify as religious, it would not be uncommon for the social worker to hear, in the course of intervention, references by a client to God's will (*insha'Allah*—God willing) or to divine predestination (*qadr Allah*—what God has destined) and to praising and thanking God (*alhamdulillah* and *shukr lillah*, respectively). Perhaps the most common misperception of a conflict between the role of religion and the U.S. value system is when the social worker believes the Arab client is fatalistic, rendering his or her healing entirely to God. Saying if God wills is an acknowledgment by the client of the omnipotence of God, but ultimately Islamic teachings especially prescribe emphasis on preventive and restorative healing measures (Husain & Ross-Sheriff, 2010).

Because the Arabs perceive the interconnectedness of religion and healing as positive, it is clear that "cultural factors stemming from religious beliefs and practices can have an intense impact on health" (Aboul-Enein & Aboul-Enein, 2010, p. 21). However, the gender differences between the client and the practitioner may adversely affect the relationship between religion and health. Thus, careful consideration should be given to the gender of the practitioner. Finally, the practitioner must always assess the degree to which religion and spirituality matter to a particular Arab client. Aloud and Rathur suggest that incorporation of religion or spirituality into treatment goals "be approached with caution in some cases, because we cannot necessarily attribute a high level of religious devotion to all Arab American clients" (Aloud and Rathur, 2009, p. 155).

COLLECTIVISM

The emphasis placed by non-Western cultures on the well-being and indeed the preferences of the family, group, or tribe is referred to as collectivism (Al-Krenawi & Graham, 2000; Haboush, 2007). This particular value is an innate part of Arab culture, transcending faith and national origin. Consider immigrants from Iraq, where the within-group diversity in terms of religion is stark, with an Iraqi Chaldean Christian, an Iraqi Jew, an Iraqi Sunni Muslim, and an Iraqi Shiite Muslim all having very different religious and spiritual outlooks. Or consider the newly arrived Syrian refugee woman who lost her husband as they fled from Syria into Turkey and now lives in the United States with her children. Nevertheless, as Arabs, each of the Iraqis and the Syrian holds in check his or her individual preferences and desires with regard to major decisions such as who to marry, where to work, and where to live—often preferring the well-being of the extended family or even giving up agency in favor of familial harmony. Al-Krenawi and Graham state that "contrary to a Western therapeutic emphasis on the individual, all interventions with Arab clients need to be couched in the context of the family, extended family, community, or tribal background" (Al-Krenawi and Graham, 2000, p. 13).

There is an increasing awareness that there must be a balance between unbending collectivism on the one hand and Western-style individualism on the other hand. Turning to one's family or group in times of crises provides a measure of security and support to the individual along with a general sense of pride in the collective identity. The practitioner can facilitate the Arab client's ability to tap into the benefits of collectivism in social work services. This strategy may have an advantage over more individualistic treatment plans, as the family may feel distanced by a social worker who appears not to value the importance of collectivism. Social workers should also appreciate the extent to which the preservation of family stability, honor, and cohesiveness is embedded in the collectivistic outlook (Haboush, 2007). Social workers should be mindful that client choices at the individual level along with interventions perceived by the family as placing their honor, stability, or cohesiveness at risk could possibly evoke feelings of intense guilt and shame in the client.

Postmigration changes to family structure may be experienced by the family unit as compromising collectivist values. For instance, Velazquez and Dettlaff note that, "following immigration, changes to previously established gender roles and expectations may occur as a result of cultural and financial pressures on the family system" (Velazquez & Dettlaff, 2011, p. 684). Whereas an educated Arab man may not be able to find employment because of a downturn in the U.S. economy, tensions may arise if his wife, who perhaps never worked outside the home or ever expected to, is able to secure work babysitting other people's children in their home. These changes may be viewed as threatening to family stability. Social workers should assess the nature of postmigration changes and the impact they may have on the family system.

A clear conflict does arise between U.S. value systems and the Middle Eastern emphasis on collectivism when one considers obligations to report instances of child abuse and neglect or sexual abuse. Compounding this problem is the possibility that the family may be undocumented and therefore fearful of any involvement with the authorities. Haboush and Alyan assert that "while the close-knit nature of Arab-American families may contribute to considerable protectiveness being extended to children, disclosure of sexual abuse may be hindered by concerns about shaming the family, particularly if the perpetrator is a family member" (Haboush & Alyan, 2013, p. 508). The more informed the social worker is about these varying and interconnected cultural values, the greater the likelihood of an efficacious intervention with Arab clients. Ultimately, the Arab "cultural constructions of family can best be used by social workers' willingness to tolerate the enmeshment so characteristic of Arab families, by educating themselves regarding Arab family values so that they can in turn sensitively educate the family about the necessary requirement for a workable helping relationship" (Al-Krenawi & Graham, 2000, p. 14).

WITHIN-GROUP DIVERSITY

The geographic span of countries classified as comprising the Middle East is vast, and the respective populations of those countries are diverse with respect to culture, race, religion, and ethnicity. Despite the nearly century-long span during which Arabs have arrived and settled in the United States, there exists much confusion about who Arabs are and the tremendous diversity that exists among them. In 1996, Suleiman wrote about the challenges educators face in teaching Arab American children and asserted even then that "the literature that provides an objective and comprehensive account about the Arab Americans is almost missing" (Suleiman, 1996, p. 9). By the turn of the twenty-first century, not much progress had been made in understanding the culture or diversity among Arabs or even among the Arab American population. So when 19 men of Arab descent were implicated in planning and executing the worst terrorist attack on American soil, the backlash and lumping together of all Arabs and the conflation of their national origin with Islam seemed all but inevitable. Given the increasing presence of clients of Arab descent within the helping professions (Abu-Ras & Abu-Bader, 2008), this section provides the reader with background information to grasp the extent of within-group diversity among Middle Easterners in the United States.

The postcolonial, modern Arab world can be divided into three distinct regions: Arabs from the Arabian Gulf region, Arabs from the Mediterranean region, and Arabs from North Africa (Al-Hazza & Lucking, 2005). People from each of these regions have maintained their indigenous dress, food, music, and dialects, but there are very obvious colonial imprints in the countries of these regions, such as the French influence on Algeria, Egypt, and Morocco. Nobles and Sciarra explain that the dialects "are all different from classical Arabic, which is spoken by educated Arabs and, as the written version of the language, is substantially the same throughout the Arab world" (Nobles & Sciarra, 2000, p. 184). For example, the Syrian dialect is different from the Lebanese dialect, and the Omani dialect is different from the Yemeni dialect. The Egyptian dialect is more commonly understood throughout the Middle East because of that nation's dominance in the entertainment market throughout the region.

There is also racial and ethnic diversity in the Middle East. Indeed, the Arab world "has always been the crossroad of civilization and, like the United States, has been enriched by the contributions of many cultures— from Greece, Rome and the ancient Near East; from Christianity, Judaism and Islam; from the Persians and the Turks, India and China; from Europe and America" (David & Ayouby, 2005, p. 17). Skin color varies from region to region, with Arabs from Lebanon and Syria who could be classified as "white," as indeed they were during the first period of migration to the United States, to Egyptians, Kuwaitis, and Yemenis, who have both white and darker complexions represented in the population. Suleiman (1996) lists, in addition to Arabs, at least eight different ethnic and racial groups, including Kurds (Iraq), Druze (Lebanon), Copts (Egypt), Assyrians (northern Iraq), Armenians, blacks, Berbers (Algeria), and Kildanis (also known commonly as Chaldeans) (Iraq). Some of the distinctions between these groups arise from racial and denominational differences within the same religion, such as Christianity for the Druze in Lebanon and Copts in Egypt.

Lastly, within-group diversity is most pronounced with regard to religion, with Christianity, Judaism, and Islam being represented throughout the Middle East. Within each major faith, there are additional differences by denomination, such as the various types of Christians represented: Assyrian, Chaldean, Copt, Druze, and Maronite. Following the creation of the state of Israel in 1948, a majority of the Jews living within the Middle East migrated to the newly established homeland. There are fewer Jews in Middle Eastern countries outside of Israel, owing both to increasing internal strife within some of these countries, such as Egypt, Iraq, and Morocco, and to continued migration either to Israel, the United States, or Europe. Descriptors such as *Mizrahi* Jews are used to refer to those Jews who trace their ancestry to Arab lands such as Egypt, Iraq, Lebanon, Syria, and Yemen, whereas *Sephardic* Jews trace their ancestry mostly to Algeria, Morocco, and Turkey (Shenhav, 2006). Even among Arabs who self-identify as Muslim, there is tremendous diversity, ranging from sects within Sunni Islam and Shi'a Islam, to levels of very conservative to progressive interpretations of Islamic teachings, to adherence to particular theological schools of thought or *madhahib*.

CHALLENGES RELATED TO CROSS-SYSTEM INVOLVEMENT

Although cross-system involvement is a laudable and to some degree inevitable part of the reality of working with Arabs, a noteworthy distinction must be made between immigrants and refugees with regard to interacting with certain systems. Because of the involvement of various government agencies and nonprofit organizations in the process of refugee entry and resettlement in the United States, at least during the first few months of their arrival, there is a greater likelihood that school-related, physical health, and mental health issues will be identified by professionals in any of those systems. A similar assertion cannot be made about immigrants, because they are self-sponsored or enter via family reunification policies and may interact with, at most, the school system, if they have school-aged children; but, their interaction with other systems is less likely. Three challenges are noteworthy: (1) varying degrees of familiarity with the various systems; (2) low participation and utilization rates in the school system and the child welfare, physical health, and mental health systems; and (3) a perceived lack of cultural competence and sensitivity on the part of the providers within the systems.

DEGREES OF FAMILIARITY WITH THE VARIOUS SYSTEMS

Several sociocultural and demographic factors combine to engender varying degrees of familiarity with helping systems among Arab immigrants and refugees (Abu-Ras, 2007; Nassar-McMillan & Hakim-Larson, 2003; Nobles & Sciarra, 2000). First, regardless of national origin or religious background, an overarching emphasis on a collectivistic outlook and the associated overreliance on family and informal support systems to address challenges in day-to-day life result in varying degrees of familiarity with external helping systems among Middle Easterners (Nassar-McMillan & Hakim-Larson, 2003). Second, even if a person were to consider seeking formal assistance, the level of education and English-language literacy of the individual immigrant or refugee will impact the degree to which he or she is able to read about or search on the Internet for available mental health and social services (Nobles & Sciarra, 2000), although even highly educated Arabs are not entirely immune to the power of the family or group in ensuring that outside help is not sought. Third, generational status, acculturation stage, and number of years of residence within the United States also impact the level of knowledge and familiarity with the availability of mental health and social services Arabs will have (Nassar-McMillan & Hakim-Larson, 2003).

LOW SERVICE-UTILIZATION RATES: CHILD WELFARE AND MENTAL HEALTH SYSTEMS

The rate of utilization of mental health and social services by Arabs is receiving increasing attention in the social sciences literature (Aloud & Rathur, 2009; Erickson & Al-Timimi, 2004; Haboush, 2007; Nobles & Sciarra, 2000). The decision to utilize services may be even more complex for undocumented immigrants, since their hesitation to involve any formal systems would be a direct result of their anxiety about having their immigration status questioned or discovered. Particular systems in which there may be especially low utilization rates are child welfare and mental health. Although not referring specifically to children of Middle Easterners, Velazquez and Dettlaff note generally that "the population of immigrant children and families who come to the attention of the child welfare system is relatively small" (Velazquez and Dettlaff, 2011, p. 680). Partly because of their collectivistic outlook, Arabs are more likely to seek out informal channels of assistance if it ever comes to their attention that a charge of child neglect or abuse is imminent. Especially because of the backlash Arabs and South Asians faced following the terrorist attacks of September 11, 2001 (Abu-Ras & Abu-Bader, 2008), parents may be apprehensive about even seeking out helpful information from a child welfare agency for fear of being misunderstood in their request at best and of being charged or jailed at worst. This apprehension is not unfounded in the case of families with either one or more members who are undocumented. In addition, lower rates of interaction with child welfare agencies may be much more reflective of efforts to prevent the family name and reputation from being tarnished than of any individual-level analysis indicating that one or both parents fell short of their responsibilities toward the child. Another challenge would be a sense of wariness on the part of the parents about the possible intersection of the child welfare system with the criminal justice system should they be charged with abuse or neglect. Cultural brokers are critically important within the child welfare system to interpret and shed light on the sociocultural basis of Arab child-rearing practices.

Low rates of utilization of mental health and social services reflect the challenges related to involvement across systems. Abu-Ras (2007) examined the relationship between cultural beliefs and mental health and legal services utilization by battered Arab immigrant women. The study found significant correlations between the espousal of traditional beliefs about gender and wife battering and the utilization of formal mental, social, and legal services among women who participated in the study. Although abuse of any kind is not sanctioned by religious teachings, an overemphasis on preserving family honor means that instances of wife battering are not likely to be reported, nor would the women be encouraged to seek out medical assistance except in cases of severe injury. To support women with signs of abuse, collaboration with cultural brokers can be instrumental in promoting an understanding of healthy relationships that is informed by religious teachings.

CULTURAL COMPETENCE, SPIRITUAL COMPETENCE, AND SENSITIVITY: HEALTH SYSTEM

Another major challenge related to cross-system involvement is the apprehension of immigrants and refugees in general, and Middle Easterners are no exception, about the level of cultural and to some degree spiritual competence and sensitivity that they will find among staff members within various systems. Such apprehension is present especially when this population deals with the health system. Aboul-Enein and Aboul-Enein assert that "healthcare professionals seem fairly unfamiliar with the distinctive cultural characteristics of Middle Easterners when they come for healthcare" (Aboul-Enein & Aboul-Enein, 2010, p. 20), and these individuals are therefore characterized as "difficult patients to work with" (Aboul-Enein & Aboul-Enein, 2010, p. 20). Depending on the generational and acculturation statuses of each individual client, their philosophy and outlook toward seeking medical treatment may be challenging for social workers to comprehend. Beyond just cultural competence, a social worker should understand in particular that a newly arrived Middle Easterner may "fear hospital admission because hospitals are considered places of bad luck where people go to die" (Aboul-Enein & Aboul-Enein, 2010, p. 21). A best practice in this type of situation includes connecting the potential patient with an Arabic-speaking medical doctor or nurse and possibly even a former patient who can bear testimony to the efficacy of the hospital admission. On the other hand, the likelihood also exists that an Arab refugee may present in the health system but with very vague physical symptoms. The absence of any evidence to substantiate those physical symptoms should alert the social worker to the existence of possible mental health symptoms for anxiety or depression, for example. Aboul-Enein and Aboul-Enein posit that Middle Easterners "lack concepts that distinguish mental states from physical states, and their experience does not allow them to carefully describe signs and symptoms as they are associated with different parts of the body" (Aboul-Enein & Aboul-Enein, 2010, p. 21).

In addition, as noted earlier, for Arabs, the overlap between religious and cultural traditions is strong, so practitioners across multiple systems have to ensure that a lack of spiritual competence does not result in low quality of care for Arab clients. Spiritual competence is a process through which

> practitioners develop expertise in three interrelated areas: (1) a growing awareness of their own value-informed spiritual worldview ... (2) an empathic understanding of the client's spiritual worldview; and (3) an ability to design and implement interventions that resonate with their client's worldview. (Hodge, 2011, p. 153)

Connecting spiritual competency to cultural competency, Hodge asserts that cultural competency "is required to select and implement spiritual interventions within the context of clients' cultures" (Hodge, 2011, p. 153). This is especially true for Arabs, whose cross-system journey in a predominantly Arab community in Dearborn, Michigan, is likely to be drastically different from the cross-system journey of Arab clients in Pontiac, Michigan, where Arabs are a minority and the likelihood of the number of health and human service staff familiar with Arab culture and traditions is also likely to be small. Part of engaging in spiritually responsive practice entails tapping into support systems such as those provided by hospital chaplains. A client self-identifying as spiritual or religious is sometimes more likely to open up, at least initially, to a priest or imam than to a health professional about their physical or mental health conditions.

IMPACT OF FEDERAL POLICIES

Middle Easterners are likely to be affected by a range of federal policies. Although analysis of the use of government assistance and welfare generally by Arab immigrants is scarce, more is known about Arab refugees since they are sponsored by the government and receive assistance during the early period of their resettlement. Iraqi refugees, for example, have been approved for resettlement mostly since the U.S. invasion in 2003; however, their actual arrival in the United States has often been delayed by complex security procedures that they must clear. As they continue to arrive, eligibility requirements for affordable health care may be difficult for them to meet, but the government has granted Iraqi refugees an exemption from the five-year bar (Rejeske, Gonzales, & Schwartz, 2014). Speaking more generally, Velazquez and Dettlaff assert that "legislative initiatives . . . restrict immigrant families' access to basic safety net services, affecting even those with legal status" (Velazquez & Dettlaff, 2011, p. 680).

This section focuses primarily on the impact of immigration policies. From the time of their arrival in the United States in the late nineteenth century, there has been evidence indicating that discriminatory practices against Arabs have been the product of interplay between racism generally, anti-immigrant sentiments, and a targeted campaign against people of Arab descent (Cainkar, 2006; Suleiman, 1996). Of particular concern is the "social distance [that] has been created and reproduced by institutions of power . . . is measurable, and is manifested in government policies" (Cainkar, 2006, p. 243).

IMPACT OF IMMIGRATION POLICIES

This section focuses primarily on immigration policies of the late twentieth and early twenty-first centuries. Essentially, the challenge of identifying people of Arab descent was never addressed by the federal government, even dating back to the late 1800s. The government categorized them as "white," and their numbers were subsumed in the national census under the white population. Even when there was an attempt to distinguish them, incorrect descriptors were used, ranging from "Turkish" to lumping them altogether under the category of "Syrian" (Haddad, 2004; Marvasti & McKinney, 2004). The efforts to allow people of Arab descent to have a distinct category of self-identification continue and are being spearheaded by organizations such as the Arab American Institute (AAI) and the Arab Anti-Discrimination Committee (AADC). Those efforts will likely continue until a decision is reached in time for the 2020 census. The category "White" on the census continues to be used to refer to people from the Middle East and North Africa or those who self-report as Arab (U.S. Bureau of the Census, 2015).

Two immigration policies, enacted in 1924 and 1965, had opposite impacts on the immigration of Arabs to the United States. The 1924 immigration reforms introduced national origin quotas and halted the immigration of any people from regions outside Northern and Western Europe. Even those residing within the United States faced complex challenges to their application for naturalization. On the one hand, their "whiteness" was questioned, as in the case of Ahmed Hassan, of Yemeni descent, whose application for naturalization was denied in 1942 because he was deemed to be of neither European nor Christian heritage (Naber, 2008). On the other hand, there is evidence to show that a naturalization application by an Arab in 1944 was approved by the federal government on the basis of the argument that his "whiteness" accorded to him the status of someone who could transmit Western civilization (Naber, 2008).

Until the 1965 immigration reforms, most Arabs arrived as refugees. Following the founding of Israel in 1948, Arabs of various religious backgrounds were displaced, and the United States enacted the "Refugee-Escapee Act of 1957 (Public Law 85-316)[, which] focused on the admission of persons fleeing communist nations or from the Middle East" (Churgin, 1996, p. 314). There is limited information available about the Arab refugees who arrived during the period between the 1940s and 1965.

Haddad (2004) connects the phasing out of the Asian Exclusion Act of the 1920s with the enactment of the 1965 Immigration and Nationality Act. This historic legislation in 1965 heralded the arrival of Arab immigrants, a critical mass of whom were "highly educated, socially mobile and professional" (Haddad, 2004, p. 5). These immigrants contributed to the development of infrastructure in major cities, joined higher education as faculty members and researchers, and held a range of positions in corporate America.

The federal government exerted intentional efforts to attract immigrants, including those from the Middle East and North Africa, among other nations that had historically lower rates of migration to the United States. Applications from Arab countries were still quite low, with Egyptians accounting for almost 29,000 visas during the period 2003 to 2012 (U.S. Department of State, 2012). The diversity visa program focuses primarily on the national origin of the applicant and whether the person can pass security clearances and less on the applicant's educational and professional backgrounds.

The most far-reaching and direct impact of federal immigration policies on Arabs has been caused by policies encoded in the USA Patriot Act, which came into being following the 9/11 terrorist attacks. Beginning just one day after September 11, 2001, the government introduced legislation directly targeting Arabs. A critical analysis of these policies can be summarized as follows:

> Twenty-five of the thirty-seven known government security initiatives implemented between September 12, 2001, and mid-2003 either explicitly or implicitly targeted U.S. Arabs and Muslims. These measures included mass arrests, secret and indefinite detentions, prolonged detention of "material witnesses," closed hearings, secret evidence, government eavesdropping on attorney/client conversations, FBI interviews, wire tapping, seizures of property, removals of aliens with technical visa violations, and mandatory special registration. (Cainkar, 2006, p. 255)

Under pressure from the public to apprehend terrorists, some "752 nonnationals were placed in custody for routine immigration violations, because they were 'presumed guilty' of links to terrorism, and were subjected to unique practices and rules not used for other visa violators" (Hall, 2004, p. 258).

Having observed the fate of some college students, professionals, and even citizens, undocumented persons of Arab descent continue to be at risk for experiencing paranoia and trauma because of fear of being detected. Attorney General John Ashcroft, for example, "removed more Arabs and Muslims (who were neither terrorists nor criminals) from the US in the past year than the total number of foreign nationals deported in the infamous Palmer raids of 1919" (Cainkar, 2003, p. 1). Starting in 2009, the Obama administration deported hundreds of thousands of undocumented immigrants, further exacerbating the anxiety of all out-of-status immigrants but particularly those of Middle Eastern descent.

CULTURALLY RESPONSIVE STRATEGIES
TO ADDRESS CHALLENGES

Although the development of culturally responsive strategies is critical for effective social work practice in general, it is especially important in the case of clients of Middle Eastern descent. Recent immigration policies thrust Arab Americans into a precarious position, with increased barriers to access of needed support services. Further complicating matters is the possibility that either one or several members of a family may be undocumented immigrants and quite wary of formal engagement with any system. Social workers are in an advantageous position to respond to their needs. The collective response should be guided by social work values of acceptance and respect for cultural diversity. This section will help to inform culturally responsive services for this population. First, evidence from successful efforts to establish culturally responsive services to serve Arabs is presented. Second, the implications of acculturation are identified in order to ensure that interventions are informed by the special needs of immigrants and refugees. Third, information is presented regarding the implications that preimmigration characteristics have for service needs. Fourth, strategies for redressing challenges related to practitioner gender are presented.

First, states with high concentrations of Arab Americans have pioneered the development of social service organizations specifically for this population. As refugees and some immigrants entered the United States following the 1967 Israeli-Arab war, Michigan was one state that experienced an increase in the existing Arab, mostly Yemeni, population. The longest continuously operating organization serving Arabs is the Arab Community Center for Economic and Social Services (ACCESS), founded in Dearborn, Michigan, in 1971. ACCESS has eight locations within Michigan and provides physical health, public health, and behavioral health services. Access California Services (AccessCAL) was founded in 1998 with one volunteer, but as of 2015 it has 30 staff members and serves nearly 11,000 Arab immigrants and refugees in Southern California. In 2006, New Jersey community leaders called for expanding the range of services available to Arab Americans in the light of increased victimization following 9/11 (Kindergarten, 2006). They subsequently founded the first nonprofit social service and mental health organization specifically designed for Arab Americans in New Jersey (Kindergarten, 2006). This had been preceded three years earlier by a similar program in New York (Kindergarten, 2006). The news coverage surrounding the launch of the New Jersey agency brought attention to the challenges that Arab Americans face in contemporary America. Kindergarten (2006) relates the following story:

> There was a girl who cut herself as a means to cope with depression, but dared not tell her parents she needed help because seeking professional mental health treatment is taboo in her culture. And the children who must cope with being called terrorists by their peers in school. There was the Muslim woman whose head scarf was pulled off by a passer-by as she walked down the street. (Kindergarten, 2006, p. A15)

The mental health implications of these traumatic incidents are clear; however, interventions should work to mobilize the multiple systems of care in support of the client. These systems should be informed by the cultural background of the Arab community.

Second, it is imperative that social workers tailor services to meet the unique needs of immigrant and refugee clients. This may require an assessment of acculturation to provide insight into the level of support that the individual requires. Acculturation involves changes at the individual and group levels of identity (McBrien, 2005). In terms of changes at the individual level, acculturation may cause one to question one's values and belief systems. This may be particularly problematic because of the centrality of religion in Arab communities (Abu-Raiya & Pargament, 2010). Organizations such as ACCESS in Dearborn, Michigan, are working closely with religious leaders to address very sensitive issues such as domestic violence and substance abuse. Clients may benefit from being connected to community and religious leaders, such as imams, who may provide guidance and support during this process by speaking authoritatively about the impermissibility of any form of domestic abuse according to religious teachings. The social worker should make referrals to Arab American community centers and organizations such as ACCESS or AccessCAL that serve to minimize the culture gap (Haboush & Alyan, 2013). However, the culturally responsive social worker should be mindful of the limits of community collaboration. Breaches in confidentiality may elicit a strong sense of shame and dishonor in the client and may result in his or her alienation from the community (Haboush & Alyan, 2013). Thus, before engagement, social workers should discuss with the client the risks and benefits of collaboration.

Third, attention should be given to the assessment of the premigration experiences of refugees and undocumented immigrants since those experiences may influence the therapeutic process. For example, Arab immigrants tend to demonstrate passive behaviors toward authority figures, and these often present in the therapeutic relationship (Al-Krenawi & Graham, 2000; Haboush, 2007). Such passivity may be attributed to conditioning as a result of cultural norms such as collectivism or a perceived loss of agency because of government control (Haboush, 2007). When such passivity is detected, social workers should be mindful that it may not necessarily be an indicator of resistance to treatment (Al-Krenawi & Graham, 2000). Furthermore, the responsive practitioner may assume a more active role in the helping process in response to such passivity (Haboush, 2007). The client therefore can be empowered to engage and actively participate in the treatment by following directives (Al-Krenawi & Graham, 2000). Indeed, research indicates that Arab clients have more success with treatment that is explanatory and instructional in nature (Al-Krenawi & Graham, 2000).

An essential component of the explanatory-instructional model of helping is the provision of information and guidance (Al-Krenawi & Graham, 2000). This function is especially important in orienting newly arrived immigrants to the helping systems. As an example, cultural notions of time are more fluid and less structured than most American helping professionals can accommodate (Al-Krenawi & Graham, 2000; Haboush, 2007). Thus, the social worker should work to educate Arab clients on the importance of meeting deadlines and being on time to appointments (Haboush, 2007). Further, many refugees experience difficulties understanding their rights and navigating through the systems of care (Ziegahn et al., 2013). Social workers can be instrumental in empowering Arab clients to learn these systems and their rights within them. Just as important is the sensitivity that must be shown toward undocumented immigrants since they may demure from ever seeking professional help because of cultural factors and their status.

In considering preimmigration factors, social workers should be mindful of the implications of trauma on the individual and the family system. Haboush (2007) indicates that Arabs displaced by the Gulf and Iraq wars are the most represented in the latest wave of immigrants. Thus, there is a high probability of exposure to trauma among this population. Moreover, in the case of refugee families, it is likely that they immigrated as a response to traumatic events (Haboush, 2007; McBrien, 2005). As such, it is essential that the social worker conduct a trauma assessment for individuals from Middle Eastern countries afflicted by war. However, social workers should be mindful that because of the influence of cultural traditions that discourage verbal displays of emotion, trauma may manifest as somatic complaints (El-Islam, 2008; Haboush, 2007). El-Islam (2008) provides two recommendations in serving Arabs that present with psychosomatic complaints. First, health professionals should listen for complaints of "chest tightness or 'heartache'" as possible indicators of psychological distress (El-Islam, 2008, p. 677). Second, service providers should work collaboratively with medical professionals to maintain the integrity of the individual and to promote health outcomes (El-Islam, 2008).

In children, intrusive thoughts and images of traumatic events may display as attention deficits (Haboush, 2007). Further, trauma symptoms may be exacerbated by social isolation and victimization in the school setting (McBrien, 2005). In fact, the synergy of trauma and postmigration stressors is attributed to accelerated school dropout rates in Middle Eastern children (McBrien, 2005). Thus, school social work is essential in identifying children who are at risk of developing trauma symptoms and in implementing appropriate interventions. Social workers should also be mindful that, although the assessment at the individual level is essential, trauma is not just a personal problem; it affects the whole family system. In parents, exposure to trauma may hinder their ability to provide emotional and social support to the child (McBrien, 2005). To address the complex needs of the family affected by trauma, a collaborative approach across systems may help optimize treatment outcomes.

Fourth, another dimension of culturally responsive services is the attention that must be given to the gender dynamics between the client and the social worker. As discussed earlier, gender roles are grounded in religious doctrine, and although there are no explicit restrictions against opposite-gender client relationships, they can be impractical (Al-Krenawi & Graham, 2000). For instance, a male client of Arab descent may find it difficult to take directives from a female social worker (Al-Krenawi & Graham, 2000). However, Arab respect for authority may open the door for a helping relationship (Haboush, 2007). Thus, it would behoove the female social worker to spend additional time developing a rapport with the male client and establishing herself as an authority in the field. On the other hand, a male social worker working with a female Arab client should maintain appropriate physical distance to avoid perceptions of impropriety

(Al-Krenawi & Graham, 2000). Moreover, male practitioners should avoid physical contact with female clients and should maintain minimal eye contact (Haboush, 2007). In addition to practitioner–client dynamics, in regard to working with families, the social worker should be respectful of power hierarchies and defer to a family spokesperson when appropriate (Aboul-Enein & Aboul-Enein, 2010). The spokesperson is frequently the father (Haboush, 2007). By paying homage to power hierarchies, the practitioner may diffuse tension and build trust with the client (Aboul-Enein & Aboul-Enein, 2010).

COLLABORATIONS ACROSS SYSTEMS

Social work practice with Arab children and families is most effective when the practitioner is deliberate in transcending system boundaries to access a broad range of resources. However, as elaborated on in more detail in earlier sections on cultural values, challenges to involvement across systems, and culturally responsive strategies, literature on improving the quality of health and human services for Arab immigrants and refugees has only recently emerged. Included in this section is information about the importance of collaborations across systems for this population and a case example of effective collaboration to serve vulnerable populations such as the children of refugees.

IMPORTANCE OF COLLABORATION ACROSS SYSTEMS FOR ARAB IMMIGRANTS AND REFUGEES

Especially for those Middle Easterners who flee their homelands to escape the devastation and destruction of war, there are prevailing concerns about physical and mental health. Impacted by the loss of loved ones and having witnessed or been victims of violence, torture, or rape, some Arabs may be unable to function in activities of daily living. Even Arab immigrants who have arrived in the United States voluntarily and with documentation could succumb to mental illness and other related issues because of the intense scrutiny and backlash against Arabs following the attacks of September 11, 2001. Hashad chronicled the impact of the societal backlash coupled with government actions, noting that "for every day that has passed since 9/11, there are dozens of painful stories borne of government-instituted discrimination and racist implementation of policy" (Hashad, 2003, p. 735). Care providers should be intentional in their interactions with such clients, making sure to use the assessment phase to dig deeper for the real source of issues. Stewart (2013) cites the importance of collaboration across systems, especially for youths of various racial and ethnic backgrounds who have experienced trauma. He states:

> Cross-system collaboration enhances the strengths of partnering agencies/ programs to promote a continuous system of services for youth and families. There is a strong connection between trauma and the need for cross-system collaboration, in that a large percentage of youth involved with any system of care has experienced some degree of trauma. (Stewart, 2013, p. 1)

Given their proclivity toward nondisclosure, especially regarding issues related to mental health, there is a greater likelihood that Middle Eastern clients of all ages may vaguely complain about physical ailments to family and friends, even when expectations of privacy are limited at best. For example, it would not be uncommon for individuals to experience panic attacks, anxiety, depression, and paranoia but lack the language to describe such mental states (Aboul-Enein & Aboul-Enein, 2010). If an Arab client did present with physical symptoms in the hospital, it would be efficacious to supplement the medical assessment team with representatives of other systems, such as social workers and religious leaders, with at least one of the latter two being able to speak Arabic.

CASE STUDY

Collaboration Across Systems: An Iraqi Refugee Child with PTSD

Although any age group could be the subject of a case study of effective collaboration across systems, the focus in this case is on an Iraqi refugee child presenting with symptoms of posttraumatic stress disorder (PTSD). As elaborated further in the example, an effective intervention consists in this case of collaboration between the school system (teacher), the behavioral health system (social worker), the child welfare system, and the juvenile justice system. Ammar is a 10-year-old Iraqi boy in the fifth grade at a local public school. Ammar was referred to the school social worker by his classroom teacher because he was having academic problems. The teacher reported that Ammar was exhibiting difficulty concentrating on his studies and completing assignments in a timely manner. She noted that he often appeared to be daydreaming in class and is startled when she approaches him. In several instances, Ammar has struck his class-mates, claiming self-defense. He has been reprimanded at school and even threatened with being referred to the juvenile justice system if he resorts to violence, but he seems unfazed by these threats. School records indicate that Ammar was placed with the school last year by a local refugee and immigrant resettlement program. He lives with his mother and father. Appreciating the pa-triarchal nature of Arab families, the social worker calls Ammar's home and speaks with his father. Because Arab families tend to respond well to home vis-its, the social worker schedules to meet with the family at their home to discuss Ammar's progress in school (Nassar-McMillan & Hakim-Larson, 2003). Thank-fully, during the weeks it takes the social worker to set up the home visit, Ammar has had no new incidents of violent outbursts. Depending on the conditions at home, the social worker knows she needs to be prepared for the possible involve-ment of the child welfare system.

At the home, the social worker is greeted by Ammar's father, who subse-quently introduces the social worker to his wife as Ammar's mother. The social worker is mindful that Arab families are traditionally hospitable and prefer to warm up to serious conversations (Aboul-Enein & Aboul-Enein, 2010). Thus, the social worker engages in light conversation, paying respect to the father as the head of the household. When the social worker feels that the parents are ready to talk about more serious matters, she addresses the father. Assuming a strengths perspective, she starts by acknowledging Ammar's accomplishments. Then, she frames the presenting problem from a pragmatic perspective, focus-ing on Ammar's academic performance. She echoes verbally the family's high regard for education and states a desire to work collaboratively with them to en-sure Ammar's success in school. When she hints at Ammar's mood swings and violent interactions with fellow students, the parents become defensive and at-tribute the incidents to misunderstandings. Ultimately, the parents are agree-able to receiving services and making arrangements for Ammar to meet with the social worker at the school. The social worker seeks to engage the family in the helping process, as Arabs tend to assume a more passive role with authority figures (Al-Krenawi & Graham, 2000; Haboush, 2007). Thus, the social worker extends an invitation to the parents to be present for some portion of the meeting. This alliance with the parents may also help to redress the cultural aversion for emotional disclosures and encourage Ammar to open up to the social worker (Al-Krenawi & Graham, 2000; Haboush, 2007). The ultimate goal of the social worker, hopefully with the support of his family, is to assemble a team representative of the various systems to track Ammar's path to full recovery from the trauma symptoms. There is evidence to show that in order "to address the underutilization of mental health services by immigrant children and certain minority groups, some initiatives aimed at providing clinical services through the school have been put forward" (Rousseau & Guzder, 2008, p. 543).

CONCLUSION

The steady increase in the population of Middle Eastern immigrants and refugees in the United States presents a tremendous opportunity for social work students, educators, researchers, and practitioners to anticipate and plan for the delivery of culturally responsive health and mental health services. Understanding Middle Eastern cultural values is imperative to ensuring that the highest-quality interventions and services are provided to this population. As this chapter makes explicit, it is not always the case that differences in the U.S. and Middle Eastern value systems will give rise to conflicts. Separating the perception of conflict from reality will involve the establishment of a rapport and trust between the practitioner and the client early in the relationship-building phase. The complex challenges Middle Eastern clients are likely to face during the acculturation process could permeate various health and human service systems that clients have to navigate on their own. Challenges related to cross-system involvement not only can be mitigated but also can be transformed into opportunities for improvement in practice with this population, as the following recommendations illustrate.

RECOMMENDATIONS FOR IMPROVING PRACTICE WITH
MIDDLE EASTERN CHILDREN AND FAMILIES

1   Not all Arabs are Muslims, and not all Muslims are Arabs, so the practitioner should assess whether religion and spirituality matter to a particular

Arab client and, if so, with which religion or spiritual tradition the client self-identifies.

2 Even as the collectivistic context is being emphasized, there is an increasing awareness that there must be a balance between unbending collectivism on the one hand and Western-style individualism on the other hand.

3 Social workers should also appreciate the almost uncompromising extent to which the preservation of family stability, honor, and cohesiveness is embedded in the collectivistic outlook (Haboush, 2007).

4 Social work practice with Middle Eastern immigrant and refugee children and families is most effective when the practitioner is deliberate in transcending system boundaries to access a broad range of resources.

5 Cultural brokers are critically important within the child welfare system to interpret and shed light on the sociocultural basis of Arab child-rearing practices.

6 It is imperative that social workers ensure that the development of interventions and services is informed by the cultural values and norms of the Arab community.

7 Concerted attention should be given to the assessment of the premigration experiences of refugees and undocumented immigrants in particular since those experiences may influence the therapeutic process.

8 It is essential that the social worker conduct a trauma assessment for individuals from Middle Eastern countries afflicted by war.

9 Middle Eastern men value expertise and specialized training, so extra time should be allocated for the female social worker to help the client admit the presenting challenge while also disclosing to him in a systematic manner why she is the person best trained and qualified to assist him.

10 Aspects of appropriate interactions for a client–social worker dyad of the opposite gender should include minimal eye contact, maintaining appropriate physical distance between the client and social worker, and integrating the family in as many of the stages of treatment as possible.

KEY TERMS

ALHAMDULILLAH Praise God.

COLLECTIVISM A cultural norm of showing preference for the good of the family or larger community over one's personal goals.

EVIL EYE The belief that good fortune may invoke jealousy in others, which gives the individual the power to inflict misfortune on the recipient.

HIJAB Traditional headdress worn by Islamic women in allegiance with cultural principles of modesty.

IMAM Islamic religious leader.

IMMIGRATION AND NATURALIZATION SERVICE SPECIAL REGISTRATION PROGRAM A component of the National Security Entry-Exit Registration System instituted by Attorney General John Ashcroft that requires call-in registration of Middle Eastern immigrants from Iran, Iraq, Libya, Syria, and Sudan.

INSHA'ALLAH God willing.

JINN Islamic folklore that attributes misfortune and illness to demons.

MADHAHIB Islamic theological schools of thought.

QADR ALLAH What God has predestined to occur.

SHUKR LILLAH Thank God.

STUDY QUESTIONS

1 What countries comprise the Middle East?
2 Why are psychosomatic symptoms more prevalent in individuals of Middle Eastern descent?
3 Describe the within-group diversity of Arab Americans.
4 What considerations must be given to the provision of treatment to Arab immigrants and refugees with regard to gender interaction?
5 How are recent Middle Eastern immigrants distinguished from earlier waves of immigrants?
6 What possible conflicts in cultural values exist between Middle Eastern and U.S. value systems?

ADDITIONAL RESOURCES

The following organizations serve Middle Eastern immigrants and refugees:

ACCESS: https://www.accesscommunity.org
Access California Services: http://www.accesscal.org/
American-Arab Anti-discrimination Committee: http://www.adc.org/
Arab-American Family Support Center of New York: http://www.aafscny.org

Arab American Institute: http://www.aaiusa.org/

Arab American Museum in Dearborn, MI: http://www
.arabamericanmuseum.org

National Network for Arab American Communities (NNAC): http://www
.nnaac.org

REFERENCES

Aboul-Enein, B. H., & Aboul-Enein, F. H. (2010). The cultural gap delivering health services to Arab-American populations in the United States. *Journal of Cultural Diversity, 17*(1), 20–23.

Abu-Raiya, H., & Pargament, K. I. (2010). Religiously integrated psychotherapy with Muslim clients: From research to practice. *Professional Psychology: Research and Practice, 41*(2), 181–188.

Abu-Ras, W. (2007). Cultural beliefs and service utilization by battered Arab immigrant women. *Violence Against Women, 13*(10), 1002–1028.

Abu-Ras, W., & Abu-Bader, S. H. (2008). The impact of the September 11, 2001, attacks on the well-being of Arab Americans in New York City. *Journal of Muslim Mental Health, 3*(2), 217–239.

Al-Hazza, T., & Lucking, B. (2005). The minority of suspicion: Arab Americans. *Multicultural Review, 14*(3), 32–38.

Al-Krenawi, A., & Graham, J. (2000). Culturally sensitive social work practice with Arab clients in mental health settings. *Health & Social Work, 25*(1), 9–22.

Aloud, N., & Rathur, A. (2009). Factors affecting attitudes toward seeking and using formal mental health and psychological services among Arab Muslim populations. *Journal of Muslim Mental Health, 4*(2), 79–103.

Arab American Institute Foundation. (2012). *Demographics.* Washington, DC: Author. Retrieved from http://b.3cdn.net/aai/44b17815d8b386bf16_vom6iv4b5
.pdf

Auclair, G., & Batalova, J. (2013). *Middle Eastern and North African immigrants in the United States.* Retrieved from http://www.migrationpolicy.org/article
/middle-eastern-and-north-african-immigrants-united-states

Brittingham, A., & De La Cruz, G. P. (2005). *We the people of Arab ancestry in the United States.* Washington, DC: U.S. Census Bureau.

Cainkar, L. (2003). Targeting Muslims, at Ashcroft's discretion. *Middle East Report Online.* Retrieved from http://epublications.marquette.edu/cgi/viewcontent.cgi
?date=1274716576&article=1014&conte t=socs_fac&preview_mode=

——. (2006). The social construction of difference and the Arab American experience. *Journal of American Ethnic History, 25*(2–3), 243–278.

Churgin, M. J. (1996). Mass exoduses: The response of the United States. *International Migration Review, 30*(1), 310–324.

David, G. C., & Ayouby, K. K. (2005). Studying the exotic other in the classroom: The portrayal of Arab Americans in educational source materials. *Multicultural Perspectives, 7*(4), 13–20.

Diouf, S. A. (1998). *Servants of Allah: African Muslims enslaved in the Americas.* New York: New York University Press.

El-Islam, M. F. (2008). Arab culture and mental health care. *Transcultural Psychiatry, 45*(4), 671–682.

Erickson, C. D., & Al-Timimi, N. R. (2004). Counseling and psychotherapy with Arab American clients. In T. B. Smith (Ed.), *Practicing multiculturalism: Affirming diversity in counseling and psychology* (pp. 234–254). Boston, MA: Allyn & Bacon.

Haboush, K. L. (2007). Working with Arab American families: Culturally competent practices for school psychologists. *Psychology in the Schools, 44*(2), 183–198.

Haboush, K. L., & Alyan, H. (2013). "Who can you tell?" Features of Arab culture that influence conceptualization and treatment of childhood sexual abuse. *Journal of Child Sexual Abuse, 22*(5), 499–518.

Haddad, Y. Y. (2004). *Not quite American? The shaping of Arab and Muslim identity in the United States* (Edmundson Lecture Series, Vol. 26). Waco, TX: Baylor University Press.

Hall, J. (2004). The treatment of asylum seekers and migrants in the context of the global "war on terror." In *Proceedings of the Annual Meeting (American Society of International Law), 98*, 258–260.

Handlin, O. (1951). *The uprooted.* New York: Grosset and Dunlap.

Hashad, D. (2003). Stolen freedoms: Arabs, Muslims, and South Asians in the wake of post 9/11 backlash. *Denver University Law Review, 81*(4), 735–747.

Hodge, D. R. (2011). Using spiritual interventions in practice: Developing some guidelines from evidence-based practice. *Social Work, 56*(2), 149–158.

Husain, A., & Ross-Sheriff, F. (2010). Cultural competence with Muslim Americans. In D. Lum (Ed.), *Culturally competent practice: A framework for understanding diverse groups and justice issues* (4th ed., pp. 358–389). Belmont, CA: Brooks/Cole.

Kindergarten, A. (2006, September 16). Clifton social services center to reach out to Arab-Americans; Tanweer to focus on mental health. *The Record* (Bergen County, NJ). Retrieved from www.lexisnexis.com/hottopics/lnacademic

Kohls, L. R. (1988). *The values Americans live by*. San Francisco, CA: San Francisco State University. Retrieved from http://www.uri.edu/mind/VALUES2.pdf

Marvasti, A. B., & McKinney, K. D. (2004). *Middle Eastern lives in America*. Lanham, MD: Rowman & Littlefield.

McBrien, J. L. (2005). Educational needs and barriers for refugee students in the United States: A review of the literature. *Review of Educational Research*, *75*(3), 329–364.

Naber, N. C. (2008). Introduction: Arab Americans and US racial formations. In A. A. Jamal & N. C. Naber (Eds.), *Race and Arab Americans before and after 9/11: From invisible citizens to visible subjects* (pp. 1–45). Syracuse, NY: Syracuse University Press.

Nassar-McMillan, S. C., & Hakim-Larson, J. (2003). Counseling considerations among Arab Americans. *Journal of Counseling & Development*, *81*(2), 150–159.

Nobles, A. Y., & Sciarra, D. T. (2000). Cultural determinants in the treatment of Arab Americans: A primer for mainstream therapists. *American Journal of Orthopsychiatry*, *70*(2), 182–191.

O'Donnell, K., & Newland, K. (2008). *The Iraqi refugee crisis: The need for action*. Washington, DC: Migration Policy Institute.

Rejeske, J., Gonzales, S., & Schwartz, S. (2014). *Overview of immigrant eligibility policies for health insurance affordability programs*. Retrieved from http://www.nilc.org/document.html?id=1138

Rousseau, C., & Guzder, J. (2008). School-based prevention programs for refugee children. *Child and Adolescent Psychiatric Clinics of North America*, *17*(3), 533–549.

Shenhav, Y. A. (2006). *The Arab Jews: A postcolonial reading of nationalism, religion, and ethnicity*. Redwood City, CA: Stanford University Press.

Stewart, M. (2013). *Cross-system collaboration*. Los Angeles, CA: National Center for Child Traumatic Stress.

Suleiman, M. F. (1996). *Educating the Arab American child: Implications for teachers*. Washington, DC: Education Resources Information Center, Department of Education. Retrieved from http://files.eric.ed.gov/fulltext/ED392864.pdf

U.S. Bureau of the Census. (2010). *American community survey*. Washington, DC: Author.

——. (2015). *State and county quickfacts*. Washington, DC: Author. Retrieved from http://quickfacts.census.gov/qfd/meta/long_RHI125213.htm

U.S. Department of State. (2012). *Number of visa issuances and adjustments of status in the diversity immigrant category.* Retrieved from http://travel.state.gov /content/dam/visas/Diversity-Visa/DV-Instructions-Translations/DV-2014 -Instructions-Translations/FY12AnnualReport-TableVII.pdf

Velazquez, S. C., & Dettlaff, A. J. (2011). Immigrant children and child welfare in the United States: Demographics, legislation, research, policy, and practice impacting public services. *Child Indicators Research, 4*(4), 679–695.

Ziegahn, I., Ibrahim, S., Al-Ansari, B., Mahmood, M., Tawffeq, R., Mughir, M., Hassan, N., DeBondt, D., Mendez, L., Maynes, E., Aguilar-Gaxiola, S., & Xiong, G. (2013). *The mental and physical health of recent Iraqi refugees in Sacramento, California.* UC Davis Clinical and Translational Science Center. Sacramento, CA: University of California- Davis.

Zolberg, A. R., & Woon, L. L. (1999). Why Islam is like Spanish: Cultural incorporation in Europe and the United States. *Politics and Society, 27*(1), 5–38.

PART 3

Practice with Immigrant and Refugee Children and Families Across Systems

Practice with Immigrant and Refugee Children and Families in the Child Welfare System

▸ ALAN J. DETTLAFF *and* ROWENA FONG

THROUGHOUT THE HISTORY of the United States, the child welfare system has evolved according to changing beliefs and attitudes about the role that government should play when children's parents are unable to provide appropriate care for them. Early interventions by the government on behalf of children needing care were centered primarily on meeting the physical needs of children who were orphaned or homeless. However, as public awareness of child maltreatment and the damage it caused grew, the importance of protecting children from abuse and neglect received greater attention by state and federal governments. As awareness grew, the first state laws to protect children from abuse and neglect were passed in the early 1900s, and the Social Security Act of 1935 authorized the first federal funding for child welfare services. Over the next several decades, the definition of child welfare services, which had historically focused solely on the placement of children in foster homes in response to abuse or neglect, was expanded to include a broader range of services, including the prevention of maltreatment.

The current service array offered by the child welfare system is designed to ensure the safety, permanency, and well-being of children who come to the attention of this system following abuse or neglect. Services range from the investigation of child maltreatment to family preservation, out-of-home care, specialized foster care, and adoption of children. Downs, Moore, McFadden, and Costin (2008) identify four primary groups of services provided to children and families by the child welfare system: (1) protective services, which focus on the investigation of suspected maltreatment to assure a child's safety and improve family functioning to prevent removal from the home; (2) supportive services, which include programs that focus on preventing maltreatment and strengthening families' abilities to provide adequate care of their children; (3) foster care services, which are designed to assist families in resolving issues of safety following removal from the home so that children can be reunited with their families as quickly as possible; and (4) adoption services, which focus on providing a permanent home for children when parents have relinquished their rights to the child or the court has terminated parental rights.

The goal of these child welfare services is to ensure children's safety, to provide children with permanent homes, and to facilitate positive outcomes in areas of well-being that include children's physical health, mental health, and educational needs. Yet, despite the limited body of knowledge examining the experiences of immigrant and refugee children and families involved in this system, it is clear that immigrant and refugee families face a number of challenges that may impede service delivery and the achievement of positive outcomes in the areas of safety, permanency, and well-being, particularly when it is necessary for children to enter substitute care. For example, although all children are eligible for child welfare services regardless of their citizenship status, many children live in mixed-status families, where the children are U.S.-born citizens but one or both parents are undocumented immigrants. When parents are undocumented, this may impact their access to and receipt of services necessary to resolve the issues leading to their involvement with the child welfare system. Children who are undocumented are eligible for foster care services and may also be eligible for Special Immigrant Juvenile Status (SIJS), which was created by Congress in 1990 as a legal remedy for undocumented children who are juvenile court dependents as a result of abuse, abandonment, or neglect. However, this remedy can only be sought once a court has found that reunification with one or both parents is not possible, which may impact the process of permanency planning for undocumented children.

This chapter will address the population of immigrant and refugee children and families involved in the child welfare system, the growing awareness of their unique needs, efforts to address these needs, barriers to system change, cross-system efforts to respond to this population, and future directions for promoting positive outcomes for immigrant and refugee children and families involved in the child welfare system.

IMMIGRANT AND REFUGEE CHILDREN AND FAMILIES
IN THE CHILD WELFARE SYSTEM

Data on the involvement of immigrant and refugee children and families involved in the child welfare system have historically been limited, as these data have not been collected uniformly by any national or state child welfare reporting system. This has resulted in a limited ability to determine the extent to which immigrant children and families become involved in this system, as well as the extent of their risk exposure and experience of child maltreatment. However, following the completion of the first national study of children who come to the attention of the child welfare system, the National Survey of Child and Adolescent Well-being (NSCAW), some light has been shed on immigrant children and families' experiences with this system, as NSCAW collected information on parent and child nativity. In the first study to examine the involvement of immigrant children and families in the child welfare system, Dettlaff and Earner (2012) found that children living with at least one foreign-born parent comprised 8.6 percent of all children who come to the attention of the child welfare system in the United States. This suggests that children of immigrants are considerably underrepresented among children who become involved with the child welfare system, given that children with at least one foreign-born parent represent nearly 23 percent of the total child population in the United States. More than two thirds (67.2 percent) of children of immigrants involved in the child welfare system are Hispanic, followed by non-Hispanic white (14.8 percent), non-Hispanic black (10 percent), and non-Hispanic Asian (7.5 percent). Consistent with the national population of children of immigrants, more than four out of five (82.5 percent) children of immigrants involved in the child welfare system are U.S.-born citizens.

Although this study provided the first national data available on the presence of foreign-born families in the child welfare system, a limitation remains that the proportion of these families who are refugees cannot be determined. Although it is likely that refugee families comprise a portion of the foreign-born families served by child welfare agencies, data to support this remain unavailable. As a result, the unique differences between immigrant families and refugee families cannot be determined.

UNACCOMPANIED REFUGEE MINORS AND THE OFFICE
OF REFUGEE RESETTLEMENT

Unaccompanied refugee minors are children under 18 who are identified by the State Department as eligible for resettlement in the United States but do not have a parent available to provide for them. These children are placed in the Office of Refugee Resettlement's Unaccompanied Refugee Minors (URM) program and receive foster care services. Because "refugee" is a legal status, unaccompanied refugee minors enter the United States legally and can apply for permanent residence within one year and citizenship within five years. Since the URM program was established in the early 1980s, nearly 13,000 refugee minors have entered the program. Currently, approximately 700 minors are in the care of the program. The majority of these children are placed in licensed foster homes, although they may also be placed in specialized foster care sites, including therapeutic foster homes or group homes. The goal of the URM program is to assist these youths in developing the skills necessary to enter adulthood and achieve independence. Therefore, URMs are eligible for all of the services that are available to all foster children in the state in which they reside, including housing, food, clothing, and medical care; independent living skills training; mental health services; English-language training; and educational and career counseling. Although the goal of the URM program is to transition unaccompanied refugee minors to independence, these minors may also be reunited with their parents or placed with other appropriate relatives if this is determined to be in the minor's best interests.

Maltreatment Patterns Among Immigrant Families

In addition to identifying the presence of immigrant children and families involved in the child welfare system, several studies have used data from NSCAW to examine the maltreatment patterns and risk factors among children in immigrant families, as well as how they differ from those of children in U.S.-born families. The study by Dettlaff and Earner (2012) found no significant differences in overall rates of maltreatment between children with immigrant parents and children with U.S.-born parents. However, children of immigrants were found to be more likely than children of U.S.-born parents to experience emotional abuse. Although definitions of emotional abuse vary widely across states, this could be the result of cultural differences in parenting styles or expectations among some immigrants that may be considered inappropriate by child welfare caseworkers unfamiliar with diverse cultures. For example, research indicates that children in Mexican immigrant families often hold significant responsibilities, including performing basic household tasks, caring for younger siblings, and providing financial support (Orellana, 2001). Supporting such practices may be viewed by some as having inappropriate developmental expectations and as being emotionally harmful to children (Jambunathan, Burts, & Pierce, 2000).

Studies have also shown that children of immigrants from certain racial or ethnic backgrounds may be vulnerable to specific types of maltreatment. For example, Dettlaff, Earner, and Phillips (2009) found that Latino children of immigrants were more than 5 times more likely to experience sexual abuse compared with Latino children of U.S.-born parents. Chang, Rhee, and Weaver (2006) found that children in immigrant Korean families were more likely to come to the attention of the California child welfare system for physical abuse compared with children in other ethnic groups. Similarly, Rhee, Chang, Weaver, and Wong (2008) found that children in immigrant Chinese families were more likely to experience physical abuse compared with the general child welfare population. Yet, although these studies have begun to shed light on the unique maltreatment patterns and experiences among children in immigrant families, it is important to caution that much additional research is still needed to fully understand these patterns and draw accurate conclusions.

The need for more research also applies to refugee children and families. Studies have reported maltreatment occurring in refugee camps and during migration journeys to the United States. This can have lingering effects, which social workers in public child welfare systems need to consider in their assessments (Dumbrill, 2008; Mason & Pulvirenti, 2013; Schmidt, 2006). Thus, child welfare caseworkers need to understand the context of the migration journey and its impact on the parenting practices of refugees when they settle in the United States. Concerns about adjusting discipline practices (Dumbrill, 2008) have caused refugee parents to work with public child welfare workers to better understand their settlement challenges and to develop child welfare policies and services that better fit refugee needs and adjustments.

Risk Exposure Among Children in Immigrant Families

Although most studies examining immigrant children's involvement with the child welfare system have focused on identifying patterns of maltreatment, a small number of studies have examined the risk factors associated with maltreatment among these families. These studies have consistently found that risk factors are more likely to be present in families with U.S.-born parents than in those with immigrant parents. Using data from NSCAW, Dettlaff and Earner (2012) found that U.S.-born parents were 3 times more likely than immigrant parents to be actively abusing alcohol or drugs and were significantly more likely to have a physical or cognitive impairment or recent history of arrests. Notably, the researchers found no significant differences in the prevalence of several risk factors often associated with immigrant families, including the use of excessive discipline, active domestic violence, low social support, and difficulty meeting their family's basic needs. Subsequently, a small number of studies have produced consistent findings concerning the presence of risk. Dettlaff and Johnson (2011) used the NSCAW data to examine differences in maltreatment patterns and risk based on the *child's* nativity and found that U.S.-born Latino children were significantly more likely to be living in homes with active alcohol and drug abuse, active domestic violence, and a recent history of parental arrest. In another recent study, Johnson-Motoyama, Dettlaff, and Finno (2012) found that Latino children with U.S.-born parents were significantly more likely to be living in homes with active alcohol and drug abuse, recent history of parental arrest, history of maltreatment of the primary caregiver, and family difficulty meeting basic needs when compared with Latino children with foreign-born parents *and* Latino children with parents of mixed nativity (one U.S.-born and one foreign-born parent).

Placement Experiences of Children in Immigrant Families

Because of very limited data, little is known about the placement patterns of children in immigrant families and how they may differ from those of children in U.S.-born families. One study examining Latino children involved in the Texas child welfare system found that immigrant children and children of immigrants were significantly less likely than children of U.S.-born parents to be placed with relatives, and that immigrant children were more likely than other children to be placed in group homes and institutions. Additionally, immigrant children were less likely than U.S.-born children to have case goals of reunification or adoption by relatives and were more likely to have goals of long-term foster care or independent living (Vericker, Kuehn, & Capps, 2007). These findings raise concerns, given the previously cited research that demonstrated lower rates of risk exposure among immigrant families, which raises the possibility that issues such as immigration status or biases against immigrant families may be interfering with decisions made by child welfare professionals. However, much additional research is needed to understand why these differences exist and to determine whether these patterns hold true in other jurisdictions.

UNIQUE NEEDS OF IMMIGRANT AND REFUGEE CHILDREN AND FAMILIES IN THE SYSTEM

Children in immigrant and refugee families have historically been considered at increased risk for maltreatment as a result of the challenges experienced by their families following immigration (Earner, 2007; Roer-Strier, 2001; Segal & Mayadas, 2005). Research on families' experiences following immigration cites several sources of risk, including financial challenges, loneliness, isolation, language difficulties, fear, and hopelessness (Earner, 2007; Finno, Vidal de Haymes, & Mindell, 2006; Maiter, Stalker, & Alaggia, 2009). Many of these challenges are also factors associated with child maltreatment (Cadzow, Armstrong, & Fraser, 1999; Miller, Fox, & Garcia-Beckwith, 1999). Additional pressures resulting from acculturation can lead to a variety of strains on family systems, as parents and children experience changing cultural contexts along with the loss of previously established support systems (Finno et al., 2006; Rumbaut, 1999). Combined with possible cultural differences in parenting styles and expectations (Jambunathan et al., 2000; Mendez, 2006), as well as in child discipline (Fontes, 2002; Newell, 2002), these factors can affect the safety and well-being of children in immigrant families. As a result, professionals working with children involved in this system need to understand the impact that immigration and acculturation have on immigrant families to provide services that adequately respond to these underlying issues.

THE MIGRATION EXPERIENCE

Beginning with the migration process, immigrant families experience numerous challenges that may affect their ability to function, meet the needs of their children, and provide for their safety and well-being. Although circumstances leading to immigration vary among families, most families choose to migrate because the financial or political situation in their own country has left them with no other option (Segal & Mayadas, 2005). For families living in poverty in their country of origin, the decision to migrate is often based on financial necessity, with families migrating in search of greater wages and increased job opportunities in order to improve the living conditions of the family (Jennissen, 2007). Migration often occurs in several phases, resulting in extended periods of separation between children and their parents, as well as between spouses and sibling groups. For undocumented immigrants, the process of entering the United States can be considerably dangerous, with some experiencing violence, robbery, and sexual assault (Espin, 1987; Solis, 2003). The stress associated with this initial transition period may result in depression or anxiety, and individuals who experience significant trauma during migration may develop symptoms of posttraumatic stress disorder (Finno et al., 2006).

This experience differs for refugees, who flee their countries of origin because of persecution and do not have the option of returning to their homelands. Within this category of refugees are asylees—individuals who are legally permitted to enter a host country but, once admitted, change their request to seek permanent residence and asylum in the host country. Refugees and asylees may be looking for refuge from their home countries because of threats of persecution and torture for political reasons, racial discrimination, or economic oppression. Since 1975, the United States has resettled more than 3 million refugees from all over the world and in all 50 states (U.S. Department of State, 2013). Cross-system services are required for this trauma-driven population because critical health and legal services are necessary during the initial period of resettlement and culturally responsive mental health services are necessary for the transitioning of refugee children and families as they adapt to the United States.

ACCULTURATION AND ACCULTURATIVE STRESS

The process of acculturation refers to the internal process of change experienced by all immigrants and refugees upon exposure to a new culture (Dumbrill, 2008; Padilla & Perez, 2003; Schmidt, 2006). Early theoretical literature suggested that acculturation occurs when individuals from one culture are continuously exposed to another culture, with this exposure resulting in changes to the original cultural and behavioral patterns of the group (Redfield, Linton, & Herskovits, 1936). Later theorists explored the psychological processes involved in acculturation, describing it as a process involving not only behavioral changes but also changes to value systems, developmental processes, and cultural norms. How individuals acculturate and the level to which they do so were described as being a function of the value systems, roles, personality styles, and developmental processes of the individual (Furuto, 2004; Social Science Research Council, 1954; Teske & Nelson, 1974). These later conceptualizations were important to the understanding of acculturation as the inclusion of value systems, roles, and cultural norms, suggesting that the process of acculturation might differ among populations as a result of cultural differences. Current literature suggests that acculturation is a complex process that is dependent on a multitude of individual and cultural factors, including ethnicity, gender, age, religious beliefs, family structure, language, and personality (Fong, 2004; Furuto, 2004; Padilla & Perez, 2003).

Acculturative stress is distinct from acculturation and refers to the stress that results directly from the acculturative process (Berry, Kim, Minde, & Mok, 1987; Fong, 2004). Upon migration, individuals are faced with a multitude of challenges as they attempt to navigate the new culture. Acculturative stress results when individuals lack the means to interact and be successful in the new environment (Berry et al., 1987). For many immigrants, the acculturative stress experienced following migration is lifelong, pervasive, and intense (Smart & Smart, 1995). Although acculturative stress among all immigrants and refugees is supported in the literature, this literature suggests that acculturation is more difficult for those immigrants and refugees who are more distinct from the host culture in factors such as ethnicity, religion, and language (Leon & Dziegielewski, 1999; Padilla & Perez, 2003; Zuniga, 2004). When significant differences exist between the country of origin and the host culture, the process of acculturation becomes more challenging as a result of the cultural negotiation that must occur, as these immigrants and refugees must cope with the societal standards and traditions of the new culture while making decisions about the level to which they will integrate into the host culture. For immigrants and refugees of different religious and cultural backgrounds, this often involves giving up previously valued cultural traditions or feeling pressured to accept certain changes to their traditions.

Thus, immigrants and refugees who are more distinct from the host culture in ethnicity, religion, and language are more likely to experience social discrimination and prejudice as a result of the factors that identify them as different from the majority (Fong, 2004; Padilla & Perez, 2003; Smart & Smart, 1995). Accented speech, unfamiliar customs, and differences in skin color are all factors that identify immigrants as outsiders to those in the new culture. These immigrants may experience additional stress, as members of the host culture may question their motives and limit their opportunities for involvement in the new culture (Padilla & Perez, 2003). When this occurs, some immigrants and refugees feel forced to undergo certain changes rather than choosing the level to which they acculturate, further contributing to stress.

CHANGING CULTURAL CONTEXTS

Related to acculturation and acculturative stress, changes in cultural contexts that follow migration can result in sources of family conflict that may impact children's safety and well-being. For example, following migration, cultural and financial pressures often result in changes to previously established gender roles and expectations (Coltrane, Parke, & Adams, 2004; Ross-Sheriff & Husain, 2004). Financial stressors often necessitate that women enter the workforce, which may require men to accept additional responsibilities for child care and housework (Coltrane et al., 2004). Although immigrant and refugee women who are employed in the United States generally experience greater autonomy and independence, men may experience the opposite (Pessar, 1999). Research indicates that outside employment of wives and unemployment of men are both significantly associated with domestic violence among immigrant couples (Aldarondo, Kaufman, & Jasinski, 2002; Cunradi, Caetano, & Schafer, 2002; Mason & Pulvirenti, 2013). Further, because undocumented immigrants can be deported upon arrest, many cases of domestic violence go unreported, as women are afraid of the resulting effects on the family (Aldarondo et al., 2002; Earner, 2010).

Differences in acculturation levels may also produce significant tension between parents, who adhere to traditional cultural values, and children, who adapt more rapidly to the social norms of their new cultural environment (Fontes, 2002; Quinones-Mayo & Dempsey, 2005). Increased parenting stress is common among immigrant and refugee parents, who feel they are no longer able to control their children. As parents struggle to maintain discipline, they may become more harsh and rigid in their attempts to regain authority (Bacallao & Smokowski, 2007; Dumbrill, 2008).

POVERTY AND ACCESS TO BENEFITS

Immigrant and refugee families with children are more likely than U.S.-born families to have incomes below the federal poverty level (FPL). In 2008, 21 percent of immigrant families had incomes below the FPL, compared with 15 percent of U.S.-born families (Chaudry & Fortuny, 2010). Children of immigrants also were more likely to live in low-income families (defined as family incomes less than twice the FPL). Nearly half (49 percent) of immigrant families were low income, compared with 35 percent of U.S.-born families (Chaudry & Fortuny, 2010). Overall, immigrant families are approximately 40 percent more likely than U.S.-born families to be poor or low income. However, significant differences exist among immigrant groups. European, East Asian, and Middle Eastern families have incomes 60 percent to 80 percent higher than the mean immigrant family income, whereas Mexican and Central American families have incomes significantly below the average (Chaudry & Fortuny, 2010).

Related to the overall lower rates of family income among immigrant and refugee families, children in immigrant and refugee families are at greater risk than children of U.S.-born parents for inadequate nutrition. In 2008, 25 percent of children of immigrants lived in food-insecure households, compared with 21 percent of children of U.S.-born parents. Children of immigrants are also more likely to live in crowded housing, defined as more than two people per bedroom (7 percent of children of immigrants compared with 2 percent of children of U.S.-born parents) (Chaudry & Fortuny, 2010). Yet, despite these higher rates of poverty and economic hardship, immigrant families are less likely to receive public benefits (e.g., Temporary Assistance for Needy Families [TANF], Supplemental Nutrition Assistance Program [SNAP]) (Chaudry & Fortuny, 2010), and children of immigrants are less likely than children of U.S.-born parents to have health insurance (Capps & Fortuny, 2006).

PARENTING STYLES AND EXPECTATIONS

Particularly relevant to vulnerability for contact with the child welfare system, differences in parenting styles and expectations may place children in some immigrant and refugee families at additional risk. Parenting styles are influenced by a number of factors, including culture, class, education, individual family practices, and personality. For immigrant and refugee families, parenting styles are further influenced by their level of acculturation and the unique goals and experiences of each family (Dumbrill, 2008; Mendez, 2006). Parenting styles are based on cultural practices and attitudes, such as beliefs about the value of punishment and the use of punitive disciplinary strategies to correct behavior. Although norms concerning acceptable child rearing and punishment vary by culture, a number of studies have documented the use of authoritarian parenting styles and corporal punishment as a disciplinary strategy prevalent among immigrant parents (Frias-Armenta & McCloskey, 1998; Park, 2001; Tajima & Harachi, 2010). When combined with other stressors, such as poverty and acculturative stress, this parenting style may result in harsh physical discipline that can lead to involvement with the child welfare system (Earner, 2007; Rhee et al., 2008).

PROTECTIVE FACTORS

Despite high levels of economic hardship and other risks, strengths within immigrant family systems, as well as their extended networks, may serve as buffers against some of the potential negative consequences resulting from migration. Most important among these strengths may be immigrant and refugee families' culture and connections to their countries of origin. Although learning to function in a new culture may serve as a source of stress for many immigrant and refugee families, researchers have suggested that adherence to cultural values and beliefs is a significant source of strength that allows individuals to maintain flexibility and cohesion in the face of a changing environment (Falicov, 2005; Fong, 2004; Hancock, 2005). Additional studies have found that identification with core values and beliefs rooted in their native culture may protect immigrants from experiencing many negative outcomes, including substance use and mental health problems (De La Rosa, 2002; Holleran & Waller, 2003).

The presence of two-parent households, a strength of many immigrant families, may provide a family structure that reduces the risk of involvement with the child welfare system. In studies examining the incidence of child maltreatment, children living with married biological parents have the lowest overall rates of child abuse and neglect (Sedlak et al., 2010). Children in immigrant families are considerably more likely than children with U.S.-born parents to live in two-parent households (76 percent vs. 62 percent), with children of Middle Eastern and East Asian origin having the highest rates of two-parent families, at more than 85 percent (Chaudry & Fortuny, 2010). Children in immigrant families are also more likely to live in families with three or more adults, including parents and other adult relatives. Members of the extended family serve as additional sources of support and may provide additional resources for the family system.

Immigrant and refugee families' reasons for migration may also serve as a protective factor for their children. Undertaking a long, expensive, and uncertain journey to a foreign country requires determination, strength, and a strong sense of personal and family responsibility. For many immigrant and refugee families, the desire for a better life for their children, which is often associated with their reasons for migration, can be a powerful strength and motivating factor. Additional characteristics often found in immigrant and refugee families, including strong parental supervision, religious beliefs, and supportive community networks, may serve as further protective factors (Dettlaff et al., 2009; Fong, 2004).

BARRIERS TO SYSTEM CHANGE

Once immigrant and refugee children and families become involved in the child welfare system, they face unique barriers and challenges that threaten the system's ability to respond to their unique needs, as well as to facilitate positive outcomes related to their safety, permanence, and well-being. Primary among them is the lack of understanding among many child welfare practitioners of the unique needs of immigrant and refugee families that result from their experiences with immigration, migration journeys, and acculturation. Although considerable efforts have been made over the past two decades to increase cultural competence within child welfare agencies and among child welfare staff, these efforts have largely focused on U.S.-born racial and ethnic groups (Dettlaff & Lincroft, 2010). This lack of cultural awareness is of particular concern when children enter foster care. In these instances, foster care is always a temporary solution, and the goal is to facilitate permanency for children while ensuring their ongoing safety and well-being. Permanency is best achieved when children are reunited with their parents following services that reduce the risk of maltreatment or otherwise resolve the conditions that warranted placement of the child into foster care. Yet, achieving reunification largely depends on the child welfare system's ability to provide family services that effectively address the issues that led to this placement, as well as the parents' meaningful participation and engagement in these services. If child welfare professionals fail to discern and address cultural factors in their assessment of families' service needs, their cultural biases or misunderstandings can affect service delivery. Cultural values shape the ways in which families view their problems, accept responsibility, and respond to interventions. Failure to understand these elements has been cited as the primary barrier to adequate assessment and effective intervention in cases of child maltreatment among immigrant and refugee families (Fong, 2004; Shor, 1999). Thus, the accuracy of assessments and the effectiveness of interventions for immigrant and refugee families depend on both the accuracy of caseworkers' insights into the families' cultural backgrounds and how their culture and child-rearing traditions influence their thoughts and actions.

A related barrier for child welfare systems serving immigrant and refugee children and families is the provision of services in families' preferred language (Ayón, 2009; Barrios, Suleiman, & Vidal de Haymes, 2004). Language barriers can result in miscommunication and misunderstandings, which can considerably affect families' ability to respond to interventions. Language barriers can also result in delays in service delivery, which can affect parents' abilities to complete required services and place them at risk for termination of parental rights because of the time frames mandated by the Adoption and Safe Families Act (ASFA) of 1997 (Ayón, 2009; Committee for Hispanic Children and Families, 2003), which calls for permanency decisions to be made within 12 months and requires the filing of petitions for termination of parental rights for children who have been in substitute care for 15 of the last 22 months. These mandates have resulted in more rapid proceedings of child welfare cases and increased terminations of parental rights.

Beyond language, immigration status can create additional delays or barriers to reunification, as noncitizen parents may be unable to obtain employment or participate in certain mandated services. Undocumented parents may also be ineligible for certain supportive services that could facilitate reunification. This is largely because of eligibility restrictions set in place through the 1996 Personal Responsibility and Work Opportunity Reconciliation Act (PRWORA). Before 1996, documented immigrants (including legal permanent and legal temporary residents) were eligible for the same public benefits as citizens if they met the eligibility criteria (e.g., income, family composition). However, in addition to denying unauthorized immigrants access to most public benefits, PRWORA restricted documented immigrants' access to most means-tested benefits, including TANF, SNAP, Medicaid, and SSI. Given these barriers, the expedited process required by ASFA may place immigrant families at a disadvantage in meeting case requirements, thus placing them at greater risk for termination of parental rights.

For immigrant and refugee children in foster care, a lack of culturally or linguistically appropriate services can also limit their ability to receive services needed to address both their physical and mental health needs (Dettlaff & Cardoso, 2010; Schmidt, 2006). Further, funding for services for immigrant children may be limited by restrictions within Title IV-E of the Social Security Act, the primary source of federal child welfare funding to states. This funding source allows states to receive federal matching funds for the care of children in state custody, but receipt of Title IV-E funds is restricted to children who meet eligibility requirements, including U.S. citizenship. Undocumented immigrant children do not meet the eligibility requirement, so states must bear the total burden of the cost of substitute care. In times of shrinking resources for public child welfare systems, this burden may limit a state's ability to adequately care for ineligible immigrant children.

IMMIGRATION ENFORCEMENT AND CHILDREN'S INVOLVEMENT IN THE CHILD WELFARE SYSTEM

Although an emerging body of research has begun to shed some light on the involvement of immigrant children and families in the child welfare system, what remains unknown is the extent to which immigration enforcement activities have affected this involvement. A recent study conducted by the Applied Research Center (2011) estimates that as many as 5,100 children currently in foster care have parents who have been either detained or deported. Although this study could not determine whether these children entered foster care as a direct result of their parents' detention or deportation, anecdotal information suggests that this is indeed a growing problem in many states. The growing evidence of this is of concern because these children typically have not been maltreated and have entered foster care solely because the apprehension of their parents left them without anyone responsible for their care. And although courts that handle child welfare cases operate under statutes requiring that children's best interests be considered in decisions regarding their custody and placement (Child Welfare Information Gateway, 2010), immigration law does not recognize children's interests as a valid factor in the immigration decisions concerning their parents, which can lead to profound implications for families with mixed immigration statuses.

Immigration enforcement activities conducted by Immigration and Customs Enforcement (ICE) have increased significantly over the past decade. The period between 2005 and 2008 saw a particularly large increase in enforcement efforts, most notably with several large, highly publicized worksite enforcement operations. These worksite enforcement activities were largely halted in 2008 by the new Obama administration in response to harsh criticism by child advocates. Following the attention generated by these raids, ICE developed a set of humanitarian guidelines that applied to enforcement actions involving more than 150 arrests (this was later reduced to actions involving more than 25 arrests). These guidelines include developing a plan to identify individuals who are the sole caregivers of minor children or who have other humanitarian concerns, including individuals with serious medical conditions, nursing mothers, pregnant women, or caregivers of spouses or relatives with serious medical conditions. To implement this plan, ICE is charged with coordinating enforcement actions with the U.S. Department of Health and Human Services Division of Immigration Health Services or with an appropriate state or local social service agency such as the public child welfare system. Recent evidence suggests that, when administered appropriately, these guidelines have been effective in preventing or minimizing parent–child separations (Chaudry et al., 2010). The guidelines do not, however, apply to enforcement actions targeting individuals or small groups, including home raids and other small criminal justice operations, leaving children vulnerable to experiencing not only separation from their parents but also the possibility of child welfare system intervention when relatives or other adult caregivers are not immediately available.

Although worksite raids were suspended under the Obama administration, the first Obama administration oversaw the highest number of deportations in the United States in recent history. In 2009, more than 600,000 apprehensions were made, and ICE detained a record total of 383,524 immigrants. Additionally, more than 393,000 immigrants were removed from the United States in 2009, the seventh consecutive record yearly total (U.S. Department of Homeland Security, Office of Immigration Statistics, 2010). In large part, these record numbers can be attributed to increased cooperation between local law enforcement and the Department of Homeland Security (DHS). Beginning in 2007, a new strategy was adopted to prioritize the apprehension of immigrants who have committed criminal offenses. This resulted in the merger of several programs under the ICE Agreements of Cooperation in Communities to Enhance Safety and Security (ACCESS) initiative. One of the most well known of these programs is the 287(g) program, which establishes collaborations between ICE and local officials that allow local police to be deputized to enforce immigration laws. Currently, ICE has 287(g) agreements with 68 law enforcement agencies in 24 states, and ICE officers have certified more than 1,500 local officers to enforce immigration law (U.S. Department of Homeland Security, 2012). A related program, Secure Communities, uses local jails to identify immigrants for deportation by forwarding fingerprint data from the FBI to ICE, which determines the arrested person's immigration status. If the arrested person is identified as a noncitizen, ICE can request that local authorities detain that person until ICE moves him or her to an immigration detention center.

The stated goal of these programs is the removal of individuals who pose a threat to national security and public safety. This includes, in order of priority, immigrants convicted of an aggravated felony or multiple felonies (Level 1), those convicted of a felony or multiple misdemeanors (Level 2), or misdemeanors (Level 3). However, recent data have demonstrated that Secure Communities has resulted in the deportation of thousands of immigrants who do not fall into these priority areas. More than one quarter of deportees who come to the attention of ICE through Secure Communities have no criminal convictions at all. Another 30 percent are Level 2 or 3 offenders, which include people charged with misdemeanors such as driving without a license (U.S. Immigration and Customs Enforcement, 2012a). In fact, data from ICE indicate that less than 30 percent of individuals who have been deported since the implementation of Secure Communities were convicted of Level 1 offenses (U.S. Immigration and Customs Enforcement, 2012a). Nevertheless, Secure Communities operates as a partnership between local law enforcement and ICE throughout the country and is in the process of being fully implemented throughout the country.

Although the exact number of children who become involved in the child welfare system as a result of immigration enforcement is unknown, it is clear that children have been impacted by these efforts. Statistics made available from ICE in late 2012 showed that between July 1, 2010, and September 30, 2012, ICE removed 204,816 parents of U.S. citizen children from the United States (U.S. Immigration and Customs Enforcement, 2012b). No data were provided on the whereabouts of the children from these families or the consequences they faced as a result of their parent's deportation. For children who enter the child welfare system solely because of an immigrant parent's arrest or apprehension, the complexities of these cases can be enormous. Parents detained in immigration facilities face considerable challenges, which may prevent them from meaningfully participating in a reunification plan. In some cases, child welfare staff cannot locate parents, making their participation in decisions concerning their children unlikely. Detained parents are also unlikely to be able to participate in court proceedings related to their children's care and custody (Cervantes & Lincroft, 2010). Deportation proceedings and decisions may last longer than the timeframes under which child welfare agencies must make decisions, further complicating the agencies' ability to act in children's best interests (Cervantes & Lincroft, 2010).

When children are U.S. citizens, the prospect of parental deportation poses a uniquely difficult situation for families and for child welfare systems. Children may remain in the United States and be permanently separated from their parents—or they can leave their home and all they have known to move to an unfamiliar country to remain with their family. Although this has been described as a "choiceless choice" for immigrant parents (Thronson, 2006), best practice would call for deported parents' decisions regarding their children to be honored when maltreatment is absent. However, the extent to which parents' and children's voices are meaningfully heard remains unknown.

CASE STUDY: THE POTENTIAL IMPACT OF IMMIGRATION ENFORCEMENT

Sylvia came to the United States 10 years ago as a teenager with her parents, who were in search of better opportunities for their children. Sylvia is now a single mother of two U.S.-born children, ages 2 and 4. Six months ago, Sylvia's children were placed into foster care as a result of neglect. Sylvia had been leaving her children unattended in their home overnight while she worked, as she was not able to afford child care. Since her children were placed in foster care, Sylvia has been engaged with the child welfare system and has been working to reunite with her children. While completing her case plan requirements, Sylvia was apprehended by immigration enforcement, placed in detention, and ultimately deported to Mexico. During this time, she was not able to get in touch with her caseworker, and the caseworker was unable to obtain any information on Sylvia's whereabouts. By the time Sylvia was able to contact her caseworker, the goal for this case had shifted to termination of parental rights, which would allow Sylvia's children to be adopted by another family. Sylvia wants her children returned to her care in Mexico, but her caseworker is reluctant to consider this, as she believes the children would have better opportunities in the United States with an adoptive family.

1 What concerns do you have for Sylvia's children?
2 What factors should the child welfare system consider in this case?
3 How should Sylvia's wishes for her children be considered?
4 What could the child welfare system do to prevent a situation like this from occurring?
5 What could the immigration enforcement system do to prevent a situation like this from occurring?

EMERGING PRACTICES AND PREVENTIVE INTERVENTIONS

Given the rapidly growing immigrant population and the persistent refugee population, a small number of child welfare agencies have begun to develop or adapt practices to more effectively serve this population. Because of the high proportion of Latino immigrants in these jurisdictions, many of these emerging practices have been specific to this population. However, they may be appropriate for adaptation to other immigrant and refugee populations and in other jurisdictions.

CULTURAL MEDIATOR PROGRAMS

Cultural mediator programs typically involve the use of lay community members, although they may also involve staff of community-based organizations. These individuals are specially trained to provide education and outreach to immigrant families within their communities. Cultural mediators serve as mentors and coaches to immigrant and refugee families involved in child welfare services to bridge the cultural gap by communicating differences and similarities between cultures. Cultural mediators may be assigned to specific cases and work in tandem with a designated caseworker throughout the life of the case, or they may serve as mediators to specific populations (e.g., nonresident fathers) or at a specific point of service delivery (e.g., to help families understand the court process).

Cultural Brokers

The concept of cultural brokering originated in the health care field, where it has been well documented as a valuable approach in delivering health care services to culturally diverse populations. The concept of cultural brokering is based on principles of cultural and linguistic competence, particularly as they concern collaboration with natural, informal support systems among diverse populations. Within child welfare, the use of cultural brokering emerged from an initiative to promote parent engagement in Fresno County, California, where the model was used as a method to address the overrepresentation of African American children. In this model, cultural brokers received initial and ongoing training by independent consultants and trainers and accompanied social workers at the point of initial contact. Although initially applied to practice with African American families, it has since been expanded in several counties with large Latino immigrant populations as a model to facilitate communication and promote culturally responsive practice.

Promotoras Programs

The concept of *promotoras* originates from the use of community health workers in medical settings to provide community education to rural populations, and it has been practiced with Latino populations since the mid-1960s. Historically, *promotoras* have been lay Latino community members who received specialized training to provide basic health education in the community, although they are not professional health care workers. *Promotoras* also provide guidance in accessing community resources. Thus, they serve as liaisons between their community, health professionals, and social service organizations. Although they are typically volunteers, they may also be paid staff. Within child welfare settings, *promotoras* play a role similar to that of cultural brokers, acting as a coach and mentor to Latino immigrant families throughout the life of a case.

SPOTLIGHT: COLLABORATION ACROSS SYSTEMS

In California, *promotoras* play a large role in the provision of services in Placer County, where the *promotoras* program is run by the Latino Leadership Council, an independent nonprofit organization that was created to advocate for culturally responsive services to Latino families in the county. *Promotoras* provide services to youths and families across social service systems, including child welfare, health, juvenile justice, and education. Within the child welfare system, results from an evaluation of the *promotoras* program found that families were more engaged in planning for services, demonstrated better follow-through, and reported greater satisfaction with services. In addition, staff reported a workload reduction because the *promotoras* provided additional support and links to services that allowed them to focus on other aspects of service delivery.

SPECIALIZED STAFF

Practices that employ specialized positions and/or units involve the use of dedicated staff that have specialized knowledge of unique issues that may affect immigrant and refugee children and families, such as issues related to immigration status or international collaboration. Specialized staff are typically bilingual and bicultural. Staff in these positions receive specialized training on culturally responsive practices and/or special issues that may arise during a case in order to ensure culturally responsive service provision. These staff may serve as primary caseworkers or as liaisons to assist in specific areas, such as complex immigration issues or to facilitate international collaboration.

For example, international or immigration liaisons are used in a number of jurisdictions with large immigrant populations and serve as the point of contact with foreign agencies and representatives to ensure compliance with international treaties, policies, and laws. Liaisons are typically assigned to any case involving a foreign-born child and collaborate with child welfare staff to facilitate repatriation of minors in a foreign country and manage requests from foreign consulates. Liaisons also assist staff with coordination and notification when staff must travel to and from another country, and they serve as resource persons to staff regarding all international issues that affect services to immigrant families, as well as identify training needs among staff. Liaisons also assist caseworkers in identifying children who may be eligible for forms of immigration relief such as Special Immigrant Juvenile Status, and they assist staff in processing these applications.

SPOTLIGHT ON PROMISING PRACTICE: SPECIAL SKILLS WORKERS

Special skills workers are used in Sacramento County, California, to facilitate culturally responsive service provision to Latino immigrant families. Special skills workers are defined as staff that demonstrate specialized knowledge of the Latino culture, as well as specialized knowledge of immigration issues. Caseworkers who are interested in serving as special skills workers must apply for these positions and interview in front of a panel of current special skills workers to demonstrate their knowledge of Latino culture and immigration issues. Special skills workers also hold quarterly meetings to identify emerging issues impacting Latino immigrant families and to make policy and practice recommendations to the agency administration. Special skills workers also meet quarterly with staff from the Mexican consulate to review cases and address issues of collaboration across agencies.

ADOPTIVE AND FOSTER PARENT RECRUITMENT PROGRAMS

Adoptive and foster parent recruitment programs typically provide targeted education and outreach to immigrant and refugee communities to promote adoption and/or foster parenting. Activities typically include community engagement, such as hosting or participating in community events, targeted advertising on adoption and foster parenting opportunities within immigrant communities, and ensuring that bilingual materials and information concerning adoption and foster parenting are provided. For example, Nuestros Niños Adoptions is an adoption program used in San Diego County, California. The program serves as the point of entry for the Spanish-speaking immigrant population in order to recruit and approve Latino immigrant families to provide adoption services.

COLLABORATIONS ACROSS SYSTEMS

When children from immigrant and refugee families become involved in the child welfare system, collaboration across systems is essential in meeting the complex needs of these families. Often, service delivery to immigrant and refugee families is complex and fragmented, resulting in families who do not receive needed services. When working with immigrant and refugee families, it is important that immediate crises and concerns be addressed so families can concentrate on the issues that led to their involvement with the child welfare system. For many families, these immediate concerns involve their immigration status. Service delivery can be aided through collaborative relationships between child welfare agencies and immigrant service providers, who work as a team to meet the complex needs of these families.

Of particular concern when providing services to children in immigrant and refugee families are the transnational dimensions that often arise, which require collaboration between child welfare and human services systems in both the sending and receiving countries. Collaboration and coordination between the respective agencies is needed to effectively carry out a number of transnational case transactions. These include obtaining birth certificates from the country of origin for immigrant children, obtaining home studies by local child welfare authorities for transnational family placements, and obtaining documentation needed to complete applications for immigration relief. However, such collaboration and coordination between most states and countries is lacking.

SPOTLIGHT ON PROMISING PRACTICE: MEMORANDA OF UNDERSTANDING
WITH FOREIGN CONSULATES

Memoranda of Understanding (MOUs) with foreign consulates were developed to address the best interests of children and families who are foreign nationals and involved in the child welfare system. They typically specify the roles and responsibilities of the local child welfare system and the consulate when foreign children are placed in foster care, and the ways in which the respective entities agree to collaborate to ensure the best interests of children. Memoranda of Understanding may also specify the role of the foreign child welfare agency (e.g., Sistema Nacional para el Desarrollo Integral de la Familia, DIF, in Mexico) in collaborating with the consulate and the local child welfare agency. Additional provisions that may be addressed in MOUs include interviews with parents or children by consular staff, staff travel provisions, consular attendance at court hearings, appointment of counsel, and exchange of information. In addition to MOUs, policies may be developed that address consular notification and other procedures for communicating and collaborating with a foreign consulate.

FUTURE DIRECTIONS

Given the increasing numbers of immigrant and refugee children and families in the child welfare system, it is imperative that child welfare systems develop culturally responsive strategies to meet the needs of this population. At the most fundamental level, culturally responsive practice requires that services be provided in the native language of immigrant and refugee children and families. Although some families may be able to speak English, they may be more comfortable speaking in their native language, particularly when addressing issues concerning their children's well-being. It is also important to recruit staff who are bicultural and bilingual in order to respond more appropriately to children and families from diverse cultures. Improved cultural understanding can lead to improved engagement, more thorough assessments, and more effective service delivery.

Given the concerns resulting from immigration enforcement efforts, child welfare agencies may need to develop relationships within immigrant communities to create a climate where reporting of maltreatment can take place without fear of deportation or other negative consequences to families. Agencies can also develop collaborations with community-based service providers in immigrant and refugee communities to facilitate education about cultural norms related to maltreatment and to dispel fears about reporting. Beyond this, to improve cultural responsiveness and reduce the potential for bias, child welfare professionals need training that provides information on the experiences of immigrant and refugee children and families. Child welfare professionals need to understand the effects of immigration and acculturation on immigrant family systems in order to conduct adequate assessments and provide interventions that adequately respond to their needs. Professionals who are unfamiliar with the issues affecting immigrant families may filter information and make decisions through their own cultural lens, resulting in misunderstandings and errors in judgment. Once children in immigrant and refugee families become involved in the child welfare system, practitioners need to be familiar with resources and programs available for immigrant and refugee children and families in order to provide comprehensive services that meet the needs of these families. Practitioners also need to be familiar with federal and state policies that affect immigrant and refugee children and families and to understand how those policies may affect service delivery.

Much additional research is also needed to facilitate the provision of culturally responsive services. Although research has begun to identify the presence of immigrant and refugee children and families in the child welfare system, research is needed that provides information on interventions that facilitate positive outcomes of safety, permanency, and well-being for immigrant and refugee children and families. Interventions that have historically been used with nonimmigrant populations may not be effective with immigrant and refugee children and families because of their cultural differences, as well as differences in the underlying issues that brought them to the attention of this system. In order to facilitate positive outcomes, interventions need to consider the cultural influences and experiences in immigrant and refugee families, as well as how these influences affect service delivery.

Finally, child welfare systems need to recognize that culturally responsive practice with immigrant and refugee children and families is not an issue that can be addressed in isolation. Many immigrant and refugee families are likely to intersect with multiple systems, and a coordinated community response is necessary to promote the overall health and well-being of this rapidly growing population. This response should include involvement from community members and community service providers, as well as law enforcement, the courts, schools, juvenile justice, and health and mental health systems. To be successful, a strategic plan for engagement with these systems should be developed through a coalition of child welfare administrators and key community stakeholders to facilitate a coordinated and multidisciplinary response.

RECOMMENDATIONS FOR CULTURALLY RESPONSIVE PRACTICE IN THE CHILD WELFARE SYSTEM

1 Ensure that all children, including those who are undocumented, receive appropriate and comprehensive child welfare services.
2 Ensure that immigrant families receive services in their preferred language.
3 Ensure that children in foster care are placed, when possible, with relatives or other kin caregivers to preserve cultural and familial ties and reduce trauma.
4 Establish procedures to ensure that parents can meaningfully participate in court cases related to their children's care and custody.
5 Establish procedures to ensure that immigrant parents have access to immigration attorneys who can provide them with appropriate legal counsel related to their immigration case.
6 Ensure that possible biases favoring legal permanent residency are not overriding or interfering with the wishes of immigrant parents or their children.

KEY TERMS

CHILD MALTREATMENT A broad term used to describe all forms of abuse and neglect of a child under 18 years of age by a parent, caretaker, or another person responsible for the care or custody of a child.

FOSTER CARE A temporary living situation provided by states for children who have been removed from their families, typically as a result of child maltreatment. Foster care can include placement in a home environment or in settings such as group homes, residential care facilities, and emergency shelters. Foster care can also refer to the services provided to children in this living situation.

KINSHIP CARE A broad term used to refer to the care of children by relatives or close family friends (often referred to as fictive kin). Kinship care may be a form of foster care, or it may be used as a form of family preservation to prevent a child from entering foster care.

PERMANENCY Within the context of the child welfare system, permanency typically refers to a safe and permanent living situation for children who have been removed from their families and placed into foster care. When this occurs, reunification with family is the preferred permanency outcome for children. Other permanency options may include relatives, adoptive families, or guardians.

PROTECTIVE FACTORS Attributes or conditions within individuals and families that mitigate or eliminate risk factors that may contribute to child maltreatment.

STUDY QUESTIONS

1 What is acculturative stress, and how might it contribute to the risk of maltreatment within immigrant families?

2 What strengths may be present within immigrant families that can serve as protective factors against child maltreatment?

3 Why is it important for immigrant families to receive child welfare services in their preferred language?

4 What can child welfare systems do to address barriers to culturally responsive practice?

5 What can child welfare systems do to facilitate collaboration across systems?

ADDITIONAL RESOURCES

Administration for Children and Families information memorandum: Case planning and service delivery for families with parents and legal guardians who are detained or deported by Immigration Enforcement: http://www .acf.hhs.gov/programs/cb/resource/im-15-02

Center on Immigration and Child Welfare: http://www.cimmcw.org

Child Welfare Information Gateway issue brief: Immigration and child welfare: https://www.childwelfare.gov/pubs/issue-briefs/immigration/

First Focus Center for the Children of Immigrants: http://firstfocus.org /issues/children-of-immigrants/

Office of Refugee Resettlement: http://www.acf.hhs.gov/programs/orr

REFERENCES

Aldarondo, E., Kaufman, G. K., & Jasinski, J. (2002). A risk marker analysis of wife assault in Latino families. *Violence Against Women, 8*, 429–454.

Applied Research Center. (2011). *Shattered families: The perilous intersection of immigration enforcement and the child welfare system*. Retrieved from http://arc.org/shatteredfamilies

Ayón, C. (2009). Shorter time-lines, yet higher hurdles: Mexican families' access to child welfare mandated services. *Children and Youth Services Review, 31*, 609–616.

Bacallao, M. L., & Smokowski, P. R. (2007). The costs of getting ahead: Mexican family system changes after immigration. *Family Relations, 56*, 52–66.

Barrios, L., Suleiman, L., & Vidal de Haymes, M. (2004). Latino population trends and child welfare services: Reflections on policy, practice, and research from the Latino Consortium roundtable discussions. *Illinois Child Welfare, 1*, 106–114.

Berry, J. W., Kim, U., Minde, T., & Mok, D. (1987). Comparative studies of acculturative stress. *International Migration Review, 21*, 491–511.

Cadzow, S., Armstrong, K., & Fraser, J. (1999). Stressed parents with infants: Reassessing physical abuse risk factors. *Child Abuse & Neglect, 23*, 845–853.

Capps, R., & Fortuny, K. (2006). *Immigration and child and family policy*. Washington, DC: Urban Institute.

Cervantes, W., & Lincroft, Y. (2010). *The impact of immigration enforcement on child welfare*. Washington, DC: First Focus.

Chang, J., Rhee, S., & Weaver, D. (2006). Characteristics of child abuse in immigrant Korean families and correlates of placement decisions. *Child Abuse & Neglect, 30*, 881–891.

Chaudry, A., Capps, R., Pedroza, J. M., Castaneda, R. M., Santos, R., & Scott, M. M. (2010). *Facing our future: Children in the aftermath of immigration enforcement*. Retrieved from Urban Institute website: http://www.urban.org/publications/412020.html

Chaudry, A., & Fortuny, K. (2010). *Children of immigrants: Family and parental characteristics*. Retrieved from Urban Institute website: http://www.urban.org/publications/412132.html

Child Welfare Information Gateway. (2010). *Determining the best interests of the child: Summary of state statutes*. Retrieved from http://www.childwelfare.gov/systemwide/laws_policies/statutes/best_interest.cfm

Coltrane, S., Parke, R. D., & Adams, M. (2004). Complexity of father involvement in low-income Mexican American families. *Family Relations, 53*, 179–189.

Committee for Hispanic Children and Families. (2003). *Creating a Latino child welfare agenda: A strategic framework for change*. New York, NY: Author.

Cunradi, C. B., Caetano, R., & Schafer, J. (2002). Socioeconomic predictors of intimate partner violence among white, black, and Hispanic couples in the United States. *Journal of Family Violence, 17*, 377–389.

De La Rosa, M. (2002). Acculturation and Latino adolescents' substance use: A research agenda for the future. *Substance Use & Misuse, 37*, 429–456.

Dettlaff, A. J., & Cardoso, J. B. (2010). Mental health need and service use among Latino children of immigrants in the child welfare system. *Children and Youth Services Review, 32*, 1373–1379.

Dettlaff, A. J., & Earner, I. (2012). Children of immigrants in the child welfare system: Characteristics, risk, and maltreatment. *Families in Society: The Journal of Contemporary Social Services, 93*, 295–303.

Dettlaff, A. J., Earner, I., & Phillips, S. D. (2009). Latino children of immigrants in the child welfare system: Prevalence, characteristics, and risk. *Children and Youth Services Review, 31*, 775–783.

Dettlaff, A. J., & Johnson, M. A. (2011). Child maltreatment dynamics among immigrant and U.S. born Latino children: Findings from the National Survey of Child and Adolescent Well-being (NSCAW). *Children and Youth Services Review, 33*, 936–944.

Dettlaff, A. J., & Lincroft, Y. (2010). Issues in evaluation and program planning with immigrant children and families in the child welfare system. *Evaluation and Program Planning, 33*, 278–280.

Downs, S. W., Moore, E., McFadden, E. J., & Costin, L. B. (2008). *Child welfare and family services: Policies and practice*. Needham Heights, MA: Pearson.

Dumbrill, G. (2008). Your policies, our children: Messages from refugee parents to child welfare workers and policymakers. *Child Welfare, 88*, 145–168.

Earner, I. (2007). Immigrant families and public child welfare: Barriers to services and approaches to change. *Child Welfare, 86*(4), 63–91.

——. (2010). Double risk: Immigrant mothers, domestic violence and public child welfare services in New York City. *Evaluation and Program Planning, 33*, 288–293.

Espin, O. M. (1987). Psychological impact of migration on Latinas. *Psychology of Women Quarterly, 11*, 489–503.

Falicov, C. J. (2005). Mexican families. In M. McGoldrick, J. Giordano, & N. Garcia-Preto (Eds.), *Ethnicity and family therapy* (3rd ed., pp. 229–241). New York, NY: Guilford.

Finno, M., Vidal de Haymes, M., & Mindell, R. (2006). Risk of affective disorders in the migration and acculturation experience of Mexican Americans. *Protecting Children, 21*(2), 22–35.

Fong, R. (Ed.). (2004). *Culturally competent practice with immigrant and refugee children and families.* New York, NY: Guilford.

Fontes, L. A. (2002). Child discipline and physical abuse in immigrant Latino families: Reducing violence and misunderstanding. *Journal of Counseling and Development, 80,* 31–40.

Frias-Armenta, M., & McCloskey, L. A. (1998). Determinants of harsh parenting in Mexico. *Journal of Abnormal Child Psychology, 26,* 129–139.

Furuto, S. (2004). Theoretical perspectives for culturally competent practice with immigrant children and families. In R. Fong (Ed.), *Culturally competent practice with immigrant and refugee children and families* (pp. 19–38). New York, NY: Guilford.

Hancock, T. U. (2005). Cultural competence in the assessment of poor Mexican families in the rural southeastern United States. *Child Welfare, 84,* 689–711.

Holleran, L. K., & Waller, M. A. (2003). Sources of resilience among Chicano/a youth: Forging identities in the borderlands. *Child and Adolescent Social Work, 20,* 335–350.

Jambunathan, S., Burts, D. C., & Pierce, S. (2000). Comparisons of parenting attitudes among five ethnic groups in the United States. *Journal of Comparative Family Studies, 31,* 395–406.

Jennissen, R. (2007). Causality chains in the international migration systems approach. *Population Research and Policy Review, 26,* 411–436.

Johnson-Motoyama, M., Dettlaff, A. J., & Finno, M. (2012). Parental nativity and the decision to substantiate: Findings from a study of Latino children in the second National Survey of Child and Adolescent Well-being (NSCAW II). *Children and Youth Services Review, 34,* 2229–2239.

Leon, A. M., & Dziegielewski, S. F. (1999). The psychological impact of migration: Practice considerations in working with Hispanic women. *Journal of Social Work Practice, 13,* 69–82.

Maiter, S., Stalker, C. A., & Alaggia, R. (2009). The experiences of minority immigrant families receiving child welfare services: Seeking to understand how to reduce risk and increase protective factors. *Families in Society, 90,* 28–36.

Mason, G., & Pulvirenti, M. (2013). Former refugees and community resilience. *British Journal of Criminology, 53*, 1–18.

Mendez, J. A. O. (2006). Latino parenting expectations and styles: A literature review. *Protecting Children, 21*(2), 53–61.

Miller, B., Fox, B., & Garcia-Beckwith, L. (1999). Intervening in severe physical child abuse cases. *Child Abuse & Neglect, 23*, 905–914.

Newell, P. (2002). Global progress towards giving up the habit of hitting children. In B. Franklin (Ed.), *The new handbook of children's rights*. London: Routledge.

Orellana, M. F. (2001). The work kids do: Mexican and Central American immigrant children's contribution to households and schools in California. *Harvard Educational Review, 71*, 366–389.

Padilla, A. M., & Perez, W. (2003). Acculturation, social identity, and social cognition: A new perspective. *Hispanic Journal of Behavioral Sciences, 25*, 35–55.

Park, M. S. (2001). The factors of child physical abuse in Korean immigrant families. *Child Abuse & Neglect, 25*, 945–958.

Pessar, P. R. (1999). Engendering migration studies: The case of new immigrants in the United States. *American Behavioral Scientist, 42*, 577–600.

Quinones-Mayo, Y., & Dempsey, P. (2005). Finding the bicultural balance: Immigrant Latino mothers raising "American" adolescents. *Child Welfare, 84*, 649–667.

Redfield, R., Linton, R., & Herskovits, M. J. (1936). Memorandum for the study of acculturation. *American Anthropologist, 38*, 149–152.

Rhee, S., Chang, J., Weaver, D., & Wong, D. (2008). Child maltreatment among immigrant Chinese families: Characteristics and patterns of placement. *Child Maltreatment, 13*, 269–279.

Roer-Strier, D. (2001). Reducing risk for children in changing cultural contexts: Recommendations for intervention and training. *Child Abuse & Neglect, 25*, 231–248.

Ross-Sheriff, F., & Husain, A. (2004). South Asian Muslim children and families. In R. Fong (Ed.), *Culturally competent practice with immigrant and refugee children and families* (pp. 163–182). New York, NY: Guilford.

Rumbaut, R. G. (1999). Assimilation and its discontents: Ironies and paradoxes. In J. DeWind, C. Hirschman, & P. Kainitz (Eds.), *Handbook of international migration: The American experience* (pp. 172–195). New York, NY: Russell Sage Foundation.

Schmidt, S. (2006). *Refugees and the U.S. child welfare system: Background information for service providers.* Washington, DC: Bridging Refugee Youth and Children's Services.

Sedlak, A. J., Mettenburg, J., Basena, M., Petta, I., McPherson, K., Greene, A., & Li, S. (2010). *Fourth national incidence study of child abuse and neglect (NIS–4): Report to Congress.* Washington, DC: U.S. Department of Health and Human Services, Administration for Children and Families.

Segal, U., & Mayadas, N. (2005). Assessment of issues facing immigrant and refugee families. *Child Welfare, 84,* 563–583.

Shor, R. (1999). Inappropriate child rearing practices as perceived by Jewish immigrant parents from the former Soviet Union. *Child Abuse & Neglect, 23,* 487–499.

Smart, J. F., & Smart, D. W. (1995). Acculturative stress of Hispanics: Loss and challenge. *Journal of Counseling and Development, 73,* 390–396.

Social Science Research Council. (1954). Acculturation: An exploratory formulation. *American Anthropologist, 56,* 973–1000.

Solis, J. (2003). Re-thinking illegality as a violence against, not by, Mexican immigrants, children, and youth. *Journal of Social Issues, 59,* 15–31.

Tajima, E. A., & Harachi, T. W. (2010). Parenting beliefs and physical discipline practices among Southeast Asian immigrants: Parenting in the context of cultural adaptation to the United States. *Journal of Cross-Cultural Psychology, 41,* 212–235.

Teske, R. H., & Nelson, B. H. (1974). Acculturation and assimilation: A clarification. *American Ethnologist, 17,* 218–235.

Thronson, D. B. (2006). Choiceless choices: Deportation and the parent–child relationship. *Nevada Law Journal, 6,* 1165–1214.

U.S. Department of Homeland Security. (2012). *2011 yearbook of immigration statistics.* Washington, DC: U.S. Government Printing Office. Retrieved from http://www.dhs.gov/yearbook-immigration-statistics

U.S. Department of Homeland Security, Office of Immigration Statistics. (2010). *Immigration enforcement actions: 2009.* Washington, DC: Author.

U.S. Department of State. (2013). *Refugee admissions.* Retrieved from http://www.state.gov/j/prm/ra/

U.S. Immigration and Customs Enforcement. (2012a). *Secure Communities: Monthly statistics through April 30, 2012.* Retrieved from http://www.ice.gov/doclib/foia/sc-stats/nationwide_interop_stats-fy2012-to-date.pdf

———. (2012b). *Deportation of parents of U.S. citizen children July 1, 2010–September 30, 2012*. Retrieved from http://colorlines.com/archives/2012/12/deportations_of _parents_of_us-born_citizens_122012.html

Vericker, T., Kuehn, D., & Capps, R. (2007). *Foster care placement settings and permanency planning: Patterns by child generation and ethnicity*. Retrieved from Urban Institute website: http://www.urban.org/publications/311459.html

Zuniga, M. (2004). Latino children and families. In R. Fong (Ed.), *Culturally competent practice with immigrant and refugee children and families* (pp. 183–201). New York, NY: Guilford.

Practice with Immigrant and Refugee Children and Families in the Juvenile Justice System

▸ ANGIE JUNCK *and* RACHEL PRANDINI

DESPITE VARIATIONS among different states, the juvenile justice system is largely grounded in the concept of youth rehabilitation (U.S. Department of Justice, 2013). Although juvenile court proceedings are similar to adult criminal proceedings in many ways, they are civil proceedings, avoiding many of the negative and stigmatizing consequences of an adult criminal record (American Bar Association, 2012). Significantly, the U.S. Supreme Court has acknowledged in recent years that developments in psychology and neuroscience demonstrate fundamental differences between children and adults, which are especially important in the context of violations of the law. In particular, the Supreme Court has recognized that juveniles are more capable of change than adults, with greater possibility for reform, and that juveniles lack maturity and are vulnerable to negative influences and outside pressures (*Graham v. Florida*, 2010). All of these realities confirm the need for a separate system for youths and continue to inform how they should be treated by our legal system.

Immigrant youths who come into contact with the juvenile justice system face not only that vast and complex institution but also potentially our nation's federal immigration system. This is true despite the fact that many of the immigrant youths involved in the juvenile justice system were brought to this country at a young age, have limited or no memory of their country of origin, and consider this country to be their only home. These youths, though often not responsible for their presence in this country, live with the burdensome threat of deportation that drives them and their families into the shadows, marginalized by the need to remain invisible. If immigrant youths come into contact with the juvenile justice system, they may experience a very different reality than youths who are U.S. citizens.[1] Although immigration law, similar to state laws governing juveniles, acknowledges the vulnerability of children and their need for different treatment under the law, both systems often still fail to meet the needs of immigrant youths in their systems.

This chapter will address the population of immigrant and refugee children and families involved in the juvenile justice system, their unique needs, barriers to effecting change in the juvenile justice system, examples of efforts to bring change and cross-system collaboration, and future directions for promoting positive developments to better assist immigrant and refugee families in the juvenile justice system.

BACKGROUND ON THE JUVENILE JUSTICE SYSTEM IN THE UNITED STATES

The juvenile justice system in the United States was founded on the principle that youths are more likely to rehabilitate successfully than adults and therefore should be treated differently when they break the law. While remaining true to that principle, the system has undergone significant changes in response to evolving societal attitudes and concerns about juveniles. Early in the history of the United States, children were often treated the same as adults when they violated the law. The nineteenth-century juvenile justice movement, however, sought to change the perception of children from smaller versions of adults to persons with less developed cognitive and moral capacities by establishing separate juvenile courts (U.S. Department of Justice, 1999). These juvenile courts were established by state governments, with the first completely separate juvenile court in the United States being established in Illinois in 1899 (Shepherd, 1999).

Beginning in the mid-twentieth century, serious concerns arose about the overuse of detention and the ability of the juvenile justice system to rehabilitate youths. In the 1960s, the U.S. Supreme Court issued a series of decisions that required the juvenile court system to adopt more formal procedures to ensure that children received due process of law (U.S. Department of Justice, 1999). These reforms included, for example, the right of youths to receive notice of the charges against them, to present and question witnesses, and to have an attorney when they faced possible confinement (U.S. Department of Justice, 1999).

The 1980s and 1990s saw a swing in the other direction, with a focus on cracking down on juveniles who committed serious crimes by increasing the consequences and requiring that some juveniles be handled as adult criminals in criminal court. For example, the number of children detained in juvenile justice facilities between 1985 and 1995 rose by 74 percent (The Annie E. Casey Foundation, Juvenile Detention Alternatives Initiative, 1999). In the 1990s, however, the Juvenile Detention Alternatives Initiative, a national effort to reduce detention of youths involved with juvenile court, led the charge to substitute community-based alternatives to detention, a movement that continues to the present day (The Annie E. Casey Foundation, Juvenile Detention Alternatives Initiative, 1999). Today, there are 51 distinct juvenile justice systems, and each system is guided by its own laws, policies, and manner of providing services for juveniles (King, 2006).

INTERSECTION OF THE JUVENILE JUSTICE SYSTEM AND IMMIGRATION SYSTEM

Immigrant and refugee children in the juvenile justice system may face significant barriers to receiving its rehabilitative services. In some cases, for example, juvenile probation officers may depart from their department's well-established protocols and practices because they believe that a child is a suspected noncitizen and may be subject to federal immigration laws. In such cases, probation officers will elicit information from a youth and then proceed to share his or her personal information, including place of birth and/or immigration status, with federal immigration officials. These local law enforcement officers may believe that because the federal government's top immigration enforcement priority is immigrants in the criminal justice system, youths in the juvenile justice system are likewise a priority, and that officers are not bound by the same confidentiality requirements for immigrant youths as they are for citizen youths. In this way, local law enforcement officers treat youths the same as adults when immigration issues come into play. The practical result is that many immigrant youths, rather than receiving the rehabilitative services they need, are detained by federal immigration officials and placed in deportation proceedings, an outcome that is clearly at odds with the goals of the juvenile justice system since it may result in additional detention, separation from family, and deportation.

Even when probation departments do not report youths to immigration officials, they may not be equipped to address the unique and complex needs of these youths. For example, many immigrant youths experience linguistic and cultural barriers to interacting with the juvenile justice system. Further, many immigrant youths have experienced trauma, either in their home country, in their journey to the United States, or within the United States, which can affect how they interact with the system and respond to rehabilitative services. Funding restrictions based on immigration status may also hinder efforts to provide adequate services to immigrant youths.

IMMIGRANT YOUTHS IN THE JUVENILE JUSTICE SYSTEM

There are no reliable data on the number of immigrant youths involved in the juvenile justice system because most jurisdictions do not formally collect or analyze these data. Even sites actively engaged in addressing racial disparities in the justice system do not routinely collect such data (W. Haywood Burns Institute, 2009). The reasons for the lack of data include, among other things, budget constraints, inability of juvenile justice officials to determine immigration status, and concerns about the misuse of data.[2] This lack of data results in a limited understanding of the extent to which immigrant youths interact with the juvenile justice system, as well as limited information about the major barriers they experience when trying to access services.

Despite the lack of formal data, juvenile justice professionals have informally reported a steep increase in the number of immigrant youths involved in the delinquency system (Junck & Wilber, 2014). It is impossible to verify this perception; however, it is consistent with overall population trends in the United States. In 2010, approximately 7.3 percent of the population in the United States were foreign born and not U.S. citizens (encompassing both documented and undocumented immigrants), compared with only 6.6 percent of the population in 2000 (U.S. Bureau of the Census, 2000, 2010). In 2010, 8.9 percent of the foreign-born population—or approximately 2 million individuals—were between the ages of 5 and 17 years (U.S. Bureau of the Census, 2010).

The perception of an increase of immigrant youths in the juvenile justice system is also consistent with the reported increase in the number of immigrant youths being reported to immigration authorities by juvenile probation officers and other juvenile justice officials (Junck, Domingo, & Beasley, 2013). In fact, a 2013 report by the Center on Juvenile and Criminal Justice confirmed that many immigrant youths are unnecessarily detained for immigration authorities in local juvenile detention facilities in response to Immigration and Customs Enforcement (ICE) hold requests, which are requests that local law enforcement agencies continue to hold an individual so that ICE (the federal agency responsible for interior enforcement of federal immigration laws) can assume custody before the person's release (Teji, 2013).[3] In California alone, the Center on Juvenile and Criminal Justice found that there were 697 ICE hold requests for immigrant youths during the 41-month period from October 1, 2009, to February 10, 2013 (Teji, 2013). However, this report does not account for all immigration enforcement efforts conducted by local law enforcement officials. Because of differing local and federal practices and policies across California, some immigrant youths in the juvenile justice system are never subject to ICE holds and/or picked up by immigration authorities. Accordingly, the number of youths subject to ICE holds may not be an accurate reflection of the number of immigrant youths in the juvenile justice system overall.

Many of the immigrant youths in the juvenile justice system were brought to the United States at a very young age, grew up almost entirely in the United States, and consider this country to be their only home. Some of them do not know the language spoken in their native country and have no memories of that country. As first-generation immigrants, these youths often experience a lack of parental control or involvement in their lives because their parents work long hours to make ends meet and because of the language barriers that many parents experience when engaging with systems in the United States. Some of these youths may also become involved with criminal street gangs as a result of lack of parental supervision and because of the economic constraints that force many immigrants to live in high-crime neighborhoods. It is also not uncommon for immigrant youths to reside in single-parent homes, often because of abandonment, abuse, or neglect by the noncustodial parent.

Other children and youths involved in the juvenile justice system may be immigrants who arrived more recently and therefore be completely unfamiliar with the legal system and customs in the United States. Some immigrant children come to the United States with a parent or an adult relative, whereas others arrive unaccompanied, without their parents or a legal guardian. Some receive the assistance of smugglers or "coyotes." Others are the victims of illegal labor or sex trafficking.

Some immigrant youths in the juvenile justice system are unaccompanied children.[4] These youths have often endured unspeakably traumatic experiences in their countries of origin. Many of these children feel that they face certain death in their home countries and that even a dangerous journey north would give them a chance at survival (Women's Refugee Commission, 2012). Notably, a United Nations High Commissioner for Refugees (UNHCR) study found that most unaccompanied children were motivated to migrate north by two main factors: violence by gangs and violence in the home (United Nations High Commissioner for Refugees, 2013). The trauma of this population is compounded by separation from their families and communities as they travel alone on a dangerous journey to the United States.

IMMIGRATION CONSEQUENCES OF INTERACTIONS WITH THE JUVENILE JUSTICE SYSTEM

Although lack of data places limits on the understanding of the number of immigrant and refugee children in the juvenile justice system, several notable consequences of interacting with the system that are specific to immigrant children have nonetheless emerged. First, an immigrant youth's confidential information may be shared with immigration authorities in order to alert them to the youth's potential unlawful presence in the United States, which can lead to additional detention and the threat of deportation. Further, confidential information about such youths may be used by immigration authorities later to deny an immigration benefit to an immigrant youth. Additionally, although youths in the juvenile justice system are supposed to receive a range of supportive services to assist in their rehabilitative process and to ensure that they transition successfully into adulthood, immigrant youths typically are not given any assistance in accessing immigration legal services. This is true even though immigration assistance could be the most important component to an immigrant youth's rehabilitation and successful transition into adulthood.

Consequences of Reporting Immigrant Youths
to Federal Immigration Authorities

For a range of reasons, including political pressure, lack of informed conversation at the local level, and pressure from the federal government, some jurisdictions report the presence of suspected immigrant youths in the juvenile justice system to immigration authorities. This involvement in federal immigration enforcement may result in violation of a youth's confidentiality, detention of a youth whereas a similarly situated U.S. citizen youth may have never been detained, and, once detained, being held longer than U.S.-citizen counterparts. This collaboration then may lead to the arrest, detention, and deportation of the youth by federal immigration authorities.

Whereas immigration policy and enforcement is an exclusively federal area, the federal government has created several programs that facilitate the voluntary cooperation of such local law enforcement. In the juvenile justice system, immigration enforcement is typically implemented through information sharing (juvenile intake information) coupled, at least in the past, with the use of "immigration detainers," also known as "ICE holds."[5] When an ICE hold is in place, rather than releasing youths from a juvenile detention facility upon completion of a sentence or by order of the juvenile court, local law enforcement may hold them for additional time to allow ICE to pick them up and transfer them to the custody of the federal government.[6] ICE holds have likely resulted in immigrant youths being subjected to longer periods of detention than similarly situated U.S. citizen youths (Junck & Wilber, 2014).[7]

Although there are various stages at which immigrant youths in the juvenile justice system can be reported to immigration authorities, including by police at arrest, prosecutors at charging, and juvenile courts at disposition, reporting is typically performed by a probation department following an initial intake screening with the youth, wherein the probation officer elicits personal information from the youth.[8] However, disclosure of this personal history may then be used directly against these youths and in some cases their families as well. Some probation departments share this information with immigration authorities despite the fact that in many states information about juveniles is strictly protected by confidentiality laws and that sharing information to facilitate deportation is against the best interests of the youth.[9] Further, such information sharing leads to additional detention and family separation for the youth, factors that further destabilize the youth's life and may lead him or her to go deeper into the system.[10]

CASE STUDY: ANGEL'S STORY

Angel was brought to the United States by his mother when he was only 2 years old. He has no memory of his home country of Mexico or his journey to the United States. He has only met his father once in his life and has no idea of his father's current whereabouts. Angel's mother works two jobs to try to provide for Angel and his sisters. From a young age, Angel had been left unsupervised after school and started to spend time with some older boys in his neighborhood, an area known for its high criminal activity. At 14, Angel was arrested for residential burglary. The probation officer doing his intake asked Angel where he was born and if he had legal status in the United States. Angel's information was then shared with immigration authorities, and he was detained by local authorities as a result of immigration's issuance of an ICE hold. An immigration officer was later sent in to speak to Angel. Upon completion of his time in juvenile hall, Angel was picked up by ICE officers and sent to an immigration detention center located three hours from his home. In the months that followed, he was transferred to various immigration detention centers all over the country. His mother, a monolingual Spanish speaker, struggled to follow what was happening to her son. No one in the juvenile justice system followed up with Angel's mother to explain to her what was happening to him. Months later, Angel was finally released back to his mother's care by immigration authorities. However, after his extended absence at home, he had to re-enroll in school, get back on course with his probation requirements, fight his deportation case, and try to rebuild his now strained relationship with his mother, who feared that she might be at risk of deportation because of her son's interaction with local and federal authorities. His mother fled an abusive relationship in Mexico, and the heightened fear prompted by her son's interaction with immigration authorities has caused this trauma to resurface for her. Angel's arrest by local authorities also brought back memories of his mother's prior interactions with law enforcement in Mexico, when she was scoffed at for trying to report the domestic abuse she suffered. For Angel, instead of his receiving rehabilitative services that could have benefited him, his rehabilitation was thwarted by his referral to immigration authorities. Not only did he not receive supportive services that could have helped steer him onto a better path, he was also placed in deportation proceedings as a result and now faces the prospect of fighting his deportation case in court without a lawyer—an almost impossible feat—with the added complication of his newly acquired delinquency history making his case even more difficult to win.

When youths are reported to immigration authorities, there are a myriad of consequences. As illustrated by Angel's story, most youths who are reported to immigration authorities are subject to additional detention although they have served their time in the local juvenile justice system. After initially being transferred and detained by ICE, the vast majority of youths apprehended are transferred to another federal entity, the Office of Refugee Resettlement (ORR).[11] Although custody by ORR is preferred over ICE custody because ORR generally takes a child welfare approach rather than an enforcement approach, ORR lacks familiarity with youths involved with the juvenile justice system. As a result, many of these youths are subject to more secure settings than are likely necessary. For example, in the Yolo County, California, juvenile detention facility, a contract facility for ORR, youths in deportation proceedings are mixed with youths who are awaiting the outcome of their local juvenile proceedings or serving their juvenile sentences.

Often, these youths do not return to their communities until after they have been transferred to immigration detention facilities in remote areas, where they have suffered the trauma of lengthy separation from their homes and communities and the isolating and frightening experience of immigration detention. However, most youths eventually return to their communities—in fact, in approximately 90 percent of cases, youths are reunited with family members. For youths involved with the juvenile justice system, this detention can last anywhere from a few months to years, typically much longer than for youths not involved with the juvenile justice system. Although reports to ICE also result in the initiation of deportation proceedings against a youth, many immigrant youths are not ultimately deportable, because they are eligible for a defense against deportation and can obtain legal status in the United States. However, even when youths can defend themselves against deportation, it is very challenging for them to obtain legal status when they are separated from their family and are navigating a complex system on their own. Many other consequences also result from the detention experience, such as gaps in education, familial discord, and stress caused by fear of deportation, as well as former trauma being exacerbated by prolonged detention.

Immigration Consequences of Delinquency on Defense Against Deportation and Obtaining Legal Status

Interactions with the juvenile justice system can also act as a barrier to obtaining lawful immigration status. Delinquency is treated differently from criminal convictions under immigration law. In fact, youths are eligible for many avenues for obtaining legal status in spite of delinquency. In this sense, immigration law acknowledges the diminished guilt of youths and their increased capacity for rehabilitation. Nonetheless, delinquency can affect immigrant children's immigration status in two important ways. First, specific delinquency adjudications, or the conduct on which they are based, may prevent youths from maintaining or achieving lawful immigration status. For example, the government may find that a child with refugee status who is applying for lawful permanent residence (a green card) is ineligible because there is "reason to believe" that the child engaged in drug trafficking. Under federal law, this would prevent a child from obtaining a "green card." Second, the government may exercise its discretion to deny an immigration benefit to an applicant based on its determination that the youth is not the type of upstanding individual who deserves the benefit. Because obtaining immigration relief from deportation is discretionary, immigration authorities may consider any potentially negative factor in an application for lawful status, including a history of juvenile delinquency.

Beyond these specific legal consequences, reporting immigrant youths in the juvenile justice system to ICE also puts these youths into a defensive posture where they are in adversarial proceedings, with opposing counsel charging them with illegal conduct, often far away from family members, and without access to immigration legal counsel. In this context, it is exceedingly difficult for youths to assert a viable defense against deportation. On the other hand, if youths can submit an immigration application affirmatively, before they have been reported to ICE, there is no opposing party or adversarial process. This greatly increases their chances of obtaining legal status. That a youth's success in obtaining immigration relief may depend more on the procedural posture of their case than the particular facts of their case evidences not only the flawed nature of the immigration system but also the disparate treatment that can result for immigrant youths who have been involved in the juvenile justice system.

Failings of the Juvenile Justice System in Assisting Immigrant Youths in Obtaining Legal Status

Congress has created various avenues for certain immigrant youths, even those involved with the juvenile justice system, to obtain lawful immigration status in the United States. Under current law, youths may be eligible for various forms of relief from deportation, including Special Immigrant Juvenile Status (for abused, neglected, or abandoned children under state court jurisdiction) and U nonimmigrant status (for victims of serious crimes). Obtaining immigration status permits young people to live and work openly in their communities, to remain with their families, to pursue future employment or higher education, and to gain access to resources and services that are essential to their well-being.

Juvenile justice officials, juvenile defense attorneys in particular, are often the first and last reliable individuals these youths may see who may be able to help them resolve their immigration situation. In fact, criminal defense attorneys—including juvenile defense attorneys—have a duty to inform their clients of the possible immigration consequences of their pending criminal or juvenile cases in order to assist them in maintaining or obtaining legal status (*Padilla v. Commonwealth of Kentucky*, 2010). However, the extremely complicated and technical nature of immigration law makes it challenging for juvenile defenders to understand all of the possible immigration consequences of a delinquency adjudication or criminal conviction. As a result, juvenile defenders may struggle to fulfill their duties to their immigrant clients. Accordingly, many immigrant youths are not even aware of the possible immigration consequences of their delinquency adjudications and do not receive effective assistance of counsel in understanding and mitigating those consequences, much less assistance in understanding what their options may be for defense from deportation.

The predominant action of the juvenile justice system toward immigrant youths is to report them and/or not do anything to help them navigate a complex immigration system. In particular, even when immigrant youths are not reported to immigration authorities, the juvenile justice system often fails to assist youths in stabilizing their immigration situation, notwithstanding the fact that this is crucial to their overall rehabilitation and successful transition into adulthood. This failure may come in the form of not identifying a youth's potential eligibility for legal status, not making a referral to a legal resource, and/or not proactively helping them pursue legal immigration options. The latter is particularly true where certain forms of immigration relief require cooperation from state courts or law enforcement in order for a youth to even apply before the federal government.

There is a need not only for juvenile justice officials to help youths to access immigration assistance but also for juvenile justice officials to cooperate with the procedures set out by federal immigration law to allow immigrant youths to apply for immigration relief. For example, in the context of Special Immigrant Juvenile Status, many state court judges have been reluctant to sign orders making the necessary findings that would allow the youth to apply for this form of relief for fear that they would be rewarding and incentivizing bad behavior.

Unfortunately, many juvenile justice professionals, whether in the courts or law enforcement, are not fully informed of the practical consequences for immigrant children of the positions and practices they adopt. These potentially damaging practices and positions can have severe consequences for immigrant and refugee children and run counter to the overall goals of the juvenile justice system of keeping families together, protecting juvenile confidentiality, and ensuring a youth is rehabilitated and successfully transitions into adulthood.

UNIQUE NEEDS OF IMMIGRANT AND REFUGEE CHILDREN AND FAMILIES IN THE JUVENILE JUSTICE SYSTEM

Many immigrant children and families confront significant obstacles when interacting with systems in the United States, including fear of engaging with law enforcement, language and cultural barriers, and ineligibility for services as a result of their immigration status. These realities make it particularly difficult for immigrant and refugee children and families to successfully interface with local juvenile justice systems.

Mistrust of Law Enforcement by the Child Immigrant Population

The juvenile justice system relies heavily on establishing a relationship of trust with youths' families so that they can work together to help the child. Unfortunately, immigrant and refugee children and their families often live with the constant fear of deportation and understand that most deportations result from contact with law enforcement. In fact, programs aimed at enforcing federal immigration law through local law enforcement have contributed significantly to the record number of deportations during the Obama administration (American Civil Liberties Union, 2014). Youths and families often know other individuals, including family and friends, who have been deported as a result of contact with law enforcement. The stress of worrying about their own or their family's immigration status and the possible effects of a report to immigration authorities can add an additional layer of concern to a youth's interaction with the juvenile justice system and impede his or her ability to form a trusting, open relationship with juvenile justice professionals.

Many youths and their families also come from cultures where law enforcement is extremely corrupt, or they live in communities in the United States that are subject to over-policing, which may further cause them to lack trust in law enforcement. Many immigrant children are also survivors of trauma. Young people who have experienced trauma often struggle to enter into trusting relationships. Thus, the relationship of trust that is so crucial to best serve youths involved with the juvenile justice system can often be particularly difficult to establish with immigrant and refugee children and their families.

Consequences of Fear and Mistrust of Law Enforcement for Immigrant Youths

The fear of deportation and the lack of trust in law enforcement may be most evident during the intake, detention, and release process for immigrant youths. All local juvenile justice systems have some process by which they determine whether an individual youth should be released or detained pending his or her initial hearing. This typically encompasses a risk assessment to determine the youth's threat to public safety and likelihood that the youth will appear at the detention hearing. Part of the risk assessment usually involves ascertaining whether youths have parents or legal guardians that can assume responsibility for them pending their initial court appearance. Some immigrant youths fear that disclosure of their family's or guardian's identity and whereabouts will expose them to risk of deportation, and accordingly, they do not supply family information even when parents are close by. This can lead to immigrant youths being detained when they would otherwise be released. Further, some jurisdictions also require the parent or guardian to present a driver's license or social security number to verify his or her identity when picking up their child. As a practical matter, these requirements prevent undocumented parents, who may not possess these documents or who may fear presenting themselves to law enforcement, from coming forward to assume custody of their children. Although these verification procedures might be based on legitimate concerns and applied evenly to all youths, this method of screening parents adversely impacts immigrant youths and unnecessarily subjects them to detention and separates them from their families.

Research shows that children placed in detention have reduced chances of rehabilitation and greater chances of recidivism (Plumer, 2013). A study by Aizer and Doyle of youths in delinquency proceedings found that children who were detained were 13 percent less likely to graduate high school and 22 percent more likely to end up in prison as adults than youths who went to court but were returned home with monitoring (Aizer and Doyle, 2013). It is clear that juvenile justice professionals need to understand and address the trust concerns that may exist in immigrant and refugee communities, and the very real fears on which they are grounded, in order to provide services that are responsive to these underlying concerns.

SPOTLIGHT ON PROMISING PRACTICE: SANTA CRUZ COUNTY

In Santa Cruz County, California, nonparents are required to provide a form of photo identification before a youth can be released to them, but a consular ID or a green card are acceptable forms of identification. This makes it possible for people who are undocumented or who are lawful permanent residents to pick up youths while the Santa Cruz County Probation Department's Juvenile Division is still able to verify their identity. The department also recognizes that, in many other cultures, ideas of family often extend beyond the nuclear family, and therefore they are more open about who they will release a youth to rather than requiring a parent or legal guardian.

Trauma in Immigrant Child Populations

Posttrauma symptoms can influence immigrant children and families' interactions with juvenile justice officials. Many immigrant and refugee children have experienced a history of trauma, including exposure to abuse or violence in their home country or in the United States. A 2013 study of unaccompanied immigrant children recently arrived in the United States, for example, revealed that 48 percent had been personally affected by violence from drug cartels, gangs, or state actors, and that 21 percent experienced violence in their homes in their country of origin (United Nations High Commissioner for Refugees, 2013). In addition, 38 percent of children from Mexico had been recruited into and exploited by human smuggling rings (United Nations High Commissioner for Refugees, 2013). Immigrant youths often have also endured traumatic journeys to the United States.

Young people who were brought to the United States at a very young age and are later involved in the juvenile justice system often lack parental supervision, have suffered abandonment, abuse, or neglect from a parent, and/or have been exposed to criminal street gangs. By virtue of arriving in the United States with refugee status, refugee children have necessarily fled their home countries because of persecution they experienced or the threat of future persecution. Many refugee children have also resided in refugee camps for extended periods of time and have lost loved ones.

According to the National Child Traumatic Stress Network, when a child feels intensely threatened by an event that they are involved in or witness, that event constitutes a trauma. Some children react to such a traumatic event with child traumatic stress (CTS), which can have effects long after the traumatic event has ended. Children affected by CTS may experience "intense and ongoing emotional upset, depression, anxiety, behavioral changes, difficulties at school, problems maintaining relationships, difficulty eating

and sleeping, aches and pains, withdrawal, substance abuse, dangerous behaviors, or unhealthy sexual activity among older children" (National Child
Traumatic Stress Network, 2005, p. 3). Since many immigrant youths have
witnessed or been subject to abuse both inside and outside the home, it follows that at least some youths would experience these symptoms.

Consequences of Trauma for Immigrant Youths

As the symptoms suggest, traumatic stress may contribute to a youth's juvenile justice involvement and may also further complicate or frustrate the
youth's rehabilitation. For example, immigrant youths who have experienced traumatic events such as abuse in the home may exhibit violent behavior themselves or turn to controlled substances as a way of coping. A
youth who because of a past traumatic event struggles to maintain relationships may experience problems in forming a trusting relationship with his
or her juvenile probation officer, even when that officer only has the child's
best interests in mind. Juvenile justice professionals need to be attuned to
the likelihood of trauma in an immigrant child's life and understand how
past trauma may have influenced the youth's delinquent behavior as well as
their response to rehabilitative services.

Discrimination Against Immigrant and Refugee Children

Inside the United States, immigrant and refugee children and families frequently experience discrimination. Undocumented immigrants in particular may experience guilt and shame and be treated as second-class citizens
(Flores & Kaplan, 2009). Research shows that experiences of discrimination "may lead to symptoms of depression and anxiety among some immigrant populations" (Flores & Kaplan, 2009, p. 6). Despite the high levels of
trauma experienced by immigrant youths, immigrant parents are often
hesitant to access critical public assistance for their children for fear of detection or of being perceived as a public charge when applying for citizenship (Flores & Kaplan, 2009).

Linguistic Barriers

Many immigrant youths in the juvenile justice system are limited English
proficient (LEP).[12] The juvenile justice system often fails to meet the needs

of these youths. Meaningful communication between youths and intake staff is essential to making sound detention and release decisions. Youths facing linguistic barriers encounter additional challenges to understanding the juvenile justice process, which can undermine their success. Further, it can be difficult for youths to build trust when they are not completely comfortable expressing themselves in English, which may result in young people sharing less information than they otherwise would.

Consequences of Linguistic Barriers

Youths may be reluctant to disclose the identity or whereabouts of their parents or caretakers unless they understand that the agency's goal is to release them, if possible, rather than subject them or their parents to the risk of deportation. This may lead to detention of immigrant youths whereas similarly situated citizen youths would be released. Youths may also fail to receive necessary services, such as counseling services, when such services are not available in their language. Linguistic barriers not only exist between youths and juvenile justice officials but also frequently arise for youths whose parents have limited English proficiency. In 2010, 61.6 percent of the population of individuals who were foreign born and not U.S. citizens spoke English less than "very well" (U.S. Bureau of the Census, 2010), indicating that linguistic barriers may exist in a large number of cases. A 2007 report by the Vera Institute of Justice found that language barriers did impact the treatment of youths. For example, the report found that parents who cannot read court documents that are only available in English may not attend important meetings and hearings affecting a child's detention status; that a parent's limited English proficiency may prevent him or her from understanding the possible benefits of agreeing to an out-of-court alternative; that a police officer may decide to leave a child overnight in a detention center because neither parent speaks English and is unable to respond to questions in English; or that a probation officer or health care clinician determining whether a parent is capable of supervising a child may recommend an out-of-home placement because an interpreter did not accurately translate the parent's responses (Vera Institute of Justice, 2007). As discussed earlier, unnecessary detention of youths can significantly affect their chances of future success (Aizer & Doyle, 2013).

Where linguistic barriers exist, youths can also end up in the uncomfortable position of serving as the translator between their parent and juvenile justice professionals. This arrangement can create a dynamic in which parental authority is undermined (Arya, Villarruel, Villanueva, & Augarten, 2009).

Cultural Barriers

Immigrant and refugee children and families often face significant cultural barriers to interacting with the juvenile justice system. For example, one study notes that although looking down in the presence of an authority figure is an indication of embarrassment at inappropriate behavior in many Latino cultures, judges may interpret this as a sign of disrespect or an indication of guilt (Villarruel et al., 2000). As that example demonstrates, cultural differences can influence every aspect of a juvenile case, even those as fundamental as the court's adjudication of guilt.

Cultural competence has been defined as "a system's, agency's or organization's ability to have attitudes, behaviors, policies, practices, procedures, and fiscal and personnel resources that enable them to work effectively in cross-cultural situations" (Arya et al., 2009, p. 55). In the context of the juvenile justice system, cultural competence may include providing training to juvenile justice personnel in how cultural beliefs influence their approach to interacting with clients, providing services that incorporate cultural values and traditions, and hiring and retaining staff who belong to the racial and ethnic groups that the agency serves (Arya et al., 2009). Cultural responsiveness, a different but related concept, is a more individualized approach that involves using the cultural knowledge and experiences of diverse clients to inform the ways in which the professional engages, assesses, and intervenes with them. Applied to the juvenile justice context, it acknowledges that the probation officer or other juvenile justice personnel does not have a full understanding of the youth's culture and positions him or her to learn from the youth about the youth's culture and to use this information in his or her practice. It also acknowledges the legitimacy and importance of the youth's culture and unique cultural experiences.

Consequences of Cultural Barriers

A lack of cultural competence and responsiveness can result in miscommunications and misunderstandings. For example, juvenile justice professionals may assume that clients who are nodding and remaining silent understand the information being provided to them. Such clients could just as easily be trying to be polite while not understanding what is being told to them, because of linguistic or cultural barriers.

One particular area in which cultural competence and responsiveness are critical is with respect to alternatives to detention. Because detaining children has been shown to be counterproductive in many cases, alternatives to detention are extremely important to achieving the goals of the juvenile justice system. Community-based programs provide an important alternative to detention for youths by allowing youths who do not require secure detention to be supervised in the community or diverted from formal processing. This is important because if courts do not have alternatives to detention at their disposal, officials may choose to detain too many youths (DeMuro, 1999). In fact, those jurisdictions that have been most successful in reducing the use of detention have developed a range of community-based services with different degrees of supervision depending on the particular risk factors of the youths awaiting adjudication, such as nonsecure shelters or day or evening reporting centers (DeMuro, 1999).

Although these alternatives to detention can be incredibly helpful, they must meet the cultural and linguistic needs of immigrant and refugee children. A major factor in the success of community-based alternatives to detention has been whether they are "culturally competent, relevant, and accessible to the youth they serve" (DeMuro, 1999, p. 14). A survey of successful community-based programs noted that "[m]any of these organizations developed programs that responded to the self-identified needs of the community and explicit efforts were made to strengthen the community's own ability to develop and support programs that work with youth" (Arya et al., 2009, p. 63). If alternatives to detention are not culturally and linguistically responsive, immigrant and refugee children and families may not succeed in these alternative arrangements, which could lead to unnecessary and counterproductive detention of youths.[13]

REFUGEE YOUTHS INTERACTING WITH THE JUVENILE JUSTICE SYSTEM

Refugee youths may experience many of the same barriers as undocumented youths when trying to interact successfully with the juvenile justice system. These include lack of trust in law enforcement, histories of trauma, and language and cultural barriers. One major difference for refugee children is that they are in

REFUGEE *(CONTINUED)*

a different situation with respect to their immigration status. Children who come to the United States with refugee status already have temporary legal status and within one year of entry are eligible to apply for permanent legal status in the form of a "green card." Thus, they may not have the same fear of being reported to immigration authorities as undocumented youths. Nonetheless, youths with refugee status could be fearful of losing that status, as certain kinds of bad behavior, such as drug trafficking, evidenced by juvenile delinquency adjudications, could make such a child vulnerable to losing his or her status and facing deportation.

BARRIERS TO CHANGE ACROSS SYSTEMS

When immigrant and refugee children and families become involved in the juvenile justice system, they may face distinct policy-related barriers that threaten or compromise their ability to obtain services that ensure they are rehabilitated and can successfully transition into adulthood. Because immigration is a political issue and local governments do not always understand the law or their role, local systems often defer to the federal government and look to deportation as the answer. There is also little informed discussion and few guidelines about the proper role of the juvenile justice system in immigration matters, including immigration enforcement, which can leave localities vulnerable to pressure from federal immigration authorities. Even in localities where immigrant and refugee children are more welcome, localities may face the challenge of restricted funding to provide services to undocumented youths. Accordingly, immigrant and refugee children in the juvenile justice system suffer the effects of the lack of informed, systematic policies and practices for best responding to their needs.

Political Pressure

Local immigration policy is often driven by politics rather than best practice. In the context of the juvenile and criminal justice systems, many localities are fearful of the political repercussions of having immigrant-friendly practices that involve working with and providing services to immigrants instead of reporting them to immigration authorities for deportation. Driving this fear is the threat that an undocumented immigrant released to the community rather than reported to immigration authorities will go on to commit violent or serious crimes for which local law enforcement will later be blamed. Increasingly, however, because of important legal changes and the lack of federal immigration reform, more states and localities are distancing themselves from federal immigration enforcement efforts by enacting policies that limit local law enforcement collaboration with immigration authorities (Junck & Wilber, 2014).

Lack of Standardized Best Practices and Policies for Treatment of Immigrant Children in the Juvenile Justice System

Because immigration is often seen as ancillary to the juvenile justice system, many local systems across the country have not prioritized informed discussions about the proper role of the system in immigration matters. The vast majority of localities therefore take an uninformed or ad hoc approach to immigration issues that varies from case to case, with few standardized practices and policies on the treatment of immigrant youths. Even those systems that have prioritized this issue and have adopted best policies and practices for working with immigrant youths often fear sharing these practices publicly or documenting them in writing because of potential political backlash.

Policies and practices in the field vary dramatically—both between and within jurisdictions. On one end of the spectrum are jurisdictions that treat youths equally regardless of their immigration status. These jurisdictions generally do not interact with federal immigration officials. For example, in Santa Clara County, California, the probation department has a stated policy against enforcing immigration holds against all youths (Cabrera, 2014). Many jurisdictions, however, have responded to the federal government's call for collaboration with local law enforcement to target immigrants. A number of these jurisdictions routinely report to the federal government youths they suspect are undocumented. For example, until recently, the Orange County, California, Juvenile Probation Department had a policy of investigating immigration status and reporting to immigration authorities all suspected immigrant youths in its care (University of California Irvine School of Law Immigrant Rights Clinic, 2013). Numerous jurisdictions fall somewhere in the middle of these two approaches. For example, these jurisdictions selectively report undocumented youths who are repeat offenders of serious crimes or who appear to have no ties to the United States. Finally, some jurisdictions have no policies at all, resulting in an ad hoc approach that depends primarily on the particular probation officer.

Apart from the Juvenile Detention Alternatives Initiative (JDAI), which has hosted immigration workshops at its annual conferences since 2007 and in 2014 published a best practices guide for juvenile justice professionals working with immigrant youths, there has been little space for having deliberate conversations on the appropriate role of the juvenile justice system in immigration matters at both the local and national levels. Consequently, juvenile justice personnel are often left to try to understand complicated laws and policies at this intersection alone. For example, in Orange County, California, the probation department had a written procedure for processing undocumented youths that relied on an inaccurate interpretation of the law (University of California Irvine School of Law Immigrant Rights Clinic, 2013). This procedure gave an ICE liaison deputy probation officer almost unfettered authority to refer youths to ICE when there were any signs of a questionable immigration status and permitted the ICE liaison to provide ICE with all relevant information on the youth. The authority for this broad policy was based on a provision of law that had been declared illegal in California (University of California Irvine School of Law Immigrant Rights Clinic, 2013). This misguided policy evidences the serious issues that can result from a lack of informed conversation at the local level, as it led the probation department to turn over extensive confidential information about youths in its care and in doing so refer to ICE the highest number of immigrant youths in the state of California (University of California Irvine School of Law Immigrant Rights Clinic, 2013). Those youths suffered not only violations of their privacy rights but also short- or long-term separation from their families, the terrifying threat of deportation, and in some cases actual deportation.

Even in jurisdictions where probation officials do not routinely report youths to immigration authorities, many such officials do not assist youths with immigration issues by referring them to providers of legal services or assisting them in compiling evidence for their immigration applications. This is true even though juvenile courts routinely order youths on probation to obey all laws. Naturally, it would flow from this court-ordered mandate that probation departments should help youths comply with all laws, including federal immigration laws. One way to do this would be to refer youths to immigration legal services providers so that they can explore immigration relief options if eligible.

Funding Restrictions for Undocumented Youths

Even when local law enforcement, like juvenile probation departments, is willing to serve youths, funding restrictions are a barrier to providing the full scope of services that an immigrant youth may need. However, it is in both the youth's and the public's best interests when youths, regardless of immigration status, receive rehabilitative services.

A youth's immigration status may determine his or her eligibility to access appropriate services. Primary sources of state funding for local law enforcement agencies may be unavailable to undocumented individuals. For example, undocumented individuals in California are ineligible for Medi-Cal, which is the main funding source for California probation departments. Immigrant youths who are not undocumented but rather have some documented immigration status may or may not be eligible for Medi-Cal. For example, youths with refugee status are eligible for Medi-Cal. In general, undocumented youths are also ineligible for federal benefits, such as Medicaid and SSI (National Immigration Law Center, 2013). Some youths are also unable to access local community services because of funding restrictions. Lack of immigration status therefore may hinder efforts to serve immigrant youths.

One such story comes out of Arizona, where an undocumented youth in desperate need of rehabilitative services was not able to access the services he needed because of his immigration status. In this case, the youth was arrested for assault but was determined to be incompetent in juvenile court because of emerging signs of schizophrenia. The youth's mother had legal status in the United States but returned to Mexico after the youth's stepfather was incarcerated in the United States and then deported to Mexico. This left the youth without any family support and in need of major services. Although the probation department sought to provide mental health services to the youth, they were unable to identify a funding source for the services and felt that their hands were tied. The Mexican consulate became involved in the case and tried to assist financially, but the need was greater than they could accommodate. Further, although the Mexican consulate was able to arrange for the youth's receipt of services in Mexico City, immigration authorities in the United States would not cooperate with requests to transfer the youth to Mexico. Thus, this child was left in limbo and was not able to receive services he gravely needed because of the funding restrictions that the probation department experienced.

SPOTLIGHT ON PROMISING PRACTICE: SANTA CRUZ COUNTY
PROBATION DEPARTMENT, JUVENILE DIVISION–PART 1

The Santa Cruz County Probation Department works hard to ensure that undocumented youths in the juvenile justice system have access to the services they need to support their rehabilitation. Within the Santa Cruz County Probation Department Juvenile Division's wraparound program, they have two spots for undocumented youths. Under their wraparound services model, the department also typically submits Permanent Residence Under Color of Law (PRUCOL)[14] applications as a means of obtaining Medi-Cal reimbursement for undocumented youths, which somewhat expands the number of undocumented youths they can serve. Although submitting these PRUCOL applications requires eliciting personal information from immigrant youths and families, including immigration status, the department makes clear to families that the information will not be used against them and rather will only be used to help them. The department also draws on county funds to provide services for mental health only. These funds can be used to provide services for approximately three undocumented youths at any given time. Although the department strives to provide all services necessary regardless of immigration status, the reality remains that its access to funding for undocumented youths is limited.

Federal Pressure

Contributing to the lack of systematic best practices and policies is not only a lack of informed discussion at the local and national levels but also confusion and disagreement among professionals regarding the appropriate role of the juvenile justice system with respect to enforcing civil immigration laws and inherent pressure from the federal government. Until recently, the federal government was not transparent about whether collaboration between local law enforcement authorities and immigration authorities was voluntary or mandatory (Junck & Wilber, 2014). Although programs aimed at collecting information about individuals who may be deportable through state and local law enforcement are technically voluntary, the federal government's relationship with state and local law enforcement undoubtedly includes an element of pressure. As the National Immigration Law Center reports, these policies "are based on meeting I[mmigration &] C[ustoms] E[nforcement]'s needs and may be imposed despite strong opposition from local communities" (National Immigration Law Center, 2014, p. 2). Thus, juvenile justice professionals often feel pressure from the federal government to report and hold youths for deportation.

SYSTEM EFFORTS TO ADDRESS THE UNIQUE NEEDS OF IMMIGRANT AND REFUGEE CHILDREN AND FAMILIES: EMERGING PRACTICES AND PREVENTIVE INTERVENTIONS

New juvenile justice system efforts to address the specific needs of immigrants, and in particular undocumented children, are emerging. There is no national consensus on promising practices in this arena. However, Santa Cruz County, California, is an example of a jurisdiction that has effectively responded to immigration issues in a way that takes into account the special needs of this population while also striving to pursue rehabilitation for these youths as they would for any other similarly situated citizen youths.

SPOTLIGHT ON PROMISING PRACTICE: SANTA CRUZ COUNTY
PROBATION DEPARTMENT, JUVENILE DIVISION–PART 2

Santa Cruz County, located in a coastal area of Northern California, has seen a growing immigrant population in recent decades. Data from 2011 indicated that 36 percent of youths in the general population were white, 1 percent were black, 54 percent were Latino, 4 percent were Asian or Pacific Islander, and 1 percent were Native American. Nonetheless, the juvenile caseload of the probation department at that time was comprised largely of Latino males.[15] Department personnel also estimated that 10 percent to 20 percent of their overall caseload consisted of undocumented youths.

Santa Cruz County is one of four model sites in the Juvenile Detention Alternatives Initiative, whose reform work has been replicated nationwide. Employing evidence-based practices, its reform efforts have resulted in positive outcomes both for its community members and for the youths it serves. These results include cost savings in the millions, reduction of the juvenile hall population by more than half, and reduction of juvenile felony arrests by 48 percent and misdemeanor arrests by 43 percent. Santa Cruz has also significantly narrowed the gap between Latino youth representation in the general population and representation in the juvenile hall population, in large part by working with the W. Haywood Burns Institute to understand how certain policies and practices contribute to racial disparities.

Through JDAI, the probation department undertook development of a set of organizational values based on the principle that all youths should be treated equally. Recognizing that youths have better chances at rehabilitation when they are not detained, this set of values holds that youths should not be detained unnecessarily, that out-of-home placements and institutions are not a good substitute for family, and that intake and probation practices should be bias-free and race-neutral. Their approach to bias-free and race-neutral intake procedures is built on a recognition that citizenship is not a good predictor of the risk of either reoffense of a youth or appearance in court. Rather, immigration status only becomes relevant when the department is seeking to provide appropriate services for youths within the system and needs to creatively structure its funding.

To put these values into practice, the department strives to employ a staff that is representative of the community it serves. In 2014, the department employed a staff that was 39 percent Latino, most of whom were also bilingual and bicultural. The department has found that having their staff be representative of the community they serve not only facilitates communication but also helps the department to understand and empathize with youths and their families and to approach their clients with compassion. In addition, the department places high importance on having staff in leadership positions that reflect the community they serve, as staff in leadership positions influence policies and practices. Further, the department provides culturally relevant training to its staff and makes it clear to the community that they do not report to immigration authorities. This assists in building relationships of trust where youths and families can feel comfortable sharing information with probation staff. The department also provides referrals for immigration legal services to immigrant youths and engages with an array of culturally responsive community-based services for Latino youths and families, many of whom also hire staff that reflect community demographics.

As part of the process of implementing its organizational values, the department deliberately engaged two immigration advocacy organizations to conduct a review of current practices and policies through an analysis of department manuals and written policies and interviews with staff, providing a half-day mandatory immigration training session to the department, and connecting the immigration organizations with community-based organizations to provide another source of immigration training and resources. All of this work culminated in the development of a clear written policy to govern intake procedures for suspected immigrant youths. This policy recognizes the crucial role of confidentiality in the juvenile justice system—that in order to be true to the founding ideals of the system, the probation department must protect the personal information of youths and, in particular, not turn over this information to immigration authorities. The policy also highlights some key provisions of law about which there has been much confusion among juvenile justice professionals. These include that

(1) the Juvenile Justice and Delinquency Prevention Act expressly prohibits detaining a juvenile solely because he or she is undocumented;

(2) that inquiries by ICE to hold youths are not court orders but merely requests, enforceable at the discretion of local officials; and

(3) that sharing confidential juvenile information and files with ICE without first obtaining a court order is a violation of California law.

The policy further recognizes that immigration status is not relevant to the purpose of the juvenile justice system, as it does not pertain to investigating or responding to delinquent behavior or supporting youths through rehabilitation. On that ground, the policy makes it clear that it is not the responsibility of probation staff to ask or attempt to determine the immigration status of a juvenile, and that intake procedures for youths suspected to be immigrants are to be handled in the same manner as any other intake.

The probation department has also taken steps to actively assist undocumented youths in stabilizing their immigration situation. For example, the department has developed a referral system to assist youths in finding immigration legal services. Currently, the department is also supporting a youth on their caseload in his application for Deferred Action for Childhood Arrivals (DACA). In that case, it was pointed out by an outside partner that the youth may be eligible for DACA. The youth's placement probation officer agreed to assist in any way possible. The probation department plans to have this officer document and share his experience with the rest of their staff so that they can replicate the assistance. In other cases, the department has helped youths formerly involved in the juvenile justice system by writing letters in support of their DACA applications. In this way, the Santa Cruz County Probation Department, Juvenile Division, provides a model for how juvenile justice personnel can positively engage with youths regarding their immigration status, ultimately contributing to the long-term stability and educational and career prospects of an immigrant youth involved with the juvenile justice system.

Finally, as noted, the Santa Cruz County Probation Department, Juvenile Division, has also taken steps to provide its services in a culturally responsive manner by employing bilingual and bicultural staff, training staff in a culturally responsive manner, and cultivating relationships with an array of culturally responsive community-based organizations providing services for Latino youths and their families. To further serve immigrant youths in its care, the department has also developed creative funding strategies to allow it to provide necessary services to undocumented youths and works hard to make it clear to the immigrant community that the department does not report youths to immigration authorities in order to facilitate trusting relationships between immigrant youths and families and juvenile justice officials.

COLLABORATIONS ACROSS SYSTEMS: HOW IMMIGRATION SYSTEMS AND JUVENILE JUSTICE STAKEHOLDERS COLLABORATE

For juvenile justice systems to best serve immigrant and refugee children and families, collaboration across systems is essential. Sadly, the primary manner in which immigration and juvenile justice systems currently interact is through reports to immigration authorities for deportation. These policies and practices that result in the initiation of deportation proceedings decrease the likelihood that youths will rehabilitate, remain with their families, and successfully transition into adulthood. Importantly, they also decrease the likelihood that eligible youths will achieve legal status. Despite this trend, limited examples of collaborations across systems are emerging in the fields of immigration and juvenile justice.

Collaborations Across Systems: Education, Immigration, and the Juvenile Justice System

The South Asian organizing center DRUM is a multigenerational, membership-led organization of low-wage South Asian immigrant workers and youths in New York City. Through their Dignity in Schools campaign, they are working to change the New York City Student Discipline Code to require schools to use restorative justice, peer mediation, and positive behavior support programs instead of suspensions and arrests. For example, DRUM has been working with Newtown High School in Elmhurst, Queens, to reduce suspensions and increase graduation rates through a student-run peer mediation program. Where effective, this effort allows immigrant youths to avoid entering the juvenile justice system following school-based incidents, thereby sidestepping the myriad negative consequences that can result when immigrant youths come into contact with the juvenile justice system.

Collaborations Across Systems: Juvenile Justice and Mental Health

Given the range of traumas that immigrant youths may have experienced, it follows that many immigrant youths involved with the juvenile justice system may have mental health needs. Collaboration has emerged between the juvenile justice system and mental health providers in the form of Juvenile Mental Health Courts. These courts divert mentally ill youths from juvenile halls to community-based mental health services by providing intensive case management and supervision rather than relying on the normal adversarial process (National Center for Youth Law, 2011). For example, in Alameda County, California, the Juvenile Mental Health Court (known as the Collaborative Court) strives to work toward positive outcomes for youths that focus on the strengths of the youth, are centered on the family, and are culturally appropriate (National Center for Youth Law, 2011). The potential for immigrant youths to benefit from this collaboration is immense.

CONCLUSION

As discussed in this chapter, immigrant children and families face unique issues and barriers in interacting with the juvenile justice system, such as possible referrals to immigration authorities, lack of assistance in obtaining immigration status, fear of engaging with law enforcement, language and cultural barriers, and ineligibility for services because of immigration status. In order to address systematic barriers that immigrant and refugee children and families encounter when interacting with the juvenile justice system, professionals need to develop informed policies that strive to achieve the following:

1 Minimize unnecessary detention or separation of immigrant youths from their families and communities.
2 Ensure that detention practices do not unfairly prejudice immigrant youths.
3 Eliminate the potentially devastating immigration consequences for immigrant youths of their involvement in the juvenile justice system.
4 Preserve the ability of immigrant youths to pursue immigration relief under federal law.

Whereas being reported to federal immigration authorities can begin a long, traumatic, and potentially devastating process for an immigrant youth, undermining the youth's rehabilitation and successful transition into adulthood and eroding community trust and cooperation with law enforcement, reporting that same youth to immigration legal and other community resources could begin a life-changing process of providing stability and hope in the youth's life. Further, establishing a clear policy against reporting immigration status to federal immigration authorities allows the community to establish trust with juvenile justice officials and feel safer when they are interacting with the juvenile justice system. As demonstrated in Santa Cruz County, juvenile justice agencies can and should develop partnerships with immigration advocates to make informed policies on immigration issues and to develop networks of vital resources from which immigrant youths may benefit. In cases where youths involved with the juvenile justice system are able to receive immigration and related assistance and it leads to lawful status in the United States, it can provide a brighter future in terms of educational and job prospects, and contribute to their overall success.

KEY TERMS

ALTERNATIVES TO DETENTION   Alternatives to placement in a secure facility, such as home confinement or day reporting.

CHILD TRAUMATIC STRESS (CTS)   A child's potential reaction to feeling intensely threatened by an event that they are involved in or witness, which can have effects long after the trauma has ended.

ICE HOLD   A voluntary request that a local law enforcement agency with custody over an individual hold the individual for 48 hours (except weekends and federal holidays) after the person is otherwise eligible for release under state law in order for the Department of Homeland Security to arrange to assume custody for the purposes of arresting and removing the person. ICE holds are also referred to as "immigration detainers."

IMMIGRANT CHILDREN   Youths who are not U.S. citizens, including both documented and undocumented youths.

IMMIGRATION AND CUSTOMS ENFORCEMENT (ICE)   The federal agency within the U.S. Department of Homeland Security that is responsible for interior enforcement of federal immigration laws.

UNACCOMPANIED ALIEN CHILD   An individual under the age of 18 who has no lawful immigration status in the United States and does not have any parent or legal guardian in the United States who is willing or able to provide care and physical custody (6 U.S.C. § 279(g)(2) (2015)).

STUDY QUESTIONS

1 What are some of the consequences that result when local law enforcement reports undocumented youths in their care to ICE?
2 What are the potential ways in which juvenile justice involvement can affect a youth's chances of fighting deportation or obtaining legal status?
3 What is the major difference between undocumented youths and refugee youths?
4 What are the main reasons that local law enforcement in the juvenile justice system might report a youth to ICE?

5   What are some of the best practices for working with immigrant youths
that have been demonstrated by the Santa Cruz County Probation
Department?

ADDITIONAL RESOURCES

The Annie E. Casey Foundation (for resources on alternatives to detention
for youth): http://www.aecf.org
Immigrant Legal Resource Center (for information on immigration relief for
children): http://www.ilrc.org/info-on-immigration-law/remedies-for
-immigrant-children-and-youth
Junck, A., Domingo, C., & Beasley, H. (2013). Two-tiered justice for
juveniles. In S. D. Phillips, W. Cervantes, Y. Lincroft, A. J. Dettlaff, &
L. Bruce (Eds.), *Children in harm's way: Criminal justice, immigration
enforcement, and child welfare* (pp. 31–40). Washington, DC: The
Sentencing Project and First Focus. Retrieved from http://www.sentencing
project.org/doc/publications/cc_Children%20in%20Harm%27s%20Way
-final.pdf
Transactional Records Access Clearinghouse (for data on immigration
enforcement and the immigration system): http://trac.syr.edu
/immigration/

NOTES

1   The term "immigrant children" refers to youths who are not U.S. citizens, and it can
include both documented and undocumented youths. The term "refugee children"
refers to a subset of the immigrant population and describes youths who were admitted to the United States with refugee status. Persons admitted as refugees are eligible
to apply to become permanent residents ("green card" holders) one year after they are
admitted to the United States.
2   On the other hand, the lack of data also protects against its misuse by anti-immigrant
groups who attack government spending on undocumented children. An example of
such a misuse was the 2011 anti-immigrant law in Alabama, House Bill 56 (HB 56),
modeled after Arizona's infamous Senate Bill 1070 (SB 1070). This law included a provision requiring the Alabama Department of Education to track the number of its
students who were undocumented, and it was justified on the grounds that one of the
state's largest costs was education for undocumented children (Reyes, 2012). The ab-
sentee rate of Latino children initially shot up, as parents kept children at home rather
than expose them to potential risk (Reyes, 2012). Less than two weeks after HB 56

went into effect, a federal appeals court temporarily halted its requirement that schools ask about students' legal status (Sarlin, 2013). The provision was later permanently blocked through a settlement agreement between civil rights groups and the state (American Civil Liberties Union, 2013).

3   On November 20, 2014, President Obama announced executive reforms to the immigration system, including changes to immigration enforcement policies. One major change is that ICE stated that it will stop using ICE holds because of constitutional concerns except in "special circumstances." This means that in most cases jails and juvenile detention facilities will not be asked to hold individuals for ICE past the time they should otherwise be released. ICE has stated that holds will be replaced with requests for notification of release dates, so that ICE agents can continue to track immigrants.

4   Federal law defines the term "unaccompanied alien child" as an individual under the age of 18 who has no lawful immigration status in the United States and does not have any parent or legal guardian in the United States who is willing or able to provide care and physical custody (6 U.S.C. § 279(g)(2) (2015)).

5   An ICE hold is a voluntary request that a local law enforcement agency with custody over an individual hold the individual for 48 hours (except weekends and federal holidays) after the person is otherwise eligible for release under state law in order for the Department of Homeland Security to arrange to assume custody for the purposes of arresting and removing the youth. The legal authority for ICE holds is in 8 U.S.C. § 1357(d) (2015), and the law implementing ICE holds is found in the Code of Federal Regulations at 8 C.F.R. § 287.7 (2016).

6   Notably, in 2014, the constitutionality of ICE holds and the ability of local law enforcement to hold individuals subject to them past the time they would otherwise be released under state law was questioned (*Miranda-Olivares v. Clackamas County*, 2014). Further, on November 20, 2014, President Obama announced executive reforms to the immigration system, including changes to immigration enforcement policies (see note 3). It remains to be seen, however, how these new policies will play out.

7   The Center on Juvenile and Criminal Justice found that immigration enforcement in the California juvenile justice system subjects youths to unnecessary prolonged detention, costing taxpayers an estimated $127,978 per year (Teji, 2013). At least two studies have also found that ICE hold requests result in an average of 21 days longer in custody than custody periods without ICE holds (Greene, 2012; White & Dwight, 2012).

8   During this intake, a probation officer will ask a youth a range of questions about his or her personal history, family information, and sometimes also his or her immigration status and history, generally under the auspices that a full understanding of a youth's social history is required to make adequate decisions about his or her care and custody and for submission in a social report to the juvenile court.

9   For example, in California, Section 827 of the Welfare & Institutions Code states that "juvenile court records, in general, should be confidential," a mandate that extends to reports of a probation officer and all other documents filed in the case or made available to the probation officer. The only mechanism by which nonauthorized parties (such as immigration authorities) may access these juvenile court records is by filing a

petition in state court and receiving permission from the court to access specified documents. If such a petition is filed, the court must determine whether the need for disclosure outweighs the policy considerations favoring confidentiality (Cal. Welf. & Inst. Code § 827 & 828 (2016).

10 The law also does not support the reporting of youths to immigration authorities. There is no duty under federal law for state or local law enforcement officials to ask about immigration status or report immigrants to federal immigration agencies. In fact, the federal government cannot require state or local officials to enact or enforce federal laws or regulations (*New York v. United States*, 1992; *Printz v. United States*, 1996). State or local law enforcement officials may report suspected immigrants to immigration authorities, but such reporting is always voluntary and in some cases occurs in contravention of state laws, such as juvenile confidentiality laws.

11 ORR is under the umbrella of the U.S. Department of Health and Human Services, Administration for Children and Families.

12 A person is classified as limited English proficient if he or she has a limited ability to read, write, speak, or understand English [Guidance to Federal Financial Assistance Recipients Regarding Title VI Prohibition Against National Origin Discrimination Affecting Limited English Proficient Persons, 67 Fed. Reg. 117, 41457 (June 18, 2002)].

13 Another way in which alternatives to detention can benefit immigrant and refugee children is that they may allow the child to sidestep the stage of their interaction with the juvenile justice system at which they may have been reported to immigration authorities. Most jurisdictions that make reports to immigration authorities do so once a youth arrives at the juvenile hall for intake and processing. When immigrant youths are diverted from secure detention, this not only may increase their likelihood of a successful rehabilitation but may also allow the youth to avoid being reported to immigration authorities.

14 Federal statutes that define eligibility criteria for public benefits allow payment of benefits not only for lawful residents but also to persons "permanently residing under color of law." Permanently residing under color of law means that U.S. Citizenship and Immigration Services is aware of the person's unlawful presence but is not actively pursuing his or her deportation.

15 Based on interviews conducted with the Santa Cruz County Juvenile Probation Department as part of the Immigrant Youth Justice Initiative Survey Report in December 2011.

REFERENCES

6 U.S.C. § 279(g)(2) (2015).

8 C.F.R. § 287.7 (2016).

8 U.S.C. § 1357(d) (2015).

Aizer, A., & Doyle, J. (2013). *Juvenile incarceration, human capital and future crime: Evidence from randomly-assigned judges.* Retrieved from http://nber.org/papers/w19102

American Bar Association. (2012). *The history of juvenile justice*. Retrieved from http://www.americanbar.org/content/dam/aba/migrated/publiced/features /DYJpart1.authcheckdam.pdf

American Civil Liberties Union. (2013). *Civil rights coalition victorious against Alabama's anti-immigrant law*. Retrieved from https://www.aclu.org/immigrants -rights/civil-rights-coalition-victorious-suit-against-alabamas-anti-immigrant-law

———. (2014). *ACLU recommendations to DHS to address record-level deportations*. Retrieved from https://www.aclu.org/sites/default/files/assets/14_5_14_aclu _recommendations_to_dhs_to_address_record-level_deportations_final.pdf

The Annie E. Casey Foundation, Juvenile Detention Alternatives Initiative. (1999). *The JDAI story: Building a better juvenile detention system*. Baltimore, MD: Author. Retrieved from http://www.aecf.org/m/resourcedoc/AECF -TheJDAIStoryOverview-1999.pdf

Arya, N., Villarruel, F., Villanueva, C., & Augarten, I. (2009, May). *America's invisible children, Latino youth and the failure of justice*. Washington, DC: Campaign for Youth Justice & National Council of La Raza.

Cabrera, Y. (2014, June 3). Court case is changing policies on immigration holds. *Voice of OC*. Retrieved from http://www.voiceofoc.org/countywide/county _government/article_355d6d06-eafc-11e3-b4ce-0019bb2963f4.html

Cal. Welf. & Inst. Code § 827 & 828 (2016).

DeMuro, P. (1999). *Pathways to detention reform, Vol. 4: Consider the alternatives: Planning and implementing detention alternatives*. Baltimore, MD: Annie E. Casey Foundation. Retrieved from www.aecf.org

Flores, L., & Kaplan, A. (2009). *Addressing the mental health problems of border and immigrant youth*. Los Angeles, CA: National Center for Child Traumatic Stress. Retrieved from http://www.nctsn.org/sites/default/files/assets/pdfs /BorderlandersSpecialReport_Final_0.pdf

Graham v. Florida, 130 U.S. 2011, 2026 (2010).

Greene, J. A. (2012). *The cost of responding to immigration detainers in California, preliminary findings*. Brooklyn, NY: Justice Strategies.

Guidance to Federal Financial Assistance Recipients Regarding Title VI Prohibition Against National Origin Discrimination Affecting Limited English Proficient Persons, 67 Fed. Reg. 117, 41457 (June 18, 2002).

Junck, A., Domingo, C., & Beasley, H. (2013). Two-tiered justice for juveniles. In S. D. Phillips, W. Cervantes, Y. Lincroft, A. J. Dettlaff, & L. Bruce (Eds.), *Children in harm's way: Criminal justice, immigration enforcement, and child welfare* (pp. 31–40). Washington, DC: The Sentencing Project and First Focus. Retrieved from http://

www.sentencingproject.org/doc/publications/cc_Children%20in%20Harm%
27s%20Way-final.pdf

Junck, A., & Wilber, S. (2014). *Noncitizen youth in the juvenile justice system.* Baltimore, MD: The Annie E. Casey Foundation, Juvenile Detention Alternatives Initiative.

King, M. (2006). *Guide to the state juvenile justice profiles.* Pittsburgh, PA: National Center for Juvenile Justice, Technical Assistance to the Juvenile Court Bulletin.

Miranda-Olivares v. Clackamas County, No. 3:12-cv-02317 (D. Or. April 11, 2014).

National Center for Youth Law. (2011). *Improving outcomes for youth in the juvenile justice system.* Retrieved from http://www.youthlaw.org/policy/advocacy/jmhcs/

National Child Traumatic Stress Network. (2005). *Understanding child traumatic stress.* Retrieved from http://www.nctsn.org/sites/default/files/assets /pdfs/understanding_child_traumatic_stress_brochure_9-29-05.pdf

National Immigration Law Center. (2013). *A quick guide to immigrant eligibility for ACA and key federal means-tested programs.* Retrieved from http://nilc.org /access-to-bens.html

——. (2014). *How ICE uses local criminal justice systems to funnel people into the detention and deportation system.* Retrieved from http://nilc.org/localjusticeandice.html

New York v. United States, 505 U.S. 144, 166 (1992).

Padilla v. Commonwealth of Kentucky, 559 U.S. 356 (2010).

Plumer, B. (2013, June 15). Throwing children in prison turns out to be a really bad idea. *The Washington Post.* Retrieved from http://www.washingtonpost.com /blogs/wonkblog/wp/2013/06/15/throwing-children-in-prison-turns-out-to -be-a-really-bad-idea/

Printz v. United States, 521 U.S. 898, 927 (1996).

Reyes, P. (2012, March 1). "It's just not right": The failures of Alabama's self-deportation experiment. *Mother Jones.* Retrieved from http://www.mother jones.com/politics/2012/03/alabama-anti-immigration-law-self-deportation -movement

Sarlin, B. (2013, December 16). How America's harshest immigration law failed. MSNBC. Retrieved from http://www.msnbc.com/msnbc/undocumented -workers-immigration-alabama

Shepherd, R. (1999). The juvenile court at 100 years: A look back. *Juvenile Justice, 6*(2), 13–21. Retrieved from https://www.ncjrs.gov/html/ojjdp/jjjournal1299/2.html

Teji, S. (2013). *The unnecessary detention of undocumented youth.* San Francisco, CA: Center on Juvenile and Criminal Justice. Retrieved from http://www.cjcj .org/uploads/cjcj/documents/cjcj_juvenile_ice_hold_factsheet.pdf

United Nations High Commissioner for Refugees. (2013). *Children on the run.* Retrieved from: http://www.unhcrwashington.org/sites/default/files/1_UAC _Children%20on%20the%20Run_Full%20Report.pd

University of California Irvine School of Law Immigrant Rights Clinic. (2013). *Why Orange County probation should stop choosing deportation over rehabilita- tion for immigrant youth.* Retrieved from http://www.law.uci.edu/academics /real-life-learning/clinics/UCILaw_SecondChances_dec2013.pdf

U.S. Bureau of the Census. (2000). *Census 2000 foreign-born profiles.* Retrieved from http://www.census.gov/population/foreign/data/stp-159-2000.html

——. (2010). *American Community Survey. Selected characteristics of the native and foreign-born populations.* Retrieved from http://factfinder.census.gov /faces/tableservices/jsf/pages/productview.xhtml?pid=ACS_14_1YR_S0501 &prodType=table

U.S. Department of Justice, Office of Justice Programs, Office of Juvenile Justice and Delinquency Prevention. (1999). *Juvenile justice: A century of change.* Re- trieved from https://www.ncjrs.gov/pdffiles1/ojjdp/178995.pdf

——. (2013). *OJJDP statistical briefing book.* Retrieved from http://www.ojjdp.gov /ojstatbb/structure_process/qa04205.asp?qaDate=2012

Vera Institute of Justice. (2007). *If parents don't speak English well, will their kids get locked up?* Retrieved from http://www.vera.org/sites/default/files/resources /downloads/Language_Barriers_and_Disproportionate_Minority_Contact _in_the_Juvenile_Justice_System.pdf

Villarruel, F., Walker, N., Minifee, P., Rivera-Vazquez, O., Peterson, S., & Perry, K. (2000). *Donde esta la justicia? A call to action on behalf of Latino and Latina youth in the U.S. justice system.* East Lansing: Building Blocks for Youth, Michigan State University Institute for Children, Youth, and Families. Retrieved from http://cclp.org/documents/BBY/Donde.pdf

W. Haywood Burns Institute. (2009). *The keeper and the kept.* San Francisco, CA: Author. Retrieved from http://www.uchastings.edu/academics/faculty/adjunct /onek2/docs/TheKeeper-and-the-Kept3-7-13.pdf

White, K. A., & Dwight, L. (2012). *Misplaced priorities: SB90 & the costs to local communities.* Denver: The Colorado Fiscal Institute.

Women's Refugee Commission. (2012). *Forced from home: The lost boys and girls of Central America.* Retrieved from https://womensrefugeecommission.org /component/zdocs/document?id=844-forced-from-home-the-lost-boys-and -girls-of-central-america

Practice with Immigrant and Refugee Children and Families in the Education System

▸ *LYN MORLAND and DINA BIRMAN*

SINCE 1965, the United States has been experiencing the highest influx of immigrants in its history, and no institution has been as directly affected by these demographic changes as the public schools. Today, more than one in four children in the United States has a foreign-born parent, and these children of immigrants and refugees are the fastest-growing portion of the U.S. child population. For the first time in history, white children now constitute the minority in U.S. schools, a change largely driven by the ethnic and racial diversity of this new immigration (Hussar & Bailey, 2014). Although today's immigrants are far more diverse than ever before in U.S. history, they must also adapt to a very structured school system—with its own policies and financial constraints—that is expected to prepare them to be part of a highly competitive and technological society. At the same time, schools must adapt to their changing communities, meet the special needs of children in immigrant families, and help prepare all children to live successfully in a diverse country and global economy.

This chapter addresses the issues that first- and second-generation immigrant and refugee children and families encounter in the U.S. education system, from pre-kindergarten to secondary. In addition to the challenges experienced by children, families, and schools, we describe a number of education models and programs under way for students with the greatest needs. Finally, we look to the future, including current research priorities and new directions that can support immigrant and refugee children's success in education.

INCREASING DIVERSITY

There are currently in the United States 18.7 million children under the age of 18 whose parents are immigrants, including nearly 3 million first-generation immigrants (foreign born) and 16 million second-generation immigrants (U.S. born, with at least one immigrant parent) (Child Trends, 2014; Zong & Batalova, 2015). The number of children of immigrants has grown by more than 50 percent over the past 20 years, largely as a result of the increase in U.S.-born children of immigrants. In 2014, more than half (55 percent) of all first- and second-generation immigrant children lived in families who migrated from Latin America (with the vast majority from just one country, Mexico), and children from different parts of Asia (primarily India, China, and the Philippines) made up 17 percent of all first- and second-generation immigrant children (Child Trends, 2014; Zong & Batalova, 2015). In all, immigrants represent well over 130 countries today and are settling in virtually all U.S. states. Although immigrants are still concentrated in the traditional gateway states of California, New York, Texas, Florida, and New Jersey, the states newest to immigration, such as North Carolina and Tennessee, have the fastest-growing populations (Zong & Batalova, 2015). Together, these immigration trends mean that children from diverse immigrant families can be found in school systems throughout the United States.

Although many newcomers are highly educated, speak English, and come to the United States on visas to join family or to work, many others arrive from rural farming backgrounds or refugee camps, often with limited or interrupted formal education, and may not be literate in their native languages (Birman & Tran, 2015; Dryden-Peterson, 2015; Morland, Birman, Dunn, Adkins, & Gardner, 2013). Although the majority of immigrants enter this country legally, 11.7 million immigrants are currently living in the United States without legal documentation, and many U.S.-born children live in mixed-status families, meaning they live with an undocumented parent. Undocumented children migrating alone from Central America and Mexico to the United States drew national attention in 2014 when the number apprehended at the U.S.-Mexico border suddenly shot up to more than 68,000 in one year (U.S. Department of Homeland Security, 2015). This surge drew particular attention to the extreme conditions of violence, poverty, and lack of educational opportunities many were fleeing (United

Nations High Commissioner for Refugees, 2014; U. S. Government Accountability Office, 2015).

Refugees, who are escaping persecution and are admitted to the United States under a special humanitarian program, represent another immigrant group with various backgrounds. Although newly arrived refugees represented only a small proportion (69,900, or less than 4 percent) of the immigrant population in 2014, they came from more than 80 different countries and spoke 288 different languages (Capps & Newland, 2015). Many refugees, particularly those from Burma, Bhutan, and Somalia, have spent years in refugee camps, with few opportunities for education or work. There is tremendous diversity within refugee groups as well; for example, Burmese in the United States speak 61 different languages, and Somalis speak 31 different languages (Capps & Newland, 2015). The diversity in backgrounds, cultures, and languages among immigrants and refugees today is unprecedented in U.S. history. For example, data from Virginia's Fairfax County Public Schools showed that nearly half of the almost 100,000 students enrolled in its elementary schools spoke one of 170 different languages at home (Fairfax County, Virginia, Public Schools, n.d.). Public school systems across the United States are understandably experiencing a number of challenges in successfully serving students and families from such diverse backgrounds.

DIVERSITY IN ACADEMIC ACHIEVEMENT

A university press release recently declared that, "Children of immigrants are outperforming children whose family trees have deeper roots in the United States, learning more in school and then making smoother transitions into adulthood" (Hao & Woo, 2012; Lunday, 2012). Indeed, there has been an accumulation of evidence indicating that, on multiple measures of school achievement, many first- and second-generation children of immigrants outperform children of U.S.-born parents. Since this educational advantage holds despite higher than average rates of poverty and other disadvantages experienced by immigrant families, it is often described as an "immigrant paradox" in education (Crosnoe & Lopez Turley, 2011; García Coll & Marks, 2012; Hao & Woo, 2012; Portes & Rumbaut, 2001; Suarez-Orozco, Rhodes, and Milburn, 2009).

At the same time, there is a high degree of variance in academic performance and high school completion rates among immigrant and refugee children as a group, which is not surprising, given the great diversity among immigrants and refugees, as well as the complexity of factors involved in academic achievement for all children. In a recent volume on the growing diversity in U.S. schools, Glick and Bates state, "Perhaps one of the easiest conclusions to draw about children of immigrants in the United States today is that they are a diverse group with considerable variation in academic performance and subsequent educational attainment. Perhaps one of the most difficult tasks, therefore, is to draw substantive conclusions about the determinants of immigrant children's paths through school" (Glick & Bates, 2010, p. 112). In order to better understand these variations, researchers have examined educational attainment by generation, country of origin, and the experiences of immigrant families and children before, during, and after migration (Crosnoe & Lopez Turley, 2011; Glick & Bates, 2010; Portes & Rumbaut, 2001; Zhou, 1997). Most of this research has been conducted thus far on first- and second-generation youths in secondary school in the United States. However, there is a small but growing body of research on premigration and migration experiences, as well as on young children of immigrants in the United States.

PREMIGRATION AND MIGRATION PATTERNS

In the general U.S. population, school success has been associated with children's parental education level, particularly the mother's. Studies of premigration characteristics of immigrants to the United States have found that many tend to be among the more highly educated in their country. For example, Feliciano (2005) found that for all but one of 32 countries and territories examined, those migrating to the United States had achieved a higher level of education relative to others in their country, with an emphasis on *relative*. For example, in countries where many do not have a high school diploma, having one may be quite meaningful and indicate a higher social status. Even for immigrants who do not attain the same level of social status after arriving in the United States, these comparatively higher levels of education positively influence the educational trajectories of their children. In other words, the higher the previous social status of the parents within their country of origin, the higher the achievement of their children in the United States. Two of the largest immigrant groups in the United States— those from India and the Philippines—tend to fit this pattern. In addition, immigrants from African countries have tended to be more highly educated (relative to their country of origin), and their children are also more likely to be successful in school (Capps & Fix, 2012; Crosnoe, 2013; Kao, 1999; Zhou & Kim, 2006).

Immigrants to the United States from Latin America, with the largest populations being from Mexico and El Salvador, are also diverse in education background. However, those with less formal education and fewer means tend to be more vulnerable to the effects of poverty, organized crime, and gangs in their country of origin. Even before the existence of a border or immigration laws, there was a long tradition of crossing the Mexico-U.S. border for work, and many U.S. businesses continue to depend largely on migrant labor today. Immigrants from these regions, then, are more likely to migrate to the United States for work, safety, and to join family members. When older youths migrate, either alone or with their families, they often must work to survive in the United States, and the prospect of attending and graduating from high school given their lack of English and educational preparation may be daunting and simply not a priority, so they never enroll in school. In addition, 58 percent of immigrants from Mexico are currently in the United States without documentation (Zong & Batalova, 2015). Although they and their children still have the right to attend school, their undocumented status typically means living in fear of discovery, limits their access to public services, and generally affects their children's healthy development and prospects for higher education (Suárez-Orozco, Yoshikawa, Teranishi, & Suárez-Orozco, 2011; Yoshikawa & Kholoptseva, 2013).

Many refugees, as forced migrants, come from politically persecuted and relatively well-educated classes, whereas other refugees are from rural backgrounds and may have spent years in refugee camps. These latter groups in particular may arrive in the United States with comparatively low levels of formal education, literacy, and English proficiency. As a result of persecution, many refugees will have endured violence, lost family members, and experienced severe deprivation before and during their migration journeys, further challenging their ability to adjust to a new land.

A recent study by Dryden-Peterson (2015) documented the opportunities for education among refugee children in countries of origin and first asylum (where they first flee for safety) and before their arrival in the United States. She found that refugee children's education had been interrupted for multiple reasons, sometimes for years. When children did attend school, it was generally considered temporary, was often of low quality, and used a style that valued memorization over asking questions. Furthermore, Dryden-Peterson found that schools in countries of first asylum could be places of bullying and discrimination against refugees by local residents, reflecting the ambivalence of the societies providing refuge. Likewise, many of the Central American and Mexican children traveling alone and apprehended at the U.S. border have had limited opportunities for quality education in their home countries, particularly past elementary school (U.S. Government Accountability Office, 2015). These earlier educational experiences by the parents of first- and second-generation children, as well as by migrant children themselves, heavily influence the experiences and achievement of children of immigrants and refugees in the U.S. school system (Birman & Tran, 2015).

POSTMIGRATION PATTERNS

Family Patterns

Immigrant families bring with them a number of cultural strengths that have been shown to support their children's achievement in school. These include a strong sense of family cohesion, high value placed on education as a path to success, and optimism regarding their children's future socioeconomic mobility (Kao & Tienda, 2010; Suárez-Orozco, Gaytán, Bang, Pakes, & Rhodes, 2010). Immigrant families in the United States are more likely to have two parents present in the home and a father who is employed, both of which are consistently linked to better education outcomes for children (Suárez-Orozco et al., 2010). Households are also more likely to include extended family members and other adults who can provide more guidance and emotional support to children, or such adults may at least live nearby (Suárez-Orozco et al., 2010). A number of researchers have found immigrant parent attitudes toward education important to children's success. Kao and Tienda (2010) found strong optimism among immigrant parents regarding their children's achievement important to their educational attainment. Similarly, Fuligni (1997) found that success by first- and second-generation immigrant students in both math and English classes was related primarily to the strong emphasis that the students, their parents, and their peers place on education. Furthermore, Hao and Bonstead-Bruns (1998) found that agreement between immigrant parents and their children regarding the importance of education enhanced children's success, and that maintaining the home language increased communication and the likelihood of agreement between parents and children.

Parents' involvement in their children's education, which consistently has been found to affect success in school both among immigrants and among the general U.S. population, is heavily influenced by a parent's education level. Researchers have found that parents with higher levels of education are more likely to seek information about the school systems in the United States and to feel more comfortable interacting with teachers. Parents who have less formal education, particularly when they have limited English proficiency, are less likely to be engaged in their children's schools. Often, these parents also work long hours at low-paying jobs that do not provide the flexibility needed for attending school meetings. They may also be less aware of and accustomed to parental roles in children's education in the United States. In addition, they may be more likely to feel intimidated and misunderstood by teachers and principals (Portes & Rumbaut, 2001; Suárez-Orozco et al., 2009, 2010).

However, some researchers have found that immigrant parents increase their involvement in their children's schools from kindergarten through the early elementary school years, and that their children do benefit. For example, attendance at open house events and parent–teacher conferences was associated with positive math scores in a recent study (Glick & Bates, 2010). On the other hand, immigrant parents support their children's education in culturally specific ways. For example, Chinese immigrant parents may send their children to specialized Chinese schools in the afternoons and on weekends, and Latino parents may emphasize encouraging their children's social and emotional development and building good character (Crosnoe & Lopez Turley, 2011; Zhou & Kim, 2006).

Poverty, Neighborhoods, and Schools

Almost one third of first-generation immigrant children live in poverty, compared with one quarter of second-generation children and about one fifth of children in U.S.-born families. These poverty rates are most strongly related to a parent's level of education (Borjas, 2011; Child Trends, 2014). Although poverty is associated with poorer school performance and decreased graduation rates among the general U.S. population, the impact on children of immigrants is not as clear (Borjas, 2011). However, level of income does determine where immigrants can afford to live, and higher rates of poverty mean that more immigrants will live in neighborhoods with underresourced schools. Such schools tend to be associated with ethnic and racial segregation; linguistic isolation; low school district resources; low teacher expectations and achievement test outcomes; higher than average dropout rates; and limited information, support, and resources for transitioning to college (Suárez-Orozco et al., 2010).

A recent study by Glick and Bates (2010) suggests that academic achievement is strongly predicted by a combination of family background characteristics, parental involvement in schools, and the different school contexts experienced by children of immigrants. In this study, underresourced schools with a high concentration of English language learners had a detrimental effect on children's academic progress over time. In addition, Han (2008) found that, in terms of academic trajectories, children from families of Latin American origin, as well as those from Vietnam, Thailand, Cambodia, and Laos, were more likely to be influenced by school-level factors than were children from India, China, and the Philippines, who were more likely to respond to child and family background factors. This means that newcomer students from families with more disadvantaged backgrounds are more vulnerable when schools are underresourced. At the same time, they are the students most likely to require additional support as they learn English, adjust to a new educational system, and attempt to fill any gaps in their education.

The effects of poverty, discrimination, and underresourced schools on children's achievement, particularly for those with parents who arrive with lower education levels and resources, may help explain the declining achievement of some immigrant groups over subsequent generations. At the same time, segregation in strong coethnic communities, even those primarily low-income, can have positive effects for children, including increased social and emotional support, continued connection to their native language, and enforcement of cultural values around family cohesion and school achievement. Such enclaves can therefore help protect children from the effects of poverty and discrimination (Portes & Rumbaut, 2001; Portes & Zhou, 1993). Efforts to ameliorate the impact of the negative effects of segregation, then, will need to focus on supporting these family and community connections while diminishing the impacts of poverty and discrimination on the educational achievement of all U.S. children.

English and Native Language Proficiency

Proficiency in English is a significant predictor of academic achievement for students from immigrant families (Portes & Rumbaut, 2001; Suárez-Orozco et al., 2009). However, the process of acquiring oral proficiency is often quite different from that for academic proficiency, although both can take more time than might be expected. Depending on a student's background (including formal education, literacy in their native language, and previous exposure to English), oral English proficiency typically takes 1–3 years but can take as long as 10 years. The average for learning academic English (which includes content vocabulary and is more formal and complex than oral or conversational English), however, tends to be higher, 5–7 years on average, and can be as long as 10 years (Thomas & Collier, 2002). Academic English in particular is essential in order to understand and respond to questions, including those on written tests, to read and understand narrative, and to be able to speak and write clearly and persuasively. English proficiency also affects the degree of belonging students feel toward their school, as well as their sense of connection with teachers and what goes on in their classes (Kia-Keating & Ellis, 2007; Marks, 2000; National Research Council, 2004).

Current research also supports the benefits of maintaining native languages while learning English. For example, developing skills (such as grammar) in a first language facilitates learning a second language, improves problem solving, supports a positive ethnic identity, and enables ongoing connections with members of the family and community, who can continue to share positive values regarding education. Maintaining the native language is positively associated with academic achievement (August & Shanahan, 2006; Bialystok & Feng, 2010; Suárez-Orozco et al., 2010).

SPOTLIGHT: THE MASSACHUSETTS REFUGEE SCHOOL
IMPACT PROGRAM

With support from the federal Office of Refugee Resettlement, the Massachusetts Refugee School Impact (RSI) program has developed partnerships between refugee service providers and public school districts in areas of high refugee concentration in the state in order to collaboratively serve refugee children of middle school and high school age. The range of activities includes after-school and summer programs to support academic skills and promote high school completion; outreach and engagement of refugee families to increase their involvement in their children's education; and promotion of language access by hiring interpreters and bilingual and bicultural aides who speak refugee languages (Massachusetts Executive Office of Health and Human Services, n.d.).

YOUNG CHILDREN OF IMMIGRANTS

Although the majority of studies on children of immigrants have focused on youths in secondary school, there is a growing body of research on younger children in the United States. The pre-kindergarten and elementary school years are especially critical to a child's development and preparation for learning at higher levels. Recent research indicates that high-quality early childhood education (ECE) confers a number of benefits on children of immigrants, including improved English proficiency and reading and math skills (Crosnoe, 2013; Golden & Fortuny, 2010; Karoly & Gonzalez, 2011). In addition, quality early education programs, such as Head Start, can offer comprehensive services, including physical health, mental health, and family support services. Such preparation has been shown to ease children's transition to kindergarten, improve academic performance, and support parents' engagement in their children's education (Magnuson, Lahaie, & Waldfogel, 2006; Park & McHugh, 2014). However, rates of enrollment in ECE programs are lower among immigrant families than among the U.S. born (Karoly & Gonzalez, 2011; Matthews & Ewen, 2006; Neidell & Waldfogel, 2009). Recent studies have identified barriers to participation for immigrant parents that include limited English proficiency; low formal education, including limited literacy; and different cultural beliefs regarding child care for young children (Crosnoe, 2013; Gelatt, Adams, & Huerta, 2014; Park & McHugh, 2014). With the recent emphasis on developing a federal and state infrastructure in ECE, it will be particularly important to incorporate models that address these barriers and promote immigrant participation in high-quality ECE programs (Morland, Ives, McNeely, & Allen, 2016).

UNIQUE NEEDS OF IMMIGRANT AND REFUGEE CHILDREN AND FAMILIES IN THE EDUCATION SYSTEM

English Language Learners (ELLs): Newcomers, Long-Term ELLs, Students with Interrupted Formal Education (SIFE) or Limited Formal Education (LFE)

According to the U.S. Department of Education (DOE), there are currently 4.6 million English language learners (ELLs) enrolled in U.S. schools (U.S. Department of Education, National Center for Education Statistics, 2014). These students (also referred to as English learners, ELs, or limited English proficient, LEP) are children who need specialized or modified instruction in order to learn the English language in addition to academic content (U.S. Department of Education, National Center for Education Statistics, 2014). Although children of immigrants and ELLs are not exactly the same populations (some immigrants speak English well and some ELLs grow up with U.S.-born parents who speak another language at home), the vast majority of ELLs are first- or second-generation immigrants. ELLs are a diverse group and include new arrivals, who may or may not have had formal schooling, as well as long-term ELLs, who are typically U.S. born, have been learning English for six years or more, and are at risk of not completing high school (Calderon, Slavin, & Sanchez, 2011).

Students with interrupted formal education (SIFE) are a special subgroup of newcomer ELLs. Most are newly arrived adolescents who know little English, and many have limited literacy. For example, the education of refugee children may have been disrupted because of war, flight from persecution, multiple moves, and years in refugee camps (Birman, 2005; Dryden-Peterson, 2015). Some of these students may have had limited access or no access at all to formal education (LFE) before their arrival in the United States. For example, a qualitative longitudinal study documented the experiences of Somali Bantu refugee children in the Chicago Public Schools, many of whom had never learned a written language or experienced a formal education setting (Birman & Tran, 2015). Other immigrants may have had limited access to education for economic or cultural reasons. For example, one of the reasons for the recent surge in migration of children and youths to the United States from El Salvador, Honduras, and Guatemala is the lack of access to and the poor quality of education. Many in the Western

Highlands of Guatemala do not have access to a secondary education, and the quality of education available in El Salvador often does not prepare youths for employment (U.S. Government Accountability Office, 2015).

The bottom line is that these students must learn English simultaneously with core content areas while adjusting to a new education system and culture. In addition, SIFE and LFE students are making up for years of lost schooling, often including learning the basic building blocks of literacy. Regardless, they are held to the same accountability standards as other students, and they have a limited amount of time (usually four years) to catch up on credits and requirements and graduate from high school (Short & Boyson, 2012). This can be particularly challenging given the number of years it takes to learn English, especially academic English.

SPOTLIGHT: U.S. CIVIL RIGHTS IN EDUCATION

U.S. federal laws mandate equal and meaningful access to a free elementary and secondary education for all children in the United States regardless of language spoken or immigration status. Under Title VI of the Civil Rights Act of 1964 and the Equal Educational Opportunities Act of 1974, public schools must ensure that ELL students can participate meaningfully and equally in educational programs. Title VI specifically prohibits discrimination on the basis of race, color, or national origin by recipients of federal funding, and these requirements have been clarified through a series of federal policy memos and case laws.

The 1970 memorandum on "Identification of Discrimination and Denial of Services on the Basis of National Origin" clarifies Title VI requirements that school districts provide equal educational opportunities to all children, regardless of national origin and language. This memo also supports the right of parents to be provided with information on school activities in a language other than English. In 1974, the U.S. Supreme Court upheld this interpretation as valid in the key decision *Lau v. Nichols*. Also in 1974, the landmark U.S. Supreme Court case *Plyler v. Doe* held that no child could be denied a public education based on immigration status. Even if a child is in the United States illegally, he or she has the right to an education. Since then, a number of memos have been issued offering guidance on school district requirements with regard to serving ELL students and addressing immigration status.

Finally, the Individuals with Disabilities Education Act (IDEA) requires districts to provide high-quality interpretation and translation when communicating with non-English-speaking parents. The U.S. Department of Education (DOE) and the U.S. Department of Justice (DOJ) issued joint letters and memos in 2014 to remind state and local education agencies of these laws regarding national origin discrimination and their obligation to ensure that ELL students can participate meaningfully and equally in educational programs (U.S. Department of Education, Office for Civil Rights, n.d.).

Social and Emotional Needs

The majority of children of immigrants and refugees are resilient and adjust well over time. However, these children are also likely to experience social and emotional needs specifically related to their and their parents' migration experiences and adjustment to the United States, and it is helpful for educators, school social workers, counselors, and psychologists to be aware of them. In a recent study of newcomer programs for ELLs, educators reported their concerns over two issues affecting their students' emotional adjustment and learning: traumatic stress and family-related stress (Short & Boyson, 2012).

Particularly among refugees, families and children may have been forcibly uprooted from their homes and may have experienced traumatic violence, deprivation, and loss of family and friends. These extreme disruptions may have been acute or chronic (American Psychological Association, 2010; Lustig et al., 2003). Some flights to safety involve multiple relocations, and refugees such as the Bhutanese, Burmese, and Somalis have often spent years and even decades in makeshift refugee camps (Capps & Newland, 2015).

Children traveling alone to the United States from Central America also report experiences of violence and severe stress before, during, and after their journeys (U.S. Government Accountability Office, 2015; United Nations High Commissioner for Refugees, 2014). Many of these children are joining parents or other family members in the United States after years of separation. These family reunifications can be both joyous and stressful, with a child sometimes needing to adjust to a new step-parent and siblings, to living in a family setting after being on his or her own, and to rebuilding relationships with parents after a long separation (Suárez-Orozco, Bang, & Kim, 2011).

Children also experience acculturative stress. As children and their families adapt to life in the United States, children generally acculturate more quickly than their parents, as they spend more time in school and with peers. Often, children begin to lose their native language as they learn English, adding to the challenges of communicating with their parents. This differential acculturation can cause a gap in understanding between parents and their children, which can result in conflict within the family (Ho & Birman, 2010). Intergenerational conflict in immigrant families has been consistently related to poor adjustment in children (Birman, 2006).

Furthermore, immigrants today are ethnically, racially, and religiously diverse, many are lesbian, gay, bisexual, or transgendered (LGBT), and the vast majority are people of color. In the United States, they may for the first time experience bullying and discrimination based on these differences, or they may have been persecuted in their home countries and/or during their migration journeys for similar reasons. Such experiences can exacerbate previous trauma. Recent research has documented the negative impact of perceived discrimination on the mental health of refugee and immigrant children (Ellis, MacDonald, Lincoln, & Cabral, 2008), as well as the positive effects of a sense of school belonging on the social and emotional adjustment of refugee children (Kia-Keating & Ellis, 2007). It is particularly crucial for educators to promote trauma-informed schools that can support a sense of safety, including taking a culturally responsive, strengths-based approach with a focus on fostering resilience (Morland et al., 2013).

SPOTLIGHT: COLLABORATION BETWEEN MENTAL HEALTH PROVIDERS, BICULTURAL FAMILY LIAISONS, AND THE SCHOOLS

Caring Across Communities (CAC) was a three-year initiative (2007–2010) of the Robert Wood Johnson (RWJ) Foundation that addressed the mental health needs of immigrant and refugee children through school-linked services. All 15 CAC projects, located in eight states, worked together with their communities to integrate four components: family engagement, basic needs, cultural orientation, and emotional and behavioral support. Those programs that successfully engaged parents and integrated these components used bicultural family liaisons trusted by the families, who worked hand-in-hand with mental health providers. These liaisons helped families by providing language interpretation, cultural orientation, information on the U.S. school system, and assistance obtaining resources to meet their basic needs (McNeely, Sprecher, & Bates, 2010).

BARRIERS TO CHANGE ACROSS SYSTEMS

The Elementary and Secondary Education Act (ESEA), reauthorized in 2002 as No Child Left Behind (NCLB), is currently the primary source of funding for educating all children in the United States, including those in immigrant families. No Child Left Behind provides the structural framework for education in this country, creating some opportunities for change across systems together with barriers to change. The Obama administration has proposed changes to NCLB in anticipation of reauthorization, although it is uncertain as to when and if this will happen. We present in the next section basic information on the main parts of NCLB that relate to children of immigrants. We then highlight the barriers to change across systems.

Background: No Child Left Behind (NCLB)

Both Title I and Title III of NCLB currently provide more support to children of immigrants than at any time in the past. Many children of immigrants receive assistance under Title I of NCLB, aimed at low-income children in high-poverty schools, whereas Title III funds English language acquisition programs. Title I is one of the most flexible sources of funding and can be used to support a broad range of activities that help children who live in high-poverty areas succeed academically. In addition to supporting instruction in English, Title III provides additional funding to school districts that have experienced a significant increase in immigrant students regardless of whether such children are English learners. These funds can be used for a broad range of activities, which include improving instruction, providing tutoring and intensified instruction, and conducting community participation programs. For both Title I and Title III, NCLB outlines information that must be provided to students' families "to the extent practicable, in a language parents can understand" (U.S. Department of Education, 2004, p. 5). In addition, under Title IV, NCLB funds 21st Century Community Learning Centers (CCLCs), including Safe and Drug-Free Schools and Communities, which supports a range of out-of-schooltime services. Although not specifically targeted toward children of immigrants, many of the CCLCs are located in low-income communities, and some programs explicitly focus on immigrant families and children.

Language Access

Despite the resources for children of immigrants provided under NCLB, however, schools in areas of high and diverse immigration typically do not have sufficient funds for the translation and interpretation services needed by immigrant families and as required by Title VI of the U.S. Civil Rights Act. This is particularly true given the broad range of languages spoken by immigrants and refugees, including low-incidence languages.

SPOTLIGHT: LANGUAGE ACCESS FOR LEP PARENTS
OF CHILDREN WITH DISABILITIES

In 2012, Advocates for Children (AFC) and New York Lawyers for the Public Interest (NYLPI) filed a complaint with the Office for Civil Rights (OCR) of the U.S. Department of Education (USDOE) against the New York City Department of Education based on local, state, and federal civil rights laws. The complaint detailed a systemic failure to provide translation and interpretation services to tens of thousands of limited English proficient (LEP) parents of children with disabilities. A representative for AFC stated, "When thousands of LEP parents are unable to read documents because they are written in English and are unable to communicate with teachers and school administrators about their children's programs and progress, they are denied their legal right to participate in their children's education. As a result, thousands of children of LEP parents may not receive the proper education placement or achieve academic success (Advocates for Children of New York & New York Lawyers for the Public Interest, 2012).

Teacher Training

No Child Left Behind requires that all teachers meet highly qualified standards when teaching core subjects (such as math) or grade levels (such as the general elementary curriculum) to all students, including ELLs. However, these higher standards do not apply to English as a Second Language (ESL) as a stand-alone subject or to ELLs as a student group. In other words, ESL teachers and other teachers must be highly qualified to teach core subjects, but teachers of core subjects or ESL are not required to have specialized skills and knowledge related to teaching ELLs (U.S. Department of Education, 2009). Many educators believe that such teacher training will increase the ability of ELLs to succeed academically (Short & Boyson, 2012).

High-Stakes Testing

For the first time, NCLB has required statewide standardized achievement testing annually for children in the third to eighth grades and once in high school, with results broken out according to ELLs, children with disabilities, ethnicity/race, and graduation rates (Center for Public Education, 2007; Short & Boyson, 2012). These data provide the first information on disparities between ELLs and other children, and enable schools to be held accountable for these disparities. Although the new testing requirements are helpful in revealing disparities in achievement between ELL and native English speakers, they have also created challenges both for the schools and for children in immigrant families. Schools are required to set goals for "Annual Yearly Progress" (AYP) and can eventually face sanctions, including a change in management or closure, if AYP is not achieved by the deadline. Although ELL scores are not counted toward AYP for one year following an immigrant child's arrival in the United States, and some children can take tests in their native language, scores are counted starting with the second year, and children must still be literate and master content (Center for Public Education, 2007). Since it can take a number of years for ELLs to master academic English as well as core content, this timeline provides very little time for ELLs, and particularly for students in the LFE and SIFE subgroups, to catch up with their peers.

In addition, this means that ELLs can be viewed as a liability regarding schools' ability to meet AYP, with some schools consequently engaging in strategies that protect their educational outcomes but violate student civil rights. For example, some districts discourage older immigrant students from enrolling in high school when it is unlikely that they will graduate on time, advising them instead to enroll in adult education and GED programs so that these students do not count against district graduation rates (U.S. Department of Education, Office for Civil Rights, n.d.).

In 2012, the Obama administration began to offer flexibility in implementing specific NCLB requirements via waivers to states while requiring them to develop rigorous and comprehensive plans to close achievement gaps, increase equity, improve instruction, and increase outcomes for all students. So far, 42 states, the District of Columbia, and Puerto Rico have qualified for this flexibility. Although NCLB has exposed achievement gaps for ELLs, most schools are still struggling to adequately address them, including meeting these waiver requirements (Migration Policy Institute, 2015).

EMERGING PRACTICES AND PREVENTIVE INTERVENTIONS

A number of emerging practices as well as tried-and-true interventions that support the academic performance of children of immigrants are currently being implemented in schools throughout the United States. Four key approaches are highlighted here.

Newcomer Programs

A number of school districts around the United States are serving newly arrived, immigrant ELLs through "newcomer programs" to help ease their entry into the English as a Second Language or mainstream classroom. In a recent survey of 63 of these programs, researchers found that virtually all newcomer programs served SIFE, that approximately 30 percent of ELLs in newcomer programs were SIFE, and that nearly all qualified for the free or reduced-price lunch program (Short & Boyson, 2012). These programs typically provide one to two years of specialized academic environments as a period of transition for ELLs who need additional support before joining regular school classes.

Newcomer programs simultaneously focus on teaching language (beginning English skills and native language literacy), providing core content instruction, and supporting students' acculturation to the new school environment. Although the impact of these programs on students and schools has not yet been formally evaluated, Short & Boyson (2012) found a number of aspects that appear to be working well. In addition to the functions noted, many successfully used extended time (after school, weekends, and summer programs), built connections with families and social services, and helped to transition newcomers into regular classes or beyond high school. In addition, these programs collected data on student progress. Challenges reported by school staff were related to the separation of ELL students from regular classes and native English-speaking peers while in the program, lack of funding for all services needed, and finding teachers skilled at working with newcomers.

Sheltered Instruction Observation Protocol (SIOP) is a research-based and validated instructional model for addressing the academic needs of English language learners and is an instructional strategy used in many newcomer programs. Its lessons aim to simultaneously develop knowledge and skills in the English language and in core content. Teachers can use the SIOP model to design and deliver lessons that meet the unique educational needs of ELLs and improve their educational outcomes (Center for Applied Linguistics, n.d.).

Mentoring

Typically defined as an adult providing assistance and support to a young person, mentoring has been shown to have positive effects in youths' lives in many cases, including increased success in school and greater likelihood of attending college (DuBois, Portillo, Rhodes, Silverthorn, & Valentine, 2011). Many schools and community programs use mentors in their programs for immigrant and refugee youths to assist with cultural orientation, English, and schoolwork, and to serve as role models. However, it is less clear how mentoring may be most helpful to children of immigrants and refugees.

Mentoring strategies may be adapted to these children and youths' cultural and migration backgrounds, as well as developmental and acculturation stages. For example, considering the strong family ties and hierarchical structure of many immigrant families, providing mentoring to the entire family may be helpful. Family mentoring may not only help address a family's concrete needs but may also help alleviate a growing acculturation gap for some parents and youths. Other forms of mentoring used with immigrant and refugee youths include group mentoring, mentoring by older peers, and intergenerational mentoring, where youths assist elders who can also help them learn about their heritage culture.

Taking acculturation stress into account, a mentor knowledgeable of the United States may be most helpful soon after a family arrives, supporting their needs for information and concrete assistance. On the other hand, when youths have been here longer and may be struggling with acculturation and identity issues, a mentor from a similar background who has learned to negotiate both the heritage and U.S. cultures might be most helpful as a role model (Birman & Morland, 2013). Regardless, mentors from U.S.-born families will benefit from training regarding immigrant and refugee cultural and migration backgrounds.

School, Family, and Community Partnerships

Also called parental involvement and family engagement, these partnerships are believed to be so key to children's success in school that NCLB includes requirements and funding specifically for improving engagement of families in their children's education. As noted, there are differences in cultural traditions regarding the roles of parents in their engagement with their children's schools, and these vary across immigrant groups. Regardless, successfully engaging immigrant and refugee parents requires culturally and linguistically responsive strategies. One of the most effective strategies has been the development of partnerships between schools and immigrant community organizations and respected community leadership (Morland et al., 2016). Such organizations can typically provide the school with information about immigrant cultures and languages, advise on outreach and engagement, and can often assist in identifying interpreters, particularly for low-incidence languages. In addition, they can relay information about the U.S. school system to parents and help create a communication pathway that flows both ways to increase mutual understanding. Another common strategy is to hire cultural or family liaisons, who essentially serve as cultural brokers between immigrant families and schools. Another effective strategy is to offer relevant needed services for immigrant families at the school, such as family literacy programs, English as a Second Language classes, and adult education classes. Some schools invite immigrant parents to provide presentations about their countries of origin and their cultures or to serve on ELL advisory committees. The more willing teachers and administrators are to learn about immigrant cultures, perspectives, and communication styles, and to develop personal relationships with families, the more engaged immigrant families and communities will become (Morland et al., 2013, 2016).

SPOTLIGHT ON PARTNERSHIPS: REFUGEE RESETTLEMENT AND HEAD START

In many communities, refugee families tend not to enroll in Early Head Start and Head Start (EHS/HS) despite their eligibility. To increase refugee participation in EHS/HS, refugee resettlement and EHS/HS programs developed a partnership in two sites: Maricopa County, Arizona, and Onondaga County, New York. Through regular meetings, staff from both services discussed mutual goals and identified barriers to refugee EHS/HS enrollment. They then worked together to develop and implement creative solutions to overcome these barriers. Participation in this initiative by local refugee leadership and ethnic community-based organizations was key to helping build refugee parents' trust in EHS/HS programs. By the end of the project, EHS/HS data showed substantially increased trends in refugee enrollment: by 200 percent in Maricopa County and by 500 percent in Onondaga County (Morland et al., 2016).

After-School Programs

After-school—or out-of-schooltime—programs have been shown to help improve students' school attendance, academic performance, behavior, and health, with the greatest benefits going to those children at risk of poor developmental outcomes (Afterschool Alliance, 2013; Durlak & Weissberg, 2007). These programs support families by providing safe, supervised environments for children before and after school and during summer months while their parents work. For example, the Department of Education's 21st Century Community Learning Centers (21st CCLC) initiative funds before-school, after-school, and summer learning programs for students attending high-poverty, low-performing schools. Activities include academic enrichment, a broad array of supplemental programs from the arts to counseling, and literacy and other programs for the families of children enrolled in the program.

Participation rates in after-school programs remain comparatively low for immigrant families, and research on their impact is limited (Wimer et al., 2006). However, many children from immigrant families do participate in after-school programs when they are aware of them, logistical barriers such as transportation are addressed, and services are provided in a culturally and linguistically responsive manner.

COLLABORATIONS ACROSS SYSTEMS

Although there are a number of individual interventions that can help address the needs of children of immigrants and refugees in education, most programs tend to combine interventions in some way. For example, newcomer programs often include after-school and summer programs, use mentors and tutors, and engage immigrant families. These interventions also frequently involve establishing collaborative relationships between the schools and different community agencies.

SPOTLIGHT: THE DES MOINES, IOWA, 21ST CENTURY COMMUNITY LEARNING CENTER (21ST CCLC)

Over the past 10 years, the number of newcomers in Des Moines has increased dramatically. Most recently, there has been an influx of refugees from Burma (Myanmar), posing a new set of challenges for the schools. The Des Moines 21st CCLC aims to bridge the gap between school, family, and community, providing comprehensive services before and after school to help ELL students succeed. The CCLC provides a central location for students and their families to learn and practice English and receive cultural orientation on the schools, daily life, and basic needs while also sharing and celebrating their cultures. Students and their families are offered transportation and classes on Saturdays. This CCLC offers advanced technology labs with learning programs designed just for newcomers, family field trips to historical sites and cultural events, and Family Nights that are focused on literacy; science, technology, engineering, and math (STEM); the arts; and other topics (Iowa Department of Education, 2012).

Schools can be viewed as community hubs and central points of access for a broad range of services to children and families—from physical health and mental health care to adult education and employment services—and there are clear advantages to this approach. First and foremost, since all children must attend school, these centers can reach most children and families in a community with essential services, including sometimes hard to reach immigrant and refugee populations. Second, such collaboratives recognize the complex range of factors involved in school success for children and therefore the need for a comprehensive approach to education.

Third, this type of approach can change the relationship between schools and immigrant and refugee families so that families begin to view schools as resources and to feel comfortable and connected there. Specific examples of these approaches include the Community Schools movement and the DOE initiative Promise Neighborhoods (Coalition for Community Schools, n.d.; U.S. Department of Education, n.d.).

In the Community Schools model, the school becomes the community center and is open to all community members at all times. The Community Schools model only requires a school's commitment and funding for a coordinator who can develop the relationships with community agencies, with the intention of bringing their services into the school. Funding can include public (such as NCLB's Titles I, III, and IV) and private sources, as well as support from community partners. The assumption behind these schools is that an integrated focus on academics, health and social services, youth, and community development will lead to increased engagement, greater learning, and healthier families and communities. Many schools are indeed demonstrating positive results in children's school readiness and academic achievement. However, since each Community School comes up with its own design in response to community needs, there appear to be a variety of models and results.

Promise Neighborhoods (a discretionary program of the Department of Education) funds cross-system collaborations aimed at improving the educational and developmental outcomes of children and youths in high-poverty, distressed communities. Promise Neighborhoods (PN) aims to build integrated "cradle-to-career" education services that include family and community supports, with public schools at the center. The most effective solutions developed by communities are then scaled up and implemented across a broader region. Promise Neighborhoods now supports projects in 20 states and the District of Columbia (U.S. Department of Education, n.d.).

SPOTLIGHT: CASA'S LANGLEY PARK PROMISE NEIGHBORHOOD

The majority of families in Langley Park, Prince George's County, Maryland, are recent immigrants from Central America. The general profile of the community is one of high risk for its children's achievement: the poverty rate is twice the rate for the state, as is the unemployment rate; two thirds of adults lack a high school diploma; and only 14 percent of the population are English proficient. The vast majority of children are children of immigrants, almost all of them U.S. born, and nearly half live in single-parent households. CASA, a nonprofit organization serving the Latino community in Maryland, partnered with the Prince George's County government to address a fragmented service system by using a Department of Education "Promise Neighborhood" grant. Through monthly community meetings, leaders are working to eliminate barriers to collaboration among services and are developing and implementing a continuum of initiatives to support children's positive developmental and educational outcomes. These include a federally qualified health center, an early learning network, a parent engagement program, a family economic success program, and a secondary community school—all within a coordinated network of services (Scott et al., 2014).

CASE STUDY: ARTURO

Arturo, a 14-year-old immigrant from Guatemala, was referred to his school's social worker, Maria, at a junior high school in a small town in North Carolina. Arturo was enrolled in ninth grade on the basis of his age and was having difficulty adjusting to school. His initial assessment found that he spoke very little English, had limited formal education and literacy, and that he spoke Spanish. He was enrolled in English as a Second Language (ESL) and literacy classes. His ESL teacher, who spoke some Spanish, reported that he was struggling with his assignments, did not seem to follow the rules, and had recently gotten into a fight with two boys who had called him names in Spanish. His teacher was also concerned that, unlike the other Spanish speakers in her class, he seemed very quiet, rarely responded to her questions, and would not look her in the eye. She thought he might have serious learning disabilities, and she was considering recommending placement in special education. Arturo seemed frustrated, and he was considering dropping out of school. His teacher had tried to contact his mother by phone and by sending notes in Spanish home with Arturo, suggesting a meeting, but his mother had never responded. His teacher assumed that she was not interested in meeting with her.

Maria, the school social worker, was a second-generation immigrant whose parents were originally from Puerto Rico, and she spoke Spanish fluently. When she met with Arturo, she quickly realized that he spoke Spanish as a second language and that his knowledge of Spanish was actually limited. She found that he and his family were originally from Quetzaltenango, Guatemala, were Mayan, and spoke Mam—a language she had never heard of. Maria scheduled another appointment and tried to find an interpreter for this meeting. However, the interpretation/translation company contracted by the school did not have a Mam interpreter.

Maria decided to contact other social workers in town for help. A colleague referred her to a respected community leader who often interpreted for families at the local hospital. Since she suspected there were more students in her school from the Mam community, she made a strong case to school administrators and was able to get this interpreter contracted by the school for a number of hours.

Once she had an interpreter, Maria decided to make a home visit to learn more about Arturo and his family. She learned that Arturo's mother, Yaneth, had come to the United States a year ago with her three children: Arturo, 12-year-old Elena, and 9-year-old Bryan. Yaneth's husband had died from an illness eight years earlier. Two years before arriving in the United States, Yaneth had reported to the local police serious domestic violence by a neighbor against his wife, a close friend of hers. The neighbor responded by threatening to kill her, and he kidnapped her and nearly beat her to death. He then threatened to kill her children. Yaneth fled with her children to a small town in the United States, where her sister lived. Her sister had lived in the United States for 15 years, had married a U.S. citizen, and they had five children together. Both families lived in their small home while Yaneth worked in a restaurant to earn enough money so she and her children could move into their own apartment.

As an indigenous Guatemalan, Yaneth had faced discrimination in her country, and neither she nor her children had access to a formal education. She felt extremely grateful that her children now had the opportunity for an education, and she was certain they would do well if only they would study and stay out of trouble; she worked long hours to support them and pushed them to work hard in school.

Although there was obviously love and mutual support in the household, Maria noticed some tensions as well. In addition to the crowded home, Yaneth shared that her sister's family seemed very "North American." Elena had become best friends with her cousins, was beginning to imitate them, and talked a lot about boys. This led to conflict with her mother. Yaneth felt Elena was no longer respectful, and she was concerned that she could no longer control Elena. In addition, although Elena was learning spoken Spanish and English quickly at school, she was still performing poorly on tests. All three children were struggling in school.

Over time, Maria began to educate herself about the Mam people and to learn about the small community near the school. She discovered a small Evangelical church and a small Catholic-style church founded by Mam members. Maria also learned that there was a national Pastoral Maya group affiliated with the Catholic Church that several of the Mam leaders worked with. She then found online resources for Mayans in the United States, including a toolkit for teachers and an interpreter network (Kennesaw State University, n.d.). She was surprised to find these resources for a group she had only recently learned existed.

As Maria learned more about the community, she met an immigration lawyer who provided education and pro bono services to the community. The lawyer believed that Yaneth and her children had a strong case for relief from deportation based on the death threats they had fled.

Maria realized that this family and other immigrants were in need of more support at their school. She invited a Mayan community leader to give a presentation to teachers and administrators about the proud and ancient history of the Maya, their culture and languages, and resources in their community. She was able to recruit the ESL teacher and others to help her start an after-school program that provided mentors and tutors to newly arrived immigrant and refugee children. They began to discuss hiring home-school liaisons from the local immigrant communities, as well as starting family literacy classes, to help families feel more comfortable coming to school. Some of the teachers integrated posters and different cultural celebrations to reflect the lives of the immigrant and refugee children in their classrooms. Maria began planning a family support group for immigrant parents to talk about the challenges of changing family roles and conflict with their teenagers. Some of the student mentors asked for leadership and conflict resolution training, and they suggested starting a soccer league.

DISCUSSION QUESTIONS

1 Discuss all the reasons that Arturo may be struggling in school. What challenges for Arturo did this school initially miss? Can you identify any cultural miscommunications between Arturo and his teacher?

2 What are the challenges that Arturo's family faces that may affect the educational experiences of their children?

3 What strengths can you identify in this family? How can Maria and other school staff build on these strengths to help Arturo and his siblings succeed in school?

4 Why is it important that the school have access to interpretation and translation services for the languages spoken by its students and their families? What challenges might schools face in providing language access?

5 Discuss all the strategies that Maria used to improve cultural and linguistic responsiveness in her practice and in the school.

6 What more could this school do to support the academic success of its immigrant and refugee students?

7 Which current legislation and policies help support the success of students like Arturo in school? Which policies might make it harder for them to succeed?

8 What policy changes would you like to see that could improve the responsiveness of our education system to today's diverse students?

CONCLUSION

In summary, immigrants and refugees in the United States today are an increasingly diverse population, and this diversity is reflected in their children's varied paths through school. In this chapter, we discussed the daunting challenges that many children in immigrant and refugee families face in school as well as the obstacles that schools may experience in providing culturally and linguistically responsive services. We also described several key interventions that improve cross-system coordination and cultural responsiveness in order to support children's learning, healthy development, and overall success in school.

Current research indicates that the most vulnerable children and families tend to be those who have experienced forced migration (such as refugees and other immigrants fleeing violence and poverty), had limited access to formal education before their arrival, and, once in the United States, live in low-income communities and attend underresourced schools. For these children in particular, limited English proficiency and discrimination based on race, ethnicity, religion, and immigration status can have profound effects on school achievement. At the same time, children in immigrant and refugee families are typically able to derive profound resilience and strength from their cultural values and traditions. Culturally responsive practice is strengths-based practice, and the interventions highlighted here can build on individual, family, community, and cultural strengths to address the unique needs of children in immigrant families.

With one quarter of all children in the United States in immigrant families—a proportion only expected to increase—schools will not only need to find ways to support children's successful adaptation to a new culture and language, but the schools must also remain flexible and adapt to the changing needs of the children and families served. In order to provide all children with the opportunity to learn and to achieve a bright future, schools will need to find ways to:

1 Ensure language access for all immigrants and refugees, including low-incidence languages.
2 Improve school readiness of young children through increased access to early childhood education that includes dual generation programming.
3 Promote partnerships between the schools and ethnic community-based organizations; the community schools and similar models seem particularly promising in this regard.
4 Expand learning time by ensuring the availability of out-of-schooltime programs; give youths arriving in their teen years at least five years before they must graduate.
5 Focus resources on high-need groups, such as LFE, SIFE, and long-term ELLs; newcomer programs seem especially promising for helping students with limited or interrupted formal education to catch up with their peers.
6 Increase requirements and professional development opportunities for all teachers with regard to teaching ELLs.
7 Ensure youths and families are provided with information, support, and guidance regarding postsecondary education and training in a manner that they can understand and use to pursue the career they want.

There is a tremendous need for more research in this field. In 2013, researchers, policy analysts, and practitioners convened a two-day meeting and conducted a national survey to identify critical gaps in basic and applied research and to prioritize the next steps with regard to supporting success in school for newly arrived refugee and immigrant youths. Remarkably, the group found strong agreement among researchers, practitioners, and policymakers in the field regarding the importance of a focus on applied research aimed at concrete strategies to improve the school success of immigrant students. As a result of the meeting and the survey, four research priorities were identified for the field: (1) evaluation of newcomer programs; (2) identifying how to engage immigrant and refugee families in their children's education; (3) identifying and reducing stressors in families, communities, and among teachers; and (4) professional development for teachers (McNeely et al., 2016). Continuing research in these directions will be essential to inform the program suggested and to support the continuing development and implementation of culturally responsive practice in the education system.

KEY TERMS

COMMUNITY SCHOOLS MODEL Describes an approach that develops a school as a community center that is open to all community members at all times. By providing an integrated focus on academics, health and social services, youth, and community development, Community Schools aim to promote engagement, greater learning, and healthier families and communities. Although many Community Schools demonstrate positive results, this approach currently includes a range of different models and results.

ELEMENTARY AND SECONDARY EDUCATION ACT (ESEA) An act passed by the U.S. Congress in 1965 as a part of President Lyndon B. Johnson's "War on Poverty." In addition to funding all public primary and secondary education in the United States, the act emphasizes equal access to education, especially for children from low-income families, and establishes standards and accountability for both students and schools. The act was most recently reauthorized in 2002 as No Child Left Behind (NCLB).

NEWCOMER PROGRAMS Specialized programs that typically provide one to two years of specialized academic environments as a period of transition for English language learners (ELLs) who would benefit from additional support before joining regular school classes. Newcomer programs simultaneously focus on teaching language (beginning English skills and native language literacy), providing core content instruction, and supporting students' acculturation to the new school environment.

SCHOOL READINESS   A primary goal of early childhood education that focuses on the healthy physical, cognitive, social, and emotional development of children from birth to age 5 so that they are ready to enter kindergarten. School readiness can also include the family's readiness to support their child's learning ("dual generation" approach), as well as ensuring that schools are ready to help children learn. Early childhood education can be especially critical for young children in immigrant and refugee families, since it can provide children with a foundation in literacy and English before starting kindergarten; orient children and families to U.S. schools; and prepare schools for immigrant children and families. School readiness has been shown to support young children's success in school as well as health and employment later in life.

STUDENTS WITH INTERRUPTED FORMAL EDUCATION (SIFE) AND LIMITED FORMAL EDUCATION (LFE)   Special subgroups of immigrant and refugee students, often adolescents, who have experienced short or long, single or multiple interruptions in their education or who may have had very limited access or no access to schooling before their arrival in the United States. These education gaps typically mean that these children arrive with limited literacy and knowledge of English, and that they must learn these skills at the same time they are learning academic content in school.

STUDY QUESTIONS

1   Which immigrant groups tend to be most at risk with regard to success in school in the United States? Why are they most at risk?

2   In what ways does No Child Left Behind (NCLB) support the needs of newcomer English language learners? In what ways does NCLB *not* support the success of newcomer students in school?

3   What are the advantages and the disadvantages of newcomer programs in addressing the academic needs of immigrant and refugee children?

4   How can partnerships between public schools and ethnic community-based organizations help meet the academic needs of newcomer students? Provide examples of models that promote partnerships between community organizations and schools.

5   Which new directions in research, policy, and practice do you believe can best help schools meet the special needs of immigrant and refugee students? Justify your answer.

ADDITIONAL RESOURCES

Bridging Refugee Youth and Children's Services (BRYCS). Schools: http:// www.brycs.org/schools.cfm

Center for Applied Linguistics (CAL). Immigrant and Refugee Integration: http://www.cal.org/areas-of-impact/immigrant-refugee-integration

¡Colorín Colorado! A bilingual site for families and educators of English language learners: http://www.colorincolorado.org/

Migration Policy Institute, Research Initiative on Young Children in Refugee Families: http://migrationpolicy.org

Office of Head Start Early Childhood Learning and Knowledge Center, National Center on Cultural and Linguistic Responsiveness: http://eclkc .ohs.acf.hhs.gov/hslc/tta-system/cultural-linguistic

REFERENCES

Advocates for Children of New York & New York Lawyers for the Public Interest. (2012). *Legal advocacy groups file complaint against the NYC Department of Education to stop discrimination against Limited English Proficient parents.* Retrieved from http://www.advocatesforchildren.org/sites/default /files/EVC%20Press%20release%20(FINAL).pdf?pt=1

Afterschool Alliance. (2013). *Afterschool outcomes.* Retrieved from http://www .afterschoolalliance.org/Afterschool_Outcomes_2013.pdf

American Psychological Association. (2010). *Resilience and recovery after war: Refugee children and families in the United States.* Washington, DC: Author. Retrieved from http://www.apa.org/pubs/info/reports/refugees-full-report.pdf

August, D., & Shanahan, T. (Eds.). (2006). *Developing literacy in second-language learners: Report of the National Literacy Panel on language-minority children and youth.* Mahwah, NJ: Erlbaum.

Bialystok, E., & Feng, X. (2010). Language proficiency and its implications for monolingual and bilingual children. In A. Durgunoglu & C. Goldenberg (Eds.), *Dual language learners: The development and assessment of oral and written language* (pp. 121–138). New York: Guilford.

Birman, D. (2005). *Refugee children with low literacy skills or interrupted education: Identifying challenges and strategies.* Denver, CO: Spring Institute for Intercultural Learning. Retrieved from http://www.springinstitute.org/Files /refugeechildrenbehavior3.pdf

———. (2006). Acculturation gap and family adjustment: Findings with Soviet Jewish refugees in the U.S. and implications for measurement. *Journal of Cross-Cultural Psychology, 37*(5), 1–22.

Birman, D., & Morland, L. (2013). Immigrant youth. In D. Dubois & M. Karcher (Eds.), *Handbook of youth mentoring* (2nd ed., pp. 355–368). Thousand Oaks, CA: Sage.

Birman, D., & Tran, D. (2015). *The academic engagement of newly arriving Somali Bantu students in a U.S. elementary school.* Washington, DC: Migration Policy Institute.

Borjas, G. (2011). Poverty and program participation among immigrant children. *The Future of Children, 21*(1), 247–266.

Calderon, M., Slavin, R., & Sanchez, M. (2011). Effective instruction for English learners. *The Future of Children, 21*(1), 103–127.

Capps, R., & Fix, M. (Eds.). (2012). *Young children of black immigrants in America: Changing flows, changing faces.* Washington, DC: Migration Policy Institute.

Capps, R., & Newland, K. (2015). *The integration outcomes of U.S. refugees: Successes and challenges.* Washington, DC: Migration Policy Institute.

Center for Applied Linguistics (CAL). (n.d.). *Sheltered Instruction Observation Protocol (SIOP).* Retrieved from http://www.cal.org/siop/lesson-plans/index.html

Center for Public Education. (2007). *What NCLB says about ELL students.* Retrieved from http://www.centerforpubliceducation.org/Main-Menu/Instruction/What-research-says-about-English-language-learners-At-a-glance/What-NCLB-says-about-ELL-students.html

Child Trends. (2014). *Immigrant children.* Retrieved from http://www.childtrends.org/?indicators=immigrant-children

Coalition for Community Schools. (n.d.). http://www.communityschools.org/

Crosnoe, R. (2013). *Preparing the children of immigrants for early academic success.* Washington, DC: Migration Policy Institute.

Crosnoe, R., & Lopez Turley, R. (2011). The K-12 educational outcomes of immigrant youth. *The Future of Children, 21*, 129–152.

Dryden-Peterson, S. (2015). *Education of refugees in countries of first asylum: What U.S. teachers need to know about the pre-resettlement experiences of refugee children.* Washington, DC: Migration Policy Institute.

DuBois, D. L., Portillo, N., Rhodes, J. E., Silverthorn, N., & Valentine, J. C. (2011). How effective are mentoring programs for youth? A systematic assessment of the evidence. *Psychological Science in the Public Interest, 12*, 57–91. doi:10.1177/1529100611414806

Durlak, J. A., & Weissberg, R. P. (2007). *The impact of after-school programs that promote personal and social skills.* Chicago, IL: Collaborative for Academic, Social, and Emotional Learning.

Ellis, B. H., MacDonald, H. Z., Lincoln, A. K., & Cabral, H. J. (2008). Mental health of Somali adolescent refugees: The role of trauma, stress, and perceived discrimination. *Journal of Consulting and Clinical Psychology, 76*(2), 184–193.

Fairfax County, Virginia, Public Schools. (n.d.). *Languages spoken at home by Fairfax County Elementary Students.* Retrieved from http://www.fairfaxcounty.gov/demogrph/languagemaps.htm

Feliciano, C. (2005). Does selective migration matter? Explaining ethnic disparities in educational attainment among immigrants' children. *International Migration Review, 39*(4), 841–871.

Fuligni, A. J. (1997). The academic achievement of adolescents from immigrant families: The roles of family background, attitudes, and behavior. *Child Development, 68,* 351–363.

García Coll, C., & Marks, A. K. (Eds.). (2012). *The immigrant paradox in children and adolescents: Is becoming American a developmental risk?* Washington, DC: American Psychological Association.

Gelatt, J., Adams, G., & Huerta, S. (2014). *Supporting immigrant families' access to prekindergarten.* Washington, DC: Urban Institute.

Glick, J. E., & Bates, L. (2010). Diversity in academic achievement: Children of immigrants in U.S. schools. In E. Grigorenko & R. Takanishi (Eds.), *Immigration, diversity, and education* (pp. 112–129). New York, NY: Routledge Taylor and Francis Group.

Golden, O., & Fortuny, K. (2010). *Young children of immigrants and the path to educational success: Key themes from an Urban Institute roundtable.* Washington, DC: Urban Institute. Retrieved from http://www.urban.org/UploadedPDF/412330-young-children.pdf

Han, W. J. (2008). The academic trajectories of children of immigrants and their school environments. *Developmental Psychology, 44*(6), 1572–1590.

Hao, L., & Bonstead-Bruns, M. (1998). Parent-child differences in educational expectations and the academic achievement of immigrant and native students. *Sociology of Education, 71,* 175–198.

Hao, L., & Woo, H. S. (2012). Distinct trajectories in the transition to adulthood: Are children of immigrants advantaged? *Child Development, 83*(5), 1623–1639.

Ho, J., & Birman, D. (2010). Acculturation gap in Vietnamese refugee families: Impact on family adjustment. *International Journal of Intercultural Relations, 34,* 22–33. doi:10.1016/j.ijintrel.2009.10.002

Hussar, W. J., & Bailey, T. M. (2014). *Projections of education statistics to 2022* (NCES 2014-051). U.S. Department of Education, National Center for Education Statistics. Washington, DC: U.S. Government Printing Office. Retrieved from http://nces.ed.gov/pubs2014/2014051.pdf

Iowa Department of Education. (2012). *Iowa after school report 2012.* Retrieved from http://www.21cclcdm.com/uploads/2/4/3/7/24372861/21cclc_iowa_afterschool _2012_final_report_2013_3_26_hng.pdf

Kao, G. (1999). Psychological well-being and educational achievement among immigrant youth. In D. J. Hernandez (Ed.), *Children of immigrants: Health, adjustment, and public assistance* (pp. 410–477). Washington, DC: National Academy Press.

Kao, G., & Tienda, M. (2010). Optimism and achievement: The educational performance of immigrant youth. In M. M. Suárez-Orozco, C. Suárez-Orozco, & D. Qin-Hilliard (Eds.), *The new immigration: An interdisciplinary reader* (pp. 331–343). New York, NY: Routledge.

Karoly, L., & Gonzalez, G. (2011). Early care and education for children in immigrant families. *The Future of Children, 21*(1), 71–101.

Kennesaw State University (KSU). (n.d.). *Maya heritage community project.* Retrieved from http://mayaproject.kennesaw.edu/

Kia-Keating, M., & Ellis, H. (2007). Belonging and connection to school in resettlement: Young refugees, school belonging, and psychosocial adjustment. *Clinical Child Psychology and Psychiatry, 12,* 29–43. doi:10.1177/1359104507071052

Lau v. Nichols, 414 U. S. 563 (1974).

Lunday, A. (2012). Children of U.S. immigrants outperforming their peers, study shows. *HUB: Johns Hopkins news network.* Retrieved from http://hub.jhu.edu /2012/09/13/immigrant-children-study

Lustig, S., Kia-Keating, M., Grant-Knight, W., Geltman, P., Ellis, H., Birman, D., ... Saxe, G. (2003). *Review of child and adolescent refugee mental health.* White Paper. Boston, MA: National Child Traumatic Stress Network Refugee Trauma Task Force.

Magnuson, K., Lahaie, C., & Waldfogel, J. (2006). Preschool and school readiness of children of immigrants. *Social Science Quarterly, 87,* 1241–1262.

Marks, H. M. (2000). Student engagement in instructional activity: Patterns in the elementary, middle, and high school years. *American Educational Research Journal, 37,* 153–184.

Massachusetts Executive Office of Health and Human Services. (n.d.). *Refugee school impact grants.* Retrieved from http://www.mass.gov/eohhs/gov/departments/ori /ori-programs/school-impact-grants.html

Matthews, H., & Ewen, D. (2006). Reaching All Children? Understanding Early Care and Education Participation Among Immigrant Families. Center for Law and Social Policy, Washington, DC. Retrieved from http://www.clasp .org/admin/site/publications/files/0267.pdf

McNeely, C. A., Morland, L., Doty, B., Meschke, L., Awad, S., & Husain, A. (2016). How schools can promote healthy transitions to adulthood for newly-arrived immigrants and adolescents: Research priorities. Manuscript submitted for publication.

McNeely, C. A., Sprecher, K., & Bates, D. (2010). *Evaluation of caring across communities: Identifying essential components of school-linked mental health services for refugee and immigrant children.* Report. Princeton, NJ: Robert Wood Johnson Foundation.

Migration Policy Institute. (2015). *Issue, action and data inputs to assist creation of national integration plan.* Memorandum to White House Domestic Policy Council. Washington, DC: Author. Retrieved from http://www.migrationpolicy .org/programs/nciip-task-force-new-americans-white-house

Morland, L., Birman, D., Dunn, B., Adkins, M., and Gardner, L. (2013). Immigrant students. In E. Rossen & R. Hull (Eds.), *Supporting and educating traumatized students.* New York, NY: Oxford University Press.

Morland, L., Ives, N., McNeely, C., & Allen, C. (2016). *Exploring collaboration between Head Start and Refugee Resettlement: Improving access to early childhood education for refugees.* Washington, DC: Migration Policy Institute.

National Research Council. (2004). *Engaging schools: Fostering high school students' motivation to learn.* Washington, DC: National Academies Press.

Neidell, M., & Waldfogel, J. (2009). Program participation of immigrant children: Evidence from the availability of Head Start. *Economics of Education Review, 28,* 704–715.

Park, M., & McHugh, M. (2014). *Immigrant parents and early childhood programs: Addressing barriers of literacy, culture, and systems knowledge.* Washington, DC: Migration Policy Institute.

Plyler v. Doe, 457 U. S. 202 (1982).

Portes, A., & Rumbaut, R. (2001). *Legacies: The new second generation.* Berkeley: University of California Press.

Portes, A., & Zhou, M. (1993). The new second generation: Segmented assimilation and its variants. *Annals of the American Academy of Political and Social Science, 530,* 74–96.

Scott, M. M., MacDonald, G., Collazos, J., Levinger, B., Leighton, E., & Ball, J. (2014). *From cradle to career: The multiple challenges facing immigrant families in Langley Park Promise Neighborhood*. Washington, DC: Urban Institute. Retrieved from http://www.urban.org/UploadedPDF/413164-From-Cradle-to-Career.pdf

Short, D. J., & Boyson, B. A. (2012). *Helping newcomer students succeed in secondary schools and beyond*. Washington, DC: Center for Applied Linguistics. Retrieved from http://www.carnegie.org/fileadmin/Media/Publications/Reporter/23/helping-newcomer-students-succeed-in-secondary-schools-and-beyond.pdf

Suárez-Orozco, C., Bang, H. J., & Kim, H. Y. (2011). "I felt like my heart was staying behind": Psychological implications of immigrant family separations & reunifications. *Journal of Adolescent Research, 21*(2), 222–257.

Suárez-Orozco, C., Gaytán, F. X., Bang, H. J., Pakes, J., & Rhodes, J. (2010). Academic trajectories of newcomer immigrant youth. *Developmental Psychology, 46*(3), 602–618.

Suárez-Orozco, C., Rhodes, J., & Milburn, M. (2009). Unraveling the immigrant paradox: Academic engagement and disengagement among recently arrived immigrant youth. *Youth & Society, 41*(2), 151–185. doi: 10.1177/0044118X09333647

Suárez-Orozco, C., Yoshikawa, Y., Teranishi, R., & Suárez-Orozco, M. (2011). Growing up in the shadows: The developmental implications of unauthorized status. *Harvard Educational Review, 81*(3), 438–472.

Thomas, W. P., & Collier, V. P. (2002). *A national study of school effectiveness for language minority students' long-term academic achievement*. Santa Cruz: Center for Research on Education, Diversity and Excellence, University of California-Santa Cruz.

United Nations High Commissioner for Refugees (UNHCR). (2014). *Children on the run: Unaccompanied children leaving Central America and Mexico and the need for international protection*. Retrieved from http://www.refworld.org/docid/532180c24.html

U.S. Department of Education. (n.d.). *Promise Neighborhoods, about*. Retrieved from http://promiseneighborhoods.ed.gov/pn/about

——. (2004). *Parental involvement: Title I, Part A, Non-regulatory guidance*. Retrieved from http://www.ed.gov/programs/titleiparta/parentinvguid.doc

——. (2009). *No Child Left Behind: A toolkit for teachers*. Retrieved from http://www2.ed.gov/teachers/nclbguide/toolkit_pg10.html

U.S. Department of Education, National Center for Education Statistics (USDOE/NCES). (2014). *The condition of education: English language learners*. Retrieved from http://nces.ed.gov/programs/coe/indicator_cgf.asp

U.S. Department of Education, Office for Civil Rights (USDOE/OCR). (n.d.). Schools' civil rights obligations to English learner students and limited English proficient parents. Retrieved from http://www2.ed.gov/about/offices/list/ocr /ellresources.html

U.S. Department of Homeland Security (USDHS), Customs and Border Protection. (2015). *Southwest border unaccompanied alien children (FY 2014)*. Retrieved from http://www.cbp.gov/newsroom/stats/southwest-border-unaccompanied -children-2014

U.S. Government Accountability Office (GAO). (2015, February). *Central America: Information on migration of unaccompanied children from El Salvador, Guatemala, and Honduras.* GAO-15-362. Washington, DC: Author. Retrieved from http://www.gao.gov/products/GAO-15-362

Wimer, C., Bouffard, S., Caronongan, P., Dearing, E., Simpkins, S., Little, P., & Weiss, H. (2006). *What are kids getting into these days? Demographic differences in youth out-of-school time participation.* Cambridge, MA: Harvard Family Research Project.

Yoshikawa, H., & Kholoptseva, J. (2013). *Unauthorized immigrant parents and their children's development: A summary of the evidence.* Washington, DC: Migration Policy Institute. Retrieved from http://www.migrationpolicy.org/ research/unauthorized-immigrant-parents-and-their-childrens-development

Zhou, M. (1997). Segmented assimilation: Issues, controversies, and recent research on the new second generation. *International Migration Review, 31*(4), 975–1008.

Zhou, M., & Kim, S. (2006). Community forces, social capital, and educational achievement: The case of supplementary education in the Chinese and Korean immigrant communities. *Harvard Educational Review, 76*(1), 1–29. Retrieved from http://www.sscnet.ucla.edu/soc/faculty/zhou/pubs/Zhou-Kim _EthnicSuppEdu2006.pdf

Zong, J., & Batalova, J. (2015). *Frequently requested statistics on immigrants and immigration in the United States.* Washington, DC: Migration Policy Institute. Retrieved from http://www.migrationpolicy.org/article/frequently -requested-statistics-immigrants-and-immigration-united-states

Practice with Immigrant and Refugee Children and Families in the Mental Health System

▸ *JODI BERGER CARDOSO* and *LIZA BARROS LANE*

MENTAL HEALTH DISORDERS are often characterized by disturbances in mood, behavior, and cognition. A "serious mental illness" is defined as any mental condition that resulted in 30 or more days of limited capacity in the past year. These illnesses can be characterized by suicidal ideation, anxiety, mood instability, psychosis, substance use, lack of impulse control, and/or violent behavior (Kessler, Chiu, Demler, & Walters, 2005). Since mental health is a central indicator of well-being, untreated mental health disorders can have devastating effects and lead to greater impairment and increased severity of episodes, which can contribute to school failure, unstable employment, homelessness, marital instability, and violence (Wang et al., 2005).

Successful treatment of mental illness depends greatly on the capacity of the mental health system to meet the needs of the community (Rosen, Nakash, & Alegría, 2014). Epidemiological data show high rates of unmet mental health needs among U.S. adults and children (Substance Abuse and Mental Health Services Administration, 2012). In the United States, roughly 40 percent of adults with a serious mental illness do not receive treatment, and more than 25 percent of individuals with a serious mental illness had a co-occurring substance abuse disorder (Substance Abuse and Mental Health Services Administration, 2012). Similar patterns of unmet mental health needs are observed in U.S. children and adolescents. Kataoka et al. (2003) found that only 23 percent of adolescents in need of mental health services had received them in the past year, whereas Merikangas et al. (2010) found that about half of youths 8 to 15 years old with a mental disorder had received treatment in the past year.

In the United States, four groups of providers deliver the majority of mental health services (Rosen et al., 2014): (1) the specialty service sector, which includes psychiatrists, psychologists, counselors, and social workers with specific training in assessment and treatment; (2) the nonspecialty sector, which includes primary care or family practice physicians who provide mental health services to clients within the context of their medical care; (3) the human services sector, which includes professionals who provide mental health services in schools, community clinics, and the justice system; and (4) the voluntary support networks, such as Alcoholics Anonymous, Narcotics Anonymous, and the National Association of Mental Illness (NAMI). The distinction between the public and private sectors is another variant in how individuals and families receive services. The public sector includes community clinics and public hospitals and often provides services to clients without insurance, whereas the private sector caters to the insured population, and care is delivered through private, for profit institutions and organizations (Rosen et al., 2014).

Adults who receive mental health services are becoming increasingly likely to receive treatment from nonspecialty service providers such as primary care physicians, community health centers, emergency rooms, schools, and correctional facilities (Wang et al., 2005) rather than specialty providers such as psychiatrists, psychologists, and social workers in private inpatient hospitals, outpatient clinics, and/or offices. From 1993 to 2003, general medical care providers were more likely to provide mental health services to U.S. adults with mental disorders than were any other type of provider (Substance Abuse and Mental Health Services Administration, 2010). This trend may have been driven by the use of general practitioners as a referral source for specialty health care providers, the shortage of specialty mental health services that are affordable, and/or health coverage barriers, such as inadequate coverage (Cunningham, 2009). Prescription medication was the most common form of treatment (32.4 percent), followed by outpatient (21.2 percent) and inpatient mental health services (3.1 percent) (Substance Abuse and Mental Health Services Administration, 2010, Table 24).

For children and adolescents, the patterns of mental health service use are slightly different from those for adults. Roughly 12 percent of youths received specialty services from outpatient psychologists, social workers, and/or psychiatrists, 12 percent received services from these providers in a school-based setting, and 4 percent received mental health services from the juvenile justice system (Substance Abuse and Mental Health Services Administration, 2012). Racial and ethnic minority youths are significantly less likely to receive mental health services than their non-Hispanic white counterparts (Kataoka et al., 2003). There is a dearth of information about the mental health needs of immigrant and refugee children, but it suggests that very few immigrant and refugee youths that need services receive them (Birman & Tran, 2008). School-based programs may provide an assessment and intervention point for youths who may otherwise not receive services, and these programs may be critical to assisting in the early identification of trauma-related disorders (e.g., PTSD, disassociate and attachment disorders) as well as depression and other anxiety disorders in children and adolescents (Birman & Tran, 2008).

UNIQUE NEEDS OF IMMIGRANT AND REFUGEE CHILDREN AND FAMILIES IN THE MENTAL HEALTH SYSTEM

The Prevalence of Disorders in Adults

Culture directly influences how individuals perceive and experience psychological symptoms (Roberts, Roberts, & Xing, 2006). There is growing attention on how the experiences before coming to the United States (premigration), during the migration journey (perimigration), and postmigration influence mental health outcomes and service utilization.

Traumatic exposure in the homeland (i.e., war, gang violence, natural disasters, and political violence) may prompt migration, and the journey itself may expose children and families to additional traumas, such as crossing rivers, homicide, rape and murder, and extended time in refugee camps (Pumariega, Rothe, & Pumariega, 2005). Children may be separated from their parents for long periods of time (Hondagneu-Sotelo & Avila, 1997) and, as a consequence, take the migration journey without their parents (Kennedy, 2014). Once in the United States, postmigration stressors related to the acculturation process, poverty, and discrimination may contribute to the immediate or delayed onset of mental health disorders (Portes & Rumbaut, 2006; Pumariega et al., 2005). Particularly for undocumented children and families, aggressive immigration enforcement increases anxiety, stress, and depression and reinforces isolation, fear, and mistrust of government institutions (Chaudry et al., 2010; Dreby, 2012; Hagan, Rodriguez, & Castro, 2011; Rodriguez & Hagan, 2004).

Before the year 2000, there was relatively little information on the mental health of immigrants in the United States. Research often focused on psychiatric disorders among nonimmigrants or included only English-speaking immigrant groups. National comparisons often were not possible, and community research included small, nongeneralizable samples. Several epidemiological surveys, such as the National Latino and Asian American Study, the National Epidemiological Survey of Alcohol and Related Conditions, and the National Longitudinal Study of Adolescent to Adult Health, have been critical in identifying the prevalence of mental disorders and have provided an unprecedented opportunity to explore how immigration-related factors and social context contribute to psychiatric diagnoses in major U.S. immigrant groups.

Research suggests that U.S.-born adults have higher rates of lifetime mood, anxiety, and substance abuse disorders than do adults who immigrate to the United States. Table 13.1 shows differences in mood, anxiety, and substance abuse disorders for aggregate U.S.-born and immigrant Latino and Asian groups. Differences in U.S.-born and immigrant groups by demographic indicators, such as country of origin, ethnicity, age of immigration, years lived in the United States, and gender, have been observed for some groups (Alegría et al., 2008; Breslau & Chang, 2006).

Disaggregating by ethnicity, Puerto Ricans have higher rates of mental health disorders compared with Mexican and Cuban immigrants (Alegría et al., 2008), Vietnamese women were less likely than Chinese women to have a lifetime depressive disorder, and Filipino men were more likely than Chinese men to have a lifetime substance abuse disorder (Breslau & Chang,

TABLE 13.1 Prevalence Rates of Mental Disorders in U.S.-Born and Foreign-Born Groups

LIFETIME PREVALENCE RATES	U.S.-BORN LATINOS[a]	FOREIGN-BORN LATINOS[a]	U.S.-BORN ASIANS[b]	FOREIGN-BORN ASIANS[b]
Mood disorders	19.8%	14.8%	16.6%	11.8%
Anxiety disorders	18.9%	15.2%	17.8%	9.1%
Substance use disorders	20.4%	7.0%	26.9%	8.0%

[a] Data on prevalence rates come from the National Epidemiological Survey of Alcohol and Related Conditions (NESARC).
[b] Data on prevalence rates come from the National Latino and Asian American Study (NLAAS).

2006). The longer an individual lives in the United States, the more at risk they are to be diagnosed with a mental disorder (Breslau & Chang, 2006; Cook, Alegría, Lin, & Guo, 2009; Takeuchi et al., 2007). Similarly, age at immigration is also associated with the onset of certain mental health disorders. For example, Asian women who arrived in the United States as adults were less likely than U.S.-born Asian women to have a mood, anxiety, or substance abuse disorder, and for Asian men the same pattern was true for substance abuse disorders (Takeuchi et al., 2007).

REFUGEES IN THE UNITED STATES

A refugee is an individual who cannot "return to his or her country because of persecution or a well-founded fear of persecution on account of race, religion, nationality, membership in a particular social group or political opinion" (Martin & Yankay, 2014, p. 1). During 2013, 69,909 refugees were granted entrance into the United States. The leading countries of nationality for refugees were Iraq (27.9 percent), Burma (23.3 percent), Bhutan (13.1 percent), Somalia (10.9 percent), and Cuba (6.0 percent).

The literature suggests that refugees have a high prevalence of mental health disorders, particularly posttraumatic stress, major depressive, and substance abuse disorders (Chu, Keller, & Rasmussen, 2013; Fortuna, Porche, & Alegría, 2008; Rasmussen, Crager, Baser, Chu, & Gany, 2012; Steel et al., 2009). In a meta-analysis of posttraumatic stress disorder (PTSD) and major depressive disorder in refugee populations, prevalence rates of these disorders were lower in national probability samples than they were in convenience samples. The weighted prevalence for posttraumatic stress disorder across 145 surveys was 30.6 percent, whereas the weighted prevalence for major depressive disorder was 30.8 percent across 117 surveys. Torture was the strongest explanatory factor for these diagnoses, and other correlates included gender, residency status, and time in the receiving country (Steel et al., 2009).

Because of their legal status, refugees have access to mental health services through resettlement programs, whereas voluntary immigrants (those that do not have official refugee status) often do not have access to services (Rasmussen et al., 2012). National data comparing the onset of PTSD and depression between refugees and voluntary immigrants are rare. The limited evidence suggests that PTSD and major depressive disorders are more frequent premigration for refugees, yet the postmigration onset of these disorders was similar for the two groups. Although refugees were more likely to report war-related traumatic exposure, non–war-related traumatic events were equally high among voluntary immigrants. Legal status and other postmigration factors explained a large part of PTSD outcomes in immigrants—above and beyond the exposure to premigration trauma (Chu et al., 2013; Rasmussen et al., 2012; Steel, Silove, Bird, McGorry, & Mohan, 1999). This highlights the importance of mental health services in attenuating the effects of postmigration trauma exposure on the development of mental health disorders for both refugees and voluntary immigrants.

The Prevalence of Disorders in Children

CHILDREN FROM EL SALVADOR, HONDURAS, AND GUATEMALA

Latin America has the highest homicide rate among children and adolescents in the world. Four out of ten global homicides occur in this region, with more than a quarter of homicide victims below the age of 20 (United Nations Office of Drugs and Crime, 2013). From October 1, 2013, to July 31, 2014, the number of unaccompanied alien children (UACs) increased from 15,949 in 2011 to 68,551 in 2014. (Rosenblum, 2015). Nearly half of the children reported a mental health diagnosis, and 33 percent reported using substances to alleviate the symptoms (U.S. Conference of Catholic Bishops, 2014).

In 2014, children who were immigrants themselves represented 3.8 percent of the total U.S. population under 18, whereas children whose parents were immigrants represented 21.5 percent (Child Trends, 2014, figure 1). Among the foreign-born children, roughly 1.1 million are unauthorized (Passel, 2011) and therefore do not have access to private, and most public, mental health services. As is the case with adults, premigration experiences and postmigration stress influence the onset of mental health disorders. The migration experience forces children to deal with stressors that are inherent to migration. Before, during, and after migration, children often experience multiple disruptions in their lives. Apart from a loss of familiar settings, children often experience ambiguous loss associated with other key interpersonal relationships (Falicov, 2005; Garcia Coll & Magnuson, 2005). For example, in a sample of 385 children, Garcia Coll and Magnuson (2005) found that 85 percent of the children lived separated from one or both of their parents. Parental separation is associated with emotional and behavioral problems, as well as depression and anxiety in children (Capps, Castañeda, Chaudry, & Santos, 2007; Chaudry et al., 2010; Heymann et al., 2009; Landale, Thomas, & Van Hook, 2011).

CHILDREN OF IMMIGRANTS INVOLVED IN THE CHILD WELFARE SYSTEM

A study using child welfare data from the second National Survey of Child and Adolescent Well-being (NSCAW II) revealed that the mental health needs for all the Latino children in the system were similar. Yet, in spite of similar levels of need, the odds of mental health service use were 67 percent lower for children of immigrant parents compared with children of U.S.-born parents and 92 percent lower for children of unauthorized parents. Although this study is limited to Latino immigrants involved in the child welfare system, it adds to an emerging concern surrounding the disparity in mental health usage for families based on immigration status (Finno-Velasquez, Berger Cardoso, Dettlaff, & Hurlburt, 2015).

Once in the United States, family dynamics often change, which can result in family conflict (Falicov, 2014). Through their interactions with the school system, children often learn the language and adapt to U.S. culture more quickly than their parents did. Family conflict, the parent–child acculturation gap, and family immigration stressors can increase stress and can compromise child well-being (Cervantes, Berger Cardoso, & Goldbach, 2015; Perreira & Ornelas, 2011). These stressors are particularly evident in undocumented families, who also have significant fears associated with detection and deportation (Berger Cardoso, Scott, & Faulkner, 2014). Additionally, experiences of prejudice, discrimination, and racism are unfortunate developmental risks for immigrant children, and these factors have been associated with increased psychological stress (Cervantes et al., 2014; Garcia Coll & Magnuson, 2005; Portes & Rumbaut, 2006; Vega & Rumbaut, 1991).

Immigrant children have lower rates of mental health and substance use disorders than do their U.S.-born counterparts (Gfroerer & Tan, 2003; Harker, 2001; Hussey et al., 2007; Peña et al., 2008; Prado et al., 2009). The prevalence of mental health and substance use disorders varies significantly across subgroups, by level of acculturation, and increases the longer immigrant children live in the United States (Gfroerer & Tan, 2003; Le, Goebert, & Wallen, 2009). Family factors, such as connectedness and parental involvement, have been identified as important protective factors in immigrant youths, whereas acculturation factors have been identified as risk factors (Le et al., 2009; Prado et al., 2009).

BARRIERS TO MENTAL HEALTH TREATMENT AND CROSS-SYSTEM CHANGE

There are many obstacles that impede access to mental health services for immigrant and refugee families. Barriers to mental health service utilization that immigrant families or their service providers report include not having funding for services (Ayon, 2013; Chen & Vargas-Bustamante, 2011; Saechao et al., 2012), documentation status (Xu & Brabeck, 2012), lack of familiarity with the mental health system in the United States (Chen & Vargas-Bustamante, 2011; Choi Wu, Kviz, & Michaels Miller, 2009), cultural and linguistic differences between service providers and clients (Ayon 2013; Cooper-Patrick et al., 1997), stigma (Nadeem et al., 2007), and challenges with time and transportation (Choi Wu et al., 2009).

Financial Considerations

Even though refugees receive social service support, limited funding for mental health services is a major barrier for immigrants (Ayon, 2013; Chen & Vargas-Bustamante, 2011; Saechao et al., 2012) who have either been legally in the United States for less than five years, are not legally authorized to be in the United States, or are members of a family with mixed documentation status. Because immigrants and refugees experience greater poverty than U.S.-born citizens (Migration Policy Institute, 2014), most immigrant and refugee families cannot afford private insurance or the out-of-pocket costs of mental health services (Kaltman, Hurtado De Mendoza, Gonzales, & Serrano, 2014; Saechao et al., 2012). In 2012, 19.2 percent of foreign-born families were below 100 percent of the federal poverty level, compared with 15.4 percent of U.S.-born families, and 24.6 percent of the foreign-born families were at the 100 percent to 199 percent federal poverty level, compared with 18.4 percent of the U.S.-born families (Migration Policy Institute, 2014).

Medicaid is a source of health care funding for individuals who are low income, have medical needs, are expectant mothers, or are children, dependent on the state. As such, it is likely that many immigrants would qualify for benefits that would help them pay for mental health services. However, the 1996 Personal Work and Responsibility Act required residence in the United States for at least five years in order for most legal immigrants to be eligible for Medicaid funding (Chen & Vargas-Bustamante, 2011). However, undocumented immigrants remain ineligible for services even after they demonstrate residency for five years. Restrictions on residency and documentation status impact access to care for immigrants at a time when they are facing many psychosocial stressors and may be at an increased risk for mental illness. Chen and Vargas-Bustamante (2011) found that immigrants were 40 percent less likely to seek treatment from a mental health service provider than those who had health insurance coverage. Delayed access to mental health services is a predictor of both the severity of the diagnosis and the likelihood that the symptoms will persist across the life cycle (Ghio, Gotelli, Marcenaro, Amore, & Natta, 2014).

Children born in the United States are eligible for federal and state health care funding, such as the Children's Health Insurance Plan (CHIP) and Medicaid, if they meet the income requirement, regardless of their parent's immigration status. Roughly 85 percent of immigrant families with children in the United States are mixed-status families. The term mixed status is used to describe families where members have different legal statuses (Fix & Zimmermann, 2001). In a household, for example, one or both parents may be undocumented, whereas the children are U.S. citizens. In families where one or both of the parents is undocumented, parents may not apply for health care coverage for the children because the parents fear deportation (Ayon, 2013; Xu & Brabeck, 2012). When parents and children are entitled to resources they do not access for fear of legal repercussions, this is frequently called a chilling effect (Borjas, 2002; Watson, 2014). Kandula, Grogan, Rathouz, and Lauderdale (2004) observed this chilling effect in Medicaid enrollment among children of immigrants. Roughly

13.8 percent of qualified children of immigrants enrolled in Medicaid (Kandula et al., 2004), a percentage that should be higher given the elevated rates of concentrated poverty experienced by children in immigrant families.

Health Care Systems in the Country of Origin

Recent immigrants often struggle to comprehend the complex service systems in the United States. The approach to mental health care in immigrants' country of origin is likely very different from what they experience in the United States, and in some cases, immigrants and refugees come from countries with no formal mental health system (Chen & Vargas-Bustamante, 2011; Saechao et al., 2012). The World Health Organization (WHO) reports on the state of mental health systems in countries around the world and provides a context for understanding how immigrants and refugees may expect to interface with the mental health system in the United States.

In 2009, 100 percent of countries with upper-middle incomes (e.g., South Africa, Chile, Panama, Uruguay, etc.) in the sample had mental health legislation, whereas 54 percent of middle-income (Bhutan, Sri Lanka, El Salvador, Kosovo, etc.) and low-income (e.g., Afghanistan, Ethiopia, Nigeria, etc.) countries did not have legislation to address the mental health needs of the population (World Health Organization, 2009). Most countries that do not have formalized mental health policies also do not allocate spending to fund mental health services. Countries with upper-middle incomes spent around 70 times more for mental health than in low-income countries and 14 times more than in countries with lower-middle incomes. Differences in mental health infrastructure and funding between countries reflect the range of experiences with formalized mental health care that immigrants and refugees have when they arrive in the United States (World Health Organization, 2009).

Cultural and Linguistic Differences

Beliefs about the nature, cause, and treatment of mental illness differ across cultures (Choi Wu et al., 2009; Saechao et al., 2012). In the United States, psychotropic medication is the most common type of treatment for mental illness (Substance Abuse and Mental Health Services Administration,

2010). However, medication as a treatment for mental illness is often resisted by immigrant and refugee communities. Ethnic minorities are more likely to believe that antidepressants are addictive (Cooper-Patrick et al., 1997), and these groups often rely on their faith and religious beliefs to cope with symptoms (Cabassa, Lester, & Zayas, 2006). Naturalized immigrants are 28 percent less likely than U.S.-born citizens to take prescription drugs for depression, and foreign-born noncitizens are 40 percent less likely than U.S.-born citizens to take drugs for mental disorders (Chen & Vargas-Bustamante, 2011). Physicians and practitioners who advocate for the use of psychotropic medication as a treatment for mental health problems with immigrants and refugees should be aware that cultural beliefs about these medications may lead to challenges in adherence. Additionally, barriers such as language and the lack of culturally responsive practitioners may increase mistrust and decrease engagement in the mental health system.

The lack of a bilingual, bicultural workforce is a significant barrier to mental health engagement in ethnic minority communities (Hogg Foundation for Mental Health & Methodist Healthcare Ministries, 2011). In 2010, approximately 25.2 million individuals, or 9 percent of the total U.S. population over age 5, reported speaking English as less than "very well." The majority of limited-English speakers in the United States are Spanish speakers (65.8 percent), followed by Chinese, Vietnamese, Korean, and Tagalog (Pandya, McHugh, & Batalova, 2011). Latinos with limited English proficiency (LEP) had significantly lower odds of mental health treatment, and differences in language and culture contributed to patients' misunderstanding of their need for mental health services and/or the treatment plan (Kim et al., 2011).

In addition to language, another barrier to treatment is the lack of providers who are a cultural match to the immigrant clients they serve. Some research suggests that clients may be more likely to engage in treatment and maintain adherence (Choi Wu et al., 2009; Saechao et al., 2012) and perceive the practitioner as competent in helping them to address their problems (Meyer, Zane, & Cho, 2011) if they are working with practitioners who share their cultural background and orientation. However, there are mixed findings in the literature, with some studies finding that the ethnic match between client and counselor had no impact on treatment outcome (Gamst, Dana, Der-Karabetian, & Kramer, 2001, 2004). Nevertheless, clients may feel more comfortable seeking and engaging in mental health treatment with practitioners from their own cultural and linguistic orientation because they may experience less perceived stigma—a significant obstacle in mental health treatment with all populations (Corrigan, 2004).

Stigma

Stigma is the perception of being damaged or defective in a socially unacceptable way (Vogel, Wade, & Haake, 2006). Stigma as a barrier to mental health service use has been well researched in different populations with severe mental illness in the United States (Corrigan, 2004). In a sample of Asian Americans, Leong and Lau (2001) found that stigma was a significant obstacle to help-seeking behavior in this community. Asian Americans have one of the lowest rates of mental health service use among immigrant populations in the United States. Other studies have yielded similar findings with different immigrant and refugee communities, such as Middle Eastern immigrant youths (Soheilian & Inman, 2009), Congolese and Somali refugee adults (Piwowarczyk, Bishop, Yusuf, Mudymba, & Raj, 2014), Asian Indian, Cambodian, Chinese, Indonesian, Korean, Taiwanese, Thai, and Vietnamese immigrant young adults (Lee et al., 2008), and African, Caribbean, and Latina immigrant women (Nadeem et al., 2007). Understanding the role of stigma in the community is a critical step to increasing engagement and treatment.

Self-stigma influences help-seeking behavior (Vogel, Wade, & Haake, 2006). Corrigan, Watson, and Barr (2006) define self-stigma as the internalization of negative beliefs about mental illness. Self-stigma increases resistance to seeking help for people with a mental illness because to seek mental health care is a confirmation of perceived weakness (Corrigan, 2004). Perhaps the acknowledgment that help is needed is perceived to be a greater threat than the mental illness itself (Vogel, Wade, & Haake, 2006). Studies have shown that self-stigma influences mental health service utilization in women with depression by lowering the desire to seek mental health treatment (Nadeem et al., 2007) and by increasing negative attitudes toward working with psychiatrists (Pattyn, Verhaeghe, Sercu, & Bracke, 2014). Together, these attitudes inhibit treatment engagement. Evidence-based interventions that implement collaborative care models to target engagement of refugees and immigrants with the mental health system have shown promise in increasing engagement and decreasing stigma.

EMERGING PRACTICES AND PREVENTIVE INTERVENTIONS

Although the majority of clinical interventions are still based on Western, middle-class samples (Antoniades, Mazza, & Brijnath, 2014), a growing number of experimental and quasi-experiential studies have tested the efficacy of mental health interventions with immigrants and refugee adults (see Antoniades et al., 2014, for a systematic review of interventions that treat depression) and children (Beehler, Birman, & Campbell, 2012; Birman et al., 2008). Interventions that include immigrants and refugees must be adapted to consider the roles of culture and context (Alegría, Atkins, Farmer, Slaton, & Stelk, 2010). Culturally responsive interventions with immigrants and refugees often involve family and friends, especially with individuals who come from collectivistic cultures that do not have much exposure to the U.S. mental health system. The delivery of these interventions can be in a family, individual, or group format and may be provided by laypersons, community health care providers, primary care physicians, teachers, and/or trained behavioral health specialists. Evidence-based practices at the individual level target specific symptom clusters and/or diagnoses, such as depression, anxiety, posttraumatic stress disorder, traumatic stress, and attention deficit disorder. In the following section, we present selected interventions that demonstrate promise or efficacy and that are implemented by laypersons, community health workers, and specialty behavioral health providers.

INTERVENTIONS THAT TARGET OUTCOMES
USING TRAINED LAYPERSONS

Tea and Families Education and Support (TAFES) (Weine et al., 2003) and Coffee and Families Education and Support (CAFES) (Weine et al., 2008) are multifamily group interventions that aim to increase engagement with the mental health system. In these approaches, multiple families are led through a curriculum, which includes six sessions of psychoeducation and group discussions that focus on increasing knowledge about mental health treatment, trauma, and the role of family support in the treatment of mental disorders—primarily posttraumatic stress disorder. The goal of these interventions is to increase the number of mental health visits and to test whether an increase in family knowledge about trauma helped explain the mental health engagement (Weine et al., 2008). Findings from the two studies suggested that these curricula can decrease the stigma of posttraumatic stress disorder, and keeping families involved increases mental health engagement. CAFES was tested with only Bosnian refugees, whereas TAFES included Kosovar immigrants. Therefore, testing the curriculum with other refugee groups is a critical next step in considering its applicability to refugees from other cultural backgrounds.

Similarly, in the Latino community, *promotoras* (also known as community health workers, health promoters, or outreach workers) have been used to increase access to health care and health education in underserved communities (Waitzkin et al., 2011). Much of the research on the efficacy of *promotoras* has focused on health outcomes such as diabetes, hypertension, cancer screening, and asthma management (Balcázar et al., 2006; Balcázar et al., 2010; Ingram et al., 2007), but there are fewer interventions that use *promotoras* to increase access to mental health information and services (Tran et al., 2014; Viswanathan et al., 2010).

ALMA (Amigas Latinas Motivando El Alma) is a *promotora*-based intervention that aims to target depression and reduce acculturative stressors among Latino immigrants (Tran et al., 2014). The ALMA curriculum focuses on increasing coping skills and is implemented in the women's social networks (*compañeras*). Women who received the *promotora* intervention within the *compañeras* framework improved on outcomes such as depressive symptoms, attitudes about treatment, acculturative stress, perceived social support, and positive coping behaviors (Tran et al., 2014). Other interventions have focused on targeting contextual factors, such as unemployment and food and housing insecurity, that may lead to mental health symptoms. Ethnographic interviews suggest that *promotoras* in community health care settings may offer some value to clients—particularly those who are underserved (Waitzkin et al., 2011).

INDIVIDUAL, GROUP, AND FAMILY THERAPEUTIC INTERVENTIONS BY SPECIALTY PROVIDERS

Traumatic exposure in the country of origin, during the migration journey, and postmigration often contributes to the onset of trauma-related mental health diagnoses. There are many interventions and modalities to treat trauma-related diagnoses. For children, exposure to violence is associated with a wide range of mental disorders, including PTSD, other anxiety disorders, depressive symptoms, dissociative disorders, and substance abuse disorders. These symptoms negatively impact children and adolescents across multiple domains, including school functioning (Hurt, Malmud, Brodsky, & Giannetta, 2001), cognition and reading ability (Delaney-Black et al., 2002), and aggressive and delinquent behavior (Farrell & Bruce, 1997). Research also suggests a strong association between trauma exposure, child abuse, and substance abuse disorders (Cohen, Mannarino, Zhitova, & Capone, 2003; Farley, Golding, Young, Mulligan, & Minkoff, 2004).

Risk factors associated with PTSD include mental health difficulties before trauma exposure, severity of the traumatic event, symptoms of disassociation, and intense negative stimuli (nightmares, fear, helplessness) (Ozer, Best, Lipsey, & Weiss, 2003). However, it is important to note that not everyone exposed to a traumatic event(s) will develop a mental health disorder. Protective factors that may promote resilience include internal characteristics of the individual, such as self-esteem, trust, sense of self-efficacy, and internal locus of control, as well as external factors such as a sense of safety, religiosity, role models, and emotional and social support (Ahmed, 2007). Although most research has been on the treatment of trauma and other disorders, there is some evidence to suggest that prevention strategies implemented early may attenuate symptoms or prevent PTSD and other disorders (Hobfoll et al., 2007).

Cognitive behavioral therapy (CBT) and its related approaches, such as exposure eye movement desensitization and reprocessing (EMDR) and exposure therapy (ET), are the most frequent treatment interventions used to address mood and anxiety disorders related to trauma. The core concepts of CBT include cognitive restructuring, behavioral modification, interpersonal skills training and stress reduction, and/or relaxation (Antoniades et al., 2014). Trauma-focused CBT (TF-CBT) also includes components of ET, particularly in treating PTSD. However, many key studies testing ET have been conducted with individuals from Western cultures, and there is some evidence that refugees and asylees may find ET hard to tolerate and that it may worsen symptoms (Hinton, Rivera, Hofmann, Barlow, & Otto, 2012). Cognitive behavioral therapy has the greatest impact on the reduction of PTSD symptoms (Bisson et al., 2007; Cloitre, 2009), as well as on co-occurring disorders such as panic disorder, serious mental illness (mood disorder, psychotic disorders, schizophrenia/schizoaffective disorders), and substance abuse disorders (Substance Abuse and Mental Health Services

Administration, 2014). These approaches may be coupled with pharmacotherapy, which can assist in relieving symptoms (Substance Abuse and Mental Health Services Administration, 2014).

The adaptation of evidence-based interventions is a critical step in providing culturally responsive services to immigrants and refugees. Several researchers have tested adapted versions of CBT interventions to treat mental disorders in diverse populations, including Latinos (Hinton et al., 2011), African refugees (Neuner, Schauer, Kjaschik, Karunakara, & Elbert, 2004), Cambodians (Hinton et al., 2009), Vietnamese (Hinton et al., 2004), and Chinese (Choi et al., 2012). However, even in light of these promising interventions, there have been few randomized trials testing other psychotherapeutic approaches with immigrants and refugees (Antoniades et al., 2014), and there is limited evidence on the effects of culture on psychotherapy for PTSD and depression with diverse populations (Substance Abuse and Mental Health Services Administration, 2014). In an effort to address this limitation in the literature, Hinton et al. (2012) illustrate how they use culturally responsive CBT (CA-CBT) for a diverse population of traumatized refugee and ethnic minority patients. They focused on emotion exposure and emotional regulation, adapting the components within the context of the individual's culture. For example, they advocate for conducting the trauma exposure component in a culturally responsive way while implementing emotional regulation techniques from the individual's religious and cultural traditions (Hinton et al., 2012).

As with adults, the efficacy of CBT is well established for the treatment of anxiety, depression, and traumatic stress in children and adolescents, and has been rated a level 1 intervention, which indicates strong support based on multiple randomized trials demonstrating efficacy (Chorpita et al., 2011). Trauma-focused CBT has demonstrated effectiveness in several randomized control trials—the most scientifically rigorous method of testing manual interventions—for treating PTSD with children and adolescents who have experienced sexual abuse (Cohen et al., 2003; Cohen & Mannarino, 1996, 1998). However, there are few documented interventions that have been tested with immigrant and refugee children and adolescents (Jaycox et al., 2002). Most research that has included racial and ethnic minorities has included samples of highly acculturated, rather than recent immigrant, youths (La Greca, Silverman, & Lochman, 2009).

For younger children, child–parent psychotherapy (CPP) is effective with children from newborns to age 5 who have been exposed to at least one traumatic event (Lieberman, Ghosh Ippen, & Van Horn, 2006; Lieberman, Van Horn, & Ghosh Ippen, 2005). Child–parent psychotherapy (CPP) is an evidence-based practice highlighted in the National Registry of Evidence-Based Programs and Practices (NREPP) by SAMHSA. It is a relationship-based treatment whereby the mental health provider works with the parent and child, together addressing the eight core components of the approach: (1) assistance with life problems through case management, (2) psychoeducational guidance to the caregiver on issues related to child development, (3) assisting caregivers in enhancing the child's physical safety, (4) assisting caregivers in enhancing the child's emotional safety, (5) collaborating to develop the family trauma narrative, (6) integrating the family's cultural norms and values, (7) engagement with the family, and (8) providing the family supportive supervision (National Child Traumatic Stress Network, 2007, 2011). The National Child Traumatic Stress Network (NCTSN) has released a brief suggesting the use of CPP with families from Latin America (National Child Traumatic Stress Network, 2011). Focusing specifically on the component "attending the family's cultural norms and values," the NCTSN identified five core skills clinicians can apply to this component: (1) linguistic matching, (2) the use of immigrant clinicians to assist families with the cultural transition, (3) broadening the caregiver's and child's expectations for interaction and the use of play, (4) integrating extended and transnational families in treatment, and (5) integration of cultural beliefs, values, and practices in dealing with trauma (National Child Traumatic Stress Network, 2011, p. 6). Although the NCTSN suggests concrete ways to integrate a culturally focused lens into the application of CPP with Latino families exposed to trauma, there have been no randomized control trials testing the efficacy of this approach with this population.

SPOTLIGHT ON PROMISING PRACTICE: CBITS WITH LATIN
AMERICAN IMMIGRANT YOUTHS IN LOS ANGELES

Kataoka et al. (2003) pilot-tested the CBITS intervention with a sample of Latino immigrants (n=152) in the Los Angeles Unified School District. Using a quasi-experimental waitlist design, they implemented eight group sessions and one individual session, targeting youths who showed symptoms of posttraumatic stress and depressive disorders. Parents as well as teachers were eligible for a psychoeducational session focusing on the impact of trauma on child mental health. Participants in the intervention group experienced a modest reduction in PTSD and depression when compared with the waitlist group. These symptoms remained lower at the three-month follow-up for youths in the intervention group. Replication studies, using an experimental design, are needed to test this intervention more rigorously with immigrant youths.

Cognitive Behavioral Intervention for Trauma in School (CBITS) is listed in the NREPP and was shown to decrease PTSD, depression, parent–child psychosocial dysfunction, and behavioral problems in a sample of sixth graders exposed to violence (Stein et al., 2003). The intervention includes 10 group sessions and one to three individual sessions with youths ranging from 11 to 15 years old who report traumatic experiences and are demonstrating symptoms related to mental health problems. CBITS, which is delivered by a mental health professional in the school environment (Jaycox, 2004), was tested by Kataoka et al. (2003) with a sample of Latino immigrant and refugee youths who reported significant symptoms of PTSD and depression. It is noteworthy that the intervention specifies the school setting, since several studies have advocated for the delivery of trauma-informed mental health services to immigrant and refugee youths in the school system, especially given the difficulty many of these youths face in accessing services (Beehler et al., 2012; Birman & Chan, 2008; Kataoka et al., 2003).

Many of the barriers to mental health treatment identified in the literature, such as inexperience with mental health care in the United States, cultural differences in understanding mental health issues and care, and stigma, point to the need for targeted engagement interventions. Beyond the educational system, connecting the mental health care system with other systems with which immigrant and refugee families regularly interact is critical to engaging this population with evidenced-based mental health treatment.

COLLABORATIONS ACROSS SYSTEMS: MODELS THAT INTEGRATE TREATMENT FOR PHYSICAL AND MENTAL HEALTH

Using the more familiar physical health care system to connect immigrants and refugees with the mental health system seems to be a promising intervention for engagement. Two models used to integrate physical and mental health care include the collaborative care model and the integrated care model.

Strosahl (1998) describes a collaborative care model as one where behavioral health care providers and primary care providers work together to monitor and treat both mental and physical health symptoms as a team after a primary care doctor has identified a mental health diagnosis. Although the team maintains close communication about client treatment plans and progress, the primary care physician remains in charge of psychotropic medication management, and the therapist on the team supports the client by providing brief therapeutic interventions and support as needed (Kaltman, Pauk, & Alter, 2011). Collaborative care, although closely related to integrated care, should not be confused with it. In an integrated health care model, behavioral health specialists work in a primary care setting and are part of the health care team (Collins, Hewson, Munger, & Wade, 2013). In contrast, in a collaborative care model, team members retain their autonomy and have the option to work as a team in the same facility or located in separate locations. Key to both of these approaches is the interdisciplinary nature of treatment with clients and understanding that biological, psychological, and social factors influence health and wellness (Collins et al., 2013).

The effectiveness of an interdisciplinary team approach to care has been demonstrated in a number of randomized control trials. Collaborative models increase treatment adherence (Gilbody, Bower, Fletcher, Richards, & Sutton, 2006; Kaltman et al., 2011; Katon & Seelig, 2008) and improve symptoms such as depression immediately following the intervention as well as five years postintervention (Gilbody et al., 2006). Although these studies have primarily included nonimmigrants, pilot studies testing community-based collaborative models in immigrant communities suggest that immigrants may be more inclined to engage in mental health services that are located within primary care settings (Kaltman, Hurtado De Mendoza, Gonzales, & Serrano, 2014).

Kaltman et al. (2011) implemented a community-based adaptation of the collaborative care approach in primary care clinics that largely serve low-income immigrant families from Central and South America. They focused on identifying co-occurring disorders that are correlated with extreme poverty and stressful life events, such as depression, panic disorder, PTSD, and generalized anxiety disorder (Kaltman et al., 2011). Additionally, they included a social service provision because of the high level of need in the population. In each clinic, the collaborative care team identified, treated, and evaluated clients. The number of clients engaging in mental health treatment rose from 71 clients in the first year to 190 clients in the fifth year of the intervention (Kaltman et al., 2011). Recognizing the value of collaboration across systems, there have also been substantial efforts at the policy level to develop collaborations between the mental health system and other service systems in order to decrease barriers for families of children with serious mental illness (Stroul, 2002). The philosophy that all systems should collaborate with the mental health system in order to serve people suffering from severe mental illness is called systems of care (Stroul, 2002).

SYSTEMS OF CARE

Historically, systems that most often serve children, such as the juvenile, educational, child welfare, and mental health systems, do not coordinate care across the social service sectors. Because families frequently have interactions with multiple systems, the lack of systemic coordination is frequently a burden to children and families (Burchard, Burchard, Sewell, & Van Den Berg, 1993). To address these systemic obstacles, the U.S. Department of Health and Human Services developed the Child and Adolescent Service System Program (CASSP) to promote collaboration across systems. Known as systems of care, this service delivery model is driven by "child-centered, family-focused, community-based, and culturally-competent" values (Dettlaff & Rycraft, 2010, p. 304). This delivery approach involves understanding each family's needs and adopting a plan that supports their individual needs. It also requires that agencies create partnerships across systems to work together toward shared goals for the family (Chuang & Lucio, 2011; Dettlaff & Rycraft, 2010; Stroul, 2002). For example, in the systems of care approach, a therapist might have the ability to meet with a student at his school because his parents cannot provide transportation, and this would be possible because of the collaboration between the educational and the mental health systems. Since service needs vary across communities and families, the systems of care approach allows for flexibility in implementation and application (Stroul, 2002).

Systems of care addresses some of the cultural barriers for immigrants by employing the philosophy of cultural sensitivity and competence with all families. However, it does not address the problem of inadequate care for immigrant children and adolescents, particularly for those without legal documentation and who are not in a special group such as victims of human trafficking. Currently, there is no formal structure in place at the policy level that provides this kind of support to immigrants in general and undocumented immigrants specifically. However, local communities have extended access through community partnerships for clients who have significant needs but are uninsured. For example, the following case study describes nongovernmental nonprofit agencies that collaborate with mental and physical health providers to facilitate access for different groups of undocumented immigrants.

CASE STUDY: COLLABORATION BETWEEN SYSTEMS

Juan, a 15-year-old Honduran boy, arrived in the United States by himself. He was left with his maternal grandmother at age 3 but then moved between caregivers at least every two to three years. When Juan was 12 years old, he was recruited by gangs and almost killed, but passersby interrupted the attack and rescued him. When he was 14, without telling anyone in Honduras or his mother in the United States, he joined a group of migrants leaving for "El Norte." No one heard from him for more than two months, until U.S. Border Control contacted his mother to let her know that he had been detained at the U.S.-Mexico border. He spent several weeks in an Office of Refugee and Resettlement shelter and was reunited with his mother—whom he had not seen since he was 3 years old. Juan demonstrates challenges with attachment and struggles with anger and feelings of intense abandonment. He demonstrates symptoms of depression, as exhibited by social isolation, guilt and shame, a loss of appetite, irritability, and profound sadness. Because Juan is undocumented, he does not qualify for traditional mental health services. However, a recent collaboration between the educational and the mental health systems has enabled Juan to partake in a school-based mental health program for newcomers. The program was directed by a major university health system that integrated physical and behavioral health care in school-based clinics. Juan receives an evidence-based cognitive behavioral intervention that is delivered by a licensed social worker who visits the different high-risk-area middle and high schools in the city.

CONCLUSION

In this chapter, we have examined the prevalence of and factors related to the mental health of immigrants and refugees in the United States. Interventions occur on different levels; for example, we presented research on therapeutic interventions at the individual and group levels but also interventions that target the mezzo-, community-level factors. Both individual-level and community-level interventions have shown promise in influencing outcomes for disorders such as depression, PTSD, and anxiety, as well as increasing mental health service use in this population. However, macro-level interventions (or policies) often negatively impact immigrants and refugees in the United States. For example, PRWORA had a negative impact on mental health service utilization by cutting health care funding for recent immigrants and for all undocumented persons (Chen & Vargas-Bustamante, 2011). We highlight future directives that aim to increase engagement, access, and practice with immigrants and refugees.

Clinical interventions often target the psychological symptoms related to trauma, such as depression and PTSD. However, there is a dearth of research on the implementation and translation of evidence-based mental health interventions in real-world settings (Antoniades et al., 2014; Kataoka et al., 2003). More research focusing on the translation of evidence-based practices is needed to improve both short-term and long-term effects of treatments and to ensure that treatment approaches are culturally responsive and meet the needs of the population.

Researchers, practitioners, and policy advocates should address the structural vulnerabilities that prevent access to mental health care by developing and implementing policies that encourage the well-being of immigrants and refugees. It is important to understand the impact of policies such as PRWORA on the mental health outcomes and needs of the community. More recently, the 2010 Patient Protection and Affordable Care Act (ACA) was implemented, and it requires that everyone in the United States have access to health insurance. Provisions in the form of tax credits and subsidies are available to families whose incomes fall between 139 percent and 400 percent of the federal poverty level. Originally, there was a mandate in the ACA for Medicaid to expand coverage to all low-income individuals regardless of whether they have children, are in serious medical need, or are an expectant mother. However, the Supreme Court ruled it was unconstitutional to force states to expand their Medicaid coverage to all low-income families, so this became optional for states. This change in the ACA resulted in a coverage gap for families making below 139 percent of the federal poverty level in the states that opted out of Medicaid expansion. Since 19.2 percent of foreign-born families' incomes are below 100 percent of the federal poverty level, this coverage gap has a direct impact on their ability to access health insurance for mental health services. A policy recommendation that could impact immigrants would be to open subsidy eligibility to all families making 139 percent or more below the federal poverty line, especially in states that opted out of Medicaid expansion, regardless of documentation status.

Although research suggests that certain individual and community interventions can increase mental health engagement and improve mental health outcomes in immigrant and refugee populations, these interventions are not sustainable unless long-term policy solutions are implemented to reduce the financial and eligibility barriers for this population. Untreated mental health problems are a public health concern and lead to a host of other health disparities that have significant financial and social costs on society. In conclusion, we present the following culturally responsive recommendations for practice with immigrants and refugees involved in the mental health system:

1   Recognize that clients from other countries may not identify a mental health disorder in themselves or a family member because of their lack of familiarity with mental health care.
2   Use culturally tailored approaches and culturally specific language to educate clients about mental disorders and mental health treatment in the United States.
3   Increase awareness of the role that mental health stigma plays in decreasing engagement with the mental health system.
4   Reassure clients about confidentiality, explaining that the communication between the client and practitioner is, in most cases, protected under the law.
5   When working with immigrants and refugees, target both previous trauma and the current psychosocial stressors impacting the client.
6   Be culturally responsive by having a diverse ethnic representation in mental health providers.

7 Involve *promotoras* and other lay community members to increase treatment engagement, adherence, and completion with immigrant and refugee populations.

8 Recognize that immigrants and refugees may prefer to receive mental health treatment at community centers that integrate physical and mental health care services.

9 Promote cross-system collaborations and other macrointerventions that increase engagement with the mental health system.

KEY TERMS

CHILLING EFFECTS Declines in benefit utilization by eligible people caused by lack of clarity regarding eligibility and fear of legal reprisal such as deportation if means-tested programs are used.

COLLABORATIVE CARE MODEL A health care model where behavioral health and primary care providers work together to monitor and treat both mental and physical health symptoms as a team after a primary care doctor has identified a mental health diagnosis.

IMMIGRANT An individual who has migrated from his or her country of origin into another country.

REFUGEE An individual who cannot "return to his or her country because of persecution or a well-founded fear of persecution on account of race, religion, nationality, membership in a particular social group or political opinion" (Martin & Yankay, 2014, p. 1). This is a political status that denotes permission to be in the United States and is conferred before entry.

TRAUMA An overwhelming life experience that leaves one unable to cope and emotionally shattered.

STUDY QUESTIONS

1 Identify the four sectors that provide mental health services in the United States, and describe the similarities and differences between these four systems.

2 How does a trauma impact mental health outcome in immigrants and refugees?

3 What is the chilling effect, and how does it impact mental health outcomes in immigrants and refugees?

4 How can the collaborative care model increase the use of mental health services in immigrant and refugee communities?

5 What evidence-based treatment approaches are implemented for the treatment of mental health disorders in immigrant and refugee communities?

ADDITIONAL RESOURCES

Center on Immigration and Child Welfare: http://cimmcw.org /mcwnnisnowcicw/

Immigrant and Refugee Research Institute: http://socialwork.buffalo.edu /social-research/institutes-centers/immigrant-and-refugee-research -institute.html

Medicaid (for a collaborative care model brief): http://www.medicaid.gov /State-Resource-Center/Medicaid-State-Technical-Assistance/Health -Homes-Technical-Assistance/Downloads/HH-IRC-Collaborative-5-13 .pdf

The National Child Traumatic Stress Network: http://nctsnet.org

Refugee Health Technical Assistance Center: http://refugeehealthta.org /physical-mental-health/mental-health/

REFERENCES

Ahmed, A. S. (2007). Post-traumatic stress disorder, resilience and vulnerability. *Advances in Psychiatric Treatment, 13*(5), 369–375. doi:10.1192/apt.bp.106.003236

Alegría, M., Atkins, M., Farmer, E., Slaton, E., & Stelk, W. (2010). One size does not fit all: Taking diversity, culture, and context seriously. *Administration and Policy in Mental Health, 37,* 48–60.

Alegría, M., Canino, G., Shrout, P. E., Woo, M., Duan, N., Vila, D., . . . & Meng, X. L. (2008). Prevalence of mental illness in immigrant and non-immigrant US Latino groups. *American Journal of Psychiatry, 165*(3), 359–369.

Antoniades, J., Mazza, D., & Brijnath, B. (2014). Efficacy of depression treatments for immigrant patients: Results from a systematic review. *BMC Psychiatry, 14*(1), 176–189.

Ayon, C. (2013). Service needs among Latino immigrant families: Implications for social work practice. *Social Work, 59,* 13–23. doi: 10.1093/sw/swt031

Balcázar, H., Alvarado, M., Hollen, M. L., Gonzalez-Cruz, Y., Hughes, O., Vazquez, E., & Lykens, K. (2006). Salud Para Su Corazon-NCLR: A comprehensive Promotora outreach program to promote heart-healthy behaviors among Hispanics. *Health Promotion Practice*, *7*(1), 68–77.

Balcázar, H. G., de Heer, H., Rosenthal, L., Aguirre, M., Flores, L., Puentes, F. A., . . . Schulz, L. O. (2010). A *promotores de salud* intervention to reduce cardiovascular disease risk in a high-risk Hispanic border population. *Preventing Chronic Disease*, *7*(2):A28, 1–10.

Beehler, S., Birman, D., & Campbell, R. (2012). The effectiveness of cultural adjustment and trauma services (CATS): Generating practice-based evidence on a comprehensive, school-based mental health intervention for immigrant youth. *American Journal of Community Psychology*, *50* (1–2), 155–168.

Berger Cardoso, J., Scott, J., & Faulkner, M. (2014). *Deportation, traumatic stress and depression in undocumented parents in Texas*. Manuscript in preparation.

Birman, D., Beehler, S., Harris, E. M., Everson, M. L., Batia, K., Liautaud, J., . . . Cappella, E. (2008). International Family, Adult, and Child Enhancement Services (FACES): A community-based comprehensive services model for refugee children in resettlement. *American Journal of Orthopsychiatry*, *78*(1), 121–132.

Birman, D., & Chan, W. Y. (2008). *Screening and assessing immigrant and refugee youth in school-based mental health programs* (Issue Brief No. 1). Washington, DC: Center for Health and Health Care in Schools.

Birman, D., & Tran, N. (2008). Psychological distress and adjustment of Vietnamese refugees in the United States: Association with pre- and post-migration factors. *American Journal of Orthopsychiatry*, *78*(1), 109–120. doi: 10.1037/0002-9432.78.1.109

Bisson, J. I., Ehlers, A., Matthews, R., Pilling, S., Richards, D., & Turner, S. (2007). Psychological treatments for chronic post-traumatic stress disorder: Systematic review and meta-analysis. *British Journal of Psychiatry*, *190*(2), 97–104.

Borjas, G. J. (2002). Welfare reform and immigrant participation in welfare programs. *International Migration Review*, *36*(4), 1093–1123.

Breslau, J., & Chang, D. F. (2006). Psychiatric disorders among foreign-born and US-born Asian-Americans in a US national survey. *Social Psychiatry and Psychiatric Epidemiology*, *41*(12), 943–950.

Burchard, J. D., Burchard, S. N., Sewell, R., & Van Den Berg, J. (1993). *One kid at a time: Evaluative case studies and description of the Alaska Youth Initiative Demonstration Project*. Washington, DC: Georgetown University Child Development Center, CASSP Technical Assistance Center.

Cabassa, L. J., Lester, R., & Zayas, L. H. (2006). "It's like being in a labyrinth": Hispanic immigrants' perceptions of depression and attitudes toward treatments. *Journal of Immigrant and Minority Health*, *9*(1), 1–16. doi:10.1007/s10903-006-9010-1

Capps, R., Castañeda, R. M., Chaudry, A., & Santos, R. (2007). *Paying the price: The impact of immigration raids on America's children*. Washington, DC: Urban Institute. Retrieved from http://www.urban.org/UploadedPDF/411566_immigration_raids.pdf

Cervantes, R., Berger Cardoso, J., & Goldbach, J. (2015). Examining differences in culturally based stress among clinical and non-clinical Hispanic adolescents. *Journal of Cultural Diversity and Ethnic Minority Psychology*, *21*, 458–467.

Chaudry, A., Capps, R., Pedroza, J. M., Castaneda, R. M., Santos, R., & Scott, M. M. (2010). *Facing our future: Children in the aftermath of immigration enforcement*. Washington, DC: Urban Institute. Retrieved from http://www.urban.org/UploadedPDF/412020_FacingOurFuture_final.pdf

Chen, J., & Vargas-Bustamante, A. (2011). Estimating the effects of immigration status on mental health care utilizations in the United States. *Journal of Immigrant Minority Health*, *13*, 671–680. doi: 10.1007/s10903-011-9445-x

Child Trends. (2014). *Immigrant children*. Retrieved from http://www.childtrends.org/?indicators=immigrant-children

Choi, I., Zou, J., Titov, N., Dear, B. F., Li, S., Johnston, L., . . . Hunt, C. (2012). Culturally attuned Internet treatment for depression amongst Chinese Australians: A randomised controlled trial. *Journal of Affective Disorders*, *136*, 459–468.

Choi Wu, M., Kviz, F. J., & Michaels Miller, A. (2009). Identifying individual and contextual barriers to seeking mental health services among Korean American immigrant women. *Issues in Mental Health Nursing*, *30*, 78–85.

Chorpita, B. F., Daleiden, E. L., Ebesutani, C., Young, J., Becker, K. D., Nakamura, B. J., ... & Starace, N. (2011). Evidence-based treatments for children and adolescents: An updated review of indicators of efficacy and effectiveness. *Clinical Psychology: Science and Practice*, *18*(2), 154–172.

Chu, T., Keller, A. S., & Rasmussen, A. (2013). Effects of post-migration factors on PTSD outcomes among immigrant survivors of political violence. *Journal of Immigrant and Minority Health*, *15*(5), 890–897.

Chuang, E., & Lucio, R. (2011). Interagency collaboration between child welfare agencies, schools, and mental health providers and children's mental health service receipt. *Advances in School Mental Health Promotion*, *4*(2), 5–15.

Cloitre, M. (2009). Effective psychotherapies for posttraumatic stress disorder: A review and critique. *CNS Spectrums*, *14*(1), 32–43.

Cohen, J. A., & Mannarino, A. P. (1996). Factors that mediate treatment outcome of sexually abused preschool children. *Journal of the American Academy of Child & Adolescent Psychiatry*, *35*(10), 1402–1410. doi:10.1097/00004583-199610000-00028

———. (1998). Factors that mediate treatment outcome of sexually abused preschool children: Six- and 12-month follow-up. *Journal of the American Academy of Child & Adolescent Psychiatry*, *37*(1), 44–51. doi:10.1097/00004583-199801000-00016

Cohen, J. A., Mannarino, A. P., Zhitova, A. C., & Capone, M. E. (2003). Treating child abuse-related posttraumatic stress and comorbid substance abuse in adolescents. *Child Abuse & Neglect*, *27*(12), 1345–1365.

Collins, C., Hewson, D. L., Munger, R., & Wade, T. (2013). *Evolving models of behavioral health integration in primary care*. New York, NY: Milbank Memorial Fund.

Cook, B., Alegría, M., Lin, J. Y., & Guo, J. (2009). Pathways and correlates connecting Latinos' mental health with exposure to the United States. *American Journal of Public Health*, *99*(12), 2247–2254.

Cooper-Patrick, L., Powe, N. R., Jenckes, M. W., Gonzales, J. J., Levine, D. M., & Ford, D. E. (1997). Identification of patient attitudes and preferences regarding treatment of depression. *Journal of General Internal Medicine*, *12*(7), 431–438.

Corrigan, P. (2004). How stigma interferes with mental health care. *American Psychologist*, *59*(7), 614–625.

Corrigan, P. W., Watson, A. C., & Barr, L. (2006). The self-stigma of mental illness: Implications for self-esteem and self-efficacy. *Journal of Social and Clinical Psychology*, *25*(8), 875–884.

Cunningham, P. J. (2009). Beyond parity: Primary care physicians' perspectives on access to mental health care. *Health Affairs*, *28*, 490–501.

Delaney-Black, V., Covington, C., Ondersma, S. J., Nordstrom-Klee, B., Templin, T., Ager, J., . . . Sokol, R. J. (2002). Violence exposure, trauma, and IQ and/or reading deficits among urban children. *Archives of Pediatrics & Adolescent Medicine*, *156*(3), 280–285.

Dettlaff, A. J., & Rycraft, J. R. (2010). Adapting systems of care for child welfare practice with immigrant Latino children and families. *Evaluation and Program Planning*, *33*(3), 303–310.

Dreby, J. (2012). The burden of deportation on children in Mexican immigrant families. *Journal of Marriage and Family*, *74*, 829–845.

Falicov, C. J. (2005). Emotional transnationalism and family identities. *Family Process, 44*(4), 399–406.

———. (2014). *Latino families in therapy* (2nd ed.). New York, NY: Guilford.

Farley, M., Golding, J. M., Young, G., Mulligan, M., & Minkoff, J. R. (2004). Trauma history and relapse probability among patients seeking substance abuse treatment. *Journal of Substance Abuse Treatment, 27*(2), 161–167.

Farrell, A. D., & Bruce, S. E. (1997). Impact of exposure to community violence on violent behavior and emotional distress among urban adolescents. *Journal of Clinical Child Psychology, 26*(1), 2–14.

Finno-Velasquez, M., Berger Cardoso, J., Dettlaff, A., & Hurlburt, M. (2015, January). *Parent nativity and legal immigration status: A national survey of barriers to mental health service use among Latino children with child welfare involvement.* New Orleans, LA: Society for Social Work and Research.

Fix, M., & Zimmermann, W. (2001). All under one roof: Mixed-status families in an era of reform. *International Migration Review, 35*(2), 397–419.

Fortuna, L. R., Porche, M. V., & Alegría, M. (2008). Political violence, psychosocial trauma, and the context of mental health services use among immigrant Latinos in the United States. *Ethnicity & Health, 13*(5), 435–463. doi: 10.1080/13557850701837286

Gamst, G., Dana, R. H., Der-Karabetian, A., & Kramer, T. (2001). Asian American mental health clients: Effects of ethnic match and age on global assessment and visitation. *Journal of Mental Health Counseling, 23*(1), 57–71.

———. (2004). Ethnic match and treatment outcomes for child and adolescent mental health center clients. *Journal of Counseling & Development, 82*(4), 457–465.

Garcia Coll, C., & Magnuson, K. (2005). The psychological experience of immigration: A developmental perspective. In C. Suarez-Orozco, M. Suarez-Orozco, & D. Baolian Qin-Hilliard (Eds.), *The immigration handbook: An interdisciplinary reader* (pp. 105–133). New York, NY: Routledge.

Gfroerer, J. C., & Tan, L. L. (2003). Substance use among foreign-born youths in the United States: Does the length of residence matter? *American Journal of Public Health, 93*(11), 1892–1895.

Ghio, L., Gotelli, S., Marcenaro, M., Amore, M., & Natta, W. (2014). Duration of untreated illness and outcomes in unipolar depression: A systematic review and meta-analysis. *Journal of Affective Disorders, 152*, 45–51.

Gilbody, S., Bower, P., Fletcher, J., Richards, D., & Sutton, A. J. (2006). Collaborative care for depression: A cumulative meta-analysis and review of longer-term outcomes. *Archives of Internal Medicine, 166*(21), 2314–2321.

Hagan, J. M., Rodriguez, N., & Castro, B. (2011). Social effects of mass deportations by the United States government. *Ethnic and Racial Studies, 34*, 1374–1391.

Harker, K. (2001). Immigrant generation, assimilation, and adolescent psychological well-being. *Social Forces, 79*(3), 969–1004.

Heymann, J., Flores-Macias, F., Hayes, J. A., Kennedy, M., Lahaie, C., & Earle, A. (2009). The impact of migration on the well-being of transnational families: New data from sending communities in Mexico. *Community, Work & Family, 12*(1), 91–103.

Hinton, D. E., Hinton, A., Chhean, D., Pich, V., Loeum, J. R., & Pollack, M. H. (2009). Nightmares among Cambodian refugees: The breaching of concentric ontological security. *Culture, Medicine, and Psychiatry, 33*, 219–265.

Hinton, D. E., Hofmann, S. G., Rivera, E., Otto, M. W., & Pollack, M. H. (2011). Culturally adapted CBT for Latino women with treatment-resistant PTSD: A pilot study comparing CA-CBT to applied muscle relaxation. *Behaviour Research and Therapy, 49*, 275–280.

Hinton, D. E., Pham, T., Tran, M., Safren, S. A., Otto, M. W., & Pollack, M. H. (2004). CBT for Vietnamese refugees with treatment-resistant PTSD and panic attacks: A pilot study. *Journal of Traumatic Stress, 17*(5), 429–433.

Hinton, D. E., Rivera, E. I., Hofmann, S. G., Barlow, D. H., & Otto, M. W. (2012). Adapting CBT for traumatized refugees and ethnic minority patients: Examples from culturally adapted CBT (CA-CBT). *Transcultural Psychiatry, 49*(2), 340–365.

Hobfoll, S. E., Watson, P., Bell, C. C., Bryant, R. A., Brymer, M. J., Friedman, M. J., . . . Ursano, R. J. (2007). Five essential elements of immediate and mid-term mass trauma intervention: Empirical evidence. *Psychiatry: Interpersonal and Biological Processes, 70*(4), 283–315. doi:10.1521/psyc.2007.70.4.283

Hogg Foundation for Mental Health & Methodist Healthcare Ministries. (2011). *Mental health workforce shortages in Texas.* Retrieved from http://www.hogg.utexas.edu/uploads/documents/Mental_Health_Crisis_final_032111.pdf

Hondagneu-Sotelo, P., & Avila, E. (1997). "I'm here, but I'm there": The meanings of Latina transnational motherhood. *Gender & Society, 11*, 548–571.

Hurt, H., Malmud, E., Brodsky, N. L., & Giannetta, J. (2001). Exposure to violence: Psychological and academic correlates in child witnesses. *Archives of Pediatrics & Adolescent Medicine, 155*(12), 1351–1356.

Hussey, J. M., Hallfors, D. D., Waller, M. W., Iritani, B. J., Halpern, C. T., & Bauer, D. J. (2007). Sexual behavior and drug use among Asian and Latino adolescents: Association with immigrant status. *Journal of Immigrant and Minority Health, 9*(2), 85–94.

Ingram, M., Torres, E., Redondo, F., Bradford, G., Wang, C., & O'Toole, M. L. (2007). The impact of promotoras on social support and glycemic control among members of a farmworker community on the US-Mexico border. *The Diabetes Educator, 33*(supplement 6), 172–178.

Jaycox, L. (2004). *Cognitive behavioral intervention for trauma in schools.* Longmont, CO: Sopri West.

Jaycox, L. H., Stein, B. D., Kataoka, S. H., Wong, M., Fink, A., Escudero, P., & Zaragoza, C. (2002). Violence exposure, posttraumatic stress disorder, and depressive symptoms among recent immigrant schoolchildren. *Journal of the American Academy of Child and Adolescent Psychiatry, 41*(9), 1104–1110. doi:10.1097/00004583-200209000-00011

Kaltman, S., Hurtado De Mendoza, A., Gonzales, F. A., & Serrano, A. (2014). Preferences for trauma-related mental health services among Latina immigrants from Central America, South America, and Mexico. *Psychological Trauma: Theory, Research, Practice, and Policy, 6,* 83–91. doi: 10.1037/a0031539

Kaltman, S., Pauk, J., & Alter, C. L. (2011). Meeting the mental health needs of low-income immigrants in primary care: A community adaptation of an evidence-based model. *American Journal of Orthopsychiatry, 81*(4), 543–551.

Kandula, N. R., Grogan, C. M., Rathouz, P. J., & Lauderdale, D. S. (2004). The unintended impact of welfare reform on the Medicaid enrollment of eligible immigrants. *HSR: Health Services Research, 39,* 1509–1526.

Kataoka, S. H., Stein, B. D., Jaycox, L. H., Wong, M., Escudero, P., Tu, W., . . . Fink, A. (2003). A school-based mental health program for traumatized Latino immigrant children. *Journal of the American Academy of Child & Adolescent Psychiatry, 42*(3), 311–318.

Kataoka, S. H., Zhang, L., & Wells, K. B. (2002). Unmet need for mental health care among US children: Variation by ethnicity and insurance status. *American Journal of Psychiatry, 159*(9), 1548–1555.

Katon, W. J., & Seelig, M. (2008). Population-based care of depression: Team care approaches to improving outcomes. *Journal of Occupational and Environmental Medicine, 50*(4), 459–467.

Kennedy, E. (2014). *No childhood here: Why Central American children are fleeing their homes.* Retrieved from http://www.immigrationpolicy.org/sites/default /files/docs/no_childhood_here_why_central_american_children_are _fleeing_their_homes_final.pdf

Kessler, R. C., Chiu, W. T., Demler, O., & Walters, E. E. (2005). Prevalence, severity, and comorbidity of 12-month DSM-IV disorders in the National Comorbidity Survey Replication. *Archives of General Psychiatry, 62*(6), 617–627.

Kim, G., Aguado Loi, C. X., Chiriboga, D. A., Jang, Y., Parmlee, P., & Allen, R. S. (2011). Limited English proficiency as a barrier to mental health service use: A study of Latino and Asian immigrants with psychiatric disorders. *Journal of Psychiatric Research, 45,* 104–110.

La Greca, A. M., Silverman, W. K., & Lochman, J. E. (2009). Moving beyond efficacy and effectiveness in child and adolescent intervention research. *Journal of Consulting and Clinical Psychology, 77*(3), 373–382.

Landale, N. S., Thomas, K. J. A., & Van Hook, J. (2011). The living arrangements of children of immigrants. *The Future of Children, 21*(1), 43–70.

Le, T. N., Goebert, D., & Wallen, J. (2009). Acculturation factors and substance use among Asian American youth. *Journal of Primary Prevention, 30*(3–4), 453–473.

Lee, S., Juon, H.-S., Martinez, G., Hsu, C. E., Robinson, E. S., Bawa, J., & Ma, G. X. (2008). Model minority at risk: Expressed needs of mental health by Asian American young adults. *Journal of Community Health, 34*(2), 144–152. doi:10.1007/s10900-008-9137-1

Leong, F. T., & Lau, A. S. (2001). Barriers to providing effective mental health services to Asian Americans. *Mental Health Services Research, 3*(4), 201–214.

Lieberman, A. F., Ghosh Ippen, C., & Van Horn, P. (2006). Child–parent psychotherapy: 6-month follow-up of a randomized controlled trial. *Journal of the American Academy of Child & Adolescent Psychiatry, 45*(8), 913–918.

Lieberman, A. F., Van Horn, P., & Ghosh Ippen, C. (2005). Toward evidence-based treatment: Child–parent psychotherapy with preschoolers exposed to marital violence. *Journal of the American Academy of Child & Adolescent Psychiatry, 44*(12), 1241–1248.

Martin, D. C., & Yankay, J. E. (2014). *Refugees and asylees: 2011.* Retrieved from http://www.dhs.gov/xlibrary/assets/statistics/publications/ois_rfa_fr_2011.pdf

Merikangas, K. R., He, J.-P., Brody, D., Fisher, P. W., Bourdon, K., & Koretz, D. S. (2010). Prevalence and treatment of mental disorders among US children in the 2001–2004 NHANES. *Pediatrics, 125*(1), 75–81.

Meyer, O., Zane, N., & Cho, Y. (2011). Understanding the psychological processes of the racial math effect in Asian Americans. *Journal of Counseling Psychology, 58*(3), 335–345.

Migration Policy Institute. (2014). *State Immigration Data Profiles.* Retrieved from http://www.migrationpolicy.org/data/state-profiles/state/income/US

Nadeem, E., Lange, J. M., Edge, D., Fongwa, M., Belin, T., & Miranda, J. (2007). Does stigma keep poor young immigrant children and U.S.-born black women and Latina women from seeking mental health care? *Psychiatric Services, 58,* 1547–1554.

National Child Traumatic Stress Network. (2007). *CPP: Child–parent psycho-therapy*. Fact sheet. Retrieved from www.nctsn.org/nctsn_assetts/pdfs/promising -practices/Child_ParentPsychotherapy

——. (2011). *Working with immigrant Latin-American families exposed to trauma*. Retrieved from http://nctsnet.org/sites/default/files/assets/pdfs/Fall_Spotlight _2011_Long_Version.pdf

Neuner, F., Schauer, M., Klaschik, C., Karunakara, U., & Elbert, T. (2004). A comparison of narrative exposure therapy, supportive counseling, and psy-choeducation for treating posttraumatic stress disorder in an African refugee settlement. *Journal of Consulting and Clinical Psychology, 72*(4), 579–587. doi:10.1037/0022-006X.72.4.579

Ozer, E. J., Best, S. R., Lipsey, T. L., & Weiss, D. S. (2003). Predictors of posttrau-matic stress disorder and symptoms in adults: A meta-analysis. *Psychological Bulletin, 129*, 52–73. doi:10.1037/1942-9681.S.1.3

Pandya, C., McHugh, M., & Batalova, J. (2011). *Limited English proficient indi-viduals in the United States: Number, share, growth, and linguistic diversity*. LEP data brief. Washington, DC: Migration Policy Institute.

Passel, J. S. (2011). Demography of immigrant youth: Past, present, and future. *The Future of Children, 21*(1), 19–41.

Pattyn, E., Verhaeghe, M., Sercu, C., & Bracke, P. (2014). Public stigma and self-stigma: Differential association with attitudes toward formal and informal help seeking. *Psychiatric Service, 65*(2), 232–238. doi:10.1176/appi.ps.201200561

Peña, J. B., Wyman, P. A., Brown, C. H., Matthieu, M. M., Olivares, T. E., Har-tel, D., & Zayas, L. H. (2008). Immigration generation status and its associa-tion with suicide attempts, substance use, and depressive symptoms among Latino adolescents in the USA. *Prevention Science, 9*(4), 299–310. doi:10.1007/ s11121-008-0105-x

Perreira, K. M., & Ornelas, I. J. (2011). The physical and psychological well-being of immigrant children. *The Future of Children, 21*(1), 195–218.

Piwowarczyk, L., Bishop, H., Yusuf, A., Mudymba, F., & Raj, A. (2014). Congo-lese and Somali beliefs about mental health services. *Journal of Nervous and Mental Disease, 202*(3), 209–216.

Portes, A., & Rumbaut, R. G. (2006). *Immigrant America: A portrait* (3rd ed.). Berkeley: University of California Press.

Prado, G., Huang, S., Schwartz, S. J., Maldonado-Molina, M. M., Bandiera, F. C., de la Rosa, M., & Pantin, H. (2009). What accounts for differences in sub-stance use among US-born and immigrant Hispanic adolescents? Results from a longitudinal prospective cohort study. *Journal of Adolescent Health, 45*(2), 118–125.

Pumariega, A. J., Rothe, E., & Pumariega, J. B. (2005). Mental health of immigrants and refugees. *Community Mental Health Journal, 41*(5), 581–597.

Rasmussen, A., Crager, M., Baser, R. E., Chu, T., & Gany, F. (2012). Onset of posttraumatic stress disorder and major depression among refugees and voluntary migrants to the United States. *Journal of Traumatic Stress, 25*(6), 705–712.

Roberts, R. E., Roberts, C. R., & Xing, Y. (2006). Prevalence of youth-reported DSM-IV psychiatric disorders among African, European, and Mexican American adolescents. *Journal of the American Academy of Child & Adolescent Psychiatry, 45*(11), 1329–1337.

Rodriguez, N., & Hagan, J. M. (2004). Fractured families and communities: Effects of immigration reform in Texas, Mexico, and El Salvador. *Latino Studies, 2*, 328–351.

Rosen, D., Nakash, O., & Alegría, M. (2014). Disproportionality and disparities in the mental health system. In R. Fong, A. J. Dettlaff, J. James, & C. Rodriguez (Eds.), *Addressing racial disproportionality and disparities in human services: Multisystemic approaches* (pp. 280–311). New York, NY: Columbia University Press.

Rosenblum, M. (2015). *Unaccompanied child migration to the United States: The tension between protection and prevention.* Washington, DC: Migration Policy Institute.

Saechao, F., Sharrock, S., Reicherter, D., Livingston, J. D., Aylward, A., Whisnant, J., . . . Kohli, S. (2012). Stressors and barriers to using mental health services among diverse groups of first-generation immigrants to the United States. *Community Mental Health Journal, 48*(1), 98–106.

Soheilian, S. S., & Inman, A. G. (2009). Middle Eastern Americans: The effects of stigma on attitudes toward counseling. *Journal of Muslim Mental Health, 4*(2), 139–158.

Steel, Z., Chey, T., Silove, D., Marnane, C., Bryant, R. A., & Van Ommeren, M. (2009). Association of torture and other potentially traumatic events with mental health outcomes among populations exposed to mass conflict and displacement: A systematic review and meta-analysis. *Journal of the American Medical Association, 302*(5), 537–549.

Steel, Z., Silove, D., Bird, K., McGorry, P., & Mohan, P. (1999). Pathways from war trauma to posttraumatic stress symptoms among Tamil asylum seekers, refugees, and immigrants. *Journal of Traumatic Stress, 12*(3), 421–435.

Stein, B. D., Jaycox, L. H., Kataoka, S. H., Wong, M., Tu, W., Elliott, M. N., & Fink, A. (2003). A mental health intervention for schoolchildren exposed to violence: A randomized controlled trial. *Journal of the American Medical Association, 290*(5), 603–611. doi:10.1001/jama.290.5.603

Strosahl, K. (1998). Integrating behavioral health and primary care services: The primary mental health care model. In A. Blount (Ed.), *Integrated Primary Care: The Future of Medical and Mental Health Collaborations* (pp. 139–166). New York, NY: W.W. Norton.

Stroul, B. (2002). *System of care: A framework for system reform in children's mental health* (Issue Brief). Washington, DC: Georgetown University Child Development Center, National Technical Assistance.

Substance Abuse and Mental Health Services Administration. (2010). *Results from the 2009 National Survey on Drug Use and Health: Volume I. Summary of national findings* (Office of Applied Studies, NSDUH Series H-38A, HHS Publication No. SMA 10-4856 Findings). Rockville, MD: Author.

——. (2012). *Mental health, United States, 2010* (HHS Publication No. SMA 12-4681). Rockville, MD: Author.

——. (2014). *Trauma-informed care in behavioral health services* (Treatment Improvement Protocol (TIP) Series 57. HHS Publication No. SMA 13-4801). Rockville, MD: Author.

Takeuchi, D. T., Zane, N., Hong, S., Chae, D. H., Gong, F., Gee, G. C., ... Alegría, M. (2007). Immigration-related factors and mental disorders among Asian Americans. *American Journal of Public Health, 97*(1), 84–90.

Tran, A. N., Ornelas, I. J., Kim, M., Perez, G., Green, M., Lyn, M. J., & Corbie-Smith, G. (2014). Results from a pilot *promotora* program to reduce depression and stress among immigrant Latinas. *Health Promotion Practice, 15*(3), 365–372. doi: 10.1177/1524839913511635

United Nations Office of Drugs and Crime. (2013). *Global study on homicide.* Retrieved from http://www.unodc.org/documents/gsh/pdfs/2014_GLOBAL_HOMICIDE_BOOK_web.pdf

U.S. Conference of Catholic Bishops. (2014). *Mission to Central America: The flight of unaccompanied children to the United States.* Retrieved from http://www.usccb.org/about/migration-policy/upload/Mission-To-Central-America-FINAL-2.pdf

Vega, W. A., & Rumbaut, R. G. (1991). Ethnic minorities and mental health. *Annual Review of Sociology, 17*, 351–383.

Viswanathan, M., Kraschnewski, J. L., Nishikawa, B., Morgan, L. C., Honeyc-utt, A. A., Thieda, P., ... Jonas, D. E. (2010). Outcomes and costs of community health worker interventions: A systematic review. *Medical Care, 48*(9), 792–808.

Vogel, D. L., Wade, N. G., & Haake, S. (2006). Measuring the self-stigma associated with seeking psychological help. *Journal of Counseling Psychology, 53*(3), 325–337.

Waitzkin, H., Getrich, C., Heying, S., Rodríguez, L., Parmar, A., Willging, C., ... Santos, R. (2011). Promotoras as mental health practitioners in primary care: A multi-method study of an intervention to address contextual sources of depression. *Journal of Community Health, 36*(2), 316–331.

Wang, P. S., Berglund, P., Olfson, M., Pincus, H. A., Wells, K. B., & Kessler, R. C. (2005). Failure and delay in initial treatment contact after first onset of mental disorders in the National Comorbidity Survey Replication. *Archives of General Psychiatry, 62*(6), 603–613.

Watson, T. (2014). Inside the refrigerator: Immigration enforcement and chilling effects in Medicaid participation. *American Economic Journal: Economic Policy, 6*(3), 313–338.

Weine, S., Kulauzovic, Y., Klebic, A., Besic, S., Mujagic, A., Muzurovic, J., Spahovic, D., Sclove, S., & Pavkivic, I. (2008). Evaluating a multiple-family group access intervention for refugees with PTSD. *Journal of Marital and Family Therapy, 34*(2), 149–164.

Weine, S. M., Raina, D., Zhubi, M., Delesi, M., Huseni, D., Feetham, S., ... Pavkovic, I. (2003). The TAFES multi-family group intervention for Kosovar refugees: A feasibility study. *Journal of Nervous and Mental Disease, 191*(2), 100–107.

World Health Organization. (2009). *Mental health systems in selected low- and middle-income countries: A WHO-AIMS cross-national analysis.* Geneva, Switzerland: World Health Organization.

Xu, Q., & Brabeck, K. (2012). Service utilization for Latino children in mixed-status families. *Social Work Research, 36*(3), 209–221. doi: 10.1093/swr/svs015

Practice with Immigrant and Refugee Children and Families in the Health Care System

▸ KRISTA PERREIRA *and* LESLIE COFIE

THE EXPERIENCES OF IMMIGRANTS in their home countries, migration experiences, and settlement experiences in the United States work together to shape immigrants' health care needs. To serve the health care needs of these new Americans, federal, state, and local governments work in collaboration with health insurers, health care providers, and community-based organizations to finance and deliver medical care for immigrants.

This chapter provides an overview of the U.S. health system and access to medical care for foreign-born noncitizens. Foreign-born noncitizens mostly consist of legal immigrants who migrate to the United States as spouses and relatives of U.S. citizens, skilled laborers, temporary workers, foreign-born students, and refugees and asylees. Foreign-born noncitizens also include unauthorized immigrants who have been unable to receive visas to legally enter, live, and work in the United States.

Immigrants who naturalize and become U.S. citizens have the same legal access to medical services and insurance as U.S.-born citizens. For U.S.-born citizens and these naturalized immigrants, access to medical care and health insurance varies primarily by age, employment, socioeconomic background, and state of residence. For foreign-born noncitizens, access to health insurance and medical care varies according to these factors as well as according to immigration status, the date of the person's arrival in the United States, and the individual's length of residency in the United States. These factors and others can also influence their health and the types of medical services they require. Emerging interventions to promote the health of immigrants have emphasized the importance of addressing the health system, the socioenvironment, and behavioral factors that influence well-being. Cross-system collaboration at federal, state, and local levels can also be further developed to enhance the health of immigrants.

OVERVIEW OF U.S. HEALTH SYSTEM AND ACCESS TO CARE FOR IMMIGRANTS AND REFUGEES

Access to medical care in the United States is determined by a patchwork of federal, state, and local policies and an individual's ability to pay for health insurance. Historically, uninsured rates among foreign-born noncitizens have been higher than among any other population group in the United States (Monger, 2009). As of 2012, 43 percent of foreign-born noncitizens (adults and children) were uninsured, compared with 18 percent of foreign-born citizens and 13 percent of U.S.-born citizens (DeNavas-Walt, Proctor, & Smith, 2013). Among children (newborns to 17 years old), uninsured rates varied from 27.4 percent for foreign-born noncitizen children to 8.4 percent and 8.7 percent among U.S.-born and naturalized citizen children, respectively (DeNavas-Walt et al., 2013).

Among foreign-born noncitizens (referred to more generally as immigrants), health insurance coverage varies substantially by age (children vs. adults) and by years in the United States (5 years or less vs. more than 5 years) (figure 14.1). Among noncitizens, the rate of health insurance coverage is higher for immigrant children than for adults (62 percent vs. 49 percent), and immigrant children (but not adults) with fewer than five years of U.S. residency have higher rates of health insurance coverage than for immigrants with more than five years of U.S. residency (65 percent vs. 58 percent) (Kenney & Huntress, 2012). Approximately 49 percent of adult immigrants are insured, regardless of the number of years of U.S. residency.

Health insurance coverage also varies substantially by state of residence and legal status. Immigrants and U.S.-born adults living in the west (76 percent), midwest (83 percent), and northeast (90 percent) regions of the United States have higher health insurance rates than those for immigrants and for U.S.-born adults living in the south (51 percent) (Shartzer, Kenney, Long, Hempstead, & Wissoker, 2014). Unauthorized immigrant adults (29 percent) and children (53 percent) have lower health insurance rates than for adults (60 percent) or children (69 percent) with legal

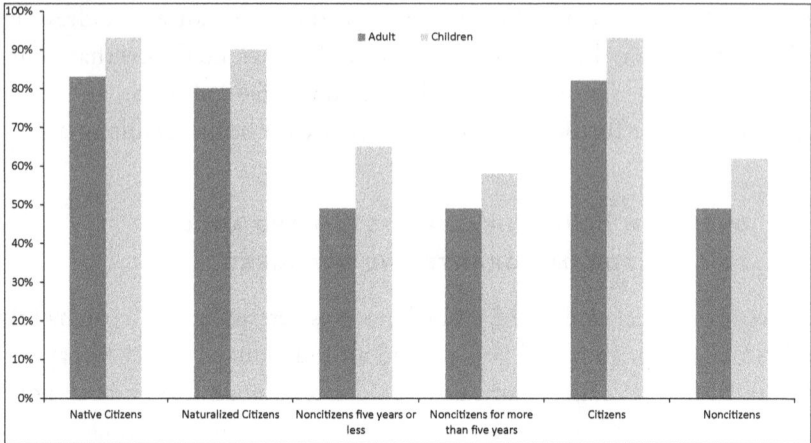

FIGURE 14.1   Health insurance estimates for adults and children
by citizenship status

permanent residency (Capps, Bachmeier, Fix, & Van Hook, 2013). Their rates of insurance coverage also vary by state or region. In the six states with the largest immigrant populations in the United States, Van Hook, Bachmeier, Coffman, & Harel (2015) estimate health insurance coverage rates among the unauthorized population of 57 percent in Illinois, 48 percent in New York, 46 percent in New Jersey, 47 percent in Florida, 43 percent in California, and 34 percent in Texas.

Access to Employer-Provided Health Insurance

These variations in health insurance coverage rates stem partially from variations in access to employer-provided insurance. Noncitizens' access to employer-provided coverage depends on the type of job they have. Noncitizens often work in low-wage jobs where employers do not offer health insurance coverage (Alker & Ng'andu, 2006; Buchmueller, Lo Sasso, Lurie, & Dolfin, 2007). Compared with U.S.-born citizens in the labor force, foreign-born noncitizens are more likely to be employed in service occupations (30 percent vs. 17 percent) or to work as laborers in natural resources, construction, or maintenance occupations (17 percent vs. 8 percent); they are less likely to work in managerial occupations (22 percent vs. 37 percent). Median annual earnings for noncitizens range from $24,492 for females to

$29,575 for males, whereas the median U.S.-born citizen earns $38,514 annually for females and $50,283 annually for males (U.S. Bureau of the Census, 2012). Lower earnings among noncitizens place them at a higher risk of poverty. In 2012, an estimated 55 percent of noncitizens lived below 200 percent of the federal poverty level (FPL), but only 34 percent of U.S.-born citizens lived below 200 percent of FPL. Although data specific to noncitizens are unavailable, analyses of trends in employer-sponsored insurance coverage in the United States show that coverage rates for this coverage have declined by 10 percentage points (from 69 percent to 59 percent) over the past decade (State Health Access Data Assistance Center, 2013). Moreover, these declines in coverage were concentrated among individuals with incomes below 400 percent of FPL (State Health Access Data Assistance Center, 2013).

Access to Public Health Insurance

In addition, these variations in health insurance rates stem from differences in access to public health insurance through Medicaid and the Children's Health Insurance Program (CHIP). Historically, Medicaid has provided health insurance coverage to low-income single parents and children. The Children's Health Insurance Program has provided health insurance coverage exclusively to children but has higher income eligibility thresholds than Medicaid does. Before the implementation of the 2010 Patient Protection and Affordable Care Act (ACA), the income eligibility threshold for Medicaid varied by state, with an average maximum income eligibility threshold of 88 percent of FPL for employed adults with dependent children and an average maximum of 170 percent of FPL for children from birth to 1 year, 144 percent of FPL for children ages 1–5, and 118 percent of FPL for children ages 6–18 (Kaiser Family Foundation, 2013a). Similarly, income eligibility for CHIP varied by state, with an average maximum of 220 percent of FPL for children from birth to 1 year, 201 percent of FPL for children ages 1–5, and 183 percent of FPL for children ages 6–18 (Kaiser Family Foundation, 2013b). Emergency Medicaid is available to low-income individuals, including unauthorized immigrants, who do not qualify for Medicaid or CHIP benefits. Although hospitals are required to provide emergency care to all persons regardless of insurance status, care for many serious conditions (e.g., cancer) does not qualify as emergency care (Gusmano, 2012). Thus, low-income individuals who do not qualify for Medicaid or CHIP are at high risk of medical bankruptcy (Gross & Notowidigdo, 2011). Moreover, health providers who care for these individuals may not receive compensation for their services (Wilensky, 1984).

CASE STUDY: ACCESS TO HEALTH CARE AND HEALTH INSURANCE
FOR REFUGEES

Refugees typically enter the United States after having lived in a refugee reset-tlement camp for several years. While in these camps, refugees receive basic medical services at no cost. Once the U.S. Department of State and U.S. Depart-ment of Homeland Security approve refugees for admission to the United States, they receive a physical examination to identify medical needs and contagious diseases such as tuberculosis. Refugees with contagious diseases are not per-mitted to enter the United States (U.S. Department of State, 2015). Once in the United States, refugees are connected to refugee resettlement agencies, who assist them with finding housing and employment, enrolling children in school, learning English, and getting additional required medical examinations, including immunizations. When refugees first arrive, they are eligible for Medicaid or CHIP and other public assistance programs in their state of residence. Refugees who do not meet Medicaid or CHIP income or other eligibility requirements in their state (typically single men) can also obtain medical care through Refugee Medi-cal Assistance (RFA) for the first eight months of their residency in the United States (Office of Refugee Resettlement, 2014a). After 12 months of residency in the United States, refugees must apply for legal permanent residency, which will give them the same access to public and private health insurance as all other legal immigrants living in the United States. However, the five-year ban on ac-cess to Medicaid or CHIP and other public assistance programs in the United States does not apply to refugees. Refugees may also apply for subsidized and unsubsidized health insurance through the Health Insurance Marketplace. After five years of residency, a refugee may apply for U.S. citizenship.

Health insurance coverage through Medicaid or CHIP has always been restricted to authorized immigrants and U.S. citizens, but the Personal Re-sponsibility and Work Opportunity Reconciliation Act of 1996 (PRWORA) created new categorical restrictions *among* authorized immigrants (see chapter 3 of this volume for additional discussion of PRWORA). Specifically, PRWORA defined two groups of authorized immigrants—qualified and nonqualified—and limited federally funded health insurance coverage to qualified immigrants who were present in the United States before August 22, 1996, or who had lived in the United States for more than five years (Fortuny & Chaudry, 2011). Qualified immigrants include legal permanent residents (LPRs), refugees and asylees, and certain other categories of immigrants qualified for public assistance on humanitarian grounds. Nonqualified immigrants include unauthorized immigrants, persons with Temporary Protected Status (TPS), and other lawfully present immigrants, such as those with temporary student, work, and tourist visas.

The passage of the Children's Health Insurance Program Reauthorization Act (CHIPRA) in 2009 loosened PRWORA eligibility restrictions slightly by allowing states to receive federal funds to cover qualified children and pregnant women under Medicaid and CHIP during the five-year ban and, under the unborn-child provisions, nonqualified pregnant women (Fortuny & Chaudry, 2012). It also allowed states to cover other nonqualified immigrants with state-only funds (Fortuny & Chaudry, 2012). As of 2011, 22 states and the District of Columbia covered both women and children during the five-year ban, five states covered only children during the five-year ban, and one state covered only pregnant women during the five-year ban (Fortuny & Chaudry, 2012) (figure 14.2). Fourteen states and the District of Columbia covered nonqualified pregnant women regardless of their immigration status, and 16 states used state funds to cover other nonqualified immigrants (Fortuny & Chaudry, 2012). Only five states (California, Florida, Illinois, New York, and Washington) and the District of Columbia used state-only funds to provide access to any public health insurance coverage for unauthorized immigrant children or nonpregnant adults (Fortuny & Chaudry, 2012).

The Affordable Care Act and Coverage for Immigrant Populations

Most recently, the ACA further extended access to both public and private health insurance for immigrants (Kenney & Huntress, 2012). First, the ACA reformed health insurance markets and established a variety of regulations to expand access to individual and employer-sponsored private coverage. Second, the ACA allowed state governments to extend eligibility for Medicaid coverage to more low-income families and single adults with no children.

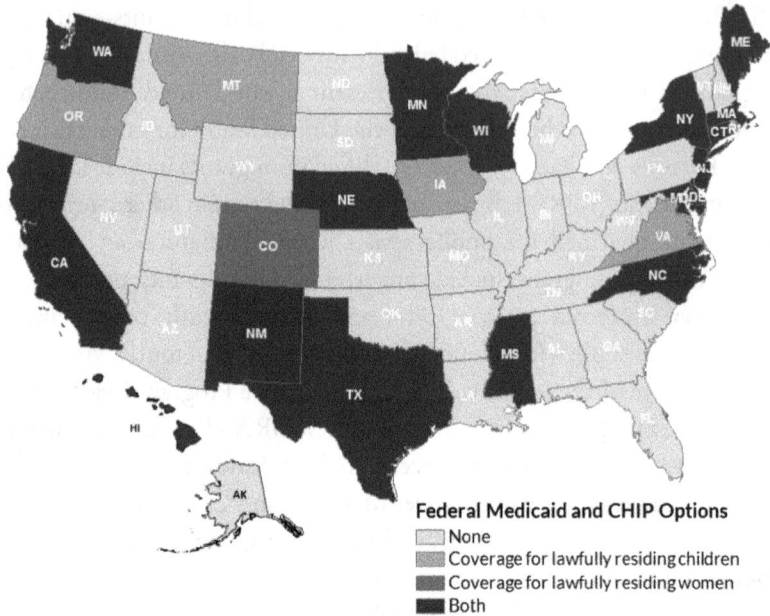

FIGURE 14.2   Federal Medicaid and CHIP coverage for immigrant
women and children

Third, the ACA created insurance markets operated through state or federal exchanges where individuals could purchase both government-subsidized and unsubsidized insurance. To encourage all U.S. residents to obtain coverage, the ACA established an individual mandate to purchase insurance and assess annual penalties to be paid by those who choose to forgo health insurance coverage for themselves or their dependents.

Regulations of the private insurance market introduced by the ACA are likely to increase coverage among immigrants in two ways. First, immigrant parents who receive insurance through their employers will be able to keep their adult children on their employer plans until age 26. Second, immigrant adults and children who have preexisting health conditions (e.g., asthma, back pain, cancer, diabetes, or depression) will be able to qualify for health insurance coverage with the same premiums as those without preexisting conditions. Before the ACA went into effect, insurers in most states could choose not to provide coverage or could charge higher premiums to persons who wanted to purchase insurance through the individual nongroup market and had a history of mental or physical health problems.

The Medicaid expansions allowed by the ACA should also increase health insurance coverage among many qualified immigrants with incomes below 138 percent of FPL. Under the ACA, states were given the option of expanding Medicaid to all individuals, including qualified immigrants, with incomes below 138 percent of FPL, and 28 states plus the District of Columbia implemented this option in 2014 (Kaiser Family Foundation, 2015). However, in these states, the five-year ban on Medicaid eligibility for most authorized immigrants who arrived in the United States after August 22, 1996, still applies and reduces the potential impact of these Medicaid expansions on rates of health insurance coverage among immigrants. Medicaid also continues to exclude immigrants who are unauthorized and those with temporary work, student, and tourist visas.

As of 2015, 22 states have chosen not to expand Medicaid coverage. For immigrants who do not qualify for Medicaid, the ACA provides an opportunity to purchase subsidized and unsubsidized health insurance through a federal or state health insurance marketplace. As of 2014, 27 states chose to use the Health Insurance Marketplace established by the federal government. The remaining 23 states and the District of Columbia chose to implement a state-based marketplace or a marketplace operated in partnership with the federal government (Kaiser Family Foundation, 2014).

In contrast to Medicaid, health insurance coverage purchased through the Marketplace is *not* limited to qualified immigrants with five or more years of U.S. residency. All noncitizens who are lawfully present in the United States are eligible to purchase both subsidized and unsubsidized insurance through the Health Insurance Marketplace. There are *no* years-of-residency restrictions on eligibility for subsidized or unsubsidized insurance purchased through the Marketplace. Lawfully present noncitizens include lawful permanent residents (LPRs) and those who have approved visa petitions to adjust their status; refugees, asylees, and other persons fleeing persecution; persons with TPS and other categories of humanitarian immigrants; survivors of domestic violence, trafficking, and other serious crimes (e.g., U-visa holders); persons with valid nonimmigrant status such as those with student visas and temporary work visas (e.g., H-1B, H-2A, and H-2B); and other longtime residents awaiting legalization (e.g., IRCA applicants). Only unauthorized immigrant children and adults are barred from purchasing insurance through the Marketplace. This includes children and adults who have received Deferred Action for Childhood Arrivals (DACA). Unauthorized immigrants, including DACA recipients, are eligible for an exemption to the individual mandate to purchase insurance (U.S. Department of Health and Human Services, 2014; Woomer-Deters, 2014).

Both for immigrants and for U.S. citizens, eligibility for subsidized insurance purchased through the Marketplace depends on the availability of employer-sponsored insurance, and it varies by income and family size. Only persons without access to employer-sponsored insurance or who are unable to afford the insurance offered by their employers are eligible to receive subsidies. Employer-sponsored insurance is considered unaffordable if the employee's annual premiums for individual coverage cost more than 9.5 percent of his or her family income (Kaiser Family Foundation, 2013c). Thus, an employee in a family earning $40,881 (the median family income among noncitizens) and having an annual premium of more than $3,884 for their employer-sponsored, individual insurance plan could choose to purchase subsidized insurance (U.S. Bureau of the Census, 2012). Eligibility for subsidized insurance also depends on where immigrants live. In the 22 states that have not expanded Medicaid, naturalized immigrants and U.S. citizens with incomes below 100 percent of FPL who do not qualify for Medicaid are not eligible for subsidies (Garfield, Damico, Stephens, & Rouhani, 2014). Because of specific provisions in the ACA for recent immigrants, this gap in subsidized insurance, called the "Medicaid Gap," does *not* apply to immigrants with five or fewer years of U.S. residency.

Health Care Coverage Through Local Health Departments and Health Centers

Uninsured immigrants and even many immigrants with insurance receive medical care through federally qualified health centers (FQHCs) and FQHC look-alikes. FQHCs and FQHC look-alikes, also called community health centers, are nonprofit health care providers that provide primary health, oral health, mental health, and substance abuse services to underserved areas or population groups (Centers for Medicaid and Medicare Services, 2013). FQHCs receive federal grant funding from section 330 of the Public

Health Services Act; FQHC look-alikes do not receive this funding (Centers for Medicaid and Medicare Services, 2013). As of 2013, there were 1,202 FQHCs and 100 FQHC look-alikes located throughout the United States. Some health centers, called migrant health centers, receive additional funding from the Health Resource and Service Administration (HRSA) to "deliver high quality, culturally-responsive preventive and primary health services to migratory and seasonal agricultural workers and their families" (Health Resources and Services Administration, 2014). As of 2013, there were 159 federally funded migrant health centers located throughout the United States (National Center for Farmworker Health, 2014). All but 15 of these were also FQHCs (National Center for Farmworker Health, 2014). Data on the number of foreign-born persons utilizing FQHCs, FQHC look-alikes, or migrant health centers are not routinely published. However, data do show that they serve a diverse population. Between 62 percent and 66 percent of those served are white, 24 percent to 28 percent are African or African American, 4 percent to 7 percent are Asian, and 35 percent to 38 percent are Hispanic/Latino of any racial background (Health Resources and Services Administration, 2013). Between 23 percent and 25 percent of patients served by FQHCs, look-alikes, and migrant health centers are best served in a language other than English (Health Resources and Services Administration, 2013).

Approximately, 2,700 county and city health departments located throughout the United States provide another source of care for low-income and vulnerable populations, including immigrants (National Association of County & City Health Officials, 2014). As required by the Immigration and Nationality Act (INA) and Public Health Services Act, these health departments are typically responsible for providing routine postarrival medical screening for all refugees entering the United States. They also provide basic preventive medical and dental care, family planning services, screening and vaccinations for communicable diseases such as AIDS and tuberculosis, lead testing, nutritional counseling, and nutritional foods under the Women, Infants, and Children (WIC) program. These services are available to all citizens and noncitizens residing in each county. At the same time, funding of local health departments varies tremendously across states, and many have difficulty meeting the needs of the populations in their service areas (Hyde & Shortell, 2012).

BARRIERS TO INSURANCE COVERAGE
AND ACCESS TO MEDICAL CARE

However, even with access to public and private health insurance, FQHC, and county health departments, immigrants can face additional barriers to obtaining insurance and receiving medical care (Arcury and Quandt, 2007; Cristancho, Garces, Peters, & Mueller, 2008; Hagan, Rodriguez, Capps, & Kabiri, 2003; Perreira et al., 2012). First, immigrants find the eligibility rules for various public benefits confusing, and applying for benefits can be daunting. Second, language, literacy, and cultural differences can create additional barriers to understanding U.S. health insurance systems and accessing medical care. Third, limited transportation and other logistical challenges (e.g., balancing work and child care demands) can prevent immigrants, especially those living in rural areas, from getting to and from the public agencies, community-based organizations, and providers that can help them. Finally, climates of fear and mistrust perpetuated by expressions of anti-immigrant sentiments in the United States, current immigration enforcement efforts in local communities, and personal experiences of discrimination can keep immigrants, regardless of their legal status, from seeking help (see chapter 4 of this volume for additional discussion of immigration enforcement efforts).

As a result of these barriers, researchers have identified a noticeable "chilling effect" on the takeup of public benefits (Kaushal & Kaestner, 2005; Van Hook, 2003). Moreover, they observe that the rate at which immigrants use health care, including emergency room services, is lower than that of U.S.-born citizens (Ku & Matani, 2001), and immigrants have lower annual health care expenditures than U.S.-born citizens for all types of care (Mohanty et al., 2005; Stimpson, Wilson, & Su, 2013).

UNIQUE HEALTH NEEDS OF IMMIGRANTS AND REFUGEES

Immigrants' low health care utilization rates reflect their low health insurance coverage rates as well as their relatively good health. Despite the stresses of migration, resettlement, and low socioeconomic status in the United States, immigrants of all racial and ethnic backgrounds have lower morbidity and mortality rates than their U.S.-born counterparts, but their health deteriorates the longer they remain in the United States. In a recent comprehensive study using eight national datasets, Singh, Rodriguez-Lainz, and Kogan (2013) showed that U.S. immigrants had a life expectancy of 80.0 years, 3.4 years longer than the life expectancy of the U.S.-born population. These differences in life expectancy occurred for all racial and ethnic groups, including whites, but were especially large for black immigrants compared with U.S.-born blacks (78.6 years vs. 71.2 years). On average, infant mortality rates were also lower for U.S. immigrants than for U.S. natives (5.17 percent vs. 7.21 percent), and these nativity differences were especially large for Asian Indians (4.02 percent vs. 7.28 percent), blacks (9.71 percent vs. 13.84 percent), and Mexicans (4.90 percent vs. 6.14 percent) (Singh et al., 2013).

Health Care Needs Among Adult Immigrants and Refugees

Although, on average, immigrants appear healthier than U.S.-born persons, some specific causes of death, infectious diseases, and chronic conditions occur more frequently among particular groups of immigrant adults (Elo, Mehta, & Huang, 2011; Markides, Salinas, & Sheffield, 2009; Prosser, Tang, & Hall, 2012; Singh, Siahpush, Hiatt, & Timsina, 2011; Singh, Yu, & Kogan, 2013a). Cardiovascular disease (CVD), stomach cancer, liver cancer, and homicides are more likely among white immigrants than among U.S.-born whites. Among Asians and Pacific Islanders, deaths from CVD, liver cancer, and suicide are more likely for female immigrants than for U.S.-born females, and deaths from liver cancer and homicide are more likely for male immigrants than for U.S.-born females. Black and Latino immigrants are more at risk of HIV infections than their U.S.-born counterparts and U.S.-born whites. In addition, older black and Latino immigrants (age 65 and older) have higher risks of depressive disorders than older U.S.-born Asians and Latinos. Some immigrant women (blacks, Asian Indians, Filipinos, Vietnamese, and Latin Americans) are also more at risk of gestational diabetes.

In addition to examining racial and ethnic differences in health among immigrants, researchers and practitioners must also consider differences in health by immigration category. In particular, refugees and unauthorized immigrants can have health risks that stem from their unique experiences before, during, and after migration. Refugees are more likely than other immigrants to report at least one chronic condition and have higher odds of arthritis, heart disease, stroke, and physical activity limitations (Yun, Fuentes-Afflick, & Desai, 2012). Poor sanitation, limited food supplies, and long internments in refugee camps before migration can also increase the risk that refugees will suffer from malnutrition and related disorders such as anemia as well as infections or parasitic diseases that are endemic to their countries of origin but uncommon in the United States (Centers for Disease Control and Prevention, 2012).

Refugees, who have often faced life-threatening experiences in their flights from their home countries, also have a high prevalence of depressive disorders and anxiety disorders such as posttraumatic stress disorder (PTSD) (Barnes, 2001; Hollifield et al., 2013; Lindert, Ehrenstein, Priebe, Mielck, & Brähler, 2009). Refugee status is a political status that can be difficult to attain. Some immigrants classified as unauthorized immigrants may in fact be fleeing political violence or migrating after having experienced natural disasters in their home countries. Others are economic migrants who can experience traumatic events during their often clandestine and arduous journeys to the United States. Thus, like refugees, unauthorized immigrants have a greater risk of exposure to trauma and the development of depressive and anxiety disorders such as PTSD (Ornelas & Perreira, 2011; Perreira & Ornelas, 2013).

Health Care Needs Among Children of Immigrants and Refugees

Among children, researchers also consistently find that the health of U.S.-born and foreign-born children of immigrants is better than that of children of U.S.-born parents (Hacker et al., 2011; Harris, 1999). U.S.-born and foreign-born children of immigrants are less likely to be diagnosed with behavioral or emotional problems, including depression, attention deficit disorder (ADD), or attention deficit hyperactivity disorder (ADHD), less likely to have chronic conditions such as asthma or diabetes, and less likely to have learning disabilities (Singh et al., 2013a, 2013b). However, the children of immigrants are more likely to be overweight or obese and more likely to report fair to poor health (Singh et al., 2013a, 2013b). These higher rates of obesity and being overweight are driven by the second-generation U.S.-born children of immigrants rather than first-generation foreign-born children of immigrants (Harris, Perreira, & Lee, 2009; Popkin & Udry, 1998). First-generation immigrant children from low-SES backgrounds and lower-income countries are also at higher risk of becoming overweight or obese after moving to the United States (Van Hook & Balistreri, 2007).

Mental health is also a particular concern for immigrant children, especially refugee children and unauthorized immigrant children. Like adult refugees, refugee children also have a potentially high risk of psychological distress, depression, and anxiety related to exposure to violence and separation from family (Lustig et al., 2004). Also, like their adult counterparts, children without authorization status to live in the United States can experience trauma and hardships associated with depression, anxiety, and PTSD (Perreira & Ornelas, 2013; Potochnick & Perreira, 2010). Thus, their likelihood of poor mental health is greater than for immigrant children with legal status. Moreover, the legal status of children's parents can threaten the health and well-being of both unauthorized and authorized immigrant children (Yoshikawa, 2011).

Understanding the Epidemiological Paradox

Often referred to as the epidemiological paradox, the good health, on average, of immigrant adults and children relative to their U.S.-born peers is thought to be the consequence of three factors. First, immigrants to the United States may be a healthier subset of the populations from their countries of origin, and immigrants who return to their home countries may be less healthy than immigrants who remain in the United States (Abraído-Lanza, Dohrenwend, Ng-Mak, & Turner, 1999; Palloni & Arias, 2004; Van Hook & Zhang, 2011). Second, immigrants to the United States may change their health behaviors and adopt less healthy behaviors as their exposure to U.S. norms and cultural practices increases (Abraído-Lanza, Chao, & Florez, 2005; Vega & Amaro, 1994). Third, immigrants may become exposed to more harmful and more stressful conditions the longer they live in the United States, and at the same time they may lose some of the protective social and cultural resources that help create resiliency in individuals (Cook, Alegría, Lin, & Guo, 2009; Vega & Amaro, 1994). Current research suggests that all three factors are at work. We focus on the latter two, which have implications for health service provision and intervention.

Many adult immigrants and their children do adopt less healthy behaviors with time in the United States. Children become less physically active, they spend more time watching TV or playing video games, and they adopt less healthy diets and eat more fast food (Gordon-Larsen, Harris, Ward, & Popkin, 2003; Singh et al., 2013a). They also smoke more, they drink alcohol more, and they engage in more risky sexual behaviors (Harris, 1999; Landale et al., 1999). Evidence of changing health behaviors with acculturation or time in the United States is less conclusive among adults and suggests differences by race or ethnicity. Nevertheless, the plurality of the evidence indicates that less acculturated adults smoke and drink alcohol less than more acculturated adults (Afable-Munsuz, Ponce, Rodriguez, & Perez-Stable, 2010; Singh et al., 2013a). However, it is unclear whether diet quality improves with time in the United States or with acculturation (Ayala, Baquero, & Klinger, 2005; Satia-Abouta, Patterson, Neuhouser, & Elder, 2002). On a positive note, physical activity among adults seems to increase with time in the United States (Abraído-Lanza et al., 2005; Afable-Munsuz et al., 2010).

Many adult immigrants and their children are also exposed to a variety of potentially stressful circumstances and lose protective social and cultural resources with time in the United States. In comparison with the U.S. born, immigrants report living in more unsafe neighborhoods, where crime and violence occur regularly (Singh et al., 2013a; Cook et al., 2009). They also report lower levels of subjective social standing (Cook et al., 2009). At the same time, they tend to report levels of discrimination that are high but lower than those of the U.S. born (Pérez, Fortuna, & Alegría, 2008; Cook et al., 2009; Yip, Gee, & Takeuchi, 2008). However, one recent study suggests that Asian and Latino immigrants may experience more discrimination than U.S.-born Asians and Latinos in health care settings (Lauderdale, Wen, Jacobs, & Kandula, 2006). As part of the process of integration into U.S. society, immigrants experience an "othering," which exposes them to greater discrimination (Viruell-Fuentes, 2007).

The negative effects of these stressors on immigrants' health are potentially offset by strong ethnic identities, family support systems, and general social support from within their ethnic communities (Chae et al., 2008; Cook et al., 2009; Mossakowski, 2003). When compared with their U.S.-born peers, both adult immigrants and their children report a stronger sense of ethnic affirmation and belonging, lower levels of family conflict, and higher levels of family cohesion (Almeida et al., 2009; Cook et al., 2009; Yip et al., 2008; Zhang & Ta, 2009). But, more general social cohesion and support are stronger among the U.S. born than among the foreign born (Almeida et al., 2009; Zhang & Ta, 2009).

EMERGING PRACTICES AND PREVENTIVE INTERVENTIONS TO PROMOTE IMMIGRANT AND REFUGEE HEALTH

To promote the health of immigrants, the adoption of salubrious health behaviors, and the maintenance of protective social and cultural resources, several interventions have been proposed. These interventions can take place at a societal or community level by making systemic changes to public policies and health care systems, and to neighborhood, school, and work environments that influence health behavior and exposure (Smedley & Syme, 2001). Alternatively, these interventions can take place at an individual level, where the focus is on modifying individuals' attitudes, beliefs, behaviors, and interpersonal relationships to promote health (Smedley & Syme, 2001). Although nascent, the literature on interventions with immigrants provides some insights into effective strategies to promote their health.

At the societal or community level, analyses of policy interventions have focused on the health consequences of immigrant enforcement activities and the implementation of the welfare reforms enacted in 1996 that restricted access to federally funded public assistance and insurance programs. Additionally, research has focused on the completion of community-based needs assessments to identify barriers to care that can be addressed through systemic changes and community-based partnerships. Lastly, research has focused on the development of culturally responsive health care systems. Although community health centers such as FQHCs are important sources of care for immigrant populations, no research that we could identify has systematically evaluated how geographic expansion in the availability of community health centers or increases in their funding can improve health care utilization patterns and the health of immigrants. However, a number of studies suggest that individuals who receive care at community health centers have lower costs for medical care, use emergency room care less frequently, and have lower rates of hospitalization (Dievler & Giovannini, 1998; Ku et al., 2010).

Immigration Enforcement and Health

Policy research on immigrant enforcement activities within the United States (see chapter 4 of this volume) suggests that these activities have had a negative effect on the health and well-being of immigrants, especially children. In the early 2000s, U.S. Immigration and Customs Enforcement (ICE) increased worksite and community-based enforcement activities (Capps, Castaneda, Chaudry, & Santos, 2007). Additionally, Congress empowered local law enforcement to collaborate with ICE to perform immigration law enforcement functions (U.S. Immigration and Customs Enforcement, 2014a). These activities led to increased deportations of unauthorized immigrants and had an immediate impact on the noncitizen and citizen children of deported immigrant parents, who were faced with the sudden disappearance of a parent. Research has documented the economic and psychological stress caused by these deportations not only on children whose parent(s) were deported but also on spouses left behind and children who feared that their parent(s) might be at risk of deportation (Capps et al., 2007; Dreby, 2012; Hacker et al., 2011; Satinsky, Hu, Heller, & Farhang, 2013). These studies strongly suggest the need for coordination between ICE, public schools, state and local governments, and community-based organizations to protect the well-being of children of immigrants (Chaudry et al., 2010; Dettlaff, 2012).

Access to Public Assistance Programs and Health

Also at the societal level, research on the effects of restrictions in eligibility for public assistance programs and public health insurance suggests that access to these programs can profoundly influence the health of immigrant adults and their children. Public assistance programs include programs such as the Supplemental Nutritional Assistance Program (SNAP) and Temporary Assistance for Needy Families (TANF) (see chapter 3 of this volume). Public health insurance, as discussed, includes programs such as Medicaid and the Children's Health Insurance Program (CHIP). In their analyses of the consequences of eligibility restrictions for SNAP, Van Hook and Balistreri (2006) found that after reforms were implemented in 1996, the children of immigrants experienced "more persistent and higher levels of food insecurity" than did the children of citizens. Similarly, evaluations of the implementation of TANF reforms have indicated that TANF receipt among the children of immigrants declined after 1996 (Fix & Passel, 2002; Kaestner & Kaushal, 2007; Lofstrom & Bean, 2002). As a result, public health insurance coverage among low-income foreign-born single women and their children declined, and these women delayed medical care for themselves, but not their children, because of cost (Hagan et al., 2003; Kaushal & Kaestner, 2005, 2007).

Although no studies have directly linked these declines in TANF participation, SNAP participation, and public health insurance coverage to poorer health among immigrant women and children, such declines have been associated with increasing poverty rates among these groups (Borjas, 2011). States that chose to use state funds to maintain coverage of immigrant women and children after federal welfare reforms, and states with more generous public assistance and public insurance benefits, had lower poverty rates among immigrant women and children (Borjas, 2011). Poverty and a lack of health insurance coverage have been associated with low health care utilization rates among immigrant women and children, especially those who are unauthorized immigrants (Bustamante et al., 2012; Ku & Matani, 2001). Moreover, improvements in health care access have been found to increase preventive health care screenings, diagnoses, and the treatment of health problems among immigrants and their children (Antecol & Bedard, 2006; Carrasquillo & Pati, 2004). Together, these studies suggest that efforts to improve access to public assistance and public insurance can improve the health of immigrants and their children (Derose, Escarce, & Lurie, 2007).

Community-Based Interventions to Improve Health

Moving from state and federal policy interventions to community-based interventions, we identified a wealth of interventions. Typically, these interventions result from needs assessments that lead to partnerships between health providers, faith-based organizations, and immigrant-serving community-based organizations. The widespread emphasis on developing community-based partnerships reflects the belief that social service and health providers can best improve the health of immigrants by building trusting relationships with them and their families and empowering them to develop grassroots solutions. However, primarily because of funding limitations, few partnerships have included systematic evaluations.

Two examples of community-based partnerships include the Midwest Immigrant Health Project and the Refugee Health Assessment Program. The Midwest Immigrant Health Project was established in 2007 to identify and improve barriers to safety and health care for the growing number of immigrants in the rural midwest (Robert Woods Johnson Foundation, 2013). The project established health action councils in 12 communities in Missouri, Iowa, and Minnesota that consisted of meat packing and poultry workers, community organizers, and faith congregations, who worked together to improve transportation to medical facilities, hire interpreters in medical facilities, and, in collaboration with the federal Occupational Safety and Health Administration (OSHA), provide training in workplace safety (Robert Woods Johnson Foundation, 2013).

THE REFUGEE HEALTH ASSESSMENT PROGRAM

In Massachusetts, the state's Department of Public Health worked with community health centers (mostly FQHCs) to establish the Refugee Health Assessment Program (RHAP). The RHAP established a preferred provider network to complete required medical screenings for refugees settling in the state, and those in the RHAP were given an exclusive contract, with payments from multiple federal funding streams (i.e., Medicaid, preventive health grants from the U.S. Office of Refugee and Resettlement, and Refugee Medical Assistance) bundled together and paid on a per capita basis. The establishment of the RHAP helped to ensure consistency and availability of services for refugees. This public–private collaboration led to more rapid needs assessments of new immigrant populations, improved the completion of health screenings for refugees, and improved knowledge of refugee health concerns among providers (Geltman & Cochran, 2005). As stated by Geltman and Cochran (2005), "this program demonstrated that public health authorities can successfully implement public–private partnerships using a preferred provider network model for conducting refugee health services."

Another set of community-based interventions focuses on improving the cultural competence of health care systems by (1) establishing programs to recruit and retain staff members who reflect the cultural diversity of the community served, (2) establishing interpreter services or employing bilingual providers for clients with limited English proficiency, (3) training health care providers in cultural competence, and (4) creating linguistically and culturally appropriate health education materials (Anderson, Scrimshaw, Fullilove, Fielding, & Normand, 2003; Beach, Price, Gary, & Robinson, 2005; Cooper, Hill, & Powe, 2002). Although some research suggests that these strategies will improve the quality of health care services for immigrants (Beach et al., 2005), other reviews of the literature have found that studies provided insufficient or inconclusive evidence on the effectiveness of these programs (Anderson et al., 2003; Cooper et al., 2002). In general, small samples, the absence of control groups, and poor measurement of resource inputs and health outcomes has limited the usefulness of these evaluations (Cooper et al., 2002).

Individual-Level Interventions to Improve Health

Although few high-quality studies of societal- and community-level interventions to improve the health of immigrants have been completed, studies of individual-level interventions are more numerous, with more rigorous designs. Individual-level interventions consist of efforts to develop interventions through community-based participatory research (CBPR), to tailor clinical interventions and outreach materials to specific immigrant populations, and to use lay health advisers to educate immigrants about health issues and promote appropriate health care utilization.

Community-based participatory research (CBPR) is "a collaborative research approach . . . designed to ensure and establish structures for participation by communities affected by the issue being studied, representatives of organizations, and researchers in all aspects of the research process" (Viswanathan et al., 2004). Researchers who employ CBPR have argued that, by enhancing trust and communication, this technique improves participation rates, decreases loss to follow-up, increases the external validity of results, and empowers individuals and communities to create and sustain interventions (Arcury, Quandt, & Dearry, 2001; Stein et al., 2002; Viswanathan et al., 2004). CBPR techniques with immigrant populations have been successfully employed in mental health, obesity, and HIV or STD interventions as well as efforts to reduce the health effects of environmental hazards (Barnes, 2001; Calzada & The Bridges Program Development Team, 2007; Rhodes et al., 2006; Wieland et al., 2012).

These CBPR studies typically begin by bringing together immigrant members of the community, community leaders, and researchers to discuss particular health problems and generate ideas about solutions. The CBPR team then works to design and implement a culturally responsive intervention informed by the community's feedback and to evaluate the intervention using both qualitative focus group data and survey data. Upon completion of the intervention, evaluations are shared with the community, with a focus on determining the next steps to sustain and expand the interventions. Although CBPR interventions with immigrants are too numerous to discuss in detail, these interventions have included home-based screening for mental health concerns among refugees (Barnes, 2001), school-based training of teachers to develop sensitivity to the immigration experiences and mental health needs of immigrant children (Calzada & The Bridges Program Development Team, 2007), women's fitness and nutrition programs supported by child care and transportation services among Latina immigrants (Wieland et al., 2012), and lay health adviser training among men leading local soccer teams (Rhodes et al., 2006).

In addition to employing CBPR techniques, researchers working with immigrants commonly focus on tailoring outreach materials and clinical interventions to specific immigrant populations. Aside from facing language barriers, immigrant populations frequently have low levels of literacy and numeracy, as well as different beliefs about disease causation and appropriate treatment, and come from countries with very different health systems. Thus, to be successful, interventions and outreach materials must address the health literacy needs of immigrant populations (Burke et al., 2011; Cabrera, Morisky, & Chin, 2002; Kreps & Sparks, 2008). Culturally responsive health education messages disseminated through videos, pamphlets, and lay health advisers have proven effective for promoting cancer and hepatitis screenings (Lam et al., 2003; Luque, Mason, Reyes-Garcia, Hinojosa, & Meade, 2011; Perumalswami et al., 2013; Wang et al., 2008), for promoting treatment adherence for tuberculosis (Ailinger, Martyn, Lasus, & Lima Garcia, 2010; Hovell et al., 2003), and for reducing the stigma associated with the use of antidepressants and mental health services (Unger, Cabassa, Molina, Contreras, & Baron, 2013). Through randomized control trials, culturally responsive clinical interventions have also been proven effective for treating depressive symptoms and trauma in immigrant women and children (Beeber et al., 2010; Beehler, Birman, & Campbell, 2012; Birman et al., 2008; Ellis et al., 2013).

In combination with tailoring health information and clinical interventions, interventions with immigrant populations also commonly use lay health advisers (LHAs): "LHAs are community members whom others naturally turn to for advice, emotional support, and tangible aid" (Rhodes et al., 2007). They receive specialized training to play the role of culture brokers who educate their communities about health issues, help their peers navigate the U.S. health care system, and advocate on behalf of their communities (Diaz-Perez, Farley, & Cabanis, 2004; Heuer, Hess, & Batson, 2006; Wilson, Wold, Spencer, & Pittman, 2000). Evaluations of LHAs in immigrant communities find that they can be effective in increasing knowledge about health issues such as diabetes, cancer, and hepatitis and in promoting the adoption of preventive behaviors such as cancer screening, vaccinations, physical activity, and healthy eating behaviors (Bird et al., 1998; Juon et al., 2008; Lujan, Ostwald, & Ortiz, 2007; Luque et al., 2011; Navarro et al., 1998; Taylor et al., 2002, 2009; Vincent, Pasvogel, & Barrera, 2009).

CROSS-SYSTEM COLLABORATIONS AND BARRIERS TO CHANGE

Health promotion among immigrants and their children requires coordination between multiple systems, including health care, education, public assistance, child welfare, immigration enforcement, and legal systems. Partnerships among these systems occur mostly at the local and state levels, and they are often possible because of the work of nonprofit community-based organizations (CBOs) that serve immigrant communities (Crosnoe et al., 2012; Yoshikawa, Kholoptseva, & Suárez-Orozco, 2013). Here we provide examples of local-, state-, and national-level collaborations between health systems, social services systems, and other immigrant-serving CBOs.

Local Health System Collaborations

At the local level, hospitals and insurers partner with FQHCs and CBOs to better coordinate the provision of health care with other social services. For example, in New York, New York Presbyterian Hospital created the Regional Health Collaborative to help reduce health disparities in Washington Heights, a neighborhood with a significant Hispanic immigrant population (Carrillo et al., 2011). Their collaborative involved a partnership between the hospital and community health centers to develop patient-centered medical homes with improved cultural responsiveness among health providers and integrated information systems across care sites. The initial results demonstrated significant declines in emergency department visits for ambulatory care and a decrease in hospitalizations (Carrillo et al., 2011).

Local Legal System Collaborations

As another example, the Boston Medical Center formed the first medical legal partnership (MLP), which brought together health care providers, family advocates, and legal practices to incorporate legal advocacy into health care teams as a means of improving the quality of care (Cohen et al., 2010). Medical legal partnerships provide training to health care providers and social workers, who are then better able to assist immigrants and other vulnerable population groups with obtaining public assistance, social services, and medical services for which they qualify. Several health systems across the country now use the MLP model to address health-related concerns of underserved populations (Cohen et al., 2010; Paul et al., 2009).

EL FUTURO

Protecting the Mental Health of Immigrants Through Culturally Responsive Care

Although, on average, first-generation immigrants have risks of mental health and substance abuse problems that are lower than for U.S.-born natives (Cook et al., 2009), those who need mental health care can face substantial barriers to care, including the availability of mental health providers with the linguistic skills and cultural humility to provide appropriate services. To address the need for culturally responsive care in North Carolina, community members and clinicians worked together to establish a nonprofit behavioral health clinic, El Futuro, focused on serving Latino immigrant children and their families (Perreira & Smith, 2007). The organization of El Futuro's clinical services recognizes the need for multilevel treatment, which involves family, schools, and community organizations and takes into account the multiple contexts—cultural, family, work, economic, and legal—that can shape immigrants' access to care. For example, to build trust and confidence in their services, El Futuro hosts weekly activity groups for families that provide a safe place to form friendships, share struggles, and get to know more about the resources available at the clinic. To ensure openness in communication and care, El Futuro also works to educate and build liaisons between its clinicians and nontraditional healers within the Latino immigrant community. To account for the lack of health insurance and discretionary income among their clients, El Futuro provides services on a sliding scale. To account for inflexible work schedules, El Futuro provides evening and weekend clinics for its clients (see http://elfuturo-nc.org).

Local School-System Collaborations

At the local level, cross-system collaborations also involve partnerships between health providers and school districts to increase immigrant children's access to medical care and social services. In Texas, the Austin Independent School District trains school personnel to screen families for eligibility for federal public assistance programs and county social services. In addition, it contracts with a local hospital to hire school nurses who can screen children for Medicaid and CHIP eligibility (Crosnoe et al., 2012). In the Los Angeles Unified School District, the Emergency Immigrant Education Program (EIEP) was established to provide medical and dental screening, as well as mental health services, to immigrant students (Stein et al., 2002).

Collaborations with Health and Human Service Systems

At the state level, health and human service agencies partner with CBOs to provide outreach about the availability of services and to assist with enrolling immigrants into services for which they qualify. Since immigrant-serving CBOs are embedded within local communities and have established trusting relationships with immigrants living in these communities, their staff can effectively bridge cultural and linguistic divides between immigrants and state agencies responsible for the provision of Medicaid, SNAP, TANF, and other health and human services (Crosnoe et al., 2012; Yoshikawa et al., 2013). In some states, CBO staff receive training from state health and human services agencies to learn the eligibility rules for various programs and application procedures. The staff can then directly assist immigrants with the completion of their applications. In other states, eligibility workers from various health and human service agencies locate their offices within key CBOs (Crosnoe et al., 2012; Yoshikawa et al., 2014). Immigrants who might be afraid of going to a state agency location can then obtain assistance with applications and services in a location that is both more convenient and more approachable for them. Finally, partnerships between health and human service agencies and CBOs in various states can be more informal and involve coordination strategies such as monthly meetings in specific communities with large immigrant populations to discuss difficult cases or systemwide policies and practices (Crosnoe et al., 2012; Yoshikawa et al., 2014).

State and National Collaborations Between Community-Based Organizations

In several states with long histories of receiving immigrants, CBOs also partner with each other to create umbrella organizations that coordinate contracts with state agencies and can engage in broader advocacy to change policies and practices that create barriers to services and to advance the interests of immigrants and refugees. Their work helps to reduce barriers to services related to transportation, language, complex application rules, requirements for documentation, and fears about immigration-related consequences of using public assistance and other social service benefits.

One such umbrella organization is the Illinois Coalition for Immigrant and Refugee Rights (ICIRR). The ICIRR has partnered with the Illinois Department of Human Services (DHS) and 37 CBOs across Illinois to form the Immigrant Family Resource Program (Quinones & Rashid, 2013). Through the program, the CBOs receive funding to serve as culture brokers who conduct outreach, manage social service cases, and provide professional interpretation and translation services. The Illinois DHS benefits from improved communication with immigrant communities, as the ICIRR helps inform DHS administrators about immigrant-related issues, and DHS in turn informs ICIRR about upcoming policy changes concerning immigrants. This exchange of information facilitates the development and implementation of new policies. Another notable statewide immigrant coalition is the New York Immigrant Coalition, a policy and advocacy coalition of about 200 CBOs (Dodge, Ospina, & Sparrow, 2004).

Nationally, the capacity of CBOs to coordinate with state agencies and to effectively advocate for policy change when needed has been strengthened by the formation of cross-state coalitions. For example, the Catholic Collaborative Refugee Network (CCRN) was developed in conjunction with the Catholic Health Association, Catholic Charities U.S.A., and the U.S. Catholic Conference's Office of Migration and Refugee Services in order to improve services provided to refugees in different areas of the country (McGuire, 2005). The CCRN has partner sites in 12 cities across the country, including Phoenix, Cleveland, Pittsburgh, Portland, and Los Angeles. Similarly, the National Council of La Raza (NCLR) provides capacity-building assistance to a network of nearly 300 affiliated CBOs. NCLR's assistance helps affiliated CBOs share promising practices and obtain the financial, legal, and technical support they need to improve health and human services in their states and local communities.

As a result of the advocacy efforts of these state and national coalitions of CBOs and others, some programs and policies have been developed to encourage cross-system collaborations at a national level. Within the Administration of Children and Families (ACF), the Office of Refugee Resettlement (ORR) collaborates with federal and state agencies and CBOs across the country to provide support programs for new refugees. These programs include application assistance for public benefits, interpretation services, and employment training programs.

Most recently, as a result of state and national advocacy efforts, Immigration and Customs Enforcement (ICE) established humanitarian guidelines to be applied to local enforcement actions involving more than 25 arrests, and it expanded guidelines to encourage the use of prosecutorial discretion in detention cases with humanitarian considerations (Chaudry et al., 2010; Dettlaff, 2012; U.S. Immigration and Customs Enforcement, 2011). These guidelines encourage ICE to identify individuals whose well-being might be placed at risk as a result of the detention of a spouse or primary caregiver (e.g., minor children) and to coordinate enforcement actions with state and local health and human service agencies. Recent evidence suggests that these coordination strategies have helped to prevent or minimize harm to the dependents of detained immigrants (Chaudry et al., 2010).

Despite efforts to improve service provision for immigrants through cross-system collaborations, a number of barriers hinder the work and partnerships of nonprofit CBOs and public agencies. First, nonprofit CBOs rely heavily on private donations and revenue from government grants and contracts (Pettijohn, Boris, De Vita, & Fyffe, 2013; Portes, Escobar, & Radford, 2007). Especially during economic recessions, CBOs continually struggle to raise the money needed to sustain their organizations and meet the demands of their communities (Crosnoe et al., 2012; Pettijohn et al., 2013). Without sustainable funding, they must make tough choices to cut back on the number of people they serve, reduce their hours of operation, and reduce the services provided. Second, many CBOs lack the human resources and infrastructure needed to effectively partner with government agencies and for-profit organizations to serve the health and human services needs of their communities. Government grants and contracts often limit the availability of funds for administrative expenses considered "overhead" costs (Pettijohn et al., 2013). These include expenses such as administrative staff time, rental costs, and basic operating expenses for computer equipment, phone, and Internet services. Without coverage for these expenses, CBOs cannot build capacity, and they have difficulty meeting the many accountability and reporting requirements for grants and contracts (Pettijohn et al., 2013; White House Office of Faith-Based and Neighborhood Partnerships, 2010). Third, employees in both public and nonprofit health and human service agencies encounter considerable stress as they aim to serve with limited resources the many needs of their clients (Lipsky, 2010; Perreira et al., 2012). As a result, burnout and turnover can be high. This further reduces the capacity of CBOs and public agencies to sustain their partnerships. Lastly, both CBOs and public agencies encounter political barriers to the sustainability of their programs and partnerships. Polarized political climates on immigration, health, and poverty issues can lead to mixed messages across public agencies with regard to their missions and the feasibility of collaborating with each other or community-based organizations. To more effectively take advantage of the potential for cross-system collaborations, each of these barriers to sustainability must be addressed.

CONCLUSION

In this chapter, we described the U.S. health care system, the unique health needs of immigrant and refugee families, and challenges they experience in accessing care in the U.S. health system. We also described emerging practices, interventions, and cross-system collaborations designed to better promote immigrant and refugee health. Our review suggests avenues for future research and the potential for changes in policies and practices to improve immigrant and refugee health.

Although most immigrants begin their lives in the United States in good health, researchers have consistently found that the health of immigrants deteriorates with time in the United States and across immigrant generations. Yet, we still understand little about how to prevent this deterioration. Future research exploring how social, cultural, and environmental resources can be used to protect the health of immigrants is critical for identifying specific points for intervention (e.g., modifying psychological, social, and physical conditions) to improve immigrants' health.

One key point of intervention that we have noted is in improving access to the health care system for immigrants who have relatively low health insurance rates and low health care utilization rates. Most foreign-born noncitizens are legal immigrants with access to a variety of public and private health insurance programs. However, the complexity of the U.S. health care system and eligibility rules for public health insurance programs such as Medicaid and CHIPRA can hinder their access. Immigrants would greatly benefit from a simplified system that removes the five-year ban on access to Medicaid and CHIPRA, expands Medicaid coverage in all states as allowed under the ACA, and provides sustained access to subsidized health insurance through federal, state, and partnership Health Insurance Marketplaces established by the ACA.

In the absence of policies to simplify our health care system and eligibility rules for immigrants' access to public insurance benefits, immigrants and their families require substantial assistance from community health centers (including FQHCs), county health departments, and community-based organizations, which provide outreach and help them to navigate these complex health systems. These organizations, however, have limited funds and resources for the services they provide. Consequently, there is a need for private and government agencies to recognize them as essential partners, provide comprehensive reimbursement for their services, and collaborate on the development of sustainable funding mechanisms.

Community-based organizations that serve immigrant families have also been central to the development and implementation of interventions and cross-system collaborations designed to improve health. They have developed strategies to build trust with immigrant communities, capitalize on social networks within immigrant communities to disseminate information, integrate and streamline access to multiple programs, and make services to immigrants more accessible through cultural, linguistic, and logistical (e.g., transportation or child care) adaptations. At the same time, many of these innovative strategies of service delivery have not been formally evaluated. Thus, additional research is needed to help develop and disseminate these innovative and effective service delivery strategies.

In conclusion, to improve access to health care for immigrants and their families, we recommend that:

1   Research should be conducted to evaluate interventions that use social, cultural, and environmental resources in immigrant communities to protect and improve immigrant health.
2   Eligibility rules for immigrants' access to Medicaid and CHIPRA should be simplified and Medicaid coverage should be expanded in all states as allowed under the ACA.
3   Funding and resources for community health centers (including FQHCs), county health departments, and immigrant-serving CBOs should be expanded.
4   Formal evaluations should be developed to test the effectiveness of innovative strategies for health care service delivery and cross-system collaborations.

As argued by Hiroshi Motomura, immigrants and refugees are "Americans in waiting" (Motomura, 2006). After one to five years of residency in the United States, most immigrants and refugees will become eligible for citizenship. When we make policy choices to restrict their access to health care, we make choices that hinder their integration into U.S. society and reduce their capacity to contribute to the economic well-being of the United States. By investing in immigrants and their health, we can invest in the future of America.

KEY TERMS

EPIDEMIOLOGICAL PARADOX   Sometimes called the immigrant paradox, this
    term refers to the finding that, on average, immigrants have similar or better
    health than U.S.-born persons of the same race or ethnicity despite the fact

that immigrants also have lower socioeconomic status than U.S.-born persons.

FEDERALLY QUALIFIED HEALTH CENTER (FQHC) FQHCs and FQHC look-alikes, also called community health centers, are nonprofit health care providers that provide primary health, oral health, mental health, and substance abuse services to underserved areas or population groups (Centers for Medicaid and Medicare Services, 2013). Migrant health centers are a specialized type of FQHC that receives additional funds to deliver high-quality, culturally responsive preventive and primary health services to migratory and seasonal agricultural workers and their families (Health Resources and Services Administration, 2014).

LAY HEALTH ADVISERS "Community members whom others naturally turn to for advice, emotional support, and tangible aid" (Rhodes et al., 2007) and who work in their communities to help improve health and access to health services. They are often referred to as *"promatoras"* in Spanish-speaking communities.

MEDICAID A federal and state-funded public insurance program enacted in 1965 to provide access to medical insurance for certain categories of low-income persons residing in the United States.

PATIENT PROTECTION AND AFFORDABLE CARE ACT (ACA) Referred to as the Affordable Care Act (ACA), this 2010 health reform law enacted during the Obama administration aims to expand the availability of private and public health insurance and control health care spending.

STUDY QUESTIONS

1 What are three potential reasons for the existence of the epidemiological paradox among immigrants residing in the United States?
2 What categories of immigrants are eligible for subsidized health insurance coverage available through the Health Insurance Marketplace?
3 Since 1996, how long must legal permanent residents reside in the United States before they become eligible for federally funded Medicaid benefits?
4 Why might immigrants choose not to take public assistance benefits for which they qualify or access health services in their communities?
5 What types of programs have federal, state, and local service providers implemented to address the health needs of immigrant populations?

ADDITIONAL RESOURCES

Centers for Disease Control, Immigrant and Refugee Health: http://www
.cdc.gov/immigrantrefugeehealth/

Kaiser Family Foundation Resources on Health Reform: http://kff.org
/health-reform/

Migration Policy Institute Resources on Health and Welfare Benefits:
http://www.migrationpolicy.org/topics/health-welfare-benefits

University of California at Berkeley, Health Initiatives of the Americas:
http://hia.berkeley.edu/

Urban Institute Center on Labor, Human Resources, and Population:
http://www.urban.org/policy-centers/center-labor-human-services-and
-population

REFERENCES

Abraído-Lanza, A. F., Chao, M. T., & Florez, K. R. (2005). Do healthy behaviors
decline with greater acculturation? Implications for the Latino mortality paradox. *Social Science & Medicine, 61*(6), 1243–1255.

Abraído-Lanza, A. F., Dohrenwend, B. P., Ng-Mak, D. S., & Turner, J. B. (1999).
The Latino mortality paradox: A test of the "salmon bias" and healthy migrant
hypotheses. *American Journal of Public Health, 89*(10), 1543–1548.

Afable-Munsuz, A., Ponce, N. A., Rodriguez, M., & Perez-Stable, E. J. (2010). Immigrant generation and physical activity among Mexican, Chinese & Filipino
adults in the US. *Social Science & Medicine, 70*(12), 1997–2005.

Ailinger, R. L., Martyn, D., Lasus, H., & Lima Garcia, N. (2010). The effect of a
cultural intervention on adherence to latent tuberculosis infection therapy in
Latino immigrants. *Public Health Nursing, 27*(2), 115–120.

Alker, J., & Ng'andu, J. (2006). *The role of employer-sponsored health coverage for
immigrants: A primer.* Menlo Park, CA: Kaiser Family Foundation.

Almeida, J., Molnar, B. E., Kawachi, I., & Subramanian, S. V. (2009). Ethnicity
and nativity status as determinants of perceived social support: Testing the
concept of familism. *Social Science & Medicine, 68*(10), 1852–1858.

Anderson, L. M., Scrimshaw, S. C., Fullilove, M. T., Fielding, J. E., & Normand, J.
(2003). Culturally competent healthcare systems. *American Journal of Preventive Medicine, 24*(3), 68–79.

Antecol, H., & Bedard, K. (2006). Unhealthy assimilation: Why do immigrants converge to American health status levels? *Demography, 43*(2), 337–360.

Arcury, T. A., & Quandt, S. A. (2007). Delivery of health services to migrant and seasonal farmworkers. *Annual Review of Public Health, 28*, 345–363.

Arcury, T. A., Quandt, S. A., & Dearry, A. (2001). Farmworker pesticide exposure and community-based participatory research: Rationale and practical applications. *Environmental Health Perspectives, 109*(supplement 3), 429–434.

Ayala, G. X., Baquero, B., & Klinger, S. (2008). A systematic review of the relationship between acculturation and diet among Latinos in the United States: Implications for future research. *Journal of the American Dietetic Association, 108*(8), 1330–1344.

Barnes, D. M. (2001). Mental health screening in a refugee population: A program report. *Journal of Immigrant Health, 3*(3), 141–149.

Beach, M., Price, E., Gary, T., & Robinson, K. (2005). Cultural competency: A systematic review of health care provider educational interventions. *Medical Care, 43*(4), 356–373.

Beeber, L. S., Holditch-Davis, D., Perreira, K., Schwartz, T. A., Lewis, V., Blanchard, H., Canuso, R., & Goldman, B. D. (2010). Short-term in-home intervention reduces depressive symptoms in early head start Latina mothers of infants and toddlers. *Research in Nursing & Health, 33*, 60–76.

Beehler, S., Birman, D., & Campbell, R. (2012). The effectiveness of cultural adjustment and trauma services (CATS): Generating practice-based evidence on a comprehensive, school-based mental health intervention for immigrant youth. *American Journal of Community Psychology, 50*(1–2), 155–168.

Bird, J. A., McPhee, S. J., Ha, N. T., Le, B., Davis, T., & Jenkins, C. N. (1998). Opening pathways to cancer screening for Vietnamese-American women: Lay health workers hold a key. *Preventive Medicine, 27*(6), 821–829.

Birman, D., Beehler, S., Harris, E. M., Everson, M. L., Batia, K., Liautaud, J., . . . & Cappella, E. (2008). International Family, Adult, and Child Enhancement Services (FACES): A community-based comprehensive services model for refugee children in resettlement. *American Journal of Orthopsychiatry, 78*(1), 121–132.

Borjas, G. J. (2011). Poverty and program participation among immigrant children. *The Future of Children, 21*(1), 247–266.

Buchmueller, T. C., Lo Sasso, A. T., Lurie, I., & Dolfin, S. (2007). Immigrants and employer-sponsored health insurance. *Health Services Research, 42*(1p1), 286–310.

Burke, N. J., Do, H. H., Tablot, J., Sos, C., Svy, D., & Taylor, V. M. (2011). Chumn-guh thleum: Understanding liver illness and hepatitis B among Cambodian immigrants. *Journal of Community Health, 36*, 27–34.

Bustamante, A. V., Fang, H., Garza, J. J., Carter-Pokras, O., Wallace, S. P., Rizzo, J. A., & Ortega, A. N. (2012). Variations in healthcare access and utilization among Mexican immigrants: The role of documentation status. *Journal of Immigrant and Minority Health, 14*, 146–155.

Cabrera, D. M., Morisky, D. E., & Chin, S. (2002). Development of a tuberculosis education booklet for Latino immigrant patients. *Patient Education and Counseling, 46*(2), 117–124.

Calzada, E. J., & The Bridges Program Development Team. (2007). *Bridges: A training manual for school-based mental health services*. New York: New York University.

Capps, R., Bachmeier, J. D., Fix, M., & Van Hook, J. (2013). *A demographic, socio-economic and health coverage profile of unauthorized immigrants in the United States* (Issue Brief No. 5). Washington, DC: Migration Policy Institute.

Capps, R., Castaneda, R. M., Chaudry, A., & Santos, R. (2007). *Paying the price: The impact of immigration raids on America's children*. Washington, DC: Urban Institute.

Carrasquillo, O., & Pati, S. (2004). The role of health insurance on Pap smear and mammography utilization by immigrants living in the United States. *Preventive Medicine, 39*, 943–950.

Carrillo, J. E., Shekhani, N. S., Deland, E. L., Fleck, E. M., Mucaria, J., Gui-mento, R., . . . & Corwin, S. J. (2011). A regional health collaborative formed by New York Presbyterian aims to improve the health of a largely Hispanic community. *Health Affairs, 30*(10), 1955–1964.

Centers for Disease Control and Prevention (CDC). (2012). *General refugee health guidelines*. Washington, DC: U.S. Department of Health and Human Services. Retrieved from http://www.cdc.gov/immigrantrefugeehealth/pdf /general.pdf

——. (2014). *Reported tuberculosis in the United States, 2013*. Atlanta, GA: Author.

Centers for Medicaid and Medicare Services (CMS). (2013). Federally Qualified Health Center, Rural Fact Sheet Series. Washington, DC: U.S. Department of Health and Human Services. Retrieved from http://www.cms.gov/Outreach -and-Education/Medicare-Learning-Network-MLN/MLNProducts/down loads/fqhcfactsheet.pdf

Chae, D. H., Takeuchi, D. T., Barbeau, E. M., Bennett, G. G., Lindsey, J. C., Stoddard, A. M., & Krieger, N. (2008). Alcohol disorders among Asian Americans: Associations with unfair treatment, racial/ethnic discrimination, and ethnic identification (the National Latino and Asian Americans study, 2002–2003). *Journal of Epidemiology and Community Health, 62,* 973–979.

Chaudry, A., Capps, R., Pedroza, J., Castaneda, R. M., Santos, R., & Scott, M. M. (2010). *Facing our future: Children in the aftermath of immigration enforcement.* Washington, DC: Urban Institute. Retrieved from http://www.urban.org/publications/412020.html

Cohen, E., Fullerton, D. F., Retkin, R., Weintraub, D., Tames, P., Brandfield, J., & Sandel, M. (2010). Medical–legal partnership: Collaborating with lawyers to identify and address health disparities. *Journal of General Internal Medicine, 25,* 136–139.

Cook, B., Alegría, M., Lin, J. Y., & Guo, J. (2009). Pathways and correlates connecting Latinos' mental health with exposure to the United States. *American Journal of Public Health, 99*(12), 2247–2254.

Cooper, L. A., Hill, M. N., & Powe, N. R. (2002). Designing and evaluating interventions to eliminate racial and ethnic disparities in health care. *Journal of General Internal Medicine, 17*(6), 477–486.

Cristancho, S., Garces, D. M., Peters, K. E., & Mueller, B. C. (2008). Listening to rural Hispanic immigrants in the midwest: A community-based participatory assessment of major barriers to health care access and use. *Qualitative Health Research, 18*(5), 633–646.

Crosnoe, R., Pedroza, J. M., Purtell, K., Fortuny, K., Perreira, K. M., Ulvestad, K., . . . & Chaudry, A. (2012). *Promising practices for increasing immigrants' access to health and human services* (Issue Brief). Washington, DC: Urban Institute and U.S. Department of Health and Human Services, Assistant Secretary for Planning and Evaluation. Retrieved from http://aspe.hhs.gov/hsp/11/immigrantaccess/practices/rb.shtml

DeNavas-Walt, C., Proctor, B. D., &, Smith, J. C. (2013). *U.S. Census Bureau, current population reports (Income, poverty, and health insurance coverage in the United States: 2012)* (pp. 60–245). Washington, DC: U.S. Government Printing Office.

Derose, K. P., Escarce, J. J., & Lurie, N. (2007). Immigrants and health care: Sources of vulnerability. *Health Affairs, 26*(5), 1258–1268.

Dettlaff, A. (2012). Immigrant children and families and the public child welfare system: Considerations for legal systems. *Juvenile and Family Court Journal, 63*(1), 20–30.

Diaz-Perez, M. D. J., Farley, T., & Cabanis, C. M. (2004). A program to improve access to health care among Mexican immigrants in rural Colorado. *Journal of Rural Health, 20*(3), 258–264.

Dievler, A., & Giovannini, T. (1998). Community health centers: Promise and performance. *Medical Care Research and Review, 55*(4), 405–431.

Dodge, J., Ospina, S., & Sparrow, R. (2004). *Making partnership a habit: Margie McHugh and the New York Immigration Coalition.* New York, NY: Synergos Institute. Retrieved from http://www. synergos.org/bridgingleadership /casestudies/margie_mchugh.pdf

Dreby, J. (2012). The burden of deportation on children in Mexican immigrant families. *Journal of Marriage and Family, 74*(4), 829–845.

Ellis, B. H., Miller, A. B., Abdi, S., Barrett, C., Blood, E. A., & Betancourt, T. S. (2013). Multi-tier mental health program for refugee youth. *Journal of Consulting and Clinical Psychology, 81*(1), 129–140.

Elo, I. T., Mehta, N. K., & Huang, C. (2011). Disability among native-born and foreign-born blacks in the United States. *Demography, 48*(1), 241–265.

Fix, M., & Passel, J. (2002). *The scope and impact of welfare reform's immigrant provisions.* Washington, DC: Urban Institute. Retrieved from http://www.urban. org/publications/410412.html

Fortuny, K., & Chaudry, A. (2011). *A comprehensive review of immigrant access to health and human services: A report submitted to Department of Health and Human Services, office of assistant secretary for planning and evaluation.* Washington, DC: Urban Institute.

——. (2012). *Overview of immigrants' eligibility for SNAP, TANF, Medicaid, and CHIP.* Washington, DC: Office of Assistant Secretary for Planning and Evaluation, Department of Health and Human Services.

Garfield, R., Damico, A., Stephens, J., & Rouhani, S. (2014). *The coverage gap: Uninsured poor adults in states that do not expand Medicaid—an update* (Issue Brief). Retrieved from http://kff.org/health-reform/issue-brief/the-coverage -gap-uninsured-poor-adults-in-states-that-do-not-expand-medicaid-an -update/

Geltman, P., & Cochran, J. (2005). A private-sector preferred provider network model for public health screening of newly resettled refugees. *American Journal of Public Health, 95*(2), 196–200.

Gordon-Larsen, P., Harris, K. M., Ward, D. S., & Popkin, B. M. (2003). Acculturation and overweight-related behaviors among Hispanic immigrants to the US: The National Longitudinal Study of Adolescent Health. *Social Science & Medicine, 57*(11), 2023–2034.

Gross, T., & Notowidigdo, M. J. (2011). Health insurance and the consumer bankruptcy decision: Evidence from expansions of Medicaid. *Journal of Public Economics, 95*(7–8), 767–778.

Gusmano, M. K. (2012). *Undocumented immigrants in the United States: U.S. health policy and access to care.* Garrison, NY: The Hastings Center.

Hacker, K., Chu, J., Leung, C., Marra, R., Pirie, A., Brahimi, M., . . . & Marlin, R. P. (2011). The impact of immigration and customs enforcement on immigrant health: Perceptions of immigrants in Everett, Massachusetts, USA. *Social Science & Medicine, 73*(4), 586–594.

Hagan, J., Rodriguez, N., Capps, R., & Kabiri, N. (2003). The effects of recent welfare and immigration reforms on immigrants' access to health care. *International Migration Review, 37*(2), 444–463.

Harris, K. M. (1999). The health status and risk behaviors of adolescents in immigrant families. In D. J. Hernandez (Ed.), *Children of immigrants: Health, adjustments, and public assistance* (pp. 286–347). Washington, DC: National Academy Press.

Harris, K. M., Perreira, K. M., & Lee, D. (2009). Obesity in the transition to adulthood: Predictions across race/ethnicity, immigrant generation, and sex. *Archives of Pediatrics & Adolescent Medicine, 163*(11), 1022–1028.

Health Resources and Services Administration (HRSA). (2013). *2013 health center data.* Retrieved from http://bphc.hrsa.gov/uds/lookalikes.aspx?state=national &year=2013

——. (2014). *Primary care: Health center program, special populations.* Retrieved from http://bphc.hrsa.gov/about/specialpopulations/

Heuer, L. J., Hess, C., & Batson, A. (2006). Cluster clinics for migrant Hispanic farmworkers with diabetes: Perceptions, successes, and challenges. *Rural Remote Health, 6*(1), 469–478.

Hollifield, M., Verbillis-Kolp, S., Farmer, B., Toolson, E. C., Woldehaimanot, T., Yamazaki, J., . . . & SooHoo, J. (2013). The Refugee Health Screener-15 (RHS-15): Development and validation of an instrument for anxiety, depression, and PTSD in refugees. *General Hospital Psychiatry, 35*(2), 202–209.

Hovell, M. F., Sipan, C. L., Blumberg, E. J., Hofstetter, C. R., Slymen, D., Friedman, L., . . . & Vera, A. Y. (2003). Increasing Latino adolescents' adherence to treatment for latent tuberculosis infection: A controlled trial. *American Journal of Public Health, 93*(11), 1871–1877.

Hyde, J. K., & Shortell, S. M. (2012). The structure and organization of local and state public health agencies in the US: A systematic review. *American Journal of Preventive Medicine, 42*(5), S29–S41.

Juon, H. S., Strong, C., Oh, T. H., Castillo, T., Tsai, G., & Oh, L. D. H. (2008). Public health model for prevention of liver cancer among Asian Americans. *Journal of Community Health, 33*(4), 199–205.

Kaestner, R., & Kaushal, N. (2007). Welfare reform and immigrants: Does the five year ban matter? *Research in Labor Economics, 25*(2): 311–347.

Kaiser Family Foundation (KFF). (2013a). *Adult income eligibility limits at application as a percent of the federal poverty level.* Retrieved from http://kff.org/medicaid/state-indicator/income-eligibility-low-income-adults/

———. (2013b). *Income eligibility limits for children's regular Medicaid and children's CHIP-funded Medicaid expansions as a percent of the federal poverty level.* Retrieved from http://kff.org/medicaid/state-indicator/income-eligibility-fpl-medicaid/

———. (2013c). *Summary of the Affordable Care Act.* Retrieved from http://kff.org/health-reform/fact-sheet/summary-of-the-affordable-care-act/

———. (2014). *State decisions for creating health insurance exchanges in 2014.* Retrieved from http://kff.org/health-reform/state-indicator/health-insurance-exchanges/

———. (2015). *State decision on Health Insurance Marketplaces and the Medicaid expansion.* KFF State Health Facts. Retrieved from http://kff.org/health-reform/state-indicator/state-decisions-for-creating-health-insurance-exchanges-and-expanding-medicaid/

Kaushal, N., & Kaestner, R. (2005). Welfare reform and health insurance of immigrants. *Health Services Research, 40*(3), 697–722.

———. (2007). Welfare reform and health of immigrant women and their children. *Journal of Immigrant and Minority Health, 9*(2), 61–74.

Kenney, G., & Huntress, M. (2012). *The Affordable Care Act: Coverage implications and issues for immigrant families.* Washington, DC: Office of the Assistant Secretary for Planning and Evaluation.

Kreps, G. L., & Sparks, L. (2008). Meeting the health literacy needs of immigrant populations. *Patient Education and Counseling, 71,* 328–332.

Ku, L., & Matani, S. (2001). Left out: Immigrants' access to health care and insurance. *Health Affairs, 20*(1), 247–256.

Ku, L. C., Richard, P., Dor, A., Tan, E., Shin, P., & Rosenbaum, S. J. (2010). *Strengthening primary care to bend the cost curve: The expansion of community health cen-*

ters through health reform (Policy Research Brief No. 19). Washington, DC: Geiger Gibson/RCHN Community Health Foundation Research Collaborative.

Lam, T. K., McPhee, S. J., Mock, J., Wong, C., Doan, H. T., Nguyen, T., . . . & Luong, T. N. (2003). Encouraging Vietnamese-American women to obtain Pap tests through lay health worker outreach and media education. *Journal of General Internal Medicine, 18*(7), 516–524.

Landale, N. S., Oropresa, R. S., Gorman, B. K. (1999). Immigration and infant health: Birth outcomes of immigrant and native-born women. In D. J. Hernandez (Ed.), *Children of immigrants: Health, adjustments, and public assistance* (pp. 244–285). Washington, DC: National Academy Press.

Lauderdale, D. S., Wen, M., Jacobs, E. A., & Kandula, N. R. (2006). Immigrant perceptions of discrimination in health care: The California Health Interview Survey 2003. *Medical Care, 44*, 914–920.

Levitt, L., & Claxton, G. (2015). *Insurance markets in a post-King world.* Retrieved from http://kff.org/health-reform/perspective/insurance-markets-in-a-post-king-world/

Lindert, J., Ehrenstein, O. S. V., Priebe, S., Mielck, A., & Brähler, E. (2009). Depression and anxiety in labor migrants and refugees—a systematic review and meta-analysis. *Social Science & Medicine, 69*(2), 246–257.

Lipsky, M. (2010). *Street-level bureaucracy: Dilemmas of the individual in public services, 30th anniversary expanded edition.* New York, NY: Russell Sage Foundation.

Lofstrom, M., & Bean, F. D. (2002). Assessing immigrant policy options: Labor market conditions and postreform declines in immigrants' receipt of welfare. *Demography, 39*(4), 617–637.

Lujan, J., Ostwald, S. K., & Ortiz, M. (2007). Promotora diabetes intervention for Mexican Americans. *The Diabetes Educator, 33*(4), 660–670.

Luque, J. S., Mason, M., Reyes-Garcia, C., Hinojosa, A., & Meade, C. D. (2011). Salud es vida: Development of a cervical cancer education curriculum for promotora outreach with Latina farmworkers in rural Southern Georgia. *American Journal of Public Health, 101*(12), 2233–2235.

Lustig, S. L., Kia-Keating, M., Knight, W. G., Geltman, P., Ellis, H., Kinzie, J. D., . . . & Saxe, G. N. (2004). Review of child and adolescent refugee mental health. *Journal of the American Academy of Child & Adolescent Psychiatry, 43*(1), 24–36.

Markides, K. S., Salinas, J., & Sheffield, K. (2008). The health of older immigrants. *Generations, 32*(4), 46–52.

McGuire, T. P. (2005). A warm welcome for refugees. *Health Progress (Saint Louis, Mo.), 86*(1), 18–21.

Mohanty, S. A., Woolhandler, S., Himmelstein, D. U., Pati, S., Olveen Carras-quillo, O., & Bor, D. H. (2005). Health care expenditures of immigrants in the United States: A nationally representative analysis. *American Journal of Public Health, 95*, 1431–1438.

Monger, R. (2009). *The foreign-born component of the uninsured population.* Washington, DC: U.S. Department of Homeland Security. Retrieved from http://www.dhs.gov/xlibrary/assets/statistics/publications/uninsured_fs_2007.pdf

Mossakowski, K. N. (2003). Coping with perceived discrimination: Does ethnic identity protect mental health? *Journal of Health and Social Behavior, 44*, 318–331.

Motomura, H. (2006). *Americans in waiting: The lost story of immigration and citizenship in the United States.* London, England: Oxford University Press.

National Association of County & City Health Officials (NACCHO). (2014). *About NACCHO.* Retrieved from http://www.naccho.org/about/

National Center for Farmworker Health (NCFH). (2014). *About community and migrant health centers.* Retrieved from http://www.ncfh.org/?sid=37

Navarro, A. M., Senn, K. L., McNicholas, L. J., Kaplan, R. M., Roppé, B., & Campo, M. C. (1998). Por La Vida model intervention enhances use of cancer screening tests among Latinas. *American Journal of Preventive Medicine, 15*(1), 32–41.

Office of Refugee Resettlement (ORR). (2014a). *About cash and medical assistance.* Retrieved from http://www.acf.hhs.gov/programs/orr/programs/cma/about

———. (2014b). *About unaccompanied children's services.* Washington, DC: U.S. Department of Health and Human Services. Retrieved from http://www.acf.hhs.gov/programs/orr/programs/ucs/about

Ornelas, I., & Perreira, K. M. (2011). The role of migration in the development of depressive symptoms among immigrant parents. *Social Science & Medicine, 73*(8), 1169–1177.

Palloni, A., & Arias, E. (2004). Paradox lost: Explaining the Hispanic adult mortality advantage. *Demography, 41*(3), 385–415.

Paul, E., Fullerton, D. F., Cohen, E., Lawton, E., Ryan, A., & Sandel, M. (2009). Medical–legal partnerships: Addressing competency needs through lawyers. *Journal of Graduate Medical Education, 1*(2), 304–309.

Pérez, D. J., Fortuna, L., & Alegría, M. (2008). Prevalence and correlates of everyday discrimination among US Latinos. *Journal of Community Psychology, 36*(4), 421–433.

Perreira, K., Crosnoe, R., Fortuny, K., Pedroza, J. M., Ulvestad, K., Weiland, C., . . . & Chaudry, A. (2012). *Barriers to immigrants' access to Health and Human Services.* Washington, DC: U.S. Department of Health and Human Services, Office of the Assistant Secretary for Planning and Evaluation.

Perreira, K., & Ornelas, I. (2013). Painful passages: Traumatic experiences and post-traumatic stress among immigrant Latino adolescents and their primary caregivers. *International Migration Review, 47*(4), 976–1005.

Perreira, K., & Smith, L. (2007). A cultural-ecological model of migration and development: Focusing on Latino immigrant youth. *The Prevention Researcher, 14*(4), 6–9.

Perumalswami, P. V., Factor, S. H., Kapelusznik, L., Friedman, S. L., Pan, C. Q., Chang, C., . . . & Dieterich, D. T. (2013). Hepatitis Outreach Network: A practical strategy for hepatitis screening with linkage to care in foreign-born communities. *Journal of Hepatology, 58*(5), 890–897.

Pettijohn, S. L., Boris, E. T., De Vita, C. J., & Fyffe, S. (2013). *Nonprofit-government contracts and grants: Findings from the 2013 National Survey.* Retrieved from http://www.urban.org/publications/412962.html

Popkin, B. M., & Udry, J. R. (1998). Adolescent obesity increases significantly in second and third generation US immigrants: The National Longitudinal Study of Adolescent Health. *Journal of Nutrition, 128*(4), 701–706.

Portes, A., Escobar, C., & Radford, A. E. (2007). Immigrant transnational organizations and development: A comparative study. *International Migration Review, 41*(1), 242–281.

Potochnick, S., & Perreira, K. M. (2010). Depression and anxiety among first-generation immigrant Latino youth: Key correlates and implications for future research. *Journal of Nervous and Mental Disease, 198*(7), 470–477.

Prosser, A. T., Tang, T., & Hall, H. I. (2012). HIV in persons born outside the United States, 2007–2010. *Journal of the American Medical Association, 308*(6), 601–607.

Quinones, L., & Rashid, A. (2013). Affordable Care Act implementation in Illinois: Overcoming barriers to immigrant health care access. Chicago, IL: Illinois Coalition for Immigrant and Refugee Rights. Retrieved from http://illinoishealthmatters.org/wp-content/uploads/2013/05/ICIRR-Report.-v2.May-2013.pdf

Rhodes, S. D., Foley, K. L., Zometa, C. S., & Bloom, F. R. (2007). Lay health advisor interventions among Hispanics/Latinos: A qualitative systematic review. *American Journal of Preventive Medicine, 33*(5), 418–427.

Rhodes, S. D., Hergenrather, K. C., Montaño, J., Remnitz, I. M., Arceo, R., Bloom, F. R., . . . & Bowden, W. P. (2006). Using community-based participatory research to develop an intervention to reduce HIV and STD infections among Latino men. *AIDS Education & Prevention, 18*(5), 375–389.

Robert Woods Johnson Foundation. (2013). *The Midwest Immigration Health Project: Community and faith-based approach to improving social services in immigrant-dense rural communities.* Retrieved from http://www.rwjf.org/content/dam/farm/reports/program_results_reports/2013/rwjf70293

Satia-Abouta, J., Patterson, R. E., Neuhouser, M. L., & Elder, J. (2002). Dietary acculturation: Applications to nutrition research and dietetics. *Journal of the American Dietetic Association, 102*(8), 1105–1118.

Satinsky, S., Hu, A., Heller, J., & Farhang, L. (2013). *Family unity, family health: How family-focused immigration reform will mean better health for children and families.* Oakland, CA: Human Impact Partners.

Shartzer, A., Kenney, G. M., Long, S. K., Hempstead, K., & Wissoker, D. (2014). *Who are the remaining uninsured as of June 2014?* Washington, DC: Urban Institute.

Singh, G. K., Rodriguez-Lainz, A., & Kogan, M. D. (2013). Immigrant health inequalities in the United States: Use of eight major national data systems. *Scientific World Journal, 213,* 1–21.

Singh, G. K., Siahpush, M., Hiatt, R. A., & Timsina, L. R. (2011). Dramatic increases in obesity and overweight prevalence and body mass index among ethnic-immigrant and social class groups in the United States, 1976–2008. *Journal of Community Health, 36*(1), 94–110.

Singh, G. K., Yu, S. M., & Kogan, M. D. (2013). Health, chronic conditions, and behavioral risk disparities among US immigrant children and adolescents. *Public Health Reports, 128*(6), 463–479.

Sixta, C. S., & Ostwald, S. (2008). Texas-Mexico border intervention by promotores for patients with type 2 diabetes. *The Diabetes Educator, 34,* 299–309.

Smedley, B. D., & Syme, S. L. (2001). Promoting health: Intervention strategies from social and behavioral research. *American Journal of Health Promotion, 15*(3), 149–166.

State Health Access Data Assistance Center. (2013). *State-level trends in employer-sponsored health insurance: A state-by-state analysis*. Retrieved from http://www.shadac.org/files/shadac/publications/ESI_Report_2013.pdf

Stein, B. D., Kataoka, S., Jaycox, L. H., Wong, M., Fink, A., Escudero, P., & Zaragoza, C. (2002). Theoretical basis and program design of a school-based mental health intervention for traumatized immigrant children: A collaborative research partnership. *Journal of Behavioral Health Services & Research, 29*(3), 318–326.

Stimpson, J. P., Wilson, F. A., & Su, D. (2013). Unauthorized immigrants spend less than other immigrants and US natives on health care. *Health Affairs, 32*(7), 1313–1318.

Taylor, V. M., Carey Jackson, J., Yasui, Y., Kuniyuki, A., Acorda, E., Marchand, A., . . . & Thompson, B. (2002). Evaluation of an outreach intervention to promote cervical cancer screening among Cambodian American women. *Cancer Detection and Prevention, 26*(4), 320–327.

Taylor, V. M., Hislop, T. G., Tu, S.-P., Teh, C., Acorda, E., Yip, M.-P., . . . & Yasui, Y. (2009). Evaluation of a hepatitis B lay health worker intervention for Chinese Americans and Canadians. *Journal of Community Health, 34*(3), 165–172.

Unger, J. B., Cabassa, L. J., Molina, G. B., Contreras, S., & Baron, M. (2013). Evaluation of a fotonovela to increase depression knowledge and reduce stigma among Hispanic adults. *Journal of Immigrant and Minority Health, 15*(2), 398–406.

U.S. Bureau of the Census. (2012). *S0501: Selected characteristics of the native and foreign-born populations, 2012 American Community Survey 1-year estimates*. Retrieved from http://factfinder2.census.gov

U.S. Department of Health and Human Services. (2014). *Exemptions from the fee for not having health coverage*. Retrieved from https://www.healthcare.gov/exemptions/

U.S. Department of State. (2015). *U.S. Refugee Admissions Program*. Retrieved from http://go.usa.gov/R3Pz

U.S. Immigration and Customs Enforcement (ICE). (2011). *Memorandum on exercising prosecutorial discretion consistent with the civil immigration enforcement priorities of the agency for the apprehension, detention, and removal of aliens*. Washington, DC: U.S. Department of Homeland Security. Retrieved from http://www.ice.gov/doclib/secure-communities/pdf/prosecutorial-discretion-memo.pdf

——. (2014a). *Delegation of Immigration Authority Section 287 (g) Immigration and Nationality Act*. Retrieved from http://www.ice.gov/news/library/factsheets/287g.htm

———. (2014b). *Secure Communities*. Retrieved from http://www.ice.gov/secure_communities/

Van Hook, J. (2003). Welfare reform's chilling effects on noncitizens: Changes in noncitizen welfare recipiency or shifts in citizenship status? *Social Science Quarterly, 84*(3), 613–631.

Van Hook, J., Bachmeier, J. D., Coffman, D. L., & Harel, O. (2015). Can we spin straw into gold? An evaluation of immigrant legal status imputation approaches. *Demography, 52,* 329–354.

Van Hook, J., & Balistreri, K. S. (2006). Ineligible parents, eligible children: Food Stamps receipt, allotments, and food insecurity among children of immigrants. *Social Science Research, 35*(1), 228–251.

———. (2007). Immigrant generation, socioeconomic status, and economic development of countries of origin: A longitudinal study of body mass index among children. *Social Science & Medicine, 65*(5), 976–989.

Van Hook, J., & Zhang, W. (2011). Who stays? Who goes? Selective emigration among the foreign-born. *Population Research and Policy Review, 30,* 1–24.

Vega, W. A., & Amaro, H. (1994). Latino outlook: Good health, uncertain prognosis. *Annual Review of Public Health, 15,* 39–67.

Vincent, D., Pasvogel, A., & Barrera, L. (2007). A feasibility study of a culturally tailored diabetes intervention for Mexican Americans. *Biological Research for Nursing, 9*(2), 130–141.

Viruell-Fuentes, E. A. (2007). Beyond acculturation: Immigration, discrimination, and health research among Mexicans in the United States. *Social Science & Medicine, 65*(7), 1524–1535.

Viswanathan, M., Ammerman, A., Eng, E., Gartlehner, G., Lohr, K. N., Griffith, D., . . . & Whitener, L. (2004). *Community-based participatory research: Assessing the evidence.* Summary, Evidence Report/Technology Assessment No. 99 (prepared by RTI–University of North Carolina Evidence-based Practice Center under Contract No. 290-02-0016) (AHRQ Publication No. 04-E022-1). Rockville, MD: Agency for Healthcare Research and Quality.

Wang, J. H., Liang, W., Schwartz, M. D., Lee, M. M., Kreling, B., & Mandelblatt, J. S. (2008). Development and evaluation of a culturally tailored educational video: Changing breast cancer-related behaviors in Chinese women. *Health Education & Behavior, 35*(6), 806–820.

White House Office of Faith-Based and Neighborhood Partnerships. (2010). A new era of partnerships: Report of recommendations to the president. Washington, DC: Author. Retrieved from http://www.whitehouse.gov/sites/default/files/microsites/ofbnp-council-final-report.pdf

Wieland, M. L., Weis, J. A., Palmer, T., Goodson, M., Loth, S., Omer, F., . . . & Sia, I. G. (2012). Physical activity and nutrition among immigrant and refugee women: A community-based participatory research approach. *Women's Health Issues, 22*(2), e225–e232.

Wilensky, G. R. (1984). Solving uncompensated hospital care: Targeting the indigent and the uninsured. *Health Affairs, 3*(4), 50–62.

Wilson, A. H., Wold, J. L., Spencer, L., & Pittman, K. (2000). Primary health care for Hispanic children of migrant farm workers. *Journal of Pediatric Health Care, 14*(5), 209–215.

Woomer-Deters, J. (2014). *Immigrants in North Carolina and the Affordable Care Act*. Raleigh: North Carolina Justice Center.

Yip, T., Gee, G. C., & Takeuchi, D. T. (2008). Racial discrimination and psychological distress: The impact of ethnic identity and age among immigrant and United States-born Asian adults. *Developmental Psychology, 44*(3), 787–800.

Yoshikawa, H. (2011). *Immigrants raising citizens: Undocumented parents and their young children*. New York, NY: Russell Sage Foundation.

Yoshikawa, H., Kholoptseva, J., & Suárez-Orozco, C. (2013). The role of public policies and community-based organizations in the developmental consequences of parent undocumented status. *Social Policy Report, 27*(3), 1–17.

Yoshikawa, H., Weiland, C., Ulvestad, K., Fortuny, K., Perreira, K., & Crosnoe, R. (2014). *Improving access of low-income immigrant families to Health and Human Services: The role of community-based organizations*. Retrieved from http://www.urban.org/UploadedPDF/2000011-Improving-Access-of-Low-Income-Immigrant-Families-to-Health-and-Human-Services.pdf

Yun, K., Fuentes-Afflick, E., & Desai, M. M. (2012). Prevalence of chronic disease and insurance coverage among refugees in the United States. *Journal of Immigrant and Minority Health, 14*(6), 933–940.

Zhang, W., & Ta, V. M. (2009). Social connections, immigration-related factors, and self-rated physical and mental health among Asian Americans. *Social Science & Medicine, 68*, 2104–2112.

PART 4

Advocacy and Future Directions

CHAPTER 15

Advocacy for Immigrant and Refugee Children and Families

▸ YALI LINCROFT, ALEXANDRA SALGADO,
  and ROWENA FONG

> From pioneering activities in the 1920s that provided nutrition literature trans-
> lated into numerous languages, to programs for unaccompanied children evacu-
> ated from Europe during World War II . . . Today, child welfare workers face many
> of the same—as well as some new—challenges in helping immigrant children and
> their families.
> —Child Welfare Information Gateway, 2015

IMMIGRATION POLICY in the United States is marked by two competing philosophies—an open door philosophy that seeks to satisfy economic demand for labor and provide relief to vulnerable populations versus an exclusionary philosophy centered on securing borderlands and limiting immigration. There are three primary legal forms of immigration to the United States: family-based sponsorship, employment-based immigration, and refugee and humanitarian relief options (Hipsman & Meissner, 2013). The most common form of legal immigration is family-based sponsorship, which provides immigration preference for close relatives of U.S. citizens and lawful permit residents.

The Immigration Nationality Act of 1952 is the primary body of law governing current immigration policy, including providing for a world-wide limit on the annual number of permanent immigrants, various visa programs, and refugee and asylum processes (Rome, 2012). The Immigration Reform and Control Act (IRCA) of 1986 addresses unauthorized immigration by prohibiting the hiring of undocumented immigrants, strengthening sanctions against employers, and denying certain welfare benefits to undocumented immigrants. The 1996 Personal Responsibility and Work Opportunity Reconciliation Act (welfare reform) made legal permanent residents ineligible for federal benefits, including food stamps and supplemental security income. In passing the Illegal Immigration Reform and Immigrant Responsibility Act of 1996 (IIRIRA), Congress further rolled back protection for undocumented immigrants and introduced expedited ways to deport noncitizens (Rome, 2012). These laws codify the federal government's exclusive power in determining immigration status.

Ultimately, and particularly in the last two decades, these federal laws have been incapable of fully controlling the powerful forces that drive unauthorized immigration—primarily the country's labor market needs (Hipsman & Meissner, 2013). The 1990s saw the longest period of sustained economic growth in the United States since World War II. Authorized and unauthorized immigration to the United States grew dramatically during that decade, not just to traditional destination states like New York, Texas, and California but to newer areas such as the southeast, midwest, and mountain states. Employment opportunities—particularly in agriculture, food manufacturing, and construction—fueled the new settlement patterns. With their lower cost of living, states like Georgia and Nevada became the growth destination states for new immigrants.

Recent immigration trends are distinct not only because of the number of immigrants but also because of the diversity of the immigrant population. Unlike previous periods of U.S. immigration, which involved mostly migrants from Europe, new immigrants are far more diverse, with the largest proportion of them coming from Latin America, Asia, the Middle East, and Africa. These new immigrants often do not share the Judeo-Christian religious background of earlier immigrants and have settled in states with little experience integrating immigrants. It is these recent and distinctive migration patterns that help explain why immigration has become an issue of national political concern and debate in recent decades.

Despite a self-proclaimed identity as a nation of immigrants, the United States has adjusted its immigration policies only rarely, largely because of the divisive nature of the politics surrounding the issue. When changes have been made to federal immigration law, they have generally taken years to legislate. The issues of legal and illegal immigration streams, border control, policies on refugees and asylum seekers, and immigration integration efforts have been central topics of debate in Congress during both the George W. Bush and Obama administrations. These debates have repeatedly ended in failed legislation, most recently with the failure of Senate Bill 744, the Border Security, Economic Opportunity, and Immigration Modernization Act (S. 744, 2013). Although this bill, which provided for comprehensive immigration reform policies, was approved with bipartisan support in the Senate, it stalled in the House of Representatives. As a result of such inaction and the rapid growth in immigration in the last 20 years, many states have become increasingly frustrated with what they perceive to be inadequate federal leadership on immigration policies.

A new dynamism has developed in immigration federalism that complicates the federal government's exclusionary immigration policy. This dynamism is characterized by greater involvement across multiple levels of government and political actors, including advocates and activists, and state and local governments assuming powers on immigration matters to compensate for federal inaction (Suro, 2015). States like Arizona and Alabama have enacted legislation in the past decade to increase state and local governments' ability to enforce immigration laws—most commonly by authorizing state and local law enforcement officials to question the immigration status of residents. Others, like California and New York, have passed laws to grant undocumented immigrants access to services and benefits, such as in-state tuition and legal representation. Whereas gridlock in Congress has thwarted efforts to pass comprehensive reform solutions, state lawmakers have enacted ample legislation on the topic, including 171 laws and 117 resolutions in 2014 (National Council of State Legislatures, 2015). These laws varied across a broad range of policy areas, including appropriations, education, health, welfare benefits, law enforcement, employment, driver's licenses, and human trafficking. States have either attempted to enhance federal enforcement practices to crack down on unauthorized immigration or, conversely, have passed laws to "mitigate the punitive effects of being unauthorized under federal rules" (Suro, 2015, p. 1). The federal government remains the exclusive power in determining an individual's immigration status, but these state and local laws have served to "define the practical consequences of that status" (Suro, 2015, p. 2).

Coexisting with these proactive legislative approaches by both pro-immigrant and anti-immigrant states, a second condition has come to define the impacts of state and local governments on immigrants. State and local policymakers generally lack a substantive understanding of the federal immigration system (Dettlaff & Fong, 2012; Rome, 2012). With limited comprehension of the implications of an individual's immigration status, policymakers are likely to pursue laws and regulations that do not consider the impact on the undocumented population (Fong & Earner, 2015; Zayas, 2015). These laws cover a broad range of topics—housing, health care, criminal justice, labor, and education—that significantly influence outcomes for undocumented immigrants. Even in states that prioritize immigrant integration, these laws can have unintended consequences that exclude undocumented immigrants from benefits and programming or expose them to harm, such as the increased likelihood of deportation or criminal prosecution (Rome, 2012; Zayas, 2015).

For undocumented children and families, these state and local policies can lead to a deprivation of services that are necessary for their livelihoods. The public child welfare system in the United States operates under the mission statement that all children deserve to have safe, stable, and permanent homes (Dettlaff & Fong, 2012; Fong, McRoy, & Hendricks, 2006). Child welfare professionals are committed to the safety and well-being of children, whether they are native born, immigrant, refugee, citizen, or noncitizen. Citizen children in mixed-status families, whose parents are noncitizens, as well as children who are unaccompanied refugee minors, are all entitled to receive public child welfare services that promote their safety and enhance their well-being (Fong, 2004; Zayas, 2015). However, securing services for these children and their families can be a challenging and complicated process given the complexities of irregular immigration statuses.

This chapter will address micro- and macro-level advocacy in the context of immigration policy. Specifically, it will discuss the important role of child welfare professionals in addressing the aforementioned policy deficiencies across all levels of government, with a particular focus on efforts in California to promote immigrant rights. The chapter will also cover collaborations with community-based organizations and coalition-building initiatives.

PROMOTING IMMIGRANT RIGHTS
IN THE CHILD WELFARE SYSTEM

As the gateway state for the past century, California exemplifies the enormous political and economic clout of immigrants. California is home to a quarter of all foreign-born people in the United States, including more than 2.5 million unauthorized immigrants (Public Policy Institute of California, 2013). The vast majority of children of immigrants in California are U.S.-born citizens. Most immigrants in California are from Latin America, but recent arrivals have been primarily from Asia (Public Policy Institute of California, 2013). Latino and Asian entrepreneurs (both foreign born and native born) own more than one quarter of all businesses in the state, and Latino and Asian consumers account for nearly one third of the state's total purchasing power (American Immigration Council, 2015). California immigrants are more likely to be on either end of the education spectrum. Whereas only 9 percent of U.S.-born California residents age 25 and older have not completed high school, that number is substantially higher for California immigrants, at 37 percent. However, recent immigrants and immigrants from Asia tend to have very high levels of educational attainment, with almost 47 percent of foreign-born residents who came to California between 2007 and 2011 having bachelor's degrees or higher (Public Policy Institute of California, 2013).

Promoting immigrant rights in California has been a priority for state legislators, as evidenced by the recent onslaught of laws to reduce barriers and support access to benefits for the millions of immigrants living in the state. California is one of a handful of states where an undocumented individual can obtain a driver's license, apply for a number of health and welfare programs, pay in-state tuition to go to a public university, and obtain professional licenses (Suro, 2015). In 2014, California legislators passed what is arguably some of the most supportive legislation for undocumented immigrants, including access to low-cost auto insurance, a new loan program to help students in postsecondary education, and $3 million in funding for legal representation for unaccompanied minors facing deportation (*Orange County Register*, 2014). In June 2015, the state budget included funding for Medi-Cal coverage for undocumented children and $15 million for implementation of Deferred Action for Childhood Arrivals (DACA) and Deferred Action for Parents of Americans and Lawful Permanent Residents (DAPA), as well as naturalization services.

Children of parents illegally residing in the United States face unique stressors because of a constant fear of discovery and separation through deportation (Dettlaff & Earner, 2010). Acculturation experiences of children and parents, characterized by a lack of social support, inadequate financial assistance, language barriers, and discrimination experiences, can foster acculturative stress (Dettlaff & Cardoso, 2010; Dettlaff & Fong, 2012). The need for culturally responsive child welfare services becomes critical when children are cared for by stressed immigrant parents, who often feel powerless and experience wrongful judgments based on assumptions about their ethnicity or immigration status rather than their actual parenting abilities (Dettlaff, 2012). Recent research has found that children experience negative emotional and behavioral outcomes after a parent is detained or deported (Koball & Capps, 2015). Family members have problems communicating with detained parents because of the great distances to detention centers, strict visiting rules, and high cost of phone calls from detention centers (Koball & Capps, 2015). Additionally, child welfare agencies experience difficulty providing services to families with detained and deported parents, including locating parents in custody and conducting home visits with family members who may also be unauthorized or living outside the United States (Koball & Capps, 2015).

Given the complex array of immigration laws in the United States, which impact the lives of immigrants at many levels, including daily activities such as employment, education, transportation, and housing, it is the responsibility of social workers and case managers to understand the unique circumstances immigrant families face because of their unauthorized immigration status. Immigrant families tend to be poorer or have lower incomes than U.S.-born families, are at greater risk for inadequate nutrition, may live in crowded housing situations, and are less likely to receive public benefits because of eligibility restrictions and fear of discovery (Dettlaff, 2012; Fong, 2004). Social service agencies often lack sufficient resources, expertise, and experience to meet the needs of children whose parents are deported or detained, particularly in places with smaller, less established immigrant communities such as in the southern states (Koball & Capps, 2015). These hardships warrant targeted advocacy for the strained immigrant parent or child so that basic needs can be met, and survival is made possible through the public child welfare system or other systems providing services to immigrant clients.

Child welfare professionals have been active in the movement toward providing greater equity and access to immigrants residing in California—both at a client level and through broader advocacy efforts. The history of the child welfare profession is based on a code of ethics to help marginalized populations access resources. That history provides a strong foundation to justify the role of child welfare professionals as social activists, as well as for the concept of client self-advocacy and empowerment (McLaughlin, 2009).

MICRO-LEVEL CLIENT ADVOCACY

Micro-level advocacy is central to the effective execution of systemic changes. Like the "canary in the coal mine," micro-level client advocacy can signal when existing policy is ineffective in addressing societal problems. The power of micro-level advocacy lies in the ability of social workers to tell their clients' stories and illustrate a policy or bureaucratic failure that needs to be addressed.

Telling the client's story is grounded on the commitment of social work to advocate on behalf of and to protect vulnerable populations. The social work profession in the United States has some of its earliest historical roots in working with immigrant children and families. Early social work leaders, such as Jane Addams with the Settlement House Movement in Chicago, developed the profession's philosophy to protect and empower the vulnerable and disadvantaged by working in the crowded immigrant neighborhoods of industrial cities more than 100 years ago (Addams, 1990). The historical context of the social work profession's commitment to marginalized populations is encapsulated in its professional code of ethics. In 1960, the National Association of Social Workers (NASW) developed its code of ethics, which officially held social workers responsible for "pursu[ing] social change with and on behalf of vulnerable and oppressed individuals and groups of people" (Stewart, 2012). Additionally, the NASW's code of diversity specifically states that, "discrimination and prejudice directed against any groups are damaging to the social, emotional, and economic well-being of the affected group and of society as a whole" (National Association of Social Workers, 2008). Furthermore, international norms and standards such as the United Nations Convention on the Rights of the Child, though nonbinding in the United States absent congressional ratification, identify globally accepted policies and practices for the child welfare profession (United Nations Office of the High Commissioner for Human Rights, 1989).

Despite strong advocacy efforts for social justice, the United States has a lower rate of social welfare investment than in most other developed countries. This lack of safety net support is evident in the strains and vulnerabilities faced by low-income communities (Morgan, 2013). Conditions are further exacerbated in low-income immigrant communities because of the implications of immigration status. In many California counties that have experienced the large-scale influx of new immigrant populations, social workers are involved in helping families address the stressors of immigration, including economic hardships and linguistic and cultural difficulties associated with acculturation. An experienced social worker understands the complex, profound relationship between the clients' personal struggles and the broader environmental forces that affect them. Researchers have found that immigration-related fears have resulted in a reluctance to seek cash or food assistance programs by noncitizen parents, even when they have U.S. citizen children who are eligible for services (Speiglman, 2013). Social workers see firsthand the difficulties faced by immigrant clients who lack the resources for maintaining the basic human needs for themselves and their families.

CASE STUDY: JUANA REYES

The case of the arrest of Juana Reyes, "the tamale lady," in Sacramento, California, illustrates the important role of micro-level client advocacy by social workers (CNN, 2012). For more than two years, Juana Reyes prepared and sold tamales outside a Wal-Mart in Sacramento. The 46-year-old single mother sold the tamales at $1 each to supplement her modest income and pay her $750 monthly rent. As Reyes explained to reporters, "I am fighting and selling tamales to get my family ahead." Reyes had been living in the United States as an undocumented immigrant for more than 16 years, and two of her children had been born and raised in the United States and were attending Sacramento public schools.

On June 28, 2012, a Sacramento County sheriff's deputy told Reyes she could no longer sell tamales outside Wal-Mart. Reyes was confused. According to her attorney, she had sold tamales at the location for so long that even Wal-Mart employees purchased her tamales. To avoid trouble, Reyes left the location with her 7-year-old daughter and 10-year-old son and headed to a different shopping mall. However, Reyes soon returned to the Wal-Mart because business was better at that location.

Since Reyes saw other women selling tamales in the Wal-Mart parking lot, she assumed it was now safe for her to return to her regular location.

According to her attorney, the sheriff's deputies returned and arrested Reyes. The deputy also placed both of Reyes's children in his patrol cruiser along with Reyes. The deputy cited Reyes for trespassing, which normally would have resulted in a warning to leave the premises, but in this case Reyes was arrested and taken into custody. Meanwhile, despite the fact that Reyes's friends, family, and neighbors had converged on the scene and asked to take the children, Child Protective Services (CPS) was called to take custody of the children. As Reyes recounted, one deputy allegedly told Reyes's son that "they are going to send your mom to Mexico and you will never see her again."

After her kids were taken by CPS and she was transported to the main jail, Reyes was unable to provide proof of identification, which to the Sacramento sheriff signaled that she was undocumented. Through a federal program called Secure Communities, which forwards local arrest records to U.S. Immigration and Customs Enforcement (ICE), the federal government learned of Reyes's arrest. Although she had no previous entanglements with the law, ICE began to target her for deportation by placing a "hold" on her release. Reyes spent 13 days in jail, without an attorney, on an immigration hold, before being released on July 10. Her first immigration court date was scheduled for a month later, and during that time, her children remained in the county's foster care system.

Reyes's arrest took hold in the Spanish-language media, as the public became outraged at the arrest of the Wal-Mart "tamale lady." Following interviews with *La Opinion* and Univision, Reyes became a symbol in the community of America's broken immigration system.

A pro bono attorney took Reyes's case, using public outrage as the primary tactic for fighting the deportation. The attorney fought against the trespassing charge, arguing that there had been "implied consent" for Reyes to be at Wal-Mart since she was a familiar face to Wal-Mart employees and had been selling on the premises for years. The arresting deputy's explanation was that the Sheriff's Department had received three prior complaints about Reyes and felt her trespassing was "likely to continue," which is why she was arrested. The attorney countered, arguing that the particular area of the parking lot had numerous other street food vendors who were not arrested. The attorney also argued that Reyes's case was "blatant racial profiling," especially in light of the alleged comment directed at Reyes's son by the arresting deputy. Multiple well-publicized rallies were held in front of the Wal-Mart location, organized by faith-based leaders and community activist groups, such as the California Immigration Policy Center (CIPC) and the Coalition for Humane Immigration Rights of Los Angeles (CHIRLA). Speakers at Reyes's rallies included Sacramento city council candidate Rob Kerth, who argued that her case is an extreme interpretation of immigration law.

Ultimately, Reyes was reunited with her children, and her removal proceeding was dismissed by ICE using "prosecutorial discretion." Each year, ICE is allowed to use this discretion in a few thousand cases based on many factors, including a clean arrest record and strong community ties.

Reyes's story ultimately became a key compelling argument for passage of the TRUST Act (Assembly Bill 4, California Statutes of 2013, Chapter 570), which was designed to stop the separation of families by prohibiting local law enforcement from holding individuals on the basis of immigration "holds" in nonserious and nonviolent cases. The TRUST Act sought to address the fact that many of the people being deported through Secure Communities were not threats to public safety. Less than one-third of the roughly 80,000 people deported from California through Secure Communities since the state joined the program in 2009 were convicted of serious felonies. In many cases, people had been deported for minor offenses where charges had actually been dropped (*Los Angeles Times*, 2012).

MACRO-LEVEL ADVOCACY

Dedicated community leaders and effective community practice are important in the social work profession so that macro-level change and advocacy for children and families can occur. Although only a small percentage of the country's social workers count advocacy as their primary job duty, all social workers carry a philosophical charge to protect and empower the vulnerable and disadvantaged. Besides direct case advocacy, social workers also have a variety of other advocacy tools available, including writing op-ed pieces, organizing local protests, and working with their legislators to change laws that adversely affect immigrant clients.

Through macro-level advocacy, laws have been changed in the public child welfare system to better provide for the needs of children in mixed-status families and for unaccompanied minors. Unaccompanied refugee minors and unaccompanied immigrant children are under the age of 18 years and have come to the United States alone, without a parent or guardian. They come under the custody of the Department of Health and Human Services, Office of Refugee Resettlement, which is the federal agency charged with the care and custody of unaccompanied minors. To accommodate finding safe and stable homes for these children and youths, the public child welfare system has changed its policies and laws to allow these non-citizens to be eligible for long-term foster care placements.

Another population found in the public child welfare system consists of immigrant adolescents who have been abused, abandoned, or neglected. If they qualify, they receive Special Immigrant Juvenile Status (SIJS), which allows them an adjusted status to lawful permanent residency, enables them to live and work permanently in the United States, qualifies them for federal financial aid and other benefits, and permits them to travel in and out of the United States.

The development of the SIJS legislation in the 1990s provides an example of macro-level advocacy in the delivery of public child welfare services to adolescents and how the influence of one client-level advocate can lead to systemic policy change.

CASE STUDY: SPECIAL IMMIGRANT JUVENILE STATUS

In 1986, President Ronald Reagan signed the Immigration Reform and Control Act (IRCA), which reformed U.S. immigration law. It allowed amnesty for millions of undocumented immigrants to legalize their status. At that time, Ken Borelli was a supervising social worker for the Immigration Services Unit at the Department of Family and Children's Services in Santa Clara County, California (Lincroft, 2015). He had many children in his caseload who were undocumented and who were unlikely to be reunited with their parents because of abuse and neglect charges. Borelli began filing immigration applications under the IRCA amnesty for these undocumented children. After approximately seven of these applications had been approved, federal immigration officials ordered him to stop this practice, given that he was not the "parent" of these children. Borelli believed firmly that it was the state's responsibility, as the legal "surrogate parent" for these children, to apply for immigration relief. As a result, he approached San Jose representative Don Edwards, who assigned his then legislative aide and future congresswoman Zoe Lofgren to address this problem. The Special Immigrant Juvenile Status (SIJS) Act, a bill that gave undocumented children in the state foster care system their own path to lawful permanent residency, was ultimately introduced and approved in 1990. Because SIJS was developed by and for child welfare workers, the legislation is truly child centered, unlike all other forms of immigration relief (Jackson, 2012). It incorporates the "best interest of the child" standard, an internationally recognized, essential child welfare philosophy, which is woefully lacking in most other immigration proceedings.

COMMUNITY-BASED ORGANIZATIONS
AND COALITION BUILDING

Although public child welfare agencies and other public social service systems should strive to ensure "the best interest of the child," children and families are better served through partnerships between public actors and community groups. Effectively addressing the multitude of social, financial, and spiritual needs of immigrant populations is best done through extensive collaboration with community-based organizations, particularly those located near or within immigrant communities.

Community-based organizations, and the social workers and case managers that staff them, play a crucial role in delivering services to immigrant families and building communities to empower immigrants. Beyond those traditional roles, community-based organizations are uniquely positioned to serve as a platform for the needs of immigrants in order to influence immigration policy. Community-based organizations play a central role in strengthening the understanding of lawmakers. As such, their involvement in the political and policy realms is critical, particularly as the interplay between federal and state governments becomes ever more complex.

Community-based organizations that work closely with immigrants have a precise understanding of the ways states and local laws discriminate against undocumented immigrants. That understanding allows them to bring to light situations that would otherwise be overlooked. Immigrants, for example, face heightened barriers in the child welfare system because of a lack of understanding about their status. Thousands of children from immigrant families are trapped in the child welfare system because their parents are under immigration custody or have been deported. When children enter the child welfare system, social workers prioritize family reunification if it is in the best interest of the child. However, many immigrant families are not given the opportunity for family reunification because of detention or deportation. As described in the Applied Research Center report *Shattered Families*, noncitizen parents are frequently unable to access services and meet requirements set out by dependency courts to regain custody of their children (Wessler, 2011). Although immigrant relatives may be willing to take custody of a child when a parent is detained or deported, social workers or the courts may incorrectly assume that children cannot be placed with undocumented parents and relatives.

To address this issue, California passed Senate Bill 1064 (Statutes of 2012, Chapter 845), a law authored by Senate President pro Tempore Kevin de León, which affords expanded rights to detained immigrant parents and their children (Lincroft, 2013). When Senate Bill 1064 (SB 1064) was proposed in California in 2012, there was limited quantifiable research on the number of parents in immigration detention and the number of deported parents. The anecdotal information that was available was gathered directly from immigrant rights organizations, many of them providing legal services and other assistance to immigrant families. As immigration attorneys fought deportation orders and sought relief for their clients, they also had to address the very real possibility that parental rights would be severed if child welfare processes were not followed. These experts shared their experiences with legislators, providing technical assistance to craft the appropriate solution, which was ultimately signed into California law. Similar legislation based on California SB 1064 was also introduced in Illinois, Arizona, and New York in 2013 (Rogerson, 2013). These state legislative initiatives have individually relied on the experience of direct service providers to inform the dialogue.

Community-based organizations vary in mission, services, client base, capacity, and level of engagement with the policy realm. Although some organizations have the ability to fully engage with policy processes at the local, state, and federal levels, others primarily focus on service delivery. That is why immigrant rights advocates and service providers have built dynamic and far-reaching coalitions to leverage each other's resources for immigration reform initiatives.

The impact of this strong coalition building has been felt across the country. One significant achievement was the efforts of advocates and activists to convince President Obama to use executive action to grant relief to a portion of the undocumented immigrant population. In 2012, the White House announced its Deferred Action for Childhood Arrivals (DACA) program, protecting from deportation many undocumented individuals who arrived as children and granting them work authorization. Although immigrant rights groups hailed the program, frustrations continued to mount as Congress failed to pass comprehensive immigration reform in 2013. As 2014 progressed and it became increasingly clear that comprehensive immigration reform was unlikely, advocates refocused their efforts on promoting the president's use of administrative discretion to grant some relief for the millions of undocumented immigrants living in the United States.

DEFERRED ACTION FOR CHILDHOOD ARRIVALS (DACA)

This program grants protection from deportation and provides work authorization to certain unauthorized immigrant youths who came to the United States as children, have pursued an education, and have not committed serious crimes or posed a threat to national security. Many states, such as California, have also allowed successful DACA applicants to be eligible for a driver's license or other state-determined benefits, including health care. Since the plan was announced in December 2012, more than 580,000 young immigrants have successfully received DACA status (MSNBC, 2014).

Immigrant advocates faced much criticism for this approach because of a strong concern that it would hamper efforts to achieve sweeping reform. However, it was the ability of the various immigrant coalitions across the country to bring forth the daily struggles of undocumented immigrants—of their desperation for some semblance of legality—that ultimately prompted the White House to announce an expansion of DACA and the creation of the Deferred Action for Parents of Americans and Lawful Permanent Residents (DAPA).

The implementation of these new programs has been halted while the courts determine the legality of President Obama's executive actions. Nevertheless, it is clear that the adoption of both DACA and DAPA, and similar efforts at the state and local levels, have depended on the development of broad-based coalitions that provide legal and policy expertise to craft policy proposals, mobilize large groups of immigrants and allies in support, and neutralize opponents' arguments. It is also these same coalitions that ultimately will monitor the implementation of the policy changes to ensure that they are meeting the intended goals.

CONCLUSION

Immigration policy and the need for comprehensive reform will continue to be subjects of debate in the foreseeable future. Although it is difficult to anticipate how soon federal legislative action will be politically viable, and whether it will deliver broad reform, it is clear that state and local governments will continue to pursue their own solutions to immigration challenges. In order to promote inclusive policies that promote the well-being of immigrant families, advocacy both at the micro and macro levels is crucial. State and local policies must be informed by child welfare professionals, community-based organizations, and legal advocates with client-informed understandings to systemically address the barriers faced by children and their immigrant families.

Social workers interacting with clients on a daily basis must be able to navigate the child welfare system with a clear understanding of the unique challenges immigrants face in order to truly serve the best interests of children. They must also come to recognize the power of telling clients' stories to shed light on unaddressed barriers, particularly in jurisdictions that may not be as favorable toward immigrants.

Besides individual efforts on behalf of specific clients, child welfare professionals should be aware of and be encouraged to use macro-level advocacy tools to promote systemic change for immigrant children and families. Past involvement by social workers has been instrumental in the development of policies and practices, and partnerships with community-based organizations and coalitions have led to important progress that can be replicated at the local, state, and federal levels.

KEY TERMS

BEST INTEREST OF THE CHILD A doctrine used by most courts to determine a wide range of issues related to the well-being of children.

DEFERRED ACTION FOR CHILDHOOD ARRIVALS (DACA) A program approved by President Obama in 2012 that gives certain youths who arrived in the United States as children a reprieve from deportation and work authorization. Eligibility for the program was expanded in 2014.

DEFERRED ACTION FOR PARENTS OF AMERICANS AND LAWFUL PERMANENT RESIDENTS (DAPA) A program that provides a reprieve from deportation and work authorization to parents of children who are U.S. citizens or legal permanent residents.

DEPORTATION When the federal government orders that a noncitizen be removed from the United States, typically after an individual breaks immigration law, overstays their temporary visa, and/or violates criminal law.

SPECIAL IMMIGRANT JUVENILE STATUS (SIJS) An immigration status for immigrant adolescents who have been abused, abandoned, or neglected that allows them to be eligible to have their status adjusted to become lawful permanent residents.

STUDY QUESTIONS

1 Describe how new waves of immigration in the 1990s differed from previous migration patterns into the United States.

2 What are the three primary legal forms of immigration to the United States?

3 What challenges make it difficult to adjust immigration policies in the United States?

4 How was public outrage and media used in the "tamale lady" incident to facilitate passage of the TRUST legislation?

5 Give examples of recent state legislation enacted in the past decade to increase local ability to enforce immigration law and to grant undocumented immigrants access to services and benefits.

6 How did publicly bringing forth the daily struggles of individual undocumented immigrants help encourage the White House to announce an expansion of Deferred Action programs (DACA and DAPA)?

ADDITIONAL RESOURCES

Center on Immigration and Child Welfare: http://cimmcw.org
First Focus Center for the Children of Immigrants: https://firstfocus.org /issues/children-of-immigrants/

Helms, J. B. (2011). *Niño's: A guide to help you protect your US-born child in the event you are detained or deported.* Montgomery, AL: Legal Services Alabama. Available at http://www.jdsupra.com/legalnews/ nios-a-guide-to-help-you-protect-your-64376/

Rabin, N. (2011). *Disappearing parents: A report on immigration enforcement and the child welfare system.* Tucson, AZ: University of Arizona, Bacon Immigration Law and Policy Program, James E. Rogers College of Law. Available at https://law2.arizona.edu/depts/bacon_program/pdf /disappearing_parents_report_final.pdf

Women's Refugee Commission. (2010). *Torn apart by immigration enforcement: Parental rights and immigration detention.* New York, NY: Author. Available at https://womensrefugeecommission.org/resources/document /667-torn-apart-by-immigration-enforcement-parental-rights-and -immigration-detention

REFERENCES

Addams, J. (1990). *Twenty years at Hull House.* Chicago: University of Illinois Press.

American Immigration Council. (2015). *New Americans in California: The economic power of immigrants, Latinos, and Asians in the Golden State.* Retrieved from http://www.immigrationpolicy.org/sites/default/files/docs/new_ameri cans_in_california_2015.pdf

Child Welfare Information Gateway. (2015). *Immigration and child welfare.* Washington, DC: U.S. Department of Health and Human Services, Children's Bureau.

CNN. (2012, August 1). Don't deport the Tamales Lady. Retrieved from http:// www.cnn.com/2012/08/01/opinion/navarrett-deportation-sacramento/

Dettlaff, A. (2012). Immigrant children and families in child welfare. In A. Dettlaff & R. Fong, *Child welfare practice and immigrant children and families* (pp. 1–12). New York, NY: Routledge.

Dettlaff, A. J., & Cardoso, J. B. (2010). Mental health need and service use among Latino children of immigrants in the child welfare system. *Children and Youth Services Review, 32,* 1373–1379.

Dettlaff, A. J., & Earner, I. (2010). *Children of immigrants in the child welfare system: Findings from the National Survey of Child and Adolescent Well-Being* [Research brief]. Englewood, CO: American Humane Association. Retrieved from http:// cimmcw.org/wp-content/uploads/2013/03/pc-childofimmigrantpdf.pdf

Dettlaff, A., & Fong, R. (2012). *Child welfare practice and immigrant children and families*. New York, NY: Routledge.

Fong, R. (Ed.). (2004). *Culturally competent practice with immigrant and refugee children and families*. New York, NY: Guilford.

Fong, R., & Earner, I. (2015). Multiple traumas of undocumented immigrants: Crisis reenactment play therapy. In N. B. Webb (Ed.), *Play therapy with children in crisis: Individual, group, and family treatment* (4th ed., pp. 372–394). New York, NY: Guilford.

Fong, R., McRoy, R., & Hendricks, C. (2006). *Intersecting child welfare, substance abuse, and family violence: Culturally competent approaches*. Alexandria, VA: Council on Social Work Education.

Hipsman, F., & Meissner, D. (2013). *Immigration in the United States: New economic, social, political landscapes with legislative reform on the horizon*. Washington, DC: Migration Policy Institute.

Jackson, K. (2012). Special status seekers. *Los Angeles Lawyers*, pp. 20–26.

Koball, H., & Capps, R. (2015). *Health and social service needs of U.S.-citizen children with detained or deported immigrant parents*. Washington, DC: Urban Institute & Migration Policy Institute.

Lincroft, Y. (2013). The Reuniting Immigrant Families Act—A case study of California's Senate Bill 1064. Brief. Washington, DC: First Focus Center for the Children of Immigrants. Retrieved from http://childwelfaresparc.org/the-reuniting-immigrant-families-act-a-case-study-of-californias-senate-bill-1064/

———. (2015). Email from Ken Borelli to Yali Lincroft regarding his role in creating the SIJS legislation.

Los Angeles Times. (2012, August 25). Sheriff Baca may defy proposed law easing immigration enforcement. Retrieved from http://articles.latimes.com/2012/aug/25/local/la-me-trust-act-20120825

McLaughlin, A. (2009). Clinical social workers: Advocates for social justice. *Advocates in Social Work*, *10*(1), 51–68.

Morgan, K. (2013). America's misguided approach to social welfare—How the country could get more for less. *Foreign Affairs*, *92*(1), 153–164.

MSNBC. (2014, December 29). Immigration action lessons learned from DACA. Retrieved from http://www.msnbc.com/msnbc/immigration-action-lessons-learned-daca

National Association of Social Workers. (2008). *Code of ethics*. Washington, DC: Author.

National Council of State Legislatures. (2015). States pass 171 immigration laws in 2014. Retrieved from http://www/ncsl.org/press-room/states-pass -171-immigration-laws-in-2014.aspx

Orange County Register. (2014, December 28). New laws in 2015 to benefit undocumented immigrants. Retrieved from http://www.ocregister.com/articles /california-646538-state-immigrants.html

Public Policy Institute of California. (2013). *Just the facts: Immigrants in California.* Retrieved from http://www.ppic.org/main/publication_show.asp?i=258

Rogerson, S. (2013). Lack of detained parents' access to the family justice system and the unjust severance of the parent–child relationship. *Family Law Quarterly, 47*(2), 141–172.

Rome, S. (2012). Promoting family integrity: The Child Citizen Protection Act and its implications for public child welfare. In A. Dettlaff & R. Fong (Eds.), *Child welfare practice and immigrant children and families* (pp. 21–38). New York, NY: Routledge.

Speiglman, R. (2013). Welfare reform's ineligible immigrant parents: Program reach and enrollment barriers. *Journal of Children and Poverty, 19*(2), 91–106.

Stewart, T. (2012). Undocumented immigrants and policy advocacy: Reasserting the activist roots of social work. *Columbia Social Work Review, 5*, 33–42.

Suro, R. (2015). California dreaming: The new dynamism in immigration federalism and opportunities for inclusion on a variegated landscape. *Journal of Migration and Human Security, 3*(1), 1–25.

United Nations Office of the High Commissioner for Human Rights. (1989). *Convention on the Rights of the Child.* New York, NY: Author.

Wessler, S. (2011). *Shattered families: The perilous intersection of immigration enforcement and the child welfare system.* New York, NY: Applied Research Center.

Zayas, L. (2015). *Forgotten citizens: Deportation, children, and the making of American exiles and orphans.* New York, NY: Oxford University Press.

CHAPTER 16

Future Directions

▸ *ROWENA FONG and* ALAN J. DETTLAFF

IMMIGRANT AND REFUGEE POPULATIONS, documented and undocumented, in the United States continue to grow in population and face complex and challenging problems. Immigrants and refugees experience difficult migration journeys to the United States, and they often manifest psychological trauma during or before their journeys. Stressful mental health problems can be exacerbated by threats and the fear of being deported. The migration journeys of immigrants and refugees are typically motivated by severe financial or political stressors in their home countries, but religious differences have resulted in persecutions that create compelling reasons for leaving their home countries to seek refuge in host countries like the United States.

Migration patterns show that immigrant populations that typically have been concentrated in urban areas are moving to suburban and rural communities. As Dettlaff reports in chapter 5 of this volume, one of the consequences has been that "over the past 10 years, states in the Midwest, Rocky Mountains, and Southeast have experienced more than a 200 percent increase in their immigrant populations" (Fortuny, Capps, Simms, and Chaudry, 2009). Whether they are dwelling in rural or urban areas, immigrant and refugee children and families are often frightened and overwhelmed as they settle. Poverty is common for immigrant and refugee children in the United States, and many of their homes are marked by hardship and strife. Many have hopes of getting a better education and better-paying jobs, but they experience a gap between their aspirations and achievements. Others are socially isolated, without social networks.

PRACTICE-FOCUSED CHALLENGES

The authors of chapters 5 through 9 in this book write about problems that challenge nearly all populations of immigrants and refugees. Common problems facing these populations relate to practice issues and the need for culturally responsive practices. Training for practitioners is needed so they understand that cultural values play a key role in the assessments and intervention planning for these tradition-bound families. Indigenous interventions that include spiritual/religious, family, and community values are important. As stated by Vakalahi, Hafoka, and Fong in chapter 6, immigrant and refugee families live with dual value systems. Many immigrant and refugee families, whether they are documented or undocumented, cling to traditional values and need to know, understand, and adjust to Western values in the United States. Likewise, American social workers need to be culturally responsive and know, understand, and adjust to the ethnic cultural values the immigrants and refugees honor and uphold as fabrics of their societies. For example, in chapter 9, Husain, Nashwan, and Howard remind readers that not all Muslims are Arabs and not all Arabs are Muslims. Culturally responsive practitioners are aware of these differences and ensure that families receive culturally responsive services respectful of their faith and religious practices.

Legal status plays a key role in the well-being of immigrant and refugee children and families, and today there is a growing population of mixed-status families, in which some members are documented and others are not. These are typically families whose parents are undocumented but the children are U.S.-born citizens, entitled to all the rights of citizenship. But for these "forgotten" children and families, as researcher and author Luis Zayas writes in his book *Forgotten Citizens: Deportation, Children, and the Making of American Exiles and Orphans*, their life can be one of "fright, fight, and flight" (Zayas, 2015, p. 85). These terms signal the need for practitioners, educators, policymakers, and advocates to better understand the complex trauma these children and families commonly experience in their journeys to this country, when settling in, and in trying to make a life in the United States.

SYSTEM-FOCUSED CHALLENGES

Although not every immigrant or refugee experiences the hardships described in these chapters, it is commonly understood that undocumented populations are at greater risk of discrimination and oppression, experiencing many kinds of social injustices. Some of these are micro-aggressions, but others are macro-aggressions caused by larger social service systems. These get manifested through bureaucratic barriers in service delivery and policies in social service systems, as discussed in chapters 10 through 14, in child welfare, juvenile justice, education, mental health, physical health, and other organizational systems. Advocacy needs to be done in systems so that changes in macro-level practices and policies can be made with a concentration on mixed-status families and the rights of citizen children and their undocumented parents.

Advocacy might be difficult because these cross systems have their own unique challenges and barriers, although they share common problems. Common macro-level problems include the lack of linguistically appropriate services and cultural brokers across systems. Practitioners working with immigrants and refugees attentive to the multicultural aspect of competent practice even at the macro-level will provide care with cultural humility (Gallardo, 2014). Culturally responsive services start where the client is, as stated in chapter 7, but also provide guidance that is culturally responsive to the ethnic client's cultural context. Understanding the historical context of migration journeys and sharing that knowledge across systems is necessary within a system of care framework. Trauma-informed practices need to be provided throughout the child welfare, physical health, mental health, education, and justice systems that work with these families.

POLICY-FOCUSED CHALLENGES

At the policy level, services are dictated by attitudes reflected in policies established at the agency, state, and federal levels. These attitudes do not reflect the fact that the immigration system is in dire need of reform. More advocacy is needed for policy changes in the federal legal system as well as human service systems. The authors of chapters 2, 3, and 4 describe common concerns in practice, policy, and research. Practice issues at the micro-, mezzo-, and macro-levels emphasize the need for more in-depth attention to culturally responsive services, with cultural humility reflected throughout. Federal, state, organizational, and agency policies need more attention to attitudes that are aimed at making undocumented citizens fear deportation so that they refuse to use the social services they desperately need. Immigration laws need to focus more on family integrity and safety. Mixed-status families are entitled to some federal and state benefits, but those policies at the state level are not often communicated to immigrant and refugee families, so they do not know about these resources.

RESEARCH-FOCUSED CHALLENGES

Research needs more focused attention on research designs and methodologies that use cultural translators and reflect cultural equivalents so measures of well-being can be appropriately selected. There needs to be more research on needs assessments that facilitate an understanding of the trauma that immigrants and refugees experience in their migration journeys and initial settlement in the United States. Evaluations of culturally responsive services offered to immigrant and refugee families need to be conducted, as well as program evaluations using social, cultural, and religious resources in the community.

CHANGING THE MODEL: THE NEED FOR A PARADIGM SHIFT

The assumption has always been that majority culture in the United States is white and both nonimmigrant and nonrefugee. Demographics, philosophies of life, attitudes, and beliefs are Western oriented, grounded in individualism, not collectivism. Social service providers need to shift from an orientation that assumes Western values, frameworks, and principles are exclusively used to guide work with immigrant and refugee populations living in the United States today. A paradigm shift needs to occur so that a broader, more multicultural, and more culture-specific perspective that exhibits cultural humility and accounts for the complexity of trauma in cross-cultural contexts is adopted. Major shifts need to occur in the areas of practice, research, and advocacy.

SOCIAL WORK PRACTICE

Social work practice needs a shift in worldview. It needs to move away from the framework of what used to be defined as people of color as a minority culture. The majority culture is becoming filled with immigrants and refugees, many of whom are nonwhite. A new language is needed for minority/majority frameworks. The majority/minority divide is a misnomer based on current demographic trends. Immigrants and refugees are a growing population in the United States and should not be referred to as minority groups.

Language in assessing client problems should also be more inclusive of clients' strengths. Immigrants and refugees had skills and strengths before coming to the United States. Culturally responsive clinicians and practitioners should be able to learn about diverse backgrounds and settings so they will acknowledge clients' strengths and accomplishments before coming to the United States, preserving their dignity and worth. Culturally responsive clinicians and practitioners will also work with their clients' cultural beliefs and religious perspectives, such as Muslim families' collective frame of work and more definite concepts of gender differences, being aware that such cultural values can be both protective and risk factors.

Using culturally responsive practices with immigrants and refugees incorporates cultural knowledge and skills with cultural humility. In part, this means incorporating clients' strengths based on their cultural values, which immigrant and refugees themselves consider vital to their well-being. Since cultural responsiveness requires effort and learning, culturally responsive training will need to become a priority for clinicians and practitioners in many social service agencies.

Micropractice

Micropractice must start with the premise that immigrant and refugee groups and their differences merit a practitioner's respect, but also that the diversity in spoken language, religious beliefs, values, and customs within a single ethnic group may be no less sharply defined than the differences that distinguish ethnic groups from one another. In chapters 5 through 9, the authors make the point that families exhibit diversity not only among races but also within the many ethnic groups within a single race. This awareness of differences within and between groups affects assessment practices. Thorough assessments about migration journeys and the trauma collected along the way are critical to the practitioner's understanding that offering social services to the same immigrant or refugee group may not account for differences within groups. A more systematic approach to assessment that recognizes diversity within a group is needed.

Mezzopractice

Social work practice with immigrant and refugee families needs to incorporate interventions that are based on family-oriented roles and processes.
For example, understanding cultural values is crucial in conducting assessments and intervention planning for a practitioner working with
Middle Eastern families, where collective well-being is more important
than Western-style individualism. Cultural diversity plays out in parenting
practices, too, when immigrants and refugees relocate to the United States.
Their native parenting practices or expectations may not conform to acceptable practices as viewed by social service systems such as the child welfare
system. Practitioners who learn and respect such differences in cultural values are better equipped to assess their immigrant and refugee families.

Knowing cultural equivalents in concepts and using cultural translators
can help practitioners use indigenous interventions at the mezzolevel with
families. To understand indigenous interventions, a systematic approach
grounded in cultural responsiveness is needed. Establishing what kind of
intervention worked well in the home country can help identify compatible
Western interventions and promote a "biculturalization of interventions"
(Fong, 2004).

Macropractice

Macro-level social work practice works with organizations and agencies
serving immigrants and refugees. The chapter authors advance several sug-
gestions for improving macropractice with these populations. Throughout
the chapters, the authors pointed to the need for more training. In social
service agencies providing macroservices, all staff need to be better trained
in working with clients for whom English is a second language. Training on
trauma-informed practice is also necessary in assessments and intervention
implementation when working with immigrant children and families.

Macrosystems also need more newcomer programs, where children,
youths, and families can absorb all the changes and new information
learned. There needs to be a developmental model of cultural orientation.
Basic orientation and advanced orientation need to be spread out over a
period of time. The pressure to learn English language skills causes opportunities to be missed that would allow newcomers to discover their skills
and strengths that are not demonstrated through oral language. Practical

skills tests are needed to determine the strengths of the individual clients and their families.

Cross-System Practices

Culturally responsive practice needs to include cross-system practices that create a climate where maltreatment can be reported without fear of deportation. It is necessary to implement policies and practices that do not separate children from families and where children and youths can obtain federal relief. Improvements are needed to help workers find ways to support successful adaptation of children; practice in schools needs to improve school readiness via dual-generation programing of the children, youths, and possibly even adults they serve.

Currently, in the juvenile justice system, it has been reported that immigrant and refugee youths are receiving harsher punishments than other youths. In the physical health and mental health systems, immigrants and refugees are less likely to have health insurance. There needs to be more collaborative efforts to address problems in a nonpunitive way and without exposing an individual's undocumented status. Because social services are complex and fragmented, there needs to be better coordination between systems. Linking data would be helpful so that cross-system services can be made comprehensive, consistent, and coherent.

There needs to be more of an emphasis and work on cross-system practice because cross-system relationships are important. Also important is the relationship between systems and the communities they are located in or the communities in which the immigrants and refugees live. In summary, culturally responsive practice at the macro-, mezzo-, and micro-levels needs strengthening in working with immigrant and refugee children and families, in using cultural values as strengths, recognizing diversity within groups, obtaining more training to understand diverse cultural values, and coordinating cross-system practices to be more coherent and responsive.

CREATING A CULTURALLY RESPONSIVE FRAMEWORK

In conducting research, there have been many concerns that research designs are not sensitive to the ethnic populations being studied. Theories of change are based on conceptual frameworks that may not fit the cultural values of the persons being interviewed or surveyed. Many ethnic groups are family or community based, and research designs that do not factor in these orientations are not capturing well-designed logic models or evaluable interventions that are culturally responsive to the ethnic group the research seeks to portray in its findings.

In working with immigrants and refugees, it may be worth considering using a framework for developing, testing, adapting, and replicating evaluable interventions that allows theory of change and intervention development to happen as a stage development approach, as can be seen in a new framework disseminated recently by the Children's Bureau (2014) to "design, test, spread, and sustain effective practice in child welfare" (see figure 16.1). This stage approach can be applied to other disciplines to develop evidence-supported interventions in mental health, physical health, juvenile justice, and schools through a culturally responsive lens. This is a practical framework that describes a process for improving the building of evidence in child welfare at each step along the continuum of designing, testing, adapting, and sustaining interventions.

At the identify and explore stage (see figure 16.1), researchers need to consider cultural values and their fit as protective and risk factors in developing the research design for the intervention. This stage emphasizes a stepwise process to develop an intervention that can be done in a culturally responsive manner:

Step 1 Identify the problem through the ethnic and cultural values of the client.

Step 2 Understand the problem by including the trauma acquired during migration journeys.

Step 3 Construct a theory of change at the micro-, mezzo-, and macro-levels using critical race theory.

Step 4 Research solutions that reflect "dual values" of East/West social environments.

Step 5 Choose interventions that include biculturalization of interventions (Fong, 2004), including indigenous and Western interventions.

At the develop and test stage, researchers develop interventions that reflect a "biculturalization of interventions" (Fong, 2004) that would incorporate indigenous and Western interventions to accommodate the treatment to the various ethnic populations. At the compare and learn stage, researchers can

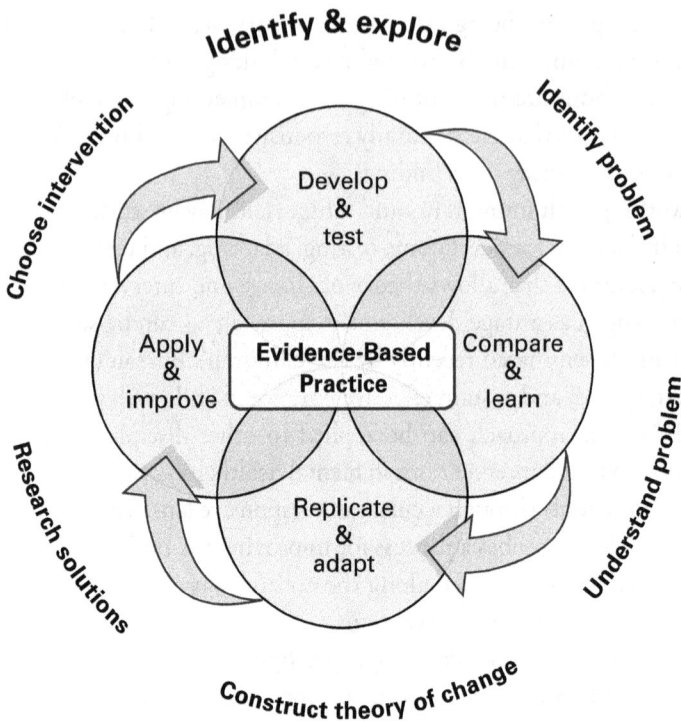

FIGURE 16.1   A framework to design, test, spread, and sustain
effective practice in child welfare

compare the evidence-supported interventions to different ethnic groupings within the same race. At the replicate and adapt stage, modifications
would be made to account for ethnic diversity based on race, religion, age,
gender, sexual orientation, and political status. Finally, at the apply and improve stage, the evaluable, evidence-supported intervention could be improved based on the application to the new cohorts of immigrants and refugees arriving in the United States annually.

CONCLUSION

Much advocacy needs to be done with and for the population of immigrant and refugee children and families. Cross-system practices can become more coherent if administrators can link data across systems, have
collaborative team meetings to assess problems, and find appropriate cul-

turally responsive interventions that reflect a biculturalization of interventions. More staff training about English language learners (ELL) needs to occur, and better coordination needs to happen to create cross-system newcomer programs where the explanation of policies and practices can occur simultaneously rather than in a silo approach.

Immigration reform is needed, and further advocacy is needed to change attitudes. Zayas (2015) strongly advocates that children in mixed-status families are citizen children. These children should have priorities and privileges just like the children who have citizenship. These children should have their rights and entitlements better explained to them by social service providers. This could be facilitated by having clearer and more accessible policies and laws aimed at helping immigrants and refugees navigate these complex systems. These agency policies should foster more trust among immigrant and refugee families rather than foster fears and anxieties.

In conclusion, immigrant and refugee children and families, especially mixed-status families, are a vulnerable group and need the supports and social services they deserve. However, attitudes, policies, and practices need to change at the federal, state, and organizational levels so that micro-, mezzo-, and macro-practices can be culturally responsive, reflecting shifts in policy and practice paradigms within and across systems.

REFERENCES

Children's Bureau. (2014). *A framework to design, test, spread, and sustain effective practice in child welfare.* Washington, DC: Children's Bureau, Administration for Children and Families, U.S. Department of Health and Human Services, Child Welfare Research & Evaluation Framework Workgroup.

Fong, R. (Ed.). (2004). *Culturally competent practice with immigrant and refugee children and Families.* New York, NY: Guilford.

Fortuny, K., Capps, R., Simms, M., & Chaudry, A. (2009). *Children of immigrants: National and state characteristics.* Retrieved from Urban Institute website: http://www.urban.org/publications/411939.html

Gallardo, M. (Ed.). (2014). *Developing cultural humility: Embracing race, privilege, and power.* Los Angeles, CA: Sage.

Zayas, L. (2015). *Forgotten citizens: Deportation, children, and the making of American exiles and orphans.* New York, NY: Oxford University Press.

EDITORS

ALAN J. DETTLAFF is Dean and Maconda Brown O'Connor Endowed Dean's Chair at the Graduate College of Social Work, University of Houston. His research focuses on improving cultural responsiveness and reducing racial disparities in the public child welfare system. In particular, his research has focused on understanding and addressing the unique needs of immigrant Latino children who come to the attention of this system. He received his PhD in social work and his MSW from the University of Texas at Arlington. Before joining academia, he worked for several years in the public child welfare system as a practitioner and administrator, where he specialized in investigations of child maltreatment. He has published extensively on children's services and immigrant Latino children, and he is co-editor of *Racial Disproportionality and Disparities: Multisystemic Approaches*, and *Child Welfare Practice with Immigrant Children and Families*. He was recently honored with induction into the 2015 Class of Fellows of the Society for Social Work and Research. He serves as chair of the Commission on Educational Policy for the Council on Social Work Education, which develops the policy that guides social work education. He also sits on the editorial boards of *Child Welfare*, *Child Abuse & Neglect*, and *Journal of Public Child Welfare*.

ROWENA FONG is the Ruby Lee Piester Centennial Professor in Services to Children and Families in the School of Social Work at the University of Texas at Austin. She is the past president of the Society for Social Work and Research and is a member of the American Academy of Social Work and Social Welfare. She received her BA in Chinese studies and psychology from Wellesley College, her MSW in children and families from the University of California at Berkeley, and her EdD in human development from Harvard University. Her areas of research are focused on adoptions and child welfare, transracial adoptions and ethnic identity formation of Chinese adoptive children and families, domestic and international victims of human trafficking, and racial disproportionality in public child welfare. She has numerous publications, including nine books: *Transracial and Intercountry Adoption Practices and Policies: A Resource for Educators and Clinicians* (2016, with R. McRoy), *Addressing Racial Disproportionality and Disparities in Human Services* (with A. Dettlaff, J. James, & C. Rodriguez), *Child Welfare Practice with Immigrant Children and Families* (with A. J. Dettlaff), *The Church Leader's Counseling Resource Book: A Guide to Mental Health and Social Problems* (with C. Franklin), *Intersecting Child Welfare, Substance Abuse, and Family Violence: Culturally Competent Approaches* (with R. McRoy & C. Ortiz Hendricks), *Culturally Competent Practice with Immigrant and Refugee Children and Families*, *Children of Neglect: When No One Cares* (with M. Smith), *Culturally Competent Social Work Practice: Skills, Interventions and Evaluation* (with S. Furuto), and *Multisystem Skills and Interventions in School Social Work Practice* (with E. Freeman, C. Franklin, G. Shaffer, & E. Timberlake). She received the 2008 Distinguished Recent Contributions in Social Work Education Award of the Council on Social Work Education, the 2007 Texas Exes Teaching Award of the University of Texas at Austin, the 2001 Regent's Teaching Award of the University of Hawaii at Manoa, and the 2001 Social Worker of the Year in Education and Training of the National Association of Social Workers, Honolulu chapter. She has served on the editorial boards of *Social Work, Journal of Social Work Education, Research and Social Work Practice*, and *Journal of Ethnic and Cultural Diversity in Social Work*, and she is currently serving on the boards of *Child Welfare, Journal of Public Child Welfare, Religion and Childhood*, and *Journal of Social Work Education*.

AUTHORS

LIZA BARROS LANE transitioned to social work after being a bilingual teacher and received her MSW in 2013. She is currently a social work doctoral student and is studying the relation between financial strain and behavioral health outcomes in Latinos, with hopes of using financial capability as a mental health intervention.

DINA BIRMAN is associate professor of educational and psychological studies and director of the community well-being PhD program at the University of Miami. Her research has primarily focused on the complex process of acculturation for immigrant and refugee adolescents, families, and communities. She holds a PhD in clinical/community psychology.

JODI BERGER CARDOSO is assistant professor at the University of Houston Graduate College of Social Work. Her research focuses on trauma exposure, stress, and mental health and substance abuse outcomes in Latino immigrants and their children. Before receiving her doctorate, she worked as a bilingual mental health clinician serving Latino immigrant families in the Houston area.

WENDY CERVANTES is vice president of Immigration and Child Rights Policy at First Focus and the director of the Center for the Children of Immigrants. She holds an MA in Latin American studies and political science from the University of New Mexico and a BA in communications from the University of Southern California.

LESLIE COFIE is a doctoral candidate in health behavior at the University of North Carolina-Chapel Hill Gillings School of Global Public Health. His research in migration and health focuses on examining changes in the health status of U.S. immigrants over time. His work aims to increase understanding of various factors that influence the health status of African immigrants and their families and contribute to developing evidence-based interventions to prevent diseases that are highly prevalent among this population.

ELIZABETH FRANKEL is the associate director of the Young Center for Immigrant Children's Rights. She has taught immigration law at the Young Center's Immigrant Child Advocacy Clinic at the University of Chicago Law School. She received her JD from New York University School of Law and her BA from Middlebury College.

OFA KU'ULEI LANIMEKEALOHA HAFOKA is a Pacific Islander born and raised in Hawaii. She is a doctoral candidate in counseling psychology at Brigham Young University. Her research interests include multicultural psychology, psychological well-being, and adjustment among Pacific Islander American communities in the United States.

STEPHENIE HOWARD is a doctoral student at Howard University. She has a background in child welfare. Her research interests include the neurological underpinnings of the stress response in children and the development of maladaptive behaviors.

ALTAF HUSAIN is an associate professor in the School of Social Work at Howard University. His research interests include the mental health of displaced populations, immigration policy and its impact on the family, cultural and spiritual competence, and the development of faith-based social services.

MICHELLE JOHNSON-MOTOYAMA is associate professor at the University of Kansas School of Social Welfare. Her research focuses on community-based approaches to child maltreatment prevention and the elimination of disparities in child health and child welfare. She completed her PhD at the University of California at Berkeley and her BS and MSW from the University of Illinois at Urbana-Champaign.

ANGIE JUNCK is a supervising attorney at the Immigrant Legal Resource Center. She specializes in the immigration consequences of crime and delinquency, immigration enforcement, and immigrant youth issues. She sits on the American Bar Association's Immigration Commission and is the co-chair of the Immigration Committee of the ABA's Criminal Justice Section.

YALI LINCROFT is a program officer with the Walter S. Foundation. She has been a child welfare policy consultant to the Annie E. Casey Foundation and First Focus, a bipartisan Washington, D.C., children's advocacy organization. She helped First Focus develop federal and state legislation helping immigrant families, including the California Reuniting Immigrant Families Bill. She received her BA from the University of California–Berkeley and MBA from the University of California–Davis.

MARGARET LOMBE is an associate professor at the Boston College School of Social Work. She is also a faculty associate at the Center for Social Development at Washington University in St. Louis. Her area of expertise is international social development, with an emphasis on social inclusion/exclusion and capacity building.

HARRIET MABIKKE is the executive director of Hope Networks International, a U.S.-based nonprofit organization dedicated to improving the livelihoods of women and children in Africa. She holds a bachelor's degree in social sciences from Uganda's Makerere University and a master's degree in social work from Boston College's Graduate School of Social Work.

E. SUSANA MARISCAL is a senior research assistant at the University of Kansas School of Social Welfare. She has a Licenciatura from the Catholic University of Bolivia and a PhD and MSW from the University of Kansas.

LYN MORLAND is research Fellow for the Center for Culturally Responsive Practice, Bank Street College of Education. For more than 30 years, she has worked to improve the cultural and linguistic responsiveness of service systems. She earned an MSW from Catholic University of America, an MA in anthropology and medical behavioral sciences from the University of Kentucky, and is a

Tomlinson Fellow in the McGill University School of Social Work PhD program.

CHIEDZA MUFUNDE has worked on research and policy development with A World At School, a global education campaign mobilizing various public and private institutions and partners on finishing the education goal of Millennium Development Goals. She is currently employed by the World Bank. She holds an MSW with a focus on global practice and policy from the Boston College School of Social Work.

AYAT NASHWAN serves as an assistant professor in the Department of Sociology and Social Work at Yarmouk University. Her primary areas of research interest include social work practice with Arab American, Muslim, and Middle Eastern immigrant families and communities across the lifespan and acculturative stress among Arab American children and adolescents.

CAITLIN O'GRADY is a PhD candidate in social work at the University of Illinois at Chicago. She received her BA from Kenyon College in 2007 and her MSW from the University of Denver in 2009. As a doctoral candidate, she is pursuing research aimed at identifying strategies for promoting the health and well-being of Latino youths.

KRISTA PERREIRA is professor of public policy at the University of North Carolina-Chapel Hill. She is a health economist and social demographer, and her research combines qualitative and quantitative methodologies to study migration and its health and educational consequences. Through her research, she aims to develop programs and policies to improve the well-being of immigrant families and their children.

RACHEL PRANDINI is the Unaccompanied Minor Law Fellow and attorney at the Immigrant Legal Resource Center. Previously, she represented unaccompanied minors in removal proceedings at the Esperanza Immigrant Rights Project. She has also worked as an associate at Paul Hastings, LLP. She received her JD from the University of California-Davis School of Law and her BA from Westmont College.

ALEXANDRA SALGADO is legislative aide to California Senator Kevin de Leon. She received a BA in political science from Stanford University in 2012.

UMA A. SEGAL is a professor at the University of Missouri-St. Louis and Fellow in International Studies and Programs. Her research focus is on immigrant and refugee integration. She was a 2013–2014 Fulbright Scholar and was editor-in-chief of the *Journal of Immigrant & Refugee Studies* from 2004 to 2012.

DAVID B. THRONSON is associate dean for experiential education and professor
   of law at the Michigan State University College of Law, where he was co-founder of
   the Immigration Law Clinic. His research explores the intersection of family
   and immigration law, with a particular focus on children.

HALAEVALU F. OFAHENGAUE VAKALAHI is a Pacific Islander immigrant of
   Tongan descent who was born in Tonga and raised in Hawaii. She earned her
   PhD in social work and a master's in educational administration from the
   University of Utah and an MSW from the University of Hawaii-Manoa. She is
   professor and associate dean in the School of Social Work at Morgan State
   University in Baltimore, Maryland. Her two areas of scholarship are Pacific
   Islander culture and community and women of color in academia.

GPSR Authorized Representative: Easy Access System Europe, Mustamäe tee
50, 10621 Tallinn, Estonia, gpsr.requests@easproject.com

www.ingramcontent.com/pod-product-compliance
Lightning Source LLC
Chambersburg PA
CBHW060017030426
42334CB00019B/2078